Contemporary Issues in Cost and Managerial Accounting

Contemporary Issues in Cost and Managerial Accounting

· · ·

A Discipline in Transition

Third Edition

Edited by

Hector R. Anton
University of California, Berkeley

Peter A. Firmin
University of Denver

Hugh D. Grove
University of Denver

HOUGHTON MIFFLIN COMPANY · BOSTON

Dallas · Geneva, Illinois · Hopewell, New Jersey · Palo Alto · London

To Our Wives —

Lois, Jean, and Nancy

Library of Congress Catalog Card Number: 77–074383

ISBN: 0–395–25435–3

Contributors

AMERICAN ACCOUNTING ASSOCIATION
COMMITTEE ON HUMAN RESOURCE ACCOUNTING

MEMBERS: ROGER H. HERMANSON, CHAIRMAN, *Georgia State University*

R. LEE BRUMMET, *University of North Carolina at Chapel Hill*

NABIL ELIAS, *University of Manitoba*

ERIC G. FLAMHOLTZ, *University of California, Los Angeles*

ROBERT R. IRISH, *University of Toledo*

CARL G. KRETSCHMAR, *University of South Carolina*

GARY A. LUOMA, *Emory University*

JOSHUA RONEN, *New York University*

MICHAEL J. VERTIGAN, *University of Alberta*

AMERICAN ACCOUNTING ASSOCIATION
COMMITTEE ON MANAGERIAL DECISION MODELS

MEMBERS: CHARLES T. HORNGREN, CHAIRMAN, *Stanford University*

HECTOR R. ANTON, *Haskins and Sells, New York, and Professor Emeritus, University of California, Berkeley*

HAROLD BIERMAN, JR., *Cornell University*

EUGENE H. BROOKS, JR., *University of North Carolina at Chapel Hill*

PETER A. FIRMIN, *University of Denver*

ELLSWORTH MORSE, JR., *U.S. General Accounting Office*

THOMAS H. WILLIAMS, *University of Texas at Austin*

ZENON ZANNETOS, *Massachusetts Institute of Technology*

RUSSELL L. ACKOFF
University of Pennsylvania

JOHN V. BAUMLER
Ohio State University

GEORGE J. BENSTON
University of Rochester

JACOB G. BIRNBERG
University of Pittsburgh

EDWIN H. CAPLAN
University of New Mexico

ABRAHAM CHARNES
University of Texas at Austin

W. W. COOPER
Harvard University

JOEL DEMSKI
Stanford University

NICHOLAS DOPUCH
University of Chicago

THOMAS R. DYCKMAN
Cornell University

NATWAR M. GANDHI
University of Pittsburgh

LAWRENCE A. GORDON
University of Kansas

v

HUGH D. GROVE
University of Denver

DAVID B. HERTZ
McKinsey & Company, Inc., New York

CHARLES T. HORNGREN
Stanford University

YUJI IJIRI
Carnegie-Mellon University

JEFFREY E. JARRETT
University of Rhode Island

ROBERT S. KAPLAN
Carnegie-Mellon University

JAMES C. KINARD
Ohio State University

ROBERT A. KNAPP
General Electric, Johnson City, New York

JAMES S. LABICK
Arthur Andersen & Company, New York

FERDINAND K. LEVY
Georgia Institute of Technology

JOHN L. LIVINGSTONE
Georgia Institute of Technology

DANNY MILLER
McGill University

WAYNE J. MORSE
Duke University

E. W. NETTEN
Price Waterhouse & Company

MOHAMED ONSI
Syracuse University

PETER A. PYHRR
Texas Instruments Incorporated

JOSHUA RONEN
New York University

JAMES E. SORENSEN
University of Denver

GARY L. SUNDEM
University of Washington

FRANK C. SURGES
Fidelity Union Trust Company, Newark, New Jersey

GERALD L. THOMPSON
Carnegie-Mellon University

DOUGLAS VICKERS
University of Western Australia

DAVID J. H. WATSON
University of Queensland

H. MARTIN WEINGARTNER
University of Rochester

JEROME D. WIEST
Rice University

Contents

Part Three

Part Four

Part Five

Part Six

Part Seven

Preface

The theme of the third edition of our cost and managerial accounting readings book is a familiar one: a discipline in transition. The readings again reflect behavioral-science, information-system, and quantitative-method analyses of cost and managerial accounting problems. The final section of the book further develops emerging trends, information system design, human resource accounting, social accounting, and operational not-for-profit performance evaluation techniques.

Increasing concern for efficiency and public accountability in the not-for-profit sector of the economy makes the concepts and techniques of managerial accounting quite relevant to public administration, management, and social work.

We have attempted to include articles that reflect the "frontier" of existing knowledge in the cost and managerial accounting disciplines. The articles cover such "frontier" issues as: using zero-base budgeting techniques to justify an organization's existence; using expectancy theory to analyze behavioral impacts on budgeting; tracking cost variances with cusum charts; applying standard costs to a service industry (for example, incorporating them into a bank's information system); using organization theory to solve the transfer pricing problem of decentralized entities; and linking nonmonetary outcome measurements to costs in an interdisciplinary perspective to provide nonprofit performance evaluations.

The articles appear in the following seven-part sequence: a perspective in managerial accounting; forecasting, budgeting, and responsibility accounting; capital budgeting; cost estimation and cost-volume-profit analysis; standard costs and performance evaluation; cost allocation and decentralization; and emerging areas in managerial accounting. The perspective developed in Part One considers information system, decision model, and behavioral science concepts. Within this perspective we will view the specific managerial accounting topics covered in Parts Two through Six. The emerging areas in Part Seven reflect the extension of these concepts in recent cost and managerial accounting developments.

The thirty articles in this book reflect various degrees of quantitative application ranging from a mere mention of method to the development or application of specific quantitative techniques. In selecting the latter type of article, we have chosen, as much as possible, "self-contained" articles with sufficient explanations of quantitative techniques that the reader will not have to consult other sources. The degree of self-containment depends upon the background of the reader, however, and some may wish to study certain quantitative techniques in greater depth. A list of such supplemental sources, keyed to various articles used in the text, is given in the Appendix.

The editors again extend their gratitude to the authors of the articles included and to the publishers who kindly consented to allow the reprints.

We appreciate the special contribution of Barbara Wihera and Joyce Frakes, graduate students who participated in the literature review and helped select the articles from their unique and crucial point of view: usefulness and accessibility to the student. We also express our appreciation to Robert Hamilton, of the University of Minnesota, and Roger Roemmich, of the University of Georgia, who reviewed the original manuscript and made valuable comments.

H.R.A.

P.A.F.

H.D.G.

Contemporary Issues in Cost and Managerial Accounting

PART ONE

A Perspective

in Managerial Accounting

Cost and managerial accounting, like accounting in general, are dynamic, evolving disciplines. Traditional cost accounting has dealt largely with the accumulation and allocation of factory costs and product for inventory valuation and income determination. The discipline is now more generally designated as managerial accounting to emphasize its conceptual expansion in order to provide relevant accounting data to decision-makers. These conceptual developments include the consideration of management information systems, decision models, behavioral science, budgeting, cost estimation and control, not-for-profit performance evaluation, internal pricing, and various decision-oriented problem areas. Part One introduces the general development and integration of management information systems, decision models, and behavioral science in the managerial accounting discipline.

Horngren outlines the scope, content, and method of management accounting in a management information system context. He distinguishes financial accounting from ". . . internal reporting for managers for planning, controlling current operations . . . [and] for making special decisions and formulating long-range plans." He also develops objectives and informational requirements for decision-makers. Although it stresses management accounting, the Horngren article applies equally to not-for-profit organizations. Indeed, cost and management accounting are increasingly being recognized as relevant to hospitals, government, and other fiduciary organizations. Horngren also foresees many later developments such as decision analysis, divisional reporting problems, and flexible organizational systems for the managerial accounting discipline.

In providing relevant information to decision-makers, managerial accounting starts with the examination of actual decision models that indicate specific types of desired accounting information. The "Report of the

1

Committee on Managerial Decision Models" of the American Accounting Association develops the investigation of various decision models and interactions with accounting and information systems. The report begins with an exploration of the general nature of decision models and general attributes of information for decision models. It then elaborates implications of decision models and information systems for managerial accounting. Finally, the report explores specific decision models to develop the types of information desired. With a cost-benefit perspective, the reader may then assess the difference between information traditionally provided by managerial accounting and that which should be provided.

Another major development in managerial accounting has been the long overdue recognition of the great impact of the behavioral sciences on accounting. This impact has been reflected in extensive non-accounting literature in the areas of motivation, behavior, and organizational theory. Benston provides a good survey of the literature and applies these concepts to accounting systems. As one of the earlier articles on behavior and accounting, it serves as an introduction to the area.

Caplan then expands the role of behavioral science in managerial accounting by specifying and comparing behavioral assumptions from the classical and modern behavioral viewpoints. The design of the management and accounting information systems depends heavily on which viewpoint management follows. If the modern behavioral viewpoint predominates, then the traditional accounting information system, which corresponds to the classical behavioral viewpoint, must also evolve into a modern system to provide relevant information. The differences between the two behavioral schools of thought are elaborated in four categories of assumptions — organization goals, participant behavior, management behavior, and the role of management accounting. The challenging implication is that traditional managerial accounting systems may be mismatched with modern behavioral viewpoints and information requirements.

1   *The scope and content of financial accounting is well known. In this article the author defines the scope of managerial accounting and contrasts it with financial accounting. The objectives of management accounting and the types of information requirements are clearly outlined.*

The main purposes are given as routine reporting of financial data or "score-keeping"; routine reporting to management for planning and control or "attention-directing"; and special reporting to management for non-recurring decisions or "problem-solving." Any guide to management accounting must pay major attention to relevancy of information and its timeliness. Accuracy, while important, may be non-relevant. Future accounting information systems' needs are clearly outlined including structuring, cost-behavior rules, and responsibility accounting.

Choosing Accounting Practices for Reporting to Management*

Charles T. Horngren†

Objectives of Management Accounting

MANAGEMENT ACCOUNTING — ITS DISTINCTIVE PURPOSES

The accounting system is the major formal information system in almost every organization. An effective accounting system provides information for three broad purposes: (1) external reporting to stockholders, government,

* *From* NAA Bulletin, *Vol. XLIV, No. 1 (September, 1962), pp. 3–15. Reprinted by permission of the publisher.*

† I am indebted to the members of the Workshop in Accounting Research, Institute of Professional Accountancy, Graduate School of Business, University of Chicago — especially Professors Sidney Davidson, David Green, Jr., Richard Lindhe, and George H. Sorter — for constructive criticism.

and other outside parties, (2) internal reporting to managers for planning and controlling current operations, and (3) internal reporting to managers for making special decisions and formulating long-range plans.

Management (internal parties) and external parties share an interest in all three important purposes, but the emphasis of financial accounting and management accounting differs. Financial accounting has been mainly concerned with the first purpose and has traditionally been oriented toward the historical, stewardship aspects of external reporting. The distinguishing feature of management accounting is its emphasis on the second and third purposes.

The job of serving both internal and external demands can be an imposing one. Conventional accounting systems have tended to grow primarily in response to external forces. Management accounting, on the other hand, attempts to implement a more balanced, multi-goaled perspective. The widespread problem that management accountants must face has been aptly described as follows:

> Very few people in business have had the opportunity to reflect on the way in which the accounting model developed, particularly on how an instrument well adapted to detect fraud and measure tax liability has gradually been used as a general information source. Having become accustomed to information presented in this form, business people have adapted their concepts and patterns of thought and communication to it rather than adapting the information to the job or person. When one suggests the reverse process, as now seems not only logical but well within economic limits, he must expect a real reluctance to abandon a pattern of behavior that has a long history of working apparently quite well.[1]

A management accounting planning and control system should be designed to spur and help executives in searching for and selecting short-run and long-run goals, formulating plans for attaining those goals, implementing plans, appraising performance and pin-pointing deviations from plans, investigating reasons for deviations, reselecting goals, etc. Management accounting is concerned with accumulating, classifying, and interpreting costs and other information that induce and aid individual executives in fulfilling organizational objectives as revealed explicitly or implicitly by top management.

TYPES OF INFORMATION SUPPLIED BY MANAGEMENT ACCOUNTING

What information should the management accountant supply? The types of information needed have been neatly described by Simon *et al.* as a result

---

[1] William R. Fair, "The Next Step in Management Controls," in Donald G. Malcom and Alan J. Rowe, (ed.), *Management Control Systems* (New York: John Wiley & Sons, Inc., 1960), pp. 229–230.

of their study of seven large companies with geographically dispersed operations. The approach of the Simon research team would probably be fruitful in any company:

> By observation of the actual decision-making process, specific types of data needs were identified at particular organizational levels — the vice presidential level, the level of the factory manager, and the level of the factory head, for example — each involving quite distinct problems of communication for the accounting department.[2]

The research team found that three types of information, each serving a different purpose, often at various management levels, raise and help answer three basic questions:

1. Score-card questions: "Am I doing well or badly?"
2. Attention-directing questions: "What problems should I look into?"
3. Problem-solving questions: "Of the several ways of doing the job, which is the best?"

Score-card and attention-directing uses of data are closely related. The same data may serve a score-card function for a foreman and an attention-directing function for his superior. For example, many accounting systems provide performance reports through which actual results are compared to predetermined budgets or standards. Such a performance report often helps answer score-card questions and attention-directing questions simultaneously.

Furthermore, the "actual results" collected can help fulfill not only control purposes but also the traditional needs of financial accounting. The answering of score-card questions, which mainly involves collection, classification, and reporting, is the task that has predominated in the day-to-day effort of the accounting function.

Problem-solving data may be used to help in special nonrecurring decisions and long-range planning. Examples include make-or-buy, equipment replacement, adding or dropping products, etc. These decisions often require expert advice from specialists such as industrial engineers, budgetary accountants, statisticians, and others.

MANAGEMENT ACCOUNTING AND THE OVERALL INFORMATION SYSTEM

These three uses of data may be related to the broad purposes of the accounting system. The business information system of the future should be a single, multi-purpose system with a highly-selective reporting scheme. It will

[2] H. A. Simon, *Administrative Behavior* (2nd ed.; New York: The Macmillan Company, 1957), p. 20. For the complete study see H. A. Simon, H. Guetzkow, G. Kozmetsky, and G. Tyndall, *Centralization vs. Decentralization in Organizing the Controller's Department* (New York: Controllership Foundation, Inc. 1954). This perceptive study is much broader than its title implies.

be tightly integrated and will serve three main purposes: (1) routine reporting on financial results, oriented primarily for external parties (score-keeping); (2) routine reporting to management, primarily for planning and controlling current operations (score-keeping and attention-directing); and (3) special reporting to management, primarily for long-range planning and nonrecurring decisions (problem-solving). Although such a system can probably be designed in a self-contained, integrated manner to serve routine purposes simultaneously, its special decision function will always entail much data that will not lie within the system.

USES OF DATA AND ORGANIZATION OF THE ACCOUNTANT'S WORK

The Simon study also emphasized that ideally the management accountant's staff should have its three distinct functions manned by full-time accountants: (1) score-keepers, who compile routine data and keep the information system running smoothly; (2) attention-directors, who attempt to understand operating management's viewpoint most fully and who spotlight, interpret, and explain those operating areas that are most in need of attention; and (3) problem-solvers, who search for alternatives, study the probable consequences, and help management follow an objective approach to special decisions.

If one accountant bears responsibility for more than one of these three functions, his energies are prone to be directed to (1), then to (2), and finally to (3). If this occurs, his two foremost values, as far as management is concerned, are likely to be dissipated.[3]

Guides to Selection of Management Accounting Practices

RELEVANT INFORMATION — THE BASIC NEED

The National Association of Accountants' Research Planning Committee has stated: "Guides are needed by the management accountant to aid him in selecting practices from among the many alternatives. These guides provide assurance that practices chosen will yield data *relevant to the recipient's purposes*." [Emphasis supplied.] Any guide, therefore, must be concerned with the concept of relevancy, because the assembly and interpretation of relevant data is the management accountant's fundamental task.

Relevant data may be defined broadly as that data which will lead to an optimum decision. The distinction between *relevancy* and *accuracy* should be kept in mind. Ideally management accounting data should be relevant (valid, pertinent) and accurate (precise). However, figures can be precise but irrelevant, or imprecise but relevant. But relevancy is basic to manage-

[3] Simon, *et al.*, *op. cit.*, p. 5.

ment accounting. Although accuracy is always desirable and often extremely important, it is really a subobjective in any conceptual approach to gathering data for planning and control.

Some executives have implied that many accountants have a twisted orientation regarding accuracy and relevancy. That is, many accountants are preoccupied with accuracy and are little concerned with relevancy. This is a reflection of the product costing and income determination goal of industrial accounting that so often overrides other important goals. What may be accurate with respect to the product costing goal may be entirely irrelevant with respect to management decisions. For example, scrupulous determinations of bases for overhead allocation may yield seemingly "accurate" results for product costing purposes but may be wholly misleading for planning and control purposes. Reverence for accuracy, while admirable, may narrow the horizons and usefulness of the industrial accountant.

Now we shall examine the meaning of relevancy as it bears on the two broad purposes of management accounting.

OBJECTIVE OF PLANNING AND CONTROLLING OPERATIONS

THE KEY QUESTIONS

The directing of attention, the providing of clues, the raising of pertinent questions, the inducing of desired behavior — these are the principal tasks of accounting for planning and controlling operations. The accountant's role here includes score-keeping and attention-directing.

Some guides to management accounting practice in this area have been described profusely in the accounting literature. For example, it has become almost self-evident that appropriate budgets and standards have wide usefulness in the execution of the accountant's attention-directing function. Much of the literature on standard costs[4] gives the impression that they are always based on sound engineering studies and rigorous specifications. Although this approach is often useful, it should be stressed that less scientific standards provide a forceful way of presenting information in order to stimulate corrective action. An accounting system is effective when it automatically calls management's attention to the areas that most sorely need investigation. Accuracy of standards, while desirable, is not as basic to successful management accounting as the more fundamental notion — that of the relevancy of using some predetermined targets as a means of implementing management by exception.

Another example of an obvious guide is the frequent need to sacrifice precision for promptness in reporting. The need for timely data is so acute

[4] Consider the definition by the 1951 Committee on Cost Concepts, American Accounting Association, *The Accounting Review*, (April, 1952), p. 177, "Standard costs are *scientifically* predetermined costs." (Emphasis supplied.)

in many cases that it should be fulfilled promptly in a flash report, even if the wanted data ordinarily are only part of a more complete formal report. Thus, an effective management accounting system is designed to supply reports on a highly selective basis; relevancy often overrides accuracy in these score-keeping and attention-directing areas. That is, highly accurate but stale data are irrelevant, because they have no bearing on the decisions then facing the recipient.

This notion of relevancy provides the cornerstone in constructing guides for the purpose of planning and controlling current operations. The logical questions to be asked are:

1. What are the objectives of the organization as a whole?
2. Who are the executives who are expected to seek such objectives? What are their spheres of responsibility?
3. What data can be provided to help them toward making individual decisions that will harmonize with and spur them toward overall company objectives?

Assuming that the answers to question (1) are available,[5] we turn to the questions under (2).

TAILORING THE SYSTEM TO THE ORGANIZATION — RESPONSIBILITY ACCOUNTING

Our initial guide is as follows: *Focus the basic design of the accounting system upon the responsibility centers of individual managers.* The accounting system must cohesively reflect the plans and actions of all responsibility centers in the organization — from the smallest to the biggest. This basic idea is being implemented on a wide scale in the form of so-called *responsibility accounting, profitability accounting,* or *activity accounting* systems.[6]

Ideally, particular revenues and costs would be recorded and automatically traced to the one individual in the organization who shoulders primary responsibility for the item. He is in the best position to evaluate and to influence a situation. For example:

> The sales department requests a rush production. The plant scheduler argues that it will disrupt his production and cost a substantial though not clearly

[5] Profitability is generally regarded as the prime objective. A discussion of organizational objectives, such as profitability, growth, power, or social service, is beyond the scope of this paper. See Wm. Travers Jerome III, *Executive Control — The Catalyst* (New York: John Wiley & Sons, Inc., 1961), Chapters 4 and 14.

[6] Martin N. Kellogg, "Fundamentals of Responsibility Accounting," *N.A.A. Bulletin* (April, 1962), pp. 5–16. John A. Higgins, "Responsibility Accounting," *The Arthur Andersen Chronicle* (April, 1952). The term *activity accounting* is used by Eric Kohler and may be used interchangeably with *responsibility accounting.* See Kohler, *A Dictionary for Accountants* (2nd ed.; New York: Prentice-Hall, Inc., 1957), pp. 22–23.

determined amount of money. The answer coming from sales is: "Do you want to take the responsibility of losing the X Company as a customer?" Of course the production scheduler does not want to take such a responsibility, and he gives up, but not before a heavy exchange of arguments and the accumulation of a substantial backlog of ill feeling.

Analysis of the payroll in the assembly department, determining the costs involved in getting out rush orders, eliminated the cause of the argument. Henceforth, any rush order was accepted with a smile by the production scheduler, who made sure that the extra cost would be duly recorded and charged to the sales department — "no questions asked." As a result, the tension created by rush orders disappeared completely; and, somehow, the number of rush orders requested by the sales department was reduced to an insignificant level.[7]

Practically, the diffusion of control throughout the organization complicates the task of collecting relevant data by responsibility centers.[8] The organizational networks, the communication patterns, and the decision-making processes are complex — far too complex to yield either pat answers or *the* ideal management accounting system.[9]

HARMONY OF OBJECTIVES

Our next guide is: *Study and delineate individual manager needs in relation to his sphere of responsibility and the objectives of the organization as a whole.*

This sweeping guide has many subguides in the area of planning and controlling current operations. We have already seen that the individual manager requires score-card and attention-directing data. But what data are relevant? To be relevant, the data should impel the manager toward decisions that will harmonize with top management objectives. It follows that the management accountant must evaluate the influence of the accounting system on the motivations of individuals. The example of rush orders cited above shows how the accounting system can affect management behavior.

The trouble here is that conflicts arise between individual goals and top management goals. We all know of instances where a manager's attempt to "look good" on a performance report resulted in action detrimental to the best interest of the organization as a whole. Examples include tinkering with

[7] Raymond Villers, "Control and Freedom in a Decentralized Company," *Harvard Business Review*, Vol. XXXII, No. 2, p. 95.

[8] One of the major difficulties here is that the organization structure itself is often only vaguely understood. Problems of organization are discussed in many management texts. See Pfiffner and Sherwood, *Administrative Organization* (Englewood Cliffs, N. J.: Prentice-Hall, Inc., 1960); March and Simon, *Organizations* (New York: John Wiley & Sons, 1958).

[9] Any thorough study of an information system is likely to disclose points of strength and weakness in the organization. No management accounting system by itself can cure basic weaknesses in executive talent or organization structure. However, it can pinpoint areas that demand attention.

scrap and usage reports, encouraging false timekeeping on the part of subordinates, reducing costs by lowering quality or by causing higher costs in other departments and, in general, doing "a little monkey business to come out right."

These examples do not necessarily imply nefarious behavior on the part of the individual manager. Often it is merely a matter of faulty cost analysis that is engendered by the accounting system. For example, the use of *net* assets as an investment base for judging managerial efficiency may encourage incorrect decisions by divisional management. If assets are replaced or scrapped before they are fully depreciated, the division may have to show a loss. Even though such a loss is irrelevant to replacement decisions (except for its impact on the timing of future income tax outlays), it does affect the division's immediate profit and could wrongly influence the division manager's decision.[10]

The successful use of budgets, standards, and various other measuring sticks is largely dependent on their value as motivating devices — as mechanisms that will influence managers and subordinates to act in accordance with the desires of top management. For example, different types of motivation may result when maintenance costs are charged to a responsibility center on the basis of (1) a rate per maintenance labor hour, (2) a rate per job, or (3) a single amount per month.[11] Anthony has commented on the motivational approach as follows:

> The usefulness of such a motivational approach becomes apparent when the concepts are applied to a practical control problem. Without such an approach, one can easily become immersed in pointless arguments on such matters as whether rent should be allocated on the basis of square footage or cubic footage. There is no sound way of settling such disputes. With the notion of motivation, the problem comes into clear focus. What cost constructions are most likely to induce people to take the action that management desires? Answering this question in a specific situation is difficult. . . .[12]

Although the views on these matters are far from settled,[13] most accountants and executives probably would agree with the following summary observations on costs for motivation:

[10] For an interesting discussion of how division managers' interests can conflict with the interests of the company as a whole, see John Dearden, "Problem in Decentralized Profit Responsibility," *Harvard Business Review* (May-June, 1960), pp. 79–86.

[11] Report of the 1955 Committee on Cost Concepts, American Accounting Association, *The Accounting Review* (April, 1956), p. 189. Also see Norton M. Bedford, "Cost Accounting as a Motivation Technique," *N.A.(C.)A. Bulletin* (June, 1957), pp. 1250–1257.

[12] Robert N. Anthony, "Cost Concepts for Control," *Accounting Review* (April, 1957), p. 234. Anthony has suggested that a control technique can be judged in two ways: by the *direction* and by the *strength* of its motivation. See his *Management Accounting* (rev. ed.; Homewood, Ill.: Richard D. Irwin, Inc., 1960), p. 317.

[13] For a provocative view, see Andrew Stedry, *Budget Control and Cost Behavior* (Englewood Cliffs, N. J.: Prentice-Hall, Inc., 1960).

Interview results show that a particular figure does not operate as a norm, in either a score-card or attention-directing sense, simply because the controller's department calls it a standard. It operates as a norm only to the extent that the executives and supervisors, whose activity it measures, accept it as a fair and attainable yardstick of their performance. Generally, operating executives were inclined to accept a standard to the extent that they were satisfied that the data were *accurately recorded*, that the standard level was *reasonably attainable*, and the variables it measured were *controllable* by them.[14]

The above quotation centers on three guides that are basic to the management accountant's work in this area:

1. Score-keeping data should be *accurate*.
2. Budgets or standards should be *understood* and *accepted* as reasonably attainable goals.
3. The items used to judge performance must be *controllable* by the recipient.

IMPORTANCE OF ACCURACY: THE SCORE-KEEPING FUNCTION

The success of the score-keeping function in management accounting depends heavily on accuracy. Earlier we saw that relevancy and accuracy were both important but that accuracy was a subobjective in any conceptual approach to management accounting. This in no way meant that accuracy was unimportant. An accounting system will not mean much to management if the score-keeping function is haphazard. This problem of having source documents reflect physical realities is immense and pervasive.

For example, Scharff[15] had a study made of the accuracy of time reporting in the shops of a large steel and alloy plate fabricator. Each workman reported his own time. The findings revealed that the time reported against any job could vary as much as 15 or 20 percent from actual time without this circumstance being detected by the foreman's checking of time cards at the end of the day or by other checks, such as comparing estimated with actual hours, etc. The two most glaring sources of error were, first, inadvertently charging time to the wrong job and, second, willfully charging time to the wrong job when it was obvious that a given job was running over the estimated hours. In all, some twenty-five sources of error were identified. Scharff believes that the average accountant should be more sensitive to possible errors, more aware of the futility of trying to get time reported accurately in small increments, and more conscious of the natural tendency of individuals to report their activities so as to minimize their individual bother and maximize their personal showing.

---

[14] Simon, *et al., op. cit.*, p. 29.
[15] Sam E. Scharff, "The Industrial Engineer and the Cost Accountant," *N.A.A. Bulletin* (March, 1961), pp. 17–18.

Understanding the Acceptance of Goals:
The Attention-Directing or Interpretative Function

Score-keeping is essential for cost accumulation, but attention-directing is the key to augmenting management's appreciation of the accounting function. The accountant's "staff" role includes being an attention-director (interpreter and analyst) and a score-keeper (cost accumulation and reporter — a policeman of sorts). However, these two roles often clash. Therefore, as mentioned earlier, the accounting department should divorce attention-directing from score-keeping. Otherwise, the day-to-day routine, the unending deadlines, and the insidious pressures of cost accumulation will shunt attention-directing (with the accompanying frequent contacts between accountants and operating people) into the background and, most likely, into oblivion.

The attention-directing roles (for example, explaining variances) should be occupied by capable, experienced accountants who, at least to some degree, can talk the line manager's language. Indeed, the attention-directors are the individuals who will largely establish the status of the controller's department in the company. Close, direct, active contacts between accountants and operating managers strengthen understanding and acceptability of the standards, budgets, and reports that are the measuring devices of performance.[16]

Controllability of Items: The Importance of
Cost Behavior Patterns

Management accountants are increasingly aware of the desirability of distinguishing between controllable and uncontrollable items on a performance report. From the viewpoint of planning and controlling operations, little is accomplished by mixing controllable and uncontrollable items in the same report; in fact the indiscriminate listing of such costs often leads to confusion and discouragement on the part of the departmental manager. Again, the motivational impact should provide the guide here. For example, some top managements assign central research costs and facilities to divisions, not because the resulting divisional rates of return can be defended but because the division manager's resentment sparks an interest in central research activities. On the other hand, many accountants confine performance reports to controllable items only.

This fundamental idea that individuals should be charged only with costs subject to their control is conceptually appealing. Practically, however, there is still much to be learned about interpreting and using the following guides:

[16] Simon *et al.*, *op. cit.*, pp. 45–56.

There are few, if any, elements of cost that are the sole responsibility of one person. Some guides in deciding the appropriate costs to be charged to a person (responsibility center) are as follows:

a. If the person has authority over both the acquisition and the use of the services, he should be charged with the cost of such services.

b. If the person can significantly influence the amount of cost through his own action, he may be charged with such costs.

c. Even if the person cannot significantly influence the amount of cost through his own action, he may be charged with those elements with which the management desires him to be concerned, so that he will help to influence those who are responsible.[17]

OBJECTIVE OF LONG-RANGE PLANNING AND SPECIAL DECISIONS

NEED FOR A GENERAL APPROACH

Management accounting has a clear need for a general approach to accounting for special decision-making purposes. Existing literature and practice are characterized by diversity of general approaches and by disjointed efforts to meet very specific needs. Managerial economists, operations researchers, and statistical decision theorists perhaps have made more progress than accountants in attempting to formulate general quantitative approaches to special decisions. The rise of operations research as a distinct field may indicate that not enough practicing accountants have responded to the management need for aid in tackling these business problems.

The area of long-range planning and special decisions offers very imposing problems for executives. Management accountants need to keep abreast of the growing body of knowledge and standards concerning the decision-making process. For example, the general superiority of discounted cash flow approaches in capital budgeting decisions is being increasingly acknowledged.[18] The correct application of relevant cost analysis, discounted cash flow techniques, and possibly statistical probability theory will help management toward intelligent decision-making. All of these techniques can easily be deemed to fall within the province of the management accountant's problem-solving function.

At the same time, the need for a team approach to these decisions is well recognized. The effective management accountant knows when to call upon

---

[17] Report of 1955 Committee on Cost Concepts, *op. cit.*, p. 189.
[18] N.A.A. Research Report No. 35, *Return on Capital as a Guide to Managerial Decisions* (New York: National Association of Accountants, 1959).

appropriate specialists such as mathematicians, statisticians, industrial engineers, and others.[19]

There are two joint guides for the accountant in this area: (1) an awareness of what constitutes relevant data for special decisions and (2) a recognition of the conflicts existing between certain accounting concepts and purposes.

RELEVANT DATA FOR SPECIAL DECISIONS

The isolation and measurement of *relevant* revenue and cost factors are by far the most challenging chores in the area of special decisions. Business decision-making entails choosing between alternative courses of action. The alternative actions take place in the future, whether it be five seconds or many years ahead; hence, the decision will be influenced by the expected results under the various alternatives. The financial ingredients of the forecast must necessarily be based on expected future data. Consequently, to be relevant for these purposes, all data must be expected future data.

But *all* future data are not necessarily relevant to a given decision; only those data that will be *different* under alternatives are relevant. For example, relevant costs for special decisions are those *future* costs that will be *different* under available alternatives. The key question in determining relevancy is, "What difference will it make?"

For example, assume that a company is thinking of rearranging its plant facilities. Accounting records show that past direct labor costs were $2.00 per unit. No wage rate changes are expected, but the rearrangement is expected to reduce direct labor usage by 25 percent. Direct material costs of $6.00 per unit will not change under either alternative. An analysis follows:

	Relevant Costs per Unit	
	Do Not Rearrange	Rearrange
Direct labor	$2.00	$1.50

The cost comparison above is one of *expected future costs* that will *differ* under alternatives. The $2.00 direct labor charge may be the same as in the past, and the past records may have been extremely helpful in preparing the $2.00 forecast. The trouble is that most accountants and managers view the $2.00 past cost as the future cost. But the crucial point is that the $2.00 is an expected future cost, not a past cost. *Historical costs in themselves are*

---

[19] Although the electronic computer has enlarged the accountant's opportunities, it has also accelerated a challenge — the threat of other quantitative specialists. The management accountant should view accounting broadly and learn how allied disciplines pertain to his job. Otherwise, the management scientists, the statisticians, and the operations researchers may nibble away at his job and gradually devour it — leaving for the accountants only the routine duty of score-keeping for income statements and balance sheets.

irrelevant though they may be the best available basis for estimating future costs.

The direct material costs of $6.00 per unit are expected future costs, not historical costs. Yet these future costs are irrelevant because they will not differ under alternatives. There may be no harm in preparing a comparative analysis that includes both the relevant direct labor cost forecast and the irrelevant direct material cost forecast:

	Cost Comparison per Unit	
	Do Not Rearrange	*Rearrange*
Direct material	$6.00	$6.00
Direct labor	2.00	1.50

However, note that we can safely ignore the direct material cost, because it is not an element of difference between the alternatives. The point is that irrelevant costs may be included in cost comparisons for decisions, provided that they are included properly and do not mislead the decision-maker. A corollary point is that concentrating solely on relevant costs may eliminate cluttersome irrelevancies and may sharpen both the accountant's and the manager's thinking regarding costs for decision-making.

In summary, Exhibit 1 shows that relevant costs for decisions are expected future costs, that will differ under alternatives. Historical costs, while helpful in predicting relevant costs, are always irrelevant costs *per se.*

EXHIBIT 1

Past Costs		*Expected Future Costs*	
(often used as a guide for prediction)		*Do Not Rearrange*	*Rearrange*
Direct material	$6.00	$6.00*	$6.00*
			------- *Second* line of demarcation
Direct labor	2.00	2.00	1.50

First line
of
demarcation in a conceptual
approach to distinction between
"relevant" and "irrelevant"

* Although these are expected future costs, they are irrelevant because they are the same for both alternatives. Thus, the second line of demarcation is drawn between those costs that are the same for the alternatives under consideration and those that differ; *only* the latter are relevant costs *as defined here.*

The basic approach to relevant cost analysis provides a common thread among all special decisions. The accountant or executive who develops an understanding of the concept of relevancy has taken a giant stride toward being able to analyze properly the quantitative aspects of any special decision, whether it be make or buy, the special order, buy or rent, equipment replacement, and so forth.

Note, too, that the area of special decisions again demonstrates the contrast between relevancy and accuracy. For example, the conventional ledgers amass data that are, in varying degrees, considered accurate or at least objectively determinable. Yet in long-range planning and special decisions, all the key data employed are necessarily expected future data. No general ledger system yet devised can possibly produce such data *per se*. Admittedly, much historical ("accurate") data may be helpful in predicting the appropriate future (relevant) data. But, in exercising his problem-solving function, the management accountant looks at the future first. He then selects the forecasting procedure that seems best under the circumstances.

Here we see that management accounting's scope is not limited by whatever accounting system design is used for routine data compilation, no matter how impressive and responsive the system may be. The problems of management accounting are too broad and too deep to be jammed into a single systems design, even if it is attuned to multi-purpose uses.

CONFLICT OF CONCEPTS AND PURPOSES

Heavy spending on capital assets since World War II has been accompanied by a hearty interest on the part of economists, financial analysts, and accountants in management approaches to these capital budgeting decisions. Space does not permit an expanded discussion of the technical issues here.

Much of the uproar has arisen because conventional accounting practices have not been aimed at the needs of the specific decision-making process. Regarding the relative merits of capital budgeting techniques, N.A.A. Research Report No. 35 rightly favors the discounted cash flow technique. The discounted cash flow method is more objective because its answer is not directly influenced by decisions as to depreciation methods, capitalization versus expense decisions, and conservatism. Erratic flows of revenue and expenses over a project's life are directly considered under discounted cash flow but are "averaged" under the financial statement (conventional) method. "The financial statement method utilizes concepts of capital and income which were originally designed for the quite different purpose of accounting for periodic income and financial position."[20]

[20] *Ibid.*, p. 64.

COST BEHAVIOR AND OVERALL REPORTING

The need for knowledge of cost behavior patterns pervades all functions of management accounting. For example, we have already seen the need for distinguishing between controllable and uncontrollable costs. In addition, so-called *breakeven analysis* cannot be conducted effectively without assurance that the cost-volume-profit relationships depicted are valid and reasonably accurate. So, while he recognizes the importance of cost accounting for compiling costs of product, the management accountant is also concerned with a host of other cost concepts. He realizes that no single cost concept is pertinent for all purposes. He has what may be called a *relevant costing* viewpoint.

Accounting reports should be designed to highlight the relevant data approach that has been supported here. For example, as a minimum, the income statement should be designed to facilitate its possible use for many purposes, not just one. As Exhibit 2 demonstrates, the income statement for management use should no longer aim at producing one income figure. Modern needs have made a singular concept of income obsolete.

The model income statement focuses on the appropriate data for overall appraisals of current performance. Also, special decisions such as pricing, dropping or adding products, advertising and promoting specific products, and selecting distribution channels are more likely to be based on relevant information. The conventional income statement often fails to distinguish between fixed and variable costs; controllable and uncontrollable costs; and joint (common) and separable costs. These distinctions are vital for judging performance and for various marketing, manufacturing, and financial decisions.

Examples of how different figures in Exhibit 2 may be relevant for various purposes follow (numbers refer to those at left of exhibit):

1. Contribution margin: This is particularly helpful in selecting which products to push and in quickly estimating the changes in profits that will ensue from fluctuations in volume or product mix.[21]

2. Performance margin: This version of income is probably most appropriate for judging performance by division managers or product managers. It is superior to the contribution margin for this purpose because these managers can influence certain fixed costs, which are sometimes called *programmed* or *managed* costs. (Note that while certain programmed costs, such as salesmen's salaries, may be easily traced to divisions, they may not be directly traceable to products.)

3. Segment margin: This is computed after deducting the directly identifiable fixed costs that are generally considered uncontrollable in the

[21] For a number of examples of the usefulness of the contribution margin see N.A.A. Research Report 37, *Current Application of Direct Costing*, 1961.

short run. Although this figure may be helpful as a crude indicator of long-run segment profitability, it should ordinarily not influence appraisals of current performance.

4. Net income before income taxes: This may sometimes be a helpful gauge of the long-run earning power of a whole company. However, the attempt to refine this ultimate measure by breaking it into segments (and still have the whole equal the sum of the parts) seldom can yield meaningful results. Here again, we see where relevancy is a more fundamental concept than accuracy. It is difficult to see how segment performance can be judged on the basis of net income after deductions for a "fair" share of general company costs over which the segment manager exerts no influence. Examples of such costs would be central research and central administrative costs. Despite the example of allocation to Divisions A and B, unless the general company costs are clearly separable, the usefulness of such allocation is questionable.

Responsibility for Selecting Management Accounting Practices

An enlightened chief management accountant, working with top management and qualified internal or external consultants, should bear primary responsibility for selecting company management accounting practices. He should tap all resources, including the industry trade associations, the professional accounting bodies, outside auditors, government agencies, friends in the industry, and the growing literature on management and management accounting.

The biggest danger here is probably the temptation to superimpose a sample management accounting system on a company without making a tough-minded appraisal of the underlying needs of the organization and its individual executives.

Despite the obvious need for the tailor-making of management accounting systems, outside groups have an opportunity to propel the progress of management accounting. There is a continuing need for research and education, such as that conducted by the N.A.A., to describe current practices that are effective for specified purposes. Most important, there is a burgeoning mass of fundamental knowledge that should be conveyed by the N.A.A., other associations, and educational institutions if management accounting is to thrive.[22]

---

[22] Critics of conventional education in accountancy basically maintain that too much effort is given to preparing scorekeepers and not enough to educating attention-directors and problem-solvers. See Herbert F. Taggart, "Cost Accounting Versus Cost Bookkeeping," *Accounting Review* (April, 1951), pp. 141–151.

EXHIBIT 2 The Relevant Costing Approach: Model Income Statement by Segments* (In thousands of dollars)

	Company as a Whole	Company Breakdown into Two Divisions		Possible Breakdown of Division B Only				
		Division A	Division B	Not Allocated	Product 1	Product 2	Product 3	Product 4
Net sales	1,500	500	1,000	0	300	200	100	400
Variable manufacturing cost of sales	780	200	580	0	120	155	45	260
Manufacturing contribution margin	720	300	420	0	180	45	55	140
Variable selling and administrative costs	220	100	120	0	60	15	25	20
1. Contribution margin	500	200	300	0	120(40%)	30(15%)	30(30%)	120(30%)
Fixed expenses directly identifiable with divisions:								
Programmed** fixed costs (certain advertising, sales promotion, engineering, research, management consulting, and supervision costs)	190	110	80	45***	10	6	4	15
2. Performance margin	310	90	220	(45)	110	24	26	105
Other fixed costs (generally uncontrollable, such as depreciation, property taxes, insurance, and perhaps the division manager's salary)	70	20	50	20	3	15	4	8
3. Segment margin	240	70	170	(65)	107	9	22	97
Joint fixed costs (not clearly or practically allocable to any segment except by some questionable allocation base)	135	45	90	(no allocations attempted beyond Divisions A and B)				
4. Net income before income taxes	105	25	80					

* There are two different types of segments illustrated here: *divisions* and *products*. A *segment* is any line of activity or subdivision of the business for which separate determination of costs and sales is wanted. Examples might be divisions, products, customers, plants, territories, and so forth.
** Programmed costs are those relatively fixed costs arising from policy decisions of management; they may have no particular relation to any base of activity. These are controllable at least when they are planned.
*** Only those costs clearly identifiable with particular products within a division should be allocated.

Conclusion

An understanding of the overall purposes and functions of the accounting system is basic to choosing effective accounting practices for reporting to management. The business information system of the future should be a multi-purpose system with a highly selective reporting scheme. It will be highly integrated and will serve three main purposes: (1) routine reporting on financial results, oriented primarily for external parties (score-keeping); (2) routine reporting to management, primarily for planning and controlling current operations (score-keeping and attention-directing); and (3) special reporting to management, primarily for long-range planning and non-recurring decisions (problem-solving).

Any guide to management accounting must aim at supplying relevant information — the basic need. Relevant data may be defined broadly as that data which will lead to an optimum decision, a decision that will best aid individuals toward overall organizational objectives.

With regard to the objective of planning and controlling operations, some of the more important guides center about responsibility accounting, accounting techniques for motivation in harmony with organizational goals, accurate score-keeping, full-fledged attention-directing, and careful classifying of controllable items.

With regard to long-range planning and special decisions, there is an evident need for a general, future-oriented approach that de-emphasizes historical revenues and costs, and there is a need for recognizing the conflict between the purposes and methods of conventional accounting and management accounting.

The accounting reports themselves should be structured to highlight relevant data. The need for knowledge of cost behavior patterns pervades all functions of management accounting. Reports at various management levels should distinguish between controllable and uncontrollable costs, variable and fixed costs, and joint (common) and separable costs.

The chief management accountant, working with top management and qualified internal or external consultants, should bear primary responsibility for the selection of company management accounting practices. In order to execute this responsibility, he needs to keep abreast of the growing body of fundamental knowledge in management accounting. Moreover, he must see that his staff receives training and experience in attention-directing and problem-solving as well as score-keeping, if the role of management accounting is to flourish in the organizations of tomorrow.

2 *The charge of this committee is to review standard managerial decision models for the purpose of making recommendations regarding the preparation and reporting of accounting information needed to implement the models, with reference to the standards for accounting information suggested in the American Accounting Association Statement of Basic Accounting Theory. This document is a tentative statement along the long road to a full understanding of how accounting and decision models should fit together. The report advocates a modern interpretation of accounting — one that responds to the broad needs for managerial information. It concentrates on how accounting systems may best identify, measure, record, and then report the results of decisions that must be made.*

Report of Committee
on Managerial
Decision Models*

*American Accounting Association
Committee on Managerial Decision Models†*

Some soothsayers, including even a few accountants, have predicted that management accounting, as we know it, will vanish by the end of the century. Accountants will be strictly data collectors, scorekeepers in the most mundane sense. According to these merchants of gloom, a new breed of information specialists will take over the accountant's existing attention-directing and problem-solving functions as a part of their very broad duties.

* *From* The Accounting Review, *Vol. XLIV, No. 1 (Supplement, 1969), pp. 42–76 excerpted. Reprinted by permission of the American Accounting Association.*

† Membership: Charles T. Horngren, Chairman, Stanford University; Hector R. Anton, University of California; Harold Bierman, Jr., Cornell University; Eugene H. Brooks, Jr., University of North Carolina; Peter A. Firmin, Tulane University; Ellsworth Morse, Jr., U.S. General Accounting Office; Thomas H. Williams, University of Texas; Zenon Zannetos, Massachusetts Institute of Technology.

21

The likelihood of such an event is directly dependent on how accountants view their role as providers of information to management. This report advocates a modern interpretation of accounting that responds to the broad needs for management information.

The accountant must obtain the necessary qualifications for playing a larger rather than a smaller role in information systems. Many accountants are distressed by the prospective narrowing of their work as operations researchers and similar specialists obtain some control over information systems. However, if accountants are to maintain or increase their position, they must understand where decision models relate to the planning and controlling functions.

We have decided to concentrate on how accounting systems may best identify, measure, record, and report the relevant data needed to implement decision models and then report the results of the decisions that are made. Too often, decision model information is considered as being separate and distinct from management accounting information; each set of information may be accumulated and used without ever being viewed as interlocking sub-parts of a cohesive over-all information system. This is undesirable and wasteful. Our major objective is to fuse the two, to link the best concepts and practices in management accounting with the power of the decision models now available . . .

I. General Overview

A. The Nature of Decision Models

Accountants continually work with accounting systems and financial reports, which are financial models of company operations. Models are useful because they provide a conceptual representation of realities, enabling the decision maker to anticipate and measure the effects of alternative actions. In this section, we briefly discuss the general characteristics of decision models.

A *model* is a depiction of the relationships among the recognized factors in a particular situation; it emphasizes the key interrelationships and frequently omits some unimportant factors. Models have many forms and purposes: they may be descriptive or predictive; mathematical, physical or verbal; dynamic or static, and so on.

Decision making is choosing among alternatives; it occurs as managers conduct their planning and controlling functions. A decision model is one which, in effect, performs management's planning and control functions — but only to the extent that management delegates when the model is constructed and implemented. For example, management may decide that inventory levels should be regulated by a system based on a decision model that specifies when to order, how much to order, how much safety stock to carry, and so forth. From that point on, the system can fully perform the delegated inventory planning and control functions unless management explicitly intervenes.

Of course, a mathematical decision model may indicate a choice which is rejected by management because of more dominant legal, sociological, psychological, political, and other considerations not included in the specific model. In such instances, the output of the mathematical model is only one input into a more complicated decision model which includes qualitative as well as quantitative dimensions.

The outputs of many decision models are often used as the relevant inputs to higher-level decision making. The Department of Defense provides an example. Simulation or capital budgeting or other models may present evaluations of a vast array of alternatives. These evaluations are considered along with other factors not contained in the specific models before a final decision is made.

In mathematical decision models, the following steps are usually taken:

1. Specify an organizational objective which can be expressed quantitatively. This objective can take many forms. For brevity, we shall assume in this report that the objective is either to maximize profit or minimize cost. Other objectives are also possible, singly or in combination (for example, maximize market share, employee satisfaction or, in the case of governmental services, output).
2. Identify and describe the mathematical relationships between the relevant variables which affect the profit (cost or other objective). These variables are of two types: environmental and decision variables. The decision variables are subject to control of the decision maker, while environmental variables are not.
3. Perform the necessary mathematical operations, using the values identified in (2). The solution consists of finding the combination of values for the decision variables that maximizes profit (or minimizes cost), given the values for the environmental variables.

In almost every case, the objective to be maximized by the model is only one of several objective criteria important to the organization. In a business organization, for example, the goal of organizational survival usually may be regarded for practical purposes as a distinct constraint. In such a situation, any maximization of one objective must be carried out subject to constraints or the introduction of penalties. In addition, the optimal solution provided by the model should be regarded as merely one of a large family of optima which might result from varying the constraints. An over-all optimum would be possible where the constraints could be fully specified and the objectives fully described; however, in practice, we can only approach such a result.

To illustrate, consider a linear programming problem with a profit maximization objective subject to a constraint on supervisory time available. The solution provided by the model may be optimal if supervisory time is considered completely fixed, while in fact more supervisory time could be made available by having supervisors work overtime. In such a case, the maximum possible profit could vary with the amount of supervisory time regarded as available, and it would be logical to fix the time constraint by comparing the profit per incremental hour with the costs of obtaining the time. The principal difficulty would be that the cost of the policy described probably should include a reduction in "employee morale" because of more overtime. The question then becomes how much employee morale (a function of overtime hours) we are willing to trade for dollar profits.

The judicious use of decision models supplements intuition and implicit guides with explicit assumptions and criteria. If the decision can be depicted by a mathematical model, and if the model builder captures within his model the critical factors bearing on the decision, the resulting model is likely to lead to decisions that are more consistent with a firm's objectives.

Mathematical model building is sometimes criticized because the process of abstraction may drastically simplify the problem and overlook significant underlying factors or difficulties. Such a danger exists. Nevertheless, numerous examples of successful applications can be cited. Consider the widespread use of linear programming in scheduling production, blending raw materials, and selecting shipping routes. The test of success is not whether mathematical models are the perfect answers to the manager's needs, but whether such models provide better answers than would have been achieved via alternative techniques. (Of course, the relative costs and benefits of using various techniques are also important.)

The vastness and complexity of the entire management process preclude a complete takeover of management by mathematical decision models. Still, mathematical decision models are being increasingly used for planning and controlling operating activities. Examples include inventory control, transportation, and production scheduling models. This more widespread use of mathematical models has also prompted attempts to program parts of the management process formerly considered unprogrammable. To "program" means to describe a process in explicit step-by-step detail so that pre-determined rules can govern day-to-day performance. In a sense, the design and implementation of mathematical models require this transformation of unprogrammed activities into programmed activities. This suggests a close relationship between accounting and mathematical models because the more highly programmed the activity, the more essential it is for an accounting system to provide the needed information (see *Statement,* p. 47). To the extent that the models relieve the manager of his programmable tasks, he can concentrate on more complex management models at a higher level.

B. Behavioral Factors and Decision Models

The most widely used decision models are rooted in the tools and assumptions of economics. Their implementation, however, is apt to be affected by behavioral complications which sometimes are so complex that the original economic decision models must be drastically altered before they are used. Although we are aware of the cardinal importance of these behavioral considerations, we can do little here beyond underscoring the need for more research and stressing that an overwhelming amount of research on decision models and accounting is based on the flimsy assumption that the user is an economic man. The latter assumption is often necessary for productive analysis that supplies normative answers *which must then either be implemented or modified in light of attempts at implementation.*

Implementation is frequently a behavioral problem. Economic analysis, then, is not wrong or undesirable; it is simply incomplete. In his role as a supplier of information, the accountant must be concerned with both the economic decision models and their implementation as an entire package.

The trouble at this point is that our knowledge of behavioral effects is too fragmented. The information produced by decision models and accounting systems is supposed to "exert influence or have the potential for exerting influence on the designated actions" (*Statement,* p. 9). Little systematic evidence is available concerning the complex effects of decision models and accounting information on user behavior. Instead, the relationship is either overlooked or it is described by over-simplified assertions. Too often, the assertions or generalizations seem to be valid in one organization but not in another, usually because they are not based on any rigorously compiled evidence that permits *prediction* rather than *explanation.*

Because accounting information is aimed at users (external users as well as internal), hardly any major accounting issue can be resolved without making some assumptions about behavior. We need more evidence to find out which assumptions are valid. Behavioral considerations need intensive research of a fundamental kind. For example, the *Statement* assertion that "accounting information could usefully be expressed in probabilistic terms" (p. 55) contains the implicit assumption that the user will be more likely to make "better" decisions with probabilistic rather than with deterministic information. Certainly a more complete decision model may be specified using probabilities, but do users deal with probabilities in a consistent, "rational" way, as every good "economic man" should? The information specialist should know the answers to such questions before giving unqualified support to any particular timing, summarization, format, or configuration of information.

The increasing use of mathematical decision models has some intriguing behavioral ramifications. Dehumanization of specific planning and controlling functions occurs when mathematical models and computers are used.

Therefore, at least for the specific activities being analyzed, the human problem disappears as activities are finely programmed and computerized. But there are still many behavioral problems. How does the use of more rules and models affect the organization as a whole and the managers who determine the inputs to the models?

C. Relationships of the Statement Standards to Information for Decision Models

1. The Standard of Relevance. Relevance is clearly the dominant standard. Relevant information is that which bears upon or is useful to "the action it is designed to facilitate or the result it is desired to produce" (p. 9). For management planning, relevant costs (and relevant revenues) are those expected future costs (and revenues) which will be *different* for one or more of the alternatives under consideration. Information about these relevant costs and revenues has value only if it may change a decision from what it would have been had the information not been received.

Historical costs may be the basis for predicting expected future costs, but the latter are the necessary inputs to the relevant cost and decision models. This point is demonstrated in Exhibit 1 . . .

EXHIBIT 1

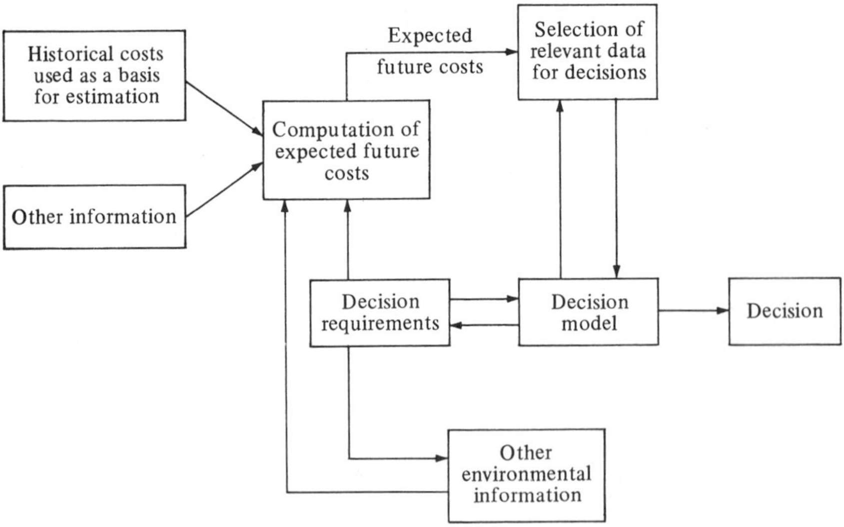

Relevant and irrelevant data are often intermingled; ordinarily, they should be sharply distinguished. Irrelevant information may do damage by contributing to confusion, error, and inefficiency, particularly if the irrelevance is not detected.

The "other information" flowing into the decision model box in Exhibit 1 includes all behavioral and social considerations. The relevant economic cost is not the only concern of management. Psychological and public policy considerations also frequently affect the actual decision.

The concept of cost as the forgoing of a benefit (the opportunity cost concept) is implicit in decision models. This view differs from the traditional idea that considers sacrifice as a "using up" or expiration of historical cost. The increased use of model-related, future-oriented opportunity costs may liberalize accountants' attitudes regarding the appropriate uses of alternatives to historical cost.

Although the standard of relevance is indisputably fundamental in spanning the gaps between accounting and decision models, it represents only the conceptual beginning. That is, the standard of relevance must be used to find answers to the questions of what inputs belong in the models and how the inputs should be measured. But that does not get us very far when we consider the overwhelming practical problems of preparing and reporting accounting information for implementing decision models. For example, in particular instances we may know that opportunity costs are relevant, but we may not know how to obtain reliable measurements of such costs. Furthermore, even if such measurements are possible, the accountant usually does not have a practical cost-and-value-of-information model which assures him that the potential benefits from making such measurements will exceed their costs.

2. The Standard of Verifiability. Verifiability aims at protecting the user from arbitrary subjective judgments by those who generate the data. The standard of verifiability must be regarded as important but less crucial for internal reporting purposes than for external reporting. Internal users are more often concerned with expected future data rather than historical data. Also, because managers usually are familiar with the underlying events, they are often in a better position to judge the validity of the accounting information . . .

Verifiability has long been regarded as more important for control and evaluation than for planning. The increasing use of decision models employing future costs and benefits will increase the importance of verifiability in the planning phases of internal accounting. Management audits, which stress the use of correct decision-making procedures by management, will focus on both planning and controlling. For this reason, evidence must be accumulated not only on day-to-day control activities, but on the procedures used for various planning decisions, and the relevance and accuracy of data employed. As aspects of planning and control become increasingly programmed, the information used therein may have to be sufficiently verifiable to allow qualified individuals (or machines) to develop essentially similar measures or conclusions from an examination of the same evidence . . .

Despite its desirability, verifiability must be traded for relevance in many instances. For example, it may be relatively easy to estimate the out-of-pocket costs of a research project that has resulted in a new product. Such costs may be verifiable but are irrelevant if a manager is seeking to estimate the value of the research project. The value would depend on estimates of future revenues and costs, items that may be impossible to verify objectively at the instant of the decision . . .

Quantitative decision models have in some cases provided the means for obtaining relevant information with increased verifiability. A linear programming model, for example, may display opportunity costs and may specify the range of outputs and inputs over which those costs are relevant . . .

3. The Standard of Freedom from Bias. It is difficult to relate clearly the standard of freedom from bias to information for decision models. Two kinds of bias are identified (but not defined). "Statistical" bias is said to result from the use of inappropriate techniques of measurement; "personal" bias apparently encompasses conscious manipulation of information for personal gain. In fact, however, deliberate manipulation of information might be implemented by selecting "statistically" biased measures . . .

Bias, although used in many contexts, is generally defined as the amount of the displacement from some "true value". As used in the field of statistics, for instance, bias generally represents the amount of difference between the expected value of some estimate (statistic) obtained by sampling and the true value of the parameter in the universe being estimated. In everyday usage, a biased opinion is one which can be expected to differ in a systematic manner (in a particular direction) from the typical or "average" opinion on the subject regarding the "true value".

Because bias is defined as a difference from some true value, it is not possible to deal in an operational manner with that concept without first specifying what the true value is or how it can be derived. One type of bias in accounting information can be usefully defined as the difference between the expected value of measurements produced by some set of measurement rules (such as absorption inventory costing) and the corresponding measurement of those values which would produce optimal decisions when introduced into a user's decision model (perhaps, in a particular case, direct costing). Because this difference is a result of the measurement rules employed, we will call it *measurement system bias.*

Obviously, when accounting bias is defined in terms of users' decision models, bias has no operational meaning until the decision models are specified. Also, a particular measurement or type of measurement may be unbiased for certain users or uses and biased for others . . .

On the other hand, in many instances deliberate bias may be beneficial if it is not personal. Deliberate impersonal bias would arise where the consensus of informed opinion would favor the insertion of bias. Management may report historical and predictive information in such a way as to motivate desired action in users. Setting of sales forecasts and various cost targets (standards or budgets) may be conditioned by their motivational impact. Standard costs, for example, might properly be set at a level which represents a biased estimate of actually attainable costs. Choice of methods for displaying historical information also may be guided by motivational considerations.

The distinction between the insertion of bias in information for motivating and in information about actual performance is subtle but important. Deliberate bias, in the context of information for motivating, may properly relate to the specification of *content* of input data. For example, should the budget be tight or loose? In the context of reporting actual performance, however, such bias will usually relate to selection of *procedures* for reporting and display . . .

Unavoidable personal bias exists almost universally because the accountant must make subjective judgments of a professional nature. In some instances, management may not prescribe formats for displaying either historical or predictive information. Managers may not even stipulate the information they need for their own decision models. In such cases, the accountant, as the expert in measurement, must often present information which in *his* judgment is proper input for the decision model or operation in question. In such cases, the introduction of personal bias in the information system may be unavoidable because our knowledge of optimal decision techniques is insufficient. This is why proper documentation for verification is necessary . . .

In summary, accounting, as a measurement process, attempts to reach unbiased estimates of particular values (even though bias may be deliberately introduced later). Unbiased estimates, in turn, require objective procedures based upon clearly defined inputs to known decision models. Bias can be substantially reduced where subjective judgments can be eliminated from the information process. The use of standard decision models has great potential in this area.

In order to develop accounting information which is relatively free of bias, therefore, it will be necessary to move further in the direction of tying accounting to quantifiable decision models.

4. The Standard of Quantifiability. We are unsure whether quantifiability is a standard in the same sense as the other standards. A particular item of information is either quantifiable, or it is not. Accounting information is often regarded as quantitative by definition. Under this view, the standard of quantifiability may be regarded as redundant — as not being subject to the same trade-offs that are frequently made among relevance, verifiability, and freedom from bias.

However, if we think of information in general, quantifiability can be viewed as a standard that may be traded off against other standards. Accounting is not necessarily confined to reporting quantitative information. For example, the concept of full disclosure in annual reports stipulates that non-quantitative information be included in financial statements where required to make them not misleading.

Moreover, quantifiability can be a misleading standard to the extent that it may contribute to the tendency for accountants and managers to weigh the quantifiable, less relevant item more heavily than the nonquantifiable, more relevant item. This is particularly graphic where short-range objectives dominate because they are easily measurable and because they may fit snugly into an over-all system. The tendency to over-emphasize short-run profits is an example . . .

In short, qualitative information may be relevant, and quantitative information may be irrelevant, or at least less useful.

The point is that accountants should seek to quantify as much important information as seems feasible. Quantification can systematically capture information that may otherwise be overlooked. This is a desirable strength of accounting, as long as such quantification does not distract from other information that may be more important but less precise . . .

5. The Standard of Economic Feasibility. As every manager and accountant knows, there are often heavy costs associated with the improvement of information systems. The potential benefits must exceed these costs if a prospective change in a system is to be justified on economic grounds . . . Economic feasibility must be a part of the trade-offs among relevance, freedom from bias, and verifiability. Economic feasibility may be measured by using cost and value of information models, the least developed but most universally important models for making decisions about the design of information systems . . .

D. General Implications of Decision Models for Accounting Systems and Accountants

1. The Accountant's Role and the Need for Integrated Information Systems. Many types of information[1] are required by decision models. What types of information should be considered as falling within the domain of accounting? There are no clear-cut answers to this difficult question, but we choose to view accounting information and accounting systems broadly as encompassing all economic data bearing on the affairs of a given entity . . .

The objective of the internal accountant has always been to generate useful information for management. As the usefulness of quantitative decision models becomes more widely understood by managers, the demand

---

[1] "Information" and "data" have a variety of meanings in both the technical and popular literature. Information is often conceived of as that subset of data which is useful for a particular purpose. A rigorous distinction in this terminology is not necessary for our purposes.

for information as model inputs will grow. Such a demand can be satisfied in many ways. For example, separate data-gathering systems can exist for each model. However, proliferation of systems would probably be wasteful because of the likely duplication of effort. Organizations and management can generally gain by combining the conventional accounting system and the other data-gathering functions necessary for decision models. Therefore, the accounting system should be designed to insure ready accessibility to the information required by the models as well as to present types of accounting information.

A major disadvantage of multiple information systems is the likelihood of "overlap". Different data libraries and different basic assumptions may produce different and sometimes contradictory information bearing on the same decision, leading to confusion and possibly to the use of irrelevant data. The various techniques used for capital budgeting are an example, particularly where discounted cash flow approaches are used for subsequent evaluation of performance. (See Section II for an elaboration.)

A contrasting disadvantage of multiple systems is the problem of "information gaps". None of the competing systems may provide the total information needed. If a company is considering hiring additional salesmen, for example, the market research group may supply the necessary estimates of incremental revenues, while the accounting system may supply out-of-pocket costs of hiring new salesmen. However, no accurate estimate of the incremental costs of selecting, training, and supervising additional salesmen may be available from either source . . .

Accountants, because of their experience and skills in systematic data gathering, should be able to provide needed information efficiently and economically. However, to do so, the accountant must be familiar with the assumptions of the mathematical decision models. If the accountant does not possess such understanding, there is a serious danger that the model builders will obtain erroneous or irrelevant data. The need for accountants to obtain adequate understanding of decision models is critical, not only for the future role of the accountant in organizations, but also for the increased success of managers and quantitative specialists who build and utilize the models . . .

2. The Raw Material of the Information System: The Data Library. A problem which has long been of primary concern to accountants is that of identifying and measuring costs and benefits with sufficient verifiability (or objectivity) to insure the reliability of the information process. Historical exchange-based data have been favored because these are frequently single-valued and generally are easily verified. Such emphasis may work within limited objectives, but its scope is far too narrow for an over-all information system.

Accounting information deals with economic events and their effects on an entity. Accounting has traditionally focused on explicit transactions.

The accountant has scrutinized many events, has selected certain kinds of formal recording, and has labeled these as accounting transactions. Accounting in the future probably will have to broaden the kinds of events which are recorded to satisfy an increasing variety of objectives. Accounting information probably should incorporate some events or transactions not now recorded. It should be multi-dimensional, encompassing both the past and projections of the future . . .

Data generated by the routine operations of the organization usually can be collected relatively quickly and inexpensively. In contrast, the generation of special or nonroutine data often requires extensive planning and considerable additional expense. For these reasons, accounting systems have often been unable to supply needed but nonroutine information. Users frequently have had to transform the available information to their particular uses as best they could, or gather information in clumsy, error-prone ways, or go without crucial information.

New, less expensive data gathering, storage, and accessibility capabilities of computers will enhance the feasibility of having a system that essentially contains a library of raw data in as elementary, unstructured but well-defined form as possible, properly indexed for subsequent retrieval and stored so as to facilitate a wide variety of manipulation, classification, and aggregation. Such data may include many events which have not been traditionally recorded . . .

3. Internal vs. External Data. Decision models, to be effective, often must use information originating outside the organization. External information must be systematically obtained to supply the inputs for operation of the model. The pricing strategies of competitors, for example, might be considered important in competitive bidding and in determining the demand factor for use in an inventory model. To incorporate such a factor in the model, it would probably be necessary to monitor the selling prices of competitive products for a period of time to ascertain the functional relationships between these prices and the demand for products.

Accountants should be aware of the trend toward the greater use of external data. Decision models may need such information as industry output trends; regional production and sales by product classifications; relationships of sales to disposable income, population trends, or birth and death rates; competitor or industry advertising costs, research costs, or other measures. They should be prepared to incorporate such data in the accounting system wherever feasible and desirable . . .

Unless the collection of external data is incorporated as a routine part of information gathering, it tends to be neglected. No manager seems to miss anything, but at the same time many opportunities are not exploited because nobody has observed a shift in the environmental parameters soon enough for action.

4. The Problem of Uncertainty. Many quantitative decision models must deal in some manner with the problem of uncertainty. Control models must allow for the effects of random variations and measurement errors, while planning models are faced with the additional difficulty of accurate forecasting where the consequences of over- and under-estimation often differ. The traditional accounting attitude often regards past events as facts leading to unique measures of economic activities. The increased use of decision models may spur a statistical approach which regards each estimation as having a range of possible values . . .

To provide information for planning models, the accounting system should be structured to obtain useful information from unusual events. A shortage of raw material caused by highly unusual weather conditions, for example, might allow new understanding of certain cost relationships by producing observations of a low area of the production curve. This might result in substantial alterations of routine input data for planning models.

Planning techniques involving models typically deal with uncertainty either through the use of expected values (explicitly weighing possible outcomes by their probabilities of occurrence), or through sensitivity analysis (in which the values of possible alternative outcomes are compared). In either case, it is helpful to have reliable estimates of the probabilities of future states. Such information is often very difficult to obtain, but the organization of the accounting system so as to give information about the past can be of great help in assigning probabilities. For example, accounting systems frequently collect and report data on sales activities by season, month, or even day-of-week. Many organizations routinely use daily cash flow and cash position reports. Such information can be used to establish historical frequency distribution of sales and cash flow data which can be helpful in assigning probabilities to these types of events.

A central problem in using decision models for control is the effect of random events. Here again, the design of the accounting system may play an important part. The systematic use of supplementary measures (often related to externally generated data) can go far toward reducing the limitations of conventional data . . .

5. Incremental Measures and Problems of Classifying Information. Almost all data-gathering processes involve some degree of aggregation. The economics of information accumulation usually necessitates a level of aggregation that results in a considerable loss of detail and information potential. As a result, accounting information typically specifies average relationships over specified segments of some variable (such as time), whereas usually the optimization criteria of managerial decision models logically require incremental data. The supplying of average and incremental measures is a key need in adapting accounting systems to decision models; a data library should be able to provide both types of information. Classifications of accounts should be expanded to incorporate other characteristics, particularly those which help to identify cost behavior patterns.

E. SUMMARY AND CONCLUSION

Mathematical decision models will probably be used increasingly in all types of organizations. These models require the routine collection and analysis of data not previously processed. The accounting system should provide the information required by the models to the greatest extent feasible because the maintenance of separate information systems is likely to be uneconomic, and because accountants are well suited for the task. A fundamental reorientation of the accounting system will be required if accountants are to continue as major suppliers of information for planning and controlling.

Decision models are typically based on the assumption that their users are economic men. But the implementation of decision models is heavily affected by behavioral considerations. As a supplier of information, the accountant must be concerned with both the models themselves and their implementation. No practical plans for linking decision models and accounting can afford to ignore these behavioral complexities.

The standard of relevance provides the conceptual first step to coordinating accounting and decision models and to determining the appropriate inputs and how to measure them. As a practical matter, various perceptions of and trade-offs between the standards of quantifiability, relevance, verifiability, freedom from bias, and economic feasibility will determine the shape of the information systems.

As the specific models described in Section II illustrate, the data must encompass both the historical and the predictive. They must facilitate incremental analysis and projection, include non-monetary items, embrace external factors, include interval estimates and probability distributions, and range over several levels of aggregation. Such diverse needs, coupled with modern computer technology, point toward the information system of the future as being based on a data library containing raw data in a very elementary form codified for subsequent retrieval, manipulation, classification, and aggregation.

But capturing masses of raw data is not the only job of the accountant. He must necessarily examine how his classifications, aggregations and reports influence the validity of the models and the ultimate decision-making process. Accountants have often classified cost by object of expenditure, by function, and by cost behavior patterns. Now decision models will generate their own unique needs which must be transformed by the accountant into new classification systems.

We have focused largely on the types of data needed to facilitate the use of decision models. Future research must necessarily pursue this avenue further. However, there are two other major areas that also deserve the attention of researchers in accounting. The first area was mentioned earlier: the need to consider the behavioral implications of implementing the models. The second area, which is perhaps a facet of the first, is the need to base performance evaluation (control standards) on the planning models used.

As mathematical decision models become more widely utilized, accountants and managers will be confronted with some serious problems in coordinating the models and the accounting reports that are commonly used for evaluating management performance. That is, planning and control decisions will be made using concepts of incremental costs, cash flows, and opportunity costs. Unless subsequent performance reports are prepared on a consistent basis, the manager may be inclined to make decisions which will bolster his performance as monitored by the conventional accounting model. This may often lead to dysfunctional decision making. A primary example is capital budgeting, where the manager's decision may be more heavily affected by how his present and near-future income statements will appear than by the long-run merits of the decision as shown by a discounted cash flow model. Another example is inventory control. The heaviest cost of carrying inventory is usually the cost of funds invested, which is often an imputed cost. Unless performance reports recognize such a cost, managers will be confronted by an evaluation system which is inconsistent with the decision model.

A major challenge for the accountant is to devise a system for reporting performance that will be consistent with the models used to make decisions. This will mean modifying the traditional accrual full-cost statements based on historical transactions. Sometimes, as in capital budgeting, the performance report may be based on cash flows and may impute opportunity costs. In other instances, as in linear programming, the performance report must be geared to a "contribution to profit" basis accompanied by a limited amount of cost allocations. In any case, the scope and flexibility of the accountant must widen if accounting is to strengthen its aid to management.

In many organizations within the past fifteen years, the posture of accounting systems has shifted from a basic orientation toward external users to a primary orientation toward internal users. For example, consider the rise of responsibility accounting, market-based transfer prices, contribution margin reporting, and profit centers. This trend will probably accelerate and bring with it a de-emphasis of the conventional accounting model geared toward external reporting. The latter should be a sub-set of the accounting system. The overall product should be a tightly-knit system that feeds the best available decision models and supports them via performance reports consistent with the models. But this progress cannot occur without a major commitment by management to use available technology and by researchers to investigate such difficult problems — problems that have both economic and behavioral implications.

II. Specific Decision Models

A. Cost and Value of Accounting Information Models

A rational decision-maker must determine which information to collect. He should obtain information where the expected value of the incremental information exceeds its expected cost. The cost and value of information models are the most general in the sense that their objective is often to decide whether some other model (such as capital budgeting or inventory models) is economically feasible. That is, the cost and value of information models answer the question of whether the value of the additional information generated by the other specific models exceeds its costs. Frequently, value depends on the use to be made of the information as input to other models.

Certain fundamental cost-benefit relationships in the information processing function may be established. For a given state of the art of information generation, greater precision, reliability, frequency, or timeliness of information normally can be achieved only by incurring greater costs. Whether data are collected to serve the requirements of a capital budgeting model, an inventory control model, or some other specific managerial model does not alter this fundamental relationship.

Problems of measurement currently limit the implementation of general models of value and cost of accounting information. Nevertheless, such models aid our understanding and perspective regarding the economic feasibility of many decision models.

1. Cost Models. "Cost of Information" refers to the cost of generating a specific information set which can be identified with a particular output requirement, such as a specific decision or planning model or an environmental requirement for information such as those imposed by the legal or tax authorities. Within this framework, many decisions must be made about the information generating process . . .

When management has defined a set of information reporting requirements and the related data needs, it must identify the cost of the information-generating process. Typically, the following natural elements of cost will be incurred:

1. Amounts paid for personal service, including professional fees and administrative salaries paid in connection with system design and installation, and clerical, administrative, and maintenance salaries or wages paid in connection with system operation.
2. Costs of equipment rental or usage represented by rental payments or by economic depreciation and interest.
3. Cost of supplies purchased to facilitate clerical or maintenance operations.

4. Power and other utilities.

Generally, the unit prices of the cost factors enumerated above may be treated as environmental variables.

In many cases, the òutput of a cost of information model will serve as input to another model such as a pricing model. If management wishes to determine the cost of generating information so that it may choose among alternative courses of action, the short-run incremental costs of generating the information will be one relevant input. Even in such situations, however, determining the cost of information will require decisions regarding alternative uses of the fixed resources.[2]

Some cost elements which may not be easily measured should nevertheless be considered. For example, the installation of a new electronic data processing system usually causes upheaval and disruption of routine, changes in employee morale, obsolescence of employee skills, changes in organization structure, and other phenomena. Management functions may be drastically revised, and some routine management functions may be replaced by programs in the data processing system. These and other similar changes will result in costs that should be included. Typical overhead allocation processes may not attribute the costs of such changes to the cost of generating information.

Similarly, the cost of retraining employees whose skills need updating because of new data processing systems should be considered an incremental cost of generating information. In some cases the investment in training necessitated by the installation of a new data processing system will increase the worth of the employee and result in a benefit that exceeds the cost of the training program.

2. Value Models. Value of information may be conceptualized in terms of incremental expected profit or benefit which will result from the information. We will assume that the expected value of information is the maximum amount which a rational decision-maker would be willing to pay for additional information. The after-the-fact value is not the relevant measure in deciding whether the information should have been obtained.

Some information must be gathered because the failure to do so brings such heavy costs that the decision is obvious. For example, the penalties for not filing tax returns and other reports to governmental agencies usually cause managers to place a very high value on the information needed for compliance.

Despite the difficulties of quantifying the expected value of information, we should frequently attempt to compare the expected cost of additional information with its expected value. However, because the comparison is

---

[2] Sometimes a priority of needs must be established where information is needed for several different functions.

imprecise, and the process of comparison does have a cost, it may not be an improvement over the intuitive decision-process used by most managers.

We have restricted our discussion of the value of information to concepts of expected monetary value. However, an actual decision may depend on the way decision makers incorporate attitudes toward risk and the value of non-monetary benefits. The decision maker's perceptions about the relevance of information for specific decisions will influence the information that is generated and displayed and, in turn, the data that are collected.

Value of information also depends on its timeliness. We have stated that managers should seek information as long as the perceived incremental value of the information exceeds its expected incremental cost. But management may be forced to make a decision on the basis of less information than it would like, simply because there is insufficient time to acquire additional information before the decision must be made.

It is necessary for information to be received by the manager quickly to facilitate planning or controlling . . .

III. Inventory Models

Inventory management problems exist because of the need for acquiring and storing resources, often of a substantial magnitude, in order to meet expected future demands. An inventory model abstracts the behavior of such a system in order to provide a basis for decisions regarding the optimal level and pattern of investment in inventories. In most instances, an inventory model identifies the timing and size of inventory orders and provides a solution which will minimize the costs associated with administering the inventory.

SUMMARY OF REQUIRED INFORMATION

Four basic categories of information are required in order to implement the inventory model. These categories are:

1. Determination of decision variables
2. Measurement of environmental variables
3. Determination of cost components
4. Structure of operational relationships.

The decision variables most commonly considered in an inventory model are the order quantity and the reorder point. Although the amount of safety stock to be carried is sometimes considered a relevant decision variable, this is redundant in the general model; determination of the optimal reorder level provides a basis for servicing demand during the lead time. However, in the modified, practical approach suggested later, determination of a satisfactory safety stock level will become an explicit decision variable. Other decision variables should be incorporated in the model depending upon the individual circumstance. For example, the supply source would also become a relevant decision variable when different suppliers offer different unit prices, quantity discounts and/or different lead times.

The principal environmental variables include unit purchase costs of inventory, demand rate, and order lead time. In order to achieve some reasonable correspondence with reality, each of these three variables should reflect, implicitly or explicitly, the appropriate underlying probability distribution. It is particularly important to recognize the probabilistic nature of demand in many cases. Other environmental variables may include restrictions imposed by the supplier (e.g., minimum order size).

The major independent *cost components* are carrying costs, ordering costs, shortage costs, and overstock costs . . .

Operational relationships describe the assumptions about the interacting influences among the decision variables, the environmental variables and cost components. These assumptions preferably should be based upon empirical observations. However, for purposes of initiating the analysis, intuitive assumptions may be useful . . .

ELEMENTS OF COST COMPONENTS

The following costs are explicitly considered in this model.

Carrying costs include both out-of-pocket costs and opportunity costs associated with the function of physically maintaining, or holding, a stock of goods. The major costs normally identifiable with this function are insurance, taxes, and storage. The principal opportunity cost normally included in this classification is the imputed interest on funds directly invested in inventory as measured by the rate of return that may be gained through the best alternative use of such funds . . .

Ordering costs consist of requisition costs, purchase order or setup costs, and receiving costs. Opportunity costs for this class include the imputed interest on funds expended and may also include the value of the best alternative uses of equipment and personnel utilized in ordering and receiving.

Shortage costs are those incurred when the demand rate exceeds the sales rate. Again, these costs can be classified as out-of-pocket costs and opportunity costs. Out-of-pocket costs result from special orders (expediting costs, special freight costs, etc.). Opportunity costs include both the immediate effect of the loss of sales (lost profits) and the future impact of the present out-of-stock condition (adverse customer good-will).

Overstock costs are incurred when the demand rate is less than the expected sales rate. These costs include spoilage, (including price concessions, replacement price decreases, and costs of special promotions in order to reduce overstocks), and interest on funds invested in special promotion . . .

Carrying cost and ordering cost are relevant cost components under any environmental conditions — certainty or uncertainty. On the other hand, shortage cost and overstock cost exist only under the condition of uncertainty.

MEASUREMENT OF ORDERING AND CARRYING COSTS

Identification of the cost components is only the first step toward providing the required input data for the inventory model. Measurement procedures must then be formulated and implemented.

The basic approach to the measurement problem is incremental analysis; that is, we are concerned with those costs that will be directly affected by the inventory decision, or decisions . . .

The basic form of the operational relationship to be minimized for each of the products under analysis may be summarized as follows:

Total relevant inventory cost = (Incremental carrying cost per dollar of average inventory × average inventory in dollars) + (incremental ordering costs per order × number of orders).

The essential notion in this formulation is that of "incremental cost", as measured by the change in total cost given a change in policy (order quantity or reorder point).

A. Short-Run Analysis. Measurement of incremental carrying costs involves the determination of the functional relationship between the amount of inventory and total carrying costs for the product(s) under consideration within the relevant time-frame. Estimates of out-of-pocket carrying costs may be based on past expenditures for taxes, insurance, and storage. Opportunity costs are usually more difficult to measure. Subjective judgment, tempered by empirical observation, is often the best measurement basis available . . .

Relevant ordering costs may be estimated in a similar manner, where the basic cost relationship is specified in terms of ordering cost and total orders placed.

B. Long-Run Analysis. Measurement of average cost elements implies that the scope of the model includes long-run, multi-product policy considerations. The focus is on the incremental cost of units over time. Measurement of average carrying costs per dollar of inventory may be estimated . . .

The relevant time period for determining the inclusion or exclusion of costs is somewhat amorphous. Generally, it should be coexistent with the effect of decisions. Thus, warehousing salaries might provide an example of a cost which would be excluded under a short-run approach and included under a long-run approach, as the longer time period associated with the more comprehensive policy decision enables an adjustment of the size of the work force.

Average ordering costs per order is determined by calculating a similar ratio . . .

Regression analysis may be applied to determine the relationship between the total costs and each of the two relevant independent variables (total inventories and total orders placed) . . . Whatever method is selected, however, an estimate of future cost behavior is desired, and appropriate adjustments for known or expected changes in the cost behavior pattern should be made to the historical data. To be relevant, the cost must be affected by the decision whatever the time dimension . . .

A solution derived from the inventory model in the multi-product, long-run case may indicate the present facilities and personnel are inadequate to implement the inventory levels and/or purchasing procedures provided by the model output. We then have an investment decision combined with inventory decisions.

SHORTAGE AND OVERSTOCK COSTS

. . . Under conditions of uncertainty shortage costs and overstock costs are relevant and are often substantial. The problem then becomes the measurement of those costs and the functional relationship between them and the demand and sales rates . . .

The amount of inventory held under conditions of uncertainty should be adjusted upward (essentially a larger order size and reorder point) to reduce the effects of shortages, and adjusted downward (both the order quantity and the reorder point) to reduce the effects of overstocks. The inverse behavior pattern implicit in this analysis prevents the formulation of a decision rule which minimizes the effects of these two costs on total costs. Accordingly, a practical solution divides the inventory items into two basic classes: (1) those items predominantly subject to shortage costs (staple items); and (2) those items predominantly subject to overstock costs (fashion items and items highly subject to physical deterioration). Then, some measure, or measures, of operating effectiveness — such as service level, percentage of spoilage or obsolescence, etc. — can be defined for each class . . .

The complexity of the analysis increases when overstock costs are a significant factor. However, there is evidence that many inventory management problems are primarily subject to the shortage cost element. The measure of operating effectiveness might, for example, be defined in terms of the probability of stockouts. Then, the costs of holding given quantities of safety stock may be compared with the corresponding probabilities of stockouts occurring . . .

SOURCES OF DATA INPUTS

Most of the monetary out-of-pocket costs discussed in the preceding sections can be obtained, directly or indirectly, from existing accounting records. In those instances where the accounting records are maintained in a highly summarized form, the information still can usually be extracted — although less efficiently — from the source documents underlying these summary classifications . . . The primary source of the principal opportunity cost data is usually a management decision as to the appropriate rate of return on current (or desired) investment opportunities. Where opportunity costs are involved in shortage, or out-of-stock costs, the suggested approach essentially permits a derived measure of the cost implicitly contained in the management choice from an array of cost-benefit alternatives.

Although the necessary cost information is generally available somewhere in the accounting system, it is not easily extracted from a conventional system . . .

There is, of course, the additional problem of securing the data inputs for the highly important environmental variables, such as demand forecasts. Those data often are independent of the accounting system per se. This separation may further block the timely provision of accurate data, and should also be considered in any redesign of an accounting information system oriented to the needs of managerial decision models . . .

IV. Queuing Models

STRUCTURAL SIMILARITY WITH INVENTORY MODELS

A system providing a supply of service facilities in order to satisfy random arrivals demanding these services may be generally described as a queuing system. For example, a drive-in bank must provide booths (service facilities) in order to process customers (demand) as they arrive . . . Facilities are merely an inventory of services; the queuing model is a special case of the inventory model. Many of the concepts in the section on inventory models are also applicable to queuing models.

Depending upon the number and type of service facilities established, a certain quantity of units will, at any time, be waiting in a line (queue) for access to these services; conversely, at other times, these service facilities will be idle. It should be apparent that an increase in the number of service facilities will decrease the average number of units in the queue. However, there are costs associated with the provision of each additional service facility which must be weighed against the corresponding reduction in costs incurred when units reside in the queue. The basic management problem is, therefore, the determination of the optimal number of service facilities which will minimize the sum of these costs.[3]

Summary of Required Information

The four basic categories of information required for inventory models are equally applicable to queuing models . . .

Sources of Data Inputs

Data inputs for queuing models may be extracted from the conventional accounting system. Because this information again generally resides in payroll records, material consumption cost records, equipment schedules, etc., the problems discussed in the section on inventory models relating to the availability and access time to this information are also comparable.

Certain differences should be noted, however. There are not as many individual cost elements in queuing models, and fewer of these elements are subject to questions of joint benefits. The primary joint cost problem is in the measurement of standby facility costs, where personnel are often moved from other functions as required. The service facility operating cost and standby facility cost, if appropriately defined in the basic accounting records, may usually be determined with a higher degree of accuracy than the corresponding carrying and ordering costs in the inventory model.

On the other hand, the required information for the basic environment variables (rate of demand for the services provided and the service rate of each service facility) generally poses a more significant problem than is encountered in the inventory model . . .

V. Capital Budgeting Models

There are many different methods of making capital budgeting decisions, and the information requirements are somewhat dependent on the method chosen. In this section we discuss the requirements for implementing the present value method of evaluating investments, the method being used by an increasing number of organizations.

The present value model incorporates the objectives of maximizing the present monetary value of internal investments, where that present value is

---

[3] There are many illustrations of queuing models in the literature. For example, see Miller and Starr, *Executive Decisions and Operations Research* (Englewood Cliffs, N.J., Prentice-Hall, Inc., 1969), pp. 193–97. A simpler illustration is included in Roy and MacNeill, *Horizons for a Profession* (New York: AICPA, 1967), pp. 278–79.

the sum of all expected cash flows associated with the investments, discounted to the present. Non-monetary objectives are not explicitly included in the model.

Management must decide whether to invest. The most important environment variables are the potential cash flows and the structure of interest rates confronting the organization.

The information requirements of capital budgeting decisions may be associated with:

1. The evaluation leading to a decision as to whether the asset should be acquired.
2. The accumulation of costs identified with the asset as it is acquired or constructed.
3. The evaluation of the performance of the investment after it begins operations.

1. THE DECISION TO ACQUIRE

The first step in the decision process is the identification of the decision variables: the feasible investment alternatives. Accounting information can play an important role by identifying the areas and types of investment which are presently producing high returns. Search in these areas is likely to produce more profitable investment opportunities.

After potential investments are identified, their net present value must be computed[4] . . .

Future cash flows from operations are primary inputs into the present value calculations. The accounting system cannot supply directly the necessary information but in many situations it can assist in the estimation process . . .

The amount of each type of cost associated with the investment should be determined for different levels of production. Some costs will not change as production changes; other costs will increase directly as production increases. These characteristics must be defined before we can compute the cash flows of a period. Because prices of factors of production differ if there is a new location, the manager might want the accounting system to supply the physical units of inputs as well as the dollar amounts necessary to achieve the different levels of production. Essentially, he would be utilizing the information storage capability of the accounting system at this stage of the investment process.

The decision-maker does not ordinarily need to know the average full cost per unit of product over a period of time, because such cost includes

[4] The choice of the discount factor is a complex question. Suggestions range from the use of a default-free interest rate to a weighted-average cost of capital. The crucial question is whether the discount factor used to compute present value equivalents should include an adjustment for risk.

depreciation and overhead allocations such as central office and corporate advertising expenses. These would be irrelevant inputs to the investment decision model, though this information might be of interest in other contexts.

Investment decisions are generally incremental to the overall operation of the organization. This means that the manager wants to know the incremental costs associated with the decision rather than the average costs. The average costs may be affected by factor inputs that are not affected by the decision and therefore should not affect the decision . . .

There are three additional inputs that are vital to the capital budgeting model: current disposal value of old assets, estimated disposal value of new assets, and expected useful life of new assets or projects. Accounting data cannot ordinarily provide direct help on any of these except to the extent that historical data can aid in formulating predictions. For example, managers may estimate a useful life on new equipment to be 20 years. But accounting records for similar equipment or projects may reveal that the useful life has been 10 or 12 years. Such information, along with the use of sensitivity analysis, can be of sizable help in judging the merits of capital budgeting proposals.

2. ACCUMULATION OF COSTS

When the investment is accepted and the acquisition occurs, the accountant records the investment costs as they are incurred. There is a need to control the costs incurred and to see that the project undertaken is the same as the one approved, and that the actual costs do not differ significantly from the budgeted costs. If material differences do occur, they must be explored. Here the accounting system is acting as an accumulator of information and then reporting the results of economic activity in the form of a comparison of actual and budgeted costs . . .

The cost of the capital tied up during a construction period is sometimes considered in practice to be a cost of the investment if the funds have been obtained using debt type securities. For managerial purposes (at a minimum), the principle of opportunity cost applies and the cost of the funds committed to the project should be considered to be a cost of the project, regardless of the source of the capital.

3. EVALUATION OF PERFORMANCE

The third phase of an investment project is its actual operation, and here the accounting system should be designed, where possible, to report the information necessary for evaluation of the project's performance. In situations where the investment is a small component of a larger interrelated operation, it may be difficult to evaluate the performance in terms of revenues and expenses (or in terms of net cash flows), because of the jointness of the expenses and revenues with those of other activities. A large amount of accounting effort is directed to the problem of measuring the effectiveness of the utilization of assets, and this effort may be viewed as the evaluation of the performance of an investment. Measurements of income and return on investment are extensions of the investment decision; they are relevant to the decision process because the anticipated post-investment accounting measures of performance may influence whether that investment is undertaken.

The use of traditional accrual accounting methods for evaluating performance is a critical roadblock to the implementation of present value models. Clearly, there is an inconsistency between citing present value models as being superior for capital budgeting decisions and then using entirely different concepts for tallying performance. As long as such practices persist, managers will often be tempted to make decisions which may be non-optimal under the present value criterion but optimal, at least over short or intermediate spans of time, under conventional accounting methods of evaluating operating performance . . .

If discounted cash flow approaches to decision making are being used by the firm, it is both possible and desirable that the accounting for the investment (or equivalently the accounting for assets) be consistent with the information that went into the investment's evaluation . . .

In sum, the implementation of discounted cash flow models will be facilitated if a practical means for the follow-up of decisions is devised. Among the major alternatives are:

1. Evaluating all major decisions and a sample of minor decisions by recording results on the same cash-flow basis used to make the original decision.
2. Using discounted cash-flow approaches to the decision but simultaneously preparing an accounting rate of return analysis which will be used as the basis for evaluating results.
3. Adopting depreciation and amortization patterns that more closely fit those patterns implicit in discounted cash-flow models . . .

3 *The motivation of employees to accomplish the goals of an organization has been one of management's main problems. The literature relevant to motivation is surveyed both in organization theory and the behavioral sciences areas — with the finding that the organizational structure best suited to motivation is the decentralized form. Accounting systems are examined in the light of this finding. And weight is given to responsibility accounting as preferable to budgets and standards for effective motivation. Accounting reports are seen as being in part negative contributors to motivation, although positive factors predominate. An informal structure of goals is found to be important, as is participatory budgeting.*

The Role of the Firm's Accounting System for Motivation*

George J. Benston†

Introduction

Motivating employees to work for the goals of the firm has long been one of management's most important and vexing problems. The search for methods that motivate effectively, that induce the employee to work harder

* *From* The Accounting Review, *Vol. XXXVIII, No. 2 (April, 1963), pp. 347–354. Reprinted by permission of the American Accounting Association and George J. Benston, Professor, Graduate School of Management, University of Rochester.*

† Grateful acknowledgement is due the members of the Workshop in Accounting Research of the Institute of Professional Accountancy at the University of Chicago for their helpful (though often devastating) criticism, and especially to Professor Charles Horngren for his encouragement and aid. Regrettably, they cannot be held responsible for errors in fact or opinion.

for the firm's goals, led to experimentation with a wide diversity of devices.[1] In recent years, several writers emphasized that the firm's accounting system has a direct influence on the motivation of managers.[2] This paper (a) surveys the available findings of research done in the behavioral sciences and organization theory as they bear on motivation and (b) critically examines the accounting system and reports in the light of such findings.

Part I surveys the literature related to motivation and organizational structure and concludes that the decentralized[3] form of organization provides the conditions in which effective motivation can occur. In the light of Part I and other evidence, the accounting system and reports are critically evaluated in Part II. The major conclusions of Part II are that:

1. The empirical research reinforces and justifies the recent emphasis on the virtues of responsibility accounting. Responsibility accounting provides an effective overall aid to decentralization and, hence, while indirect and not as dramatic as some proposed direct uses (such as "proper" budgets or standards), perhaps is more important for effective motivation.
2. The evidence does not support the unqualified use of accounting reports as direct motivating factors. Indeed, there is evidence that the direct use of budgets can lead to a reduction in effective motivation. Nevertheless, there are positive aspects to the direct use of accounting reports.

[1] See M. S. Viteles, *Motivation and Morale in Industry*, New York: W. W. Norton and Co., 1953.

[2] C. Argyris, *The Impact of Budgets on People*, New York: The Controllership Foundation, 1952.

"Tentative Statement on Cost Accounting Concepts Underlying Reports for Management Purposes," *The Accounting Review*, 1956, Vol. 31, p. 188.

R. Anthony, "Cost Concepts for Control," *The Accounting Review*, 1957, Vol. 32, pp. 229–234.

N. Bedford, "Cost Accounting as a Motivation Technique," N.A.C.A. Bulletin, 1957, pp. 1250–1257.

A. Stedry, *Budget Control and Cost Behavior*, Englewood Cliffs, N.J.: Prentice-Hall, 1960.

[3] Decentralization, as used in this paper and in organization theory generally, refers to the vesting of authority and responsibility in the department manager or supervisor for the day-to-day conduct of departmental operations. The department in question need not be physically or organizationally separate from the rest of firm. The title "department manager" and the organizational grouping "department," then, signify any supervisory position and work group for which authority and responsibility over specific tasks are delegated and for which accounting reports are prepared. With this system of organization, the department manager is given the authority to operate his department and supervise his employees as he would do if he were an individual entrepreneur.

I. Motivation and Organizational Structure

The motivation of employees may be attempted by the use of a very large variety of techniques, applied in a number of ways. Among these techniques are direct wage incentives, participation schemes, goal setting, and morale boosters. These may be offered directly to the employee by the firm in a centralized fashion (by the personnel department, for example), or indirectly, by the department head in a decentralized firm.[4] Since even a cursory examination of the literature on motivation leads to the realization that the specific techniques of motivation are of almost infinite variety, this paper will concentrate on the problem of application. Indeed, the survey of the literature presented below led the writer to conclude that the organizational structure of the firm is very important for the successful application of motivation techniques, especially with respect to the ordinary worker.[5] The influence of organizational structure on motivation, then, is examined below.

Decentralization and Centralization

The organizational structure of decentralization is one in which managers and employees are in direct and continuous contact. This face-to-face relationship facilitates the manager's perception of the needs and goals of his workers. With the authority given him by decentralization, the manager can provide those specific rewards and penalties that are effective for motivating individual workers and groups. Thus, he is in a good position to persuade them to accept the goals of the firm as their own (or as not opposed to their goals) and work to achieve these ends.

In contrast, centralization and large size make perception of the workers' needs difficult. Communication between the decision makers and those who carry out their decisions becomes complicated and subject to more interference ("noise").[6] And, as a study of ten voluntary associations revealed, ordinary members become more passive and disassociated from the central purposes of the organization and leaders become further removed from the activities they plan.[7]

[4] In a small firm, these two procedures of application may merge, since the central decision maker is in direct contact with the employees.

[5] The motivation of managers and other executives similarly is affected by organizational structure. However, since published findings that dealt with the motivation of executives specifically could not be found, the major emphasis in this paper is on the motivation of the ordinary worker.

[6] T. M. Whitin, "On the Span of Central Direction," *Naval Research Logistics Quarterly,* 1954, Vol. 1, p. 27.

[7] F. S. Chapin and J. E. Tsouderos, "Formalization Observed in Ten Voluntary Associations: Concepts, Morphology, Process," *Social Forces,* 1955, Vol. 33, pp. 306–309.

In addition, research at Sears, Roebuck and Co. revealed that organizational size alone unquestionably is one of the most important factors in determining the quality of employee relationships: "the smaller the unit, the higher the morale and vice versa."[8] And, a study of two British motor-car factories demonstrated that the size factor affects productivity directly. Significant (though low) correlations were found between output and size, the smaller work groups showing consistently larger output in each factory.[9]

However, the existence of small groups, per se, is not a sufficient condition for motivation. Workers may feel a greater sense of belonging if they work in smaller, more cohesive groups, but they will not necessarily be motivated toward fulfilling the goals of the organization. Some writers, notably Argyris (who has done extensive research at Yale's Labor and Management Center) believe that it is inevitable that the ordinary worker fight the organization. He writes that the organization characterized by ". . . task specialization, unity of direction, chain of command, and span of control . . . may create frustration, conflict and failure for the employee. He may react by regressing, decreasing his efficiency, and creating informal systems against management."[10]

This tendency for informal organizations to be created has been explored extensively.[11] Selznick, for example, writes that "In every organization, the goals of the organization are modified (abandoned, deflected, or elaborated) by processes within it. The process of modification is effected through the informal structure."[12] After reviewing several empirical studies, he concludes that "the day-to-day behavior of the group becomes centered around specific problems and proximate goals which have primarily an internal relevance. Then, since these activities come to consume an increasing proportion of the time and thoughts of the participants, they are — from the point of view of actual behavior — *substituted* for the professed goals."[13]

The Motivation of Small Groups

There also is ample evidence that these informal groups can work to increase or decrease productivity, depending on whether or not the workers

[8] J. C. Worthy, "Organization Structure and Employee Morale," *American Sociological Review*, 1950, Vol. 15, p. 173.

[9] R. Marriott, "Size of Working Group and Output," *Occupational Psychology*, 1949, Vol. 23, p. 56.

[10] C. Argyris, "The Individual and Organization: Some Problems of Mutual Adjustment," *Administrative Science Quarterly*, 1957, Vol. 2, p. 1.

[11] For example see C. I. Barnard, *The Functions of the Executive*, Cambridge, Mass.: Harvard University Press, 1938; J. A. March and H. A. Simon, *Organizations*, New York: John Wiley and Sons, 1958; P. Selznick, "An Approach to a Theory of Organization," *American Sociological Review*, 1943, Vol. 8, pp. 47–54; and H. A. Simon, *Administrative Behavior*, New York: The Macmillan Co., 1947.

[12] *Ibid.*, p. 47.

[13] *Ibid.*, p. 48. (Emphasis appears in the original.)

perceive that the organization's goals are not contrary to theirs.[14] Two types of procedures have been proposed to cope with this problem. One, the direct approach, involves an immediate attempt by top management to influence the worker through direct wage incentive plans, company-wide incentive plans, and group discussions. The other, the indirect approach, gives primary responsibility and authority to the department manager to motivate his workers effectively.

The direct approach is often effective but it is also difficult to administer successfully. Direct incentive plans are not feasible generally unless a homogeneous product is produced under repetitive conditions.[15] Also, attempts to promote individual increases in productivity usually are disruptive and detrimental to efficiency where the employees' tasks are interrelated.[16] Company-wide incentive plans have had a spotty record of success.[17] They seem to work best where there is a long history of trust between labor and management or an unusual person as chief executive of the company.[18] However, efforts to impose company-wide incentive plans in other situations have been generally unsuccessful. Group discussions also do not appear to be reliable. A famous experiment conducted in an American plant on the effect of group discussions on productivity and worker acceptance of change produced negative results when replicated in Norway.[19]

The indirect approach makes the informal group's goals synonymous with the organization's goal through effective company leadership of the informal group. The firm then can take advantage of the demonstrated positive relationship between group goals and productivity (cited above).[20] Also, this approach does not rule out the use of direct techniques when and where they are deemed feasible.

[14] For example see L. Berkowitz, "Group Standards, Cohesiveness and Productivity," *Human Relations,* 1954, Vol. 7, pp. 509–19; D. Cartwright and A. Zander, "Group Pressures and Group Standards," in *Group Dynamics,* Second Edition, D. Cartwright and A. Zander, eds., Evanston, Illinois: Row, Peterson and Co., 1960, pp. 165–188; S. Schachter, N. Ellertson, D. McBride, and D. Gregory, "An Experimental Study of Cohesiveness and Productivity," *Human Relations,* 1951, Vol. 4, pp. 229–38, and W. F. Whyte and others, *Money and Motivation,* New York: Harper, 1955.

[15] W. B. Wolf, *Wage Incentives as a Management Tool,* New York: Columbia University Press, 1957.

[16] P. M. Blau, *The Dynamics of Bureaucracy,* Chicago: University of Chicago Press, 1955, Chapter IV; M. Deutch, "The Effects of Cooperation and Competition Upon Group Process," in *Group Dynamics,* Second Edition, *op. cit.* footnote 14, pp. 414–48; and E. J. Thomas, "Effects of Facilitative Role Interdependence on Group Functioning," *Human Relations,* 1957, Vol. 10, pp. 347–66.

[17] J. N. Scanlon, "Profit Sharing: Three Case Studies," *Industrial and Labor Relations Review,* 1948, Vol. 2, pp. 58–75.

[18] See J. F. Lincoln, *Lincoln's Incentive System,* New York: McGraw-Hill, 1946.

[19] L. Coch and J. R. P. French, Jr., "Overcoming Resistance to Change," *Human Relations,* 1948, Vol. 1, pp. 512–32; and J. R. P. French, Jr., J. Israel and D. As, "An Experiment on Participation in a Norwegian Factory," *Human Relations,* 1960, Vol. 30, pp. 3–19.

[20] See footnote 14.

The Role of the Department Manager

The indirect approach can be effected most readily in the decentralized firm. The department manager, who is likely to understand and accept the firm's goals,[21] can be assigned the task of leading the informal group. In assigning the department manager this role, the departmentalized firm can take advantage of the probability that the informal grouping of workers will follow the formal department organization. Task specialization and frequent interaction provide this cohesiveness.[22]

It is very important that the organization-oriented manager assume the leadership role, for when he abdicates or is incapable in his role as leader, an informal leader arises.[23] Without a management-oriented leader, the drives of workers for satisfaction are often channeled into nonproductive or destructive practices.[24] This behavior is to be expected, since the effort necessary for high production rarely is satisfying in itself. Indeed, many empirical investigations have shown that there seldom is positive, but occasionally negative, correlation between productivity and job satisfaction.[25]

The factors that are likely to make the department manager an effective leader also are a product of decentralization. Bass, who considers much of the literature on leadership, concludes that the effective supervisor satisfies the needs of his subordinates.[26] Since these needs are diverse, any number of leadership styles have been found to work in a variety of situations. Thus, the organizational structure must allow the manager the freedom and authority to reward his workers. Freedom is necessary so that the manager can adapt his methods to the particular needs of his group. And, the employees will respond to the demands of the manager only if he has enough influence to make the employees' behavior pay off in terms of actual benefits.[27]

---

[21] Research that examined the motivation of managers, as distinct from production workers, could not be found. However, managers are in more direct and continual contact with the firm's policy makers than are ordinary workers. Hence, they are likely to assume the goals of top-management (see evidence cited in footnotes 14 and 22). Also, top management can exercise control over the performance and possibly the motivation of department managers through budgets and accounting reports of performance (as discussed below).

[22] J. M. Jackson, "Reference Group Processes in a Formal Organization," *Sociometry*, 1959, Vol. 22, pp. 307–327. Also reprinted in *Group Dynamics*, Second Edition, *op. cit.*, footnote 14.

[23] R. L. Kahn and D. Katz, "Leadership Practices in Relation to Productivity and Morale," in *Group Dynamics*, Second Edition, *op. cit.*, footnote 14, pp. 554–70.

[24] W. F. Whyte and others, *op. cit.*, footnote 14.

[25] A. H. Brayfield and W. H. Crockett, "Employee Attitudes and Employee Performance," *Psychological Bulletin*, 1955, Vol. 52, pp. 396–424; and R. L. Kahn and N. C. Morse, "The Relationship of Productivity to Morale," *Journal of Social Issues*, 1951, Vol. 7, pp. 8–17.

[26] B. M. Bass, *Leadership, Psychology, and Organizational Behavior*, New York: Harper and Bros., 1960. The bibliography of this work includes 1155 items.

[27] D. C. Petz, "Influence: A Key to Effective Leadership in the First Line Supervisor," *Personnel*, 1952, Vol. 29. A similar conclusion is reached by Fiedler for

Decentralization also is effective in encouraging the manager to use a style of leadership that promotes effective motivation. It was found in several empirical studies that the fewer the restraints put upon a group (within limits), the more it produced.[28] Kahn and Katz have done extensive research on this aspect of motivation. They find that "Apparently, close supervision can interfere with the gratification of some strongly felt needs."[29] They go on to observe that "There is a great deal of evidence that this factor of closeness of supervision, which is very important, is by no means determined at the first level of supervision. . . . The style of supervision which is characteristic of first-level supervisors reflects in considerable degree the organizational climate which exists at higher levels in the management hierarchy."[30] Thus decentralization, which is characterized by the autonomy of action given the department manager by top management, serves both to allow the managers the necessary freedom and authority needed for motivation and to encourage them to supervise their workers effectively.

II. Accounting Systems and Motivation

Decentralization, which provides the motivational advantages described above, is aided by the firm's accounting system. In fact, many students of decentralization agree with E. F. L. Brech's conclusion (in a review of British experience with decentralization):

> By whatever arrangements and procedures, decentralization necessitates provision for the periodic review of performance and progress and the expression of approval.[31]

This need is met by the firm's accounting system. Top management can afford to give authority to the department manager, since it can control the basic activities of the department with the help of accounting reports of performance. Furthermore, accounting reports and budgets may serve as reliable means of communication, wherein top management can inform the manager of the goals of the firm that it expects him to fulfill.

---

military and sports groups. He concludes that ". . . leadership traits can become operative in influencing group productivity only when the leader has considerable power in the group." (F. E. Fiedler, "The Leader's Psychological Distance and Group Effectiveness," in *Group Dynamics,* Second Edition, *op. cit.,* footnote 14, p. 605). Kahn and Katz also reach this conclusion (*op. cit.,* footnote 22, p. 561), as do W. S. High, R. D. Wilson, and A. Comrey, "Factors Influencing Organizational Effectiveness VIII," *Personnel Psychology,* 1955, Vol. 8, p. 368.

[28] R. M. Stogdill, *Individual Behavior and Group Achievement,* New York: Oxford University Press, 1959, p. 272.

[29] R. L. Kahn and D. Katz, *op. cit.,* footnote 22, p. 560.

[30] *Ibid.,* p. 560.

[31] E. F. L. Brech, "The Balance Between Centralization and Decentralization in Managerial Control," *British Management Review,* 1954, Vol. 12, p. 195.

Responsibility Accounting

More specifically, the findings surveyed above reinforce the recent emphasis on responsibility accounting. In making the smallest areas of responsibility the fundamental building blocks of the accounting system, accountants facilitate effective motivation. With a system of responsibility accounting, top management can afford to widen its span of control and allow operating decisions to be made on a decentralized basis. Correlatively, assigning costs to the individual managers who have control over their incurrence is a factor in encouraging these managers to exercise effectively their authority to motivate their supervisees. The managers' performance in this regard is measured by the accounting reports, which are likely to be an incentive for the effective motivation of the managers.

Budgets and Motivation

Indeed, several writers have proposed that accounting reports be used as a direct factor for effective motivation. The most extensive examination of the use of budgets as a tool for motivation was made by Stedry, who measured the effect of various budgets on an individual's level of aspiration as a method of determining the differences in motivation on these budgets.[32] His experiment, in which the subjects attempted to solve problems for which they received budgets and were rewarded for achievement, resulted in the following determinations:

> The experimental results indicate that an "implicit" budget (where the subject is not told what goal he must attain) produced the best performance, closely followed by a "medium" budget and a "high" budget. The "low" budget, which was the only one which satisfied the criterion of "attainable but not too loose," resulted in performance significantly lower than the other budget groups.
>
> However, there is a strong interaction effect between budgets and the aspiration level determination grouping. The group of "high" budget subjects who received their budgets prior to setting their aspiration levels performed better than any other group, whereas the "high" budget group who set their aspirations before receiving the budget were the lowest performers of any group.[33]

After presenting arguments to the effect that firms probably do not operate at optimal efficiency, Stedry concludes that ". . . it seems at least reasonable to suppose that it is a proper task of budgetary control to be concerned with strategies for constant improvement in performance."[34] He

---

[32] *Op. cit.*, footnote 2.
[33] *Ibid.*, pp. 89–90.
[34] *Ibid.*, p. 147.

implies that the budget should be used to motivate department managers. The function of the budget would be to raise the manager's level of aspiration and thereby increase his level of performance, rather than to inform him of top management's goals and decisions.

Stedry briefly notes, but does not really consider, the effects of accounting reports on the setting of aspiration levels. His experiment was deliberately designed so that the subjects would not have knowledge of their performance.[35] The budget then became their primary point of reference.[36] But would this happen where the managers had knowledge of their previous performance to compare with the budget that is supposed to motivate them to new productive heights?

It is likely that department managers can make a fairly accurate estimate of their performance. The experience of time study engineers can be noted, since the setting of a rate for a particular job is analogous to the setting of a budget for a department. In both situations the attempt is made to motivate the worker to produce more by setting high standards. But, as many articles, texts, and case studies attest, the worker almost always can gauge his performance. The worker generally will fight a "tight" rate by refusing to produce efficiently, because of his fear that the "carrot" will always be pushed ahead every time he attempts to overtake it.[37] There is no reason to expect department managers to be less perceptive than factory workers.

In an actual situation, the department manager probably would compare his estimate of his performance with the budget to see how well he did. This means that the manager would have knowledge of his success or failure. Several experimenters have examined the effect of this knowledge on aspiration levels. Levin, Dembro, Festinger, and Sears, in an often quoted review and analysis of the literature to 1944 conclude that ". . . generally the level of aspiration will be raised and lowered respectively as the performance (attainment) reaches or does not reach the level of aspiration."[38]

The effects of success and failure are difficult problems for the would-be budget manipulator. Stedry's findings indicate that a high budget (one technically impossible of attainment) produced the best performance where

[35] *Ibid.*, p. 71.

[36] *Ibid.*, p. 82.

[37] See W. F. Whyte and others, *op. cit.*, footnote 14, Chapter 3, "Setting the Rate," for a delightful description of this practice.

[38] K. Levin, T. Dembro, L. Festinger, and P. Sears, "Level of Aspiration," in *Personality and the Behavioral Disorders,* Vol. I., J. McV. Hunt, ed., New York: Ronald Press, 1944, p. 337. A comprehensive test of the hypothesis stated by Levin, *et al.,* which confirmed it, was made by I. L. Child and J. W. M. Whiting, "Determinants of Level of Aspiration: Evidence from Everyday Life," *Journal of Abnormal and Social Psychology,* 1949, Vol. 44, p. 314. Similar results are reported by I. M. Steisel and B. D. Cohen, "Effects of Two Degrees of Failure on Level of Aspiration in Performance," *Journal of Abnormal and Social Psychology,* 1951, Vol. 46, pp. 78–82.

the subject received it before setting his level of aspiration. The attainable low budget produced the worst results. But in working conditions, assuming knowledge, the high budget probably will result in failure for the deparment manager and, consequently, in lowering his level of aspiration (motivation) and performance.[39] The budget manipulator, then, must either give the manager false reports about his performance or attempt to set the budget just enough above the manager's perception of his performance to encourage him.

The first alternative, false reports, is a potentially dangerous procedure and is likely to be quite expensive. Performance reports would have to be secretly prepared. This would make accounting data on the department's actual operations (needed for economic decisions) difficult to obtain, since the department manager could not be consulted. Also, this procedure must be based on the assumption that the manager will believe a cost report, even if it conflicts with his own estimates. The validity of this assumption is denied in a study by Simon, Guetzkow, Kozmetsky and Tyndall:

> Interview results show that a particular figure does not operate as a norm, in either a score-card or attention-directing sense, simply because the controller's department calls it a standard. It operates as a norm only to the extent that the executives and supervisors, whose activity it measures, accept it as a fair and attainable yardstick of their performance. Generally, operating executives were inclined to accept a standard to the extent that they were satisfied that the data were *accurately recorded,* that the standard level was *reasonably attainable,* and that the variables it measured were *controllable* by them.[40]

The second alternative open to the budget manipulator is rather difficult to effect. The manager's level of aspiration must be measured, and *his* perception of his performance level must be estimated. However, measurement of an individual's aspiration level is not a well-developed science. Some fairly successful, though crude, procedures for measuring level of aspiration have been developed. Unfortunately, they depend on the subject's verbal response to questions about the goal explicitly to be undertaken, such as the score expected (not hoped for) in a dart-throwing contest.[41] The usefulness of this technique for a work situation is limited, since the employee has an incentive to state a false, low goal and thus avoid failure. A more precise measure has been developed by Siegel,[42]

[39] This may have happened even in Stedry's experiment, since he found that the poorest performance occurred where the subjects determined their aspiration levels before they were given the high budget.

[40] H. A. Simon, H. Guetzkow, G. Kozmetsky, and G. Tyndall, *Centralization vs. Decentralization in Organizing the Controllers Department,* New York: The Controllership Foundation, 1954, p. 29. (Emphasis appears in the original.)

[41] K. Levin, T. Dembro, L. Festinger, and P. Sears, *op. cit.,* footnote 38.

[42] S. Siegel, "Level of Aspiration and Decision Making," *Psychological Review,* 1957, Vol. 64, pp. 253–63.

but the technique itself restricts it to highly artificial conditions. Thus, it is doubtful that the use of budgets for motivation can be effective except in carefully selected situations.

The direct influence of the budget on motivation may be more effective than is indicated above if the budget is a participation budget, rather than an imposed budget of the type used by Stedry. In a forthcoming article, Becker and Green present evidence and arguments to show that participation in budget-making in conjunction with the comparison and reviewing process may lead to increased cohesiveness and goal acceptance by the participants.[43] If this goal acceptance is at a higher level than previous goals, the aspiration level of the participants has been raised and should lead to increased production.[44]

Accounting Reports of Performance and Motivation

Budgets are not the only accounting reports that may be used for motivation. Accounting reports of performance also have a direct effect on motivation by giving the department manager knowledge of his performance. Most of the published experiments on this subject consider the effects of knowledge on the learning or performance of physical tasks. However, the general findings reported ought to be relevant to the effect of accounting information on the manager's performance. Ammons surveyed most of the literature in this area (to 1956) and reached the following generalizations that seem applicable to the present problem:[45]

Knowledge of performance affects rate of learning and level reached by learning.

Knowledge of performance affects motivation. The most common effects of knowledge of performance is to increase motivation.

The more specific the knowledge of performance, the more rapid improvement and the higher the level of performance.

The longer the delay in giving knowledge of performance, the less effect the given performance has.

When knowledge of performance is decreased, performance drops.

However, overemphasis of departmental cost reports may have undesirable effects, since accounting data often does not measure fulfillment of

---

[43] S. Becker and D. Green, Jr., "Budgeting and Employee Behavior," *The Journal of Business,* 1962, Vol. 35, pp. 392–402.

[44] For a fuller treatment of this subject see the Becker and Green paper, in which is discussed the conditions under which cohesiveness, goal acceptance, and productivity can be lowered as well as increased.

[45] R. B. Ammons, "Effects of Knowledge of Performance: A Survey and Tentative Theoretical Information," *Journal of General Psychology,* 1956, Vol. 54, pp. 283–290. (Emphasis appears in the original.)

the firm's goals. Ammons notes that "It is very important to keep in mind *what* the subject is motivated to do when knowledge of performance increases his motivation. Often he is motivated to score higher, not necessarily to learn the task faster and better. He may then resort to taking advantage of weaknesses in the apparatus, learning habits which are of no value or actually lead to poorer performance when he later attempts to learn a similar task."[46] Overemphasis of accounting reports has been found to result from this behavior.[47] Where the reports became the sole criteria for evaluating performance, managers resorted to such anti-productive techniques as delayed maintenance, bickering over cost allocations, and even falsification of inventories. Thus, recognition of the positive motivational aspects of accounting reports should not lead to the conclusion that they can be used without limits. Indeed, the history of the search for "the key to motivation" indicates that people's needs are too diverse and changeable to be satisfied by any single device or mechanically applied procedure.

Conclusion

Decentralization contributes to effective motivation. The firm's accounting system facilitates decentralization and hence has an indirect but important impact on motivation. The direct use of accounting reports, such as budgets, for motivation can result in reduced performance, if the budget is imposed on the department manager. However, a participation budget may be effective in increasing motivation. Also, accounting reports of activities aid motivation by giving the manager knowledge of his performance.

In short, the accounting system facilitates decentralization, which is conducive to effective motivation. Furthermore, the careful use of accounting reports can directly contribute toward effective motivation by expressing goals and by supplying knowledge of performance.

---

[46] *Ibid.*, p. 280.
[47] See C. Argyris, *op. cit.*, footnote 10; P. W. Cook, Jr., "Decentralization and the Transfer Price Problem," *Journal of Business,* 1955, Vol. 27, p. 87; and V. F. Ridgeway, "Dysfunctional Consequences of Performance Measurements," *Administrative Science Quarterly,* 1956, Vol. 1, pp. 240–47.

4 *The purpose of this article is ". . . to demonstrate that an understanding of behavioral theory is relevant to the development of management accounting theory and practice." It discusses management accounting as a behavioral process with implications for the nature and scope of management accounting systems.*

Caplan develops and compares two views of behavior, traditional and modern, from classical and modern organization theory. He identifies four conflicts in terms of assumptions concerning organization goals, behavior of participants, behavior of management, and the role of accounting. Managerial accounting systems have usually followed the traditional, or classical, view of behavior. To the extent that the modern view exists in organizations, the traditional managerial accounting system is not in harmony with management goals and needs. The author advocates further research to investigate the ". . . effectiveness with which management accounting systems do perform their functions of motivating, explaining, and predicting human behavior."

Behavioral Assumptions of Management Accounting*

Accounting has been closely associated with the development of the modern business organization. Thus, we might expect accountants to show a strong interest in recent contributions to organization theory which increase our understanding of the business firm and how it functions. An examination of accounting literature, however, suggests that (despite the steadily increasing flow of accounting articles and texts incorporating the

* From The Accounting Review, *Vol. XLI, No. 3 (July 1966)*, pp. 496–509. Reprinted by permission of the American Accounting Association and the author.

words "management" and "decisions" in their titles) accountants have been relatively unconcerned with current research in organization theory. Although the past few years have witnessed the beginnings of an effort to bridge this gap, much still remains to be done.[1] This paper attempts to demonstrate that an understanding of behavioral theory is relevant to the development of management accounting theory and practice.

The discussion to be presented here may be summarized as follows:

1. The management accounting function is essentially a behavioral function and the nature and scope of management accounting systems is materially influenced by the view of human behavior which is held by the accountants who design and operate these systems.
2. It is possible to identify a "traditional" management accounting model of the firm and to associate with this model certain fundamental assumptions about human behavior. These assumptions are presented in Table I on page 61.
3. It is also possible to postulate behavioral assumptions based on modern organization theory and to relate them to the objectives of management accounting. A tentative set of such assumptions appears in Table II on page 62.
4. Research directed at testing the nature and validity of accounting assumptions with respect to human behavior in business organizations can be useful in evaluating and, perhaps, improving the effectiveness of management accounting systems.

Management Accounting as a Behavioral Process

The management of a business enterprise is faced with an environment — both internal and external to the firm — that is in a perpetual state of change. Not only is this environment constantly changing, but it is changing in many dimensions. These include physical changes (climate, availability of raw materials, etc.), technological changes (new products and processes, etc.), social changes (attitudes of employees, customers, competitors, etc.), and financial changes (asset composition, availability of funds, etc.).

An important characteristic of "good" management is the ability to evaluate past changes, to react to current changes, and to predict future changes. This is consistent with the view that management is essentially a decision-making process and the view that accounting is an information system which acts as an integral part of this decision-making process. It is inconceivable, however, that any workable information system could

[1] See, for example: Robert T. Golembiewski, "Accountancy as a Function of Organization Theory," *The Accounting Review*, April 1964, pp. 333–341; and John J. Willingham, "The Accounting Entity: A Conceptual Model," *The Accounting Review*, July 1964, pp. 543–552.

TABLE I

Behavioral Assumptions of "Traditional" Management Accounting Model of the Firm

Assumptions with Respect to Organization Goals
A. The principal objective of business activity is profit maximization (economic theory).
B. This principal objective can be segmented into sub-goals to be distributed throughout the organization (principles of management).
C. Goals are additive—what is good for the parts of the business is also good for the whole (principles of management).

Assumptions with Respect to the Behavior of Participants
A. Organization participants are motivated primarily by economic forces (economic theory).
B. Work is esentially an unpleasant task which people will avoid whenever possible (economic theory).
C. Human beings are ordinarily inefficient and wasteful (scientific management).

Assumptions with Respect to the Behavior of Management
A. The role of the business manager is to maximize the profits of the firm (economic theory).
B. In order to perform this role, management must control the tendencies of employees to be lazy, wasteful, and inefficient (scientific management).
C. The essence of management control is authority. The ultimate authority of management stems from its ability to affect the economic reward structure (scientific management).
D. There must be a balance between the authority a person has and his responsibility for performance (principles of management).

Assumptions with Respect to the Role of Management Accounting
A. The primary function of management accounting is to aid management in the process of profit maximization (scientific management).
B. The accounting system is a "goal-allocation" device which permits management to select its operating objectives and to divide and distribute them throughout the firm, i.e., assign responsibilities for performance. This is commonly referred to as "planning" (principles of management).
C. The accounting system is a control device which permits management to identify and correct undesirable performance (scientific management).
D. There is sufficient certainty, rationality, and knowledge within the system to permit an accurate comparison of responsibility for performance and the ultimate benefits and costs of that performance (principles of management).
E. The accounting system is "neutral" in its evaluations—personal bias is eliminated by the objectivity of the system (principles of management).

provide data relative to all, or even a substantial portion, of the changes occurring inside and outside of the organization. There are several reasons for this. Many changes — particularly those that occur in the external environment — are simply not available to the information system of the firm. These changes represent "external unknowns" in a world of

TABLE II

Some Behavioral Assumptions from Modern Organization Theory

Assumptions with Respect to Organization Goals

A. Organizations are coalitions of individual participants. Strictly speaking, the organization itself, which is "mindless," cannot have goals—only the individuals can have goals.

B. Those objectives which are usually viewed as organizational goals are, in fact, the objectives of the dominant members of the coalition, subject to whatever constraints are imposed by the other participants and by the external environment of the organization.

C. Organization objectives tend to change in response to: (1) changes in the goals of the dominant participants; (2) changes in the relationships within the coalition; and (3) changes in the external environment of the organization.

D. In the modern complex business enterprise, there is no single universal organization goal such as profit maximization. To the extent that any truly over-all objective might be identified, that objective is probably organization survival.

E. Facing a highly complex and uncertain world and equipped with only limited rationality, members of an organization tend to focus on "local" (i.e., individual and departmental) goals. These local goals are often in conflict with each other. In addition, there appears to be no valid basis for the assumption that they are homogeneous and thus additive — what is good for the parts of the organization is not necessarily good for the whole.

Assumptions with Respect to the Behavior of Participants

A. Human behavior within an organization is essentially an adaptive, problem-solving, decision-making process.

B. Organization participants are motivated by a wide variety of psychological, social, and economic needs and drives. The relative strength of these diverse needs differs between individuals and within the same individual over time.

C. The decision of an individual to join an organization, and the separate decision to contribute his productive efforts once a member, are based on the individual's perception of the extent to which such action will further the achievement of his personal goals.

D. The efficiency and effectiveness of human behavior and decision making within organizations is constrained by: (1) the inability to concentrate on more than a few things at a time; (2) limited awareness of the environment; (3) limited knowledge of alternative courses of action and the consequences of such alternatives; (4) limited reasoning ability; and (5) incomplete and inconsistent preference systems. As a result of these limits on human rationality, individual and organizational behavior is usually directed at attempts to find satisfactory — rather than optimal — solutions.

Assumptions with Respect to the Behavior of Management

A. The primary role of the business manager is to maintain a favorable balance between (1) the contributions required from the participants and (2) the inducement (i.e., perceived need satisfactions) which must be offered to secure these contributions.

Table II   Some Behavioral Assumptions (*cont.*)

B. The management role is essentially a decision-making process subject to the limitations on human rationality and cognitive ability.   The manager must make decisions himself and must effectively influence the decision premises of others so that their decisions will be favorable for the organization.
C. The essence of management control is the willingness of other participants to *accept* the authority of management.   This willingness appears to be a non-stable function of the inducement-contribution balance.
D. Responsibility is assigned from "above" and authority is accepted from "below."   It is, therefore, meaningless to speak of the balance between responsibility and authority as if both of these were "given" to the manager.

Assumptions with Respect to the Role of Accounting
A. The management accounting process is an information system whose major purposes are: (1) to provide the various levels of management with data which will facilitate the decision-making functions of planning and control; and (2) to serve as a communications medium within the organization.
B. The effective use of budgets and other accounting control techniques requires an understanding of the interaction between these techniques and the motivations and aspiration levels of the individuals to be controlled.
C. The objectivity of the management accounting process is largely a myth. Accountants have wide areas of discretion in the selection, processing, and reporting data.
D. In performing their function within an organization, accountants can be expected to be influenced by their own personal and departmental goals in the same way as other participants are influenced.

---

uncertainty and limited knowledge. Further, a substantial number of changes that occur within the firm itself may not be perceived by the information system.   Thus, there exist "internal" as well as "external" unknowns.

Even if accountants were aware of all the changes which are taking place — or if they could be made aware of them — they still would not be able to reflect them all within their information system.   There must be a selection process, explicit or implicit, which permits the gathering and processing of only the most critical information and facilitates the screening out of all other data.   In the first place, many items of information would cost more to gather and process than the value of the benefits they would provide.   Also, an excessive flow of data would "clog" the system and prevent the timely and efficient passage and evaluation of more important information.[2]   Therefore, only a certain, very limited, set of data (i.e., observations about changes) can be selected for admission into the system. The essential point to be noted here is that decisions regarding what information is the most critical, how it should be processed, and who should receive it are almost always made by accountants.   In addition, they are

[2] This is the "capacity problem" discussed by Anton. See Hector R. Anton, *Some Aspects of Measurement and Accounting,* Working Paper No. 84 (Berkeley, Calif.: Center for Research in Management Science, University of Calif., 1963).

often directly involved, as participants, in the management decision-making process itself.

In carrying out these activities, accountants utilize a frame of reference that is, in effect, their view of the nature of the firm and its participation. The operation of their system requires them to be constantly abstracting a selected flow of information from the complex real world and using this selected data as the variables in their "model" of the firm. It seems clear that accountants exercise choice in the design of their systems and the selection of data for admission into them. It also seems clear that the entire management accounting process can be viewed from the standpoint of attempting to influence the behavior of others. It follows, therefore, that they must perform these functions with certain expectations with respect to the reactions of others to what they do. In other words, their model of the firm must involve some set of explicit or implicit assumptions about human behavior in organizations.

The "Traditional" View of Behavior

Once it has been demonstrated that the management accounting function does by necessity involve assumptions about behavior, the next task is to identify these assumptions. Our investigation is complicated by the fact that nowhere in the literature of accounting is there a formal statement of the behavioral assumptions of the management accounting model of the firm. It is necessary, therefore, to attempt to construct such a statement. We begin with the premise that present-day management accounting theory and practice is the product of three related conceptual forces, namely, industrial engineering technology, classical organization theory, and the economic "theory of the firm." An examination of the literature of management accounting suggests that accountants may have avoided the necessity of developing a behavioral model of their own by borrowing a set of assumptions from these other areas. If this thesis is valid, an appropriate point to begin the search for such assumptions is by an examination of the assumptions of these related models. Since much of the engineering view appears to be incorporated in the classical organization theory model,[3] it can probably be eliminated from this analysis without significant loss. Further, it appears that classical organization theory and economics do not represent two completely different views of human behavior, but rather that they share essentially a single view.

The following paragraphs will attempt to demonstrate that — with the exception of the modern organization theory concepts of recent years — there has been a single view of human behavior in business organizations

---

[3] One of the earliest, and perhaps the best, example of this consolidation can be found in the work of Taylor. See, Frederick W. Taylor, *Scientific Management* (New York: Harper & Brothers, 1911).

from the period of the industrial revolution to the present and that management accounting has adopted this view without significant modification or serious question as to its validity.

THE ECONOMIC THEORY OF THE FIRM

It has been suggested that, from the beginnings of recorded history, the traditional determinants of human behavior in organizations have been either custom or physical force.[4] As long as this was the case, there was no real need for an organization theory or economic theory to explain how and why human beings worked together cooperatively to accomplish common goals. However, the changing structure of society, which accompanied — and to an extent caused — the industrial revolution, destroyed much of the force of these traditional determinants of behavior. The new entrepreneurial class of the 18th century sought not only a social philosophy to rationalize its actions, it also sought practical solutions to the immediate problems of motivating, coordinating, and controlling the members of its organizations. The second of these needs resulted in the development of the classical organization theories which will be discussed in the following section. The first need, i.e., the question for a rationalization, ultimately led to the incorporation of the economic theory of the firm into the logic of the industrial society.

The economic theory of the firm can be summarized as follows. The entrepreneur is faced with a series of behavior alternatives. These alternatives are limited by the economic constraints of the market and the technological constraints of the production function. Within these constraints he will act in such a way as to maximize his economic profit. This behavior is facilitated by the personality characteristic of complete rationality and the information system characteristic of perfect knowledge. Finally, the individual so described is one who is entirely motivated by economic forces. A more subtle elaboration of this last point is the view that leisure has value and that a person will not work except in response to sufficient economic incentives. Thus, the classical economist specifically assumed that man was essentially "lazy" and preferred to minimize his work effort.[5]

Most modern economists would agree that the classical theory of the firm is based on several rather severe abstractions from the real world of business enterprise.[6] Nevertheless, despite these criticisms, there can be little doubt that it has had a substantial influence on the development of

---

[4] Robert L. Heilbroner, *The Worldly Philosophers* (ed. rev.; New York: Simon and Schuster, 1961), pp. 7–8.

[5] This assumption is the basis for the "backward-bending" labor supply curve found in the literature of economics.

[6] See, for example, Andreas G. Papandreou, "Some Basic Problems in the Theory of the Firm," *A Survey of Contemporary Economics,* ed. Bernard F. Haley (Homewood, Ill.: Richard D. Irwin, Inc., 1952), Vol. II, pp. 183–219.

management philosophy and practice. The explanation of human behavior offered by economists — i.e., economic motivation and profit maximization — was incorporated into the patterns of thought of the merging industrial community where it not only became established in its own right but also provided the philosophical and psychological foundations of the scientific management movement.

CLASSICAL ORGANIZATION THEORY

At the turn of the century, Fredrick W. Taylor began a major investigation into the functioning of business organizations which became known as the scientific management movement. Taylor's approach combined the basic behavioral assumptions of the economic theory of the firm with the viewpoint of the engineer seeking the most effective utilization of the physical resources at his disposal. He was concerned with men primarily as "adjuncts to machines" and was interested in maximizing the productivity of the worker through increased efficiency and reduced costs. Implicit in this approach was the belief that if men who might otherwise be wasteful and inefficient could be instructed in methods of achieving increased productivity and, at the same time, provided with adequate economic incentives and proper working conditions, they could be motivated to adopt the improvements, and the organization would benefit accordingly.[7]

March and Simon have noted that the ideas of the scientific management movement are based predominantly on a model of human behavior which assumes that "organization members, and particularly employees, are primarily *passive instruments,* capable of performing work and accepting directions, but not initiating action or exerting influence in any significant way."[8]

The scientific management movement flourished and rapidly became an important part of the business enterprise scene; in fact, for many years it virtually dominated this scene. Furthermore, even a brief glance at current management literature and practices should satisfy the reader that most of Taylor's views are still widely accepted today. Newer theories of management may have supplemented but they have never entirely replaced the scientific management approach.

About 1920, a second major pattern of organization theory, usually referred to as "principles of management" or "administrative management theory," began to develop. This body of doctrine adopted what was essentially a departmentalized approach to the problem of management. Its primary objective was the efficient assignment of organization activities to individual jobs and the grouping of these jobs by departments in such a way as to minimize the total cost of carrying on the activities of the firm.

[7] James G. March and Herbert A. Simon, *Organizations* (New York: John Wiley & Sons, Inc., 1958), pp. 12ff.
[8] Ibid., p. 6.

Writers of this school concerned themselves largely with the development of "principles of management" dealing with such subjects as lines of authority and responsibility, specialization, span of control, and unity of command.[9] This administrative management theory appears to have had a substantial and continuing influence on management theory and practice.

The work of Taylor and his scientific management successors led them into detailed studies of factory costs and provided an important stimulus for the development of modern cost and management accounting. Administrative management theory further contributed to this development through its emphasis on control and departmental responsibility and accountability. Finally, all of this occurred within the over-all setting provided by the economic theory of the firm. In summary, it seems clear that with respect to both its philosophy and techniques, much of contemporary management accounting is a product of, and is geared to, these classical theories. This is what is referred to here as the traditional management accounting model of the firm.

A Tentative Statement of the Behavioral Assumptions Underlying Present-day Management Accounting

It should now be possible to draw together the several strands of the preceding discussion and attempt to postulate some of the fundamental behavioral assumptions that appear to underlie the traditional management accounting model. These assumptions were presented in Table I above. The parenthetical notations note the major conceptual sources of the assumptions. In some cases, there appears to be a considerable overlapping of sources; however, since this is not crucial to the present investigation, the notations have been limited to the primary or most significant area.

Some Behavioral Concepts of Modern Organization Theory

The preceding paragraphs were concerned with an effort to identify a set of behavioral assumptions which could be associated with current theory and practice in management accounting. We will now attempt to develop an alternative set of behavioral assumptions for management accounting — one that is based on concepts from modern organizational theory.

Of the several different modern organization theory approaches, the "decision-making model" of the firm has been selected for use here. The basis for this choice is the close relationship which appears to exist

---

[9] Ibid., pp. 22ff.

between the "decision-making model" and the "information-system" concept of management accounting discussed earlier. The decision-making approach to organization theory effectively began with the writings of Chester I. Barnard, particularly in *The Functions of the Executive,* and was further developed by Simon and others.[10] The model is primarily concerned with the organizational processes of communication and decision making. While drawing heavily on sociology and psychology, it is distinguished from these organization theory approaches by its emphasis on the decision as the basic element of organization.

Organizations are viewed as cooperative efforts or coalitions entered into by individuals in order to achieve personal objectives which cannot be realized without such cooperation. These individuals are motivated to join the organization and contribute to the accomplishment of its objectives because they believe that in this way they can satisfy their personal goals. It is important to note that these personal goals include social and psychological, as well as economic, considerations. Thus, the survival and success of the organization depends on the maintenance of a favorable balance between the contributions required of each participant and the opportunities to satisfy personal goals which must be offered as inducements to secure effective participation.

It is common practice to speak of organization goals; however, to be completely precise, it is the participants who have goals. The organization itself is mindless and, therefore, can have no goals. In the sense that it is used here, the term organization goals is intended to mean the goals of the dominant members of the coalition subject to those constraints which are imposed by other participants and by the external environment. This view implies an organizational goal structure which is in a constant state of change as the environment and the balances and relationships among the participants change. Under such circumstances, it seems meaningless to talk of a single universal goal such as profit maximization. To the extent that any long-run over-all objective might be identified, it appears that this objective would have to be stated in very broad and general terms such as the goal of organization survival.

The decision-making process is usually described as a sequence of three steps: (1) the evoking of alternative courses of action; (2) a consideration of the consequences of the evoked alternatives; and (3) the assignment of values to the various consequences.[11]

It has been suggested that any behavioral theory of rational choice must

---

[10] Chester I. Barnard, *The Functions of the Executive* (Cambridge: Harvard University Press, 1938); Herbert A. Simon, *Administrative Behavior* (New York: John Wiley & Sons, Inc., 1947); March and Simon, *Organizations;* and Richard M. Cyert and James G. March, *A Behavioral Theory of the Firm* (Englewood Cliffs, N. J.: Prentice-Hall, Inc., 1963). The preceding works represent the principal theoretical sources for the decision-making model discussed here.

[11] March and Simon, p. 82.

consider certain limits on the decision maker.[12] These include his (1) limited knowledge with respect to all possible alternatives and consequences; (2) limited cognitive ability; (3) constantly changing value structure; and (4) tendency to "satisfice" rather than maximize. Rational behavior, therefore, consists of searching among limited alternatives for a reasonable solution under conditions in which the consequences of action are uncertain.

The behavioral concepts which flow from the decision-making model have a number of interesting implications. For example, authority is viewed as something which is accepted from "below" rather than imposed from "above."[13] In other words, there must be a *decision to accept* authority before such authority can become effective. Further, human activity is considered to be essentially a process of problem-solving and adaptive behavior — a process in which goals, perception, and abilities are all interrelated and all continually changing.

To summarize the decision-making model, the basic element of organization study is the decision. The objective of managerial decision-making is to secure and coordinate effectively the contributions of other participants. This is accomplished by influencing, to the extent possible, their perception of alternatives and consequences of choice and their value structures, so that the resulting decisions are consistent with the current objectives of the dominant members of the organization.

While the theorists of the "decision-making" school have paid substantial attention to behavioral concepts, the literature does not appear to contain a detailed and complete statement of their underlying behavioral assumptions. Accordingly, it becomes necessary, as it was with the traditional accounting model, to abstract and formulate a set of assumptions. The modern organization theory assumptions presented in Table II represent an attempt by the present writer to identify and extend the behavioral assumptions of the decision-making model in terms of the management accounting function.

Basic Conflicts Between the Behavioral Assumptions of Traditional Management Accounting and Modern Organization Theory

An examination of the two sets of behavioral assumptions developed above suggests a number of interesting questions. Answers to these questions, however, can only be found through extended empirical analysis. Thus, whatever value attaches to the foregoing discussion appears to relate to its possible contribution in providing a theoretical framework for

---

[12] Simon, pp. xxv–xxvi.
[13] Douglas McGregor, *The Human Side of Enterprise* (New York: McGraw-Hill Book Co., Inc., 1960), pp. 158–160.

future empirical research. This research might be designed to explore such questions as the following:

A. What behavioral model provides the most realistic view of human behavior in business organizations? (Accountants should, perhaps, be willing to accept the research findings of organization theorists regarding this question.)
B. Is it possible to draw any general conclusions about the view of behavior actually held by accountants (and managers) in practice?
C. What, if any, are the major differences in the behavioral assumptions of the views in A and B above?
D. What, if any, are the consequences for the organization and its participants of the differences in the behavioral assumptions of the views in A and B?
E. Is it possible to design management accounting systems which are based on a more realistic view of behavior, and would such systems produce better results than present systems?

Lacking empirical evidence, any attempt to investigate the implications of the differences between the two views of behavior discussed in this paper must be considered highly speculative. We might, however, examine briefly a few of the major differences in order to illustrate the nature of the problem. Let us assume for the moment that the decision-making model represents a more realistic view of human behavior than the traditional management accounting model. Let us further assume that the traditional model is a reasonably accurate summary of actual management accounting views in practice. Under these circumstances, what are some of the consequences for business organizations of the use of accounting systems based on the traditional management accounting model of behavior? The system of classification used in Tables I and II will also be adopted here. Thus, this analysis will concentrate on four major areas: organization goals; behavior of participants; behavior of management; and the role of accounting.

ASSUMPTIONS WITH RESPECT TO ORGANIZATION GOALS

In comparing these two sets of assumptions, the most immediately apparent difference concerns the relative simplicity and brevity of the traditional accounting assumptions as contrasted to those of the organization theory model. This should not be particularly surprising since such a difference seems to be consistent with the general philosophies of the two models. There can be little doubt that the view of human behavior associated with the scientific management movement and classical economics is much less complicated than the behavioral outlooks of modern organization theory. In fact, the principal conflict between modern and classical organization theories appears to rest precisely on this issue. Since traditional management accounting is closely related to the classical models, it seems reasonable to expect that it will also tend toward a relatively simple and uncomplicated view of behavior. For example, with respect to organization goals, the behavioral assumptions of the accounting model focus on a single universal objective of business activity. The organization theory assumptions, on the other hand, suggest a much broader and rather imprecise structure of goals.

The traditional management accounting view of organization goals, which appears to be directly related to the theory of the firm of classical economics, may be summarized as follows: The principal objective of business activity is the maximization of the economic profits of the enterprise; the total responsibility for the accomplishment of that objective can be divided into smaller portions and distributed to sub-units throughout the organization; the maximization by each sub-unit of its particular portion of the profit responsibility will result in maximization of the total profits of the enterprise.

The entire structure of traditional management accounting appears to be built around this concept of profit maximization and the related (but quite different) idea of cost minimization. Management accountants have, for the most part, limited the scope of their systems to the selection, processing, and reporting of data concerning certain economic events, the effects of which can be reduced — without too many complications — to monetary terms. This approach is justifiable only if the particular class of events under consideration can be viewed as *the* critical variables affecting the organization. Thus, accountants have been able to rationalize the importance of the data flowing through their systems by relating this data and its use directly to the assumed goal of profit maximization. However, the classical economic view of profits as the universal motivating force of business enterprises has come under substantial attack in recent years. This attack has been based on two general issues. First, questions have been raised concerning the adequacy of economic profits as the sole significant explanation for what takes place within an organization. Second, it has been suggested that limitations on the decision-making process result in behavior which is best described as satisficing rather than maximizing.

It should be particularly emphasized that the recognition of a more complex goal structure does not mean that economic profits can be ignored. Obviously, business firms cannot survive for any extended period of time without some minimum level of profits. Nevertheless, the attempt to summarize the entire goal structure of a complex business entity through the use of one index may result in an overly simplified and unrealistic view of the organization. In short, profits may represent a necessary but not a sufficient definition of the goal structure of business organizations.

The view of organization goals, suggested by the behavioral assumptions of the decision-making model, has two major aspects. First, those objectives which are commonly referred to as goals of the organization are, in fact, the goals of the dominant group of participants. Secondly, it is suggested that these goals are the result of the interaction of a set of constantly changing forces. Thus, the goal-structure of an organization is not only rather imperfectly defined at any given point in time, but it is also in a continual process of change throughout time. In order to identify any truly universal goal, it may be necessary, as suggested earlier, to generalize to the very broad — and perhaps meaningless — level of an objective such as organization survival.

In view of the complex nature of organization goals, it is possible that the profit maximization assumption unduly restricts the role of management accounting to providing a limited and inadequate range of data for decision making. It is as if the accountant were viewing the firm through a narrow aperture which permits him to observe only a thin "slice" of the total organization activity. In emphasizing this narrow view, traditional management accounting appears to ignore many of the complexities and interrelationships that make up the very substance of an organization. What is the practical implication of these observations? How would management accounting change if accountants did not concentrate exclusively on profit maximization? It is likely that this, in itself, would not involve immediate operational changes but rather a change in underlying philosophy. As this philosophy is modified, it should become apparent that a number of specific changes in procedures and systems are in order. Examples of such specific changes might be found in the departmental budgeting and accounting techniques discussed below.

The traditional accounting assumption with respect to the divisibility and additivity of the responsibility for the accomplishment of organization goals seems to warrant some additional comment. Research in organization theory has indicated that individual members of an organization tend to identify with their immediate group rather than with the organization itself. This tendency appears to encourage the development of strong sub-unit loyalties and a concentration on the goals of the sub-unit even when these goals are in conflict with the interests of the organization. The usual departmental budgeting and accounting techniques, by which management accountants endeavor to measure the success of the various sub-units within an organization in achieving certain goals, are based on the assumption that profit maximization or cost minimization at the departmental level will lead to a similar result for the firm as a whole. Thus, accounting reports tend to highlight supposed departmental efficiencies and inefficiencies. Reports of this type seem to encourage departmental activities aimed at "making a good showing" regardless of the effect on the entire organization. It appears to be common for departments within an organization to be in a state of competition with each other for funds, recognition, authority, and so forth. Under such circumstances, it is not very likely that the cooperative efforts necessary to the efficient functioning of the organization as a whole will be furthered by an accounting system which emphasizes and, perhaps, even fosters interdepartmental conflicts.

The tendency for intra-organizational conflict appears to be further compounded by some of the common management accounting techniques for the allocation and control of costs. For example, in some organizations with relatively rigid budgeting procedures, it appears to be a normal practice for departments to attempt deliberately to use up their entire budget for a given period in order to avoid a reduction in the budgets of succeeding periods. Another example is the emphasis often placed on the desirability of keeping costs below some predetermined amount. In such cases, it is likely that, even though a departmental expenditure would be extremely beneficial to an organization, it will not be undertaken if such action would cause the costs of that department to exceed the predetermined limit.

Assumptions with Respect to the Behavior of Participants

The view of the individual inherent in the behavioral assumptions associated with traditional management accounting is one which has been completely rejected by most of the behavioral scientists interested in modern organization theory. To what extent this traditional view is actually held by accountants in practice is a question which, as stated earlier, can only be answered by empirical investigation. Our own limited experience suggests that it is held by a sufficient number of management accountants to be considered at least a significant view within the profession.

It is possible that the failure of management accountants to consider the more complex motivating forces which organization theory recognizes in the individual contributes to the use of accounting systems and procedures which produce "side-effects" in the form of a variety of unanticipated and undesired responses from participants. For example, many management accounting techniques intended to control costs, such as budgeting and standard costing, may virtually defeat themselves because they help to create feelings of confusion, frustration, suspicion, and hostility. These techniques may not motivate effectively because they fail to consider the broad spectrum of needs and drives of the participants.[14]

Assumptions with Respect to the Behavior of Management

Modern organization theory encompasses a view of the management process which differs substantially from the "classical" view associated

---

[14] For a discussion of the behavioral implications of budgets, see Andrew C. Stedry, *Budget Control and Cost Behavior* (Englewood Cliffs, N.J.: Prentice-Hall, Inc., 1960).

here with management accounting. It is interesting, however, that both models appear to take essentially the same position with respect to the basic purpose of managerial activity. This purpose relates to securing effective participation from the other members of the organization. One way of emphasizing the nature of the conflict between the two models in this regard is to examine the manner in which each attempts to accomplish this basic purpose.

According to the traditional accounting model, management must control the performance of others — the principal instrument of control being authority. This model assumes that participants must be continually prodded to perform and that this prodding is accomplished through the use of authority which is applied from above. Also, it places heavy reliance on the use of economic rewards and penalties as devices to implement authority and motivate effective participation.

The decision-making model, on the other hand, assumes that management must *influence* the behavior of others. Furthermore, this approach suggests that, unless individuals are willing to accept such influence, effective participation cannot be assured regardless of the extent of the formal (classical) authority available to management. Viewed in this sense, meaningful authority cannot be imposed on a participant; rather it must be accepted by him. Finally, the decision-making model assumes that the willingness of participants to accept authority and to make effective contributions to the organization depends not only on economic considerations but also to a substantial extent on social and psychological factors.

There seems to be a very close relationship between the behavioral assumptions of traditional management accounting and those associated with the classical management view of the firm. This is evidenced not only in their historical development but also by the manner in which management and management accounting currently interact in the modern business organization. It appears reasonable to expect that the effect of this interaction is to strengthen a jointly shared philosophy with respect to human behavior and the role of management. Managers who tend toward the classical view of behavior are likely to find support from traditional accounting systems which provide the kinds of data that emphasize this view. This accounting emphasis in turn probably serves to focus the attention of management on issues and solutions which are consistent with the philosophy of the classical view. Thus, a "feedback loop" is established which appears to be an important factor in perpetuating this relatively narrow view of human behavior among both management and accountants.

Since the assumptions of the traditional accounting model are so close to classical organization theory and, in fact, appear to be a reasonably good description of the classical theory itself, it would be interesting to consider two questions. First, does the classical view of management provide an efficient solution to the problems of influencing behavior within an organization? Second, if the principal function of management accounting is to furnish relevant data for managerial decision making, should the accountant be concerned with providing the kinds of information that management should want?

With respect to the first question, this paper has attempted to demonstrate that the classical view may not be an efficient approach in motivating organizationally desirable behavior. This premise appears to be supported by a substantial amount of theoretical and empirical research in modern organization theory. In terms of the present discussion, the important point is that traditional management accounting procedures and attitudes cannot be justified solely on the basis that they are consistent with other common management practices because serious questions have been raised regarding the desirability of many of these practices themselves.

In reference to the second question posed above, it can be argued that it is the task of management accounting to provide the information desired by management and to provide it in a manner which is consistent with existing management philosophy. In other words, it is not the responsibility of the accountant to attempt to change the viewpoint of management but only to function within the framework established by this viewpoint. The difficulty with this argument is that it treats accounting as something separate from management. This paper, on the other hand, assumes that management accounting is an integral part of management. The adoption of a more realistic model of behavior by accountants could place them in the position of leading rather than passively following the changes in management philosophy which are bound to occur as a result of the impact of modern organization theory. Thus, it might be hoped that the development of more sophisticated management accounting systems would encourage the evolution of a much more sophisticated management viewpoint in general.

Assumptions with Respect to the Role of Accounting

Modern economic organizations are, of course, highly complex entities. Business managers must continually operate under conditions of uncertainty and limited rationality. In addition, management accountants are subject to the same kinds of drives and needs as are other members of the organization. All of this suggests that management accounting systems could not, even under the best of circumstances, achieve the degree of certainty, neutrality, and objectivity that is often attributed to them. To the extent that management accounting fails to live up to its image in this regard, it can be anticipated that problems will arise for the organization. For one thing, organization members are often subject to evaluations based on information produced by the accounting system. These individuals are likely to be seriously confused and disturbed by a flow of seemingly precise and exact accounting data which they cannot really understand or explain, but which nevertheless implies that they are (or are not) performing their tasks properly. The better education of organization participants regarding the limitations of accounting data, while worthwhile in its own right, does not represent an adequate solution. A much more important step would be a clearer understanding of these limitations by accountants themselves.

Also, as members of the organizations which they serve, management accountants can be expected to seek such psychological and social objectives as security, prestige, and power. In some instances, they might also be expected — as suggested by the discussion of sub-unit goals — to view the success of the accounting department and the technical perfection of the accounting process as ends in themselves. Thus, it is possible that some management accountants tend to view their function as primarily one of criticizing the actions of others and of placing the responsibility for failures to achieve certain desired levels of performance. Where this tendency exists, it may be expected to have a significant effect on motivation and be a major source of difficulty within the organization.[15]

Conclusions

This paper has attempted to postulate a set of behavioral assumptions which could be associated with the theory and practice of "traditional" management accounting. The resulting set of fifteen assumptions represents an accounting adaptation of what might be termed the classical view of human behavior in business organizations. This view emphasizes such concepts as profit maximization, economic incentives, and the inherent laziness and inefficiency of organization participants. It is a model which is structured primarily in terms of the classical ideas of departmentalization, authority, responsibility, and control. The accounting process which has emerged in response to the needs presented by this classical model appears to treat human behavior and goals essentially as given. Further, the generally accepted measure of "good" accounting seems to be one of relevance and usefulness in the maximization of the money profits of the enterprise.

In addition, we have examined a set of behavioral assumptions based on research in modern organization theory. It seems clear that a management accounting system structured around this second set of behavioral assumptions would differ in many respects from the accounting systems found in practice and described in the literature.

One should not infer that the traditional assumptions considered here are completely invalid. The very fact that they have endured for so long

---

[15] Chris Argyris, *The Impact of Budgets on People* (Ithaca, N. Y.: Prepared for the Controllership Foundation, Inc., at Cornell University, 1952).

suggests that this is not the case. It should at least be recognized, however, that in many respects the extent of their validity may be subject to question. Also, it is not argued that all accountants limit themselves at all times to this traditional view. Rather, the two sets of behavioral assumptions discussed might be considered as extreme points on a scale of many possible views. The significance of the traditional point on such a scale appears to be twofold: (a) it is likely that the traditional model represents a view of behavior which is relatively common in practice; and (b) this view seems to underlie much of what is written and taught about accounting.

If the modern organization theory model does ultimately prove to be a more realistic view of human behavior in business organizations, there is little doubt that the scope of management accounting theory and practice will need to be expanded and broadened. In particular, accountants will have to develop an increased awareness and understanding of the complex social and psychological motivations and limitations of organization participants. What is urgently needed, and what we have had very little of in the past, is solid empirical research designed to measure the effectiveness with which management accounting systems do, in fact, perform their functions of motivating, explaining, and predicting human behavior.

Supplemental

Readings

to Part One

American Accounting Association. "Report of the Committee on the Relationship of Behavioral Science and Accounting." *The Accounting Review,* XLIX (1974), 126–139.
> Concerns the organizational form of behavioral accounting research. The report addresses five main issues, e.g., Who should do the research? Who should provide the financial, institutional, and professional support that is necessary?

———. "Report of the Committee on Concepts and Standards — Internal Planning and Control." *The Accounting Review,* XLIX (1974), 78–96.
> Identifies and discusses the criteria for choosing among alternative internal accounting information systems.

Anthony, Robert N. "The Rebirth of Cost Accounting." *Management Accounting,* LVII, No. 4 (October 1975), 13–16.
> Provides a brief historical perspective of cost accounting and summarizes recent developments in the field.

Anton, Hector R. "Activity Analysis of the Firm: A Theoretical Approach to Accounting (Systems) Development." *The Journal of Business Economics,* IV (1961), 290–305.
> Discusses the need to design more general theoretical systems to satisfy the information requirements of managerial decision-making. The article also discusses the interdependency between the information structure and organizational behavior.

Bruns, William J., Jr. "Accounting Information and Decision-making: Some Behavioral Aspects." *The Accounting Review,* XLIII, No. 3 (July 1968), 469–480.
> Uses a model to identify factors that determine when accounting data affect decisions.

Caplan, Edwin H. "Behavioral Assumptions of Management Accounting — Report of a Field Study." *The Accounting Review,* XLIII, No. 2 (April 1968), 342–362.
> Investigates with a field study two models concerning management accountants' views of human behavior.

————. "Management Accounting and the Behavioral Sciences." *Management Accounting,* 50, No. 10 (June 1969), 41–45.

Presents behavioral implications of various aspects of management accounting.

Carlisle, Howard M. "Cost Accounting for Advanced Technology Programs." *The Accounting Review,* XLI, No. 1 (January 1966), 115–120.

Provides guidelines for the use of cost accounting in research programs.

Charnes, A., and W. W. Cooper. "Some Network Characterizations for Mathematical Programming and Accounting Approaches to Planning and Control." *The Accounting Review,* XLII, No. 1 (January 1967), 24–52.

Explores some of the ways in which accounting and mathematical programming might be related.

Cohrs, James C. "The Accountant's Responsibility for Effective Management Control." *Management Controls,* 12, No. 2 (February 1965), 32–37.

Examines the role of the accounting system in helping management exercise control.

Colbert, Bertram A. "The Management Information System." *The Price Waterhouse Review,* 12, No. 1 (Spring 1967), 4–14.

Provides an overview of the "what," "when," and "how" of vital management information needs.

Cramer, Joe J., Jr., and Thomas Iwand. "Financial Reporting for Conglomerates: An Economic Analysis." *California Management Review,* XI, No. 3 (Spring 1969), 25–33.

Examines proposed SEC regulations on conglomerate reporting, including a discussion of joint costs.

Devaney, C. William. "Examples of Program Budgeting for Non-profit Administrative Decisions." *The Price Waterhouse Review,* 13, No. 2 (Summer 1968), 44–53.

Illustrates planning-program-budgeting systems for nonprofit groups.

Eilon, Samuel. "What Is a Decision?" *Management Science,* 16, No. 12 (December 1969), B177–189.

Surveys aspects of the decision-making process.

Fagerberg, Dixon, Jr. "Unmeasured Costs: A Checklist." *Management Accounting,* LV, No. 8 (February 1974), 29–32.

Lists ten types of commonly unmeasured costs and discusses the psychological factors underlying the nonmeasurement and human faults often found accompanying such factors.

Field, John E. "Toward a Multi-level, Multi-goal Information System." *The Accounting Review,* XLIV, No. 3 (July 1969), 593–599.

Discusses the need to design accounting systems to facilitate control of a multilevel, multigoal organization structure.

Feltham, Gerald A. "The Value of Information." *The Accounting Review,* XLIII, No. 4 (October 1968), 684–696.

Describes a model for determining the net value of a change in the information system.

Gellerman, Saul. "Behavioral Strategies." *California Management Review,* XII, No. 2 (Winter 1969), 45–51.

Compares "traditional" cost-control strategy with one that encourages productivity.

Gibson, James L. "Accounting in the Decision-making Process: Some Empirical Evidence." *The Accounting Review,* XXXVIII, No. 3 (July 1963), 492–500.
Reports on research on management's use of accounting information in decision-making based on experience in forty-four companies.

Gonedes, Nicholas J., and Yuji Ijiri. "Improving Subjective Probability Assessment for Planning and Control in Team-like Organizations." *Journal of Accounting Research* (Autumn 1974), 251–269.
Discusses the explicit recognition of uncertainty as an emerging feature in managerial accounting. The article also discusses schemes for solving the related problems of dishonest and substantively deficient assessments.

Harrill, E. Reece. "Cost Accounting and Control — In Government." *Management Controls,* 15, No. 12 (December 1968), 265–269.
Explains the use of cost accounting in various phases of government accounting.

Harris, John K., and Jack L. Krogstad. "A Profile and Index of the CMA Examination." *The Accounting Review,* LI, No. 3 (July 1976), 637–641.
Summarizes the cost accounting problems and questions in the CMA examinations of 1971–1975.

Hitch, Charles J. "Program Budgeting." *Datamation,* 13, No. 9 (September 1967), 37–40.
Explores risk and opportunities in expanding program budgeting to nonmilitary areas.

Horngren, Charles T. "Motivation and Coordination in Management Control Systems." *Management Accounting,* 48, No. 9 (May 1967), 3–7.
Examines the question of whether budgets and responsibility accounting foster departmental orientation at the expense of total organizational orientation.

Ijiri, Yuji, Robert K. Jaedicke, and Kenneth E. Knight. "The Effects of Accounting Alternatives on Management Decisions." *Research in Accounting Measurement,* American Accounting Association, Chicago, 1966, pp. 186–199.
Explains conditions under which alternative accounting methods affect management decisions.

Johnson, Howard G. "Key Item Control." *The Price Waterhouse Review,* 11, No. 3 (Autumn 1966), 26–32.
Shows that managerial effectiveness can be increased through control of "key items."

Livingstone, J. Leslie, and Joshua Ronen. "Motivation and Management Control System." *Decision Sciences,* 6, No. 2 (April 1975), 360–375.
Presents an explicit, systematic statement of the relationships between motivation and accounting control systems through comparison and synthesis of a conventional accounting model of control and a comprehensive behavioral model of motivation.

Mattessich, Richard. "Methodological Preconditions and Problems of a General Theory of Accounting." *The Accounting Review,* XLVII, No. 3 (July 1972), 469–487.

> Discusses the difference between traditional and modern methods of accounting and emphasizes the change toward a more rigorous and systematic approach.

Mautz, Robert K., and K. Fred Skousen. "Common Cost Allocation in Diversified Companies." *Financial Executive,* 36, No. 6 (June 1968), 15–25.

> Presents various approaches to the resolution of the problem of common cost allocation in diversified enterprises.

McRae, T. W. "Opportunity and Incremental Cost: An Attempt to Define in Systems Terms." *The Accounting Review,* XLV, No. 2 (April 1970), 315–321.

> Compares "traditional" concepts of opportunity and incremental costs with a "systems" approach to the concepts.

Novick, David. "Long-range Planning Through Program Budgeting." *Business Horizons,* XII, No. 1 (February 1969), 59–65.

> Explains principles of planning-programming-budgeting systems.

Rappaport, Alfred. "Sensitivity Analysis in Decision Making." *The Accounting Review,* XLII, No. 3 (July 1967), 441–456.

> Illustrates how sensitivity analysis can improve the basis for decision-making.

Rawcliffe, G. A. "Accounting Concepts for Managerial Decision-making." *Management Accounting,* LIII, No. 10 (April 1972), 23, 24, 30.

> Stresses the importance of a multidimensional approach to decision-making. Data must be evaluated in terms of relevancy, opportunity costs, segregation of costs, time value of money, and expected monetary value.

Rickey, Kenneth R. "Control Cost Accounting." *Management Accounting,* 51, No. 10 (April 1970), 9–13.

> Discusses the basis of control cost accounting — the theory that people create all costs.

Rosen, L. S., and R. E. Schneck. "Some Behavioral Consequences of Accounting Measurement Systems." *Cost and Management,* 41, No. 9 (October 1967), 6–16.

> Reviews behavioral weaknesses of accounting measurement systems and what to do about them.

Trueblood, Robert M. "Operations Research — A Challenge to Accounting." *The Journal of Accountancy,* 109, No. 5 (May 1960), 47–51.

> Discusses how methods of operations research, implemented by computer, can help cost accountants and enhance the value of accounting information.

Usry, Milton R. "Cost Accounting in the CPA Examination — Updated." *The Accounting Review,* LI, No. 3 (July 1976), 633–636.

> Summarizes the cost accounting problems and questions in the ten examinations of 1971–1975 and compares the two previous five-year periods.

Additional
Bibliography
to Part One

American Accounting Association. "Report of the Committee on Professional Examinations." *The Accounting Review,* XLXI (1976), 1–38.

Becker, Selwyn W., Joshua Ronen, and George H. Sorter. "Opportunity costs — An Experimental Approach." *Journal of Accounting Research* (Autumn 1974), 317–329.

Beckett, John A. "A Study of the Principles of Allocating Costs." *The Accounting Review,* XXVI, No. 3 (July 1951), 327–333.

Bedford, Norton M. "The Nature of Business Costs, General Concepts." *The Accounting Review,* XXXII, No. 1 (January 1957), 8–14.

Buckley, John W. "Accounting Priorities in the Seventies." *California State University Los Angeles Accounting Colloquium,* November 1973.

Chatfield, Michael. "The Origins of Cost Accounting." *Management Accounting,* LII, No. 12 (June 1971), 11–14.

Chesley, G. R. "Elicitation of Subjective Probabilities: A Review." *The Accounting Review,* L, No. 2 (April 1975), 325–337.

Davidson, H. Justin, and Robert M. Trueblood. "Accounting for Decision-making." *The Accounting Review,* XXXVI, No. 4 (October 1961), 577–582.

Davison, Sidney. "Old Wine into New Bottles." *The Accounting Review,* XXXVIII, No. 2 (April 1963), 278–284.

Dearden, John. "Monthly Unit Costs — Are They Still Significant?" *NAA Bulletin,* XLII, No. 7 (March 1961), 83–91.

Dudick, Thomas S. "Common Errors in Costing." *The Controller,* XXIX, No. 6 (June 1961), 280–284.

Earley, James S., and Willard T. Carleton. "Budgeting and the Theory of the Firm." *The Journal of Industrial Economics,* X, No. 3 (July 1962), 165–173.

Edelman, Franz. "Accounting and Operations Research — Example of a Problem in Marketing Channels." *NAA Bulletin,* XLI, No. 6 (February 1960), 27–36.

Ferrara, William L. "Overhead Costs and Income Measurement." *The Accounting Review,* XXXVI, No. 1 (January 1961), 63–70.

———. "Relevant Costing — Two Points of View." *The Accounting Review,* XXXVIII, No. 4 (October 1963), 719–722.

———. "What Managerial Functions Does Accounting Serve?" *Financial Executive,* XXXII, No. 7 (July 1964), 27–33.

Frank, George W. "Combined Costing Procedures at Work." *NAA Bulletin,* XLIII, No. 10 (June 1962), 15–24.

Greene, Melvyn, and Richard J. Cornwell, A.C.A. "Added Value — An Important Factor in Financial Control." *The Accountant,* 150, No. 4660 (April 11, 1964), 431–433.

Griffin, Charles H. "Multiple Products Costing in Petroleum Refining." *The Journal of Accountancy,* 105, No. 3 (March 1958), 46–52.

Hesse, Rick. "Sesame Street for Decision Sciences." *Decision Sciences,* 5, No. 4 (October 1974), 654–663.

Jaedicke, Robert K. "Marketing Cost Analysis — A Reply." *NAA Bulletin,* XLIII, No. 11 (July 1962), 57–61.

Khandwalla, Pradip N. "The Effect of Different Types of Competition on the Use of Management Controls." *Journal of Accounting Research* (Autumn 1972), 275–285.

Ladin, Eugene. "The Role of the Accountant in Operation Analysis." *The Accounting Review,* XXXVII, No. 2 (April 1962), 289–294.

Management Accounting Practices Committee. "Concepts for Contract Costing." *Management Accounting,* LIII, No. 9 (March 1972), 55–57.

Manes, Rene Pierre. "Using Computers to Improve Distribution of Service Costs." *The Journal of Accountancy,* 115, No. 3 (March 1963), 57–60.

Manes, R. P., and Vernon L. Smith. "Economic Joint Cost Theory and Accounting Practice." *The Accounting Review,* XL, No. 1 (January 1965), 31–35.

Maynard, Brian A. "Productivity in the Office." *Accountancy,* LXXIV, No. 842 (October 1963), 866–874.

McLain, Robert K. "The Pool Method of Setting Overhead Rates." *NAA Bulletin,* XLI, No. 5 (January 1960), 75–83.

Mellman, Martin. "Cost Analysis for the Marketing Function." *The New York Certified Public Accountant,* XXXII, Nos. 5 and 6 (May and June 1962), 327–333, 395.

———. "Marketing Cost Analysis — Its Relationship to Factory Costing Methods." *NAA Bulletin,* XLIII, No. 5 (January 1962), 25–33.

Mepham, M. J. "Concepts of Cost." *The Accountant,* 150, No. 4648 (January 18, 1964), 61–64.

Mossman, Frank H. "Distribution Costs, Where Are They?" *The Controller,* XXX, No. 5 (May 1962), 302 ff.

Papion, Claude M. "Operations Research and Inventory Control." *The Canadian Chartered Accountant,* 82, No. 6 (June 1963), 427–432.

Raun, Donald L. "Accounting for Decisions." *The Accounting Review,* XXXVI, No. 3 (July 1961), 460–471.

Schraff, Sam E. "The Industrial Engineer and the Cost Accountant." *NAA Bulletin,* XLII, No. 7 (March 1961), 13–24.

Scott, D. R. "Accounting Principles and Cost Accounting." *The Journal of Accountancy,* 67, No. 2 (February 1939), 70–76.

Shrimpton, R. D. S. "Service to Management." *Accountancy,* LXIV, No. 834 (February 1963), 129–138.

Simon, Sidney I. "Cost Accounting and the Law." *The Accounting Review,* XXXIX, No. 4 (October 1964), 884–889.

Sorter, George H., and Charles T. Horngren. "Asset Recognition and Economic Attributes — The Relevant Costing Approach." *The Accounting Review,* XXXVII, No. 3 (July 1962), 391–399.

Spencer, Leland G. "Integrating Control and Allocation of Service Section Expense." *NAA Bulletin,* XLI, No. 5 (January 1960), 63–74.

Staubus, George J. "Direct, Relevant or Absorption Costing?" *The Accounting Review,* XXXVIII, No. 1 (January 1963), 64–74.

Watson, Robert H. "Two-variate Analysis." *The Accounting Review,* XXXV, No. 1 (January 1960), 96–99.

Wilson, J. P. "Integral Accounting." *The Accountant,* 148, No. 4604 (March 16, 1963), 308–312.

PART TWO

Forecasting, Budgeting,

and Responsibility Accounting

An initial decision problem of accounting measurement is the selection of the object (or property of an object) to be measured. Prerequisite to this decision is a definition of organizational goals, or objectives, against which performance is to be evaluated. As predictive measurements, forecasts and budgets provide the standards for subsequent control and evaluation of organizational performance. In practical applications many factors condition both the selection of measurement objects and the use of the measurements.

Forecasts are the essential starting point for the budgeting measurement process. Both forecasts and budgets should be as accurate and reliable as possible, subject to the constraint that the cost of achieving given levels of accuracy and reliability should not exceed the value of the incremental information the process yields. Some reasonable levels of accuracy and reliability are obviously necessary if forecast and budget data are to be useful standards and predictors of performance. To obtain information characteristics of accuracy and reliability, Knapp advocates the use of correlation analysis in the forecasting and budgeting process. He argues further that the resultant increased precision in budgeting measurements would increase management's sensitivity to problems of control. A brief, straightforward explanation of correlation analysis completes the article.

Increased emphasis on organizational efficiency, particularly in the public sector, suggests the appropriateness of a zero-base budgeting strategy. This strategy requires that entities or subunits of organizations justify their existence by starting from zero-base during the budgeting process. This approach is different from the traditional incremental approach where only changes (normally increases) in budget requests must be justified. Pyhrr describes the zero-base budgeting system he has applied in both private and public sector activities (Texas Instruments and the State of Georgia).

The behavioral impact of budgets is examined by Ronen and Livingstone in emphasizing the continuing interface of behavioral science and accounting. They discuss individual motivation, satisfaction, and achievement within an expectancy-theory framework. Using this framework, they analyze general assumptions in the accounting and budgeting literature concerning the impacts of budgets on behavior and indicate future effects of the budgeting process on subordinates' performance.

PERT (program evaluation and review technique) and CPM (Critical Path Method) were first developed as project-scheduling techniques, primarily in the public sector, and were later used as more generalized scheduling and budgetary tools. Many industries and government units, particularly the Department of Defense, have used these procedures. Levy, Thompson, and Wiest introduce the Critical Path Method as a technique for scheduling and budgeting and extend this discussion to the closely related PERT methods.

Because budgets should be formulated by relevant areas of responsibility, there is a need to understand and develop responsibility accounting information systems. Netten summarizes budgeting and other managerial information needs that led to the development of responsibility accounting. He introduces concepts of responsibility accounting and formulates them into an information system with guidelines for application in an organization. He also describes some planning and control benefits derived from such a system.

5 *The use of correlation analysis as a tool for forecasting, budgeting, and measurement of operating
elements is advocated. Statistical analysis offers more accurate forecasts,
capacity to predict limits of acceptable error, and the isolation of causes
of forecast error. The budget man is thus alerted to the need for a revision
of forecast, or additional or more stringent controls if random influences
and errors persist.*

*Examples are given of actual experience with the method as well as
valuable insight into the requirements for good correlations. Poor correlations experienced are also explained with some notion of the inherent
problem. Three statistical appendices explain the details of the methods
used and their properties.*

Forecasting and
Measuring With
Correlation Analysis*

Robert A. Knapp

Correlation analysis has been described as one of the most powerful tools
available for business analysis, planning, and forecasting. It is in general
use by econometricians, operations researchers and management consultants;
however, there is too little evidence of its day-to-day use as a tool for forecasting, or for budgeting and measuring the operating elements, the assets
and the liabilities of business.

Since our business operates almost 100 per cent within the defense market,
we are faced with market vagaries that prompted us to approach our application of this technique from the inside out, building experience on the

* From Financial Executive, *Vol. XXXI, No. 5 (May, 1963), pp. 13–19. Reprinted by*
permission of the publisher and the author.

simpler, more stable relationships rather than jumping right into international politics.

Our plan has been to investigate successive business elements on the basis of need and ability to discern logically the pertinent causal relationships. Our goal is to synthesize as complete a network of reliable predicting equations as possible, excluding certain program-type elements, such as, rearrangement expense, maintenance, plant and equipment expenditures, and certain tax and other accruals which, in our case, and usually, are better handled by other methods. This network will provide the basis for mechanized programs of forecasting, budgeting and measurement of performance that will be more accurate, more realistic and more perceptive, respectively, than any based on less sophisticated techniques. These attributes derive from three distinctive features of correlation analysis:

1. Individual (e.g., monthly) errors are minimized and offset one another to the maximum extent, leading to a minimum total period (e.g., year) error.

2. Statistical by-products provide the capacity to predict limits of acceptable error, or variance, both monthly and year-to-date and thus signal the need for second looks.

3. Through the predicting equation, causes for forecast error, or budget variance, can be quantitatively identified.

Correlation analysis may be indicated whenever accuracy of forecast, planning of budget, or measurement of performance need improvement. Its contribution depends on the analyst's ability to distinguish the logical complex of relationships, and on the stability and durability of these relationships in each case. So there are cases in which correlation analysis may not be considered applicable in spite of the need. However, in the many applicable cases correlation analysis provides a sensitivity to more causal factors, and a flexibility to more business situations than any of the more common methods such as experience ratios, pure extrapolation, or seat-of-pants evaluation of a mental or written list of pertinent conditions.

Table 1 provides a sample of our experience with correlation analysis as compared to other methods previously in use, or concurrently in use.

The first two lines of Column A depict performance in predicting the average investment in the largest of our asset and liability accounts respectively. Since these accounts were budgeted with predicting equations derived through correlation analysis, no parallel forecast is available for comparison.

In Column B a comparison is made with the 1961 budget and the previous two years' budget experience.

Line four provides an example of an application to an interim overhead rate revision wherein the same analysis used for line three is updated to include the latest available experience, and the accuracy of the resulting predicting equation compared to a forecast employing a combination of extrapolation and judgment. In addition to eliminating 28 per cent of the error in

TABLE 1

			A	B		
				Experienced % Error Using Other Methods		
Forecasts With Correlation Analysis			%	Previous Two Years		
Item Forecasted	Source Period of Data Correlated	Year Forecasted	Error	1961	Least	Average
Customers Receivables	Oct. 58–Oct. 60	1961	2.5	NA	23.2	41.9
Accounts Payable	Jan. 58–Oct. 60	1961	9.0	NA	16.9	27.2
Gross IME	Nov. 58–Oct. 60	1961	5.4	10.7	9.7	17.8
Gross IME	Nov. 58–Aug. 61	1961	1.6	2.3	NA	NA

the forecast actually used, this updating and prediction were accomplished in considerably less time.

Correlation analysis does not, of course, supplant an investigative procedure whereby the forecaster looks through the eyes of the people responsible for the area of operations to be forecast. Only through such a process can impending developments without historical precedent be factored into any prediction. Correlation analysis does provide the most concise expression of the historical interrelationships of the selected variables that can be derived. It offers no guarantee that the relationships will hold. But, used in combination with knowledge of operating plans and judgment of future business conditions, it can eliminate a large percentage of the error inherent in other forecasting methods.

As would be expected, month-by-month accuracy for any given item is not so great as the total year accuracy shown in Table 1. Vagaries in the occurrence and timing of events, which tend to balance out over a 12-month period, accentuate shorter-term fluctuations. A unique feature of correlation analysis, supplied by the measures of the predicting equation's capabilities, allows the forecaster to predict the amount of error that is likely to result from these short-term random influences. Errors in excess of expected signal the introduction into the business picture of unprecedented and unforeseen factors. The forecaster, or budget man, is thus alerted to the need for a second look which may suggest: (1) a revision in the forecast, or the budget itself, if the changing influences promise to be continuing and pronounced, and/or (2) that additional or more stringent controls may be required to modify the effect of these new, or more pronounced, influences.

It is also characteristic of the predicting equation derived through correlation analysis, as discussed more fully in Appendices A and B, that it will minimize the sum of the forecast errors[1] by month (or whatever the time increment of the data may be).

The closer the forecast period resembles the period from which the data correlated were obtained, the more completely will the errors offset, so that total-year error approaches 0 as a parameter. This is not an exclusive feature since, as illustrated in Appendix A, more than one approximation of the relationship between variables can be made that will minimize the sum of the errors. However, as discussed therein, there is only one such approximation that will at the same time minimize the individual (monthly) errors. This is what distinguishes correlation analysis from less sophisticated methods.

To illustrate the unique capabilities claimed for correlation analysis in the preceding two paragraphs, we forecasted our 1961 average investment in Customers Receivables (excluding retention which was handled separately) within 2.5 per cent. This represents a 90 per cent improvement over the lowest error realized in the previous two years. The measures of this predicting equation's capabilities indicated a monthly error not to exceed 14.5 per cent eight months out of twelve. Actual errors ranged from −18 per cent to +17 per cent, with errors less than 14.5 per cent eight months out of twelve. Because there were some slight differences during 1961 in the way in which the account balance responded to the chosen independent variables and random influences, these monthly errors did not balance out to 0 (as we should hardly ever expect they would in a dynamic business environment). However, total-year error was reduced substantially, and to a satisfactorily low amount. This is to be expected in the application of correlation analysis to business element prediction where relatively stable accounting procedures and business practices lend a degree of durability to historical interactions, and where, with a large amount of control centered within the business, relatively dependable plans can be considered in the analysis. In other words, we are dealing with the greater assurances inherent in a microeconomic application of correlation analysis as opposed to a macroeconomic application requiring the prediction of such things as national defense expenditures by weapon system, number of housing starts, or national employment levels.

The ±14.5 per cent in the above illustration was the approximate equivalent of one standard error of estimate. As the year progressed, had one of the monthly errors exceeded two standard errors of estimate (29 per cent) which would be expected only five times out of one hundred, or had the monthly errors not demonstrated an offsetting year to date pattern within calculable converging limits, a change in the basic relationships among the variables, or the influence of a new variable might have been indicated, and

---

[1] This is an extrapolation of the characteristic of minimizing the sum of the + and − deviations of the values of the dependent variable (element to be forecasted) estimated through the equation from the respective actual values correlated. The degree of accuracy of the statement varies with (1) the representativeness and size of the historical sample analyzed; (2) errors in the historical values not discovered and corrected in the processes of accumulation and adjustment of the data; (3) any significant dissimilarity between the sample and a normal distribution.

a re-analysis required. While neither of these eventualities are likely with the variables involved in this case, there is always a possibility that a change in environmental or accounting structure will distort historical relationships, and introduce substantial errors in a predicting equation. In contrast to less sophisticated techniques, correlation analysis provides the analytical perception needed to provide early warning of such developments.

Forecasting, budgeting and measuring with correlation analysis is a developmental process. It can be used effectively for long-range forecasting, where more popular methods leave the most to be desired, at an earlier stage of development than it can for forecasting, budgeting and measuring by month because it takes less refined correlations to promise total year accuracies well above previous standards. The farther into the future the forecast is carried, the less confidence can be placed in the endurance of historical patterns, or the continuing appropriateness of judgment adjustments. But this is a failing of all forecasting methods, and there is no reason to believe that correlation analysis does not maintain its lead over less sophisticated methods throughout the forecast period. In fact, there are numerous examples at the macroeconomic level, at least, of very satisfactory durability of correlation derived predicting equations.

The application to forecasting budgeting and measuring by month, for the year ahead, is more exacting. Here, the results form the basis for a much larger percentage of irreversible decisions that will affect the immediate economic future of the business. The greater stringency of the demands on the method employed actually enhances the attractiveness of correlation analysis. At the same time, it dictates that higher degrees of correlation be obtained since we are, in this case, concerned with monthly accuracy, and more critical total-year accuracies. This requirement multiplies the problem of adjustment of the data correlated, the significance of which is discussed more fully in Appendix C. Adjustment of raw data is the most time-consuming phase in correlation analysis. Parts of an element to be forecast or budgeted may have to be segregated, seasonal adjustments made, and the parts correlated with their respectively appropriate independent variables. While some adjustment is required for good correlations in any case, the finer adjustments required to make a good correlation better demand a thorough insight into the interactions of the variables and their seasonal behavior, which must sometimes be supplemented with trial and error.

Once a significant correlation is obtained, the judgment as to whether or not it is good enough will depend upon the experienced accuracy with other methods, the standard for accuracy that has been set, and the time available for further refinement.

Table 2 presents a sample of correlations, including the best and the weakest, that we have accepted for use for 1962.

Obviously, we are not satisfied with explanations of monthly error as incomplete as that for Accounts Payable. We are, nevertheless, employing predicting equations in such cases for both budgeting and forecasting because of the expected total-year accuracy.

TABLE 2

Element To Be Forecasted	Maximum % of Expected Error Two Out of Three Times			Independent Variables	% of Variation Explained by Independent Variables	Source Period of Data Correlated
	Monthly	Quar-terly	Total Year			
Customer Receivables	9	—	→ 0	Three classes of sales and a working-day index	78	Jan. '59–Sept. '61
Contributed Value	7	—	→ 0	Sales by product line (five)	88	Jan. '58–Oct. '61
Plant Labor Cost	3	—	→ 0	Employment and hour-ly/total employment index	98	Jan. '58–Sept. '61
Accounts Payable	25	—	→ 0	Cost of operations input, direct material input, and a working-day index	58	Jan. '58–Sept. '61
Sundry Creditors	—	3	→ 0	Plant labor cost	69	1st Q '60–3rd Q '61
Gross IME	—	—	0.7	Direct and applied labor base and direct material input	97	12 mos. ended Oct. '59–12 mos. ended Nov. '61

NOTE: → 0 = approaching 0: From our experience we expect these total-year errors to range from 0.5 per cent to 10 per cent in line with the spread of expected monthly errors.

The contribution of correlation analysis to measurement of performance is supplied by the mathematical expressions of the relationship between variables included in the predicting equation. Forecasts or budgets can be reappraised through this media in the light of actual developments (analysis of variance). Causes for error, or variance, can thus be quantitatively identified so that we are supplied with a statistical tool for apprising responsible individuals of the approximate amount of variance attributable to their performance versus the amount attributable to factors beyond their control.

Referring to our 1961 Customers Receivables experience again, the greatest monthly variance (18 per cent) occurred in July. Reappraisal through the predicting equation (substituting actual values of the independent variables) indicated that three percentage points of the 18 were caused by a higher-than-budgeted proportion of fixed-price sales, a much lower proportion of cost-recovery sales subject to interim billing, plus a slightly higher-than-budgeted total sales volume. With business volume and mix eliminated, we logically look to our collection performance for the explanation of the remaining 15 per cent. Our aged analysis of customers receivables showed an increase over the year-to-date average in receivables over 30 days old amounting to 15 per cent of the total account balance, thus accounting for the rest of the variation. In this case, the deterioration in collection performance could be attributed to an externally caused reaction in the month following the end of our customer's fiscal year and the effect of our vacation shutdown. The full combined effect of these two influences had not been experienced during the period from which the data correlated were obtained, and the seasonal adjustment was consequently inadequate.

Initiating a program of correlation analysis requires a working knowledge of, and cautious respect for, statistical tools combined with a solid financial background. Because of the need for extensive historical data, and the analysis and adjustment that is required before the actual correlation can be productive, significant results are at first slow in evolving. However, as the chain of predicting equations grows, results begin to snowball. Established correlations can be updated in a matter of minutes on the smallest computers and new predictions made in a fraction of the time required for re-analysis by more common methods, and with much greater confidence in the results. Given the predicting equations, substantial portions of the work of forecasting and budgeting can be readily mechanized, leaving more time for analysis, and making substantial last-minute revisions possible that could not otherwise be contemplated. Although at least a small computer must be occasionally available for any broad-scale program, isolated problem areas can be economically analyzed with a standard desk calculator.

Correlation analysis is more expensive than the more commonly employed methods of forecasting, budgeting and measuring, but it can more than pay for itself by providing the base for more astute planning, pricing and control of performance — in short, more profitable decision-making.

Bibliography

Spencer, Milton H. and Louis Siegelman, *Managerial Economics*, Richard D. Irwin, Inc., 1959.

Waugh, Albert E., *Elements of Statistical Methods*, Third Edition, McGraw-Hill, 1952.

Ezekiel, Mordecai and Karl A. Fox, *Methods of Correlation and Regression Analysis*, Third Edition, McGraw-Hill, 1959.

Croxton, Frederick E. and Dudley J. Cowden, *Applied General Statistics*, First Edition, Prentice-Hall, 1939.

Kenney, J. F. and E. S. Keeping, *Mathematics of Statistics*, Third Edition, D. Van Nostrand Co., Inc., 1957.

Appendix A

CORRELATION ANALYSIS

The purpose of correlation analysis is to derive a mathematical equation which best discloses the nature of the relationship that exists between a business element to be predicted (dependent variable) and one or more causal factors (independent variables). This mathematical equation is known by various names of which: (1) "predicting equation" probably best describes its role in forecasting and part of its role in budgeting, when the primary objective is the value of the dependent variable calculated by substitution of estimated or actual values of the independent variable(s) in the equation, and (2) "regression equation" most closely defines its role in the measurement of performance when the primary objective is to determine the amount and nature of variance attributable to variations in the independent variable(s). However, since the two objectives are usually intertwined, particularly in budget application, we have selected the single term "predicting equation" for this report.

The derivation of the predicting equation amounts to weighting the separate causal factors according to their individual importance in their effect upon the element to be forecast. This is accomplished most commonly by correlating historical data chosen from a period judged to be representative of the future period for which a forecast, budget and subsequent measurement of performance is desired. As discussed more fully in Appendix C, the data may require adjustment to obtain satisfactory representativeness.

This correlation process (least squares method) characteristically provides the equation of the line (simple linear correlation) that comes closest to all of the actual values used in the analysis. Unless the correlation is perfect, this line will fall below some actual values and above others. But the sum of all these + and − deviations will always equal 0, and if we square these deviations and add them together, this sum of the squares will always be less than it would be from any other line. The significance of the latter characteristic applies especially to the time segment of the data correlated and can be illustrated as in Figure 1.

FIGURE 1

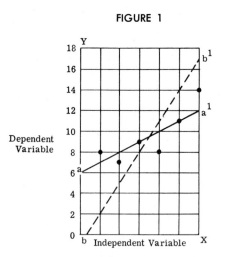

In Figure 1, the sum of the + or − deviations from either regression line equals 0. But the squared deviations are at a minimum from line aa^1 $((+1)^2 + (-1)^2 + (0)^2 + (-2)^2 + (0)^2 + (+2)^2 = 10)$. The sum of the squared deviations from bb^1 = $(+6)^2 + (+2)^2 + (+1)^2 + (-3)^2 + (-3)^2 + (-3)^2 = 68$. If we view this figure as a picture of a six-month historical period with the dots representing actual observations, line aa^1 representing the equation derived by correlation analysis and bb^1 representing another approximation of the relationship between the dependent and independent variables, we can see that either line will estimate the total or average value for the dependent variable for the six-month period as a whole with no error, since the + and − deviation cancel out. However, it is obvious that individual month's accuracy is substantially greater using the line (equation) derived by the least squares method.

It should also be apparent that should the future period for which a forecast of the dependent variable is to be made require an extrapolation of the line beyond the range of independent variable values included in the historical period, the bb^1 line (or equation representing it), or for that matter any other line but aa^1, will introduce a bias in the total or average future period prediction, in addition to failing to minimize the individual month's errors.

Although a simple linear correlation has been used to illustrate these characteristics of the least squares method, the comments apply to multiple linear and simple and multiple curvilinear correlation as well. There is a wide choice of curve types in simple (single independent variable) correlation and of combination of curve types in multiple correlation (two or more independent variables). It is difficult to conceptually present more than two independent variable correlations, but some of the one and two independent variable relationships that we have found applicable are presented in Figure 2 with their respective equations in general form.

The expeditious selection of appropriate curve type or combination of curve types is contingent upon logic and a knowledge of the business element interactions. Various methods of curve fitting are available to supplement the process.

The purpose of the preceding description has been to emphasize that (1) a wide variety of predicting equations are available to fit any logically synthesized correlation problem; (2) whether the equation is linear or curvilinear, simple or multiple, the two characteristics of offsetting individual deviations and minimized sum of the squared deviations, so valuable to the application of correlation analysis to forecasting, budgeting and measuring, are retained.

While the predicting equation is the vehicle with which we forecast, budget and quantitatively analyze variance, at least two statistics describing the capabilities of the predicting equation should be mentioned.

Correlation analysis provides the Coefficient of Determination (R^2), measuring the percentage of variation in the dependent variable explained by the independent variable(s) and the Standard Error of Estimate (S_y) which gives an idea in absolute terms of the dependability of estimates provided by the predicting equation.

The coefficient of determination helps to evaluate (1) the wisdom of the particular selection of independent variables; (2) the effectiveness of the elimination, by adjustment of the original data, of periodic fluctuations and/ or elements of the variables that should logically be analyzed separately; (3) the appropriateness of the selected curve-type.

FIGURE 2

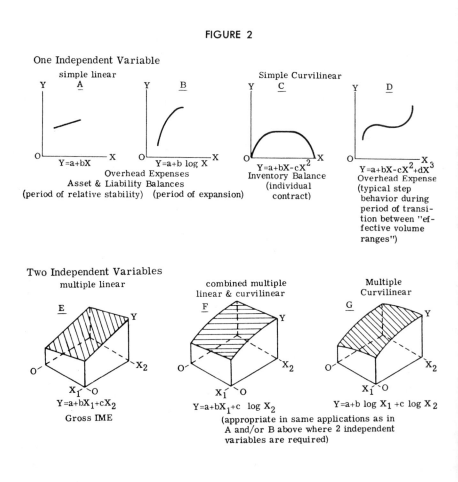

The standard error of estimate states the maximum amount of error that should be expected in two out of three estimates and allows the calculation of other maximum amounts of error to be expected with different probabilities. Thus forecasts can be made and decisions based upon them weighing the decision against measurable risk of being wrong.

We have attempted in this Appendix to convey a utility-oriented, as opposed to a mechanically oriented, feel for correlation analysis. In keeping with this goal we have used only the most essential statistical terms to avoid the clutter of definition.

Appendix B

ACCURACY OF FORECAST AND THE PRACTICAL
SELECTION OF INDEPENDENT VARIABLES

The probable forecasting error, S_1, of a predicting equation derived through correlation analysis (least squares method) is a function of (1) the standard deviation, σ (relative dispersion, or observed magnitude of variation about the arithmetic mean) of the dependent variable (element to be forecast), (2) the coefficient of determination, R^2 (amount of variation that is explained or accounted for by the independent variables), (3) the number of observations, N_1 (number of months, years, etc., of data included in the analysis[2]), and (4) the number and probable forecasting accuracy of the independent variables (forecasting bases).

The specific mathematical relationship[3] predetermines that the greater the historical variability (or instability) of the element to be forecast, the greater will be the forecasting error with a given ability to explain the variation. In establishing an acceptable maximum error, it follows that a higher standard for your ability to explain variation, R^2, will be required for a relatively unstable business element than for a relatively stable one. As a practical consideration, the standard set for forecasting accuracy may have to be lowered, remembering that an unstable element is also more difficult to forecast by other methods. Comparison of a forecast using a predicting equation with seemingly unacceptable probable accuracy to the experienced accuracy of forecasts by other methods often indicates marked improvement in forecasting ability.

The measures of forecasting ability derived through correlation analysis describe this ability in terms of the time increment of the data correlated. Thus correlation of monthly data provides measures of your ability to predict by month. The ability to forecast and budget by month are important goals. Much of their importance, however, attaches to the forecast or budget for the year in the form of supplying patterns for attainment.

With accuracy for the year the primary goal, it becomes extremely significant that predicting equations derived through correlation analysis characteristically minimize the sum of the forecast errors. Monthly errors will largely offset so that the cumulative error for the year will approximate zero given a business and accounting climate that is approximately described within the period analyzed[4] and subject to the bias of error in forecasting bases.

The job of minimizing the bias from errors in predicting the forecasting bases (independent variables) can be accomplished by practical selection of

---

[2] See Appendix C

[3] $S_1 = \sigma\sqrt{1 - R^2}$

[4] See comments in Appendix C.

variables. The independent variables chosen on the basis of logic and knowledge of business element interaction must be evaluated not only in terms of the amount of variation in the dependent variable that they explain but also (1) in terms of their own individual stabilities, the amount of their separate variabilities that can be explained, and so the probable errors in forecasting them; (2) the significance of these probable errors, or the relative bias that may be transmitted to the forecast of the dependent variable through the predicting equation[5]; and (3) the combination of variables that will supply the greatest potential offsetting error capability.

Consideration (1) above is a repetition of the same problem discussed previously in connection with the dependent variable.

Consideration (2) involves expressing the transmitted error as a percentage of the average magnitude of the element to be forecast. Such a comparison is essential to the evaluation of the predicting equation. Without this knowledge it is possible to be grossly misled in the use of a predicting equation described by acceptable statistics, i.e., satisfactorily low forecast error, an equation which includes independent variables with satisfactorily low forecast error for the purpose of forecasting these bases, the absolute amount of which, however, as transmitted to the dependent variable forecast imputes entirely unacceptable inaccuracy.

Possible solutions to this problem include:

1. Appropriate adjustment of the offending independent variable(s) to exclude elements causing the greatest variability (provided these can be forecast with acceptable accuracy, and provided their exclusion does not destroy the effective correlation to the dependent variable).

2. Substituting a second choice forecast base, one whose indicated forecasting error in relation to itself is not so good, and one which may not explain so much of the variation in the dependent variable, but whose indicated forecasting error related to the size of the dependent variable is enough smaller to more than compensate.

On the other hand, independent variables which might significantly improve the ability to explain variations in the dependent variable may be avoided because of relatively less ability to predict them when, in fact, their relatively high indicated forecasting errors as judged in relation to their own average size may, in transmission through the predicting equation and comparison with the average size of the dependent variable, prove to be insignificant.

Consideration (3), the selection of the optimum combination of independent variables, we have attacked as a problem of ± signs of coefficients

---

[5] Which may be expressed as relative forecast error through the expression

b_i = predicting equation coefficient of the independent variable

S_i = standard forecast error of the independent variable

$b_i \dfrac{S_i}{\overline{X}_1}$ = arithmetic average of the dependent variable

i = numerical designation of the independent variable $(1, 2, \ldots, n)$

in the predicting equation and positive, negative, or no interaction of the independent variables within business operations. Proper construction and evaluation of the predicting equation must allow for or take advantage of the imputed influence from (1) complementary independent variables; (2) independent variables that substitute for one another within the operations of the business; and (3) independent variables that show little or no tendency to vary either positively or negatively with changes in another.

Error in forecasting complementary independent variables will be additive in transmission through the predicting equation if the signs of their coefficients are both, or all, the same, since we should expect an increase in any one above the forecast to be accompanied by an increase in the other(s). In contrast, if the signs of their coefficients in the predicting equation are opposite, there will be an offsetting influence in transmission.

With independent variables that tend to vary in opposite directions, we can expect our forecast of one to be low if the other(s) is (are) high. Given like signs of their coefficients, the errors will tend to offset in the forecast of the dependent variable. Unlike signs in this case will, of course, cause the errors to be additive.

Whether errors transmitted from independent variables that are, for practical purposes, independent of each other will be additive or offsetting, generally speaking, is unpredictable. However, the use of such variables, given the choice, promises greater ability to explain variations in the dependent variable since correlation between or among independent variables tends to reduce this ability.

There is probably never complete freedom of choice in the combination of independent variables. The problem is to exploit the limited selection available so that the optimum combination of the least number of variables can be constructed. Given a limited number of observations, the fewer the variables the greater the dependability of the statistics, the less time will be consumed both in arriving at and using the predicting equation, and the simpler will be the analysis of variance and its interpretation to management.

Appendix C

DEPENDABILITY AND THE NUMBER AND ADJUSTMENT OF OBSERVATIONS

The dependability of a predicting equation derived through correlation analysis is a function of the number of observations and the number of independent variables.[6] Generally speaking, the greater the number of independent variables used, the greater will be the number of observations required (e.g., months of data).

---

[6] Actually the number of constants in the predicting equation which includes one for each independent variable plus one, commonly expressed in general forms as "a", representing the Y intercept, or value of the dependent variable when the value(s) of the independent variable(s) is (are) equal to zero.

Because of the predominance of complicated interrelationships in the operations of a business, requiring multiple correlation for satisfactory analysis, the number of observations becomes a critical quantity. For this reason, the shortest period for which the data are recorded should be used whenever periodic variation can be removed by appropriate averaging (e.g., converting monthly data to average weekly or average daily), and/or accounted for by the inclusion of an appropriate time variable (e.g., number of weeks or number of working days in the fiscal month).

With data subject to quarterly cycles, such as some liability accounts, which can be acceptably forecast with few variables and, therefore, the number of observations is less critical, we have found it expedient to correlate quarterly totals and estimate monthly balances as percentages of the quarterly totals, or to correlate contemporary months of each quarter separately rather than search for the sometimes very illusive time variable. Either approach, of course, cuts the number of observations by 75 per cent.

Where a 12-month cycle is predominant and cannot otherwise be adjusted for, moving 12-month totals or averages will supplement the number of observations effectively. By this means three fiscal years of data can be made to yield 25 observations, four years — 37 observations, etc. However, averaging creates the problem of adjusting for bias in the predicting equation and extends the time required for both deriving, and forecasting with, the predicting equation.

Proper adjustment of the data to be correlated is a prime prerequisite to obtaining acceptable correlation statistics. Program-type portions of the element for which a predicting equation is desired must be removed for separate treatment, as, for example, rearrangement and factory and equipment development from manufacturing overhead. Any other significant portions that do not logically vary with the independent variables selected for the total element or vary in a different manner (along a different type curve) must also be removed as, for example, retention dollars from customers receivables and assessments from manufacturing overhead. Changes in accounting practice must be either adjusted for by indexing, or the account removed and handled separately, as, for example, depreciation from manufacturing overhead due to the change from straight line to sum of the digits.

Basically, appropriate adjustment requires the recognition of the segments of operating elements which are homogeneous from an accounting standpoint but heterogeneous for correlation purposes, separating these segments for individual analysis, indexing the segments appropriately, and removing the irrelevant periodic fluctuations.

A thorough knowledge of the financial interactions and accounting practices of the business is essential in this phase of the application of correlation analysis to forecasting, budgeting and measuring. Without it correlation analysis will be sterile. On the other hand, without correlation analysis, forecasting, budgeting and measuring cannot provide its maximum contribution to management decision-making.

6 *Organizations have two kinds of expense: (a) direct expense, for materials, labor, and overhead; and (b) support expense, for everything else. It is the "everything else" that causes the worst headaches at budget time, when, for example, a management squeezed by rising costs must decide between decreasing the allocation for a major R&D project and cutting funds for executive training and development. Traditionally, problems like this boil down to one question: How should the company shift its allocations around? Rather than tinker endlessly with its existing budget, Texas Instruments prefers to start from base zero, view all its activities and priorities afresh, and create a new and better set of allocations for the upcoming budget year. TI has developed a procedure that gives management a firm grip on support allocations of all kinds, a procedure for describing all support expense minutely, classifying the alternatives to each, and sorting them all by importance and priority. The technique is simple in principle and easy to apply — and TI, finding it has worked most successfully for its staff and research budgets for 1970, is currently using it for the budgets of all its divisions for 1971. And the nonmanufacturing expenditures at TI amount to about 25% of the total budget — a significant segment by any standard.*

Zero-base Budgeting*

Peter A. Pyhrr

Two years ago Arthur F. Burns, then Counsellor to the President, addressed the Annual Dinner Meeting of the Tax Foundation on "The Control of Government Expenditures." In this speech Burns identified the basic need for what we at Texas Instruments have come to call *zero-base budgeting*. He stated that:

* Peter A. Pyhrr, "Zero-Base Budgeting." Harvard Business Review, 48, No. 12 (November–December, 1970), pp. 111–121. Copyright © 1970 by the President and Fellows of Harvard College; all rights reserved.

101

Customarily, the officials in charge of an established program have to justify only the increase which they seek above last year's appropriation. In other words, what they are already spending is usually accepted as necessary, without examination. Substantial savings could undoubtedly be realized if [it were required that] every agency . . . make a case for its entire appropriation request each year, just as if its program or programs were entirely new. Such budgeting procedure may be difficult to achieve, partly because it will add heavily to the burdens of budget-making, and partly also because it will be resisted by those who fear that their pet programs would be jeopardized by a system that subjects every . . . activity to annual scrutiny of its costs and results.[1]

Burns was advocating that government agencies start from ground zero, as it were, with each year's budget and present their requests for appropriations in such a fashion that all funds can be allocated on the basis of cost/benefit or some similar kind of evaluative analysis. TI is using this approach to budgeting in its business operations, building on cost benefit techniques, and has had a considerable measure of success with it.

The need for effective zero-base budgeting of this kind is increasingly apparent in both industry and government today, since all institutions must adapt to an environment in which the allocation of limited resources presents a constantly deepening challenge. However, as our experience at TI demonstrates, this kind of budgeting need not "add heavily to the burdens of budget-making." In fact, efficiently planned and properly managed, it can actually reduce them.

As developed at TI, this kind of budgeting separates out the basic and necessary operations from those of a more optional or discretionary character so that management can focus special attention on this second, softer group. The basic steps to effective zero-base budgeting are:

- Describe each discrete company activity in a "decision" package.
- Evaluate and rank all these packages by cost/benefit analysis.
- Allocate resources accordingly.

Naturally these steps cannot be applied quite so easily as they can be stated.

I hope the following description of TI's practices and results will help the executive who is interested in pursuing this approach to budgeting think through the problems of applying it in his own company.

Where to Use It . . .

The first thing to understand about zero-base budgeting is that it is best applied to service and support areas of company activity, rather than to manufacturing operations proper.

A corporation's level of manufacturing activity is determined by its sales

[1] New York, Plaza Hotel, December 2, 1969.

volume; and this production level, in turn, determines how much the company shall spend on labor, materials, and overhead. A decision to increase company expenditures for these items does not necessarily bring increased benefits in the form of increased sales, although it does tend to boost production volume. Hence there is not the same simple relation between costs and benefits here as there is in the service and support areas, where the manager can trade off a level of expenditure on a project against the direct returns his investment in the project will bring him.

Thus, cost/benefit analysis, which is crucial to zero-base budgeting, cannot be straightforwardly applied to decisions to increase or decrease expenditures in the manufacturing area.

In industry, then, zero-base budgeting finds its main use in areas where expenditures are not determined directly by manufacturing operations themselves—in areas, that is, where the manager has discretion to choose between different activities (and between different levels of activity) having different direct costs and benefits. These ordinarily include marketing, finance, quality control, maintenance, production planning, engineering, research and development, personnel, data processing, and so on.

In passing I might note that although areas such as quality control and maintenance may be heavily influenced by the manufacturing level or by changes in this level, the zero-base budgeting process can still be used in these areas because the manager's decision to fund quality-control or maintenance activities depends on the relative benefits he thinks these activities will ultimately provide to the central manufacturing operations.

. . . + *How to Begin*

When a company applies zero-base budgeting in its service and support areas, it must explain the *decision package concept* to all levels of management and then present guidelines for the individual manager to use in breaking his area's activities into workable packages of this kind. Next, it must set in motion a *ranking and consolidation process* whereby the packages sift upward toward the top in such a fashion that the decision packages of less importance are winnowed for top management's study and judgment. Let me now explain these two procedures in more detail.

THE DECISION PACKAGE CONCEPT

The decision package is a document that identifies and describes a specific activity in such a manner that management can (a) evaluate it and rank it against other activities competing for the same or similar limited resources and (b) decide whether to approve it or disapprove it. Management may use quantitative or subjective evaluation techniques in ranking each package (I shall discuss evaluation techniques and ranking procedures later), giving a higher priority or rank to packages that satisfy minimum operating and legal requirements and a lower rank to the more discretionary packages.

The specifications in each package must provide management with the information it needs to evaluate the activity. These may include a statement of the goals of the activity, the program by which the goals are to be achieved, the benefits expected from the program, the alternatives to the program, the consequences of *not* approving the package, and the expenditures of funds and personnel the activity requires.

There are two basic types of decision packages:

1. *Mutually exclusive packages* identify alternative means for performing the same function. The best alternative is chosen, and the other packages are discarded.
2. *Incremental packages* reflect different levels of effort that may be expended on a specific function. One package, the "base package," may establish a minimum level of activity, and others identify higher activity or cost levels.

The following example begins with a set of three mutually exclusive decision packages formulated by a production planning manager for handling the production planning of product X. Of the three, he recommends the first, which represents the current level of activity in the area, and states the other two as alternatives to be discarded. The three mutually exclusive packages are as follows:

- *Recommended package A* — Retain five production planners at a cost of $60,000. This level of effort would maintain production and shipping schedules and inventory reporting at the level the manufacturing superintendent desires.
- *Alternative package B* — Eliminate the production planners and let line foremen do their own planning. This strategy will result in zero incremental costs for foremen, but will also result in excessive inventories, inefficient production runs, and delayed shipments.
- *Alternative package C* — Combine production planning for products X, Y, and Z. This procedure eliminates two supervisors at a total cash saving of $30,000. However, this alternative entails a number of consequences. The foremen on each product line will fear lack of specialized service; peak workloads on all product lines will coincide, creating excessive burden on the foreman supervisor to manage operations effectively; and, although it is desirable to locate the planning function close to the production line, the production facilities for X, Y, and Z are so widely separated that this desirable proximity would have to be sacrificed.

Once he has defined the basic alternatives and selected the one he considers best, the manager should complete his analysis by describing the incremental variations (if any) of this chosen alternative. And, specifically, for his recommended alternative A, he should describe packages that call for more or less than five production planners for product X. In this particular case, the manager believed that he could eliminate one planner from the group and still satisfy the minimum requirements for planning. Hence, he identified these base and incremental packages for his recommended alternative, A, as follows:

- *Base package (satisfies requirements for minimum operating level):* Retain only four planners to support coordination between marketing and manufacturing and to establish production schedules and reports. Consequently, long-range planning, inventory control, and marketing support for special product modification will be reduced. The required allocation for this is $45,000.
- *Incremental package 1:* Add back one planner to the basic package. This will increase forward planning of production and shipping schedules from a two-week horizon to a four-week horizon, allow in-process inventory control reports to be updated daily rather than every other day, and help marketing management accommodate customers who require special product modification. The allocation increment required is $15,000. (This incremental package represents the status quo.)
- *Incremental package 2:* Add one OR analyst to evaluate optimal production lots versus optimal inventory levels by color and size. The allocation increment required is $15,000. (Note that savings of 1% in production cost or 5% in inventory would offset this price tag.)

This example, summarized in *Exhibit I,* roughly illustrates the format used to display decision packages at TI in its 1971 budgeting, although it omits a good deal of detail. Note that it shows both the total cost of the current level of activity ($60,000) and the cost of the level of activity that the manager considers minimal ($45,000); and that it also identifies the two discarded alternatives and another possible increment for the basic package. This kind of format encourages the manager to scrutinize each operation for all possible cost reduction and operating improvements for base and incremental packages, as well as all discretionary packages.

The Appendix to this article suggests some guidelines for identifying various categories of packages and offers a number of additional, rough examples of particular packages.

FORMULATING PACKAGES COMPANYWIDE

Decision packages are usually formulated at the "ground level." This promotes detailed identification of activities and alternatives and generates interest and participation by the managers who will be operationally responsible for the approved budget. *Exhibit II* shows the basic formulation process.

EXHIBIT I

Decision Package Format

Department: Product X Planning   Package No. 500
Package name: Base package for product X planning Manager: John Harrison

Goals:
    1. Provide minimum level of planning activities for
       199,000 units of product X.
    2. Maintain in-process and finished goods at current
       inventory level.
    3. Provide minimum marketing coordination with manufac-
       turing foremen.

Statement of program:
    1. Maintain updated production and shipping schedules for
       two weeks in advance (currently maintaining schedules
       four weeks in advance).
    2. Provide finished goods inventory reports daily, and
       in-process inventory reports every other day (currently
       being done daily).
    3. Maintain perpetual inventory system on raw material
       to maintain a two-weeks supply on hand and a two-weeks
       supply on order.

Benefits:
    This is the minimal level of planning required to deliver
    product X on schedule.
    Personnel: 4
    Cost: $45,000.

Consequences of nonapproval:
    Elimination of planners would force line foremen to do
    their own planning with zero incremental cost; but exces-
    sive inventories, inefficient production runs, and delayed
    shipments would result in an excessive, constant sales
    loss.

Incremental packages:
    1. Add back long-range planner, at $15,000
       (Recommended package).
    2. Add operations research analyst, at $15,000.

Alternative package:
    Combine production planning for departments X, Y, and Z.
    A poor logistic setup would result.

Resources required:

1969	$60,000	(Personnel: 5)
1970	$45,000	(Personnel: 4)
Change	−$15,000	−1

A logical starting point for determining next year's needs is the current year's operations. Each manager takes his area's forecasted expense level for the current year, identifies the activities creating this expense, and calculates the cost for each activity. At this stage, he should simply identify each activity at its current level and method of operation and not try to identify alternatives or increments.

EXHIBIT II

Formulation of Decision Packages at the Lowest
Operational Level, or Cost Center

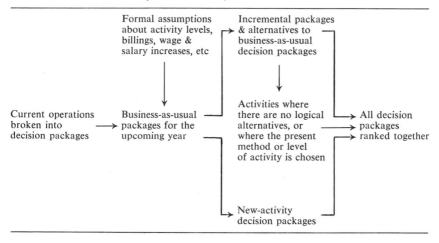

After he has broken his current operations into preliminary decision packages, the manager looks at his requirements for the upcoming year. To aid him in specifying these requirements, upper management should issue a formalized set of assumptions on the activity levels, billings, wage and salary increases, and so on, for the upcoming year. The manager needs this formalized set of assumptions primarily because it provides him and his peers with uniform bench marks for estimating their funding requirements for next year's budget. However, it fills several other important functions as well:

- It brings inaccurate assumptions or misunderstandings to light. As a consequence, it is often easier for the manager to analyze any unusual cost variances that might have occurred during the current budget year.
- It provides a focal point for reviewing and revising assumptions and indirectly helps keep the number of such revisions under control.
- It helps everyone keep track of revisions in the list of assumptions and of the changes in activity levels and costs that these revisions entail.

Once the manager has formulated his preliminary list of decision packages and has received the formalized set of assumptions about the next year's operations, he translates the packages in his list into "business as usual" packages for the upcoming year. These packages merely cast this year's operations in terms of next year's costs.

To determine next year's costs, each manager simply adjusts costs for changes in activity level, for salary and wage increases, and (on an annualized basis) for personnel and operations expenditures not incurred during the present budget year or which will not be incurred during the upcoming budget year.

Next comes the real starting point in determining next year's budget. The manager now develops his final set of decision packages from his business-as-usual packages by segmenting each of them into mutually exclusive and incremental packages wherever possible and noting the discarded alternatives as the final items on the decision-package document. If he should happen to decide that one of these alternatives is a more reasonable or realistic base package for a particular activity than the one he has listed for this activity in his business-as-usual group, he just swaps the two and develops a set of incremental packages around the new base package.

Finally, at the same time the manager is looking into his current and ongoing activities, he should identify all new activities in his area for the upcoming year, develop decision packages that handle them, and attach them to his final set.

At the conclusion of the formulation stage, then, the manager will have identified all his proposed activities for the upcoming year as follows:

1. Business-as-usual packages in which no variations are possible or justifiable, so far as he can see. Here the manager merely exhibits the present level and method of activity in decision-package format.
2. Decision packages, each consisting of a base package and incremental packages (with alternatives noted at the end), for all other ongoing activities.
3. Decision packages for new activities.

The manager is now ready to rank his packages.

The Ranking Process

The ranking process provides management with a technique to allocate its limited resources by making management concentrate on these questions: "How much should we spend?" and "Where should we spend it?"

Management constructs its answer to these questions by listing *all* the packages identified *in order of decreasing benefit to the company.* It then identifies the benefits to be gained at each level of expenditure and studies the consequences of not approving additional decision packages ranked below that expenditure level.

Theoretically, one ranking of decision packages can be obtained for an entire company and judged by its top management. But while this one, single ranking would identify the best allocation of resources, ranking and judging the high volume of packages created by describing all the discrete activities of a large company would impose a ponderous, if not impossible, task on top management. At the other extreme, ranking only at the cost-center level is obviously unsatisfactory, since it does not offer upper management any opportunity to trade off expenditures among cost centers or other, larger divisions of the company.

One can begin to resolve this dilemma by grouping cost centers together naturally, according to types of activity, and producing consolidated rankings for each grouping. The organizational width and depth of such groupings are determined by three factors:

1. The number of packages involved, and the time and effort required to review and rank them.
2. Local management's ability and willingness to rank unfamiliar activities.
3. The need for extensive review across organizational boundaries to determine trade-offs in expense levels. (This factor is particularly important when deep cuts in expense levels are required to combat poor profits.)

The initial ranking should of course occur at the cost-center level, where the packages are developed, so that each manager can evaluate the relative importance of his own activities and rank his packages accordingly.

Then the manager at the next level up the ladder reviews these rankings with the cost center managers themselves, and uses their rankings as guides to produce a single, consolidated ranking for all the packages presented to him from below. At lower levels of an organization, an individual can sometimes do the ranking without any consultation if he has detailed knowledge of the areas involved. In general, however, and particularly at higher levels of the organization, we have found that the expertise necessary to rank packages is best obtained by the use of a committee. At each ranking level the committee membership should consist of all the managers whose packages are being ranked and a manager from the next higher organizational level to serve as chairman.

As *Exhibit III* indicates, the consolidated ranking for cost centers D_1, D_2, and D_3 would be worked out by a committee chaired by the manager of C_2 with the managers of D_1, D_2, and D_3 as members. The manager of C_2, together with the managers of C_1 and C_3, would then serve as a member of a committee chaired by the manager of B_2. At these sessions all three managers from Level C would present the consolidated rankings from their areas for further consolidation. This process continues to the top. (This "consolidation" hierarchy usually corresponds to the ordinary hierarchical organization of the company, but logical groupings of similar functions may be useful even where these cut across normal organizational boundaries.)

VOTING MECHANISMS

At TI, each committee produces its consolidated ranking by voting on the decision packages presented by its members. As at the cost-center level, the most important or most beneficial packages are ranked highest

EXHIBIT III

Consolidation Levels in a Four-level Structure

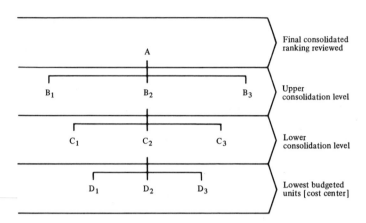

and the least important or beneficial lowest. (I should note, incidentally, that the base package is always ranked higher than the incremental packages clustered around it, so that the base can easily be retained even if the increments are rejected.)

The voting mechanism can be simple or complex, depending on the

EXHIBIT IV

A Voting Ballot

6	Packages ranked here should definitely be funded (a) to satisfy minimum operating or legal requirements or (b) because they have a high probability of significant impact.
5	
4	Packages ranked here have some muscle, but these would be the first packages to cut if the goal expenditure level were reduced.
	◄ *Decision point: goal expenditure level*
3	Packages ranked here have some muscle, and these would be the first packages to add if the goal expenditure level were increased.
2	
1	Packages ranked here should not be seriously considered, given the current expenditure goals.

number of criteria on which the packages must be evaluated, the committee's ability to rank the packages against the criteria, the number of packages, and the time allotted for the process. Three basic voting schemes are in use:

1. Each member gets one vote on a fixed scale.
2. Each member votes on several different criteria, with even or weighted values.
3. A combination of the first two schemes is used, the first to establish a preliminary ranking and the second to establish a detailed ranking around the cutoff level after one has been established.

Exhibit IV shows a voting scale. This scale was designed for overhead and support activities, but can easily be modified from qualitative to quantitative criteria if appropriate information on the packages being ranked is available.

We have found it helpful to have a review session after the detailed ranking, in which the votes of the members are displayed, misunderstandings of package content and differences of opinion are discussed, and a final ranking is established.

CONTROLLING THE VOLUME

We encountered three problems with the ranking process:

- *First,* although the consolidated rankings encompassed only two small divisions, staff and research, the number of decision packages generated overwhelmed top management's ability to evaluate them thoroughly and rank them in the allotted time. The two divisions comprised 100 cost centers, in each of which 3 to 10 packages were identified.
- *Second,* managers had conceptual difficulty in ranking packages they considered to be legally or operationally obligatory.
- *Third,* they expressed concern about their own ability to judge the relative importance of dissimilar activities, especially in areas like staff, where almost all the packages required subjective evaluation and ranking.

The second and third problems caused little or no practical difficulty, for reasons that will shortly be evident. The first problem, however — that of volume — was serious because in any application of this technique the total volume of packages was bound to increase greatly with each consolidation, at each successive level.

If the problem was serious, the solution was simple. To reduce the number of packages to be reviewed in detail by successively higher levels of management and to concentrate top management's attention on the lower ranked activities, a cutoff expense line was established at each organizational level. Management at that level then reviewed in detail and ranked only the decision packages involving expenditures below that cutoff line in any detail. This process is shown in *Exhibit V*.

EXHIBIT V

Decision Package Ranking Cycle

Lowest Budgeted Units (*cost center*)	Lower Consolidation Level		Upper Consolidation level	
	Critical Review		*Critical Review*	
All packages ranked together	List and display packages ranked above the 60% cutoff.	Review and rank together all packages below the 60% cutoff.	List and display packages ranged above the 80% cutoff.	Review and rank together all packages below the 80% cutoff.

Packages above the cutoff line were, and indeed should be, briefly reviewed at each successive level to give management a feel for the entire operation and to allow top management to verify to its own satisfaction the relative importance of the packages above the cutoff line versus the ones below it — that is, the ones being studied in detail and ranked.

Since the total number of packages to be reviewed does increase at each higher level, the cutoff line must be made more stringent at each higher level if the volume of packages to be reviewed at successive levels is to be kept under control.

SETTING THE CUTOFFS

In practice, it is best to establish the cutoff line at the highest consolidation level first, and then establish the cutoff lines for the lower levels. The most effective way to establish this first cutoff is for management at the highest consolidation level to estimate the expense that will be approved at the top level and then set the cutoff far enough below this expected expense figure to allow the desired trading-off between the divisions whose packages are being ranked. Lower consolidation levels then set less stringent cutoffs for their own use. It is important to note that *these cutoffs must be set before consolidation at any level begins.*

At the highest consolidation level, for example, management might set the cutoff at 80%. This means that at this level — call it Level B — management would glance over the package rankings handed up to it from Level C; skim off the highest ranked ones until the expenditures represented by the skimmed packages added up to 80% of last year's budget for the areas in question; review these packages for reasonableness; and then seriously scrutinize and rank the remaining, low-ranked, and more discretionary packages into a consolidated series to be passed to the top.

At Level C, let us assume, a cutoff line of 50% had been set. When

Level D had handed up its rankings, management at Level C would have glanced over all the packages; skimmed the top ones up to a total value of 50% of last year's expenditures in the areas in question; checked these for reasonableness; and then evaluated and consolidated the rest in its own, new ranking to be handed up to Level B. (Naturally, cutoff lines can be expressed just as well in absolute dollars as in percentages.)

Thus the conceptual difficulty and concern that management initially expressed over the ranking process proved to be unfounded. Managers did not concentrate their time on packages that were legally or operationally required; rather, they concentrated on discretionary activities. Note that the relative order of "required" packages is unimportant; even if these packages fall below the cutoff at one level, they will probably fall above the cutoff at the next consolidation level.

Furthermore, managers did not spend too much time worrying whether Package 4 was more important than Package 5, but only assured themselves that Packages 4 and 5 were more important than Package 15, and that Package 15 was more important than Package 25, and so forth.

The ability to achieve a list of ranked packages at any given organizational level allows management to evaluate the desirability of various expenditure levels throughout the budgeting process. Also, this ranked list provides management with a reference point to be used during the operating year to identify activities to be reduced or expanded if allowable expenditure levels change or if the organization is over or under budget during the year.

Conclusion

The decision-package ranking process is a general procedure for achieving zero-base budgeting. It provides management with an operating tool to evaluate and allocate its resources effectively and efficiently, and provides the individual manager with a mechanism for identifying, evaluating, and communicating his activities and alternatives to higher levels of management.

As this process expanded from the staff and research divisions to the manufacturing divisions within TI, the general procedure and philosophies remained the same, although some mechanical details of implementation (such as information and analysis required on each decision package, decision criteria used to evaluate and rank the packages, the level to which the packages are ranked, and so forth) have been modified to fit the specific needs of each operation.

This process was also adopted during 1970 to identify and evaluate benefits and alternative expenditure levels and cash flows for major facility projects, with the subordinate rankings consolidated into one ranking for the entire corporation.

Zero-base budgeting is a flexible and powerful tool. It has greatly simplified the budgeting procedures at TI, and brought about better resource allocation to boot. We believe it is potentially useful to a great many companies in a great many industries; and, if our success with it is any indicator, it will be applied widely in the future.

Appendix

AIDS FOR IDENTIFYING PACKAGES

To break down their department activities into packages, managers should think in terms of three broad categories: service and support; capital expenditures; and labor, material, and overhead expenses directly associated with manufacturing.

1. Service + Support Packages

These packages focus on five kinds of subjects: people, projects or programs, services received, services provided, and cost reduction.

People provide the most common subject for decision packages because they both spend money and create expenses through their wages and salaries. The subject of a package is likely to be personnel in an area where (a) costs are predominantly people-related, (b) people perform several tasks or functions and a level of personnel effort can be identified, or (c) the function of specific individuals can be condensed or eliminated. The following base package suggests a personnel reduction.

Decision Package: Combined Sales Manager for Region A and Region B.

Cost: $45,000.

Statement: Combine sales regions A and B into one region, eliminating Sales Manager A.

Benefits: Combining regions saves expenses of Sales Manager A and secretary ($40,000).

Consequences of Nonapproval: The manager for the combined region will have less time for market surveys and problem solving for smaller customers, but negative sales impact should be minimal due to sales leveling and expected economic slump for two of the largest customers in Region A.

Alternatives:

- Maintain sales manager in Region A at an additional cost of $40,000. (This might have been an incremental package.)
- Combine sales regions A and C.

Projects or programs are likely to be the package topic where costs are generated by personnel and services provided. The following package is an example.

Decision Package: Automated Inventory System.

Cost: $60,000.

Statement: A ready-access, perpetual inventory system for in-process and finished goods. Two man-years of programmer effort are required, with $30,000 expense for computer charges.

Benefits: This will reduce production and shipping delays due to stock-outs, and reduce inventory levels by 25%. The costs will be repaid in one year.

Alternatives:

- Eliminate the system. However, this would eliminate the stated benefits and waste the $20,000 already spent on development.
- Delay installation from September 1971 to April 1972, for a $30,000 savings in 1971.
- Eliminate the ready-access capability of the system ($5,000 reduction in package cost).
- Expand the system to include raw materials inventory ($15,000 additional cost).

Services received is an appropriate subject wherever costs for services received are paid to sources external to the manager's area of activity. The manager should identify separate decision packages or include these costs within other packages. For example, the following base package for a quality control activity represents a cutback to the minimal level in present service costs paid out by the product X production department.

Decision Package: Reduced Quality Control for product X.

Cost: $100,000.

Statement: Inspect 25% of finished goods for product X within one hour of assembly completion.

Benefits: This sample will identify repetitive process errors and ensure 90% probability of customer acceptance.

Consequences of Nonapproval: Greatly increased customer rejection and probable sales losses; process errors will continue if the present level of testing is reduced.

Alternatives:

- Increase sample tested to 35%. This will increase the probability of customer acceptance to 95% ($30,000 additional cost).
- Reduce sample to 20%. This will reduce probability of customer acceptance to 80% ($15,000 reduction in package cost).
- Retain present level of testing activity, but delay inspection to four hours after assembly completion to reduce peak testing loads and overtime ($10,000 delayed into next budget year).

Services provided is a helpful category wherever charges can be specified or estimated. If services are directly charged to the customers, the budget should be determined from a list of packages developed in conjunction with and approved by the customer. (In some cases, of course, customers are too numerous for individual packages to be developed for each one, or perhaps customers will not assume commitment for any planned service level because of uncertainty.) If the customer is *not* directly charged for services received, the service packages identified will follow the normal ranking and review procedures.

Cost reduction, incidentally, is a kind of package that is useful when a cost incurred for receiving or providing a service is not recovered during the same budget period. The net cost of the package should be shown as the total cost minus savings during the budget year. (If the cost is offset in the same period, the manager should incorporate the reduction in the appropriate decision package.)

2. Capital Expenditures Packages

This category is chiefly useful for breaking out major expenditures not included in other packages. This frequently occurs when (a) capital projects have a long lead time, (b) benefit will not be realized during the budget year, (c) expenditure rates can vary, (d) projects are deferrable, or (e) cash flow problems require tradeoffs between expense and capital dollars budgeted. Capital packages may also conveniently identify expenditures related to cost-reduction programs.

Capital packages frequently identify variable expenditure schedules for meeting normal operating needs. The following package is an example.

Decision Package: Expenditure Schedule for Expanding Dallas Chemical Facility.

Cost: $2 million in 1971, $1.5 million in 1972, $0.5 million in 1973.

Benefits and Consequences of Nonapproval: Marketing studies justify adding capacity at this rate.

Alternatives:

- Delay necessary plant expansion for six months by going to full-capacity operation at existing facilities on Saturdays and Sundays.
- Slip expenditure and completion schedules.
- Compress construction schedule and incur 5% to 10% acceleration premium.
- Reduce capacity on the chemical storage tanks to minimum requirements ($200,000 reduction in total project cost).

Once managers understand the formats they should use, they can begin formulating packages for their areas of activity.

3. Labor, Material, and Overhead Expenses Directly Associated with Manufacturing

Although the zero-based concept will probably not apply here, the manufacturing area may use decision packages to identify alternatives and discretionary activities, allowing management to rank these packages with packages identified for other areas.

7 *Within an expectancy theory framework, an individual behavior is influenced by expectations of satisfaction derived
from behavioral outcomes. Valences are used to scale the expected
outcomes and develop a motivational measure.*

*The authors carefully develop the theory and integrate it with
prior studies. They explain five general assumptions within the
framework concerning the effects of budgets on behavior. For given
levels of a subordinate's budget achievement, the motivational effects
of supervisors' responses are examined. Thus the expectancy model.
is useful for evaluating a subordinate's future performance as it is
affected by accounting budget reports.*

An Expectancy Theory
Approach to the
Motivational Impacts
of Budgets*

J. Ronen and J. L. Livingstone†

In this paper we discuss the implications of budgets for motivation and
behavior in the context of expectancy theory as developed in the psychology
of motivation. We argue that propositions from expectancy theory can
be used to integrate and accommodate the fragmented research findings on
budget and behavior in the accounting literature. We discuss how the
expectancy model reconciles what might appear to be contradictory findings
from prior studies.

*From The Accounting Review, Vol. L, No. 4 (October, 1975), pp. 671–685.
Reprinted by permission of the American Accounting Association and the authors.*

† The authors gratefully acknowledge the comments and helpful suggestions of
Arie Y. Lewin.

The Functions of Budgets

Budgets serve three decision-making functions: planning, control, and motivation. Budgets aid planning in that they incorporate forecasts which reflect the anticipated consequences of different combinations of plans (actions) made by management and the relevant uncontrollable events that may occur in the environment. Budgets also serve the planning function through being utilized as a tool for sensitivity analysis which includes the examination of how slight changes in management plans affect the consequences (budgets). Many budgets could be thus generated as a result of alternative plans so that the most desirable plan could then be chosen.

The control function is typically a feedback process whereby information about past performance (both anticipated and actual) is provided to those who "control," to be utilized by them for making decisions. As a motivational tool, the budget conveys information to the subordinate about expectations of superiors regarding what constitutes successful task performance and the consequent reinforcement contingencies. These characterizations of the control and motivation processes probably apply whether the budget is imposed on subordinates, whether developed through the participation of the "controlled," or whether they result from a dynamic, interlevel bargaining process over goals and resource allocations (Schiff and Lewin, 1970).

The three functions of budgets are interdependent. The motivational effect must be explicitly considered in planning and control. Similarly, knowledge by subordinates of superiors' plans and control styles have motivational effects. Furthermore, the budgeting process is likely to cause subordinates to bargain for increases in the resources they command. This may result in dysfunctional budgetary slack (Schiff and Lewin, 1970; and Williamson, 1964).

The Dysfunctional Aspects of Budgets

Budgetary slack is not the only potential dysfunctional aspect of budgets. The literature is filled with exhortations to consider the behavioral effects of standards and budgets on motivation and consequently on performance (Argyris, 1952; Benston, 1963; Becker and Green, 1962; and Usry, 1968). These effects could be either dysfunctional or positive. Many articles deal specifically with the behavioral impacts of budgets on employees; some base their conclusions on generalizations from the psychological literature, and others show findings from empirical experiments (Cherrington and Cherrington, 1973; Stedry, 1960; Stedry and Kay, 1966). Mostly, these discussions were launched in terms of specific principles taken from various areas of psychology such as aspiration level, participation, and attitude change.

To gain better understanding and insight into how these behavioral effects are created, we propose the expectancy model as a unifying framework within which the effects could be analyzed. While the universal usage of budgets implies that their benefits are perceived to exceed the possible dysfunctional effects, the latter can be minimized if the budget's behavioral impacts are better understood.

By choosing the expectancy model (a description of the model appears below) as a framework, we do not wish to imply that it accurately describes behavior even though some recent progress has been made.[1] Rather, we view it as a framework that facilitates the generation of hypotheses about the behavioral effects of budgets. The testing of these hypotheses would indicate whether subordinates' behavior is consistent with the model.

In the following section we describe the expectancy model. After that, we reinterpret the budget's behavioral implications discussed in the literature within the expectancy framework.

The Expectancy Model

The expectancy model is viewed as underlying the superior-subordinate budget relationship in two respects: (1) as the model according to which the subordinate's motivation to perform the task is influenced via the budget; and (2) as the model which the superior regards as determining the subordinate's motivation. (It is assumed that the superior can and may affect the subordinate's motivation via the budget in accordance with the expectancy model.)[2]

The particular expectancy model version that we use in this paper is the one advanced by House (1971) which in turn is derived from the Path-Goal hypotheses advanced by Georgopoulos, Mahoney, and Jones (1957) and from previous research supporting the class of expectancy models of motivation (Atkinson, 1958; Galbraith and Cummings, 1967; Graen, 1969; Lawler, 1968, 1971, 1973; Porter and Lawler, 1967; Vroom, 1964b). The basic tenet of expectancy theory is that an individual chooses his behavior on the basis of (1) his expectations that the behavior will result in a specific outcome and (2) the sum of the valences, i.e., personal utilities or satisfaction that he derives from the outcome. A distinction is made

[1] Indeed, the model has been found wanting with respect to its description power. (See, e.g., Kerr, Klimoski, Tolliver and Von Glinow, 1974.) But there is some recent evidence of progress (see footnote 4).

[2] Clearly, motivation is only one variable that is likely to affect performance. Others are the subordinate's general ability, as well as specific skills. To improve the subordinate's performance, the superior may choose to initiate training programs or take other actions to enhance the subordinate's skill, in addition to affecting his motivation.

(Galbraith and Cummings, 1967) between valences that are intrinsic to behavior itself (such as feelings of competence) and those that are the extrinsic consequences of behavior (such as pay). Behavior that is intrinsically valent is also intrinsically motivational because the behavior leads directly to satisfaction, whereas extrinsic valences are contingent on external rewards.

House's formulation can be expressed as follows:

$$M = IV_b + P_1 \left(IV_a + \sum_{i=1}^{n} P_{2i}EV_i \right), \qquad i = 1, 2, \cdots, n$$

where

M = motivation to work

IV_a = intrinsic valence associated with successful performance of the task

IV_b = intrinsic valence associated with goal-directed behavior

EV_i = extrinsic valences associated with the ith extrinsic reward contingent on work-goal accomplishment

P_1 = the expectancy that goal-directed behavior will accomplish the work-goal (a given level of specified performance); the measure's range is $(-1, +1)$

P_{2i} = the expectancy that work-goal accomplishment will lead to the ith extrinsic reward; the measure's range is $(-1, +1)$.

The individual estimates the expectancy, P_1, of accomplishing a work-goal given his behavior. For the estimate he considers factors such as (1) his ability to behave in an appropriate and effective manner and (2) the barriers and support for work-goal accomplishment in the environment. Also, he estimates the expectancy, P_2, that work-goal accomplishment will result in attaining extrinsic rewards that have valences for him such as the recognition of his superiors of his goal accomplishment. He also places subjective values on the intrinsic valence associated with the behavior required to achieve the work-goal IV_b, the intrinsic valence associated with the achievement of the work-goal IV_a, and the extrinsic valences associated with the personal outcomes that accrue to him as a result of achieving the work-goal, EV_i.

The superior can affect the independent variables of this model:

1. He partially determines what extrinsic rewards (EV_i) follow work-goal accomplishment, since he influences the extent to which work-goal accomplishment will be recognized as a contribution and the nature of the reward (financial increases, promotion, assignment of more interesting tasks or personal goals and development).
2. Through interaction, he can increase the subordinate's expectancy (P_2) that rewards ensue [from] work-goal accomplishment.

3. He can, through his own behavior, support the subordinate's efforts and thus influence the expectancy (P_i) that the effort will result in work-goal achievement.
4. He may influence the intrinsic valences associated with goal accomplishment (IV_a) by determining factors such as the amount of influence the subordinate has in goal setting and the amount of control he is allowed in the task-directed effort. Presumably, the greater the subordinate's opportunity to influence the goal and exercise control, the more intrinsically valent is the work-goal accomplishment.
5. The superior can increase the net intrinsic valences associated with goal-directed behavior (IV_b) by reducing frustrating barriers, by being supportive in times of stress, and by permitting involvement in a wide variety of tasks and being considerate of the subordinate's needs (House, 1971).

Three classes of situational variables that determine which particular superior behaviors are instrumental in increasing work motivation were hypothesized by House (1973):

(a) *The needs of the subordinate:* The subordinate views the superior's behavior as legitimate only to the extent that he perceives it either as an immediate source of satisfaction or as instrumental to his future satisfaction. For example, subordinates with high needs for social approval find warm, interpersonal superior behavior immediately satisfying and therefore legitimate. On the other hand, subordinates with high need for achievement desire clarification of path-goal relationships and goal-oriented feedback from superiors. The perceived legitimacy of the superior's behavior is thus partially determined by the subordinate's characteristics.

(b) *Environmental demands:* When the task is routine and well-defined, attempts by the superior to clarify path-goal relationships are redundant and are likely to be viewed as superfluous, externally imposed control, thus resulting in decreased satisfaction. Also, the more dissatisfying the task, the more the subordinate resents behavior by the superior directed at increasing productivity and enforcing compliance with organizational procedures.

(c) *The task demands of subordinates:* The superior's behavior is assumed to be motivational to the extent that it helps subordinates cope with environmental uncertainties, threat from others, or sources of frustration. Such behavior is predicted to increase the subordinate's satisfaction with the job content, and to be motivational to the extent that it increases the subordinate's perceived expectancies that effort will lead to valued rewards.

The Relation Between the Expectancy Model and the Accounting Budgeting Process

Budgets have long been recognized as a managerial tool of communication between superiors and subordinates with respect to the parameters of the task. As a tool of communication, the budgets are perceived by subordinates as an aspect of their superior's attitudes toward them, the task, and the work environment.

First, the budgets reflect management's expectations about what constitutes successful task performance; implicit in this is the promise of extrinsic rewards for the subordinates if the budget is accomplished. The imposition by management of a particular budget implies that its accomplishment will be recognized by management since it is in accordance with what management views as desirable goal attainment. To the extent that subordinates value the superior's recognition of their accomplishment, the budget communication constitutes a specification of the potential level of some of the extrinsic valences associated with work-goal accomplishment, (EV_i). The budgeting process, when coupled with subordinate knowledge of the external reinforcement contingencies (i.e., the set of rewards contingent on effective performance), clarifies the set of external valences associated with work-goal accomplishment or at least helps the subordinate to assess subjectively these valences.

Second, the perceived difficulty of the budget affects the expectancy of the subordinate that his effort would lead to budget achievement. Thus, the content of the budget also serves as an input for the subordinates to formulate their P_1 expectancies. Comparison of past levels of performance with past budgets generates a record of deviations which clearly influences P_1.

Third, the degree to which superiors were consistent or inconsistent in delivering the contingent rewards following budget accomplishment may induce the subordinates to revise their estimates of P_{2i}. Also, the degree to which superiors show recognition of past accomplishments will affect the subordinate's expectation of the level of future extrinsic valences (EV_i) associated with work-goal accomplishment.

The budget may also fulfill the role of providing structure to an ambiguous task as well as of coordinating activities so that merely working toward accomplishment of the budget provides satisfaction. To the extent that the budget content facilitates the derivation of this satisfaction, the budget also affects the intrinsic valence associated with the goal-directed behavior (IV_b).

Thus the budgeting process can crucially affect the parameters of the expectancy model. Consequently, we can gain insights into the effect on motivation — the dependent variable in this model — by examining the effects of the budgets on the independent variables of the model, such as the subordinate's expectations, perceived valences, etc. Such an examination should increase the likelihood of identifying the psychological mechanisms underlying the effects of budgets on work motivation. Among the psychological states of subordinates that deserve exploration are the subordinate's intrinsic job satisfaction, his expectancies that effort leads to effective performance, and his expectancies that performance leads to reward.

In the next section, it is shown that reinterpretation of previous experimental and other empirical investigations regarding the effects of budget on behavior makes it possible to integrate and reconcile the otherwise fragmented findings cited in the literature within the expectancy model framework.[3]

Integration of Prior Studies Within the Expectancy Framework

It is useful to reconcile prior findings and assumptions regarding impacts of budgets by focusing on the underlying behavioral assumptions assumed (although not necessarily valid) by accountants in the budgetary process:

A. The budget should be set at a reasonably attainable level.
B. Managers should participate in the development of budgets for their own functions in the organization.
C. Managers should operate on the principle of management by exception.
D. Personnel should be charged or credited only for items within their control.
E. Dimensions of performance that cannot be conveniently measured in monetary terms are outside the budgetary domain.

The possible invalidity of these assumptions has been extensively discussed in the accounting literature. The generalizations offered can be summarized as follows.

Achievement of budgeted performance may not satisfy the needs of the subordinates, who thus need not be motivated by the budget. Also, the individual's goals and the organization's goals may not be identical. For an individual to internalize or accept the budget, he must believe that

---

[3] Cherrington and Cherrington (1973) tested experimentally the effect of various conditions of budget participation and reinforcement contingencies on performance and on psychological states of subordinates such as satisfaction with job and perceived superior consideration. However, they did not test an expectancy model per se but merely investigated the effects of their manipulated conditions in the context of reinforcement and operant conditioning theory.

achieving it will satisfy his needs better than not achieving it. A goal that an individual has internalized is known as his aspiration level — the performance level that he undertakes to reach (see, e.g., Becker and Green, 1962). The probability that an individual will internalize the budget is influenced by his expectations of what he is able to achieve (Costello and Zelking, 1963), his past experience of success in reaching budgeted goals, and the priority that he assigns to the need for a sense of personal achievement.

These assumptions are now closely examined in an attempt to show how the expectancy model can be used to integrate findings and assertions related to them within a cohesive framework.

A. THE ASSUMPTION THAT STANDARDS SHOULD BE REASONABLY ATTAINABLE

Summary of Existing Studies. The assumption implies that as long as the standards do not exceed what is reasonably attainable, the subordinate will internalize them. If too tight, presumably the subordinate will regard the budget as unrealistic and either cease to be motivated or be negatively motivated by it. Thus, while loose standards (as opposed to reasonably attainable standards) will lead to slackening of effort, tight standards could be perceived as unrealistic and therefore fail to motivate personnel, except perhaps in a negative direction (National Association of Accountants, 1948). For example, Stedry (1960) suggested that, under certain conditions, performance could be improved if management will impose unattainable standards on subordinates. Under laboratory conditions, he found that his measurements of the subjects' aspiration levels were influenced by the level at which the imposed standards were set. He also found that performance that was significantly different from the aspiration level led to an adjustment of the aspiration level in the direction of the performance level that was actually achieved. Thus, he suggested that standards be changed from period to period so that they are met some of the time and are slightly above the attainable level the rest of the time. Hofstede (1967) also found that motivation is highest when standards are difficult to reach but are not regarded as impossible.

Other discussions and evidence in the literature support these findings. When an individual barely achieves the level of aspiration, he is said to have subjective feelings of success; subjective feelings of failure follow nonachievement of the level of aspiration (Lewin, Dembo, Festinger and Sears, 1944). In particular, Child and Whiting (1954) argue that (a) success generally raises the level of aspiration, failure lowers it; (b) the probability of rise in level of aspiration is positively correlated with the strength of success or failure; (c) changes in the level of aspiration partially depend on changes in the subject's confidence in his ability to attain goals; and (d) failure is more likely than success to lead to avoidance of setting a level of aspiration.

From their review of the literature, Becker and Green (1962) conclude that "level of aspiration not only describes a goal for future attainment but also it partially insures that an individual will expend a more than minimal amount of energy, if necessary, to perform at or above the level." Indeed, although not in a business budgeting setting, Bayton (1943) found that higher performance followed higher level of aspiration in testing the performance of 300 subjects on seven arithmetic problems. Also, Cherrington and Cherrington (1973) experimentally found that, when supervisors imposed either a minimum or a specific standard of performance, the subordinate's estimate of their performance (level of aspiration) was higher than when supervisors imposed either lenient minimum standards of performance or imposed none at all. They also found that the higher estimates of performance also were followed by higher actual performance. Cherrington and Cherrington's findings seem somewhat to contradict some of Stedry's (1960) results. In Stedry's study, one group was first given the standard and then asked to indicate its own goal for performance in the subsequent period. The second group was asked to indicate its goals *before* it knew what the experimental manager's goals were. The group setting its personal goals first set higher goals and performed better than the group which was informed of management's goals first, although it must be noted that, in Cherrington and Cherrington's study, high estimates and performance were achieved when the group also formulated its estimates before knowledge of the supervisor's imposed minimums. Thus, in a sense, the situation is not unsimilar to Stedry's except that revision of the estimate after knowledge of the supervisor's higher standards proved to be beneficial.

Reconciliation with the Expectancy Model. In terms of the expectancy model, the conclusion that standards regarded as impossible are not motivational or negatively motivational can simply be explained by the fact that P_1, the expectancy that goal-directed behavior would lead to work-goal accomplishment, was low or even negative and, to show this more clearly, Stedry's conclusions are examined in light of the expectancy model.

As indicated, Stedry found that his measurements of the subject's aspiration levels were influenced by the level at which the imposed standards were set. The results of the Cherringtons' study partially confirm Stedry's results in that the experimental group's estimate of their performance was highest under nonparticipation conditions, i.e., when high minimum standards were imposed. If the aspiration level is taken to reflect the level which the subordinate sets out to achieve, then it is understandable that (within limits) the higher the imposed standards by superiors, the higher would be the aspiration level. In comparison with other levels of attainment, P_{2i}, the expectancies that work-goal accomplishment will lead to extrinsic valences would be higher the nearer the performance level is to the imposed standard. Thus, if the subordinate's task is viewed as a selection among different aspiration levels, it is only natural that he will choose the aspiration level that maximizes the dependent variable M in the model.

However, if the imposed standards are too high, the aspiration level will lag behind since, although P_{2i} will increase, P_1, the expectancy that goal-directed behavior will lead to work-goal accomplishment, is likely to be negatively correlated with the perceived difficulty of attaining the standard.

The assessment of P_1 is also likely to be affected by feedback on past performance; P_1 will tend to be positively correlated with prior levels of performance and consequently the dependent variable and the aspiration level will tend to move in the same direction as performance. This "Expectancy Model" induced observation could explain Stedry's other finding that performance which differed significantly from the aspiration level led to the latter's adjustment in the direction of the performance level actually achieved.

It is particularly important and interesting to relate the level of aspiration conceptualization of the budgeting process with the expectancy approach. The expectancy model's dependent variable — motivation to exert effort in the task — is a direct function of the expected valences. The model's underlying assumption is that the higher the expectation of valences, the greater the effort the subordinate is likely to exert and, thus, the higher the performance level. In other words, the subordinate's effort exerted in task performance is assumed to change along a continuum as a function of the expectation of valences.

Level of aspiration, on the other hand, is operationally defined as "the goal one explicitly undertakes to reach," where "maximum effort will be exerted to just reach an aspiration goal" (Becker and Green, 1962). According to this view, effort is seen not as a continuum but as changing discretely where the level of aspiration goal of performance is that for which a maximum — a specifically defined amount of effort — is spent in order to derive the subjective feeling of success. If we attempt to interpret the meaning of the level of aspiration within the expectancy framework, it seems that it corresponds to the performance level consciously chosen by the subordinate (among alternative performance levels) so as to maximize the expectation of valences — the value of the expectancy equation. That is, the subordinate behaves as if he computes the expected values associated with different performance levels, which clearly depend on the model's parameters (P_1, P_2, IV_b, IV_a, and EV_i) and selects the one that maximizes M as the level of aspiration. The implications of this relationship between the level of aspiration and the expectancy model's dependent variable to the specification of desirable attributes of the budgetary process could be far-reaching.

B. PARTICIPATION

Summary of Existing Studies. Participation means that decisions affecting a manager's operations are, to some extent, jointly made by the manager and his superior. As such, it is more than mere consultation by which the superior informs himself of the manager's views but makes the decisions himself. The participation of subordinates in budget setting is usually regarded as effective in getting subordinates to internalize the standards embodied in the budgets and thus in achieving goal congruence (Welsch, 1971).

The role of participation can perhaps be best understood in the context of group dynamics. Aspiration levels are said partially to depend on the levels of aspiration prevailing in the groups that the individual belongs to (Lewin, 1964). The amount of influence that group members are said to have on the individual's aspiration level depends on the group's cohesiveness, i.e., the degree to which individual members value their group membership.

The value of group membership to an individual derives from the degree to which the individual believes that group membership will help him attain his own goals (Caplan, 1966 and Vroom, 1964a). Perceived value of membership seems to be correlated with the likelihood that different members in the group will have similar goals — thus the individual's likelihood of continued membership in the group. The relationship between the two appears to be reciprocal. Similarity of goals among the group's members will make membership in the group more attractive. On the other hand, if membership in the group is highly valued, the individual will tend to assimilate the group's goal to be able to maintain the valued membership. As a result of valuing his own membership and his desire to maintain it, the individual will tend to reject goals that he believes conflict with those prevailing in the group and accept those that appear to be consistent with the group's goals (Caplan, 1966 and Vroom, 1964a).

Thus, participation does not seem automatically to produce congruence between the group's goal and that of the firm. Conditions may be such that a more authoritarian managerial style will be more effective in raising the aspiration levels of subordinates. Becker and Green (1962) describe these conditions in greater specificity. Their position could be summarized as follows: if greater interaction of individuals leads to greater group cohesiveness, and if this cohesiveness plus some incentive to produce either at higher or lower levels are positively correlated, then participation can be an inducement for higher or lower levels of performance. Also, if participation at an upper level generates positive attitudes on the part of supervisors, then they will try to induce higher individual and group aspirations in the sub-group which will hopefully lead to higher rather than lower levels of performance.

There is also some evidence that participation improves morale. Coch and French (1948) found a much lower turnover rate, fewer grievances about piece rates, and less aggression against the supervisor as individual participation in planning job changes increased. Vroom (1960) argues that participation makes employees feel more a part of the activities and less dominated by a superior, more independent, and thus improves their attitude toward the job. But while participation enhanced satisfaction, it did not necessarily increase productivity. Or at least the results are ambiguous. Literature to date shows no direct correlation between participation and improved productivity (e.g., Cherrington and Cherrington, 1973; Coch and French, 1948; and French, Kay, and Meyer, 1962).

Personality variables can also affect the relation between participation and performance. For example, Vroom emphasizes the affective consequences of the degree of consistency between a person's performance and his self-concept: persons were found to perform better on tasks perceived to require highly valued ability or intelligence which they believed themselves to possess (Vroom, 1960).

Reconciliation with the Expectancy Model. It was indicated that participation tends to increase performance if interaction of individuals leads to greater group cohesiveness and if the group norms are such that they are conducive to higher levels of production. These particular effects of participation can be accommodated within the expectancy model. A group is cohesive when the individual members value their acceptance within the group. Participation in the context of a cohesive group would be a process of reaching consensus within the group on the desirable standards of performance within the group. Once such a consensus has been reached as a result of the group's participation, it would be viewed by the individual as reflecting the group's own norm. Striving to attain that goal would, therefore, increase the individual's likelihood of maintaining his acceptance in the group. In terms of the expectancy model, the existence of a cohesive group of which the subordinate is a member enhances the extrinsic valence associated with work-goal accomplishment. With the attainment of the goal, the individual achieves not only the extrinsic and intrinsic valences that exist in the absence of a group context, but in addition, he maintains his acceptance in a cohesive group which can be regarded as an extrinsic valence associated with goal-accomplishment.

In addition, participation may create intrinsic valences that are absent in nonparticipative environments. These intrinsic valences may be due to a tendency for individuals to become "ego-involved" in decisions to which they have contributed, as would be the case in participative decision-making. A similar process is suggested by evidence that participation by a single person in decision-making with a superior affects the subsequent performance of that person (Vroom, 1970).

Thus, only when groups are cohesive and their norms support the organization would participation be likely to increase motivation and hence the aspiration level and hence performance. When groups are not cohesive, no additional valence is introduced and therefore motivation is not likely to be increased, although participation may increase group cohesiveness, as stated above. In fact, participation in certain environments can lead to negative results as related, for example, by Shillinglaw (1972). The introduction of participative budgeting in a large electrical equipment factory years ago was received coldly by most of the first level supervisors. The reason offered was that foremen were reluctant to accept the risk of censure for failure to achieve targets that they had set themselves (Stedry and Kay, 1966). In terms of this expectancy model, this phenomenon can be explained in terms of the effect of undesired participation on IV_b. Since participation under this environment induced anxiety and thus a decrement in the intrinsic valence associated with goal-directed behavior, motivation and performance were likely to decline.

C. Management by Exception

Summary of Existing Studies. The fact that accountants and managers emphasize deviations (we use this term instead of variances) in accounting reports implies that, by and large, attention is merited when significant deviations are observed and not when standards are met. Such a system, however, may be perceived as emphasizing failure with only exceptional success attracting management attention. The response to favorable deviations not requiring corrective actions often seems to be weaker than that to unfavorable deviation. As a result, subordinates may be led to view the system as punitive rather than as informative. This may lead to defensiveness, overcautious behavior, and other dysfunctional effects (Sayles and Chandler, 1971). This suggests that effort should be made to emphasize positive as well as negative aspects of performance to provide "positive reinforcement" (Birnberg and Nath, 1967).

Reconciliation with the Expectancy Model. In terms of the expectancy model, it is easy to predict the effect of these practices. Nonreinforcement or mere attainment of the budget will tend to decrease P_{2i}, the expectancy goal that accomplishment leads to extrinsic valences. The same effect would be produced by relative nonreinforcement of performance that is superior to the budget. On the other hand, punitive response to unfavorable deviations, while it may accomplish some results since subordinates have no alternatives, may also result in resistance, sabotage, and other kinds of conflict. Punishment is known to have generally negative effects (Vroom, 1964a). The Cherringtons' (1973) finding that only appropriate reinforcement contingencies (i.e., when subordinates can control the performance on which rewards are contingent) were motivational can also be explained in terms of the effect on P_{2i}.

D. THE CONTROLLABILITY CRITERION

Summary of Existing Studies. Controllability refers to the ability of the subordinate to make decisions and execute them in his attempt to accomplish specified goals or a budget. A distinction must be made between *actual* control and *perceived* control. The motivational variable of interest is perceived control, which may differ from the actual degree of control that the subordinate can apply to a task. Personality as well as sociological factors can affect the degree of deviation between perceived control and actual control (Feather, 1967).

It is generally asserted that only controllable activities in the budget should constitute the basis for evaluation and reinforcement of the subordinate. For example, according to Vroom (1970, p. 213):

> the effectiveness of any system in which rewards and punishments are contingent on specified performance outcomes appears to be dependent on the degree of control which the individual has over these performance outcomes. The increment in performance to be expected from an increase in the extent to which the individual is rewarded for favorable results and/or punished for unfavorable results is directly related to the extent to which the individual can control the results of his performance.

Several sources can contribute to the lack of control over results which appears from existing evidence to reduce the effectiveness of organizationally administered reward-punishment contingencies. The first source is the existence of interpersonal and interdepartmental interdependencies within the formal organization. The jointness of the inputs in terms of subordinates' effort makes it extremely difficult to measure and assess a particular subordinate's contribution to the results. In such an interdependence set-up, only the effort of a group as a whole can be adequately evaluated and each person has but partial control over the group's outcome.

The second source for lack of control is the operation of "chance" events that perturb the otherwise one-to-one relationship between the subordinate's efforts and his accomplishments. States of nature that are beyond his control affect the results of his effort. The existence of these "chance" events is partially a function of the nature of the task itself. Shooting at a fast-moving target, for example, is subject to far more external and uncontrollable events than performing a standard manufacturing operation.

The degree of skill of a subordinate to perform a job constitutes a third source of lack of control over results. While the degree of skill tends to be inversely related to the incidence of "chance" events, the two variables (skill and chance) are usefully viewed as distinct from each other (Feather, 1967). The degree to which "chance" factors affect performance depends on the skill of the performer as well as on the nature of the task. Thus, a very competent and skillful performer may still fail because the task is subject to many external perturbances, and, at the same time, an unskilled worker may fail to perform effectively even if his task is highly structured and subject to no external disturbances.

As indicated above, the perceived and not the actual degree of control is the variable of interest from the standpoint of predicting motivation and performance. And, as suggested, perceived control may differ from actual control, and the difference can depend on personality variables such as degree of achievement motivation, risk-taking behavior, as well as on cultural variables such as blacks vs. whites, etc. (Lefcourt, 1965; Rotter, Liverant, and Crowne, 1961; and Sutcliffe, 1956.)

Reconciliation with the Expectancy Model. Using the expectancy model, it can be explained why only activities in the budget that are perceived as controllable by the subordinate should constitute the basis for evaluation and reinforcement. Only activities that are perceived as controllable are likely to be associated with a relatively high P_1. In addition, performing tasks that are perceived as controllable could be associated with higher intrinsic valences (Ronen, 1973).

Unfortunately, since it is difficult to discriminate finely between controllable and noncontrollable activities, dysfunctional decisions may result:

(1) Excluding from the evaluation basis activities that are partially controllable but classified as uncontrollable will direct the subordinate not to exert effort in those activities and eventually to jeopardize the accomplishment of the organization's goals. When basically controllable activities are excluded from the evaluation basis, the dependent variable, M, of the expectancy model operates on only some of the activities that are instrumental to the firm's over-all goal attainment and it by-passes other beneficial activities.
(2) Including in the evaluation basis activities that are perceived by the subordinate as noncontrollable can result in lowering his expectancy that effort will lead to work accomplishment, i.e., P_1.

Also, the intrinsic valence associated with goal-accomplishment may decrease if the task is perceived as partially beyond the subordinate's control. Under both cases, the subordinate's motivation to exert effort in his performance will tend to decrease.

E. THE EXCLUSION OF CRITERIA THAT ARE NOT EASILY MEASURED IN MONETARY TERMS

Summary of Existing Studies. Because of the difficulty of measuring nonmonetary dimensions of performance, the accounting structure usually restricts itself to reporting financial performance. As a result, managers may be motivated to emphasize the things that are measured to the neglect of those that are not. One suggested solution to this problem is the development of a composite measure of performance, with each dimension assigned a weight in proportion to top management's perceived priority. But this solution is deficient because the weighting schemes are implicit, difficult to translate into numerical form, and possibly non-stable over time. However, a useful step is said to be to identify the major dimensions of performance, whether measurable or not, so that they could be incorporated into the performance review process. The motivational problem involved is that the subordinates lack knowledge of the precise managerial reward structure and the weighting schemes implicit in the evaluation system.

Reconciliation with the Expectancy Model. The exclusion of nonmonetary criteria from the evaluation basis can be interpreted in terms of the expectancy model as motivating subordinates on the basis of only one dimension. In other words, the dependent variable, M, is characterized by only one dimension — the maximization of monetary profits. Since the work-goal accomplishment that is expected to secure extrinsic rewards EV_i, is only defined by the criterion of maximizing monetary profits, the kinds of effort spent by the subordinate in the task will be only directed to that, and other objectives will be neglected.

Using the expectancy model, the subordinate can be motivated to spend effort to accomplish nonmonetary objectives if these are formally introduced into the control system by: (1) making extrinsic rewards contingent on their accomplishment, (2) by facilitating their accomplishment through task clarification, (i.e., through increasing P_1), and (3) also by attempting to make the accomplishment of the nonmonetary criteria intrinsically valent to the subordinate.

As suggested by Vroom, one of the conditions needed to improve productivity by making effective performance on a task instrumental to the attainment of organizationally mediated rewards or the avoidance of punishments is that:

> There is no conflict, either actual or perceived, between those behaviors necessary to attain a short term reward (for example, higher wages this week) and those required to avoid a longer term punishment (for example, a tightening of standards) (Vroom, 1970).

However, merely introducing the nonmonetary criteria into the expectancy model through the explicit specification of effective performance via the budget does not in itself facilitate the attainment of goal congruence, unless the importance attached by top management to the attainment of various criteria is also made explicit to subordinates and internalized by them. If the weights to be attached to the criteria that are implicit in management's preference function are not made explicit to the subordinate, he may impose his own preference ordering on the criteria. That may not coincide with the management's preference ranking. In this case, goal congruence will not be attained in spite of the incorporation of the nonmonetary criteria into the model.

Summary and Conclusions

The literature on the effects of budgets on behavior is quite fragmentary and draws upon many diverse and partial areas of behavioral science. We have shown that this is the case for five general assumptions made in accounting with respect to budgets and behavior. These assumptions are:

(A) that standards should be reasonably attainable,
(B) that participation in the budgeting process leads to better performance,
(C) that management by exception is effective,
(D) that noncontrollable items should be excluded from budget reports, and
(E) that budgetary accounting should be restricted to criteria measurable in monetary terms.

We then introduced an expectancy model of task motivation within which, with some refinement, it was possible both to reconcile the fragmentary and contradictory past research findings and to explain the five assumptions in a consistent manner. To summarize, the following relations between the assumptions and variables in the expectancy model were discussed:

Standards:	P_1, P_2 (expectancies of performance and of reward)
Participation:	IV_a, IV_b, EV_i (intrinsic and extrinsic valences)
Exception Management:	P_2
Controllability:	P_1, IV_a
Monetary Criteria:	P_1, EV_i

We examined not only the budget's impact on behavior per se, but also the effects of the superiors' responses contingent on given levels of budget achievement on the part of the subordinate. Thus, the administration of extrinsic rewards contingent on successful budget achievement and the facilitation of intrinsic values are both related to the budgeting process and affect the subordinates' performance. As a result, the expectancy model could be also used as a framework for evaluating the effect of the accounting reports that compare actual performance with the budget on the subordinates' future performance.

Of course, there is a wealth of other relations which fall outside the immediate scope of this paper. The literature of expectancy theory is large, rich in empirical research, and fast-growing. We recognize that the expectancy theory and its assumptions have come under criticism and that tests of the model's predictive ability have produced ambiguous results (see footnote 1). Nonetheless, recent progress in the testing and the operationalization of the model has apparently been made.[4]

Future research should be concerned with the derivation of testable hypotheses that apply the expectancy framework to the budgeting process as well as with further improving the predictive validity of the model through better operationalization of its variables. Also, the moderating effects of situational variables that are part of the working environment on the relation between budgets and motivation should be explored and tested. These situational aspects include variables such as the needs of subordinates, the environmental pressures and demands that subordinates must cope with to accomplish work goals and satisfy their needs, and the task demands of subordinates. Another particularly promising avenue for future research is the rigorous formulation of an expectancy model version which ties in with the SEU (Subjections Expected Utility) model, and with the level of aspiration theory.

Motivation, the dependent variable in the expectancy model, can be used as an indication of the probability that the task will be performed, given the ability of the subordinate. In other words, the probability that a task will be performed is a function of motivation and ability. To the superior it is important to assess this ability in order both to evaluate the merit of competing activities and to allocate effectively people to tasks. Hypotheses generated and tested within an expectancy framework should be helpful toward that end.

References

Argyris, C., *The Impact of Budgets on People* (Controllership Foundation, 1952).

---

[4] Reviews of recent empirical studies in nonbudget context, which were designed either to test directly the expectancy model or to provide an inferential basis for assessing the model's validity indicate some empirical support for the relationships stipulated by the expectancy theory (Dessler, 1973; House and Dessler, 1973; House and Wahba, 1972; Kopelman, 1974). In fact, Kopelman (1974) observed coefficients of correlation between the model's independent variables and performance indicators as high as 0.53. Furthermore, operational tools for measuring the model's parameters are available and are in the process of being continually improved and refined (House, 1972).

Atkinson, J. W., "Toward Experimental Analysis of Human Motivation in Terms of Motives, Expectations and Incentives," in J. W. Atkinson, ed., *Motives in Fantasy, Action and Society* (Van Nostrand, 1958).

Bayton, J. A., "Inter-relations Between Levels of Aspiration, Performance, and Estimates of Past Performance," *Journal of Experimental Psychology* (1943), *33*, p. 1–21.

Becker, S. and Green, D., "Budgeting and Employee Behavior," *Journal of Business* (October 1962), pp. 392–402.

Benston, G., "The Role of the Firm's Accounting System for Motivation," *The Accounting Review* (April 1963), pp. 351–3.

Birnberg, J. G. and Nath, R., "Implications of Behavioral Science for Managerial Accounting," *The Accounting Review* (July 1967), p. 478.

Caplan, E., "Behavioral Assumptions of Management Accounting," *The Accounting Review* (July 1966), pp. 476–509.

Cherrington, D. J., and Cherrington, J. O., "Appropriate Reinforcement Contingencies in the Budgeting Process," presented at the *Accounting Empirical Research Conference,* University of Chicago (May 1973).

Child, J. L. and Whiting, J. W. M., "Determinants of Level of Aspiration: Evidence from Everyday Life," in H. Branch, ed., *The Study of Personality* (Wiley, 1954), pp. 145–58.

Coch, L. and French, J. R. P., "Overcoming Resistance to Change," *Human Relations* (1948), *1*, pp. 512–32.

Costello, T. and Zelking, S., *Psychology in Administration: A Research Orientation* (Prentice-Hall, 1963).

Dessler, G., "A Test of the Path-Goal Theory of Leadership," Doctoral Dissertation, Bernard M. Baruch College, City University of New York, 1973.

Feather, N. T., "Valence of Outcome and Expectation of Success in Relation to Task Difficulty and Perceived Locus of Control," *Journal of Personality and Social Psychology* (1967), *7,* pp. 372–86.

French, J. R. P., Kay, E., and Meyer, H. H., *A Study of Threat and Participation in a Performance Appraisal Situation* (General Electric Co., 1962).

Galbraith, J., and Cummings, L. L., "An Empirical Investigation of the Motivational Determinants of Past Performance: Interactive Effects Between Instrumentality, Valence, Motivation and Ability," *Organizational Behavior and Human Performance* (1967), *8*, pp. 237–57.

Georgopoulos, B. S., Mahoney, G. M., and Jones, N. W., "A Path Goal Approach to Productivity," *Journal of Applied Psychology* (1957), *41,* pp. 345–53.

Graen, G., "Instrumental Theory of Work Motivation: Some Empirical Results and Suggested Modifications," *Journal of Applied Psychology* (1969), *53*, pp. 1–25.

Hofstede, G. H., *The Game of Budget Control* (Assen, The Netherlands, Koninklijke Van Corcum and Comp. N. V., 1967), pp. 152–6.

House, R. J., "Some Preliminary Findings Concerning a Test of the Path Goal Theory of Leadership," (unpublished manuscript, University of Toronto, April 1972).

————, *Notes on Questionnaires Frequently Used by or Developed by R. J. House,* Faculty of Management Studies, University of Toronto, July, 1972.

————, "A Path-Goal Theory of Leader Effectiveness," *Administrative Science Quarterly* (September 1971), *16, 3,* pp. 321–38.

———— and Dessler, G., "The Path-Goal Theory of Leadership: Some Post Hoc and A Priori Tests," paper presented at the Second Leadership Symposium: Contingency Approaches to Leadership; Southern Illinois University, Carbondale, Ill., April 1973.

———— and Wahba, M. A., "Expectancy Theory as a Predictor of Job Performance, Satisfaction and Motivation: An Integrative Model and a Review of the Literature," paper presented at the American Psychological Association Meeting, Hawaii, August, 1972; Working Paper 72-21, Faculty of Management Studies, University of Toronto, 1972.

Kerr, S., Klimoski, R. J., Tolliver, J., and Von Glinow, M. A., "Human Information Processing and Problem Solving," paper presented at the Workshop in Behavioral Accounting: Annual Meeting of the American Institute for Decision Sciences, Atlanta, Ga., Oct. 30, 1974.

Kopelman, R., "Factors Complicating Expectancy Theory Prediction of Work Motivation and Job Performance," paper presented at the meeting of the American Psychological Association, 1974.

Lawler, E. E., "A Correlation Causal Analysis of the Relationship Between Expectancy Attitudes and Job Performance," *Journal of Applied Psychology* (1968), *52,* pp. 462–8.

————, *Pay and Organizational Effectiveness: A Psychological Perspective* (Wiley, 1971).

———— and Suttle, J. K., "Expectancy Theory and Job Behavior," *Organizational Behavior and Human Performance* (1973), *9,* pp. 482–503.

Lefcourt, H. M., "Risk Taking in Negro and White Adults," *Journal of Personality and Social Psychology* (1965), *2,* pp. 765–70.

Lewin, K., "The Psychology of a Successful Figure," in *Readings in Managerial Psychology,* H. S. Leavitt and L. R. Pondy, eds. (University of Chicago Press, 1964), pp. 25–31.

————, Dembo, T., Festinger, L., and Sears, P., "Level of Aspiration," in J. McV. Hunt, ed., *Personality and Behavior Disorder* (Ronald Press, 1944), *1,* pp. 338–78.

National Association of Accountants, *How Standard Costs Are Used Currently* (New York, 1948), pp. 8–9.

Porter, L., and Lawler, E. E., *Managerial Attitudes and Performance* (Irwin-Dorsey, 1967).

Ronen, J., "Involvement in Tasks and Choice Behavior," *Organizational Behavior and Human Performance* (February 1974), *2,* pp. 28–43.

Rotter, J. B., Liverant, S., and Crowne, D. P., "Growth and Extinction of Expectancies in Chance Controlled and Skill Tasks," *Journal of Psychology,* (1961), *52,* pp. 151–77.

Sayles, L. R. and Chandler, M. K., *Managing Large Systems: Organizations for the Future* (Harper & Row, 1971).

Schiff, M. and Lewin, A. Y., "The Impact of People on Budgets," *The Accounting Review* (April 1970), pp. 259–68.

Shillinglaw, G., *Cost Accounting, Analysis and Control,* 3rd ed. (Irwin, 1972).

Stedry, A., *Budgetary Control and Cost Behavior* (Prentice-Hall, 1960).

———— and Kay, E., "The Effects of Goal Difficulty on Performance: A Field Experiment," *Behavioral Science, II* (1966), pp. 459–70.

Sutcliffe, J. P., "Random Effects as a Function of Belief in Control," *Australian Journal of Psychology* (1956), *8,* pp. 128–39.

Usry, M., "Solving the Problem of Human Relations in Budgeting," *Budgeting* (Nov.–Dec. 1968), pp. 4–6.

Vroom, V. H., "Industrial Social Psychology," in *Handbook of Social Psychology* (Addison-Wesley, 1970).

————, "Some Psychological Aspects of Organizational Control," in Cooper, Leavitt & Shelly, eds., *New Perspectives in Organizational Research* (Wiley, 1964a).

————, *Work and Motivation* (Wiley, 1964b).

————, *Some Personality Determinants of the Effect of Participation* (Prentice-Hall, 1960).

Welsch, G. A., *Budgeting: Profit Planning and Control,* 3rd ed. (Prentice-Hall, 1971), pp. 17, 22–23.

Williamson, O. E., *The Economics of Discretionary Behavior: Managerial Objectives in a Theory of the Firm* (Prentice-Hall, 1964), pp. 28–37.

8 *Critical Path Method, like PERT, is a decision-making tool which can find wide appreciation at all levels of management. Both (along with other similar techniques) are methods of determining which activities in a project or task are critical to the timely completion of the total project.*

CPM is most effective within the context of well-defined, ordered jobs or tasks which may be performed independently of each other. An obvious and early application — the construction industry — is illustrated in this painstaking and thorough introduction to the methodology of CPM.

One of the significant advantages of either PERT or CPM is that the user is required to give considerable attention to planning and scheduling, which yields a return which is independent of the PERT–CPM technique.

The ABCs of the Critical Path Method*

Ferdinand K. Levy, Gerald L. Thompson,
Jerome D. Wiest†

Recently added to the growing assortment of quantitative tools for business decision making is the Critical Path Method — a powerful but basically simple technique for analyzing, planning, and scheduling large, complex projects. In essence, the tool provides a means of determining (1) which jobs or activities, of the many that comprise a project, are "critical" in their

* *Ferdinand K. Levy, Gerald L. Thompson, and Jerome D. Wiest, "The ABCs of the Critical Path Method," Harvard Business Review, 41, No. 5 (September–October, 1963), pp. 98–108.* Copyright © 1963 by the President and Fellows of Harvard College; all rights reserved.

† The preparation of this article was supported by the Office of Naval Research and the Bureau of Ships through grants to the Graduate School of Industrial Administration, Carnegie Institute of Technology. A different version of this material appears as Chapter 20 in *Industrial Scheduling*, edited by J. F. Muth and G. L. Thompson (Englewood Cliffs, New Jersey: Prentice-Hall, Inc., 1963). The job list and project graph for the house-building example were developed by Peter R. Winters.

effect on total project time, and (2) how best to schedule all jobs in the project in order to meet a target date at minimum cost. Widely diverse kinds of projects lend themselves to analysis by CPM, as is suggested in the following list of applications:

- The construction of a building (or a highway).
- Planning and launching a new product.
- A turnaround in an oil refinery (or other maintenance projects).
- Installing and debugging a computer system.
- Research and engineering design projects.
- Scheduling ship construction and repairs.
- The manufacture and assembly of a large generator (or other job-lot operations).
- Missile countdown procedures.

Each of these projects has several characteristics that are essential for analysis by CPM:

1. The project consists of a well-defined collection of jobs (or activities) which, when completed, mark the end of the project.
2. The jobs may be started and stopped independently of each other, within a given sequence. (This requirement eliminates continuous-flow process activities, such as oil refining, where "jobs" or operations necessarily follow one after another with essentially no slack.)
3. The jobs are ordered — that is, they must be performed in technological sequence. (For example, the foundation of a house must be constructed before the walls are erected.)

What Is the Method?

The concept of CPM is quite simple and may best be illustrated in terms of a project graph. The graph is not an essential part of CPM; computer programs have been written which permit necessary calculations to be made without reference to a graph. Nevertheless, the project graph is valuable as a means of depicting, visually and clearly, the complex of jobs in a project and their interrelations:

First of all, each job necessary for the completion of a project is listed with a unique identifying symbol (such as a letter or number), the time required to complete the job, and its immediate prerequisite jobs. For convenience in graphing, and as a check on certain kinds of data errors, the jobs may be arranged in "technological order," which means that no job appears on the list until all of its predecessors have been listed. Technological ordering is impossible if a cycle error exists in the job data (e.g., job *a* precedes *b*, *b* precedes *c*, and *c* precedes *a*).

Then each job is drawn on the graph as a circle, with its identifying symbol and time appearing within the circle. Sequence relationships are indicated by arrows connecting each circle (job) with its immediate successors, with the arrows pointing to the latter. For convenience, all circles with no predecessors are connected to a circle marked "Start"; likewise, all circles with no successors are connected to a circle marked "Finish." (The "Start" and "Finish" circles may be considered pseudo jobs of zero time length.)

Typically, the graph then depicts a number of different "arrow paths" from Start to Finish. The time required to traverse each path is the sum of the times associated with all jobs on the path. The critical path (or paths) is the longest path (in time) from Start to Finish; it indicates the minimum time necessary to complete the entire project.

This method of depicting a project graph differs in some respects from that used by James E. Kelley, Jr., and Morgan R. Walker, who, perhaps more than anyone else, were responsible for the initial development of CPM. (For an interesting account of its early history see their paper, "Critical-Path Planning and Scheduling."[1]) In the widely used Kelley-Walker form, a project graph is just the opposite of that described above: jobs are shown as arrows, and the arrows are connected by means of circles (or dots) that indicate sequence relationships. Thus all immediate predecessors of a given job connect to a circle at the tail of the job arrow, and all immediate successor jobs emanate from the circle at the head of the job arrow. In essence, then, a circle marks an event — the completion of all jobs leading into the circle. Since these jobs are the immediate prerequisites for all jobs leading out of the circle, they must all be completed before *any* of the succeeding jobs can begin.

In order to accurately portray all predecessor relationships, "dummy jobs" must often be added to the project graph in the Kelley-Walker form. The method described in this article avoids the necessity and complexity of dummy jobs, is easier to program for a computer, and also seems more straightforward in explanation and application.

In essence, the critical path is the bottleneck route. Only by finding ways to shorten jobs along the critical path can the over-all project time be reduced; the time required to perform noncritical jobs is irrelevant from the viewpoint of total project time. The frequent (and costly) practice of "crashing" *all* jobs in a project in order to reduce total project time is thus unnecessary. Typically, only about 10% of the jobs in large projects are critical. (This figure will naturally vary from project to project.) Of course, if some way is found to shorten one or more of the critical jobs, then not only will the whole project time be shortened but the critical path itself may shift and some previously noncritical jobs may become critical.

Example: Building a House

A simple and familiar example should help to clarify the notion of critical path scheduling and the process of constructing a graph. The project of

---

[1] *Proceedings of the Eastern Joint Computer Conference*, Boston, December 1–3, 1959; see also James E. Kelley, Jr., "Critical-Path Planning and Scheduling: Mathematical Basis," *Operations Research*, May–June, 1961, pp. 296–320.

building a house is readily analyzed by the CPM technique and is typical of a large class of similar applications. While a contractor might want a more detailed analysis, we will be satisfied here with the list of major jobs (together with the estimated time and the immediate predecessors for each job) shown in Exhibit 1.

In that exhibit, the column "immediate predecessors" determines the sequence relationships of the jobs and enables us to draw the project graph,

EXHIBIT 1

Sequence and Time Requirements of Jobs

JOB NO.	DESCRIPTION	IMMEDIATE PREDECESSORS	NORMAL TIME (DAYS)
a	START		0
b	EXCAVATE AND POUR FOOTERS	a	4
c	POUR CONCRETE FOUNDATION	b	2
d	ERECT WOODEN FRAME INCLUDING ROUGH ROOF	c	4
e	LAY BRICKWORK	d	6
f	INSTALL BASEMENT DRAINS AND PLUMBING	c	1
g	POUR BASEMENT FLOOR	f	2
h	INSTALL ROUGH PLUMBING	f	3
i	INSTALL ROUGH WIRING	d	2
j	INSTALL HEATING AND VENTILATING	d,g	4
k	FASTEN PLASTER BOARD AND PLASTER (INCLUDING DRYING)	i,j,h	10
l	LAY FINISH FLOORING	k	3
m	INSTALL KITCHEN FIXTURES	l	1
n	INSTALL FINISH PLUMBING	l	2
o	FINISH CARPENTRY	l	3
p	FINISH ROOFING AND FLASHING	e	2
q	FASTEN GUTTERS AND DOWNSPOUTS	p	1
r	LAY STORM DRAINS FOR RAIN WATER	c	1
s	SAND AND VARNISH FLOORING	o,l	2
t	PAINT	m,n	3
u	FINISH ELECTRICAL WORK	t	1
v	FINISH GRADING	q,r	2
w	POUR WALKS AND COMPLETE LANDSCAPING	v	5
x	FINISH	s,u,w	0

Exhibit 2. Here, in each circle the letter before the comma identifies the job and the number after the comma indicates the job time.

Following the rule that a "legal" path must always move in the direction of the arrows, we could enumerate 22 unique paths from Start to Finish,

EXHIBIT 2

Project Graph

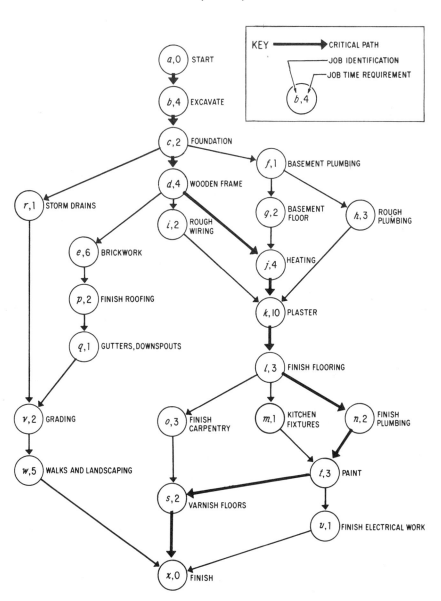

with associate times ranging from a minimum of 14 days (path *a-b-c-r-v-w-x*) to a maximum of 34 days (path *a-b-c-d-j-k-l-n-t-s-x*). The latter is the critical path; it determines the over-all project time and tells us which jobs are critical in their effect on this time. If the contractor wishes to complete the house in less than 34 days, it would be useless to shorten jobs not on the critical path. It may seem to him, for example, that the brickwork (*e*) delays progress, since work on a whole series of jobs (*p-q-v-w*) must wait until it is completed. But it would be fruitless to rush the completion of the brickwork, since it is not on the critical path and so is irrelevant in determining total project time.

SHORTENING THE CP

If the contractor were to use CPM techniques, he would examine the critical path for possible improvements. Perhaps he could assign more carpenters to job *d*, reducing it from four to two days. Then the critical path would change slightly, passing through jobs *f* and *g* instead of *d*. Notice that total project time would be reduced only one day, even though two days had been shaved off job *d*. Thus the contractor must watch for possible shifting of the critical path as he effects changes in critical jobs.

Shortening the critical path requires a consideration of both engineering problems and economic questions. Is it physically possible to shorten the time required by critical jobs (by assigning more men to the job, working overtime, using different equipment, and so on)? If so, would the costs of speedup be less than the savings resulting from the reduction in overall project time? CPM is a useful tool because it quickly focuses attention on those jobs that are critical to the project time, it provides an easy way to determine the effects of shortening various jobs in the project, and it enables the user to evaluate the costs of a "crash" program.

Two important applications of these features come to mind:

- Du Pont, a pioneer in the application of CPM to construction and maintenance projects, was concerned with the amount of downtime for maintenance at its Louisville works, which produces an intermediate product in the neoprene process. Analyzing the maintenance schedule by CPM, Du Pont engineers were able to cut downtime for maintenance from 125 to 93 hours. CPM pointed to further refinements that were expected to reduce total time to 78 hours. As a result, performance of the plant improved by about one million pounds in 1959, and the intermediate was no longer a bottleneck in the neoprene process.

  PERT (i.e., Program Evaluation Review Technique), a technique closely related to the critical path method, is widely credited with helping to shorten by two years the time originally estimated for completion of the engineering and development program for the Navy's Polaris missile. By pinpointing the longest paths through the vast maze of jobs necessary for completion of the missile design, PERT enabled the program managers to concentrate their efforts on those activities that vitally affected total project time.[2]

Even with our small house-building project, however, the process of enumerating and measuring the length of every path through the maze of jobs is tedious. A simple method of finding the critical path and, at the same time, developing useful information about each job is described next.

Critical Path Algorithm

If the start time or date for the project is given (we denote it by S), then there exists for each job an earliest starting time (ES), which is the earliest possible time that a job can begin, if all its predecessors are also started at their ES. And if the time to complete the job is t, we can define, analogously, its earliest finish time (EF) to be ES + t.

There is a simple way of computing ES and EF times using the project graph. It proceeds as follows:

1. Mark the value of S to the left and to the right of Start.
2. Consider any new unmarked job *all of whose predecessors have been marked*, and mark to the left of the new job the *largest* number marked to the right of any of its *immediate* predecessors. This number is its early start time.
3. Add to this number the job time and mark the result (EF time) to the right of the job.
4. Continue until Finish has been reached, then stop.

Thus, at the conclusion of this calculation the ES time for each job will appear to the left of the circle which identifies it, and the EF time will appear to the right of the circle. The number which appears to the right of the last job, Finish, is the early finish time (F) for the entire project.

To illustrate these calculations let us consider the following simple production process:

> An assembly is to be made from two parts, A and B. Both parts must be turned on the lathe, and B must be polished while A need not be. The list of jobs to be performed, together with the predecessors of each job and the time in minutes to perform each job, is given in Exhibit 3.
>
> The project graph is shown in Exhibit 4. As previously, the letter identifying each job appears before the comma and its job time after the comma. Also shown on the graph are the ES and EF times for each job, assuming that the start time, S, is *zero*. The ES time appears to the left of the circle representing a job, and the EF time appears to the right of the circle. Note that F = 100. The reader may wish to duplicate the diagram without these times and carry out the calculations for himself as a check on his understanding of the computation process described above.

---

[2] See Robert W. Miller, "How to Plan and Control with PERT," *Harvard Business Review*, March–April, 1962, p. 93.

EXHIBIT 3

Data for Production Process

JOB NO.	DESCRIPTION	IMMEDIATE PREDECESSORS	NORMAL TIME (MINUTES)
a	START		0
b	GET MATERIALS FOR A	a	10
c	GET MATERIALS FOR B	a	20
d	TURN A ON LATHE	b,c	30
e	TURN B ON LATHE	b,c	20
f	POLISH B	e	40
g	ASSEMBLE A AND B	d,f	20
h	FINISH	g	0

EXHIBIT 4

Calculation of Early Start and Early Finish Times for Each Job

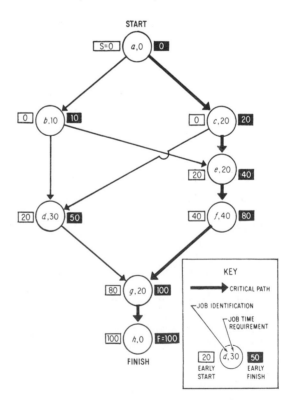

LATEST START AND FINISH TIMES

Suppose now that we have a target time (T) for completing the project. T may have been originally expressed as a calendar date, e.g., October 1 or February 15. When is the latest time that the project can be started and finished?

In order to be feasible it is clear that T must be greater (later) than or equal to F, the early finish time for the project. Assuming this is so, we can define the concept of late finish (LF), or the latest time that a job can be finished, without delaying the total project beyond its target time (T). Similarly, late start (LS) is defined to be LF $-$ t, where t is the job time.

These numbers are determined for each job in a manner similar to the previous calculations except that we work from the end of the project to its beginning. We proceed as follows:

1. Mark the value of T to the right and left of Finish.
2. Consider any new unmarked job *all of whose successors have been marked*, and mark to the right of the new job the *smallest* LS time marked to the left of any of its immediate successors.

    The logic of this is hard to explain in a few words, although apparent enough by inspection. It helps to remember that the smallest LS time of the successors of a given job, if translated into calendar times, would be the latest finish time of that job.
3. Subtract from this number the job time and mark the result to the left of the job.
4. Continue until Start has been reached, then stop.

    At the conclusion of this calculation the LF time for a job will appear to the right of the circle which identifies it, and the LS time for the job will appear to the left of the circle. The number appearing to the right of Start is the latest time that the entire project can be started and still finish at the target time T.

In Exhibit 5 we carry out these calculations for the example of Exhibit 3. Here T $=$ F $=$ 100, and we separate early start and finish and late start and finish times by semicolons so that ES; LS appears to the left of the job and EF; LF to the right. Again the reader may wish to check these calculations for himself.

Concept of Slack

Examination of Exhibit 5 reveals that some jobs have their early start equal to late start, while others do not. The difference between a job's early start and its late start (or between early finish and late finish) is called total slack (TS). Total slack represents the maximum amount of time a job may be delayed beyond its early start without necessarily delaying the project completion time.

EXHIBIT 5

Calculation of Late Start and Late Finish Times for Each Job

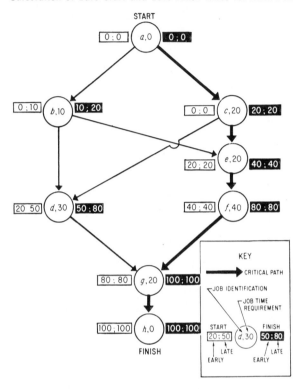

We earlier defined critical jobs as those on the longest path through the project. That is, critical jobs *directly* affect the total project time. We can now relate the critical path to the concept of slack.

FINDING THE CRITICAL PATH

If the target date (T) equals the early finish date for the whole project (F), then all critical jobs will have *zero* total slack. There will be at least one path going from Start to Finish that includes critical jobs only, i.e., the *critical path*.

If T is greater (later) than F, then the critical jobs will have total slack equal to T minus F. This is a minimum value; since the critical path includes only critical jobs, it includes those with the smallest TS. All noncritical jobs will have *greater* total slack.

In Exhibit 5, the critical path is shown by darkening the arrows connecting critical jobs. In this case there is just one critical path, and all critical jobs lie on it; however, in other cases there may be more than one critical path.

Note that T = F; thus the critical jobs have zero total slack. Job *b* has TS = 10, and job *d* has TS = 30; either or both of these jobs could be delayed by these amounts of time without delaying the project.

Another kind of slack is worth mentioning. Free slack (FS) is the amount a job can be delayed without delaying the early start of any other job. A job with positive total slack may or may not also have free slack, but the latter never exceeds the former. For purposes of computation, the free slack of a job is defined as the difference between the job's EF time and the *earliest* of the ES times of all its immediate successors. Thus, in Exhibit 5, job *b* has FS of 10, and job *d* has FS of 30. All other jobs have zero free slack.

Significance of Slack

When a job has zero total slack, its scheduled start time is automatically fixed (that is, ES = LS); and to delay the calculated start time is to delay the whole project. Jobs with positive total slack, however, allow the scheduler some discretion in setting their start times. This flexibility can usefully be applied to smoothing work schedules. Peak loads that develop in a particular shop (or on a machine, or within an engineering design group, to cite other examples) may be relieved by shifting jobs on the peak days to their late starts. Slack allows this kind of juggling without affecting project time.[3]

Free slack can be used effectively at the operating level. For example, if a job has free slack, the foreman may be given some flexibility in deciding when to start the job. Even if he delays the start by an amount equal to (or less than) the free slack, the delay will not affect the start times or slack of succeeding jobs (which is not true of jobs that have no free slack). For an illustration of these notions, we return to our house-building example.

Back to the Contractor

In Exhibit 6, we reproduce the diagram of house-building jobs, marking the ES and LS to the left, and the EF and LF to the right of each job (for example, "0;3" and "4;7" on either side of the *b*,4 circle). We assume that construction begins on day zero and must be completed by day 37. Total slack for each job is not marked, since it is evident as the difference between the pairs of numbers ES and LS or EF and LF. However, jobs that have positive free slack are so marked. There is one critical path, which is shown darkened in the diagram. All critical jobs on this path have total slack of three days.

---

[3] For a method for smoothing operations in a job shop, based on CPM and the use of slack, see F. K. Levy, G. L. Thompson, and J. D. Wiest, "Multi-ship, Multi-Shop Production Smoothing Algorithm," *Naval Logistics Research Quarterly*, March 9, 1962.

EXHIBIT 6

Project Graph with Start and Finish Times

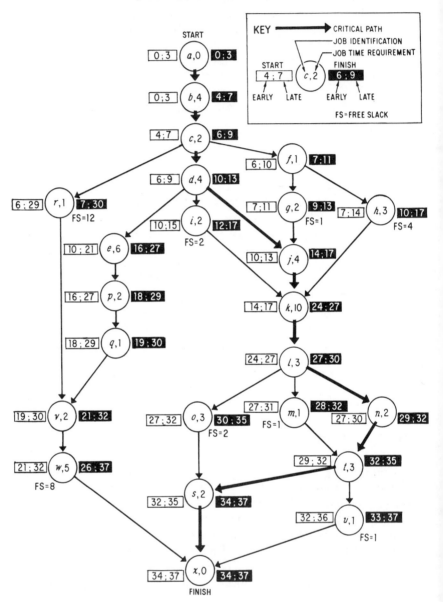

Several observations can be drawn immediately from the diagram:

1. The contractor could postpone starting the house three days and still complete it on schedule, barring unforeseen difficulties (see the difference between early and late times at the Finish). This would reduce the total slack of all jobs by three days, and hence reduce TS for critical jobs to zero.

2. Several jobs have free slack. Thus the contractor could delay the completion of *i* (rough wiring) by two days, *g* (the basement floor) by one day, *h* (rough plumbing) by four days, *r* (the storm drains) by 12 days, and so on — without affecting succeeding jobs.

3. The series of jobs *e* (brickwork), *p* (roofing), *q* (gutters), *v* (grading), and *w* (landscaping) have a comfortable amount of total slack (nine days). The contractor can use these and other slack jobs as "fill in" jobs for workers who become available when their skills are not needed for currently critical jobs. This is a simple application of work-load smoothing: juggling the jobs with slack in order to reduce peak demands for certain skilled workers or machines.

If the contractor were to effect changes in one or more of the critical jobs, by contrast, the calculations would have to be performed again. This he can easily do; but in large projects with complex sequence relationships, hand calculations are considerably more difficult and liable to error. Computer programs have been developed, however, for calculating ES, LS, EF, LF, TS, and FS for each job in a project, given the set of immediate prerequisites and the job times for each job. [4]

Handling Data Errors

Information concerning job times and predecessor relationships is gathered, typically, by shop foremen, scheduling clerks, or others closely associated with a project. It is conceivable that several kinds of errors may occur in such job data:

1. The estimated job times may be in error.

2. The predecessor relationship may contain cycles: e.g., job *a* is a predecessor for *b*, *b* is a predecessor for *c*, and *c* is a predecessor for *a*.

3. The list of prerequisites for a job may include more than the immediate prerequisites; e.g., job *a* is a predecessor of *b*, *b* is a predecessor of *c*, and *a* and *b* both are predecessors of *c*.

4. Some predecessor relationships may be overlooked.

5. Some predecessor relationships may be listed that are spurious.

How can management deal with these problems? We shall examine each briefly in turn.

---

[4] An algorithm on which one such computer program is based is discussed by F. K. Levy, G. L. Thompson, and J. D. Wiest, in Chapter 22, "Mathematical Basis of the Critical Path Method," *Industrial Scheduling*.

Job Times. An accurate estimate of total project time depends, of course, on accurate job-time data. CPM eliminates the necessity (and expense) of careful time studies for *all* jobs. Instead the following procedure can be used:

- Given rough time estimates, construct a CPM graph of the project.
- Then those jobs that are on the critical path (together with jobs that have very small total slack, indicating that they are nearly critical) can be more closely checked, their times re-estimated, and another CPM graph constructed with the refined data.
- If the critical path has changed to include jobs still having rough time estimates, then the process is repeated.

In many projects studied, it has been found that only a small fraction of jobs are critical; so it is likely that refined time studies will be needed for relatively few jobs in a project in order to arrive at a reasonably accurate estimate of the total project time. CPM thus can be used to reduce the problem of Type 1 errors at a small total cost.

Prerequisites. A computer algorithm has been developed to check for errors of Types 2 and 3 above. The algorithm (mentioned in footnote 4) systematically examines the set of prerequisites for each job and cancels from the set all but immediate predecessor jobs. When an error of Type 2 is present in the job data, the algorithm will signal a "cycle error" and print out the cycle in question.

Wrong or Missing Facts. Errors of Types 4 and 5 cannot be discovered by computer routines. Instead, manual checking (perhaps by a committee) is necessary to see that prerequisites are accurately reported.

Cost Calculations

The cost of carrying out a project can be readily calculated from the job data if the cost of doing each job is included in the data. If jobs are done by crews, and the speed with which the job is done depends on the crew size, then it is possible to shorten or lengthen the project time by adding or removing men from crews. Other means for compressing job times might also be found; but any speedup is likely to carry a price tag. Suppose that we assign to each job a "normal time" and a "crash time" and also calculate the associated costs necessary to carry the job in each time. If we want to shorten the project, we can assign some of the critical jobs to their crash time, and compute the corresponding direct cost. In this way it is possible to calculate the cost of completing the project in various total times, with the direct costs increasing as the over-all time decreases.

Added to direct costs are certain overhead expenses which are usually allocated on the basis of total project time. Fixed costs per project thus decrease as project time is shortened. In ordinary circumstances a combination of fixed and direct costs as a function of total project time would probably fall into the pattern shown in Exhibit 7. The minimum total cost (point A) would

EXHIBIT 7

Typical Cost Pattern

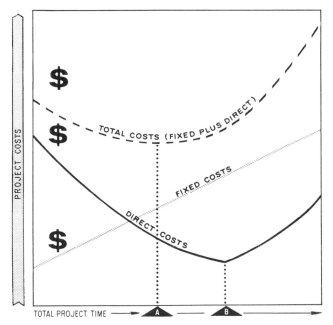

likely fall to the left of the minimum point on the direct cost curve (point B) indicating that the optimum project time is somewhat shorter than an analysis of direct costs only would indicate.

Other economic factors, of course, can be included in the analysis. For example, pricing might be brought in:

> A large chemical company starts to build a plant for producing a new chemical. After the construction schedule and completion date are established, an important potential customer indicates a willingness to pay a premium price for the new chemical if it can be made available earlier than scheduled. The chemical producer applies techniques of CPM to its construction schedule and calculates the additional costs associated with "crash" completion of jobs on the critical path. With a plot of costs correlated with total project time, the producer is able to select a new completion date such that the increased costs are met by the additional revenue offered by the customer.

New Developments

Because of their great potential for applications, both CPM and PERT have received intensive development in the past few years. This effort is sparked, in part, because of the Air Force (and other governmental agency) requirements that contractors use these methods in planning and monitoring their work. Here are some illustrations of progress made:

- One of the present authors (Wiest) has developed extensions of the work-load smoothing algorithm. These extensions are the so-called SPAR (for Scheduling Program for Allocating Resources) programs for scheduling projects having limited resources.
- A contemporaneous development by C-E-I-R, Inc., has produced RAMPS (for Resource Allocation and Multi-Project Scheduling), which is similar but not identical.
- The most recent version of PERT, called PERT/COST, was developed by the armed services and various businesses for use on weapon-systems development projects contracted by the government. Essentially, PERT/COST adds the consideration of resource costs to the schedule produced by the PERT procedure. Indications of how smoothing can be accomplished are also made. Other recent versions are called PERT II, PERT III, PEP, PEPCO, and Super PERT.

Conclusion

For the manager of large projects, CPM is a powerful and flexible tool, indeed, for decision making:

- It is useful at various stages of project management, from initial planning or analyzing of alternative programs, to scheduling and controlling the jobs (activities) that comprise a project.
- It can be applied to a great variety of project types — from our house-building example to the vastly more complicated design project for the Polaris — and at various levels of planning — from scheduling jobs in a single shop, or shops in a plant, to scheduling plants within a corporation.
- In a simple and direct way it displays the interrelations in the complex of jobs that comprise a large project.
- It is easily explainable to the layman by means of the project graph. Data calculations for large projects, while tedious, are not difficult, and can readily be handled by a computer.
- It pinpoints attention to the small subset of jobs that are critical to project completion time, thus contributing to more accurate planning and more precise control.
- It enables the manager to quickly study the effects of "crash" programs and to anticipate potential bottlenecks that might result from shortening certain critical jobs.
- It leads to reasonable estimates of total project costs for various completion dates, which enable the manager to select an optimum schedule.

Because of the above characteristics of CPM — and especially its intuitive logic and graphic appeal — it is a decision-making tool which can find wide appreciation at all levels of management.[5] The project graph helps the fore-man to understand the sequencing of jobs and the necessity of pushing those that are critical. For the manager concerned with day-to-day operations in all departments, CPM enables him to measure progress (or lack of it) against plans and to take appropriate action quickly when needed. And the under-lying simplicity of CPM and its ability to focus attention on crucial problem areas of large projects make it an ideal tool for the top manager. On his shoulders falls the ultimate responsibility for over-all planning and co-ordination of such projects in the light of company-wide objectives.

[5] See A. Charnes and W. W. Cooper, "A Network Interpretation and a Directed Sub-Dual Algorithm for Critical Path Scheduling," *Journal of Industrial Engineering,* July–August 1962, pp. 213–219.

EDITORS' NOTE: PERT differs from CPM by requiring three time estimates for each project: most optimistic, most pessimistic, and most likely. These estimates are aver-aged, with appropriate weights $\left(\text{usually } \dfrac{P + 4L + 0}{6}\right)$ to derive the time estimate utilized by the PERT algorithm. Probability distributions for the various completion time ex-pectations can also be generated, and appropriate measures of central tendency calculated.

9

"Responsibility accounting" is another of the concepts developed to serve the burgeoning needs of management for better information. Although the principle is simple — classify information on enterprise activities by responsible manager — the application often is intricate and time-consuming.

Areas of responsibility for organizational activities — and associated revenues and expenses, receipts and expenditures — must be defined. New informational needs of managers at all levels must be ascertained. Standards and other measures of performance must be developed, and appropriate data collection procedures devised.

Implementation of the responsibility accounting concept may involve integration of the accounting system with other (non-monetary) information systems, to avoid duplication of effort and to insure system effectiveness.

Responsibility Accounting
for Better Management*

E. W. Netten

In the biblical "Parable of the Talents," a businessman who was going abroad entrusted part of his capital to each of three servants. Two invested their money and doubled it, but the third was afraid of the risks and buried his. When the businessman returned he was pleased with the first two men and promoted them, but berated the third for not earning a profit and cast him into the place of wailing and gnashing of teeth.

Control and communication techniques being what they were in those days the businessman had no means of telling, while he was away, how good a job his men were doing. Nowadays, one might say that he lacked a system

* Reprinted with permission from CA magazine, published by the Canadian Institute of Chartered Accountants, Toronto, Canada.

of responsibility accounting. Nevertheless, circumstances not too dissimilar to these ancient ones exist in many enterprises today.

Need for Better Information

The impetus for development of responsibility accounting and the growing use of it by progressive enterprises, large and small, sprang from several sources. Chief among them were:
- Increased complexity of business operations. Witness the pace of technological and market changes, of diversification, mergers, and the lengthened time span between investment decisions and profit results.
- Management decentralization to grapple with this complexity and to provide a more flexible and dynamic organization structure.
- The importance of raising productivity and of tight cost control in the current competitive situation.
- Recognition of the vital role of planning and control in successful management.
- Realization that the means — the techniques and the information — available to management to exercise its planning and control functions were far from good.

These factors put heavy pressure on the accountant to reorient his work toward management's requirements. Responsibility accounting evolved in response.

What Is Responsibility Accounting?

Responsibility accounting classifies accounting and statistical information on an enterprise's activities according to the managers responsible for them. So many varied techniques are practised now under the name of responsibility accounting that really it is synonymous with management accounting. It ties accounting, reporting and budgeting to management organization and responsibilities. The techniques apply to enterprises big and small, centralized or decentralized, business, non-profit, or governmental. Information is reported, with comparisons to budgets or other standards, in the detail and at the time each manager requires it for effective planning, decision-making and control. In sum, it provides the right information to the right people at the right time.

The underlying principles are simple — deceptively so — yet their application to a specific enterprise can be intricate and time-consuming. The areas involved are:
- The determination of responsibility for each activity carried on in the enterprise and the assigning of each item of income, expense and other expenditure accordingly.
- The definition of the kind and amount of data each manager needs and the reflection of them in the account and statistical classifications.

- The use of management reports to convey the data to those who will use it, at the time they want it.
- Planning and budgeting practices made fully compatible with the reports.
- The setting up of measures of performance to be incorporated in the reports and budgets.
- Devising accounting and statistical procedures to gather and process the required data.

What Responsibility Accounting Is Not

Responsibility accounting can never be a substitute for good management. It is simply a tool, and a tool is inert until it is used. Some systems that are otherwise sound never get off the ground because the managers do not really understand them nor put them to good use.

Nor is it an accounting technique that stands or falls on the accountant's use of it. It is an integral part of the management process and the accountant's role is a technical and supporting one. This points up the great importance of careful attention to the human relations aspects; there should be full management participation in designing it and a clear understanding of its aims and uses. Unless the operating people enthusiastically support responsibility accounting and make it work, even the best-conceived system will fail.

Organization and Responsibility

Responsibility accounting is founded upon the organization structure. It must be tailor-made to the particular enterprise's distribution of responsibility and authority amongst its managers. There can be no packaged approach.

One of the more difficult tasks is the assignment of responsibility for each activity and for each corresponding item of expense, income, capital expenditure and, sometimes, asset investment. Organization charts and manuals, policy directives and similar documents provide leads but the managers concerned must participate actively if realistic assignments are to be made. Typically, there come to light many instances of fuzzy organization lines, misunderstanding of who is responsible for certain activities, overlapping of duties, authority not commensurate with responsibility, and expenses for which no one seems to be responsible. Sound organization principles must be followed if responsibility accounting is to work. Often it proves necessary to 'put the house in order' before proceeding further.

Strict Assignment of Items

Since all activities are the responsibility of someone in the enterprise, all items of income, operating costs, other expenses and capital expenditures are the responsibility of some manager. None should be left unassigned. Each expenditure should be assigned to the manager (whose unit is called a "responsibility unit") who has the authority to incur it and is therefore in the best position to control it. In most cases this will be the manager who 'spends the money' — that is, supervises the work force concerned, originates or approves personnel changes, and requisitions for materials and purchases. Expenditures should be charged to the lowest management level to which these can be directly assigned, closest to the point of action. Similarly, income controllable by a manager should be credited to his unit.

As a corollary, a manager is charged only with expenditures over which he can exercise a significant degree of direct control. Prorations and arbitrary allocations necessary for costing products or services have no place in short-term control reports. Assignment to a responsibility unit of expenses over which it has no control, if and when needed to ascertain the full cost of a department, operation or product, should be built up and reported separately.

How far down within the organization should responsibility accounting go? This depends, naturally, on the extent of delegation of authority and assignment of responsibility. Customarily, reports are provided down to the first-line supervisory level. A shop foreman, for example, is likely to be in the best position to control in the short run the efficiency of shop operations and labour and material usage, and he should receive reports on his performance in doing so.

The difference between responsibility accounting and an accounting system aligned only to product costing and inventory valuation should now be evident. For product costing, all expenses associated with a given production department may be charged directly or by proration to that department for distribution to the products processed. It is concerned with the disposition of costs. Responsibility accounting on the other hand is concerned with the origin of costs. Direct labour and material might, for example, be charged to several foremen; indirect labour and supplies to the department head; maintenance labour and materials to the maintenance superintendent; fire insurance to the treasurer; and building depreciation to the general manager.

Information Requirements

No hard and fast rules can be laid down for determining the accounting and statistical information that managers need. Our ability to produce vast amounts of raw figures mechanically or electronically has outstripped our ability to select those figures that are meaningful for planning and control. The problem is not more information but the right information. The managers concerned should play a predominant role in choosing the information to be reported to them. This is so even though most managers find it exceedingly difficult to pinpoint just what figures they want, how often they want them, and the format.

Responsibility accounting can be used with any chart of accounts simply by adding the classification by responsibility unit. Often, however, the account classification is revamped to suit new needs stemming from responsibility accounting.

Redrawing the Chart

Most conventional charts of accounts emphasize the natural classification of expenses — the numerous types of wages, salaries, materials, facilities and outside services for which funds are spent. This can be thought of as 'input' to the responsibility unit. Such charts may be inadequate because they do not distinguish the various major functions (types of work performed or 'output') in each responsibility unit and so do not provide costs of work done that can be related to the volume of the work. Therefore the chart frequently is redrawn to accumulate costs (and income if applicable) for each major function that can be compared to figures on the volume of work done, and thereby to measure performance. The natural classification, which details the resources used to carry out each function, is retained but assumes a secondary position in the chart.

Since the chart of accounts must serve many purposes a rather large number of kinds of groupings may have to be built into it. Depending on the nature of the enterprise it may be desirable to distinguish direct and indirect costs, variable, semivariable, managed and fixed costs and administrative and operating costs. Special data for planning and controlling cash, financial position, inventories, purchases and manpower will undoubtedly be needed. Beyond the basic chart of accounts, other classifications are necessary to gather detailed data such as sales by customer, salesman or distribution channel; costs by product; capital expenditures by project; and maintenance costs by facility.

Costs and Volume Matched

Due consideration should be given to the gathering of physical statistics in addition to or in place of dollar information in the accounts. Statistics on volume of work done must be in a form that can be matched with the corresponding costs in the accounts. Information expressed in man hours, units of material usage, yields, machine speeds, facilities-utilization percentages or output per man hour often is simpler and quicker to prepare, eliminates the effect of price or wage rate fluctuations and may be more easily understood. Dollars may be the only common denominator but it is possible to overemphasize them.

Expense information is expensive information. One must guard against overelaboration. To report a large amount of detail each month to each responsibility unit may increase accounting costs out of proportion to the value of the data and may overwhelm the unfortunate manager who receives a mass of indigestible figures. In most responsibility units a few operating factors, in physical or dollar terms or ratios, can be identified and reported upon. It is best to define functions and natural expense classes rather broadly, and to refine them later if really necessary. Only figures that are significant to each type of responsibility unit should be recorded separately. It is not desirable, for example, to impose a rigid natural expense classification to be applied to all units.

Responsibility Reporting

After the nature of the information required is known, thought must be given to how often it is to be reported, the amount of detail to be presented, and the format. Reports for control purposes may be produced monthly, weekly, daily or even hourly. At successively higher levels in the organizational chain, less and less time is devoted to control and more and more to planning. Foremen and first line supervisors may need considerable detail and frequent reports, often expressed in physical terms such as work performed, labour hours, materials used and machine efficiency. Reports to senior management are not so frequent, are in condensed form summarizing the results of lower levels, and are mainly expressed in dollars.

Control is centered on monthly reports, often called "responsibility reports," prepared by the accounting function for each responsibility unit. The report to each unit shows its expenses, income and capital expenditures in the detail appearing in the account classification (or some condensation of this), statistics such as volume of work, costs per unit and perhaps man-hour data and number of employees.

In selecting the contents of these reports the criterion should be: is the information important enough that action may be based on it? Care should be exercised not to clutter up the reports with reams of data when a few strategic figures will do. Each report runs to one or two pages on the average and should be released as quickly after the month end as is feasible.

Reports from Other Units

Each manager who has other units reporting to him receives a monthly summary listing the expenses, income and capital expenditures of each of these units, with pertinent statistics. He receives also a report on the activities retained under his own personal control, in the same fashion as other responsibility units do.

Since absolute figures alone are of little value, comparisons with budgets or other standards should always appear in the form of variations between actual and the standards. The variation data focus attention on items requiring action and conserve time by permitting 'management by exception.' Because the reports are aligned to the organization chart and the totals on each report appear in the detail on the report to the next higher level, it is easy to trace variations at any level back to their roots. Thus the reports achieve their prime purpose; they enable and stimulate control action.

These monthly reports should show figures for the current month and the period (year or quarter) to date. The cumulative position and trends shown by to-date figures may at times be of greater significance than the month's results. Comparisons with the previous year can safely be omitted since the purpose is to control performance to standards rather than to raise questions already thrashed out when the standards were set.

Narrative Commentaries

Narrative commentaries should be prepared to explain important variations from standards and state the remedial action taken or to be taken. These commentaries come from two sources. The accounting function provides to the responsibility unit affected, details of the composition of a variation, but only the unit itself can explain the underlying cause. For example, the accountant might trace a material-usage variation to a certain chemical in a particular process, but the unit concerned must proffer the explanation that impurities due to careless storage caused it. Desirably, the head of each responsibility unit should furnish a narrative commentary to his superior, with a copy to the accounting function, so that the latter can prepare an over-all summary for senior management.

Many other types of control reports are used in managing special activities, such as cash, inventory levels and working capital. Reports may be prepared quarterly or as required for planning, pricing or special studies; these may cut across organizational lines and contain data analyzed by account, product, territory or facility, instead of by responsibility.

Care in laying out the format of reports will be amply repaid. They should be simple, attractive and couched in terms understood by the recipients. Presentation can be in the form of statements, graphs, charts or tables, although machine processing may force a uniform format for reports turned out in volume.

Responsibility Budgeting

The planning and control cycle calls for setting objectives, developing plans to meet them, expressing the plans in figures through budgets, gathering information, preparing reports and taking corrective action. Planning and budgeting practices are a field unto themselves and will not be discussed in detail here.

Effective responsibility accounting may require more sophisticated budgets than were previously used. Each manager receiving a responsibility report should prepare or at least participate in preparing his budget since he will be held accountable for achieving it.

Since the budgets provide the means for comparing plans with actual results, the form and content of the budgets must be fully compatible with the regular control reports. For example, the account and statistical classes should be the same for both and the budget must be broken down into time periods corresponding to the periods covered by the reports. The budgets and reports are in fact two sides of the same coin.

Based on Careful Plans

Management by exception depends on a realistic budget; without a good budget there is no point in trying to use it as a yardstick. The budget must be based on carefully set objectives and operating plans, not, as someone aptly put it, on "past history eloquently defended."

Fixed budgets, flexible budgets and profit planning can all be readily incorporated into an over-all system of responsibility accounting.

Fixed budgets offer a medium for over-all planning and expression of objectives. Sometimes responsibility reports include comparisons only with fixed budgets. This is adequate if the volume of activity can be predicted accurately or if volume changes take place slowly. Where it is hard to predetermine volume and changes happen quickly — and this is typical of a manufacturing concern — fixed budgets should be supplemented by flexible budgets or standard costs. If a manager cannot control the volume of his work, it can be positively misleading to compare results at one activity level with a budget predicated on another level.

Some planning and control systems tend to emphasize the reports and relegate budgets to a supporting role of providing the yardsticks for the reports. The shoe should really be on the other foot. Preparation of carefully thought out plans that are then used as a guide to action will usually produce more benefits than the same amount of effort devoted to accounting for and reporting of actual results.

Performance Measurement

It has been said that "to measure is to control." That is an oversimplification, but without some yardstick — a budget or other standard — real control cannot be exercised. Control may be defined, indeed, as taking the action necessary to make actual results conform to a predetermined standard.

Budgets provide the principal standard for measuring performance. Other standards can also be applied in certain areas, such as standard costs, engineered physical standards, manning tables, sales quotas and share of market.

To date, responsibility accounting has concentrated on concrete financial and statistical data. Some key measures of management performance are intangible and hard to set. This would include such important determinants of organizational health as industry leadership, product creation, manager development and employee, customer, supplier and community relationships. Measurements here are in their infancy but some progress is being made in developing specific and objective standards for them.

Accounting and Data Processing

Revisions in systems and procedures are needed to collect, process and summarize the data to be reported. Information classifications and application of codes to source documents have already been discussed. Data processing equipment is by no means essential but the job of sorting and summarizing large amounts of basic data in several ways, quickly and correctly, lends itself to mechanization in medium- and large-scale enterprises.

To produce reports promptly calls for careful planning, rigid scheduling of close-off dates and the intelligent use of estimates. At times, though, the speedy release of reports becomes a fetish achieved only by great effort not warranted by the value of the action that can be taken by having the reports so quickly. Nor is a high level of accuracy always justified. Many decisions can be based just as effectively on approximations worked up in a fraction of the time taken to prepare absolutely accurate figures.

Clear Audit Trails

Clear audit trails from the reports back to the source documents must be provided to facilitate the analysis of budget variations and of actual results. Audit trail listings of the documents supporting each account may be furnished to the responsibility units concerned, but preferably should be retained in the accounting department for reference.

Control information need not emanate from the accounting department. It may, especially if it is needed hourly or daily, be more cheaply and quickly prepared in the operating department where the work is done. Duplication and overlap must be avoided, however. Many operating units have their complement of bootleg bookkeepers who produce reports that the accounting department was unable or unwilling to provide in the past. Such reports tend to linger on when replaced by responsibility reports and may be a costly drain on clerical time.

New Ways to Serve

Responsibility accounting opens up new ways for the accountant to provide valuable services to his enterprise and to take his place on the management team. Enterprise after enterprise has adopted it and has found that it brought very worthwhile benefits through more realistic planning, greater profit consciousness, clearer definition of organizational responsibilities, closer control and better management decisions.

Supplemental

Readings

to Part Two

Birnberg, Jacob G., and Louis R. Pondy. "An Experimental Study of the Allocation of Financial Resources Within Small, Hierarchical Task Groups." *Administrative Science Quarterly,* 14, No. 2 (June 1969), 192–201.
  Discusses the requirement that budgeting systems be designed to counteract, or take advantage of, the self-interested behavior of budget managers.

Bradley, Hugh E. "Setting and Controlling Budgets with Regression Analysis." *Management Accounting,* 51, No. 5 (November 1969), 31–34, 40.
  Illustrates the use of regression analysis in budgeting.

Bruns, William J., and John H. Waterhouse. "Budgetary Control and Organization Structure." *Journal of Accounting Research* (Autumn 1975), 177–203.
  Links structural and contextual organization measures to budget-related behavior in an empirical survey.

Buzby, Stephen L. "Extending the Applicability of Probabilistic Management Planning and Control Models." *"The Accounting Review,* XLIX, No. 1 (January 1974), 42–49.
  Shows that Tchebycheff-type inequalities exist that can help management apply a probabilistic approach to planning.

Comiskey, Eugene E. "Better Budgeting with Multiple Regression Analysis." *Cost and Management,* 41, No. 1 (January 1967), 14–17.
  Illustrates improvements in cost budgeting, or forecasting, through multiple linear regression.

Davis, Edward W., and James H. Patterson. "A Comparison of Heuristic and Optimum Solutions in Resource-Constrained Project Scheduling." *Management Science* (April 1975), 944–955.
  Advocates an optimal scheduling rule for PERT, based on a comparison with eight different heuristic rules on eighty-three problems.

DeCoster, Don T. "PERT/Cost—The Challenge." *Management Services,* 1, No. 2 (May–June 1964), 13–18.
  Shows that PERT/Cost, a variation of flexible budgeting, requires that accounting systems be project oriented. PERT/Cost also demands effective coordination of all management personnel involved in projects.

Ferrara, William. "Responsibility Accounting — A Basic Control Concept." *NAA Bulletin* (September 1964), 11–19.
    Describes and applies basic concepts of responsibility accounting in an industrial setting.

Ferratt, Thomas W., and Vincent A. Maber. "A Description and Application of the Box-Jenkins Methodology." *Decision Sciences,* 3, No. 4 (October 1972), 83–107.
    Illustrates the use of the Box-Jenkins methodology by analyzing the Ohio Electrical Power consumption time series. The three basic analytical steps discussed are: model identification, nonlinear estimation of parameters, and diagnostic checking.

Friedman, John. "A Conceptual Model for the Analysis of Planning Behavior." *Administrative Science Quarterly,* 12, No. 2 (September 1967), 225–252.
    Presents a model for the analysis of the planning process itself.

Gunders, Henry. "Better Profit Planning." *Management Accounting,* 46, No. 12 (August 1965), 3–24.
    Illustrates applications of operations research to all forms of budgeting.

Ijiri, Y., J. C. Kinard, and F. B. Putney. "An Integrated Evaluation System for Budget Forecasting and Operating Performance with a Classified Budgeting Bibliography." *Journal of Accounting Research,* 6, No. 1 (Spring 1968), 1–28.
    Provides a system for budget evaluation with a comprehensive bibliography of related materials.

Irvine, Bruce V. "Budgeting: Functional Analysis and Behavioral Implications." *Cost and Management,* 44, No. 2 (March–April 1970), 6–16.
    Introduces behavioral implications for budgeting.

Lewin, Arie Y., and Michael Schiff. "The Impact of People on Budgets." *The Accounting Review,* XLV, No. 2 (April 1970), 259–268.
    Explores the relationship between the controller and the controlled in the context of the budget process.

Lewin, Arie Y., and Michael Schiff. "Where Traditional Budgeting Fails." *Financial Executive,* 36, No. 5 (May 1968), 51–62.
    Examines behavioral implications of the occurrence of slack as an unintended result of the budget and control system.

Mabert, V. A., and R. C. Radcliffe. "A Forecasting Methodology as Applied to Financial Time Series." *The Accounting Review,* XLIX, No. 1 (January 1974), 61–75.
    Explains and advocates Box-Jenkins methodology over traditional forecasting methods.

Merz, C. Mike. "Measuring Sales Forecast Accuracy." *Management Accounting,* LVII, No. 1 (July 1975), 53, 54, 58.
    Applies a time-adjusted measure of relative dispersion and the coefficient of variation statistic to measure forecast accuracy.

Milani, Ken. "The Relationship of Participation in Budget-setting to Industrial Supervisor Performance and Attitudes: A Field Study." *The Accounting Review,* L, No. 2 (April 1975), 274–284.

Discusses research findings that budget-setting participation related well to attitudes but did not relate consistently to performance.

Morris, R. D. F. "Budgetary Control is Obsolete." *The Accountant,* 158, No. 4874 (May 18, 1968), 654–656.
Explains why the use of budgets for control purposes is obsolete.

Needles, Belverd E., Jr. "Budgeting Techniques: Subjective to Probabilistic." *Management Accounting,* LIII, No. 6 (December 1971), 39–45.
Applies three budgeting techniques — high, low and medium; decision tree; and statistical trend — to a hospital setting.

Onsi, Mohamed. "Factor Analysis of Behavioral Variables Affecting Budgetary Slack." *The Accounting Review,* XLVIII, No. 3 (July 1973), 535–548.
Identifies budgetary slack through a review of the literature. The article also presents the findings of a study using factor analysis to analyze the relationship between budgetary slack and managerial behavioral variables.

Rogers, Rolf E. "How Good Are Financial Performance Control Systems?" *Systems and Procedures Journal,* 18, No. 1 (January–February 1967), 17–20.
Reviews advantages and disadvantages of a responsibility accounting system in terms of organizational and managerial aspects.

Wallace, Michael E. "Behavioral Considerations in Budgeting." *Management Accounting,* 47, No. 12 (August 1966), 3–8.
Studies behavioral considerations in budgeting.

Additional Bibliography to Part Two

Armstrong, George F. "Performance Information Through Responsibility Accounting." *NAA Bulletin,* XLI, No. 7 (March 1960), 89–93.

Arnstein, William E. "The Fundamentals of Profit Planning." *The New York Certified Public Accountant,* XXXII, No. 5 (May 1962), 313–321.

Britney, Robert R. "Bayesian Point Estimation and the PERT Scheduling of Stochastic Activities." *Management Science* (May 1976), 938–948.

Buffa, Frank P. "The Application of a Dynamic Forecasting Model with Inventory Control Properties." *Decision Sciences,* 6, No. 2 (April 1975), 298–306.

Bump, Edwin A. "Effects of Learning on Cost Projections." *Management Accounting,* LV, No. 11 (May 1974), 19–24.

Cherrington, David J., and J. Owen Cherrington. "Appropriate Reinforcement Contingencies in the Budgeting Process." *Empirical Research in Accounting: Selected Studies, 1973,* 225–266.

Clark, John J., and Pieter Elgers. "Forecasted Income Statements: An Investor Perspective." *The Accounting Review,* XLVIII, No. 4 (October 1973), 668–678.

Dearden, John. "Budgeting and Accounting for R & D Costs." *Financial Executive,* XXXI, No. 12 (December 1963), 20 ff.

Demski, Joel S., and Gerald A. Feltham. "Forecast Evaluation." *The Accounting Review,* XLVII, No. 3 (July 1972), 533–548.

Doofe, Henry C. "The Profit Path as Seen Through the Budgetary Control Program." *NAA Bulletin,* XLI, No. 3 (November 1959), 47–58.

Dressel, R. L. "Input-Output Relationships as a Forecasting Tool." *NAA Bulletin,* XLIII, No. 10 (June 1962), 25–32.

Fogler, H. Russell. "A Pattern Recognition Model for Forecasting." *Management Science* (April 1974), 1178–1189.

Godfrey, James T. "Short-run Planning in a Decentralized Firm." *The Accounting Review,* XLVI, No. 2 (April 1971), 286–297.

Goodman, David A. "A Goal Programming Approach to Aggregate Planning of Production and Work Force." *Management Science* (August 1974), 1569–1575.

Gargiulo, Granville R. "Critical Path Methods." *NAA Bulletin,* XLVI, No. 5 (January 1965), 3–16.

Hanson, Ernest I. "The Budgetary Control Function." *The Accounting Review,* XLI, No. 2 (April 1966), 239–243.

Heuser, William A., Jr., and B. E. Wynne, Jr. "CPM — An Effective Management Tool — Part II." *Financial Executive,* XXXI, No. 8 (August 1963), 18 ff.

Holstrum, Gary L. "The Effect of Budget Adaptiveness and Tightness on Managerial Decision Behavior." *Journal of Accounting Research* (Autumn 1971), 268–277.

Jaedicke, Robert K. "Accounting Data for Purposes of Control." *The Accounting Review,* XXXVII, No. 2 (April 1962), 181–188.

James, John V. "Management Planning of Capital Allocations to Business Activities." *NAA Bulletin,* XLIII, No. 1 (September 1961), 5–15.

Jantsch, Erick. "Forecasting and Systems Approach: A Frame of Reference." *Management Science* (August 1973), 1355–1367.

Jodka, John. "PERT — A Recent Control Concept." *NAA Bulletin,* XLIII, No. 5 (January 1962), 81–86.

Kellogg, Martin N. "Fundamentals of Responsibility Accounting." *NAA Bulletin*, XLIII, No. 8 (April 1962), 5–16.

Kemp, Patrick S. "Accounting Data for Planning, Motivation, and Control." *The Accounting Review*, XXXVII, No. 1 (January 1962), 44–50.

Kiessling, J. R. "Profit Planning and Responsibility Accounting." *Financial Executive*, XXXI, No. 7 (July 1963), 13–15.

Koren, Alexander C. "The Critical Path Method (CPM): A Planning and Control Procedure." *The New York Certified Public Accountant*, XXXIII, No. 10 (October 1963), 697–705.

Kotiah, T. C. T., and N. D. Wallace. "Another Look at the PERT Assumptions." *Management Science* (September 1973), 44–49.

Krueger, Donald A., and John M. Kohlmeier. "Financial Modeling and 'What If' Budgeting." *Management Accounting*, LIII, No. 11 (May 1972), 25–30.

Lorek, Kenneth, Charles L. McDonald, and Dennis H. Patz. "A Comparative Examination of Management Forecasts and Box-Jenkins Forecasts of Earnings." *The Accounting Review*, LI, No. 2 (April 1976), 321–330.

Mattessich, Richard. "Budgeting Models and System Simulation." *The Accounting Review*, XXXVI, No. 3 (July 1961), 384–397.

McEwan, W. J. R. "Productivity and Profits." *The Accountant*, 150, No. 4664 (May 9, 1964), 587–590.

Most, Kenneth S. "Practical Problems in Measuring Productivity." *The Accountant*, 149, No. 4642 (December 7, 1963), 714 ff.

Neal, Dewey W. "Straight-line Projections with the Learning Curve." *NAA Bulletin*, XLII, No. 10 (June 1961), 62.

Newman, Maurice S. "The Essence of Budgetary Control." *Management Services*, 2, No. 1 (January–February 1965), 19–26.

Rushton, James H. "Pricing to Maximize Return on Investment." *The Controller*, XXIII, No. 3 (March 1955), 107–112, 132–133.

Shegda, Michael, and Hyman Weinberg. "Costs for Inventory Control and Production Planning." *NAA Bulletin*, XLV, No. 11 (July 1964), 3–12.

Swieringa, Robert J., and Robert H. Moncur. "The Relationship Between Managers' Budget-oriented Behavior and Selected Attitude, Position, Size, and Performance Measures." *Empirical Research in Accounting: Selected Studies, 1972*, 194–214.

Tasso, George J. "Responsibility Accounting." *The New York Certified Public Accountant*, XXXII, No. 12 (December 1962), 809–817.

Thompson, Howard E., LeRoy J. Krajewski. "A Behavioral Test of Adaptive Forecasting." *Decision Sciences*, 3, No. 4 (October 1972), 108–119.

Troxel, Richard B. "Variable Budgets Through Correlation Analysis: A Simplified Approach." *NAA Bulletin*, XLVI, No. 6 (February 1965), 48–55.

Wait, Donald J. "The Use of Responsibility Reporting in the Control of Costs." *Cost and Management*, XXXV, No. 11 (December 1961), 482–90, 492.

PART THREE

Capital Budgeting

T his section explores prominent capital budgeting issues. Evaluation of alternative capital investment opportunities usually involves estimating net cash or income flows for varying future periods. Risk and uncertainty are factors that must be considered carefully in the investment decision. Hertz uses probability analysis and simulation to incorporate these factors into a systematic procedure for increasing reliability and accuracy of cash-flow estimates. This procedure determines a capital investment decision model that includes the real-world problems of risk and uncertainty rather than simple, single-point estimates.

The payback model does not specifically consider such factors as risk, uncertainty, or present value. Trying to evaluate why businesses continue to use the payback model, Weingartner considers the roles of payback as a constraint, a break-even concept, and a crude measure of uncertainty. Payback is seen to imply a form of break-even that makes little sense in a world of uncertainty but can function like other rules of thumb to shorten the process of generating information and evaluating it. In another sense, payback is primarily a constraint rather than an optimizable criterion. The capital investment problems, which managers seek to attack through the use of payback, must be addressed by operational methods such as the Hertz model. If more sophisticated models are not operational and understandable, the simplistic payback method will continue to be employed.

In a companion article addressing the use of payback methods, Sundem simulates modifications of net present value and payback model performances. His results challenge the importance of the payback method. ". . . Based on a time-state preference simulation model, it has been shown that (1) there is little synergistic effect of combining a net present value objective function with a payback constraint, and (2) there is a possibility to increase greatly the performance of a net present value model by assigning projects to two or three risk classes and using a different discount rate for evaluating projects in each class." Sundem thus develops a more

170

sophisticated capital budgeting model based on operational present-value techniques.

The Dyckman and Kinard article further examines these present-value or discounted cash flow techniques by considering accounting income constraints. These constraints are developed in terms of income smoothing and income growth models. The authors then show these various models to generate different capital investment decisions. The article implies that accounting income should be measured on a cash-flow basis to harmonize financial income statement and capital investment decision goals.

10

Rate of return calculations involve three estimates: (1) estimated outlay, (2) estimated cash inflows, and (3) economic life. Use of a simple "best estimate" analysis may obscure vital information about risk — a relevant factor in any capital budgeting decision. Risk is influenced both by the odds on various events occurring and by the magnitude of the rewards or penalties which are involved when they do occur.

More accurate forecasts, empirical adjustments to estimates, "conservative" cutoff rates, three-level estimates, or selected probabilities are methods which have been used to deal with uncertainty. But rate of return analysis may be made even more sensitive to management's uncertainties about the key factors underlying the measurement. Four steps are suggested: (1) Determine the probability function for each of the significant factors, (2) Select — at random — sets of these factors according to the chances they have of turning up in the future, (3) Determine rate of return for each combination, (4) Determine probability distribution of rate of return, and base investment decisions on this distribution.

Risk Analysis in
Capital Investment*

David B. Hertz

Of all the decisions that business executives must make, none is more challenging — and none has received more attention — than choosing among alternative capital investment opportunities. What makes this kind of decision so demanding, of course, is not the problem of projecting return on investment under any given set of assumptions. The difficulty is in the assumptions and in their impact. Each assumption involves its own degree — often a high degree — of uncertainty; and, taken together these combined

* David B. Hertz, "Risk Analysis in Capital Investment," Harvard Business Review, 42, No. 1 (January–February, 1964), pp. 95–106. Copyright © 1964 by the President and Fellows of Harvard College; all rights reserved.

uncertainties can multiply into a total uncertainty of critical proportions. This is where the element of risk enters, and it is in the evaluation of risk that the executive has been able to get little help from currently available tools and techniques.

There is a way to help the executive sharpen his key capital investment decisions by providing him with a realistic measurement of the risks involved. Armed with this measurement, which evaluates for him the risk at each possible level of return, he is then in a position to measure more knowledgeably alternative courses of action against corporate objectives.

Need for New Concept

The evaluation of a capital investment project starts with the principle that the productivity of capital is measured by the rate of return we expect to receive over some future period. A dollar received next year is worth less to us than a dollar in hand today. Expenditures three years hence are less costly than expenditures of equal magnitude two years from now. For this reason we cannot calculate the rate of return realistically unless we take into account (a) when the sums involved in an investment are spent and (b) when the returns are received.

Comparing alternative investments is thus complicated by the fact that they usually differ not only in size but also in the length of time over which expenditures will have to be made and benefits returned.

It is these facts of investment life that long ago made apparent the shortcomings of approaches that simply averaged expenditures and benefits, or lumped them, as in the number-of-years-to-pay-out method. These shortcomings stimulated students of decision making to explore more precise methods for determining whether one investment would leave a company better off in the long run than would another course of action.

It is not surprising, then, that much effort has been applied to the development of ways to improve our ability to discriminate among investment alternatives. The focus of all of these investigations has been to sharpen the definition of the value of capital investments to the company. The controversy and furor that once came out in the business press over the most appropriate way of calculating these values has largely been resolved in favor of the discounted cash flow method as a reasonable means of measuring the rate of return that can be expected in the future from an investment made today.

Thus we have methods which, in general, are more or less elaborate mathematical formulas for comparing the outcomes of various investments and the combinations of the variables that will affect the investments.[1] As these

---

[1] See for example, Joel Dean, *Capital Budgeting* (New York, Columbia University Press, 1951); "Return on Capital as a Guide to Managerial Decisions," *National Association of Accountants Research Report No. 35*, December 1, 1959; and Bruce F. Young, "Overcoming Obstacles to Use of Discounted Cash Flow for Investment Shares," *NAA Bulletin*, March, 1963, p. 15.

techniques have progressed, the mathematics involved has become more and more precise, so that we can now calculate discounted returns to a fraction of a per cent.

But the sophisticated businessman knows that behind these precise calculations are data which are not that precise. At best, the rate-of-return information he is provided with is based on an average of different opinions with varying reliabilities and different ranges of probability. When the expected returns on two investments are close, he is likely to be influenced by "intangibles" — a precarious pursuit at best. Even when the figures for two investments are quite far apart, and the choice seems clear, there lurks in the back of the businessman's mind memories of the Edsel and other ill-fated ventures.

In short, the decision-maker realizes that there is something more he ought to know, something in addition to the expected rate of return. He suspects that what is missing has to do with the nature of the data on which the expected rate of return is calculated, and with the way those data are processed. It has something to do with uncertainty, with possibilities and probabilities extending across a wide range of rewards and risks.

THE ACHILLES HEEL

The fatal weakness of past approaches thus has nothing to do with the mathematics of rate-of-return calculation. We have pushed along this path so far that the precision of our calculation is, if anything, somewhat illusory. The fact is that, no matter what mathematics is used, each of the variables entering into the calculation of rate of return is subject to a high level of uncertainty. For example:

> The useful life of a new piece of capital equipment is rarely known in advance with any degree of certainty. It may be affected by variations in obsolescence or deterioration, and relatively small changes in use life can lead to large changes in return. Yet an expected value for the life of the equipment — based on a great deal of data from which a single best possible forecast has been developed — is entered into the rate-of-return calculation. The same is done for the other factors that have a significant bearing on the decision at hand.

Let us look at how this works out in a simple case — one in which the odds appear to be all in favor of a particular decision:

> The executives of a food company must decide whether to launch a new packaged cereal. They have come to the conclusion that five factors are the determining variables: *advertising and promotion expense, total cereal market, share of market for this product, operating costs,* and *new capital investment.* On the basis of the "most likely" estimate for each of these variables the picture looks very bright — a healthy 30% return. This future, however, depends on

each of the "most likely" estimates coming true in the actual case. If each of these "educated guesses" has, for example, a 60% chance of being correct, there is only an 8% chance that *all five* will be correct (.60 × .60 × .60 × .60 × .60). So the "expected" return is actually dependent on a rather unlikely coincidence. The decision-maker needs to know a great deal more about the *other* values used to make each of the five estimates and about what he stands to gain or lose from various combinations of these values.

This simple example illustrates that the rate of return actually depends on a specific combination of values of a great many different variables. But only the expected levels of ranges (e.g., worst, average, best; or pessimistic, most likely, optimistic) of these variables are used in 'formal mathematical ways to provide the figures given to management. Thus, predicting a single most likely rate of return gives precise numbers that do not tell the whole story.

The "expected" rate of return represents only a few points on a continuous curve of possible combinations of future happenings. It is a bit like trying to predict the outcome in a dice game by saying that the most likely outcome is a "7." The description is incomplete because it does not tell us about all the other things that could happen. In Exhibit 1, for instance, we see the odds on throws of only two dice having six sides. Now suppose that each die has 100 sides and there are eight of them! This is a situation more comparable to business investment, where the company's market share might become any one of 100 different sizes and where there are eight different factors (pricing, promotion, and so on) that can affect the outcome.

Nor is this the only trouble. Our willingness to bet on a roll of the dice depends not only on the odds but also on the stakes. Since the probability of rolling a "7" is 1 in 6, we might be quite willing to risk a few dollars on that outcome at suitable odds. But would we be equally willing to wager $10,000 or $100,000 at those same odds, or even at better odds? In short,

EXHIBIT 1

Describing Uncertainty — A Throw of the Dice

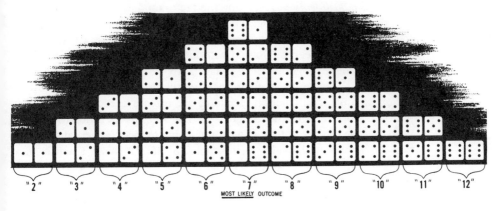

"2"　　"3"　　"4"　　"5"　　"6"　　"7"　　"8"　　"9"　　"10"　　"11"　　"12"

MOST LIKELY OUTCOME

risk is influenced both by the odds on various events occurring and by the magnitude of the rewards or penalties which are involved when they do occur. To illustrate again:

> Suppose that a company is considering an investment of $1 million. The "best estimate" of the probable return is $200,000 a year. It could well be that this estimate is the average of three possible returns — a 1-in-3 chance of getting no return at all, a 1-in-3 chance of getting $200,000 per year, a 1-in-3 chance of getting $400,000 per year. Suppose that getting no return at all would put the company out of business. Then, by accepting this proposal, management is taking a 1-in-3 chance of going bankrupt.
>
> If only the "best estimate" analysis is used, management might go ahead, however, unaware that it is taking a big chance. If all of the available information were examined, management might prefer an alternative proposal with a smaller, but more certain (i.e., less variable), expectation.

Such considerations have led almost all advocates of the use of modern capital-investment-index calculations to plead for a recognition of the elements of uncertainty. Perhaps Ross G. Walker sums up current thinking when he speaks of "the almost impenetrable mists of any forecast."[2]

How can the executive penetrate the mists of uncertainty that surround the choices among alternatives?

LIMITED IMPROVEMENTS

A number of efforts to cope with uncertainty have been successful up to a point, but all seem to fall short of the mark in one way or another:

1. *More accurate forecasts* — Reducing the error in estimates is a worthy objective. But no matter how many estimates of the future go into a capital investment decision, when all is said and done, the future is still the future. Therefore, however well we forecast, we are still left with the certain knowledge that we cannot eliminate all uncertainty.

2. *Empirical adjustments* — Adjusting the factors influencing the outcome of a decision is subject to serious difficulties. We would like to adjust them so as to cut down the likelihood that we will make a "bad" investment, but how can we do that without at the same time spoiling our chances to make a "good" one? And in any case, what is the basis for adjustment? We adjust, not for uncertainty, but for bias.

   For example, construction estimates are often exceeded. If a company's history of construction costs is that 90% of its estimates have been exceeded by 15%, then in a capital estimate there is every justification for increasing the value of this factor by 15%. This is a matter of improving the accuracy of the estimate.

---

[2] "The Judgment Factor in Investment Decisions," *Harvard Business Review* Vol. 39, No. 2 (March–April, 1961), p. 99.

But suppose that new-product sales estimates have been exceeded by more than 75% in one-fourth of all historical cases, and have not reached 50% of the estimate in one-sixth of all such cases? Penalties for overestimating are very tangible, and so management is apt to reduce the sales estimate to "cover" the one case in six — thereby reducing the calculated rate of return. In doing so, it is possibly missing some of its best opportunities.

3. *Revising cutoff rates* — Selecting higher cutoff rates for protecting against uncertainty is attempting much the same thing. Management would like to have a possibility of return in proportion to the risk it takes. Where there is much uncertainty involved in the various estimates of sales, costs, prices, and so on, a high calculated return from the investment provides some incentive for taking the risk. This is, in fact, a perfectly sound position. The trouble is that the decision-maker still needs to know explicitly what risks he is taking — and what the odds are on achieving the expected return.

4. *Three-level estimates* — A start at spelling out risks is sometimes made by taking the high, medium, and low values of the estimated factors and calculating rates of return based on various combinations of the pessimistic, average, and optimistic estimates. These calculations give a picture of the range of possible results, but do not tell the executive whether the pessimistic result is more likely than the optimistic one — or, in fact, whether the average result is much more likely to occur than either of the extremes. So, although this is a step in the right direction, it still does not give a clear enough picture for comparing alternatives.

5. *Selected probabilities* — Various methods have been used to include the probabilities of specific factors in the return calculation. L. C. Grant discusses a program for forecasting discounted cash flow rates of return where the service life is subject to obsolescence and deterioration. He calculates the odds that the investment will terminate at any time after it is made depending on the probability distribution of the service-life factor. After calculating these factors for each year through maximum service life, he then determines an over-all expected rate of return.[3]

Edward G. Bennion suggests the use of game theory to take into account alternative market growth rates as they would determine rate of return for various alternatives. He uses the estimated probabilities that specific growth rates will occur to develop optimum strategies. Bennion points out:

Forecasting can result in a negative contribution to capital budget decisions unless it goes further than merely providing a single most probable prediction. . . . [With] an estimated probability coefficient for the forecast, plus knowledge of the payoffs for the company's alternative investments and calculation of indifference probabilities . . . the margin of error may be substantially reduced,

---

[3] "Monitoring Capital Investments," *Financial Executive*, April, 1963, p. 19.

and the businessman can tell just how far off his forecast may be before it leads him to a wrong decision.[4]

Note that both of these methods yield an expected return, each based on only one uncertain input factor — service life in the first case, market growth in the second. Both are helpful, and both tend to improve the clarity with which the executive can view investment alternatives. But neither sharpens up the range of "risk taken" or "return hoped for" sufficiently to help very much in the complex decisions of capital planning.

Sharpening the Picture

Since every one of the many factors that enter into the evaluation of a specific decision is subject to some uncertainty, the executive needs a helpful portrayal of the effects that the uncertainty surrounding each of the significant factors has on the returns he is likely to achieve. Therefore, the method we have developed at McKinsey & Company, Inc., combines the variabilities inherent in all the relevant factors. Our objective is to give a clear picture of the relative risk and the probable odds of coming out ahead or behind in the light of uncertain foreknowledge.

A simulation of the way these factors may combine as the future unfolds is the key to extracting the maximum information from the available forecasts. In fact, the approach is very simple, using a computer to do the necessary arithmetic. (Recently, a computer program to do this was suggested by S. W. Hess and H. A. Quigley for chemical process investments.[5])

To carry out the analysis, a company must follow three steps:

1. Estimate the range of values for each of the factors (e.g., range of selling price, sales growth rate, and so on) and within that range the likelihood of occurrence of each value.

2. Select at random from the distribution of values for each factor one particular value. Then combine the values for all of the factors and compute the rate of return (or present value) from that combination. For instance, the lowest in the range of prices might be combined with the highest in the range of growth rate and other factors. (The fact that the factors are dependent should be taken into account, as we shall see later.)

3. Do this over and over again to define and evaluate the odds of the occurrence of each possible rate of return. Since there are literally millions of possible combinations of values, we need to test the likelihood that various specific returns on the investment will occur. This is like

---

[4] "Capital Budgeting and Game Theory," *Harvard Business Review*, Vol. 34, No. 6 (November–December, 1956), p. 123.

[5] "Analysis of Risk in Investments Using Monte Carlo Techniques," *Chemical Engineering Symposium Series 42: Statistics and Numerical Methods in Chemical Engineering* (New York, American Institute of Chemical Engineering, 1963), p. 55.

finding out by recording the results of a great many throws what per cent of "7"s or other combinations we may expect in tossing dice. The result will be a listing of the rates of return we might achieve, ranging from a loss (if the factors go against us) to whatever maximum gain is possible with the estimates that have been made.

For each of these rates the chances that it may occur are determined. (Note that a specific return can usually be achieved through more than one combination of events. The more combinations for a given rate, the higher the chances of achieving it — as with "7"s in tossing dice.) The average expectation is the average of the values of all outcomes weighted by the chances of each occurring.

The variability of outcome values from the average is also determined. This is important since, all other factors being equal, management would presumably prefer lower variability for the same return if given the choice. This concept has already been applied to investment portfolios.[6]

When the expected return and variability of each of a series of investments have been determined, the same techniques may be used to examine the effectiveness of various combinations of them in meeting management objectives.

Practical Test

To see how this new approach works in practice, let us take the experience of a management that has already analyzed a specific investment proposal by conventional techniques. Taking the same investment schedule and the same expected values actually used, we can find what results the new method would produce and compare them with the results obtained when conventional methods were applied. As we shall see, the new picture of risks and returns is different from the old one. Yet the differences are attributable in no way to changes in the basic data — *only to the increased sensitivity of the method to management's uncertainties about the key factors.*

INVESTMENT PROPOSAL

In this case a medium-size industrial chemical producer is considering a $10-million extension to its processing plant. The estimated service life of the facility is 10 years; the engineers expect to be able to utilize 250,000 tons of processed material worth $510 per ton at an average processing cost of $435 per ton. Is this investment a good bet? In fact, what is the return that the company may expect? What are the risks? We need to make the best

[6] See Harry Markowitz, *Portfolio Selection, Efficient Diversification of Investments* (New York, John Wiley and Sons, 1959); Donald E. Farrar, *The Investment Decision Under Uncertainty* (Englewood Cliffs, New Jersey, Prentice-Hall, Inc., 1962); William F. Sharpe, "A Simplified Model for Portfolio Analysis," *Management Science*, January, 1963, p. 277.

and fullest use we can of all the market research and financial analyses that have been developed, so as to give management a clear picture of this project in an uncertain world.

The key input factors management has decided to use are:

1. Market size.
2. Selling prices.
3. Market growth rate.
4. Share of market (which results in physical sales volume).
5. Investment required.
6. Residual value of investment.
7. Operating costs.
8. Fixed costs.
9. Useful life of facilities.

These factors are typical of those in many company projects that must be analyzed and combined to obtain a measure of the attractiveness of a proposed capital facilities investment.

OBTAINING ESTIMATES

How do we make the recommended type of analysis of this proposal?

Our aim is to develop for each of the nine factors listed a frequency distribution or probability curve. The information we need includes the possible range of values for each factor, the average, and some ideas as to the likelihood that the various possible values will be reached. It has been our experience that for major capital proposals managements usually make a significant investment in time and funds to pinpoint information about each of the relevant factors. An objective analysis of the values to be assigned to each can, with little additional effort, yield a subjective probability distribution.

Specifically, it is necessary to probe and question each of the experts involved — to find out, for example, whether the estimated cost of production really can be said to be exactly a certain value or whether, as is more likely, it should be estimated to lie within a certain range of values. It is that range which is ignored in the analysis management usually makes. The range is relatively easy to determine; if a guess has to be made — as it often does — it is easier to guess with some accuracy a range rather than a specific single value. We have found from past experience at McKinsey & Company, Inc., that a series of meetings with management personnel to discuss such distributions is most helpful in getting at realistic answers to the a priori questions. (The term "realistic answers" implies all the information management does *not* have as well as all that it does have.)

The ranges are directly related to the degree of confidence that the estimator has in his estimate. Thus, certain estimates may be known to be quite accurate. They would be represented by probability distributions stating, for instance, that there is only 1 chance in 10 that the actual value will be different from the best estimate by more than 10%. Others may have as much as 100% ranges above and below the best estimate.

Thus, we treat the factor of selling price for the finished product by asking executives who are responsible for the original estimates these questions:

1. Given that $510 is the expected sales price, what is the probability that the price will exceed $550?
2. Is there any chance that the price will exceed $650?
3. How likely is it that the price will drop below $475?

Managements must ask similar questions for each of the other factors, until they can construct a curve for each. Experience shows that this is not as difficult as it might sound. Often information on the degree of variation in factors is readily available. For instance, historical information on variations in the price of a commodity is readily available. Similarly, management can estimate the variability of sales from industry sales records. Even for factors that have no history, such as operating costs for a new product, the person who makes the "average" estimate must have some idea of the degree of confidence he has in his prediction, and therefore he is usually only too glad to express his feelings. Likewise, the less confidence he has in his estimate, the greater will be the range of possible values that the variable will assume.

This last point is likely to trouble businessmen. Does it really make sense to seek estimates of variations? It cannot be emphasized too strongly that the less certainty there is in an "average" estimate, *the more important it is to consider the possible variation in that estimate.*

Further, an estimate of the variation possible in a factor, no matter how judgmental it may be, is always better than a simple "average" estimate, since it includes more information about what is known and what is not known. It is, in fact, this very *lack* of knowledge which may distinguish one investment possibility from another, so that for rational decision making it *must* be taken into account.

This lack of knowledge is in itself important information about the proposed investment. To throw any information away simply because it is highly uncertain is a serious error in analysis which the new approach is designed to correct.

COMPUTER RUNS

The next step in the proposed approach is to determine the returns that will result from random combinations of the factors involved. This requires realistic restrictions, such as not allowing the total market to vary more than some reasonable amount from year to year. Of course, any method of rating the return which is suitable to the company may be used at this point; in the actual case management preferred discounted cash flow for the reasons cited earlier, so that method is followed here.

A computer can be used to carry out the trials for the simulation method in very little time and at very little expense. Thus, for one trial actually made in this case, 3,600 discounted cash flow calculations, each based on a selection of the nine input factors, were run in two minutes at a cost of $15 for computer time. The resulting rate-of-return probabilities were read out immediately and graphed. The process is shown schematically in Exhibit 2.

DATA COMPARISONS

The nine input factors described earlier fall into three categories:
1. *Market analyses.* Included are market size, market growth rate, the firm's share of the market, and selling prices. For a given combination of these factors sales revenue may be determined.
2. *Investment cost analyses.* Being tied to the kinds of service-life and operating-cost characteristics expected, these are subject to various kinds of error and uncertainty; for instance, automation progress makes service life uncertain.
3. *Operating and fixed costs.* These also are subject to uncertainty, but are perhaps the easiest to estimate.

These categories are not independent, and for realistic results our approach allows the various factors to be tied together. Thus, if price determines the total market, we first select from a probability distribution the price for the specific computer run and then use for the total market a probability distribution that is logically related to the price selected.

We are now ready to compare the values obtained under the new approach with the values obtained under the old. This comparison is shown in Exhibit 3.

VALUABLE RESULTS

How do the results under the new and old approaches compare?

In this case, management had been informed, on the basis of the "one best estimate" approach, that the expected return was 25.2% before taxes. When we ran the new set of data through the computer program, however, we got an expected return of only 14.6% before taxes. This surprising difference not only is due to the fact that under the new approach we use a range of values; it also reflects the fact that we have weighted each value in the range by the chances of its occurrence.

Our new analysis thus may help management to avoid an unwise investment. In fact, the general result of carefully weighing the information and lack of information in the manner I have suggested is to indicate the true nature of otherwise seemingly satisfactory investment proposals. If this practice were followed by managements, much regretted over-capacity might be avoided.

EXHIBIT 2

Simulation for Investment Planning

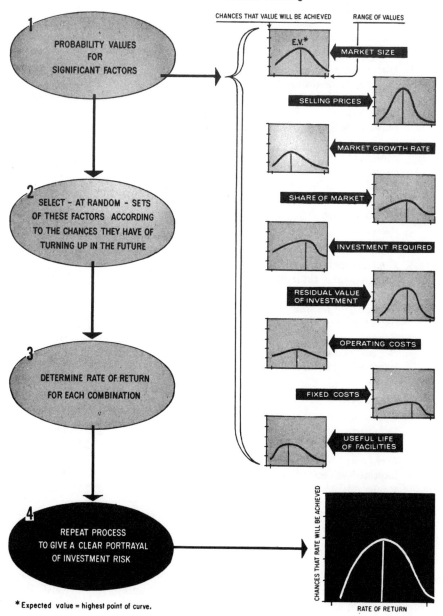

* Expected value = highest point of curve.

EXHIBIT 3

Comparison of Expected Values Under Old and New Approaches

	Conventional *"Best Estimate"* Approach	New Approach
MARKET ANALYSES		
1. *Market size*		
Expected value (in tons)	250,000	250,000
Range	—	100,000–340,000
2. *Selling prices*		
Expected value (in dollars/ton)	$510	$510
Range	—	$385–$575
3. *Market growth rate*		
Expected value	3%	3%
Range	—	0–6%
4. *Eventual share of market*		
Expected value	12%	12%
Range	—	3%–17%
INVESTMENT COST ANALYSES		
5. *Total investment required*		
Expected value (in millions)	$9.5	$9.5
Range	—	$7.0–$10.5
6. *Useful life of facilities*		
Expected value (in years)	10	10
Range	—	5–15
7. *Residual value (at 10 years)*		
Expected value (in millions)	$4.5	$4.5
Range	—	$3.5–$5.0
OTHER COSTS		
8. *Operating costs*		
Expected value (in dollars/ton)	$435	$435
Range	—	$370–$545
9. *Fixed costs*		
Expected value (in thousands)	$300	$300
Range	—	$250–$375

NOTE: Range figures in right-hand column represent approximately 1% to 99% probabilities. That is, there is only a 1 in a 100 chance that the value actually achieved will be respectively greater or less than the range.

The computer program developed to carry out the simulation allows for easy insertion of new variables. In fact, some programs have previously been suggested that take variability into account.[7] But most programs do not

[7] See Frederick S. Hillier, "The Derivation of Probabilistic Information for the Evaluation of Risky Investments," *Management Science*, April, 1963, p. 443.

allow for dependence relationships between the various input factors. Further, the program used here permits the choice of a value for price from one distribution, which value determines a particular probability distribution (from among several) that will be used to determine the value for sales volume. To show how this important technique works:

Suppose we have a wheel, as in roulette, with the numbers from 0 to 15 representing one price for the product or material, the numbers 16 to 30 representing a second price, the numbers 31 to 45 a third price, and so on. For each of these segments we would have a different range of expected market volumes; e.g., $150,000–$200,000 for the first, $100,000–$150,000 for the second, $75,000–$100,000 for the third, and so forth. Now suppose that we spin the wheel and the ball falls in 37. This would mean that we pick a sales volume in the $75,000–$100,000 range. If the ball goes in 11, we have a different price and we turn to the $150,000–$200,000 range for a price.

Most significant, perhaps, is the fact that the program allows management to ascertain the sensitivity of the results to each or all of the input factors. Simply by running the program with changes in the distribution of an input factor, it is possible to determine the effect of added or changed information (or of the lack of information). It may turn out that fairly large changes in some factors do not significantly affect the outcomes. In this case, as a matter of fact, management was particularly concerned about the difficulty in estimating market growth. Running the program with variations in this factor quickly demonstrated to us that for average annual growths from 3% and 5% there was no significant difference in the expected outcome.

In addition, let us see what the implications are of the detailed knowledge the simulation method gives us. Under the method using single expected values, management arrives only at a hoped-for expectation of 25.2% after taxes (which, as we have seen, is wrong unless there is no variability in the

EXHIBIT 4

Anticipated Rates of Return Under Old and New Approaches

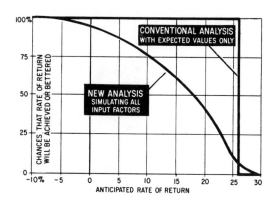

various input factors — a highly unlikely event). On the other hand, with the method we propose, the uncertainties are clearly portrayed:

Per cent return	Probability of achieving at least the return shown
0%	96.5%
5	80.6
10	75.2
15	53.8
20	43.0
25	12.6
30	0

This profile is shown in Exhibit 4. Note the contrast with the profile obtained under the conventional approach. This concept has been used also for evaluation of new product introductions, acquisitions of new businesses, and plant modernization.

Comparing Opportunities

From a decision-making point of view one of the most significant advantages of the new method of determining rate of return is that it allows

EXHIBIT 5

Comparison of Two Investment Opportunities

SELECTED STATISTICS	INVESTMENT A	INVESTMENT B
AMOUNT OF INVESTMENT	$10,000,000	$10,000,000
LIFE OF INVESTMENT (IN YEARS)	10	10
EXPECTED ANNUAL NET CASH INFLOW	$ 1,300,000	$ 1,400,000
VARIABILITY OF CASH INFLOW		
I CHANCE IN 50 OF BEING *GREATER* THAN	$ 1,700,000	$ 3,400,000
I CHANCE IN 50 OF BEING *LESS*[*] THAN	$ 900,000	($600,000)
EXPECTED RETURN ON INVESTMENT	5.0%	6.8 %
VARIABILITY OF RETURN ON INVESTMENT		
I CHANCE IN 50 OF BEING *GREATER* THAN	7.0%	15.5 %
I CHANCE IN 50 OF BEING *LESS*[*] THAN	3.0%	(4.0 %)
RISK OF INVESTMENT		
CHANCES OF A LOSS	NEGLIGIBLE	I IN 10
EXPECTED SIZE OF LOSS		$ 200,000

management to discriminate between measures of (1) expected return based on weighted probabilities of all possible returns, (2) variability of return, and (3) risks.

To visualize this advantage, let us take an example which is based on another actual case but simplified for purposes of explanation. The example involves two investments under consideration, A and B.

When the investments are analyzed, the data tabulated and plotted in Exhibit 5 are obtained. We see that:

· Investment B has a higher expected return than Investment A.
· Investment B also has substantially more variability than Investment A. There is a good chance that Investment B will earn a return which is quite different from the expected return of 6.8%, possibly as high as 15% or as low as a loss of 5%. Investment A is not likely to vary greatly from the expected 5% return.
· Investment B involves far more risk than does Investment A. There is virtually no chance of incurring a loss on Investment A. However, there is 1 chance in 10 of losing money on Investment B. If such a loss occurs, its expected size is approximately $200,000.

Clearly, the new method of evaluating investments provides management with far more information on which to base a decision. Investment decisions made only on the basis of maximum expected return are not unequivocally the best decisions.

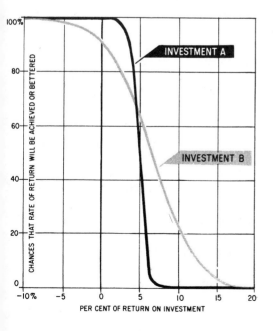

Conclusion

The question management faces in selecting capital investments is first and foremost: What information is needed to clarify the key differences among various alternatives? There is agreement as to the basic factors that should be considered — markets, prices, costs, and so on. And the way the future return on the investment should be calculated, if not agreed on, is at least limited to a few methods, any of which can be consistently used in a given company. If the input variables turn out as estimated, any of the methods customarily used to rate investments should provide satisfactory (if not necessarily maximum) returns.

In actual practice, however, the conventional methods do *not* work out satisfactorily. Why? The reason, as we have seen earlier in this article, and as every executive and economist knows, is that the estimates used in making the advance calculations are just that — estimates. More accurate estimates would be helpful, but at best the residual uncertainty can easily make a mockery of corporate hopes. Nevertheless, there is a solution. To collect realistic estimates for the key factors means to find out a great deal about them. Hence the kind of uncertainty that is involved in each estimate can be evaluated ahead of time. Using this knowledge of uncertainty, executives can maximize the value of the information for decision making.

The value of computer programs in developing clear portrayals of the uncertainty and risk surrounding alternative investments has been proved. Such programs can produce valuable information about the sensitivity of the possible outcomes to the variability of input factors and to the likelihood of achieving various possible rates of return. This information can be extremely important as a backup to management judgment. To have calculations of the odds on all possible outcomes lends some assurance to the decision-makers that the available information has been used with maximum efficiency.

This simulation approach has the inherent advantage of simplicity. It requires only an extension of the input estimates (to the best of our ability) in terms of probabilities. No projection should be pinpointed unless we are *certain* of it.

The discipline of thinking through the uncertainties of the problem will in itself help to ensure improvement in making investment choices. For to understand uncertainty and risk is to understand the key business problem — and the key business opportunity. Since the new approach can be applied on a continuing basis to each capital alternative as it comes up for consideration and progresses toward fruition, gradual progress may be expected in improving the estimation of the probabilities of variation.

Lastly, the courage to act boldly in the face of apparent uncertainty can be greatly bolstered by the clarity of portrayal of the risks and possible rewards. To achieve these lasting results requires only a slight effort beyond what most companies already exert in studying capital investments.

11

"The Payback Period has been dismissed as misleading and worthless by most writers on capital budgeting at the same time that businessmen continue to utilize this concept. This paper seeks to identify the problems which businessmen try to solve by use of the payback period, so that better tools can be provided for solving these, since neither the present value nor the internal rate of return does so.

In the course of the analysis the payback concept is considered as follows: its role as a constraint, rather than an optimizable criterion, payback and liquidity of capital assets and the liquidity requirements of the firm, payback as a break-even concept, and payback as a crude measure of the rate of resolution of uncertainty. While payback is not advocated for capital investment decisions, the reasons for its popularity need to be understood before it is possible to develop superior alternatives."

Some New Views on the Payback Period and Capital Budgeting Decisions*

H. Martin Weingartner†

While academic writers have almost unanimously condemned use of the Payback Period in capital budgeting, it continues to be one of the most

* *From* Management Science, *Vol. 15, No. 9 (August, 1969), pp. B594–607. Reprinted by permission of the publisher and the author.*

† Motivation for this paper was provided by some stimulating discussions with W. W. Cooper whose agreement with what follows must not be assumed. Myron Gordon, Michael Jensen and Merton Miller made helpful comments on an earlier draft. It was presented as an Invited Paper at the TIMS/ORSA Meeting in San Francisco on May 2, 1968.

widely applied quantitative concepts in making investment decisions.[1] It must be conceded that the payback period, i.e., the time it is expected for an investment project to recoup its initial cost, is hardly a tool which can provide the decision maker with all the information he needs. As most text-books correctly point out, the time value of money via discounting of future cash flows never enters into its calculation. Nevertheless, a serious question must be raised and answered: why is the payback period so ubiquitously used, despite its universal critics? It may be the case that the problem which managers are seeking to solve by use of payback is not, in fact, handled by the tools many text-book writers espouse.

This paper seeks to provide a better understanding of the capital investment problem by carefully analyzing the payback concept. Given the complexity of the problem of capital investment decisions and our state of knowledge with respect to the economic, psychological and organizational bases for current practice, it must be admitted that what follows should more properly be labeled as a set of conjectures. Although the plausibility of the arguments will be supported wherever possible, the objective here is to widen the perspective within which much of the discussion of investment decision methods takes place. By following an encyclopedic approach in the paper, it should not be assumed that all or even most of the suggested rationales for the use of payback are operative at the same time, or within the same individuals, parts of the organization or even firms. Rather, it is suggested that all of them are considerations at one time or another, and that the variety of problems which the payback concept attacks helps to reinforce the appeal which businessmen profess for this measure of investment value.[2] In the course of the analysis which follows we shall discuss payback as a criterion versus payback as a constraint, liquidity of capital assets versus liquidity requirements of the firm, payback as a break-even concept and finally, payback and the resolution of uncertainty.

One point should be emphasized at the outset. *We shall not end by rehabilitating payback,* for more sophisticated and precise methods are available or can be developed to deal with the issues to be raised below. Hopefully, however, we shall have learned something about the nature of the investment problem and encouraged development of alternatives.

---

[1] See for example, [12]. For some views different to those presented here, see also [19], Chapter 9. It is also interesting to observe that numbers of companies which utilize sophisticated computer programs for the evaluation of capital investments have written payback into them in one form or another.

[2] The response which private circulation of this paper has generated so far, and it was surprisingly large, has been in the form of enthusiasm from businessmen, but much less agreement from academic colleagues. While opinion sampling cannot be used to establish the truth or falsehood of a set of arguments, the fairly clear-cut division between types of respondents here is particularly interesting in that the paper's contention is that the problem which businessmen face is generally oversimplified by academic writers. Should this paper persuade some of the academicians to broaden their view of the problem, I will regard it as having served its purpose.

One disclaimer seems appropriate at the outset. In seeking to analyze the capital investment decision within firms, one ought to include also a variety of aspects whose origin lies entirely within the organizational process of decision making. On the descriptive side, this would include preparation of the underlying data for a project, its review at higher levels, etc. These considerations will not be our concern here. Nevertheless, it would be useful to point out the immense difference between a single figure of merit which is attached to a proposed project for purposes of *communication* as opposed to use of that same figure as the *sole basis* for making the accept/reject decision. At various levels of the organization a hierarchy of different considerations is brought to bear on the problem, while other aspects are presumed to have been dealt with before a proposal has reached that stage.[3] The need to communicate explicit information between groups and levels is a function of the nature of the organization and its past. When a single figure of merit is cited as being "used" by a firm in its capital investment process, as for example, the Istvan study [12] reveals, care must be taken to distinguish its use as a communications device from its application as a decision criterion. While these remarks apply to all the common text-book criteria for capital budgeting decisions, they apply with special emphasis to the payback period.

Payback as a Criterion Versus Payback as a Constraint

Some writers, notably Gordon [10], have interpreted the payback period as an indirect though quick measure of return.[4] Given a uniform stream of receipts, the reciprocal of the payback period is the discounted cash-flow rate-of-return for a project of infinite life, or a good approximation to this rate for a long-lived project. Alternatively, using annuity tables one can translate the payback period directly into the correct rate of return given the project life, again if the inflows are uniform during this life.[5]

When the scale of the investment is itself a decision variable, the above interpretation of payback has also erroneously led to its advocacy as a criterion for optimization. We refer once more to investments of the "point-input, stream-output" type, and assume a perpetual stream of receipts whose level is a function of the amount of investment, exhibiting the usual property

---

[3] An example would be the use, explicit or implicit, of a discount rate in the *design* of a project, usually encompassed in what is called engineering economics, and the subsequent use of a different discount rate in the evaluation of the merit of that project.

[4] The conclusions of Gordon are arrived at more rigorously and also generalized by V. L. Smith in [19], pp. 220–224.

[5] The Present Value of an annuity of $1 per period for n periods at an interest rate r, is given by $V(r) = (1/r) [1 - (1 + r)^{-n}]$. To find the rate r one enters the annuity tables on the line for the correct number of years, n, and seeks the value of the project's outlay/annual inflow. The interest rate where this is found is the internal or discounted-cash-flow rate-of-return.

of decreasing returns to scale. Under these assumptions, the scale of investment which maximizes the internal rate of return also minimizes the payback period.[6] Unfortunately, maximization of the internal rate of return is not an appropriate criterion. As discussed already some time ago in the debate between Boulding and Samuelson ([5] and [18]), the scale must be decided upon by reference to economic variables external to the investment, viz., the interest rate. For present purposes this implies that the optimal scale is achieved by maximization of the net present value, and is given by the point at which the marginal rate of return equals the interest rate. This, in turn, is equivalent to the point at which the payback period is equal to the reciprocal of "the interest rate" or cost of capital.[7]

Before income taxes played an important role in investment decisions, one also could see a direct similarity between the payback period and the price/earnings ratio. Taking once more a uniform stream of receipts as the first approximation for an investment project, the ratio of cost to annual receipts, which is the payback period, is of the same form as the price to earnings per share multiple for common stock. Projecting earnings to be uniform for the foreseeable future, one may interpret P/E for a company's stock as a payback period, or, alternatively, the payback period may be regarded as the project's cost expressed as a multiple of earnings (receipts). Judgement as to whether specific numerical values associated with particular alternatives are "reasonable" or desirable is made in the same way, though obviously with different numerical standards.

Such use of payback as a figure of merit may describe business practice during the last century and perhaps the early decades of the present one. It is, however, difficult to believe that these plausible reasons plus a general cultural lag explain this tool's still-current popularity. Careful consideration of the effect of taxes and depreciation rules requires distinguishing between cash flows and the more general earnings concept represented in the firm's income statement.

It is not clear that payback is used as a direct figure of merit, i.e., that it is applied to choose that project among mutually exclusive alternatives which minimizes the payback period. It *is* often (and perhaps more properly) used as a constraint: no project may be accepted unless its payback period is shorter than some specified period of time.[8] Furthermore,

---

[6] See, for example, Lutz and Lutz [14]. So long as the internal rate of return is the payback reciprocal, maximization of the rate of return is equivalent to minimization of payback.

[7] See also [14], [19] and [24].

[8] Charnes, Cooper, Devoe and Learner [7] and Byrne, Charnes, Cooper, and Kortanek [6] emphasized this difference. It also follows from selection of the optimal scale of the investment. One can translate the criterion of maximizing the net present value into expanding the scale of the investment up to the point at which its marginal rate of return is equal to the interest rate, or until the payback period is below the reciprocal of the interest rate. In this fashion, payback is also more appropriately regarded as a constraint on the acceptability of an investment, rather than as a figure of merit to be optimized. See also Smith [19].

not all projects satisfying the payback constraint are automatically accepted. They must satisfy *additional* criteria as well.[9] The foremost among these, as the writer has pointed out elsewhere ([22] and [23]), concerns the interrelationships which exist between projects because of the use they make of resources that are of limited supply in the short run such as, especially, managerial manpower. Handling such problems formally requires sophisticated methods, as discussed in the references cited.

Assuming that the desirability of projects is judged on an individual project basis, perhaps by application of an appropriate discounted cash flow (DCF) measure, the question we wish to answer is, what does the payback period tell? To answer requires taking a step backward and glancing briefly at the framework of certainty within which the common DCF criteria are usually derived.

Under the assumption of certainty and perfect capital markets, the investor may be shown to be better off whenever he commits his funds to an undertaking which yields a positive net present value after allowance for all costs. The discount rate or rates which are applied to the venture's cash flows are also the market determined trade-offs between present and future consumption, which allows the investor to choose the timing of his consumption independently of the timing of his investment. Under conditions of uncertainty, the cash flows generated by the investment as well as all other claims the investor has on future benefits are subject to random fluctuations. The appropriate discount rates themselves are uncertain and these rates might be expected to change due not only to changes in market rates for risky investments, but also because the uncertainty of the cash flows of the particular investment most probably will change over its life. It is the latter notions that need to be unravelled to make sense out of the payback period.

There is one other item in the theoretical ancestry of DCF analyses which needs to be raised in these preliminaries. Basically, it is that capital goods of which economists traditionally speak are assumed to have a market value reasonably close to their depreciated cost, so that investment is essentially a reversible process.[10] Accordingly, at any time a firm finds

[9] Even when payback is cited as the sole quantitative concept applied to investment decisions, it does not follow that desirability is expressed in qualitative terms such as "strategic" value, while payback is utilized in the form of a constraint as just described. Reading of much of the literature would lead one to believe that investment decisions should always be made on the basis of some single figure of merit, such as the present value or the discounted cash flow rate of return. When the decision is placed into its organizational setting, it should become clear that no single number can answer all the questions which need to be raised concerning the commitment of the firm's resources. For additional reasons for rejecting a single number criterion see [25]. A referee for this paper has also pointed out that in optimizations involving multiple criteria any subset of them can be regarded as constraints.

[10] The definition of reversibility used here is that of Tobin ([21], Chapter 2, p. 8). "By the reversibility [as distinct from liquidity] of an asset is meant the value of the asset to its holder expressed as a percentage of its contemporaneous cost to a buyer. For a perfectly reversible asset, this percentage would be 100%, indicating that a seller could realize in cash all that it costs a buyer to acquire the asset."

changed conditions which indicate future profitability of some investments to be impaired, the firm is assumed to be able to sell the assets at prices which, while affected by these new conditions, nevertheless are not too far from original cost less allowance for wear and obsolescence. (Put in different terms, the return to capital called rent in such a situation is at most a minor component of the total return. While this model may hold for reasonably competitive industries, firms which make careful evaluations of their capital expenditures generally believe that they face falling demand curves, in which environment selecting the best level of output in the short run and capacity in the long run are among the most important managerial problems, along with choice of the best production function.)

If the investment implies potentially substantial returns to the combination of managerial or entrepreneurial skill in the form of marketing, production or other know-how; or, alternatively, if it requires substantial non-recoverable outlays such as for site preparation, etc., the "going concern value" of the assets of the project far exceeds their market value at all times of the project's existence. Such an investment does not fit the model of completely reversible investment implied, for example, in the writing of Fisher who derived the optimality of the yield or internal rate of return criterion for investment analysis.[11]

It is the case that common, though incomplete analysis of investment projects using the present value criterion is subject to the myopia problem. That is, a project usually has as one alternative its own postponement, with consequential changes in payoffs and costs. When measured from the present it is by no means always true that the highest discounted value is associated with the earliest starting date.[12] Application of the present value criterion here, viz., the selection of that project which has the highest net present value from among the set of mutually exclusive alternatives, would still be appropriate within this framework.

The imposition of constraints on capital expenditures invalidates the present value apparatus, as has been discussed in detail in [22] and especially in [2] and [25]. That is, when the expenditure of funds on capital projects has been limited to an amount not explicitly based on the investment opportunities, it is no longer true that the present value criterion satisfies a more basic objective of investment in terms of the investor's utility and consumption possibilities.[13] Here the myopic problem of constructing an investment

[11] See Irving Fisher [9]. Recent writers have brought out the importance of reversibility assumption. See for example S. Marglin [16], and K. J. Arrow [1], and their discussion of the "Myopia Rule" for investment. It should be noted that reversibility and irreversibility are meaningful notions under certainty, being the result, primarily, of economies of scale or of less than perfect competition.

[12] For this reason the literature, as well as company practice, often refers to an "urgency rating" associated with projects.

[13] Of course, it need not be empirically true that firms *set* ceilings without regard to their opportunities for employing funds. It is nevertheless the case that once budgets have been set within a firm, those subject to the budget limitation are required to make choices among alternatives while staying within the expenditure ceiling.

project too early becomes more important in that the timing of expenditures and revenues requires internal valuation, e.g., in terms of the alternatives they open up and/or foreclose because of the capital constraints. In either of these instances the payback period contains information (in the form of a single number) regarding the timing of the inflows, which could be a warning against early commitment of funds if without its use the only choice evaluated is to accept the project now or not-at-all.

Payback and Liquidity

One consequence of insisting that each proposed investment have a short payback period is thàt, in some sense, the investments made are relatively "liquid."[14] Deferring more careful analysis of this statement for a moment, it would seem to imply that this early repayment of the invested funds is desirable in and of itself, specifically apart from the desirability measured by some DCF figure of merit. In the paper [6] referred to earlier, Byrne, et al, regard a low payback period as a way of minimizing "lost opportunity risk" so that the investor can assure himself of being restored to his initial position within a short span of time in order to be able to take advantage of additional, perhaps better investment possibilities that may come along.[15] Payback as utilized in the cited paper is applied as a constraint across all investment opportunities simultaneously, and not on a project-by-project basis, and also in a probabilistic way. Its advocacy and use there does represent a substantial departure from other recent writing.

This use of payback does raise some question about traditional project evaluation. For one thing, the investment opportunities which would have to be foregone were it not for the funds generated by the new projects, as implied there, are usually assumed to have been evaluated using an appropriate discounting rate or its equivalent. That is, if the cost of capital has been estimated, and the prospective investment yields a positive net present value after discounting at this rate, then, presumably, future investments offering a positive present value will still be available: they will yield more than they cost in terms of the combination of debt and equity capital and retained earnings which will be required to finance them. When this is not the case one might presume that either the cost of capital had changed *as a result* of making the investments, in which instance this change should have been anticipated and taken into account in the computation of present values currently. Alternatively, the particular liquidity requirement of

---

[14] Following the definitions of Tobin [21] once more, one would not want to characterize investments as liquid or illiquid. The question is not whether a long time is required to realize the value of the asset when it is for sale, but rather whether the asset yields its value in the form of product quickly or after some time.

[15] [6], p. 3.

Byrne, et al, implies that the concept of the cost of capital as the cost of foregone investment opportunities is not well defined.[16]

Put somewhat differently, the assumption of competitive capital markets, plus, perhaps the assumption that the expectations of the capital market regarding the firm's new investment are substantially the same as those of the managers of the firm itself, would guarantee that future opportunities must not be foregone for lack of funds. Additionally, growth by *internally* generated funds is by no means the only path for rapid growth. It would seem, therefore, that in this use of payback the motive of providing for the internal generation of funds from investments for future, as yet undetermined, additional investment is based more on an implicit or explicit spending limit than on an explicit limitation of risk. More directly, the usually designated speculative and/or precautionary motive of firms to hold liquid or near liquid funds[17] in order to seize upon unexpected opportunities is a *different* motive from that which requires each new investment separately to recover its original cost within a short time. Unless we assume that firms cannot plan for the generation of funds from operations generally, and from the investment program taken as a whole, we are forced to conclude that use of payback by Byrne, et al, is for purposes different from those related to an individual project payback constraint.

Payback as a Break-Even Concept

The payback period appears to be one of a common type of break-even notions frequently employed by businessmen. Generally, the break-even point is a point of indifference — with qualifications — beyond which an accounting profit is expected to be generated by the operation under analysis, and below which loss is expected. The qualifications come from use of accounting profit rather than some more meaningful economic measure which would attach a cost to the use of funds and to the application of managerial effort.

Once again, under certainty there is no significance to the break-even point. Under uncertainty, estimation of the break-even point serves to reduce the information search for resolving choices in allocation problems. The risk against which the profit potential is to be evaluated is the risk that the firm will not be "made whole again" as a result of undertaking some operation. The fact that this standard for comparison, the firm as it was before, is not the correct measure of foregone opportunities serves only to point out that the break-even measure is an oversimplification.[18]

---

[16] This question will be followed-up in a subsequent paper.

[17] See, for example, [8].

[18] Indeed, the break-even point may be primarily a tool for suboptimization by managers with asymmetric penalty functions between failing to act vs. failing by acting. See, for example, [15].

Indeed, some writers suggest that the payback period should be computed to include not only recovery of the original outlays, but also the foregone interest on the amount of capital committed to the project. Doing so would, to some degree, give expression to the requirement that under normal circumstances the firm would not stand still but would earn some "normal" rate of return. However, the essential differences between the ordinary cost-volume break-even point and the payback period as a break-even point must also be considered.

In the usual break-even analysis, the evaluation made implicitly concerns the chances that the firm would incur a loss as opposed to the chances that the particular undertaking would result in gains of varying amounts. Viewing the decision from the point of view of the decision maker, the asymmetry between payoffs and penalties can, to a first approximation, be represented

Success Failure

	Success	Failure
Accept	+	−
Reject	0	0

by a two-by-two payoff matrix which divides the world into two states, Success and Failure, and two actions, Accept the project and Reject it, as in the figure. Assuming that similar choices must be made with sufficient frequency so that *some* projects are likely to be accepted, the rejection of a particular one by the decision maker is probably neutral.

If degree of success is a refinement which plays a role secondary to the *counting* of successes in the evaluation of a manager's performance, his initial view of the decision as having two outcomes *for him* (in contrast to the outcomes for the firm) makes some sense. The question of interest then is the meaningful line of separation between Success and Failure.

The least ambiguous, even if not the most appropriate, dividing line, as already discussed, is whether the firm is ahead or not by doing the project.[19] It is not necessary to suggest that decision makers accept a minimax strategy with respect to such decisions. It is probably sufficient to say that unless the probability of "at least breaking even" is sufficient, the decision maker is likely to reject the project. Such a procedure appears to be a crude substitute for a computation which goes beyond merely the *expected* profit (in the statistical sense) to a consideration of some aspects of the *distribution* of outcomes and their consequences for the decision maker. In such a simplified short-cut procedure, the means of judging the distribution are

---

[19] It must be readily admitted that *ex post* it is seldom simple to prove that any single activity of a firm is "losing money."

combined with the measure itself. This is intended to take the place of a much more elaborate, if correct, two-step procedure in which the distribution is first generated, then evaluated.[20] The probability of failing to reach at least the break-even point (the area under the density of outcomes up to a zero accounting profit), is compared with the probability of making a profit (the area to the right of the break-even point).

By contrast, the payback period is a point in *time* at which the firm expects "to be made whole again" (except for foregone interest) after making an investment. When the life of the project's stream of revenues is subject to substantial uncertainty, the payback period focuses on the period of time over which the project is expected to generate a "profit." That is, assuming for simplicity that net revenues are constant through time and only the project's life is a random variable, the aggregate (undiscounted, i.e., accounting) profit is proportional to the life of the project after the payback period has elapsed. Prior to then the stream of net revenues has been used to offset the original cost.[21]

A measure of undiscounted profit is then the project life after the payback period, and the conditional probability distribution of the project's life, given that it has reached the payback period, becomes a measure of the distribution of project profitability. In the same sense as for break-even analyses in general, the decision maker then is presumed to weigh the probability that the project's life lasts longer than its payback period to make it worthwhile for him. For a given distribution of project lives, under the assumption of uniform flows, the longer the payback period the greater are the chances of incurring an accounting loss on the project. However, a short payback period would mean a higher probability of profit, and hence the project would be more attractive.

One additional observation seems still to be in order. The shorter the payback period, given the Net Present Value (or internal rate of return) of the project, the sooner its profitability would become known.[22] A manager

---

[20] On this see also the "Plumber's daughter" in the address by Ronald Howard [11].

[21] The proportionality is only approximate because of the depreciation expense deduction for reporting profit. The effect of taxes has also been ignored here. Project life, unfortunately, enters here in two distinct ways. Aside from the above remarks that profitability depends on the project's life (especially after payback), accounting profit depends also on the rate at which depreciation expense is charged against the project's revenues. Thus a longer anticipated life yields a higher initial profit, other things remaining equal, because depreciation expense will be lower. Indeed, the life of the project may be overestimated by the proposer not only to enchance its total profitability, but also to reduce the payback period on the accounting profit basis. A bias countering this one may arise in the selection of the shortest project or asset life which the tax authorities permit to improve the actual after-tax cash-flow profitability. Cash-flow payback, the usual concept, is less affected since depreciation enters only as a tax shield. (The above qualifications to the statement in the text were suggested by Sidney Davidson.)

[22] Given the net present value, a short payback period implies that early cash flows are expected to be high relative to later ones, and/or to the investment. Actually, of course, neither cash flows nor accounting profit will be easily attributable to a given project, and initial accounting profit may, in any case, be a loss due to heavy initial depreciation expense.

therefore could also reasonably expect that his wise decision would show up early enough for the rewards (e.g., in the form of a bonus or advancement) to be received when they will still do him some good, given his high personal rate of discount. If the forecast turns out, ex post, to have been too optimistic after a number of years have elapsed, the possibility for alibi in the form of higher future returns yet to come is not lost, a circumstance which makes risk and reward in this situation once more asymmetric for the manager.

Stability of the Payback Measure

An interesting observation regarding the payback period may also reinforce the basis for some of its appeal. This concerns its relative stability under random variation in the cash flows. Projection of cash flows is, at best, an imprecise art, and the ex post results are unlikely to have been included among the projections made in advance. The correctness of the decision will be somewhat more easily assessed after the fact, since the outcomes will have turned out to have been favorable or not when compared against alternatives thought to have been available. Hence the ex ante measure of project worth should be "robust", in analogous fashion to the concept as used by statisticians. The internal rate of return, for example, is quite sensitive to variation in the underlying cash flows, as was demonstrated numerically in [20]. By contrast if it is possible to generalize from results which use the simplifying assumptions analogous to those made earlier, the payback period appears to be relatively constant.

To illustrate, we assume that net revenue is normally distributed at each moment in time, with constant expectation and constant variance over time. Under these assumptions the probability distribution of the payback period can be obtained from the following expression:[23]

$$f(T) = \frac{I}{T} \frac{1}{(2\pi kT)^{\frac{1}{2}}} \exp\left[-(I - cT)^2/2kT\right]$$

where I is the initial investment, $c(t) = c$ is the uniform stream of net revenues, with variance $\sigma^2(t) = k$, and T is the payback period.

A few sample computations have been carried out using this formula, and the results are presented in the table . . . (on the following page). In the examples the amount invested, I, was assumed to be $10. The expected cash inflow, c, assumed to be received continuously, has an expected value of $4 per year, with three different values of the variance, k: 1, 2, and 5. The table gives six points on the right-tail cumulative distribution of payback periods for each of the three values of cash-flow variance, from the ten per cent point to the 95 per cent point.

[23] See [13], p. 1007.

Table of Payback Periods (in Years) Exceeded with Probability P,
for Three Values of Cash Flow Variance k, Given Investment 1 = 10,
Average Annual Cash Flow
c = 4

P	k		
	1	2	5
.05	3¼	3½	4¼
.10	3	3¼	3¾
.33	2¾ −	2¾ −	2¾
.50	2½	2½	2½
.67	2¼ +	2¼ −	2
.90	2	1¾	1½

The expected payback period of 2½ years appears for each of the values
of *k*, the variance, in the row indicated by $P = 0.50$; i.e., fifty per cent of
the time one would expect the mean value of $T = 2½$ years to be exceeded,
while the other half of the time it would not be expected to be this high.
Approximately one third of the time the payback period here would be as
high as 2¾ years or higher, and this quantity is about the same for all three
values of cash flow variance. Ten per cent of the time it would be as large
as three years when the variance is one, 3¼ years when the variance is two,
but 3¾ years when the variance is as high as five.

Payback and the Resolution of Uncertainty

In addition to the fact that the return on capital investment projects includes substantial rewards for good management of the project and related
activities (economic rent), capital investments differ in the course of action
afforded to those making the investment in contrast to the alternatives facing
investors in other assets. To bring the differences into sharp relief it may be
useful to compare "investments" or gambles at a roulette table, investments
in bonds and stocks which are traded in a market, and capital investments.
Gambles on a roulette wheel have the characteristic that, once the wheel
stops spinning the payoff has been determined and settlement is made. The
outcome of subsequent spins is (presumed to be) independent of earlier
outcomes. Also, the bettor's wealth has already been determined at the end
of a spin, and in making his next bet he can take his new wealth position
into account. Put more directly, the bets are made sequentially with the
state of information the same at the beginning of each bet.
An investor purchasing marketable securities is essentially in the same
position as the gambler at the roulette table. At any moment in time his

decision to leave funds in an investment may be interpreted to be a reinvestment of the funds which the market value of his securities represents. The fact that the variability of outcomes is smaller for shorter intervals of time than for longer ones is unimportant here. The only significant discontinuities in this investment-disinvestment decision process are introduced by brokerage costs which are avoidable by leaving funds invested in the same securities. Another, though minor qualification, is that outcomes are not precisely known until the decision to liquidate the investment is actually carried out.[24] However, since a market price is quoted at all times, an investor knows his wealth position with only a small degree of uncertainty and can take this into account in making decisions with respect to the continued commitment of his funds. Additionally, the decision to make the commitment does not affect the outcome in a noticeable way. Given a reasonably broad market, an individual investor's decision to make a transaction does not affect the price of the security more than trivially. Thus it is not surprising that no one computes a payback period for, say, a bond, which is expected to generate a known income stream when held to maturity.

An extreme contrast with the preceding situations would be an investment in a space flight which is expected to last several years, and which is expected to bring back valuable objects from another planet. The space ship is presumed to be the first of its kind, and to be on a mission the scope of which had never before been attempted. It is assumed to be unable to communicate with the earth (or its outposts) during almost the entire duration of its voyage. Thus the outcome of the investment will not be known until some substantial time after the original commitment of funds, and little if any additional information is assumed to be generated in the interval to alter the subjective probabilities of the recovery of the space craft, or its success in bringing back the valuable cargo.

Under these rather extreme assumptions[25] the investor in this venture has tied up some of his capital for a potentially long time, with the interval to the time when the returns come in being itself a random variable. To analyze the investor's attitude to such an investment, we see that it can be broken down into two distinct components which, in turn, may be clarified by referring back to the roulette wheel.

First, suppose that the investor could place a bet today on one of two roulette wheels, the first being spun today, while the second is not spun until one year from today. If the odds were the same for the two wheels, a risk-averting bettor would prefer the first wheel to the second, assuming only that the availability of gambles next year is not expected to be curtailed or

---

[24] Even on securities listed on the New York Stock Exchange a stop-loss order becomes a market order when certain conditions are met, and the investor is not *guaranteed* a stipulated price.

[25] See also [3] for a related example.

yield less favorable odds. (It is important that in either case the bet is made today, and the chips are paid for today.) Reasons for preferring the present over the deferred payoff would include a) the bettor might not be alive next year, and his utility for a bequest may not be the same as his utility for consumption while alive; b) until the outcome is known, the bettor's wealth is uncertain and he cannot adjust to the preferred consumption based on his wealth *during* the year with the second wheel; and c) even if the gamble is for an objective in the distant future, e.g., retirement, by repeating similar gambles to the first wheel, the bettor can achieve the same expected payoff, but with a lower variance of payoff.[26] Selection of the second wheel would generally require more favorable odds.

Suppose now alternatively that the first wheel is still one which is spun today, but that a third wheel, physically identical to the second one, is not spun until some randomly selected time interval has passed, as might be determined by an auxiliary process. If the *expected* outcome of the auxiliary process, which determines the timing of the spin of the third wheel, were exactly one year, would the investor be indifferent between this deferred spin or the earlier one (the second wheel) for which the spin is slated to take place one year from now? Most likely not. Obviously, the nature of the auxiliary process would enter into the choice between the second and the third wheel.

The space venture resembles the third wheel here, since both the payoff and its timing are uncertain. The investor's consumption decisions until the return of the space craft are constrained in the following sense. The investor may be able to sell some or all of his shares in the venture, and, indeed, a market for them may exist. Prices for the shares may fluctuate in response to changes in expectations regarding the final outcome, its timing as well as its amount. For any given set of expectations regarding the amount of payoff, the elapse of time would presumably result in an increase in the price of the shares since the actual payoff is then closer.[27]

Alternative to selling his shares, the investor may prefer to borrow against them. While he could always lever himself generally, by pledging his other assets or earning power against a loan, the shares themselves do not lend themselves to bank borrowing in the form of the common demand note with the shares as collateral. From the nature of the probability distribution of outcomes facing the *lender,* the latter would find himself in a position with more than trivial risk. Of course, such a risk may fit the portfolio of some lenders, so that at some high enough rate of interest (contingent upon there being a payoff at all) the lender would advance

---

[26] These results are developed rigorously in a forthcoming paper.

[27] My colleague Myron Gordon steered me away from the incorrect conclusions implied by the results of Robichek and Myers in [17] which would be that the values of the shares, given constant expectations, would rise at the pure (i.e., riskless) rate of interest.

some or all of the required funds.[28] To make a loan attractive to both borrower and lender requires their utility functions to be of different shape, assuming that their expectations of the outcome are the same and the composition of their portfolios is otherwise similar. The size of the residual risk, however, precludes banks operating with the funds supplied by depositors from making loans of this type.[29]

In the preceding example the uncertainty arising from the delayed knowledge of the outcome is resolved all at once, at the end of the venture. The only time of relevance is the interval until the voyage is over. Capital investment projects of the ordinary kind represent a situation between the simple roulette wheel or security and the space venture with respect to the resolution of uncertainty. Cash flows are projected at the time the investment is first contemplated, and at least implicitly, the cash flows are considered to be subject to random deviation from their expected values. As time passes and some of the anticipated cash flows are realized, information is generated thereby as to the subsequent outcomes of the whole project. Each time such information is received, the "investor" may take any corrective managerial action he deems necessary to realize his expectations. For example, he may commit additional resources in the form of advertising, further product or process development, and especially assign additional or different managerial supervision to the project. More important, however, he is in a better position to make decisions with respect to his current consumption and with respect to other investment alternatives which present themselves. Thus the evolving information on the project's outcome is extremely valuable to him for making subsequent decisions.[30]

A natural scaling of the importance of the information content of the initial cash inflows might be the size of the original commitment of funds. In looking at the investment entirely *ex ante,* the rate at which the uncertainty devolving around the outcome is expected to be resolved may be measured, at least crudely, by the relation between the series of cumulated expected cash inflows and the amount of the investment. In terms of a standardized measure, the time interval required for the cumulated expected

---

[28] The detailed development of these arguments parallel fairly closely those contained in a forthcoming paper by Karl Borch [4] which came to my attention while this paper was being revised. They will therefore be omitted.

[29] An analogy would be the position of an individual expecting a potentially large legacy: The legator may change his will, he may outlive his heir (with a substitute heir and not the original heir's estate), or the legator may lose his fortune. In all these events the individual gets nothing or substantially less than expected. Based on these prospects, would a commercial bank lend him any funds? Clearly the bank's position would be different if the property were held in trust for him or for his estate.

[30] To the extent that motivations of potentially mobile managers differ from those of the firm, managers would choose projects for which the wisdom of their choices is *expected* to be revealed early, as was discussed before.

inflows exactly to equal the original investment is a measure of the rate at which the project's uncertainty is *expected* to be resolved. But this measure is precisely the Payback Period.

Conclusion

In this review of different ways in which the payback period can be interpreted, we have seen that only the first, the payback reciprocal as a measure of the rate of return of a project, had significance in the context of certainty. Even with this interpretation it is more appropriate to regard payback as a constraint which a project must satisfy than as a criterion which is to be optimized. The use of payback as a measure of the "liquidity" of an asset, essentially as the reciprocal of the capital turnover ratio, but computed separately for each proposed project, was found to be substantially different from a liquidity requirement for the firm as a whole.

Payback was seen to imply a form of break-even analysis, which makes no sense in a world of certainty, but which can function like many other "rules of thumb" to shortcut the process of generating information and then evaluating it. Thus it was shown that payback reduces the information search by focussing on that time at which the firm expects to "be made whole again" in some sense, and hence it allows the decision maker to judge whether the life of the project past the break-even point is sufficient to make the undertaking worthwhile. The fact that this break-even notion is both naive and incorrect does not alter the fact of its use in the absence of other simple measures which serve the same purpose. To this must be added the appeal of payback for the decision maker, rather than for his firm, in that it indicates how rapidly he can expect confirmation that he has made a good choice, and for which he can expect to benefit personally.

Finally, the paper discussed some of the inherent differences between financial investments and investments in capital projects by firms. While the choice of the investor in the former case revolves purely around the decision to withdraw the funds from an investment or to leave them, the situation is different with investments in physical assets. Not only is the market value of the assets substantially below the "going concern" value of the project at almost all times during the life of the project, but the range of alternatives available with respect to the project are quite different. Additional resources can be committed to alter the outcome of a project after it has been initiated, or less funds can be devoted to it than was originally contemplated. The randomness of both the size and timing of the outcomes themselves focus on the financial restrictions within which the firm is forced to operate. For both these reasons, information of a certain kind is extremely important to the decision maker. This is the rate at which he can expect the uncertainty devolving around a project to be resolved. While once more no single number can convey the necessary information, the payback period does provide some idea of the relevant data.

As the detailed discussion above makes abundantly clear, the payback concept is an oversimplification in each case. However, the problems which managers seek to attack by its use will not disappear simply by arguing that payback is not meaningful. Rather, it is necessary to face up to these problems, and to employ methods which solve them.

References

1. Arrow, Kenneth J., "Optimal Capital Policy with Irreversible Investment," Stanford University Institute for Mathematical Studies in the Social Sciences, Technical Report No. 146, December 14, 1966.

2. Baumol, W. J., and Quandt, R. E., "Mathematical Programming and the Discount Rate Under Capital Rationing," *Economic Journal* (June 1965), pp. 317–329.

3. Boness, A. James, "A Pedagogic Note on the Cost of Capital," *Journal of Finance* (March 1964), pp. 99–106.

4. Borch, Karl, "Equilibrium, Optimum and Prejudices in Capital Markets," *Journal of Financial and Quantitative Analysis* (forthcoming).

5. Boulding, Kenneth, "The Theory of a Single Investment," *Quarterly Journal of Economics* (May 1935), pp. 475–494.

6. Byrne, R., Charnes, A., Cooper, W. W., and Kortanek, K., "A Chance Constrained Approach to Capital Budgeting with Portfolio Type Payback and Liquidity Constraints," *Journal of Financial and Quantitative Analysis* (December 1967), pp. 339–364.

7. Charnes, A., Cooper, W. W., Devoe, J. K., and Learner, D. B., "DEMON: Decision Mapping via Optimum Go-No-Go Networks," *Management Science,* Vol. 12, No. 11 (July 1966), pp. 865–887.

8. Duesenberry, James S., "The Portfolio Approach to the Demand for Money and other Assets," *Review of Economics and Statistics,* Vol. 45, Supplement (February 1963).

9. Fisher, Irving, *The Theory of Interest,* Reprints of Economic Classics, Augustus Kelly, New York, 1961.

10. Gordon, Myron J., "The Payoff Period and the Rate of Profit," *Journal of Business* (October 1955), pp. 253–261.

11. Howard, Ronald, "The Practicality Gap," *Management Science,* Vol. 14, No. 7 (March 1968), pp. 503–507.

12. Istvan, Donald F., *Capital-Expenditure Decisions: How They Are Made,* Bureau of Business Research, Indiana University, Bloomington, Ind. 1961.

13. Keilson, Julian, "The First Passage Time Density for Homogeneous Skip-Free Walks on the Continuium," *Annals of Mathematical Statistics,* (September 1963), pp. 1003–1011.

14. Lutz, F. and Lutz, V., *The Theory of Investment of the Firm,* Princeton University Press, Princeton, N.J., 1951.

15. Mansefield, E. and Wein, H., "A Study of Decision-Making Within the Firm", *Quarterly Journal of Economics* (November 1958), pp. 515–536.

16. Marglin, Steven, *Approaches to Dynamic Investment Planning,* North-Holland, Amsterdam, 1963.

17. Robichek, A. and Myers, S., "Risk Adjusted Discount Rates", *Journal of Finance* (December 1966), pp. 727–730.

18. Samuelson, Paul A., "Some Aspects of the Pure Theory of Capital," *Quarterly Journal of Economics* (May 1936), pp. 469–496.

19. Smith, Vernon L., *Investment and Production,* Harvard University Press, Cambridge, Mass., 1961.

20. Solomon, Martin B., Jr., "Uncertainty and Its Effects on Capital Investment Analysis," *Management Science,* Vol. 12, No. 8, (April 1966), pp. B334–339.

21. Tobin, James, Unpublished (but widely circulated) manuscript, 1959, Chapter 2.

22. Weingartner, H. Martin, *Mathematical Programming and the Analysis of Capital Budgeting Problems,* Prentice-Hall, Inc., Englewood Cliffs, N.J., 1963, reissued by Markham Publishing Company, Chicago, 1967.

23. ———, "Capital Budgeting of Interrelated Projects," *Management Science,* Vol. 12, No. 7 (March 1966), pp. 485–516, reprinted in the Markham edition of [22].

24. ———, "Equipment Replacement Analysis: A Note on the Optimum Investment Period," *Industrial Management Review,* (Fall 1965), pp. 47–51.

25. ———, "Criteria for Programming Investment Project Selection," *Journal of Industrial Economics,* Vol. 15, No. 1 (November 1966), pp. 65–76, reprinted in the Markham edition of [22].

12

Sundem analyzes net present value (NPV) criterion with a payback constraint and a net present value model with the discount rate dependent on the proposed project's risk as models that perform at a level high enough to be potentially cost-benefit efficient for many firms. He simulates an environment with a time-state preference model to evaluate the two models. It appears that the use of a payback period as a secondary criterion in capital budgeting is not totally irrelevant, though it leaves much to be desired. Also, the dominant use of the NPV model seems justified in certain circumstances; and the NPV-replacement cost model gives decisions nearly as accurate as some of the most sophisticated models. Finally, it is important to realize that there is no one model that is best for every firm.

Evaluating Simplified Capital Budgeting Models Using a Time-state Preference Metric*

Gary L. Sundem†

Sophisticated models for capital investment decisions have been prominent in the accounting and finance literature during the past decade. Many operations research techniques were incorporated in these models, especially techniques designed explicitly to recognize the risk of proposed investments. It has been shown that in simulated environments where considerable uncertainty about the future exists the decisions from some of these sophisticated models are clearly superior to the decisions from a

* *From* The Accounting Review, *Vol. XLIX, No. 2 (April, 1974), pp. 306–320. Reprinted by permission of the American Accounting Association and the author.*

† The author wishes to thank the Puget Sound Power and Light Company and the Graduate School of Business Administration, University of Washington, for their support of this research.

naive application of net present value or payback models.[1] However, a recent survey by Klammer indicates that simplified models are used most often, discounted cash flow being by far the most popular primary criterion for evaluating proposed capital budgeting projects, and payback continuing a sizable (though decreasing) popularity as a primary criterion and an almost equally large (and increasing) popularity as a secondary criterion.[2]

There are at least two possible explanations for the gap between the advocacy of sophisticated models in the theoretical literature and the use of highly simplified models in practice. First, managers may not yet be acquainted with the new, sophisticated techniques. Even though sophisticated models are superior, it may take time for them to gain acceptance. Second, the net present value model or payback model (possibly with some embellishments) may be the most cost/benefit efficient model for capital budgeting for many firms. If sophisticated models were actually better (in a cost/benefit sense) than the presently used simplified models, firms would be forced to adopt these models in order to survive. Since widespread adoption of sophisticated models has not been observed, the added cost of applying these models may be greater than the added benefit derived from their use.

This paper explores the possibility that some form of net present value or payback model has a performance level high enough to be potentially cost/benefit efficient for many firms. Two variations of net present value and payback models are explored: (1) Net present value criterion with a payback constraint and (2) net present value model with the discount rate dependent on the proposed project's risk.

To evaluate these models, a metric model based on time-state preference theory is first developed. Many more parameters, especially risk parameters, are included in this model than in the simplified models being evaluated. This model provides a set of simulated environments and an ideal investment decision within each environment. The decisions of the two simplified models are then compared to the ideal decisions. The result of the comparison is a quantitative measure of the value given up by using the simplified model in a given environment. If this value is not great, there exists a great potential for the simplified model to be cost/benefit efficient.

Part I describes briefly the simulated environments in which these models are evaluated. The environments are defined so that market-based values are established for every proposed capital budgeting project in each environment. The ideal decision is to accept all projects with a positive value. Part II presents each of the two simplified models, and it describes

---

[1] See Sundem, Gary L., "Evaluating Capital Budgeting Models in Simulated Environments" (unpublished working paper, 1972).

[2] Klammer, Thomas, "Empirical Evidence of the Adoption of Sophisticated Capital Budgeting Techniques," *Journal of Business* (July 1972), pp. 387–397. The category of discounted cash flow models includes internal rate of return and net present value models, which are nearly identical for practical purposes.

the method by which it accepts and rejects projects. Each simplified model is then used to select a set of accepted projects in each environment, and the value of that set of projects is calculated. The results consist of comparisons of the values of the sets of projects selected by the simplified models with the value of the set of all projects with positive value in each environment. Finally, Part III summarizes the findings and points the direction for future research.

I. The Simulated Environment[3]

The basis for the simulated environmnents is the time-state preference model of Arrow and Hirshleifer.[4] The firm is the decision-making agent, choosing among proposed capital budgeting projects with an objective of maximizing the utility of its stockholders. Each project is a set of claims, $(c_{jts}, t \in T, s \in S_t)$, where c_{jts} is the cash flow from project j to be received if state s occurs at time t; T is the set of all possible times; and S_t is the set of all possible states of the world that could occur in time period t. Under an assumption of complete and perfect (cash-mediated) markets,[5] equilibrium prices for unit claims to net cash flow in time t and state s, $\{\phi_{ts}\}$, are determined by the market.[6]

If we assume time and state independence and time preferences that do not vary over time,[7] the utility of individual i for a cash flow of c_{its} in period t and state s is $u_{is}(c_{its})/(1 + r_i)^t$, where u_{is} is a state dependent utility function for cash flow and r_i is a time preference discount rate. Each individual will then adjust his holdings of claims by trading in the market until prices meet the following requirement for each individual:

---

[3] More detailed descriptions of the environment are found in Sundem, Gary L., *Simplification in Capital Budgeting Models* (Unpublished Ph.D. Dissertation, Stanford University, 1971).

[4] Arrow, Kenneth J., "The Role of Securities in the Optimal Allocation of Risk Bearing," *Review of Economic Studies* (April 1964), pp. 91–96, and Hirshleifer, Jack, *Investment, Interest, and Capital* (Prentice-Hall, 1970).

[5] Because aggregation over utility functions of individual stockholders is likely to be impossible, these assumptions are introduced to allow separation of the investment decision from an explicit consideration of utility functions. Under complete markets every time-state claim is a marketable commodity. Under perfect markets every actor is a price taker, and there are no external drains on the system. In a cash-mediated market all transactions are carried out with securities rather than consumptive commodities. When consumption is desired, securities are traded directly for the desired consumptive goods.

[6] An elegant proof of the existence of such an equilibrium is found in Debreu, Gerard, *Theory of Value: Cowles Foundation for Research in Economics at Yale University, Monograph No. 17* (Wiley, 1959). The details of the establishment of a market equilibrium are described in Hirshleifer, and a summary of the most important details is found in Sundem, *Simplification in Capital Budgeting Models*, pp. 19–25.

[7] Time (state) independence means that the utility of claims in one period (state) is independent of claims in other periods (states). Time preferences that do not vary imply that the same discount factor for time preference is applied in each period.

(1) $$\phi_{ts} = [\pi_{its} du_{is}(c_{its})/dc_{its}]/(1+r_i)^t$$

where π_{its} is the probability assigned by individual i to the occurrence of state s in period t, and $du_{is}(c_{its})/dc_{its}$ is the derivative of the individual's state preference function. With prices thus established, and with c_{jts} being the net cash flow from project j in period t if state s occurs and c_{jo} being the certain current net cash flow, the value of project j is[8]

(2) $$V_j = c_{j0} + \sum_{t \in T} \sum_{s \in St} c_{jts} \phi_{ts}$$

If and only if $V_j > 0$, the wealth of each stockholder of a firm will increase if project j is undertaken by that firm. Assuming nonsatiation and either quasi-concave utility functions or a large number of actors in the market all with a relatively small wealth,[9] such an increase in wealth will increase an individual's utility.

This model for specifying the value of project j is heralded for its generality, not its operationality.[10] To use it for assigning dollar values to projects, the state (s), the market price function (ϕ_{ts}), and the relation between project cash flows and the state (c_{jts}) must be operationally defined. The values assigned to these variables will specify the characteristics of the environment. Because different firms operate in different environments, a range of values for some of the variables will be examined.

STATE

The state variable summarizes all environmental influences on cash flow claims. Once the state variable in period t is known, all cash flows in period t from all projects become known with certainty. In period t, the relevant elements of the state variable for project j are $(\hat{s}_{1t}, \hat{s}_{2t}, s_{jt})$, where $\hat{s}_{1t}$ is an index of aggregate (market) wealth in period t; $\hat{s}_{2t}$ is an index of industry well-being; and s_{jt} is a state variable that affects period t cash flows from project j only. One can think of high values of $\hat{s}_{1t}$ as representative of large aggregate wealth (boom) and low values as small aggregate wealth (depression). These conditions affect both returns from the projects, where cash flow from most projects is greater the higher the value of $\hat{s}_{1t}$, and the utility (or market price) of those returns, where utility of a dollar of cash flow is smaller the higher the value of $\hat{s}_{1t}$. Because there will be some commonality beyond market factors in all projects undertaken by a given

---

[8] Note that this is a partial equilibrium analysis that assumes prices would be unaffected by implementing project j.

[9] See Arrow, footnote 1, p. 96.

[10] Use of this model as a metric is justified because it contains finer partitions over states and actions than the models being evaluated. See Feltham, Gerald A., *Information Evaluation, American Accounting Association Studies in Accounting Research 5* (American Accounting Association, 1972).

firm, the s_{2t} factor accounts for this. However, this affects only cash flows and not the utility of the cash flows because it can be diversified at a market level. The s_{jt} term summarizes all variation in return that is unique to project j; thus, it is completely diversifiable by both the firm and the market.

The values of s_{1t}, s_{2t}, and s_{jt} over time possess similar (though independent) statistical qualities. They follow a random walk with zero drift. Let s_t' represent any of the state vector elements with $s_0' = 0$ the known current state. Then $s_t' = s_{t-1}' + \tilde{e}_t$, where $\tilde{e}$ is a continuous random variable with $E(\tilde{e}_t) = 0$, $\sigma^2(\tilde{e}_t) = \sigma_t^2$, and $\sigma(\tilde{e}_t, \tilde{e}_{t'}) = 0$ for $t \neq t'$.[11] The expected state in period t is the state in period $t - 1$; it is not dependent on the sequence of states before period $t - 1$. It is easily shown that

$$\sigma^2(s_t') = \sum_{i=1}^{t} \sigma^2(\tilde{e}_i);$$

consequently, $\sigma^2(s_t') \geq \sigma^2(s_{t'}')$ if $t > t'$. This indicates increasing uncertainty the further into the future s_t' is predicted, an intuitively desirable quality.

To complete this specification, one needs values for $\{\sigma^2(\tilde{e}_i), i = 1, 2, \cdots, T\}$. The higher the values of $\sigma^2(\tilde{e}_i)$, the greater the uncertainty about the future states. It is assumed that $\sigma^2(\tilde{e}_i) = \sigma^2(\tilde{e}_{i'})$ for all i and i'. Four values of $\sigma^2(\tilde{e}_i)$ will be analyzed (representing four levels of uncertainty in the environment): $\sigma^2(\tilde{e}_i) = 0.5, 1.0, 1.5$, and 2.0 for all i. The resulting distributions of s_t' are normal with mean of zero and variance of $t\sigma^2(\tilde{e}_i)$.

MARKET PRICE FUNCTION

The market price function, 0_{ts}, indicates the equilibrium value placed on one dollar of cash flow in period t and state s by market participants. From the individual optima conditions of time-state preference theory presented earlier, recall that[12]

$$\emptyset_{ts} = [\pi_{its} du_{is}(c_{its})/dc_{its}]/(1 + r_i)^t \qquad \text{for all } i$$

To create a market-based function from these individual conditions, a social (market) utility function is substituted for u_{is} and social time preference for r_i:

(3) $$\emptyset_{ts} = [\pi_{ts} du_s(C_{ts})/dC_{ts}](1 + r)^t$$

---

[11] This makes s_t' a continuous random variable while in theory it must be discrete. However, since the sum over discrete partitions approaches the integral over a continuous variable as the discrete partitions become finer, we will use the integral as an approximation to the sum over the underlying discrete partitions.

[12] See equation (1).

where π_{ts} is a consensus (social) probability for state s in period t; u_s is a generalized (social) preference function for cash flow; r is a social (risk-free) time preference discount rate; and C_{ts} is aggregate available cash flow in period t and state s. Since s_{1t} is also aggregate available cash flow, it can be substituted for C_{ts}. Finally, using a commonly accepted utility function as the form of u_s, namely $u_s(s_{1t}) = 1 - (1/k) \exp(-ks_{1t})$, the market price function is[13]

$$(4) \qquad 0_{ts} = \pi_{ts}(1+r)^{-t} \exp(-ks_{1t})$$

The values of π_{ts} and s_{1t} are determined by the probability distribution over future states which was specified in the previous section. The value of r is assumed to be 0.05 (or 5%) in all environments. The value of k reflects the effect of the price function on project values, and four values of k will be examined: $k = 0.03, 0.06, 0.09,$ and 0.12.

STATE RETURN RELATIONSHIPS

Projects will be accepted and rejected from a proposed set of thirty independent projects. The net cash flow from project j in period t if state s_t occurs is assumed to be

$$(5) \qquad c_{jt}(s_t) = \mu_{jt} + \alpha_{1j}s_{1t} + \alpha_{2j}s_{2t} + \alpha_{3j}s_{jt}$$

where μ_{jt} is expected cash flow and α_{1j}, α_{2j}, and α_{3j} are coefficients indicating the magnitude of the effect of each state factor on project returns.[14]

The expected cash flows for all projects are adapted from Weingartner[15] and are shown in Table 1. These projects represent a variety of sizes, lives, and patterns of cash flows. The diversity of these projects is also indicated by some familiar parameters of the projects shown in Table 2. The values of α_1, α_2, and α_3 were randomly selected for each project from normal distributions with means of 5.0, 1.0, and 4.0 and standard deviations of 5.0, 1.0, and 4.0 respectively, and they are shown in Table 3 [p. 214]. The means are consistent with King's[16] findings about market, industry, and unique effects on firms' returns.

---

[13] This function for 0_{ts} satisfies the criterion expressed in Arrow, Kenneth J. and Mordecai Kurz, *Public Investment, the Rate of Return, and Optimal Fiscal Policy* (Johns Hopkins Press, 1970), p. 7, that "the price of a claim in state s is relatively higher than the actuarial value for adverse conditions, and vice versa."

[14] See Sundem, *Simplification in Capital Budgeting Models*, for analysis of other functional forms of the relationship.

[15] Weingartner, H. Martin, *Mathematical Programming and the Analysis of Capital Budgeting Problems* (Markham Publishing Co., 1967), p. 180.

[16] King, Benjamin, "Market and Industry Factors in Stock Price Behavior," *Journal of Business*, Part II (January 1966), pp. 139–190.

TABLE 1 Expected Net Cash Flows

Project	0	1	2	3	4	5	6	7	8	9	10	11	12	13	14	15	16	17	18	19	20	21	22	23	24	25
1	-100	20	20	20	19	19	18	16	14	11	6	-8														
2	-100	20	18	18	18	18	14	14	14	14	14	10	10	10	10	10	6	6	6	6	6					
3	-100	15	15	15	15	15	13	13	13	13	13	11	11	11	11	11	9	9	9	9	9					
4	-100	20	6	11	7	16	5	14	18	3	20	2	22	8	10	18	6	9	14	24						
5	-100	-60	-60	80	74	66	56	44	30	14	20															
6	-200	25	25	25	25	25	25	25	25	25	25	25	25	25	25	25	25	25	25	25	25	25	25	25	25	25
7	-80	20	20	20	19	17	14	10	6	2																
8	-60	-30	-10	45	34	25	16	12	8	-20	21	16														
9	-120	25	25	30	35	30	25	20	15	10	5	16	12	9	7											
10	-100	18	17	15	12	8	-10	18	17	15	12	20	-10													
11	-150	20	20	20	20	20	20	20	20	20	20	18	16	14	12	10	8	4								
12	-100	18	18	16	14	12	10	4	-20																	
13	-150	-75	-75	60	60	55	50	44	38	36	35	34	33	30	25	17	9									
14	-50	-100	-175	50	55	60	65	60	50	40	30	20	10	-25												
15	-100	-150	-100	10	20	30	40	60	60	60	60	60	60	60	60	60	60	60	60	60	60					
16	-95	-60	47	42	37	31	24	18	13	9	6	4	3													
17	-175	50	45	35	25	10	-60	45	35	25	40	32	25	19	14	10	7	5								
18	-250	45	45	40	30	25	20	15	10	15	15	5														
19	-75	-75	-40	40	40	40	35	35	30	25	15	5	13	17	11	14										
20	-180	20	12	16	13	11	19	17	17	12	19	6	13	14	17	20										
21	-80	18	16	14	12	10	4	16	14	3																
22	-85	20	20	16	15	13	10	7	3																	
23	-270	-100	125	115	105	80	60	35	25	15	10															
24	-40	15	13	9	7	5	2	9	25	15	10															
25	-50	10	10	9	7	4	-14	50	40	30	20	10	3	-16	8	4										
26	-200	60	40	30	15	-25	-25	25	9	8	6	3	10													
27	-70	15	13	11	10	9	7	25	15	6	4	5	2													
28	-355	60	70	80	70	55	40	25	20	15	-75	35	30	25	20	15	10	5								
29	-275	40	45	45	40	35	30	15	20	15	18	16	13	10	6	-25	16	16	14	11	8	5				
30	-140	20	20	18	16	14	11	8														2				

213

TABLE 2

Information about the Expected Net Cash Flows

Project	Internal Rate of Return (%)	NPV ($) @ 5%	NPV ($) @ 10%
1	11.0	25.36	3.60
2	14.1	66.41	23.09
3	11.9	57.03	11.73
4	10.0	45.74	0.03
5	12.7	72.54	21.65
6	11.7	152.39	26.99
7	13.8	26.32	9.96
8	12.5	42.81	11.30
9	15.7	57.25	26.02
10	9.0	28.99	−5.53
11	7.0	16.14	−20.08
12	8.5	21.32	−6.97
13	8.8	72.94	−18.88
14	9.2	84.83	−11.75
15	10.8	286.06	26.81
16	10.5	34.50	2.73
17	5.8	5.23	−22.75
18	5.3	3.61	−50.41
19	6.7	15.65	−24.16
20	5.2	3.44	−52.46
21	9.4	15.42	−1.93
22	6.1	3.01	−9.31
23	11.9	98.94	23.95
24	10.2	5.02	0.16
25	4.7	−0.80	−10.66
26	4.2	−6.48	−40.97
27	3.5	−3.78	−13.99
28	4.7	−3.57	−55.98
29	4.6	−5.05	−60.92
30	4.9	−0.62	−37.58

DECISION ENVIRONMENTS

A decision environment in this research is specified by the values of $\sigma^2(\tilde{e}_i)$ and k described earlier. There will be sixteen decision environments, and each will be referred to by a two-digit figure, "*ab*", where "*a*" relates to the value of $\sigma^2(\tilde{e}_i)$ and "*b*" relates to the value of k. The number "*ab*" will signify the following:

$$a = 1 \Rightarrow \sigma^2(\tilde{e}_i) = 0.5 \qquad b = 1 \Rightarrow k = 0.03$$
$$a = 2 \Rightarrow \sigma^2(\tilde{e}_i) = 1.0 \qquad b = 2 \Rightarrow k = .06$$
$$a = 3 \Rightarrow \sigma^2(\tilde{e}_i) = 1.5 \qquad b = 3 \Rightarrow k = .09$$
$$a = 4 \Rightarrow \sigma^2(\tilde{e}_i) = 2.0 \qquad b = 4 \Rightarrow k = .12$$

Environments of the form $1b$ indicate that the future is relatively certain, while environments of the form $4b$ indicate a relatively uncertain future. An $a1$ environment reflects a relatively small influence of the state on project valuation, while an $a4$ environment represents a relatively large state effect.

TABLE 3

Coefficients for Project Returns

Project	α_{1j}	α_{2j}	α_{3j}
1	3.773	.731	.365
2	9.921	.081	4.349
3	13.806	1.607	1.836
4	6.707	.228	−.498
5	5.782	.027	5.475
6	8.091	1.865	2.231
7	.891	2.329	8.619
8	2.640	−1.009	4.760
9	−.075	2.222	5.192
10	11.621	−.662	5.516
11	6.074	1.345	−3.846
12	6.447	.665	9.036
13	9.089	.272	−2.626
14	8.950	1.690	−1.566
15	2.598	2.183	6.799
16	−.080	3.744	6.211
17	5.508	.509	6.082
18	4.196	1.042	5.493
19	5.040	1.431	7.180
20	11.027	1.811	6.085
21	−1.877	1.190	3.699
22	−3.718	−1.671	8.055
23	9.488	1.742	−1.870
24	−1.516	.267	7.867
25	8.939	1.377	5.375
26	3.558	1.550	.411
27	11.950	−.504	4.331
28	8.532	2.273	−1.456
29	6.838	.810	2.558
30	2.355	1.065	.144

There is no guarantee that these environments span all possible real world environments. However, trends in model performance as each parameter changes are easily discernible; consequently, extrapolation may be made confidently. Only additional research will indicate which specific environment is appropriate for a given firm.

VALUATION BY THE TIME-STATE PREFERENCE MODEL

The values assigned to a project by the time-state preference (TSP) model are assumed to be the same as the values assigned by the market at equilibrium. The value of project j is

(6)
$$V_j = \sum_t \int_{T_t} S_{s_t} \pi_{st} [\mu_{jt} + \alpha_{1j}\hat{s}_{1t} + \alpha_{2j}\hat{s}_{2t} + \alpha_{zj}s_{jt}]$$
$$\cdot \exp(-k\hat{s}_{1t})(1+r)^{-t} ds_t$$
$$= \sum_{t=0}^{T} (1+r)^{-t} \exp(\tfrac{1}{2}k^2\sigma_t^2)(\mu_{jt} - \alpha_{1j}k\sigma_t^2)$$

where σ_t^2 is the variance of $\hat{s}_{1t}$, π_{st} is the probability density function for s_t, and all other variables are as previously defined.[17] The project parameters affecting value are μ_{jt} and α_{1j}, and the environmental parameters affecting value are r, k, and σ_t^2. Notice that greater expected returns, μ_{jt}, means greater value while the more returns vary with the market index, indicated by α_{1j}, the smaller the value.

If the TSP model could be used for capital budgeting decisions, every project with $V_j > 0$ would be accepted and all others rejected. The maximum possible increase in value for the firm that can be achieved through the capital budgeting decision is the sum of the V_j's for all projects with $V_j > 0$. This is the value attributed to the TSP model.

II. The Simplified Models

The performance of two often-used capital budgeting models is evaluated in this section. The first model is a net present value model with a payback constraint (NPV–PBK), and the second model is a net present value model that uses a discount rate dependent on the risk class of the proposed project (NPV–RC). Each model selects a set of projects to be implemented in each decision environment, and the value attributed to the model is the increase in the value of the firm due to implementing the set of projects selected, which is the sum of the values of the selected projects. The amount by which this value falls short of the value of the TSP model

---

[17] The second form of equation (6) is derived from the first using moment generating functions. For the steps involved see Sundem, *Simplification in Capital Budgeting Models*, pp. 63–64.

in each environment is the amount paid for the simplifications in the model.

Predictions of project and environmental parameters are required in applying any capital budgeting model. Project parameters (e.g., the expected cash flow from project *j* in period *t*) are initially assumed to be predicted perfectly, and environmental parameters (e.g., appropriate discount rate) are selected ex post in each decision environment to optimize model performance. These assumptions allow each model to perform as well as possible in each environment, allowing model comparisons under identical ground rules. These assumptions do not allow consideration of the sensitivity of the performance of the models to the accuracy of parameter predictions. These assumptions are quite critical to assessing the performance of the NPV–RC model, and some attempt has been made to examine the effect of relaxing the assumptions on both project and environmental parameters. However, this area needs further research.

THE NPV–PBK MODEL

The performance of both the net present value model and the payback model in the simulated environments described in Part I has been presented elsewhere,[18] and the results are summarized in part of Table 4. The figures in Table 4 are both the increase in the value of the firm obtained by using a given model and the percent of the maximum possible increase in value for each model. The results come from a relatively naive application of the models where the required rate of return or maximum allowable payback period is the same for all projects in a given environment. Use of the NPV model provides quite good performance in environments where uncertainty and state effects are small. However, in environments with high uncertainty and where the effect of the state on valuation is large, performance is not very good. In fact, only 12% of the potential increase in value of a firm is realized with the NPV model in environments 43 and 44. The performance of the payback model is likewise much less than optimal in many environments, decreasing quickly in performance level as moderate uncertainty arises, but not reaching as low a level of performance as the NPV model in very uncertain environments.

It has been suggested by Weingartner,[19] among others, that use of the payback model as a primary standard for capital budgeting is not tremendously appealing, but using it as a constraint with an NPV model as the primary standard has much appeal. This view accepts the present value of a proposed project as its profitability and suggests that the payback period could be used as a surrogate measure of its riskiness. All projects with

---

[18] See Sundem, "Evaluating Capital Budgeting Models in Simulated Environments."
[19] Weingartner, H. Martin, "Some New Views on the Payback Period and Capital Budgeting Decisions," *Management Science* (August 1969), pp. B594–B607.

TABLE 4
Model Performance: NPV–PBK Model

Decision Environ- ment	Model Values				Model Value as a Percent of TSP Model Value		
	TSP	NPV	Payback	NPV– Payback Combined	NPV	Payback	NPV– Payback Combined
11	1097	1097	1045	1097	100	95	100
12	974	973	890	973	100	91	100
13	889	861	747	861	97	84	97
14	829	758	612	758	91	74	91
21	962	960	876	960	100	91	100
22	785	712	560	712	91	71	91
23	696	539	315	539	77	45	77
24	651	401	308	401	62	47	62
31	854	825	705	825	97	83	97
32	669	514	306	514	77	46	77
33	596	302	288	302	51	48	51
34	610	97	278	278	16	46	46
41	763	689	534	698	90	70	90
42	592	352	286	352	59	48	59
43	572	70	263	263	12	46	46
44	598	69	258	253	12	42	42

long payback periods are rejected. Because distant returns are most risky, and since the payback model ignores returns after the payback period, this model may separate, in an ad hoc fashion, risky from relatively risk-free projects. The increasing use of the payback criterion as a secondary standard for project selection while it is being replaced by the NPV model as the primary standard[20] indicates that the NPV–PBK combined model may be finding increasing use in practice as well as being advocated in the literature.

The NPV–PBK model was applied to select a set of projects to implement in each decision environment. The expected cash flows used in the simulation of project values were used as the assumed certain cash flows in applying both the NPV criterion and payback constraint. The appropriate discount rate for the NPV model and maximum allowable payback period for each environment were determined after the fact; each relevant rate and period were tested, and that combination which selected the set of projects with the highest value was used. This approach ignores the problems of the ex ante selection of these parameters, allowing the model to perform as if these parameters could be perfectly predicted.

[20] See Klammer.

RESULTS: NPV–PBK MODEL

The increases in the value of the firm from applying the NPV–PBK model (i.e., the value of the model) in each environment are shown in Table 4. Also shown is the value of the NPV–PBK model as a percent of the value of the TSP model value; this indicates the percentage of potential increase in value given up by using the NPV–PBK model.

The most significant result is the lack of synergistic effect of the NPV criterion and the payback constraint. The value of the NPV–PBK model is merely the highest of the values of the NPV model or payback model applied separately. In fact, the payback constraint changes the decision of the NPV model in only those three environments (34, 43, and 44) where the value of the payback model exceeds the value of the NPV model, and the value of the NPV–PBK model in those environments is equal to the value of the payback model. The NPV–PBK model is apparently better (in terms of performance) than either the NPV or payback models, but its level of performance in environments with high uncertainty and a large state effect on valuation is still much less than the possible maximum level, with a performance level under 50% in three environments.

THE NPV–RC MODEL

It has been contended that a normative capital budgeting model should be based on a positive theory of market valuation.[21] The NPV–RC model is based on such a theory, namely, the capital asset pricing model of Sharpe and Lintner.[22] This theory states that, under appropriate assumptions,[23] the expected return on risky financial assets is

$$(7) \qquad \overline{R}_i = R^* + \lambda_i(\overline{R}_m - R^*)$$

[21] See Litzenberger, Robert H. and Alan P. Budd, "Corporate Investment Criteria and the Valuation of Risk Assets," *Journal of Financial and Quantitative Analysis* (December 1970), pp. 395–420, for a development and empirical specification of this view.

[22] Sharpe, William F., "Capital Asset Prices: A Theory of Market Equilibrium Under Conditions of Risk," *The Journal of Finance* (September 1964), pp. 425–42; Lintner, John, "The Valuation of Risk Assets and the Selection of Risky Investments in Stock Portfolios and Capital Budgets," *The Review of Economics and Statistics* (February 1965), pp. 13–37.

[23] A complete set of assumptions is found in Beaver, William H., "The Behavior of Security Prices and its Implications for Accounting Research (Methods)," *Supplement to the Accounting Review* (1972), pp. 407–37. Briefly, these assumptions are: (1) Perfect capital markets, (2) homogeneous expectations, (3) investors who are risk-averse, one-period utility of wealth maximizers, (4) utility which is expressed totally as a function of the mean and variance of the rate of return over the investment period, and (5) the existence of a risk-free asset.

where

$\overline{R}_i$ = the expected rate of return on asset i,

R^* = the risk-free interest rate,

$\overline{R}_m$ = the expected rate of return on the market portfolio,

$\lambda_i = r_{im}\sigma_i/\sigma_m$ = the systematic risk of asset i,

r_{im} = the correlation coefficient of the rates of return on asset i and the market portfolio,

σ_i = the standard deviation of the rate of return on asset i, and

σ_m = the standard deviation of the rate of return on the market portfolio.

The systematic risk, λ_i, measures the sensitivity of the rate of return on asset i to changes in the rate of return on the market portfolio.

This capital asset pricing model applies to financial assets, and additional assumptions are necessary in applying the model to real assets.[24] For strict application of the model, it must be assumed that there is no bankruptcy risk, no expected changes in purchasing power or interest rates, and that the component of valuation reflecting future investment opportunities at rates above the cost of capital is independent of the component of value attributed to present and past opportunities. These conditions are sufficient to conclude that the pay-out ratio (or dividend policy in general) has no effect on valuation.

From these assumptions it has been shown[25] that the cost of capital for capital budgeting project j is

(8) $$d_j = R^* + \lambda_j(\overline{R}_m - R^*)$$

Notice that this cost of capital not only is different for different projects proposed by the same firm, but it in no way depends on the firm which is considering the investment.[26] The common textbook notion that the cost of capital is equal to the expected return on a firm's existing assets is true only for projects with the same risk per dollar invested as that of existing assets. This does not seem to be a logical presumption for most projects. Even if returns from all proposed projects and all existing assets are perfectly correlated, the cost of capital will differ for projects if they do not have identical variances of their rate of return.

This theoretical model, despite quite binding and somewhat unrealistic assumptions, enhances one's prior beliefs that assigning proposed projects

---

[24] See Litzenberger and Budd or Hamada, R. S., "Portfolio Analysis, Market Equilibrium, and Corporate Finance," *Journal of Finance* (March 1969), pp. 95–108, for more details about the assumptions.

[25] See either Hamada or Litzenberger and Budd.

[26] See Schall, Lawrence D., "Asset Valuation, Firm Investment, and Firm Diversification," *Journal of Business* (January 1972), pp. 11–28, for a rigorous development of this point.

to risk classes and using risk-class dependent discount rates for determining projects' net present values may provide a relatively good, practical capital budgeting model. The fact that its assumptions do not completely hold in the real world is not necessarily crucial in deciding whether to use the model; the performance of a model is much more important than its theoretical validity.[27] The NPV–RC model represents models based on the Sharpe-Lintner capital asset pricing model, and its performance in the environments described in Part I is presented next.

In applying the NPV–RC model to select among the thirty projects described in Part I, the cost of capital, d_j, for each project in each environment was determined. This cost of capital is the discount rate that equates a project's net present value to its value under the TSP model.[28] From equation (8) it is clear that ranking projects by d_j is equivalent to ranking them by λ_j because R^* and $\bar{R}_m$ are public parameters that are the same for all projects. Therefore, ranking by d_j is a ranking in terms of riskiness.

From the ranking of projects obtained, it is easy to assign projects to risk classes. First, assume that all risk assignments can be perfectly made. At one extreme, N projects could be assigned to N risk classes, and using the appropriate discount rate for the project in each risk class (i.e., d_j) and accepting those projects with positive value, the accepted set of projects would be the same as the set accepted by the TSP model. At the other extreme, using only one risk class and consequently using the same discount rate for all projects, the accepted set of projects would be the same as the set accepted by the NPV model.

The significant issue is how the NPV–RC model performs when more than one but less than N risk classes are used and one discount rate is applied to all projects in a given risk class. Situations with two, three, five, and six risk classes were examined. When two risk classes are used, the fifteen most risky projects are placed in one risk class and the fifteen least risky in another risk class. A discount rate was selected for each risk class so that the subset of the fifteen projects accepted using that rate has a higher value than the subset selected using any other rate. Of course, the appropriate discount rate for the high risk class was greater than the rate for the low risk class. The value of the NPV–RC model with two risk classes is the sum of the values of the accepted projects in both risk

---

[27] Of course, one would expect a positive correlation between a model's performance and its theoretical validity.

[28] This approach ignores the prediction error involved in predicting d_j from estimates of R^*, $\bar{R}_m$, and λ_j. However, it is consistent with the approach of using perfect parameter predictions. In a real world application one must be concerned with errors in predicting λ_j (which is analyzed briefly later) and errors due to incompatibility of the Sharpe-Lintner model and the TSP model. Previous research has shown that the valuation of these two models is quite compatible, though not identical, both in theory and practice. See Sundem, "Evaluating Capital Budgeting Models in Simulated Environments."

classes. This is the amount by which the value of the firm would increase because of using this particular capital budgeting model.

When three risk classes were examined, ten projects were placed into each of the three risk classes, and the appropriate rate for each risk class was again selected ex post. A similar method was used for determining the value of five and six risk class models.

RESULTS: NPV–RC MODEL

Table 5 summarizes the values of the NPV–RC model in each environment depending on the number of risk classes into which projects are divided, and also listed is a comparison of these values with the values for the TSP model. For instance, in environment 23 the value of the one risk class model is 539 which is 77% of the value of the TSP model, while the two risk class model has a value of 602 which is 86% of the value of the TSP model.

From the results in Table 5 it is evident that there is a very significant increase in performance of the two risk class model over the one risk class (i.e., straight NPV) model. This is especially dramatic in the highly uncertain environments. For instance, in environments 34, 43, and 44 the

TABLE 5

NPV–RC Model: Perfect Risk Class Assignment

| Decision Environ-ment | TSP | Model Values | | | | | Model Value as a Percent of TSP Model Value | | | | |
| | | Number of Risk Classes | | | | | Number of Risk Classes | | | | |
		1	2	3	5	6	1	2	3	5	6
11	1097	1097	1097	1097	1097	1097	100	100	100	100	100
12	974	973	973	973	974	974	100	100	100	100	100
13	889	861	861	877	889	889	97	97	99	100	100
14	829	758	761	795	829	829	91	92	96	100	100
21	962	960	960	960	962	962	100	100	100	100	100
22	785	712	717	750	785	785	91	91	96	100	100
23	696	539	602	688	688	688	77	86	99	99	99
24	651	401	617	631	651	651	62	95	97	100	100
31	854	825	825	842	854	854	97	97	99	100	100
32	669	514	588	619	663	669	77	88	93	99	100
33	596	302	581	596	596	596	51	97	100	100	100
34	610	97	585	610	610	610	16	96	100	100	100
41	763	689	698	728	763	763	90	91	95	100	100
42	592	352	556	578	592	592	59	94	98	100	100
43	572	70	547	572	572	572	12	96	100	100	100
44	598	69	560	598	598	598	12	94	100	100	100

performance as a percent of TSP model performance improves from 16%, 12%, and 12% for the one risk class model to 96%, 96%, and 94% when there are two risk classes. A smaller but still evident increase in value occurs in most environments with movement to a three risk class model rather than the two risk class model. The largest increase in performance here is in environment 23 where the performance level is 86% with two risk classes and 99% with three risk classes. With more refinement in the model to five and six risk class models, only small increases in performance are observed, the largest being from 93% to 99% in environment 32 when moving from three to five risk classes. The six risk class model has a performance level equal to that of the TSP model in every environment but one. A possible conclusion from this analysis is that it is likely to be cost/benefit efficient to use a two or three risk class model rather than the one risk class model, but added refinements may not be worth their added cost.

NPV–RC MODEL WITH IMPERFECT PARAMETER PREDICTIONS

So far this analysis has assumed perfect assignment of projects to risk classes and perfect selection of the appropriate discount rate for each risk class. This section briefly examines the sensitivity of model performance to predictions of both project and environmental parameters. This will give some indication of possible consequences of imperfect parameter predictions.

First, consider the prediction of the appropriate discount rate for each risk class. The two and three risk class models were examined to determine what range of discount rates would yield optimal decisions for each risk class in each environment. These ranges are presented in Table 6. In 67% of the cases in Table 6 the optimal range is at least 1.0% and in only 11% is the range less than 0.5%.

These results are dependent both on the simulated environments and on the number of proposed projects. As the number of projects evaluated increases, the optimal range of discount rates will decrease. However, while not being conclusive as to optimal ranges, these numbers do give an intuitive feel for the prediction accuracy needed.

Another use of these data is to examine the different optimal rates for different risk classes. Notice that the rates do not vary much across risk classes in low uncertainty environments; consequently the improvement in performance by using different risk classes is slight. In highly uncertain environments, much different rates are optimal for different risk classes. These situations provide the greatest potential for improved performance through using different risk classes.

A second type of prediction error examined is the assignment of projects to risk classes. Consider a situation where all projects were not perfectly assigned to risk classes, but some were assigned at random to one of two

TABLE 6

Range of Optimal Discount Rates: NPV–RC Model

Decision Environ- ment	2 Risk Classes		3 Risk Classes		
	Low	*High*	*Low*	*Middle*	*High*
11	5.3–6.1%	5.2–5.8%	4.7–6.1%	5.3– 5.8%	5.2– 8.5%
12	5.3–6.1	5.8–7.0	4.7–6.1	5.8– 6.7	5.2– 8.5
13	5.3–6.1	5.8–7.0	4.2–6.1	5.8– 6.7	5.2– 8.5
14	5.3–6.1	8.5–8.8	4.2–6.1	5.8– 6.7	9.0–10.0
21	5.3–6.1	5.8–7.0	4.2–6.1	5.8– 6.7	5.2– 8.5
22	5.3–6.1	8.5–8.8	4.2–6.1	5.8– 6.7	9.0– 9.2
23	5.3–6.1	14.1–∞	4.2–6.1	7.0– 8.8	14.1–∞
24	5.8–6.1	14.1–∞	4.2–6.1	9.2–11.0	14.1–∞
31	5.3–6.1	5.8–7.0	4.2–6.1	5.8– 6.7	9.0–10.0
32	5.3–6.1	14.1–∞	4.2–6.1	7.0– 8.8	14.1–∞
33	5.8–6.1	14.1–∞	4.2–6.1	9.2–11.0	14.1–∞
34	7.0–9.4	14.1–∞	4.2–6.1	11.0–12.5	14.1–∞
41	5.3–6.1	9.0–9.2	4.2–6.1	5.8– 6.7	9.0– 9.2
42	7.0–9.4	14.1–∞	4.2–6.1	9.2–11.0	14.1–∞
43	7.0–9.4	14.1–∞	4.2–6.1	11.0–12.5	14.1–∞
44	6.7–9.4	14.1–∞	4.2–6.1	12.5–∞	14.1–∞

risk classes. Assume that projects are ranked from one (most risky) to thirty (least risky). For the three risk class model, projects 1–6 were assigned to a high risk class, 13–18 to a medium risk class, and 25–30 to a low risk class. Projects 7–12 were randomly assigned to high and medium risk classes (with an equal probability of being assigned to each), and projects 19–24 were randomly assigned to medium and low risk classes. Fifty sets of random assignments were generated, and the average and minimum model values in each environment over the fifty trials are listed in Table 7. The related percentages of TSP model value are in Table 8. Comparison of the average values to the values in Table 5 shows a very small decrease in value due to random assignment. There is also little difference between average and minimum project values.

A more extensive analysis of the effect of random assignment was carried out on the two risk class model. Four sets of randomly assigned projects were tested: 13–18, 11–20, 9–22, and 7–24. For example, when projects 13–18 were randomly assigned, projects 1–12 were assigned to the high risk class, 19–30 to the low risk class, and 13–18 assigned randomly to either class. These results are also in Tables 7 and 8. When only six projects (20% of the projects) were randomly assigned, the performance of the model is not much below the performance with perfect assignment. But with random assignment of eighteen projects (60%)

TABLE 7

NPV–RC Model: Partially Random Risk Class Assignment

	Model Values									
	Two Risk Class Model								*Three Risk Class Model*	
	No. of Projects Randomly Assigned								*12 Projects Randomly Assigned*	
Decision Environ-ment	*6*		*10*		*14*		*18*			
	Ave.	*Min.*	*Ave.*	*Min.*	*Ave.*	*Min.*	*Ave.*	*Min.*	*Ave.*	*Min.*
11	1097	1097	1097	1097	1097	1097	1097	1097	1097	1097
12	973	973	973	973	973	973	973	973	973	973
13	867	861	864	861	865	861	865	861	877	877
14	775	761	771	758	779	758	775	758	794	789
21	960	960	960	960	960	960	960	960	961	960
22	733	717	731	714	734	714	733	712	751	746
23	596	576	636	578	627	571	602	549	635	608
24	604	584	602	584	579	536	547	508	633	625
31	833	825	830	825	831	825	832	825	842	842
32	573	556	585	556	595	551	583	529	617	588
33	567	555	567	555	533	496	507	456	588	583
34	579	573	581	573	532	467	477	367	597	592
41	710	698	709	695	715	695	709	689	730	726
42	548	537	552	537	529	488	502	462	571	563
43	544	536	546	536	498	433	433	330	559	552
44	559	547	562	547	449	372	438	323	578	563

there is a noticeable drop in performance. However, note that even with eighteen projects randomly assigned the average and minimum values of the model are greater than the value of the one risk class model. This is especially evident in highly uncertain environments and where the effect of the state factor is great. The lowest average and minimum levels of performance are 73% and 54% respectively in environment 44, while the performance level of the one risk class model in that environment is only 12%.

From the results of the NPV–RC model it is evident that there is a likelihood of tremendous improvement in model performance if different discount rates are used for different risk classes of projects in applying the net present value model rather than using the same rate for all projects. This conclusion holds even if the assignment of projects to risk classes is imperfect. However, it assumes that the assignment to risk classes is on

TABLE 8

NPV–RC Model: Partially Random Risk Class Assignment

Model Values as a Percent of TSP Model Value

Decision Environ-ment	Two Risk Class Model								Three Risk Class Model	
	No. of Projects Randomly Assigned								12 Projects Randomly Assigned	
	6		10		14		18			
	Ave.	Min.	Ave.	Min.	Ave.	Min.	Ave.	Min.	Ave.	Min.
11	100	100	100	100	100	100	100	100	100	100
12	100	100	100	100	100	100	100	100	100	100
13	98	97	97	97	97	97	97	97	99	99
14	93	92	93	91	94	91	93	91	96	95
21	100	100	100	100	100	100	100	100	100	100
22	93	91	93	91	94	91	93	91	96	95
23	86	83	91	83	90	82	86	79	91	87
24	93	90	92	90	89	82	84	78	97	96
31	98	97	97	97	97	97	97	97	99	99
32	86	83	87	83	89	82	87	79	92	88
33	95	93	95	93	89	83	85	77	99	98
34	95	94	95	94	87	77	78	60	98	97
41	93	91	93	91	94	91	93	90	96	95
42	93	91	93	91	89	82	85	78	96	95
43	95	94	95	94	87	76	76	58	98	97
44	93	91	94	91	75	62	73	54	97	94

the basis of systematic risk only. The ability of the decision maker to assess risk on this basis will greatly affect the efficiency of the model.[29]

III. Summary and Conclusions

Based on a time-state preference simulation model, it has been shown that (1) there is little synergistic effect of combining a net present value objective function with a payback constraint and (2) there is a possibility to increase greatly the performance of a net present value model by assign-

[29] A recent research project gives encouragement that such an assessment on an intuitive basis may be possible. See Kim, Kee Sang, *Predicting Riskness for Capital Budgeting Decisions* (Unpublished MBA research report, University of Washington, 1973).

ing projects to two or three risk classes and using a different discount rate for evaluating projects in each risk class.

From this, several tentative conclusions may be drawn. First, the increasing use of a payback period as a secondary criterion in capital budgeting is not completely irrational since it does improve the decisions of a straight NPV model in highly uncertain environments. However, the NPV–PBK model in general leaves much room for improvement. Second, the dominant use of the NPV model seems warranted, provided different discount rates are used for different risk classes of projects. From the performance levels when only two or three risk classes are used, it appears that the NPV–RC model provides decisions nearly as good as even the most sophisticated models. There is no reason to believe that lack of knowledge is the reason that sophisticated models are not used more. This could easily be due to the cost/benefit efficiency of the relatively simple NPV–RC model. Third, there is no reason to believe that there exists one model that will be the best model for all firms. The striking differences in performance of the models (even though the ranking of the models stays quite constant) across different environments indicate that two firms facing different environments may well find different capital budgeting models to be most cost/benefit efficient in their environment.

Even though the NPV–RC model has a great potential for being cost/benefit efficient, consideration must be given to the added cost of the required risk assessment before selecting it as superior to the NPV model for a given firm. The costs of assigning each proposed project to a risk class and the cost of determining multiple discount rates to be used in the different risk classes must be predicted. Only if the added benefit from the better decisions of the NPV–RC model are greater than these costs should the NPV–RC model be used instead of a straight NPV model.[30]

These conclusions point a direction for further research in capital budgeting different from that which many researchers are taking. We may not need as extensive an effort as presently exists in the area of developing new models. We do need much research in the area of parameter prediction and cost estimation for the NPV–RC model. How sensitive is model performance to cash flow predictions? How well can risk class assignments be made? On what basis are they made? How can we improve the method of risk class assignment? How is an appropriate discount rate for a risk class predicted? Which parameters are most critical to model performance, and how can the prediction techniques for these parameters be improved? What are the added costs involved with using an NPV–RC model? These are but a few of the questions that must be answered by future research.

---

[30] The model selection problem ideally consists of the maximization of the difference between total benefits and total costs over all possible decision models. However, in practice, the comparison of two models (likely the model presently used and a proposed alternative model) is a common simplified model selection method.

13

This article extends current management accounting literature concerning the use of discounted cash flow (DCF) calculations in making capital budgeting decisions. The authors develop four variations of the accounting income constrained model. These variations are based on accounting income growth goals, including income smoothing.

Using a DCF numerical example, the authors compare the four variations to the accounting income constrained model, the accounting income model without constraints, and the well-known DCF model. The authors emphasize trade-offs in present value for the various accounting income pattern constraints. To analyze changes in income patterns, the article also develops shadow prices for the seven models. The importance of accounting income patterns in capital investment decisions leads to the intriguing possibility that the DCF basis should also be used for financial income purposes in order to harmonize managerial and financial accounting income reporting.

The Discounted Cash Flow Investment Decision Model with Accounting Income Constraints*

Thomas R. Dyckman and
James C. Kinard†

In an article initially published in the *Harvard Business Review* and later reprinted in slightly revised form, Professors Lerner and Rappaport

* *From* Decision Sciences, *Vol. 4, No. 3 (July, 1973), pp. 301–313. Reprinted by permission of the editor.*

† The authors wish to express their thanks to the accounting workshop at Carnegie-Mellon University for helpful comments.

of Northwestern University propose an investment decision model with important implications for accounting theory and practice.[1]

They cite data[2] that indicates a large proportion and probably a majority of even the largest firms do not employ discounted cash flow (DCF) calculations in making capital budgeting decisions despite its wide support among theorists.[3] Rejection of the DCF approach does not surprise Lerner and Rappaport because they perceive a good reason for this rejection. They observe that "the DCF method tends to favor projects which, though most profitable in the long run, would often produce erratic accounting income from year to year."[4] For this reason, Lerner and Rappaport propose a modification of the DCF approach that maximizes the present value of the total selected investments subject to a constraint on accounting income (see their Exhibit VII in the original article). The proposed constraint requires that accounting income grow at a stipulated rate per period.

The significant aspect of the proposal is that income as reported by accountants is the constraint measure. The reason given for this choice by Lerner and Rappaport is that this measure is the *general purpose earnings measure* about whose growth the firm is concerned and which is reported to and presumably used by outside decision makers.[5] This constraint produces an interdependence between the accounting external-reporting model and a particular decision model. This type of interdependence is very different from that which some financial accounting theorists seek: to make the accounting external-reporting model congruent with the decision model.

The model as proposed by Lerner and Rappaport is meant to be descriptive rather than normative.[6] As such we find it a very provocative suggestion although its descriptive validity has not to our knowledge been empirically tested. Unfortunately, we believe the model was misspecified, the illustrative example is in error at several places,[7] and the important

---

[1] E. M. Lerner and A. Rappaport, "Limit DCF in Capital Budgeting," *Harvard Business Review,* (September–October, 1968), pp. 133–139. Reprinted in *Information for Decision Making: Quantitative and Behavioral Dimensions,* edited by A. Rappaport, Prentice-Hall, Englewood Cliffs, N. J., 1970, pp. 301–308.

[2] The study cited by Lerner and Rappaport reports that less than one-half of a sample of firms from Fortune's 500 use a pure DCF approach. See A. A. Robichek and J. G. McDonald, *Financial Management in Transition,* Stanford Research Institute, Menlo Park, California, 1965, p. 7.

[3] Lerner and Rappaport, *op. cit.,* p. 133.

[4] *Loc. cit.*

[5] For some recent evidence of the relevance of earnings measures to investors see W. H. Beaver, P. Ketler, and M. Scholes, "The Association Between Market Determined and Accounting Determined Risk Measures," *The Accounting Review,* October, 1970, pp. 654–682; and T. R. Dyckman, *Investment Analysis and General Price Level Adjustments: A Behavioral Study* (Evanston, Illinois, American Accounting Association, 1969), pp. 28–30.

[6] Letter of December 10, 1968 from Professor Rappaport.

[7] We were not able to reproduce the Lerner-Rappaport results exactly. In trying to use their data in our formulation, we discovered several apparent errors in the present-

behavioral implications of the model were substantially ignored. Recognizing the debt we owe to the authors for their idea, we intend to develop the ideas and their implications afresh.

Alternate Formulations of the
Lerner-Rappaport Model

Several possible formulations of the basic concept in the Lerner-Rappaport article are possible. It is not clear exactly which of these formulations is the model they intended to specify, although all of the formulations are consistent with their basic concept.

FORMULATION A

The model presented in this subsection is the one which most nearly fits Lerner's and Rappaport's published intentions and the one they were attempting to specify and illustrate with their numerical example. Their model is consistent with a growth-rate constraint that applies to each year in relation to the prior years. In other words, the increase in income from year t to year $t + 1$ must be at least equal to the product of the total accounting income reported in year t multiplied by the required inter-year growth rate, g, which is the same for all years in the planning horizon. Using this interpretation of the growth-rate constraint, adding a term E'_t to represent earnings in each year t of the accounting income planning period $t = 1, 2, \ldots, r$ for a particular decision point, as determined by previous investment decisions at earlier decision points and making several other minor adjustments to the original model, we reformulate the basic model as:[8]

Maximize
$$\sum_{j=1}^{M_a} \sum_{t=1}^{N_j} \left[\frac{A_{j,t}}{(1+k)^t} X_j \right]$$

Subject to

(a_A)

$$\left[E'_t + \sum_{j=1}^{M} E_{j,t} X_j \right] - (1+g) \left[E'_{t-1} + \sum_{j=1}^{M} E_{j,t-1} X_j \right] \geqslant 0, t = 1, 2, \ldots, r$$

value calculations (their Exhibit V), total yearly accounting income over the five-year planning period, and the optimal proportion of projects to adopt (their Exhibit VI). Some, but not all, of these errors are corrected in the reprinted version. The data in their Exhibits I and II as given in the original article are used in all our calculations. Our Formulation A of the AIC–DCF model most nearly duplicates Lerner's and Rappaport's numerical example. (See the results in the reprinted version.)

[8] Lerner's and Rappaport's model is specified mathematically in Exhibit VII of their original article.

(b) $$0 \leqslant X_j \leqslant 1, j = 1, 2, \ldots, M$$

and

$$E_{j, t} = 0 \text{ for } t < 1 \text{ and } t > r$$

(c) $$A_{j, t} = 0 \text{ for } t < 1 \text{ and } t > N_j;$$

where

$k =$ is the cash-flow discount-rate at decision point;
$A_{j, t} =$ is the cash flow from project j_a in period t;
$X_j =$ is the proportion of the jth project adopted;
$E'_t =$ is the accounting income for year t other than that due to projects under consideration;
$j =$ is the project index, $j = 1, 2, \ldots, M$;
$t =$ is the period index, $t = 1, 2, \ldots, N$;
$E_{j, t} =$ is the accounting income of project j in period t;
$M =$ is the number of projects available at the decision point;
$N_j =$ is the life of project j;
$g =$ is the required accounting income growth rate; and
$r =$ is the length of the accounting income planning horizon.

The following three formulations are modifications of Formulation A.

FORMULATION B

This formulation would be appropriate if management preferred an exact growth rate from year to year. This formulation might be preferred since in the previous model (Formulation A), a large percentage income growth in the income planning period could make it difficult to satisfy the growth constraint in future planning periods. The reformulation requires only that an equality replace the inequality in constraint (a_A).

$$(a_B) \qquad \left[E'_t + \sum_{j=1}^{M} E_{j, t} X_j \right] - (1 + g) \left[E'_{t-1} + \sum_{j=1}^{M} E_{j, t} X_j \right] = 0$$

A recent report in the *Wall Street Journal* suggests that at least one firm does make its accounting income conform to this formulation.[9] The article reports that "McCulloch Oil has had year-to-year gains in net income of about 30% for '14 to 15 consecutive quarters.'" The executive (a vice president) quoted in the article said, "the figure of '30% is tattooed on everyone's brain.' He explained that the company can fairly predict ahead of time what it will earn from its oil and gas operations and then it sells just enough land to reach the 30% increase."

[9] "McCulloch Oil says 1st Quarter Net Climbed: Gain of 30% Has Been Realized for Seven Consecutive Years; Growth Rate 'Tattooed on Brain,'" *The Wall Street Journal*, April 27, 1971, p. 14 ("Two Star" Edition).

FORMULATION C

A third possible formulation poses a more modest constraint on accounting income, namely that it exhibit, at least in the long run, a compounded growth rate of g. Growth is not constrained to a year-to-year relationship requirement. This model requires that the Formulation A constraint-inequality (a_A) be rewritten as follows:

$$(a_C) \qquad \left[E'_t + \sum_{j=1}^{M} E_{j,t} X_j \right] - (1+g)^t (E^*) \geqslant 0$$

where E^* is the level of accounting income relative to which the compound growth rate is applied.

FORMULATION D

The most conservative, and therefore perhaps the most attractive, model specification is one that involves compounding at an exact growth rate. This specification, as was previously mentioned in Formulation B, mitigates against accounting income fluctuations: accounting income is "smoothed" and a continuous compounded growth rate based on some initial value E^* maintained (assuming satisfactory investments are available). This reformulation of the model is achieved simply by altering the inequality (a_C) in Formulation C to an equality.[10]

$$(a_D) \qquad \left[E'_t + \sum_{j=1}^{M} X_j E_{j,t} \right] - (1+g)^t (E^*) = 0$$

---

[10] If $E^* = E'_0$ then the constraint sets in Formulations B and D, and hence the two models, are identical. This may be shown as follows:

The Formulation B type (a) constraint is

$$\left[E'_t + \sum_{j=1}^{M} E_{j,t} X_j \right] - (1+g) \left[E'_{t-1} + \sum_{j=1}^{M} E_{j,t-1} X_j \right] = 0, t = 1, 2, \ldots, r,$$

which is equivalent to

$$\left[E'_t + \sum_{j=1}^{M} E_{j,t} X_j \right] = (1+g) \left[E'_{t-1} + \sum_{j=1}^{M} E_{j,t-1} X_j \right], t = 1, 2, \ldots, r.$$

This last equation is a recursive expression thereby allowing any period t constraint to be stated as

$$\left[E'_t + \sum_{j=1}^{M} E_{j,t} X_j \right] = (1+g)^t \left[E'_0 + \sum_{j=1}^{M} E_{j,0} X_j \right], t = 1, 2, \ldots, r,$$

but by definition $E_{j,0} = 0$, and the expression further reduces to

$$\left[E'_t + \sum_{j=1}^{M} E_{j,t} X_j \right] = (1+g)^t (E'_0), t = 1, 2, \ldots, r.$$

The Formulation D type (a) constraint set form is

$$\left[E'_t + \sum_{j=1}^{M} E_{j,t} X_j \right] - (1+g)^t (E^*) = 0, t = 1, 2, \ldots, r$$

which differs from the previous constraint only by $E'_0 = E^*$.

Alternative Models

There are several alternative models which are reasonable in place of the DCF decision model with accounting income constraints. Three are offered here. The first is a possible competitor as a description of management behavior. The second and third offer benchmark results for comparison purposes. Other more naive models are also possible, including the simple "do at least as well as last year" approach.

THE ACCOUNTING-INCOME-CONSTRAINED ACCOUNTING-INCOME INVESTMENT DECISION MODEL

Perhaps management behavior is best described as having the objective of maximizing total accounting income over the income planning period subject to a constraint of the type proposed earlier on the inter-period relationship of accounting incomes. If one chooses the Formulation A type of constraint, the model is formally stated as:

Maximize
$$\sum_{j=1}^{M} \sum_{t=1}^{r} E_{j,t} X_j$$

subject to the same constraint set as Formulation A of the DCF models.

This model denies the place of DCF considerations in the decision process. Such a model is not inconsistent with the data about management decision-making cited in both the Lerner-Rappaport article and this article.

Two similar models which are offered as standards of comparison are presented next.

AN ACCOUNTING-INCOME INVESTMENT DECISION MODEL

To round out the obvious income-model possibilities, it is of interest to ask what results would be obtained in the investment decision situation if the objective were merely to maximize accounting income over the income planning horizon, without any yearly income constraints. In symbols:

Maximize
$$\sum_{j=1}^{M} \sum_{t=1}^{r} E_{j,t} X_j, \qquad \text{subject to } 0 \leqslant X_j \leqslant 1.$$

A DCF MODEL

Finally, the well known pure (i.e., unconstrained) DCF investment decision model is stated using the same symbols for comparison purposes.

Maximize
$$\sum_{j=1}^{M} \sum_{t=1}^{N_j} \left[\frac{A_{j,t}}{(1+k)^t} X_j \right], \text{ subject to } 0 \leqslant X_j \leqslant 1.$$

A Numerical Example

The above models are examined next in terms of the numerical example contained in the Lerner-Rappaport article.[11] The hypothetical data provided in Exhibits I and II of the original Lerner-Rappaport articles will be used. The necessary present values and other calculations are based on these data. The additional parameter values required to obtain numerical example solutions for the various models are repeated here for completeness:[12] $k = .2; E_0' = \$7,000; E_1' = \$10,000; E_2' = \$9,500; E_3' = E_4' = \$9,000; E_5' = \$8,000; g = .05$ and $r = 5$. A value for E^* of \$5,000 was assumed for model Formulations C and D.

The revised present values obtained from a double-precision Fortran-language computer program are given in Table 1. The solutions to the four formulations of the accounting income constrained DCF criterion

TABLE 1

Project Present Values (in Hundreds of Dollars)

Project	Present Value	Project	Present Value	Project	Present Value
1	(34.46684)	6	186.90311	11	151.74394
2	96.96425	7	31.93173	12	138.41843
3	33.19615	8	72.13710	13	(12.20167)
4	(10.63963)	9	45.02450	14	185.27449
5	(29.46910)	10	(9.18039)	15	32.86426

[11] In order to algebraically restate the models for linear programming algorithm computer program solution, it is useful to note that several expressions in model A can be simplified. For example, using V_j to represent the present value of project j,

$$\left(\sum_{t=1}^{N_j} \frac{A_{j,t}}{(1+k)^t} \right),$$

in the objective function, rearranging constraint (a_A) and letting the income growth terms — namely $[E_{j,\,t} - (1+g)\,E_{j,\,t-1}]$ and $[E_t' - (1+g)\,E_{t-1}']$ — be represented by $G_{j,\,t}$ and G_t' respectively, the objective function and constraint (a_A) of model Formulation A can be more compactly (and perhaps more understandably) written as:

Maximize $\sum_{j=1}^{M} V_j\,X_j$, subject to $\sum_{j=1}^{M} G_{j,\,t}\,X_j \geqslant -G_t'$, $t = 1, 2, \ldots, r$.

[12] The value of E_0' is not available in the original article but was communicated to us in the Rappaport Letter, *op. cit.* We note that a figure of \$7,350 is supplied in the reprint (Rappaport, *op cit.*, p. 303), but since this figure fails to satisfy the growth constraint we conclude it is in error and most likely reflects the reported earnings in year one (see Table 2).

model, the accounting income constrained–accounting income criterion model, the unconstrained accounting income criterion model, and the unconstrained DCF criterion model are given in Table 2.

Although there are several important structural differences between the Lerner-Rappaport specification of the model and our Formulation A, and some differences in intermediate calculations (e.g., present value), the results (i.e., investments chosen) are very similar.[13]

Observations on the Models

An examination of the reported accounting earnings and the total present value of the projects accepted in Table 2 will give the reader some feeling for the trade-off in present value for the various income-pattern constraints that are required by each of the models. In general, a more binding accounting-income growth-rate constraint reduces reported total accounting income. But note that Formulation A shows not only the required steady growth in accounting income but also larger total income for the five-year period than the DCF model which has no accounting income constraint. This may surprise the reader. One reason, as Lerner-Rappaport state, is that the accounting income constrained DCF criterion model is constrained by only the next five years' incomes in selecting projects while the criterion considers present values for the entire project life, which for all of the 15 projects exceeds the five-year planning period. Further, to some extent there is a trade-off in reported total accounting income and present values, but a simple relationship between the models cannot be stated. For a given model, the solution of the dual linear programming formulation provides shadow prices which indicate the trade-off between the model criterion and the constraints.

The shadow prices for each model are given in Table 3 [p. 238] for each constraint. The two interpretations of the shadow prices are related to the two basic types of constraints in the specification of the model.

The constraints on yearly income in those models where maximizing present value is the objective, if binding on the optimal solution (i.e., income is equal to the constraining value), yield non-zero shadow prices which indicate the rate at which the present value of the solution would increase as the constraint is relaxed.

This type of constraint is stated in terms of an amount of accounting income. Thus the shadow price refers to the marginal rate of change in the objective function value per dollar of accounting income. One could state any dollar change in a constraint amount in terms of the implicit change in the growth rate for that constraint in the particular year under consideration. It is much more difficult, however, to state the impact of a uniform

---

[13] Rappaport, *op. cit.,* especially pages 306 and 307.

TABLE 2

Proportion of Projects Adopted, Total Yearly Accounting
Earnings; and Total Present Value of Capital Investments
Accepted for Each Model

| | Project | Accounting Income Constrained DCF-Model | | | |
		A	*B*	*C*	*D*
Proportion	1	1.0000	1.0000	.0000	1.0000
of Project	2	.0000	.0000	.4969	.4097
Adopted	3	.1625	.1625	.0000	.4315
	4	.0000	.0000	.0000	.0000
	5	.0000	.0000	.0000	.0000
	6	.8975	.8975	1.0000	.7772
	7	.0503	.7273	.1443	1.0000
	8	1.0000	.5769	1.0000	.3869
	9	1.0000	1.0000	1.0000	.7423
	10	.7179	.9598	.0000	1.0000
	11	1.0000	1.0000	1.0000	1.0000
	12	1.0000	1.0000	1.0000	1.0000
	13	.0000	.0000	.0000	.0000
	14	1.0000	1.0000	1.0000	1.0000
	15	1.0000	1.0000	1.0000	1.0000
Accounting	*Year*				
Earnings	1	$ 7,350.000	$ 7,350.000	$ 8,757.813	$ 5,250.000
Reported	2	7,717.500	7,717.500	5,512.500	5,512.500
	3	8,103.375	8,103.375	5,788.130	5,788.130
	4	16,705.965	8,508.544	19,064.128	6,077.530
	5	17,541.263	8,933.971	7,705.252	6,381.430
	Total	$57,418.103	$40,613.390	$46,836.823	$29,009.590
Present Value of Projects Accepted		$75,915.229	$74,802.633	$86,515.104	$75,723.295

change in the required growth rate for all years in the income planning horizon. Such a sensitivity analysis would require more analysis than simply considering the shadow prices on constraints for one growth rate.

The other type of constraint — on the proportion of a project which may be accepted (in those models where maximizing present value is the objective), if binding on the optimal solution (i.e., all of the project is being

Table 2 (cont.)

Acctg. Income Constrained Acctg. Income Model	Acctg. Income Model	DCF- Model
1.0000	1.0000	.0000
.0000	.0000	1.0000
.1625	1.0000	1.0000
.0000	.0000	.0000
.0000	.0000	.0000
.8975	1.0000	1.0000
.0000	.0000	1.0000
1.0000	1.0000	1.0000
1.0000	1.0000	1.0000
.0000	.0000	.0000
.0000	.0000	1.0000
1.0000	1.0000	1.0000
.0000	.0000	.0000
.0000	.0000	1.0000
.0000	.0000	1.0000
$ 7,350.000	$ 4,000.000	$ 3,500.000
7,717.500	5,000.000	500.000
8,355.000	7,500.000	2,000.000
32,600.000	42,000.000	27,000.000
64,052.500	74,000.000	19,000.000
$120,075.000	$132,500.000	$48,000.000
$39,425.309	$44,121.243	$97,445.794

used in the optimal solution) — yields a shadow price indicating the rate at which the present value of the solution would increase if the scale of the project could be increased (or additional identical projects made available). This point may be illustrated by considering the constraint shadow price on X_1 (i.e., $X_1 \leq 1$) in the AIC-DCF model, Formulation A, which has a shadow price of $19,742.43. If this single constraint is changed to

TABLE 3

Shadow Prices for the Constraints* (in Hundreds of Dollars)

	Accounting Income Constraint DCF-Model			
	A	B	C	D
Income Constraint				
Year 1	4.7205	4.2431	.0000	5.2387
2	12.2559	12.2107	1.9451	5.6822
3	.6544	.5747	.6386	.2985
4	.0000	.1357	.0000	.5160
5	.0685	.0125	.0000	.2221
Project Proportion Constraint				
1	197.4243	201.5872	.0000	67.6558
2	.0000	.0000	.0000	.0000
3	.0000	.0000	.0000	.0000
4	.0000	.0000	.0000	.0000
5	.0000	.0000	.0000	.0000
6	.0000	.0000	199.0913	.0000
7	.0000	.0000	.0000	66.7800
8	26.2942	.0000	21.0463	.0000
9	41.7348	30.4717	38.6382	.0000
10	.0000	.0000	.0000	20.9930
11	145.2354	166.5058	151.7439	247.7636
12	155.7173	142.0435	138.4184	119.7963
13	.0000	.0000	.0000	.0000
14	171.5724	187.7784	185.2745	229.6958
15	26.0132	34.1162	32.8643	55.0749

* The values in the table indicate the improvement in the criterion measure that can be obtained by moving the constraint in the proper direction.

$X_1 \leqslant 1.01$, then the present value becomes $76,112.65, which is what one would predict based on the shadow price (i.e., the present value of projects accepted under the first constraint value, $75,915.23, plus the amount by which the constraint is relaxed [.01 times the shadow price], $19,742.43, equals the present value of project accepted under the modified constraint value, $76,112.65).

For both constraint types in the two models where maximizing accounting income is the objective, the shadow prices indicate the rate at which total accounting income would increase. These values are particularly im-

Table 3 (cont.)

Acctg. Income Constrained Acctg. Income Model	Acctg. Income Model	DCF-Model
5.5000	↑	↑
7.5000		
.0000	Not	Not
.0000	Applicable	Applicable
.0000		
	↓	↓
165.0000	80.0000	.0000
.0000	.0000	96.9643
.0000	130.0000	33.1961
.0000	.0000	.0000
.0000	.0000	.0000
.0000	150.0000	186.9031
.0000	.0000	31.9317
220.0000	220.0000	72.1371
140.0000	140.0000	45.0245
.0000	.0000	.0000
.0000	.0000	151.7439
150.0000	150.0000	138.4184
.0000	.0000	.0000
.0000	.0000	185.2745
.0000	.0000	32.8643

portant to calculate for the model being used by an organization, since they indicate the marginal advantage to be gained if the constraint is or can be relaxed.

In the example, the optimal solutions to most of the models described involve investments with negative present values; for example, Projects 1 and 10 in model Formulation A (see Tables 1 and 2). Extending the conditions that produce this result leads to the possibility of including an investment which involves only net cash outflows (so long as these are accompanied with some positive accounting income over the income planning horizon). Moreover, not only are the fluctuations in the trend in an individual year's reported accounting incomes in the income-planning-period reduced — in comparison to the result for the pure DCF model — by the accounting-income constraint, but in most of the formulations total reported accounting income over the planning period is also increased by selection of projects with negative present values.

There are two ways that the acceptance of negative-present-value projects could be avoided. The most obvious approach is to exclude all negative-present-value projects when defining the set of projects (whose order is M). If negative-present-value projects are included in the set of projects under consideration, a constraint of the form

(d)
$$\sum_{t=1}^{N_j} \left[\frac{A_{j,\,t}}{(1+k)^t} \right] [X_j] \geqslant 0$$

could be added to the accounting income constrained DCF criterion formulations to avoid acceptance of such projects.

The models as specified are single-period decision models. A more sophisticated multi-period model would require a dynamic programming specification for solution. In either the single-period or multi-period model formulation, the selection of the accounting-income planning period r and the DCF horizon (the largest N_j) constitute important management decisions for the model. Subsequent investment decisions, using any of the formulations of the basic model, are influenced by the decisions made previously. This is particularly true in Formulations A and C. This effect occurs because optimal decisions depend on accounting-income levels as established by existing investments. Further, when the DCF horizon exceeds the accounting-income planning horizon, as is true in the Lerner-Rappaport example, projects accepted now will affect reported accounting-income beyond the accounting-income planning horizon. Hence, the acceptance of future investments will be affected by previous investments, even when they are independent, because of the effect of both on reported income. One conclusion based on these observations is that if the same set (in terms of cash flows and accounting incomes) of 15 independent investment opportunities were again available at the next decision point, the optimal immediate solution to any of the income constrained models would probably not be an optimal solution at the next decision point. This issue is unimportant only for a firm with other income that yields an income growth rate substantially higher than the imposed constraint.

Using the model, a firm which has a pre-existing income growth-rate substantially in excess of the rate used as a constraint would have greater latitude to invest in projects that could have short-run negative effects on accounting income. This would give such firms a wider field of action and permit, and even perhaps encourage, them to invest in projects that might have a very favorable effect on cash flows (considering present values), although such projects might be deemed unacceptable by firms more tightly constrained by their pre-existing earnings. Many attractive investment opportunities could be of this type. Firms with low or negative pre-existing earnings patterns might be forced to reject such investments due to their short-run impact on reported earnings. Such firms might well find themselves cut off from the very investments which would most enhance their long-term future position. For the "firm" in the example, with the slightly unfavorable "other" earnings pattern (see the E'_t figures), Project 2 provides an example of a "good" (in discounted cash flow terms) project with "bad" short-run accounting income. Note that despite a positive net present value, it does not appear in the optimal solution to Formulation A.

One should also note that the AIC models are valid only when accounting income is positive. It is possible to alter the formulation by changing the specification of the constraints to force a loss to decrease (i.e., use $1 - g$ in place of $1 + g$), but such a model will not produce a gain. This limitation suggests that formulations involving amounts of accounting income growth (or declines in losses) instead of growth rates might prove worthy of consideration.

The models as specified are deterministic models. We do not relax that assumption here despite the appeal of alternative formulations involving uncertainty. The implications of a certainty approach are two in number. First, projects available at a given decision point must be accepted (in the solution proportion) or rejected at that point. The "contract for projects available now must be signed" on these projects now. If this assumption were relaxed, projects should not be considered until either the cash or income flows are non-zero. Second, within the DCF and accounting income horizon, income and cash flows are known or at least treated as if known with certainty.

Further, instead of focusing on total yearly accounting income, the constraints could have been formulated in terms of other accounting variables such as revenue, contribution margin, funds flow, etc. Finally, the assumption that projects may be adopted in any proportion may in practice be invalid for at least some alternatives. The effects of procedures which require integer solutions are not considered either in this paper or in the original Lerner and Rappaport paper. Further, the refinement of the present model to handle this point is not central to the points we wish to make.

The Model's Descriptive Power

Lerner and Rappaport advance their model as a descriptive hypothesis and, as we have said, the descriptive power has not been tested. Nevertheless we have had some personal experiences that are consistent with the basic behavioral thrust — namely that accounting measures used in reports to outsiders are capable of influencing, in general adversely, internal decisions. Consider the following sketchy data from our experiences.

The vice president of a major industrial corporation with an extremely rapid earnings growth rate indicated recently, in conversation with one of our colleagues, that his firm intended to reject an investment that everyone concerned believed was sure to provide a return on investment of over fifty per cent. The reason he gave was that generally accepted accounting methods would require an almost immediate expensing of the investment, while the return would be spread out over a ten-year period. The effect on the externally reported financial condition of the firm would be such that the firm felt compelled to reject the investment. (It is interesting to note that here even a very successful firm rejected a profitable project that was to its long-run advantage, because of the short-run impact on income.)

An indirect example of decisions that might be consistent with a broadened interpretation of the Lerner-Rappaport idea (i.e., beyond just capital budgeting decisions) is supplied by Lev.[14] He concludes in his empirical study that firms tend to make decisions which in effect adjust their financial ratios to coincide with industry-wide averages. We would anticipate that choices between selling (or buying) and leasing, bond-refunding decisions, choices of merger candidates and the accompanying financial acquisition strategy, and many other decisions may be made under constraints imposed by the accounting methods and figures that appear in external reports. This should not be surprising. If investors are interested in and act on the basis of certain data, then it can be expected that management will consider these perceptions as important to their decision making and incorporate the relevant perceptual variables in their models.[15]

Empirical testing of the behavioral hypotheses suggested and consistent with the mathematical formulations in this paper would probably be quite difficult. While the basic notion remains valid, different versions of the model may describe the behavior of different segments of an organization at different points in time (and of two different segments at the same point in time). There are also problems of obtaining data. An initial attempt, which would also be useful in reducing the number of viable hypotheses about the models being used, might be made through examining the reasonableness of a time series of simulation-generated income patterns reflecting different behavioral assumptions. Another possible line of attack would be a controlled field study of decisions made on capital investment projects under different information sets.

One must also consider, for empirical testing purposes, the fact that management may be satisfied so long as the reported income figure is within a pre-specified range. This can be accomplished by modifying the income constraint as follows:

[14] B. Lev, "Industry Averages as Targets for Financial Ratios," *Journal of Accounting Research,* Autumn, 1969, pp. 290–299.

[15] The point reflects the view of Gordon. See M. J. Gordon, "Postulates, Principles and Research in Accounting," *The Accounting Review,* April, 1964, pp. 251–263.

$$(a_E) \qquad L_t \leqslant \left[E'_t + \sum_{j=1}^{M} E_{j,t} X_j \right] \leqslant U_t$$

where L_t and U_t represent the lower and upper bounds, respectively, for accounting income in period t.

We also suspect that an even more complex model of the variables available which management might use to manipulate reported income — including not only the selection of investment projects as discussed in this paper but also reporting (e.g., income concepts) and computation (e.g., lifo vs. fifo) variables in the financial accounting model — might provide a viable behavioral hypothesis.

We have argued that if the original Lerner-Rappaport model or one of the alternative formulations is valid descriptively (and we believe it may be for many organizational decisions), the accounting measurement process creates serious problems. At least one conclusion that might be drawn from this state of affairs is that accounting methods are as yet inadequate in determining earnings for certain uses. Methods of determining earnings to be reported to outsiders that are more nearly in harmony with the underlying decision-making process are in order.[16] One possibility would be to adopt a DCF basis for income measurement. An advantage is that the planning-horizon issue is resolved for income purposes when it is settled for decision purposes. Still another alternative is to reduce the perceived importance of the earnings and earnings-per-share figures. This might require an almost total revamping of present reporting procedures — an unlikely event. At any rate the challenge of these models to the accounting profession is clear. Because the Lerner and Rappaport article raised the issue again, we owe them a debt of thanks for the reminder.

[16] For similar arguments see, for example, H. Bierman, "A Further Study of Depreciation," *The Accounting Review,* (April, 1966), pp. 271–274.

Supplemental

Readings

to Part Three

Berczi, Andrew, and Jose Ventura. "A Proposal of Risk Analysis." *The Canadian Chartered Accountant*, 95, No. 2 (August 1969), 88–93.
  Presents a reconciliation of internal rate of return and net present value concepts, allowing for the risk factor.

Brown, Victor H. "Rate of Return: Some Comments on Its Applicability in Capital Budgeting." *The Accounting Review*, XXXVI, No. 1 (January 1961), 50–62.
  Elaborates some advantages of rate of return method.

Burkert, Ronald L. "Recognizing Inflation in the Capital Budgeting Decision." *Management Accounting*, LIII, No. 5 (November 1971), 40–46.
  Discusses a capital budgeting decision that is not one of choosing among alternative investments but rather a go/no-go investment decision with returns depending on pricing structures.

Denholm, John A. "Investment by Simulation." *The Journal of Management Studies*, 6, No. 2 (May 1969), 167–180.
  Presents a model relating various investment decisions to present and future firm position.

Edge, C. G. "Capital Budgeting: Principles and Projection." *Financial Executive*, 33, No. 9 (September 1965), 50–59.
  Presents six basic principles of capital budgeting.

Finerty, James J. "Product Pricing and Investment Analysis." *Management Accounting*, LIII, No. 6 (December 1971), 15–18.
  Discusses a two-step approach to investment analysis that involves analysis of economic variables to determine optimum selling price and a mathematical approach for considering various investment alternatives.

Fogler, H. Russell. "Ranking Techniques and Capital Budgeting." *The Accounting Review*, XLVII, No. 1 (January 1972), 134–143.
  Examines the efficiency of both simple and multidimensional ranking techniques as project selection procedures in capital budgeting.

Gynther, R. S. "Using Return on Capital for Management Control." *Accountancy*, LXXIV, Nos. 841 and 843 (September, November 1963), 768–775, 971–976.
  Stresses the need for implementing concepts of direct costing and responsibility accounting for measuring divisional performance. The au-

thors devote special attention to the effect of financial leases and price level movements on return on investment.

Huefner, Ronald J. "Analyzing and Reporting Sensitivity Data." *The Accounting Review,* XLVI, No. 4 (October 1971), 717–732.
   Reviews established methods for presenting sensitivity data, presents a new approach based on the isoquant concept, and illustrates this new approach with an example of capital budgeting analysis.

Kennedy, Miles. "Risk in Capital Budgeting: An Interactive Sensitivity Approach." *Industrial Management Review,* 9, No. 3 (Spring 1968), 121–140.
   Presents a unified analysis encompassing Monte Carlo simulation, sensitivity analysis, and user-controlled intuitive explorations.

Klammer, Thomas. "The Association of Capital Budgeting Techniques with Firm Performance." *The Accounting Review,* XLVIII, No. 2 (April 1973), 353–364.
   Discusses a study that showed there was no consistent significant association between performance and capital budgeting techniques.

Kravitz, Bernard J., and Robert J. Monteverde. "An O. R. Approach to Capital Budgeting." *Management Controls,* 16, No. 3 (March 1969), 67–69.
   Considers operations research approaches to capital budgeting.

Lerner, Eugene M., and Alfred Rappaport. "Limit DCF in Capital Budgeting." *Harvard Business Review,* 46, No. 5 (September–October 1968), 133–139.
   Presents a discounted cash flow approach employing an accounting income constraint.

Lewellen, Wilbur G., and Michael S. Long. "Simulation Versus Single-value Estimates in Capital Expenditure Analysis." *Decision Sciences,* 3, No. 4 (October 1972), 19–33.
   Concludes that the information provided by simulation is, at best, no better than that generated by the traditional single-point, present-value approach and, in one important respect, is markedly inferior.

Rappaport, Alfred. "The Discounted Payback Period." *Management Sciences* (July–August 1965), 30–35.
   Analyzes the continued use of the payback method and offers a discounting modification.

Van Horne, James C. "The Analysis of Uncertainty Resolution in Capital Budgeting for New Products." *Management Science,* 15, No. 8 (April 1969), B-376–B-386.
   Uses a capital budgeting framework to develop a method for resolving uncertainty in new product decisions.

Vernon, Thomas H. "Capital Budgeting and the Evaluation Process." *Management Accounting,* LIV, No. 4 (October 1972), 19–24.
   Discusses several capital budgeting methods of analysis and illustrates summaries of project rankings.

Weingartner, H. Martin. "Capital Budgeting of Interrelated Projects: Survey and Synthesis." *Management Science,* 12, No. 7 (March 1966), 485–516.
   Presents a survey of techniques available to handle project interrelationships.

Wilson, Charles J. "The Operating Lease and the Risk of Obsolescence." *Management Accounting*, LV, No. 6 (December 1973), 41–44.

    Offers a mathematical model that accounts for risk of obsolescence when comparing the cost of the operating lease to the cost associated with purchasing.

Wright, F. K. "Investment Criteria and the Cost of Capital." *The Journal of Management Studies*, 4, No. 3 (October 1967), 253–269.

    Provides useful investment criteria for producing approximate solutions to the optimizing problem.

Additional
Bibliography
to Part Three

Anthony, Robert N. "Some Fallacies in Figuring Return on Investment." *NAA Bulletin,* XLII, No. 4 (December 1960), 5–13.

Backer, Morton. "Additional Considerations in Return on Investment Analysis." *NAA Bulletin,* XLIII, No. 5 (January 1962), 57–62.

Beranek, William. "A Note on the Equivalence of Certain Capital Budgeting Criteria." *The Accounting Review,* XXXIX, No. 4 (October 1964), 914–916.

Brief, Richard P., and Joel Owen. "Present Value Models and the Multi-asset Problem." *The Accounting Review,* XLVIII, No. 4 (October 1973), 690–695.

Chasteen, Lanny G. "Implicit Factors in the Evaluation of Lease vs. Buy Alternatives." *The Accounting Review,* XLVIII, No. 4 (October 1973), 764–767.

Clayton, Henry L. "How to Handle Product Evaluation Procedure." *NAA Bulletin,* XLII, No. 6 (February 1961), 55–61.

Coughlan, John W. "Accounting and Capital Budgeting." *The Business Quarterly,* XXVII, No. 4 (Winter 1962), 39–48.

———. "Contrast Between Financial-statement and Discounted-cash-flow Methods of Comparing Projects." *NAA Bulletin,* XLI, No. 10 (June 1960), 5–17.

Davidson, H. Justin, and Robert M. Trueblood. "Accounting for Decision-making." *The Accounting Review,* XXXVI, No. 4 (October 1961), 577–582.

Dougall, Herbert E. "Payback as an Aid in Capital Budgeting." *The Controller,* XXIX, No. 2 (February 1961), 67–72.

Fraser, R., and M. S. Henderson. "Uncertainty in Capital Budgeting — The Simulation Approach." *Cost and Management,* 44, No. 2 (March–April 1970), 47–50.

Grant, Robert B. "Mathematically Influenced Decision-making." *NAA Bulletin,* XLII, No. 5 (January 1961), 33–44.

Gregory, John C. "Capital Expenditure Evaluation by Direct Discounting." *The Accounting Review,* XXXVII, No. 2 (April 1962), 308–314.

Haidinger, Timothy P. "The Case for Continuous Discounting." *Management Accounting,* 49, No. 6 (February 1968), 57–61.

247

Hetrick, James C. "Mathematical Models in Capital Budgeting." *Harvard Business Review,* 39, No. 1 (January–February 1961), 49–64.

Jaedicke, Robert K. "Rate of Return Verification by Follow-up Reporting on a Project Basis." *NAA Bulletin,* XLI, No. 10 (June 1960), 59–64.

Johnson, Herbert W. "Measuring the Earning Power of Investment — A Comparison of Methods." *NAA Bulletin,* XLIII, No. 5 (January 1962), 37–55.

Kieser, William F. "Product Cost Brought into Focus by Comparative Analysis." *NAA Bulletin,* XLII, No. 6 (February 1961), 73–79.

Kilpatrick, Ivan J. "A Problem of Disinvestment." *The Canadian Chartered Accountant,* 94, No. 4 (April 1969), 235–238.

Lawson, Gerald H. "Capital Investment Criteria in Business." *The Accountant,* 148, Nos. 4608–4610 (April 13, 20, and 27, 1963), 448–452, 491–496, 544–547.

Madison, Jim. "The 'Make or Buy' Decision." *Management Accounting,* LIV, No. 8 (February 1973), 32–34.

Merrett, A. J. "Investment in Replacement: The Optimal Replacement Method." *The Journal of Management Studies,* 2, No. 2 (May 1965), 153–166.

Moore, Carl L. "The Concept of the P/V Graph Applied to Capital Investment Planning." *The Accounting Review,* XXXVII, No. 4 (October 1962), 721–729.

Pollack, Gerald A. "The Capital Budgeting Controversy: Present Value vs. Discounted Cash Flow Method." *NAA Bulletin,* XLIII, No. 3 (November 1961), 5–19.

Satchell, Roy C. "Fallacies in Capital Investment Decisions." *Financial Executive,* 34, No. 8 (August 1966), 36–42.

Schuba, Kenneth F. "Make-or-Buy Decisions — Cost and Non-cost Considerations." *NAA Bulletin,* XLI, No. 7 (March 1960), 53–66.

Taussig, Russell. "Information Requirements of Replacement Models." *Journal of Accounting Research,* 2, No. 1 (Spring 1964), 67–69.

Vatter, William J. "Does the Rate of Return Measure Business Efficiency?" *NAA Bulletin,* XL, No. 5 (January 1959), 33–48.

Wellington, Roger. "Capital Budgeting." *The Journal of Accountancy,* 115, No. 5 (May 1963), 46–53.

PART FOUR

Cost Estimation

and Cost-Volume-Profit Analysis

$\mathbf{M}$anagement must know the cost process to evaluate the control, planning, and related performance of such cost processes. Determining the behavior of costs is the subject of the article by Benston. He advocates the statistical method of regression analysis as a primary method for management to investigate and estimate cost behavior. In this "self-contained" article, he thoroughly explains and illustrates with examples multiple regression analysis. He also explains cost-recording implications from the use of regression analysis.

Cost-volume-profit (CVP) is a technique helpful in analyzing basic relationships for business decisions. The technique, though useful, of course does not make the decisions. It does, however, permit the evaluation of predictions based on cost-volume-profit assumptions that relate cost and profit behavior to volume. Traditionally, cost accountants have considered relationships to be mainly linear within the normal operations of the firm for both cost and revenue relative to volume. They have normally represented costs by linear fixed and variable portions, while they have considered revenues completely linearly variable with volume.

Vickers argues that these linearity assumptions ignore economic theorems that emphasize non-linear cost and revenue behavior. He recommends that industrial break-even charts be adapted and brought into closer conformity with economics and that both economists and accountants devote attention to reinterpreting cost-volume-profit relationships to clarify the true empirical behavior. As Benston discussed previously, this linear–non-linear argument can be empirically investigated by regression analysis to determine the actual cost and revenue relationships in specific situations.

In the third article, Charnes, Cooper, and Ijiri rely on linear relationships in exploring the applications of linear and goal programming to break-even analysis. They develop linear and goal-programming techniques to generate break-even opportunity cost data. A unique matrix method known as *spread-sheet analysis* constructs journal entries and summarizes financial information as an alternative to double entry accounting and as a basis for linear programming applications.

Jarrett extends CVP analysis to consider the existence of uncertainty. Jarrett discusses certain factors such as price, unit sales, and unit variable costs that are not constant but have expected values in recognition of the uncertainty involved in measuring them. As in the Hertz article, probability distributions are determined and expected profits calculated for a CVP decision on the production of alternative products. In the latter part of the article, Jarrett further expands CVP analysis with Bayesian decision theory to deal with uncertainties in the production decision. He compares the cost of additional information provided by survey research to the value of reduced uncertainty for the production decision.

14

Cost estimation is essential to cost control: The behavior of costs must be understood before such costs can be effectively controlled. Benston contrasts commonly used methods of cost analysis with the multiple regression method and introduces types of cost decision problems. He argues that multiple regression analysis is ". . . particularly useful in estimating costs for recurring decisions."

The author explains the statistical tool of multiple regression analysis so thoroughly that no other statistical sources need be consulted; that is, the article is "self-contained." The requirements of multiple regression have cost-recording implications for the following factors: length of time periods, number of time periods, range of observations, specification of cost-related factors, measurement errors, correlations among the explanatory variables, and distribution of the non-specified factors. A straightforward example completes the article.

Multiple Regression
Analysis of Cost Behavior*

George J. Benston

Accountants probably have always been concerned with measuring and reporting the relationship between cost and output. The pre-eminence of financial accounting in this century resulted in directing much of our attention towards attaching costs to inventories. However, the recent emphasis on decision making is causing us to consider ways of measuring the variability of cost with output and other decisions variables. In this

* *From* The Accounting Review, *Vol. XLI, No. 4 (October, 1966), pp. 657–672. Reprinted by permission of the American Accounting Association and George J. Benston, Professor, Graduate School of Management, University of Rochester.*

paper, the application, use, and limitations of multiple regression analysis, a valuable tool for measuring costs, are discussed.[1]

A valid objection to multiple regression analysis in the past has been that its computational difficulty often rendered it too costly. Today, with high speed computers and library programs, this objection is no longer valid: most regression problems ought to cost less than $30 to run. Unfortunately, this new ease and low cost of using regression analysis may prove to be its undoing. Analysts may be tempted to use the technique without adequately realizing its technical data requirements and limitations. The "GI-GO" adage, "garbage in, garbage out," always must be kept in mind. A major purpose of this paper is to state these requirements and limitations explicitly and to indicate how they may be handled.

The general problem of cost measurement is discussed in the first section of this paper. Multiple regression analysis is considered first in relation to other methods of cost analysis. Then its applicability to cost decision problems is delineated. Second, the method of multiple regression is discussed in nonmathematical terms so that its uses can be understood better. The third section represents the "heart" of the paper. Here the technical requirements of multiple regression are outlined, and the implications of these requirements for the recording of cost data in the firm's accounting records are outlined. The functional form of the regression equation is then considered. In the final section, we discuss some applications for multiple regression analysis.

The General Problem

In his attempts to determine the factors that cause costs to be incurred and the magnitudes of their effects, the accountant is faced with a formidable task. Engineers, foremen, and others who are familiar with the production process being studied usually can provide a list of cost-causing factors, such as the number of different units produced, the lot sizes in which units were made, and so forth. Other factors that affect costs, such as the season of the year, may be important, though they are more subtle than production factors. The accountant must separate and measure the effects of many different causal factors whose importance may vary in different periods.

---

[1] The use of statistical analysis for auditing and control is outside the scope of this paper. Excellent discussions of these uses of statistics may be found in Richard N. Cyert and H. Justin Davidson, *Statistical Sampling for Accounting Information* (Prentice-Hall, 1962), and Herbert Arkin, *Handbook of Sampling for Auditing and Accounting,* Volume I: Methods (McGraw-Hill, 1963).

COMMONLY USED METHODS OF COST ANALYSIS

Perhaps the most pervasive method of analyzing cost variability is separation of costs into two or three categories: variable, fixed and sometimes semivariable. But this method does not provide a solution to the problem of measuring the costs caused by each of many factors operating simultaneously. In this "direct costing" type of procedure, output is considered to be the sole cause of costs. Another objection to this method is that there is no way to determine whether the accountant's subjective separation of costs into variable and fixed is reasonably accurate. Dividing output during a period into variable cost during that period yields a single number (unit variable cost) whose accuracy cannot be assessed. If the procedure is repeated for several periods, it is likely that different unit variable costs will be computed. But the accountant cannot determine whether the average of these numbers (or some other summary statistic) is a useful number. Another important short-coming of this method is the assumption of linearity between cost and output. While linearity may be found, it should not be assumed automatically.

A variant of the fixed-variable method is one in which cost and output data for many periods are plotted on a two-dimensional graph. A line is then fitted to the data, the slope being taken as variable cost per unit of output. When the least-squares method of fitting the line is used, the procedure is called simple linear regression. Until the recent advent of computers, simple regression was considered to be quite sophisticated.[2] While it was recognized that its use neglects the effects on cost of factors other than output, it was defended on the then reasonable grounds that multiple regression with more than two or three variables is too difficult computationally to be considered economically feasible.

MULTIPLE REGRESSION

Multiple regression can allow the accountant to estimate the amount by which the various cost-causing factors affect costs. A very rough description is that it measures the cost of a change in one variable, say output, while holding the effects on cost of other variables, say the season of the year or the size of batches, constant. For example, consider the problem of analyzing the costs incurred by the shipping department of a department store. The manager of the department believes that his costs are primarily a function of the number of orders processed. However, heavier packages are more costly to handle than are lighter ones. He also

---

[2] National Association of Accountants, *Separating and Using Costs as Fixed and Variable,* June, 1960.

considers the weather an important factor; rain or extreme cold slows down delivery time. We might want to eliminate the effect of the weather, since it is not controllable. But we would like to know how much each order costs to process and what the cost of heavier against lighter packages is. If we can make these estimates, we can (1) prepare a flexible budget for the shipping department that takes account of changes in operating conditions, (2) make better pricing decisions, and (3) plan for capital budgeting more effectively. A properly specified multiple regression equation can provide the required estimates.

A criticism of multiple regression analysis is that it is complicated, and so would be difficult to "sell" to lower management and supervisory personnel. However, the method allows for a more complete specification of "reality" than do simple regression or the fixed-variable dichotomy. Studies have shown that supervisors tend to disregard data that they believe are "unrealistic," such as those based on the simplification that costs incurred are a function of units of output only.[3] Therefore, multiple regression analysis should prove more acceptable to supervisors than procedures that require gross simplification of reality.

The regression technique also can allow the accountant to make probability statements concerning the reliability of the estimates made.[4] For example, he may find that the marginal cost of processing a package of average weight is $.756, when the effects on cost of different weather conditions and other factors are accounted for. If the properties underlying regression analysis (discussed below) are met, the reliability of this cost estimate may be determined from the standard error of the coefficient (say $.032) from which the accountant may assess a probability of .95 that the marginal cost per package is between $.692 and $.820 (.756±.064).

Multiple regression analysis, then, is a very powerful tool; however, it is not applicable to all cost situations. To decide the situations for which it is best used, let us first consider the problem of cost estimation in general and then consider the sub-class of problems for which multiple regression analysis is useful.

TYPES OF COST DECISION PROBLEMS

In general, cost is a function of many variables, including time. For example, the cost of output may be affected by such conditions as whether

[3] H. A. Simon, H. Guetzkow, G. Kozmetsky, and G. Tyndall, *Centralization versus Decentralization in Organizing the Controllers Department* (New York: The Controllership Foundation, 1954).

[4] This and the following statements are made in the context of a Bayesian analysis, in which the decision maker combines sample information with his prior judgment concerning unknown parameters. In the examples given, a jointly diffuse prior distribution is assumed for all parameters.

production is increasing or decreasing, the lot sizes are large or small, the plant is new or old, the White Sox are losing or winning, and so forth. Since there is *some* change in the environment of different time periods or in the circumstances affecting different decisions, it would seem that the accountant must make an individual cost analysis for every decision considered.

However, the maximization rule of economics also applies to information technology: the marginal cost of the information must not exceed the marginal revenue gained from it. The marginal revenue from cost information is the additional revenue that accrues or the losses that are avoided from not making mistakes, such as accepting contracts where the marginal costs exceed the marginal revenue from the work, or rejecting contracts where the reverse situation obtains. The marginal cost of information is the cost of gathering and presenting the information, plus the opportunity cost of delay, since measurement and presentation are not instantaneous.[5] Since these costs can be expected to exceed the marginal revenue from information for many decisions, it usually is not economical to estimate different costs for each different decision. Thus, it is desirable to group decision problems into categories that can be served by the same basic cost information. Two such categories are proposed here: (1) recurring problems and (2) one-time problems.

Recurring decision problems are those for which the data required for analysis are used with some regularity. Examples are determining the prices that will be published in a catalogue, preparation of output schedules for expected production, the setting of budgets and production cost standards, and the formulation of forecasts. These decisions require cost data in the form of schedules of expected costs due to various levels of activity over an expected range.

One-time problems are those which occur infrequently, unpredictably, or are of such a magnitude as to require individual cost estimates. Examples of these problems are cost-profit-volume decisions, such as whether the firm should take a one-time special order, make, buy, or lease equipment, develop a new product, or close a plant. These decisions require that cost estimates be made which reflect conditions especially relevant to the problem at hand.

These categories present different requirements for cost estimation. Recurring problems require a schedule of *expected* costs and activity. Since these problems are repetitive, the marginal cost of gathering and presenting data each time usually is expected to be greater than the marginal revenue from the data. Thus, while the marginal cost of additional production, for example, will differ depending on such factors as whether overtime is required or excess capacity is available, in general it is more

---

[5] These two costs are related since delay can be reduced by expending more resources on the information system.

profitable to estimate the amount that the marginal cost of the additional production may be, on the average, rather than to take account of every special factor that may exist in individual circumstances.

In contrast, one-time problems are characterized by the economic desirability of making individual cost estimates. We do not rely on average marginal costs because the more accurate information is worth its cost. This situation may occur when the problem is unique, and average cost data are therefore not applicable. Or the decision may involve a substantial commitment of resources, making the marginal revenue from avoiding wrong decisions quite high.

Multiple Regression Analysis

Regression analysis is particularly useful in estimating costs for recurring decisions.[6] The procedure essentially consists of estimating mathematically the *average* relationship between costs (the "dependent" variable) and the factors that cause cost incurrences (the "independent" variables). The analysis provides the accountant with an estimate of the expected marginal cost of a unit change in output, for example, with the effects on total cost of other factors accounted for. These are the data he requires for costing recurring decisions.

The usefulness of multiple regression analysis for recurring decisions of costs can be appreciated best when the essential nature of the technique is understood. It is not necessary that the mathematical proofs of least squares or the methods of inverting matrices be learned since library computer programs do all the work.[7] However, it is necessary that the assumptions underlying use of multiple regression be fully understood so that this valuable tool is not misused.

Multiple regression analysis presupposes a linear relationship between the contributive factors and costs.[8] The functional relationship between these factors, $x_1, x_2, \cdots, x_n$, and cost, C, is assumed in multiple regression analysis to be of the following form:

$$(1) \qquad C_t = \beta_0 x_{0,t} + \beta_1 x_{1,t} + \beta_2 x_{2,t} + \cdots + \beta_n x_{n,t} + \mu_t,$$

where

β_0 is a constant term ($x_0 = 1$ for all observations and time periods), the β's are fixed coefficients that express the marginal contribution of each x_i to C, and

---

[6] Indeed, its use requires the assumption that the past costs used for a regression analysis are a sample from a universe of possible costs generated by a continuing, stationary, normal process.

[7] The mathematics of multiple regression is described in many statistics and econometrics texts.

[8] A curvilinear or exponential relationship also can be expressed as a linear relationship. This technique is discussed below.

μ is the sum of unspecified factors, the disturbances, that are assumed to be randomly distributed with a zero mean and constant variance, and

$t = 1, 2, \cdots, m =$ time periods.

The β coefficients are estimated from a sample of C's and x's from time periods 1 through m. For example, assume that the cost recorded in a week is a function of such specified factors as $x_1 =$ units of output, $x_2 =$ number of units in a batch, and $x_3 =$ the ratio of the number of "de luxe" units to total units produced. Then the right hand side of equation (2) is an estimate of the right hand side of equation (1), obtained from a sample of weekly observations, where the b's are estimates of the β's and u is the residual, the estimate of μ, the disturbance term:

(2) $$C_t = b_{0,t} + b_1 x_{1,t} + b_2 x_{2,t} + b_3 x_{3,t} + u_t.$$

If the values estimated for coefficients of the three independent variables, x_1, x_2, and x_3, are $b_0 = 100$, $b_1 = 30$, $b_2 = -20$, and $b_3 = 500$, the expected cost ($\hat{C}$) for any given week (t) is estimated by:

$$\hat{C} = 100 + 30x_1 - 20x_2 + 500x_3.$$

Given estimates of the β's, one has, in effect, estimates of the marginal cost associated with each of the determining factors. In the example given above, the marginal cost of producing an additional unit of output, x_1, is estimated to be \$30, with the effects or costs of the size of batch (x_2) and the ratio of the number of de luxe to total units (x_3) accounted for. Or, β_2, the marginal reduction in total cost of increasing the batches by 3 units, given fixed values of the number of units and the relative proportions of de luxe units produced, is estimated to be $-\$60$ (\$$-20$ times 3).

It is tempting to interpret the constant term, b_0, as fixed cost. But this is not correct unless the linear relationship found in the range of observations obtains back to zero output.[9] This can be seen best in the following two-dimensional graph of cost on output. The line was fitted with the equation $C = b_0 + b_1 x_1$, where the dots are the observed values of cost and output. The slope of the line is the coefficient, b_1, an estimate of the marginal change in total cost (C) with a unit change (z) in output (x_1). The intercept on the C axis is b_0, the constant term. It would be an estimate of fixed cost if the range of observations included the point where output were zero, and the relationship between total cost and output were linear. However, if more observations of cost and output (the x's) were available, it might be that the dashed curve would be fitted and b_0 would be zero. Thus the value of the constant term, b_0, is not the costs that would be expected if there were no output; it is only the value that is calculated as a result of the regression line computed from the available data.

---

[9] Fixed cost is defined here as avoidable cost related to time periods and not to output variables.

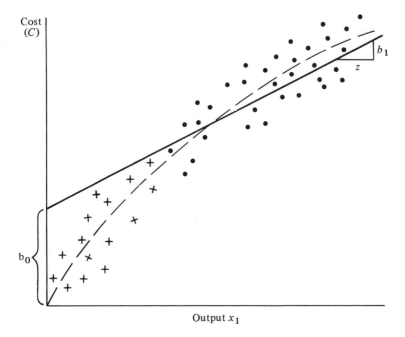

Output x_1

The data for the calculations are taken from the accounting and production records of past time periods. The coefficients estimated from these data are averages of past experience. Therefore, the b's calculated are best suited for recurring cost decisions. The fact that the b's are averages of past data must be emphasized, because their use for decisions is based on the assumption that the future will be like an average of past experience.

The mathematical method usually used for estimating the β's is the least-squares technique. It has the properties of providing best, linear, unbiased estimates of the β's. These properties are desirable because they tend "to yield a series of estimates whose average would coincide with the true value being estimated and whose variance about that true value is smaller than that of any other unbiased estimators." [10] While these properties are not always of paramount importance, they are very valuable for making estimates of the expected average costs required for recurring problems.

Another important advantage of the least-squares technique is that when it is combined with the assumptions about the disturbance term (μ_t) that are discussed in point 7 below, the reliability of the relations between the explanatory variables and costs can be determined. Two types of reliability estimates may be computed. One, the standard error of estimate, shows how well the equation fits the data. The second, the standard error of the regression coefficients, assesses the probability that the β's estimated are within a range of values. For example, if a linear cost function is used, the coefficient (b_1) of output (x_1) is the estimated marginal cost

[10] J. Johnston, *Statistical Cost Analysis* (New York: McGraw-Hill, 1960), p. 31.

of output. With an estimate of the standard error of the coefficient, s_{b1}, we can say that the true marginal cost, β_1, is within the range $b_1 \pm s_{b1}$, with a given probability.[11]

Requirements of Multiple Regression and Cost Recording Implications

Although multiple regression is an excellent tool for estimating recurring costs, it does have several requirements that make its use hazardous without careful planning.[12] Most of the data requirements of multiple regressions analysis depend on the way cost-accounting records are maintained. If the data are simply taken from the ordinary cost-accounting records of the company, it is unlikely that the output of the regression model will be meaningful. Therefore, careful planning of the extent to which the initial accounting data are coded and recorded is necessary before regression analysis can be used successfully. This section of the paper is organized into four groupings that include several numbered subsections in which the principal technical requirements are described, after which the implications for the cost system are discussed. In the first group, (1) the length and (2) number of time periods, (3) the range of observations, and (4) the specification of cost-related factors are described, following which their implications for cost recording are outlined. In the second group, (5) errors of measurement and their cost recording implication are considered. The third group deals with (6) correlations among the explanatory variables and the important contribution that accounting analysis can make to this problem. Finally, (7) the requirements for the distribution of the nonspecified factors (disturbances) are given. The implications of these requirements for the functional form of the variables are taken up [beginning on p. 269].

1. LENGTH OF TIME PERIODS

(a) The time periods $(1, 2, 3, \cdots, m)$ chosen should be long enough to allow the bookkeeping procedures to pair output produced in a period with the cost incurred because of that production. For example, if 500 units are produced in a day, but records of supplies used are kept on a weekly basis, an analysis of the cost of supplies used cannot be made with shorter than weekly periods. Lags in recording costs must be corrected or adjusted. Thus, production should not be recorded as occurring in one week while indirect labor is recorded a week later when the pay checks are written.

---

[11] The interpretation of the confidence interval is admittedly Bayesian.

[12] Proofs of the requirements described may be found in many econometrics textbooks, such as Arthur S. Goldberger, *Econometric Theory* (Wiley, 1964), and J. Johnston, *Econometric Methods* (McGraw-Hill, 1963).

(b) The time periods chosen should be *short* enough to avoid variations in production within the period. Otherwise, the variations that occur during the period will be averaged out, possibly obscuring the true relationship between cost and output.

2. NUMBER OF TIME PERIODS (OBSERVATIONS)

For a time series, each observation covers a time period in which data on costs and output and other explanatory variables are collected for analysis. As a minimum, there must be one more observation than there are independent variables to make regression analysis possible. (The excess number is called "degrees of freedom.") Of course, many more observations must be available before one could have any confidence that the relationship estimated from the sample reflects the "true" underlying relationship. The standard errors, from which one may determine the range within which the true coefficients lie (given some probability of error), are reduced by the square root of the number of observations.

3. RANGE OF OBSERVATIONS

The observations on cost and output should cover as wide a range as possible. If there is very little variation from period to period in cost and output, the functional relationship between the two cannot be estimated effectively by regression analysis.

4. SPECIFICATION OF COST-RELATED FACTORS

All factors that affect cost should be specified and included in the analysis.[13] This is a very important requirement that is often difficult to meet. For example, observations may have been taken over a period when input prices changed. The true relationship between cost and output may be obscured if high output coincided with high input due to price-level effects. If the higher costs related to higher price levels are not accounted for (by inclusion of a price index as an independent variable) or adjusted for (by stating the dependent variable, cost, in constant dollars), the marginal cost of additional output estimated will be meaningful only if changes in input prices are proportional to changes in output and are expected to remain so.

---

[13] Complete specification is not mandatory if requirement 7 (below) is met. However, requirement 7 is not likely to be fulfilled if the specification is seriously incomplete.

IMPLICATIONS FOR COST RECORDING OF 1, 2, 3, AND 4

In general, the time period requirements (1a, 1b and 2) call for the recording of production data for periods no longer than one month and preferably as short as one week in length. If longer periods are chosen, it is unlikely that there will be a sufficient number of observations available for analysis because, as a bare minimum, one more period than the number of explanatory variables is needed. Even if it is believed that only one explanatory variable (such as units of output) is needed to specify the cost function in any one period, requirement 4 (that all cost related factors be specified) demands consideration of differences among time periods. Thus, such events as changes in factor prices and production methods, whether production is increasing or decreasing, and the seasons of the year might have to be specified as explanatory variables.

The necessity of identifying all relevant explanatory variables such as those just mentioned, can be met by having a journal kept in which the values or the behavior of these variables in specific time periods is noted. If such a record is not kept, it will be difficult (if not impossible) to recall unusual events and to identify them with the relevant time periods, especially when short time periods are used. For example, it is necessary to note whether production increased or decreased substantially in each period. Increases in production may be met by overtime. However, decreases may be accompanied by idle time or slower operations. Thus, we would expect the additional costs of increases to be greater than the cost savings from decreases.[14]

Other commonly found factors that affect costs are changes in technology, changes in capacity, periods of adjustment to new processes or types of output, and seasonal differences. The effect of these factors may be accounted for by including variables in the regression equation, by specific adjustment of the data, or by excluding data that are thought to be "contaminated."

The wide range of observations needed for effective analysis also argues against observation periods of longer than one month. With long periods, variations in production would more likely be averaged out than if shorter periods were used (which violates requirement 1b). In addition, if stability of conditions limits the number of explanatory variables other than output that otherwise would reduce the degrees of freedom, this same stability probably would not produce a sufficient range of output to make regression analysis worthwhile. Thus, weekly or monthly data usually are required for multiple regression.

---

[14] A dummy variable can be used to represent qualitative variables, such as $P = 1$ when production increased and $P = 0$ when production decreased. From the coefficient of P, we can estimate the cost effect of differences in the direction of output change and also reduce contamination of the coefficient estimated for output.

5. Errors of Measurement

It is difficult to believe that data from a "real life" production situation will be reported without error. The nature of the errors is important since some kinds will affect the usefulness of regression analysis more than others will. Errors in the dependent variable, cost, are not fatal since they affect the disturbance term, μ.[15] The predictive value of the equation is lessened, but the estimate of marginal cost (β_1) is not affected.

But where there are errors in measuring output or the other independent variable $(x\text{'s})$, the disturbance term, μ, will be correlated with the independent variables.[16] If this condition exists, the sample coefficient estimated by the least-squares procedure will be an underestimate of the true marginal cost. Thus, it is very important that the independent variables be measured accurately.

The possibility of measurement errors is intensified by the number of observations requirement. Short reporting periods increase the necessity for careful classification. For example, if a cost caused by production in week 1 is not recorded until week 2, the dependent variable (cost) of both observations will be measured incorrectly. This error is most serious when production fluctuates between observations. However, when production is increasing or decreasing steadily, the measurement error tends to be constant (either in absolute or proportional terms) and hence will affect only the constant term. The regression coefficients estimated, and hence the estimates of average marginal cost, will not be affected.[17]

Another important type of measurement error is the failure to charge the period in which production occurs with future costs caused by that production. For example, overtime pay for production workers may be paid for in the week following their work. This can be adjusted for easily. However, the foreman may not be paid for his overtime directly. Rather, many months after his work he might get a year-end bonus or a raise in pay. These costs cannot easily be associated with the production that caused them but will be charged in another period, thus making both periods' costs incorrect.[18] This type of error is difficult to correct. Usu-

---

[15] Let γ stand for the measurement errors in C:

$$C + \gamma = \beta_0 + \beta_1 x_1 + \mu$$
$$C = \beta_0 + \beta_1 x_1 + \mu - \gamma.$$

[16] In this event, where ψ stands for the measurement error in x_1:

$$C = \beta_0 + \beta_1(x_1 + \psi) + \mu$$
$$C = \beta_0 + \beta_1 x_1 + \beta_1 \psi + \mu.$$

The new disturbance term $\beta_1 \psi + \mu$, is not independent of x_1 because of the covariance between these variables.

[17] If the error is proportionally constant (i.e., 10 per cent of production), transformation of the variables (such as to logarithms) is necessary.

[18] Actually, the present value of the future payment should be included as a current period cost.

ally, all that one can do is eliminate the bonus payment from the data of the period in which it is paid and realize that the estimated coefficient of output will be biased downward. Average marginal costs, then, will be understated.

A somewhat similar situation follows from the high cost of the careful record keeping required to charge such input factors as production supplies to short time periods. In this event, these items of cost should be deducted from the other cost items and not included in the analysis. If these amounts are large enough, specific analysis may be required, or the decision not to account for them carefully may be re-evaluated.

This separation of specific cost items also is desirable where the accountant knows that their allocation to time periods bears no relation to production. For example, such costs as insurance or rent may be allocated to departments on a monthly basis. There is no point in including these costs in the dependent variable because it is known that they do not vary with the independent variables. At best, their inclusion will only increase the constant term. However, if by chance they are correlated with an independent variable, they will bias the estimates made (requirement 7a). This type of error may be built into the accounting system if fixed costs are allocated to time periods on the basis of production. For example, depreciation may be charged on a per unit basis. The variance of this cost, then, may be a function of the accounting method and not of the underlying economic relationships.[19]

6. Correlations Among the Explanatory (Independent) Variables

When the explanatory variables are highly correlated with one another, it is very difficult, and often impossible, to estimate the separate relationships of each to the dependent variable. This condition is called multicollinearity, and it is a severe problem for cost studies. When we compute marginal costs, we usually want to estimate the marginal cost of *each* of the different types of output produced in a multiproduct firm. However, this is not always possible. For example, consider a manufacturer who makes refrigerators, freezers, washing machines, and other major home appliances. If the demand for all home appliances is highly correlated, the number of refrigerators, freezers and washing machines produced will move together, all being high in one week and low in another. In this situation it will be impossible to disentangle the marginal cost of producing refrigerators from the marginal cost of producing freezers and washing machines by means of multiple regression.[20]

---

[19] Depreciation is assumed to be time, not user, depreciation.

[20] However, the computed regression can provide useful predictions of total costs if the past relationships of production among the different outputs are maintained.

Problems similar to that of our manufacturer can be alleviated by dis-aggregation of total cost into several sub-groups that are independent of each other. Preanalysis and preliminary allocations of cost and output data may accomplish this disaggregation. This is one of the most important contributions the accountant can make to regression analysis.

If the total costs of the entire plant are regressed on outputs of different types, it is likely that the computed coefficients will have very large standard errors and, hence, will not be reliable. This situation may be avoided by first allocating costs to cost centers where a single output is likely to be produced. This allows a set of multiple regressions to be computed, one for each cost center. The procedure (which may be followed anyway for inventory costing) also reduces the number of explanatory variables that need be specified in any one regression.[21] Care must be taken to assure that the allocation of costs to cost centers is not arbitrary or un-related to output. For example, allocation of electricity or rent on a square footage basis can serve no useful purpose. However, allocation of the salary of the foremen on a time basis is necessary when they spend varying amounts of time per period supervising different cost centers.

A further complication arises if several different types of outputs are produced within the cost centers. For example, the assembly department may work on different models of television sets at the same time. In most instances, it is neither feasible nor desirable to allocate the cost center's costs to each type of output. Cost, then, should be regressed on several output variables, one for the quantity of each type of output. If these independent variables are multicollinear, the standard errors of their re-gression coefficients will be so large relative to the coefficients as to make the estimates useless. In this event, an index of output may be constructed, in which the different types of output are weighted by a factor (such as labor hours) that serves to describe their relationship to cost. Cost then may be regressed on this weighted index. The regression coefficient com-puted expresses the average relationship between the "bundle" of outputs and cost and cannot be decomposed to give the relationship between one output element and cost. However, since the outputs were collinear in the past, it is likely that they will be collinear in the future, so that knowl-edge about the cost of the "bundle" of outputs may be sufficient.

A valid objection to the allocation of costs to cost centers is that one can never be sure that the allocations are accurate. Nevertheless, some allocations must be made for multicollinearity to be overcome. Therefore, the statistical method cannot be free from the accountant's subjective judgment; in fact, it depends on it.

A limitation of analysis of costs by cost centers also is that cost exter-nalities among cost centers may be ignored. For example, the directly

---

[21] The author used this procedure with considerable success in estimating the mar-ginal costs of banking operations. See "Economies of Scale and Marginal Costs in Banking Operations," *National Banking Review,* 1965, pp. 507–549.

chargeable costs of the milling department may be a function of the level of operations of other departments. The existence and magnitude of operations outside of a particular cost center may be estimated by including an appropriate independent variable in the cost center regression. An overall index of production, such as total direct labor hours on total sales is one such variable. Or, if a cost element is allocated between two cost centers, the output of one cost center may be included as an independent variable in the other cost center's regressions. The existence and effect of these possible inter-cost center elements may be determined from the standard error of the coefficient and sign of this variable.

Some types of costs that vary with activity cannot be associated with specific cost centers because it is difficult to make meaningful allocations or because of bookkeeping problems (as discussed above). In this event, individual regression analyses of these costs probably will prove valuable. For example, electricity may be difficult to allocate to cost centers although it varies with machine hours.[22] A regression can be computed such as the following:

$$(3) \qquad E = b_0 + b_1 M + b_2 S_1 + b_3 S_2 + b_4 S_3$$

where

$\quad E =$ electricity cost
$\quad M =$ total machine hours in the plant
$\quad S =$ seasonal dummy variables

where

$\quad S_1 = 1$ for summer, 0 for other seasons
$\quad S_2 = 1$ for spring, 0 for other seasons
$\quad S_3 = 1$ for winter, 0 for other seasons
$\qquad b_0, b_1, b_2, b_3,$ and b_4 are the computed constants and coefficients.

If the regression is fully specified, with all factors that cause the use of electricity included (such as the season of the year), the regression coefficient of M, b_1, is the estimate of the average marginal cost of electricity per machine hour. This cost can be added to the other costs (such as materials and labor) to estimate the marginal cost of specific outputs.

For some activities, physical units, such as labor hours, can be used as the dependent variable instead of costs. This procedure is desirable where most of the activity's costs are a function of such physical units and where factor prices are expected to vary. Thus, in a shipping department, it may be best to regress hours worked on pounds shipped, percentage of units shipped by truck, the average number of pounds per sale, and other

---

[22] Machine hours may not be recorded by cost center although direct labor hours are. If machine hours (M) are believed to be proportional to direct labor hours (L), so that $M_i = k_i L_i$, where k is a constant multiplier that may vary among cost centers, i, $k_i L_i$ is a perfect substitute for M_i.

explanatory variables. Then, with the coefficients estimated, the number of labor hours can be estimated for various situations. These hours then can be costed at the current labor rate.

7. Distribution of the Non-specified Factors (Disturbances)

(a) *Serial Correlation of the Disturbances.* A very important requirement of least squares that affects the coefficients and the estimates made about their reliability is that the disturbances not be serially correlated. For a time series (in which the observations are taken at successive periods of time), this means that the disturbances that arose in a period t are independent from the disturbances that arose in previous periods, t-1, t-2, etc. The consequences of serial correlation of the disturbances are that (1) the standard errors of the regression coefficients (b's) will be seriously underestimated, (2) the sampling variances of the coefficients will be very large, and (3) predictions of cost made from the regression equation will be more variable than is ordinarily expected from least-squares estimators. Hence, the tests measuring the probability that the true marginal costs and total costs are within a range around the estimates computed from the regression are not valid.

(b) *Independence from Explanatory Variables.* The disturbances which reflect the factors affecting cost that cannot be specified must be uncorrelated with the explanatory (independent) variables ($x_1, x_2, \cdots, x_n$). If the unspecified factors are correlated with the explanatory variables, the coefficients will be biased and inconsistent estimates of the true values. Such correlation often is the result of bookkeeping procedures. For example, repairs to equipment in a machine shop is a cost-causing activity that often is not specified because of quantification difficulties. However, these repairs may be made when output is low because the machines can be taken out of service at these times. Thus, repair costs will be negatively correlated with output. If these costs are not separated from other costs, the estimated coefficient of output will be biased downward, so that the true extent of variableness of cost with output will be masked.

(c) *Variance of the Disturbances.* A basic assumption underlying use of least squares is that the variance of the disturbance term is constant; it should not be a function of the level of the dependent or independent variables.[23] If the variance of the disturbance is nonconstant, the standard errors of the coefficients estimated are not correct, and the reliability of the coefficients cannot be determined.

When the relationship estimated is between only one independent vari-

[23] Constant variance is known as homoscedasticity. Non-constant variance is called heteroscedasticity.

able (output) and the dependent variable (cost), the presence of non-constant variance of the disturbances can be detected by plotting the independent against the dependent variable. However, where more than one independent variable is required, such observations cannot be easily made. In this event, the accountant must attempt to estimate the nature of the variance from other information and then transform the data to a form in which constant variance is achieved. At the least, he should decide whether the disturbances are likely to bear a proportional relationship to the other variables (as is commonly the situation with economic data). If they do, it may be desirable to transform the variables to logarithms. The efficacy of the transformations may be tested by plotting the independent variables against the residuals (the estimates of the disturbances).

(d) *Normal Distribution of the Disturbances.* For the traditional statistical tests of the regression coefficients and equations to be strictly valid, the disturbances should be normally distributed. Tests of normality can be made by plotting the residuals on normal probability paper, an option available in many library regression programs. While requirement 7 does not have implications for the accounting system, it does determine the form in which the variables are specified. These considerations are discussed in the following section.

Functional Form of the Regression Equation

Thus far we have been concerned with correct specification of the regression equation rather than with its functional form. However, the form of the variables must fit the underlying data well and be of such a nature that the residuals are distributed according to requirement 7 above.

The form chosen first should follow the underlying relationship that is thought to exist. Consider, for example, an analysis of the costs (C) of a shipping department. Costs may be a function of pounds shipped (P), percentage of pounds shipped by truck (T), and the average number of pounds per sale (A). If the accountant believes that the change in cost due to a change of each explanatory variable is unaffected by the levels of the other explanatory variables, a linear form could be used, as follows:

$$(4) \qquad C = a + bP + cT + dA.$$

In this form, the estimated marginal cost of a unit change in pounds shipped (P) is $\partial C/\partial P$ or b.

However, if the marginal cost of each explanatory variable is thought to be a function of the levels of the other explanatory variables, the following form would be better:

$$(5) \qquad C = aP^b T^c A^d.$$

In this case, a linear form could be achieved by converting the variable to logarithms:

$$(6) \qquad \log C = \log a + b \log P + c \log T + d \log A.$$

Now, an approximation to the expected marginal cost of a unit change in pounds shipped (P) *is* $\partial C/\partial P = baP^{b-1}\overline{T}^c\overline{A}^d$, where the other explanatory variables are held constant at some average values (denoted by bars over the letters). Thus, the estimated marginal cost of P is a function of the levels of the other variables.

The logarithmic form of the variables also allows for estimates of non-linear relationships between cost and the explanatory variables. The form of the relationships may be approximated by graphing the dependent variable against the independent variable. (The most important independent variable should be chosen where there is more than one, although in this event the simple two-dimensional plotting can only be suggestive.) If the plot indicates that a non-linear rather than a linear form will fit the data best, the effect of using logarithms may be determined by plotting the data on semi-log and log-log ruled paper.

If the data seem curvilinear even in logarithms, or if an additive rather than a multiplicative form describes the underlying relationships best, polynomial forms of the variables may be used. Thus, for an additive relationship between cost (C) and quantity of output (Q), the form fitted may be $C = a + bQ + cQ^2 + cQ^3$. If a multiplicative relationship is assumed, the form may be $\log C = \log a + \log Q + (\log Q)^2$. Either form describes a large family of curves with two bends.

When choosing the form of the variables, attention must always be paid to the effect of the form on the residuals, the estimates of the disturbances. Unless the variance of the residuals is constant, not subject to serial correlation, and approximately normally distributed (requirement 5), inferences about the reliability of the coefficients estimated cannot be made. Graphing is a valuable method for determining whether or not these requirements are met. (The graphs mentioned usually can be produced by the computers.) Three graphs are suggested. First, the residuals should be plotted in time sequence. They should appear to be randomly distributed, with no cycles or trends.[24] Second, the residuals can be plotted against the predicted value of the dependent variable. There should be as many positive or negative residuals scattered evenly about a zero line, with the variance of the residuals about the same at any value of the predicted dependent variable. Finally, the residuals should be plotted on normal probability paper to test for normality.

If the graphs show that the residuals do not meet the requirements of

---

[24] A more formal test for serial correlation is provided by the Durbin-Watson statistic, which is built into many library regression computer programs. (J. Durbin, and G. J. Watson, "Testing for Serial Correlation in Least-Squares Regression," Parts I and II, *Biometrica,* 1950 and 1951.)

least squares, the data must be transformed. If serial correlation of the residuals is a problem, transformation of the variables may help. A commonly used method is to compute first differences, in which the observation from period $t, t-1, t-2, t-3$, etc., are replaced with $t-(t-1)$, $(t-1)-(t-2)$, $(t-2)-(t-3)$, and so forth. With first difference data, one is regressing the change in cost on the change in output, etc., a procedure which in many instances may be descriptively superior to other methods of stating the data. However, the residuals from first difference data also must be subjected to serial correlation tests, since taking first differences often results in negative serial correlations.[25]

Where non-constant variance of the residuals is a problem, the residuals may increase proportionally to the predicted dependent variables. In this event transformation of the dependent variable to logarithms will be effective in achieving constant variance. If the residuals increase more than proportionately, the square root of the dependent variable may be a better transformation.

An Illustration

Assume that a firm manufactures a widget and several other products, in which the services of several departments are used. Analysis of the costs of the assembly department will provide us with an illustration. In this department, widgets and another product, digits, are produced. The widgets are assembled in batches while the larger digits are assembled singly. Weekly observations on cost and output are taken and punched on cards. A graph is prepared, from which it appears that a linear relationship is present. Further, the cost of producing widgets is not believed to be a function of the production of digits or other explanatory variables. Therefore, the following regression is computed:

(7)
$$\hat{C} = 110.3 + 8.21N - 7.83B + 12.32D + 235S + 523W - 136A$$
$$(40.8) \quad (.53) \quad (1.69) \quad (2.10) \quad (100) \quad (204) \quad (154)$$

where

$\hat{C}$ = expected cost
N = number of widgets
B = average number of widgets in a batch
D = number of digits

---

[25] If there are random measurement errors in the data, observations from period $t-1$ might be increased by a positive error. Then $t-(t-1)$ will be lower and $(t-1)-(t-2)$ will be higher than if the error were not present. Consequently, $t-(t-1)$ and $(t-1)-(t-2)$ will be negatively serially correlated.

$S =$ summer dummy variable, where $S = 1$ for summer, 0 for other seasons

$W =$ winter dummy variable, where $W = 1$ for winter, 0 for other seasons

$A =$ autumn dummy variable, where $A = 1$ for autumn, 0 for other seasons

$R^2 = .892$ (the coefficient of multiple determination)

Standard error of estimate $= 420.83$, which is 5% of the dependent variable, cost.

Number of observations $= 156$.

The numbers in parentheses beneath the coefficients are the standard errors of the coefficients. These results may be used for such purposes as price and output decisions, analysis of efficiency, and capital budgeting.

For price and output decisions, we would want to estimate the average marginal cost expected if an additional widget is produced. From the regression we see that the estimated average marginal cost, $\partial C/\partial N$ is 8.21, with the other factors affecting costs accounted for. The standard error of the coefficient, .53, allows us to assess a probability of .67 that the "true" marginal cost is between 7.68 and 8.74 $(8.21 \pm .53)$ and .95 that it is between 7.15 and 9.27 (8.21 ± 1.06).[26]

The regression also can be used for flexible budgeting and analysis of performance. For example, assume that the following production is reported for a given week:

$W = 532$
$B = 20$
$D = 321$
$S =$ summer $= 1$

Then we expect that, if this week is like an average of the experience for past weeks, total costs would be:

$100.3 + 8.21(532) - 7.83(20) + 12.32(321) + 235.3(1) = 8511.14.$

The actual costs incurred can be compared to this expected amount. Of course, we do not expect the actual amount to equal the predicted amount, if only because we could not specify all of the cost-causing variables in the regression equation. However, we can calculate the probability that the actual cost is within some range around the expected cost. This range can be computed from the standard error of estimate and a rather complicated set of relationships that reflect uncertainty about the height and tilt of the regression plane. These calculations also reflect the difference between the production reported for a given week and the means of the production

---

[26] The statements about probability are based on a Bayesian approach, with normality and diffuse prior distributions assumed.

data from which the regression was computed. The greater the difference between given output and the mean output, the less confidence we have in the prediction of the regression equation. For this example, the adjusted standard error of estimate for the values of the independent variables given is 592.61. Thus, we assess a probability of .67 that the actual costs incurred will be between 2918.53 and 9103.75 (8511.14 ± 592.61) and probability .95 that they will be between 9696.36 and 7325.92 ($8511.14 \pm 2 \cdot 592.61$). With these figures, management can decide how unusual the actual production costs are in the light of past experience.

The regression results may be useful for capital budgeting, if the company is considering replacing the present widget assembly procedure with a new machine. While the cash flow expected from using the new machine must be estimated from engineering analyses, they are compared with the cash flows that would otherwise take place if the present machines were kept. These future expected flows may be estimated by "plugging" the expected output into the regression equation and calculating the expected costs. While these estimates may be statistically unreliable for data beyond the range of those used to calculate the regression, the estimates may still be the best that can be obtained.

Conclusion

The assertion has been made throughout this paper that regression analysis is not only a valuable tool but a method made available, inexpensive and easy to use by computers. The reader may be inclined to accept all but the last point, having read through the list of technical and bookkeeping problems. Actually it is the ease of computation that the library computer programs afford which makes it necessary to stress precautions and care: it is all too easy to "crank out" numbers that seem useful but actually render the whole program, if not deceptive, worthless.

But when one considers that costs often are caused by many different factors whose effects are not obvious, one recognizes the great possibilities of regression analysis, limited as it may be. Nevertheless, it is necessary to remember that it is a tool, not a cure-all. The method must not be used in cost situations where there is not an ongoing stationary relationship between cost and the variables upon which cost depends. Where the desired conditions prevail, multiple regression can provide valuable information for solving necessary decision problems, information that can put "life" into the economic models that accountants are now embracing.

15

". . . in the large area of [operational] financial and economic decision-making . . . , the marriage of the economists' concepts and the principles on which managements appear to act . . . [seems] less [than] harmonious." Break-even analysis, which ignores the economists' theorems of cost and revenue behavior, is an example of one of the sharpest expressions of this cleavage of attitudes.

Industrial break-even charts should be brought into closer conformity to economic theory, and they should be reinterpreted to clarify their true empirical significance.

". . . a key role should be played by the cost accountant, and the advanced techniques of cost accounting should be used as the bridge between theoretical concepts and real-world analysis at this point.

"Economic analysis should now take up new lines of development, based principally on quantitative studies under the auspices of firms and industrial groups."

On the Economics
of Break-Even*

Douglas Vickers

I

The practical analysis of business financial problems appears well suited to the use of the propositions and theorems of theoretical economics. But the interplay of empirical problems and the theories designed for their explanation has not yet proceeded to very great lengths. There has, of course, been a considerable progress in theoretical analysis in this area during the last three decades. And in more recent times attempts have been made to achieve more satisfying general theories of aspects of business behavior. The

* From The Accounting Review, *Vol. XXXV, No. 3, (July, 1960)*, pp. 405–412. *Reprinted by permission of the American Accounting Association and the author.*

analysis of the criteria for investment decision in the corporate enterprise, the theory of optimum capital structure, and the relative costs of differing forms of capital financing are important instances of this progress. But in the large area of financial and economic decision-making within which the enterprise operates from day to day, the marriage of the economists' concepts and the principles on which managements appear to act has been less successful and less harmonious. The economists and the businessmen have examined similar problems with the aid of differing categories of thought. There has been too little communication of ideas between them.

The purpose of this paper is to draw attention to one of the sharpest expressions of this cleavage of attitudes, and to advance some tentative suggestions for improvements in both analysis and application. This relates to the use by business of a method of cost-volume-profit analysis, and of pricing and volume adjustments, which is referred to as break-even analysis and which, *prima facie*, ignores the economists' generalized theorems of cost and revenue behavior. Other important issues which call for a similar new attack will not be raised in this paper, but many potentially fruitful lines of development may be discovered in the literature referred to in the attached bibliographical note. Our principal conclusions in the matter of break-even analysis are threefold:

(a) The components of the break-even charts as used in industry are in need of reinterpretation to bring them more closely into line with some significant suggestions of economic theory, and, at the same time, to clarify their true empirical significance.

(b) In the new analysis and reinterpretation a key role should be played by the cost accountant, and the advanced techniques of cost accounting should be used as the bridge between theoretical concepts and real-world analysis at this point.

(c) Economic analysis should now take up new lines of development, based principally on quantitative studies under the auspices of firms and industrial groups.

In the course of the discussion, some of the traditional assumptions of economic theory which inhibit its empirical applicability will be indicated.

II

The key role of the accounting function can be highlighted by noting some recent developments within the business enterprise. The traditional role of the accountant as the recorder of costs, expenses, incomes, and profits has been broken down in many businesses into several more detailed functions. Firstly, new approaches have been made to the analysis and fragmentation of costs into such categories as fixed, semi-variable, and variable. Semi-variable costs have been separated more carefully into their fixed and variable components, and costs in general have been assigned more completely and in more detail to each of the various segments of the firm's operations. Developments in these respects have been most important for the refinement and the practical value of the break-even analysis. Details of alternative cost classifications need not be given at present, as the classifications themselves will change from one enterprise situation to another, and the basic dichotomy of fixed versus variable costs will be applied in as many different ways. One interesting refinement was suggested in this connection recently by K. J. Arkwright, writing in *The Australian Accountant*, December, 1958. He suggests the following sixfold categories: (a) unitary variable costs, which increase by one cost unit with each increase of one production unit; (b) non-unitary variable costs, which change by more or less than one cost unit with each unit change of production; (c) cost of reserve capacity necessarily incurred to cater for short-term fluctuations in the level of activity; (d) irregular independent costs which are completely irregular in amount and in frequency of occurrence, for example losses arising from inventory revaluations; (e) periodical independent costs which are periodical in occurrence but not predictable as to amount, for example additional factory heating expenses depending on the severity of the winter; (f) perfectly fixed costs, or costs of being in business and which could be eliminated only by winding up the firm. Whatever methods of classification are adopted, however, the thing of practical importance is the assignment of cost elements to the various segments of the firm's operations, and for this purpose a segment can be understood as a product, a process, or a market area, depending on the characteristics of the business.

The second development of the traditional accounting function has been the construction of revenue, production-cost, and profit budgets as a background for pricing studies. Central to this procedure is the summation of segmentized costs, that is the various cost elements assigned to segments of operations as referred to above, for purposes of balancing volume, price, and profit variations in each such segment and in the enterprise as a whole.

Thirdly, there remains the more traditional accounting function of the recording of income and outlay. Depending on the stage of development of the functions already referred to, this traditional task involves increasingly also the comparison of historic income and outlay data with the budgeted standards implicit in pricing studies. Finally, these several activities are frequently co-ordinated in the hands of a financial manager for the determination of budgeted and actual return on investment. This final economic and financial datum forms the basis of advice to the directors or owners of the business on policy changes and on expansion and new financing. To this last mentioned and co-ordinating function is frequently added the supervision of the internal cash flow of the business, the financing of short term cash requirements, and the more fundamental task of advising on the timing and techniques of long term capital financing.

The significance of this increasing sophistication of the traditional accounting function is that it points clearly to more general theorems of business behavior. Firstly, the principal focus of attention is now forward-looking and prospective, rather than concentrated on historical data alone, thus opening new applications of criteria of policy choice and action; and secondly, the bases for behavior which are thus established permit clear applications of the marginal balancing of costs and incomes. This occurs via the allocations of revenues and costs, and via the comparison of segment marginal revenues and relevant marginal costs. The kernel of these new and embryonic developments in the business firm is thus the emphasis on incremental values of revenues, costs, and profits, and on the additional returns realizable from changes in production volumes. It is in the light of these developments that the soundness, strength, and relevance of the break-even analysis will be examined.

III

The break-even chart has a long history, as indicated in the literature referred to in the bibliographical note. Throughout the 1930's, while economists were developing the theories of the firm on the assumption of curvilinear cost and revenue functions, as will be referred to briefly below, industrial consultants made large headway in an analysis of similar problems based explicitly on linearity assumptions. The break-even chart was a device of the industrialists, never at that time a tool of the economists. Perhaps the latter saw these charts, as Professor Machlup recently described them, as "nothing but glamorized multiplication tables." Joel Dean, on the other hand, has given the weight of his authority to the opinion that "break-even analysis . . . provides an important bridge between business behavior and the theory of the firm."

The typical break-even chart, as indicated in Figure 1, shows total dollar values on its vertical axis (total dollar values of revenues and expenses) and total quantities of output on its horizontal axis. Variations of the form may show on the X axis either output as a percentage of capacity, or total dollar values of sales. The last mentioned form is applicable for the analysis of the break-even situations of multi-product firms. The line OZ in Figure 1 indicates the total sales revenue derivable from varying levels of output on the assumption of a given market selling price. Variations in selling price will determine the possible slopes of this revenue line. The fixed costs of the enterprise are taken as OA, and the variable costs are described by the line OV, the angle of incidence of which depends on the established relationship of variable cost per unit of output produced. The total cost line AB (parallel to OV) represents the summation of fixed and variable costs and indicates, for example, that at output and sales of OC, total costs and total revenues will be equal at CE. OC will therefore represent the enterprise break-even

FIGURE 1

Break-even Chart

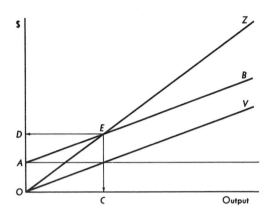

production level. If, as is useful in the case of multi-product analysis, the *X* axis is marked off in dollar values, the revenue line must take an angle of 45° and the unit selling price function is not implicit in the diagram. In other cases the unit selling price will determine the slope of the revenue line.

Before moving to consider the logical and empirical weaknesses of this popular device, a few of its principal implications can be noted. Firstly, the level of a single-product enterprise break-even point is dependent upon *both* the total revenue and the total cost characteristics. Given revenue possibilities, the level of production and sales at which an enterprise will break even will depend as much on the variable cost ratio as on the existing level of fixed charges. The level of *E* in Figure 1 will depend on the slope of *AB* as well as on the level of *A*. For the analysis of return on investment and for capital financing this has a threefold significance. Firstly, the percentage of capacity at which the firm breaks even is thus directly calculable, indicating, in other words, the level of production and sales beyond which the firm begins to penetrate what can be called its profit area, indicated by *ZEB* in Figure 1. Secondly, the relationship of forces so far envisaged determines the *rate* at which the firm penetrates its profit area after passing break-even point, or, alternatively, the rate at which losses mount up at levels of operation lower than this crucial point. Thirdly, the degree of possible fluctuations in operating incomes which are thus envisaged, depending on the severity of what can be called the firm's operational leverage, clearly contains implications for the desirable and possible structure of the firm's capitalization, thus giving rise to greater or lesser degrees of financial leverage. The manner in which this last mentioned feature affects the residual owners' or stockholders' position will not be considered at present.

In the second place, the shapes of these revenue and cost functions, while they ignore the arguments for curvi-linearity which economic theory adduces, probably do have a good deal of empirical justification, provided one important assumption is made in their use. This is the assumption that the extent of possible movements along the respective aggregate functions is limited to a fairly narrow range of output variation. In such a case, however, the break-even lines do *not* become relevant for management policy decisions throughout their entire length, but only within the distances representing possible marginal fluctuations from the level of production and sales at which the enterprise is currently operating. As soon as this is recognized, however, and as soon as it is seen that the break-even lines have empirical validity only within a narrow range of fluctuation from current output volume, the question arises whether the break-even diagram in this traditional form has any operationally significant meaning at all. For the break-even point itself, as drawn under these assumptions, has no meaning because the firm, in the normal course of events, will be endeavoring to operate *not* at break-even point, but at some volume level *above* break-even volume. The firm will, in other words normally endeavor to operate at a profit, which means, in terms of the traditional diagram as in Figure 1, somewhere in the profit area *ZEB*, or at some volume point higher than *OC*.

This does not mean that the break-even chart has no longer any potential usefulness, or that analysis of this kind can not be made to serve financial management objectives. But it does mean that a genuine reinterpretation of the break-even analysis is necessary, that a redefinition of its components and assumptions is called for, and that a recasting of the analysis should be made in terms of the assumptions which economic analysis has imported from its inspection of real-world enterprise situations. Before turning to the task of reinterpretation, it will be helpful to look briefly at the most relevant tools of theoretical economic analysis.

IV

Space does not permit an extended discussion of the economic theory of the firm. The literature referred to below, notably the works of Weintraub, Boulding, and Mrs. Robinson, set out the main points of the traditional theory. Some of the most relevant issues are summarized in Figure 2, in a form readily comparable with the break-even analysis in Figure 1.

Presented in this form, which depicts what may be called the break-even functions of the traditional theory, the total revenue and total cost functions, together with the assumption of given fixed costs, are directly analogous to the components of the business break-even analysis already examined. The analogue in the economists' tool kit is thus the *total* revenue and cost functions, and not the *average* functions in terms of which the behavior of the firm under varying competitive assumptions has frequently been analyzed.

It appears, therefore, that the functions of Figure 2, those of traditional economic theory, are formally similar to those of the break-even analysis in Figure 1. Only the shapes appear to differ. But this is not the whole of the contrast which has to be made, as will appear immediately below. A note on the shapes of the theoretical functions, however, is necessary at this point. Firstly, the total revenue function as drawn in this curvi-linear form depicts the fact that the enterprise is able to sell increasing quantities of output only at a diminishing selling price per unit, thus giving a total income which does not increase proportionally with output. This is the empirically valid assumption as to the market opportunities facing producers in conditions of what the economists refer to as imperfect or monopolistic competition. If conditions of perfect competition are assumed, on the other hand, indicating a situation in which an individual producer disposes of an undifferentiated product at a price set by the market, the total revenue curve will be linear through the origin in the manner of the total revenue function of Figure 1. This follows from the assumption that the individual producer's volume of the homogeneous commodity being supplied to the market by all producers is not sufficiently large to affect market price. The market price is therefore regarded by each producer as a parameter, or as a determinant of behavior which remains unchangeable for the length of time envisaged in his production policy decisions. Clearly, in the vast majority of non-agricultural, industrial enterprise situations this special case of perfect competition is not empirically significant. The literature cited examines fully the relevant and refined concepts of the elasticities of the functions and their sensitiveness to price and volume changes.

Equally important is the shape of the total cost function in Figure 2. The fixed cost component is taken as given in the same manner as in Figure 1. This simply indicates that a short period of time is being considered in which the capital equipment and fixed assets employed by the firm cannot be reduced or changed, and that output volume changes can be effected only by applying differing amounts of variable factors to the fixed factors already installed. In the very long run all factors are variable. In the short run some are fixed. The division between the two depends on the length of time under consideration.

The shape of the variable cost function, which again determines the shape of the total cost function, is the more significant component. This is determined by the so-called technological-economic "law of variable proportions," which states that as larger quantities of variable factors are applied to given fixed factors the resulting increase in total product, that is the marginal product, may increase for a short time but will ultimately diminish. Marginal costs per unit of output then rise rapidly. Instances of the practical reasons for this phenomenon will be familiar to industrial managers. Thus it is seen that by combining these assumptions as to the shapes of the total revenue and total cost functions, the pure theory of enterprise behavior is able to make the following definitional statements: (a) The slopes of the total cost and total revenue functions indicate respectively the marginal cost of production at any given output level, and the marginal revenue derivable from any given level of sales. (b) The equilibrium condition of the firm, that is the condition under which profits will be maximized, is that marginal cost should be equal to marginal revenue, which is the same as saying that the slopes of the total cost and revenue functions in Figure 2 should be equal. This condition is satisfied at some point such as output volume *OC*, at which the profit maximization is indicated by the maximum vertical distance between the cost and revenue functions. (c) The enterprise confronts, therefore, not one break-even point but two, indicated on Figure 2 at points *A* and *B*. Point *A* is analogous to the break-even point in Figure 1, and point *B* derives from the technological-economic laws of diminishing marginal productivity on the cost side and diminishing elasticity of demand on the revenue side.

Immediately, therefore, the economic theory goes one step further than the traditional break-even analysis, in specifying not only a *break-even* condition, but also an *equilibrium* condition. It specifies, in other words, the position *within* the profit area at which the firm should endeavor to operate. Break-even analysis, under its traditional assumptions of linearity, is able to say only that the break-even point should be passed, and it implies, what is logically and empirically untenable, that the profit area will keep on widening as production volume expands.

Can we say, then, that the cost accountants and financial managers should simply endeavor to redraw the break-even functions in such curvi-linear forms as the theory suggests, and that empirically relevant behavior lines will result, suitable to guide the management in financial decisions? It may not, unfortunately, be very meaningful to assume such a simple solution, or such a qualitative identity between the aggregate functions of theory and the empirically relevant cost and revenue curves. The curves of the theory, it is important to note, are severely static in form. They show a series of possible equilibrium positions based on the assumption of successively different, but *stable*, output rates, and they postulate smooth, continuous and *reversible* movements between alternative output positions. The curves, in other words, admit of analytical manipulations in describing comparative static

FIGURE 2

Enterprise Profit Maximization

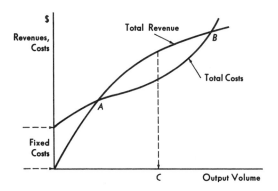

situations, and the shapes of the curves are in no sense envisaged as being alterable by the fact or degree of change.

If it is supposed that the break-even chart and the diagrams of theory *do* contain the same static assumptions, then clearly any number of alternative competitive assumptions and hypotheses can be examined and developed on the respective diagrams, for they then become in effect the very same thing. In such a case, however, we have stepped over from the field of hypothesizing about the conditions and behavior of industrial enterprises to imagining that we are actually *describing* enterprise situations. It is this gratuitous leap from hypothesis to imagined description that has invalidated much of the argument in this area.

V

Two important questions therefore arise at this point. Firstly, will the break-even lines, as applied to the analysis of practical problems, necessarily assume a linear form? And secondly, will a movement along the cost and revenue functions toward higher output levels be necessarily reversible? Logical and empirical reasons suggest that the developments envisaged would involve irreversible movements along *non-linear* functions, and it is in the clarification of these probabilities that the cost accountants and the economists can most fruitfully look for common ground.

Consider the aggregate revenue function first. Here the empirically valid economic assumption can be adduced that the elasticity of demand will diminish as producers lower price in order to increase sales, and that a curvi-linear total revenue function will result. But there exist, probably, ranges of output in which producers can sell varying amounts without any price change, and the curvi-linear total revenue function can in such a case be looked upon as made up of a series of short linear sections, the slope of each of which indicates a certain market selling price. The actual revenue function most significant for business policy decisions might then be regarded as the locus of the mid-points of such a succession of short linear sections, the revenue curve thus describing a movement-path as output moves through varying volume ranges. This may establish an empirically probable function as a basis for business decisions, but the probability and ambiguity it contains result principally from the fact that movements along the function in any direction as volume changes may not be reversible over time if volume should return to a previous level. There is no reason to believe that a rise in price following a fall in price would necessarily move the volume of market demand back to where it was before the fall. Market structures and patterns of demand might conceivably change.

On the cost side, the economists' empirically valid assumptions should again be invoked, and the phenomenon of diminishing marginal productivity can be expected to give a curvi-linear shape to the total cost function. Here again the function may be translated from the usual static form to a dynamic form in which the cost levels and cost components change as volume changes, and in which the achievable costs may not be reversible over time as output volume fluctuates. But at this point the accountants' fragmentation of costs can be intelligently employed to separate out, and allocate to the relevant segments of the enterprise, the fixed costs and the fixed elements of semi-variable costs referable to them, and to *define* a residuum of unitary variable costs in such a way as to give once again a series of short linear total cost sections as output changes. The total cost function can then be regarded as a movement-path, or locus of linear sections, analogous to the construction of the total revenue curve. But this, of course, implies fairly minute degrees of cost fragmentation and analysis. Fortunately, this is beginning to be done and gives promise of being carried further with the aid of standardized procedures in industry. Obviously, the degree of precision and sophistication which is called for or desired must depend on the size and character of the undertaking concerned.

But there remains again the question of reversibility. On the cost side the evidence for irreversibility rests mainly in two kinds of factors: firstly, changes in efficiency in the use of variable factors (wastes, methods of use, technology, etc.) can not easily be conceived to be reversible over movements between output ranges; and secondly, there is no necessary guarantee that all fixed elements of total costs which were added as output rose will be found by management to be regulatable or dispensable as output levels move again in the opposite direction. Whether the irreversibilities in the break-even cost and revenue functions would exert favorable or unfavorable effects on the level of the break-even point, or on the rapidity of penetration of the profit area, remains an issue for testing against empirical models.

Against the background of these arguments regarding the nature, shape, and reversibility of break-even cost and revenue functions, the familiar propositions depicted in Figure 1 call for reinterpretation. The analysis of industrial volume-profit experience and planning requires a more sensitive segmentized approach. Account should be taken of changes in the levels and shapes of the operative functions over as fine a variation of output ranges, or variations of intervals of time, as is administratively possible for budget and accounting purposes. It is not sufficient to argue, as is frequently done, that the case can be met by re-drawing the break-even chart of Figure 1 as often as budget changes are made, for this avoids the more fundamental issue of the nature and shape of the aggregate functions of Figure 1, and the extent of the output over which they have any empirical relevance or applicability.

It will be clear from the foregoing analysis that the conceptions which are here advanced of workable break-even models in industry have moved a good way from the naive and static models frequently relied upon in the firm itself, and which certainly have too frequently been used by the economist to caricature industry financial operations and management. The arguments which this paper has developed, however, set a program of research and development by the cost accountant, and suggest that economists now give their attention to examining the shape and stability of aggregate revenue and cost functions over time and over output ranges, applying their resources of statistical analysis to the reconstruction of empirical micro-functions and variables.

For the financial manager in industry the lesson of the analysis is that he cannot rely with the same degree of confidence on the more naive forms of his break-even charts. But the re-interpreted and reconstructed tools which are suggested to him by the economists and cost accountants should provide a firmer foundation for relevant policy decisions. This in no sense implies that the businessman should necessarily strive for the maximization of net revenue in the sense of the earlier static models of economic theory. But the indications of incremental costs applicable to production changes between or within, output ranges, such as is suggested by the analysis, should afford management clearer guidance as to the directions in which net incremental additions to income lie.

Bibliographical Note

The indispensable starting point for further theoretico-empirical work in this area is P. J. D. Wiles' *Price, Cost and Output* (Oxford, Blackwell, 1956). For the economic theory consult Sidney Weintraub, *Price Theory* (New York, Pitman, Revised edition, 1956), Joan Robinson, *The Economics of Imperfect Competition* (London, Macmillan, 1933) and Kenneth Boulding, *Economic Analysis* (New York, Harper, 3rd edition, 1955). For the development of break-even analysis in industry see Ned Chapin, "The Development of the Break-Even Chart: A Bibliographical Note" in *Journal of Business*, April 1955, and a comment on Chapin's article by Raymond Villers, *Journal of Business*, October 1955. A fairly complete exposition of break-even techniques from the industrial consultant's viewpoint appeared in Walter Rautenstrauch and Raymond Villers, *The Economics of Industrial Management* (New York, Funk and Wagnalls, 1949; 2nd Revised edition by Raymond Villers, 1957). See also the same authors' *Budgetary Control* (New York, Funk and Wagnalls, 1950.) Joel Dean's *Managerial Economics* (New York, Prentice-Hall, 1951) contains relevant sections. A critical attitude to the break-even analysis is taken by Fritz Machlup in *The Economics of Sellers' Competition* (Baltimore, Johns Hopkins, 1952).

Among the journal literature the following are important: Hans Brems, "A Discontinuous Cost Function," *American Economic Review*, Dec. 1952; Wilford J. Eiteman and Glenn E. Guthrie, "The Shape of the Average Cost Curve," *American Economic Review*, 1952; James S. Earley, "Recent Developments in Cost Accounting and the 'Marginal Analysis,' " *Journal of Political Economy*, June 1955; Sidney Robbins and Edward Foster, "Profit-planning and the Finance Function," *Journal of Finance*, Dec. 1957; K. J. Arkwright, "Marginal Costing: Reconciliation of Theory and Practice," *The Australian Accountant*, 1958; George Gibbs, "New Cost Accounting Concepts," *The Accounting Review*, Jan. 1958; Joel Dean, "Cost Structures of Enterprises and Break-even Charts," *American Economic Review Supplement*, May 1948.

16

This paper explores some applications of linear programming ... to breakeven analysis with special reference to ways in which accounting and mathematics might be joined to effect an extended and uniform approach to problems in financial and budgetary planning.

"... various physical (production) considerations [are joined] to the usual accounting rubrics of breakeven analyses ... the notion of a 'spread sheet' [is introduced] ... the relations between these approaches and the planning and projection of finished statements ... [are] indicated."

One of the important observations of this article is the suggestion that the linear programming algorithm can be used to generate an "opportunity cost" income statement which management can use to evaluate alternatives.

A basic knowledge of linear programming concepts is helpful to an understanding of this article.

Breakeven Budgeting and Programming to Goals*

A. Charnes, W. W. Cooper, and Y. Ijiri†

Capitalism without double-entry bookkeeping is simply inconceivable. They hold together as form and matter. And one may indeed doubt whether capitalism has procured in double-entry bookkeeping a tool which activates its forces, or whether double-entry bookkeeping has first given rise to capitalism out of its own (rational and systematic) spirit. — Werner Sombart[1]

* *From* Journal of Accounting Research, *Vol. 1, No. 1 (Spring, 1963), pp. 16–43. Reprinted by permission of the editor.*

† This paper was presented as part of a talk delivered to The University of Pittsburgh, Graduate School of Business, Institute in Applied Mathematics for Teachers of Business on March 9, 1962.

Part of the research underlying this paper was undertaken for the project *Temporal Planning and Management Decision under Risk and Uncertainty* at Northwestern University and part for the project *Planning and Control of Industrial Operations* at Carnegie Institute of Technology. Both projects are under contract with the U. S. Office of Naval Research. Reproduction of this paper in whole or in part is permitted for any purpose of the United States Government. Contract Nonr-1228(10), Project NR 047–021 and Contract Nonr-760(01), Project NR-047011.

[1] Werner Sombart, *Der moderne Kapitalismus* (Munchen und Leipzig: von Duncker und Humblot, 1922).

That the countries in which the science of bookkeeping made the most progress were always those in which most economic progress was being made can no doubt be explained as a mixture of cause and effect. — H. M. Robertson[2]

Introduction

This paper explores some applications of linear programming (referred to hereafter as L.P.) to breakeven analysis with special reference to ways in which accounting and mathematics might be joined to effect an extended and uniform approach to problems in financial and budgetary planning.

Accountants, economists and general students of business or finance are accustomed to the geometry and algebra of breakeven charts and, in fact, some time ago M. L. Pye showed how to effect further algebraic extensions to multiple product (mix) variations by means of simultaneous algebraic equations.[3] Because these ideas are already familiar, as is the separation of total costs into fixed and variable components,[4] there is no need to elaborate on either the general breakeven approach or the kinds of principles that apply when it is being implemented for ordinary accounting purposes.

Linear programming is relatively new, both as a branch of mathematics and as a tool for accounting. However, the mathematical techniques associated with L.P. have received widespread attention as well as some managerial applications under such names as "operations research," "management science," and the like. These, too, are now finding their way into accounting, where they have been considered as a possible alternative to the breakeven approach. Jaedicke [37], for example, has suggested that a L.P.[5] emphasis on optimizing objectives (e.g., maximum profit or minimum cost) may offer advantages over an analysis that centers on merely breaking even.

The pursuit of an optimum objective plays a prominent role in L.P. But this does not mean that *applications* are restricted to situations where optimization has been stated as an actual managerial objective. A variety of artifacts are available for use when other objectives are at issue and some of these same artifacts may be used to handle various kinds of *nonlinear*

[2] H. M. Robertson, *Aspects of the Rise of Economic Individualism* (Cambridge: University Press, 1935).

[3] See the item designated as [52] in the bibliography. See also [48].

[4] The *Encyclopaedia Britannica* credits Dionysius Lardner (1850) with being the first to make these distinctions and it also credits the ideas of profit charting and flexible budgeting to John Manger Fells (1903). W. Rautenstrach and R. Knoeppel are also mentioned as early advocates of profit-volume planning and breakeven charting. See also [64], p. 34 ff. and the references to C. A. Guilbault on pp. 59 ff. in [28].

[5] It is perhaps of interest to observe that the project graphs and PERT/PEP critical path scheduling techniques discussed in [39], can also be represented in terms of linear programming network models. This means, as will be shown later in this paper, that these new approaches to scheduling and control are immediately amenable to characterizations in terms of double entry principles. See, e.g., [8]. See also Chapter XVII in [9] for remarks on general relations between the Kirchhoff laws for networks and double-entry analyses and record keeping.

problems via mathematical models that are suitably arranged for applying any of the standard *linear* programming solution methods.[6]

These topics will be illustrated, at least in a simple way, by means of what is called a "goal programming model" in L.P. Comment will be interjected at various points to suggest how most of the objectives that have been discussed in the breakeven literature[7] can be achieved via suitable variations on this approach.

Linear programming methods have already demonstrated an ability to deal with very large management problems where many (hundreds and more) interacting variables have been involved. Furthermore, electronic computer codes have been prepared and are readily available whenever recourse to these kinds of facilities becomes necessary. It may therefore be desirable to show that L.P. can offer something more than a uniform approach to problems like mix-volume interactions, breakeven analyses, profit maximization and cost minimization. For this reason, various extensions will be essayed in the examples which are treated in this paper. First, the development will commence by joining various physical (production) considerations to the usual accounting rubrics of breakeven analyses. Second, extensions into the balance sheet accounts will be effected via the notion of a "spread sheet" or "articulation statement."[8] Finally, the relations between these approaches and the planning and projection of financial statements will be indicated.

There are still other possible developments and extensions that could be made by means of any contacts that can be established between accounting and L.P. and, only for illustration, we mention topics like the following, which have been treated by means of L.P.:[9] (1) determining transfer prices when multiple interdepartmental interactions should be taken into account; (2) obtaining statistical estimates that conform to prescribed organization arrangements and managerial policies; and (3) effecting optimum consolidations (e.g., on spread sheets) for the management decisions that are to be arranged.[10] Also of interest are the recent research reports pointed towards uses of L.P.[11] in (a) capital budgeting where complex congeries of interrelated investment decisions are involved and (b) costing or otherwise evaluating funds by reference to their alternative "best" uses for financing capital or operating expenditures, credit extensions to customers, borrowing and repayment, etc.

This very brief and incomplete summary (supplemented by the bibliography) is intended only to supply background material and a general

[6] *Vide*, e.g., [9].
[7] See the bibliography cited at the end of this article.
[8] *Vide*, E. L. Kohler [40] p. 389 for a definition and an accounting illustration of a spread sheet. See also Mattessich [47] and Richards [55].
[9] See [9], Chapters IX and X and Appendix E. See also [72].
[10] Cf. [51]. Mathematical approaches to consolidation and aggregation in other contexts may be found in [56] and [57] and [45.2].
[11] In [71] and [10].

perspective from which to judge the detailed developments that will now be undertaken.

A Breakeven Model with Production Constraints

In order to avoid recourse to abstract mathematical symbols, we shall follow the precedent of Jaedicke's article[12] and restrict the immediate presentation to a very simple numerical example that is easily graphed for further study and elucidation. Thus, let x_1 and x_2 represent the amounts of two different products that can be offered for sale under the labels "Product 1" and "Product 2," respectively. Suppose that the per unit contribution that each makes to profit and overhead is: c_1 = \$1.00 for Product 1, and c_2 = \$.50 for Product 2. Then, if the fixed cost per period is \$2.50, the following expression can be solved for the values of x_1 and x_2 that achieve the required breakeven point:

(1) $$\$1x_1 + \$\tfrac{1}{2}x_2 = \$2.5.$$

Each possible pair which satisfies this expression, like $x_1 = 2$, $x_2 = 1$ or $x_1 = 1$, $x_2 = 3$, represents a different physical product mix that will contribute \$2.50 over the variable cost of production and hence achieve the indicated breakeven level.

The equation represented in (1) is only one of several possible approaches to a breakeven analysis and, of course, a variety of refinements can be employed.[13] Since these are well known, a somewhat different course will be elected here. In particular, we shall utilize the data of Table 1 to show how certain "physical facts" of production may be studied in the context of a breakeven analysis.

The data of Table 1 are intended to have the following meanings. Each unit of Product 1 is supposed to require processing on two different machines: On Machine A this product requires 3 hours of processing time per unit and, on Machine B, 5 hours per unit. A completed unit of Product 2, on the other hand, can be secured from 2 hours of processing on Machine A. No processing is required (for this product) on Machine B and so a zero processing time (per unit) is entered in the cell where the Machine B row and the Product 2 column intersect.[14] Finally, the capacities available for each machine are shown in the right-hand column and positioned in the row where the relevant machine is designated. These are the rated capacities, of

---

[12] [37].

[13] See, for instance, the profit-graph breakeven chart in Kohler, [40] *op. cit.*, p. 65. For a discussion of possible managerial uses see Eastwood [22].

[14] Alternatively, this cell may be left blank, if desired, and this is the convention utilized in the immediately following mathematical expressions. E.g., the variable x_2 is omitted from the second expression in (2). See Charnes and Cooper, [9], Ch. I for further discussion of this and related examples.

course, stated in the hours that will be available during the period for which a breakeven analysis is being considered.

TABLE 1

Machine Processing Times and Capacities

	Machine processing times (hrs./unit)		Available machine capacities (hours)
	Product 1	*Product 2*	
Machine A.......	3	2	12
Machine B.......	5	0	10

All of these operating "facts" are now given expression in the following inequalities:

$$
\begin{aligned}
3x_1 + 2x_2 &\leq 12 \\
5x_1 &\leq 10,
\end{aligned}
$$
(2)

which are intended to mean that any values (amounts of Product 1 and Product 2) can be assigned to x_1 and x_2, *provided* that such an assignment does not yield a number to the left of the "$\leq$" which exceeds the number positioned immediately to its right. The open side of the inequality symbol, "$\leq$," indicates the side that is allowed to be larger.

The meaning of these "$\leq$" symbols can be further elucidated in another connection. It is not meaningful in this context to assign negative quantities to either x_1 or x_2. This restriction to non-negative values is given mathematical form by means of the expressions $x_1 \geq 0$, $x_2 \geq 0$ or, more briefly, $x_1, x_2 \geq 0$. The latter is the so-called "non-negativity condition" of L.P. and its meaning is "neither x_1 nor x_2 can be less than zero." (I.e., $x_1 > 0$ or $x_1 = 0$ but never $x_1 < 0$, and the same applies for the numerical values that can be assigned to x_2.)

In preparation for the following sections, we now rewrite the expression (2) in the following equivalent set of equations:

$$
\begin{aligned}
3x_1 + 2x_2 + y_1 &= 12 \\
5x_1 + y_2 &= 10 \\
x_1, x_2, y_1, y_2 &\geq 0.
\end{aligned}
$$
(3)

In this form the variables y_1 and y_2 are technically referred to as "slack" — e.g., as distinguished from x_1 and x_2 which are referred to as "structural variables." Observe that the equivalence between (3) and (2) is achieved by constraining the slack variables y_1 and y_2 (along with the structural variables x_1 and x_2) to non-negative values only. Thus, a $y_1 > 0$ — i.e., a positive value for y_1 — corresponds to idle time programmed for Machine A and a $y_2 > 0$ represents idle time on Machine B. On the other hand, $y_2 = 0$

means no idle time on Machine B and similarly, $y_1 = 0$ means no idle time is being programmed on Machine A.

Goal Programming

A combination of all of the preceding constraints can now be arranged as follows:

$$
\begin{aligned}
3x_1 + 2x_2 + y_1 \quad\quad\quad &= 12 \\
5x_1 \quad\quad\quad + y_2 &= 10 \\
x_1 + \tfrac{1}{2}x_2 \quad\quad\quad &= 2.5 \\
x_1, x_2, y_1, y_2 &\geq 0
\end{aligned}
$$

(4)

and any set of non-negative values that simultaneously satisfies all of these relations will provide (i) a breakeven volume and mix (cf. the third constraint) and (ii) a feasible machine load (cf. the first two constraints). Among the L.P. (optimization) approaches that can be used on such a problem is one called "goal programming." This approach is distinguished from others by virtue of the fact that at least one of the constraints is incorporated in the functional in such a manner that it becomes part of the objective (for maximization or minimization). This approach can also be employed to handle various kinds of nonlinearities and so it is the one that we shall elect.

In preparation for subsequent discussion, we therefore erect the following goal programming model for breakeven analysis:

$$\text{minimize } y_3^- + y_3^+$$

subject to:

$$
\begin{aligned}
3x_1 + 2x_2 + y_1 \quad\quad\quad\quad\quad\quad &= 12 \\
5x_1 \quad\quad\quad + y_2 \quad\quad\quad\quad &= 10 \\
x_1 + \tfrac{1}{2}x_2 \quad\quad\quad + y_3^- - y_3^+ &= 2.5 \\
x_1, x_2, y_1, y_2, y_3^-, y_3^+ &\geq 0.
\end{aligned}
$$

(5)

That is, the objective is to secure values for the variables which will (a) satisfy all of the constraints, including non-negativity, to which the variables have been subjected, and (b) make the sum $y_3^- + y_3^+$ a minimum.

To see what this involves, the function[15]

(6.1) $$f(y_3^-, y_3^+) = y_3^- + y_3^+$$

and the third constraint — *viz.*,[16]

---

[15] The terms "function" and "functional" are used interchangeably throughout this article to mean that the function, "*f*," assumes a unique value (number) as soon as values for both of the variables y_3^+ and y_3^- are assigned. Thus, in this case the function "*f*" is $y_3^+ + y_3^-$.

[16] This is, of course, only a rewriting of the condition

$$x_1 + \tfrac{1}{2}x_2 + y_3^- - y_3^+ = 2.5.$$

(6.2) $$y_3^- - y_3^+ = 2.5 - x_1 - \tfrac{1}{2}x_2$$

are now sequestered for further examination. It is to be emphasized, again, that only non-negative values can be assigned to the variables. Thus, in any permissible case $y_3^- + y_3^+ \geq 0$ so that the function, $f(y_3^+, y_3^-)$, can never be negative. In fact, if the breakeven level can be achieved then the minimization process will drive the function to $y_3^- + y_3^+ = 0$ and neither a positive nor a negative deviation will occur for (6.2).

This last statement will now, perhaps, help to explain the plus and minus symbols that were assigned as distinguishing superscripts for both y_3 variables. If the values assigned to x_1 and x_2 give $x_1 + \tfrac{1}{2}x_2 > 2.5$, then the mathematical procedures (if they are to be meaningful) should arrange to give $y_3^- = 0$ and $-y_3^+ = 2.5 - x_1 - \tfrac{1}{2}x_2 < 0$. In short, it is intended that $y_3^+ > 0$ should represent a positive deviation above the breakeven level. Alternatively, if $x_1 + \tfrac{1}{2}x_2 < 2.5$ occurs, then the mathematics should arrange $y_3^+ = 0$ and $y_3^- = 2.5 - x_1 - \tfrac{1}{2}x_2 > 0$ so that a negative deviation (below the breakeven level) is thereby indicated. Since it is not meaningful to admit both a negative and a positive deviation simultaneously, the constraint (6.2) must never be allowed to utilize any nonzero *pairs* for the two variables in $y_3^- - y_3^+$, which are also available, at least in principle, when $2.5 - x_1 - \tfrac{1}{2}x_2 \neq 0$ occurs.[17]

A formal mathematical statement of the condition that at least one of y_3^+ and y_3^- must be zero is rendered by the quadratic (nonlinear) constraint:

(6.3) $$y_3^+ \times y_3^- = 0,$$

which can only be satisfied when at least one of y_3^+ and y_3^- is equal to zero. The standard solution procedures of L.P., on the other hand, *always* arrange to have at least one of the pair y_3^+ and y_3^- equal to zero. Hence these solution procedures may be applied to the model (5) with assurance that the nonlinear (quadratic) constraint (6.3) will also be satisfied. Moreover, and equally important, the optimizations are automatically arranged to ensure that $y_3^- > 0$ will occur only if this provides the least possible deviation from the supposed \$2.50 breakeven level whereas if the constraints of (5) and (6.3), together, jointly admit of a still smaller deviation from the other side then $y_3^- = 0$ and $y_3^+ > 0$ will occur. In this manner the constraint (6.2) is incorporated in the functional and, without any ambiguity whatsoever, the value of the function (6.1) provides a measure of the total dollar deviation by means of the expression $y_3^- + y_3^+ \geq 0$.

Alternate Optima and Product Mix Variations

The constraints of (5) admit of a solution with $y_3^+ + y_3^- = 0$ which is certainly minimal. Hence, the methods of L.P. will bring about such a solution in this case. These methods are also extended to other purposes as well.

---

[17] The symbol "$\neq$" means "not equal to."

For instance, they can be used to locate other programs (called alternate. optima) which also minimize (6.1) with different values assigned to x_1, x_2, y_1 and y_2.

The data of this example have been arranged to bring this "alternate optima" aspect to the fore in order to show how product mix possibilities can be studied in a L.P. approach to breakeven analysis. Two such alternate optima, called "basic solutions," are, in fact, summarized in Table 2 by omitting all of the variables that have been assigned a value of zero.[18]

One reason for referring to these as "basic solutions" may be seen as follows. These two solutions are not the only ones that yield a product mix that gives $y_3^- + y_3^+ = 0$. But every product mix which will achieve the $2.50 breakeven level can be derived from suitable percentage combinations[19] of these two basic solutions. In particular, if "solution 1" is labelled "A" and "solution 2" is labelled "B" and if p is a fraction between zero and one then

$$(7) \qquad pA + (1 - p)B$$

is also an optimum for *any* $0 \le p \le 1$.

Chart 1 provides a graphic aid to understanding what is involved in the mathematical model (5) and the solutions of Table 2 and expression (7). Every point in the shaded region of Chart 1 assigns coordinate values to x_1 and x_2 which can be associated with y values that, together, satisfy all constraints in (5). Points above the line AB have values $y_3^+ > 0$ and points below this same line have values $y_3^- > 0$. Only points on the line from A to B give $y_3^- + y_3^+ = 0$. The first basic solution, with $x_2 = 5$, is shown at A and the second basic solution is shown at B (with $x_1 = 2, x_2 = 1$). Every point on the line segment between A and B can be obtained by choosing a suitable p. For instance, choosing $p = \frac{1}{4}$ gives $x_1 = 1\frac{1}{2}, x_2 = 2$, the coordinates at C, as can be seen by using the x_1 and x_2 values from solutions 1 and 2 to obtain:[20]

$$(8) \qquad \begin{aligned} x_1 &= \tfrac{1}{4} \times 0 + \tfrac{3}{4} \times 2 = 1\tfrac{1}{2} \\ x_2 &= \tfrac{1}{4} \times 5 + \tfrac{3}{4} \times 1 = 2 \end{aligned}$$

This is an alternate (derived)[21] breakeven program and every other possible breakeven program can also be derived from the basic solutions of Table 2 by simply choosing different $0 \le p \le 1$ and applying them to (7) in a wholly analogous manner. Thus, as this simple example shows, all possible product mix possibilities can be studied.

[18] E.g., column 1 of Table 2 shows the solution $x_1 = 0, x_2 = 5, y_1 = 2, y_2 = 10$ with, of course, $y_3^- + y_3^+ = 0$ so that no units of Product 1 and 5 units of Product 2 achieve the indicated breakeven level by assigning 2 hours of idle time on Machine A and 10 hours of idle time (all available capacity) on Machine B.

[19] Also called "convex combinations." *Vide* [9].

[20] The fraction $p = \frac{1}{4}$ (hence $1 - p = \frac{3}{4}$) is chosen to help in distinguishing between the two programs. Note that $p = \frac{1}{4}$ multiplies $x_1 = 0$ from solution 1 and $(1 - p) = \frac{3}{4}$ multiplies $x_1 = 2$ from solution 2. Similar remarks apply to the derivation of the x_2 coordinate for C from the previous x_2 values in A and B, respectively.

[21] I.e., it is derived from the preceding basic solutions at A and B.

CHART 1

Breakeven Points and Profit Possibilities

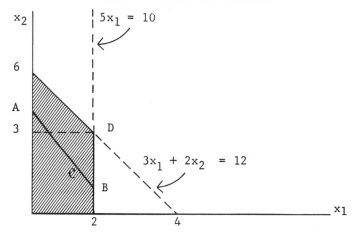

Further Extensions

It is possible, almost without pause, to extend the already achieved solution possibilities in order to explore still other topics that a breakeven analysis might suggest. Suppose, for instance, that it is desired to proceed from a breakeven analysis to a study of maximum profit possibilities. Simplifying the model (5) and reorienting the objective gives another (closely related) model which appears as follows:

$$\text{maximize } y_3^+$$

subject to:

(9)
$$
\begin{aligned}
3x_1 + 2x_2 + y_1 \quad\quad\quad &= 12 \\
5x_1 \quad\quad\quad + y_2 \quad\quad &= 10 \\
x_1 + \tfrac{1}{2}x_2 \quad\quad\quad - y_3^+ &= 2.5 \\
x_1, x_2, y_1, y_2, y_3^+ &\geq 0
\end{aligned}
$$

and the solution occurs, at point D, with $x_1 = 2$, $x_2 = 3$ so that $y_3^+ = \$1$ represents the maximum contribution (to profit) over and above the fixed costs of \$2.50. If, on the other hand, the fixed costs were at a still higher level such as, say \$4.50, then the model

$$\text{minimize } y_3^-$$

subject to:

(10)
$$
\begin{aligned}
3x_1 + 2x_2 + y_1 \quad\quad\quad &= 12 \\
5x_1 \quad\quad\quad + y_2 \quad\quad &= 10 \\
x_1 + \tfrac{1}{2}x_2 \quad\quad\quad + y_3^- &= 4.5 \\
x_1, x_2, y_1, y_2, y_3^- &\geq 0
\end{aligned}
$$

TABLE 2

Alternate Optima

Basic Solutions	
A *Solution 1*	*B* *Solution 2*
$x_2 = 5$	$x_1 = 2$
$y_1 = 2$	$x_2 = 1$
$y_2 = 10$	$y_1 = 4$

would also give $x_1 = 2$, $x_2 = 3$ while the $y_3^- = \$1$ would be a measure of the closest possibility that the constraints admit for covering all of the fixed costs — *viz.*, $y_3^- = \$4.50 - \$1x_1 - \$\frac{1}{2}x_2 = \$1.00$ means that $x_1 = 2$, $x_2 = 3$, falls \$1.00 short of covering all fixed costs. But $y_3^- = \$1.00$ is minimal. Hence there is no other product mix which will do better (i.e., come closer) to covering all fixed costs.

The models (9) and (10) are only some of the possible variants of (5). Other variants will not be covered here, however, so that we may thereby gain space to examine other uses of L.P. To conclude this section we therefore only mention the following kinds of possibilities: First, when data are in doubt — e.g., on costs, prices, machine times, etc. — there are a variety of L.P. procedures[22] that can be brought into play in order to assess the program consequences that might attend possible errors in the data. Second, additional nonlinearities may also be dealt with by L.P. methods and among these may be numbered the kinds of accounting situations that are encountered when semi-fixed or semi-variable costs occur or when volume discounts and other arrangements enter in a way that can affect the profit-and-overhead contributions that are to be accommodated with different volumes and mixes.

Spread Sheet Analyses

An entrance into the next extension may be effected by means of the simplified spread sheet example exhibited in Table 3. The transactions are recorded as they have occurred for a company that is now being organized to lease the machine facilities portrayed in Table 1 at a fixed rental of \$2.50 per period. Preparatory to completing the leasing arrangements, a balance-sheet extension of the preceding breakeven analyses is desired.

In the spread sheet approach, every relevant account is assigned two positions, a row position and a column position. (1) It is positioned in the stub (row) to reflect the debits for any transaction where this account applies and (2) it is positioned in a column (caption) to reflect the credits for any transaction where this account applies.

---

[22] This includes the so-called parameterization procedures that are available on many of the extant computer codes.

TABLE 3

Spread Sheet

Debits \ Credits	C = Cash	G = Goods	R = Raw Materials	E = Net Worth	S = Sales	Totals
C = Cash				60		60
G = Goods	10					10
R = Raw Materials	10					10
E = Net Worth	10					10
S = Sales						0
Totals	30	0	0	60	0	90

Balance Sheet
End of Period One

Cash	$30	Net Worth	$50
Goods	10		
Materials	10		
Total	$50	Total	$50

With every relevant account being thus represented, the way a spread sheet gives effect to the "double-entry principle" is illustrated by the specimen transactions of Table 3.[23] The owners have opened the books of account by investing $60 in cash, a transaction which is reflected by means of the entry in row 1, which debits Cash in this amount and, simultaneously, credits Net Worth. Next, $10 is expended to acquire "Goods" which will become "Product 1" when suitably processed on Machines A and B. This number is the first entry in column 1 showing simultaneously a credit to Cash (the column caption) and a debit to Goods (the stub designation). An analogous entry is made for "Raw Materials," the raw material which

[23] The spread sheet approach (and other related working paper forms) suggests that it is not wholly adequate to assert that "A necessary prerequisite [of double entry] is that all transactions be recorded twice, once on the debit and once on the credit side." See deRoover [44.3], p. 114. In the early periods of accounting development, however, it seems to have been customary to emphasize this. See, e.g., [11], p. 107, where Paciolo is translated to say: "All entries posted in the book must be double; that is, if you make one creditor you must make one debtor."

Machine A can process into "Product 2." Finally, a withdrawal by the owners is recorded by the $10 figure that appears in the Cash column and the Net Worth row.

No sales have been undertaken pending completion of the leasing arrangements for the machines of Table 1. Hence the cells in the S (= Sales) row and column remain vacant and the operating statement is void (or vacuous). A balance sheet can be readily prepared from these spread sheet data, however, and the one shown at the bottom of Table 3 is obtained by reference to the following considerations. Totaling any row gives the sum of all debits to the corresponding account. The total of all credits to this same account is secured by footing the appropriate column. The difference is then the net debit or credit balance in this account. For instance, row 1 yields a total of $60 in debits to Cash and column 1 yields a credit total of $30 to this same account. The net is a debit balance of $30 = $60 − $30 as shown by the figure reported for the Cash account in the balance sheet.

Evidently the other entries for the balance sheet, as exhibited, can be obtained in a precisely analogous manner. Indeed by further elaborations,[24] a spread sheet approach can be used to synthesize profit-and-loss statements, cost analyses and allocations, and other accounting reports, as wanted.[25] Although accruals and other non-cash items (credit sales and purchases) can also be accommodated in a spread sheet, this topic will not be pursued here. All transactions will be assumed to occur on a cash basis and no other expenses besides the lease rental and material costs will be incurred.[26]

Proceeding on these assumptions, the constraints for a simple instance of a spread-sheet-breakeven analysis will be elaborated, in steps, from the preceding examples. First the machine times and capacities are reproduced from (3) above:

$$(11.1) \qquad \begin{aligned} 12 &= 3x_1 + 2x_2 + y_1 \\ 10 &= 5x_1 \qquad\qquad + y_2. \end{aligned}$$

Then it is assumed that Product 1, when processed, sells for $2.50 = $5/2 per unit while Product 2 brings in $1.75 = $7/4 per unit. Because all transactions are in cash, this gives

$$(11.2) \qquad 0 = -\frac{5}{2} x_1 - \frac{7}{4} x_2 + x_{CS}$$

where x_{CS} means that the amount, x, is to be debited to C = Cash and credited to S = Sales.

---

[24] *Vide*, e.g., Kohler [40] or Richards [55] and Mattessich [46]. For a discussion of the closely related input-output approach to the national accounts see Chapter III in [9].

[25] Cf. Ijiri [35].

[26] A detailed treatment of payables, receivables, labor costs, etc. — for a firm operating in the (complex) Carnegie Tech Management Game business environment — may be found in the combined L.P. spread sheet approach used in [36].

The name-designating symbols which will be employed as subscripts are shown in the sideheadings and captions of Table 3. In every case the first letter of the subscript pair will refer to the debit entry and the second letter to the credit entry. Thus, if the unit purchase price of Goods = G is $\$1.50 = \$3/2$ and if the unit purchase price of Raw Materials = R is $\$1.25 = \$5/4$, then any transfer from inventory to Sales (= Profit and Loss) account gives

(11.3)
$$0 = \frac{3}{2} x_1 \quad - x_{SG}$$
$$0 = \quad \frac{5}{4} x_2 \quad - x_{SR}.$$

The immediate objective is to break even on all accounts so that we now impose the conditions

(11.4)
$$0 = x_{SG} \quad - x_{GC}$$
$$0 = \quad x_{SR} \quad - x_{RC}$$

to reflect the restoration to the Goods and Raw Materials inventories by means of cash purchases.[27]

Because these "breakeven conditions" give $x_{SG} = x_{GC}$ and $x_{SR} = x_{RC}$, we can next write

(11.5)
$$0 = -x_{CS} + x_{GC} + x_{RC} + x_{SE}$$

to indicate the residual entry (positive or negative)[28] which clears the net effects of these sales into $E =$ Net Worth account. Then we impose the further breakeven condition

(11.6)
$$0 = -x_{SE} + x_{EC}$$

which is to be interpreted together with

(11.7)
$$-\frac{5}{2} = -x_{EC}$$

wherein x_{EC} is the amount ($\$5/2$) to be debited to Net Worth and credited to Cash for the fixed rental of equipment.

A reason for the indicated choice of negative and positive signs on these variables will shortly be indicated. First, however, we collect all of the above constraints together:

[27] It is assumed that purchase prices do not change, but any such variations can be accommodated by rather obvious adjustments when this is not the case.

[28] That is, we do not restrict x_{SE} to non-negative values so that $x_{SE} > 0$ means a debit to Sales and a credit to Net Worth while $x_{SE} < 0$ means a credit to Sales (= Profit or Loss for period) and a debit to Net Worth. For further discussion, and other ways of handling this, see Chapter XVII in [9].

$$
(12) \quad
\begin{aligned}
12 &= 3x_1 + 2x_2 + y_1 \\
10 &= 5x_1 \qquad\qquad + y_2 \\
0 &= -\tfrac{5}{2}x_1 - \tfrac{7}{4}x_2 \qquad\quad + x_{CS} \\
0 &= \tfrac{3}{2}x_1 \qquad\qquad\qquad - x_{SG} \\
0 &= \qquad\quad \tfrac{5}{4}x_2 \qquad\qquad - x_{SR} \\
0 &= \qquad\qquad\qquad x_{SG} \qquad - x_{GC} \\
0 &= \qquad\qquad\qquad x_{SR} \qquad - x_{RC} \\
0 &= \qquad\quad - x_{CS} \qquad + x_{GC} + x_{RC} + x_{SE} \\
0 &= \qquad\qquad\qquad\qquad\qquad - x_{SE} + x_{EC} \\
-\tfrac{5}{2} &= \qquad\qquad\qquad\qquad\qquad - x_{EC}
\end{aligned}
$$

and then we impose the condition that all variables be restricted to non-negative values with the sole exception of x_{SE}.[29] Next we observe that the spread sheet variables always occur in exactly two constraints where, alternately, $+1$ or -1 appear as the coefficients of these variables. This means that the model is one of so-called incidence (or network) type[30] for which particularly efficient solution procedures can be, or have been, developed.[31]

The present article is not concerned with technical mathematical developments, and so we simply utilize these expressions in (12) to write down the network[32] shown in Chart 2. In order to interpret this network the following conventions should be accorded to its elements. Each account is assigned to a node. The links connecting these nodes represent routes for the possible transaction flows, when submitted to an accounting analysis, and the arrowheads are oriented in all cases towards the debit entry. The only exception is the link associated with x_{SE}, which has no arrowhead, because the flow can, in this case, be in either direction. Finally, the value $-$ \$2.50 points outward from the Net Worth $= E$ node to show that this amount will flow out of the system (for rentals) during the period.

We can now close this section by noting that this network could be used as a guide for accounting simulation studies on either an analogue or digital computer. Alternatively a driving function, either for optimization or (controlled) simulation purposes can be achieved by stating an appropriate objective and function which would bring the model (12) into L.P. form.

[29] See preceding footnote. If optimization were the objective we could maximize x_{SE}, either gross or net of taxes, dividends, etc., and alter $-5/2 = -x_{EC}$ to $-5/2 \geq -x_{EC}$ and proceed to adjust the model so that it would also accommodate such other constraints (e.g., on working capital) as might be required. This means that the condition $x_{SE} \geq 0$ would be superfluous since the objective would then be to make it as large as possible and, *a fortiori*, positive whenever the constraints admit such a possibility. See [29] for such an application.

[30] See remarks in footnote,[5] *supra*. See also [45.1] for still another network characterization of double-entry accounting as reached from a different kind of mathematics.

[31] See the discussion of dyadic models and subdual methods in Chapter XV of [9]. For an illustration of the way subdual algorithms (solution methods) can be generated see the example of critical path scheduling in [8].

[32] More precisely this is only part of a total network which would have to be completed by showing an input as well as an output node.

CHART 2

Graph for an Accounting Network

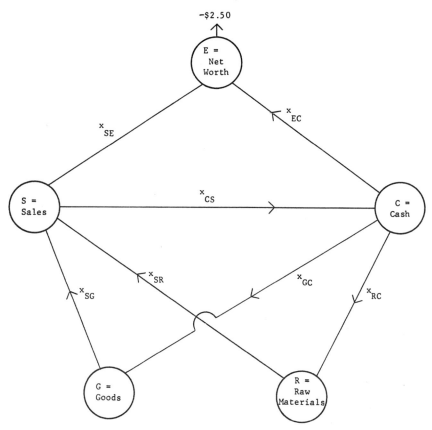

Preemptive Priorities and Breakeven Balance Sheets

Rather than repeating the previous analysis in order to extend it to the constraint system (12), we shall use a slight alteration in tactics and change the outflow at node E to $4.50 = $9/2$. The maximum net cash realization that this system will admit is still only $3.50. Cf. (12). Hence it is no longer possible to bring all accounts back up to their previous level in order, thereby, to break even on every balance sheet account.

Choices must be made under such circumstances and so it might seem natural to turn to some set of numerical weights that could reflect the relative preferences (degree of priority) which a management might want to accord to the various account balances that it would like to see maintained. This could be done whenever such a management is willing to supply the indicated weights. It is conceivable, however, that the indicated weights might not be forthcoming and, indeed, it is even conceivable that no set of numerical values will accurately reflect the wishes of some managements.

Simply to illustrate the latter point, we will replace (11.7) by

$$-\frac{9}{2} = -x_{EC}$$ (13.1)

so that there can be no solution (set of x and y values) which can simultaneously satisfy all of the other constraints, along with (13.1) — i.e., no solution is possible within the allowances imposed by non-negativity. Then we will replace (11.5) by

(13.2) $0 = -x_{CS} + x_{SG} + x_{SR} - y_{RC} - y_{GC} + x_{SE}$

wherein the variables y_{RC}, $y_{CG} \geq 0$ are entered to absorb any deficiencies which occur when the total debits to cash, arising from sales, are inadequate to cover the cost of merchandise sold, $x_{SG} + x_{SR}$, and the additional debit arising from the rental $x_{EC} = \$4.50$.

Now we assume that management imposes the following *preemptive*[33] priorities on inventory replenishment: First, replace all "Goods" inventory to the maximum possible extent. Second, with any remaining funds restore the "Raw Materials" inventory, so far as possible. Finally, and even more urgently, do not draw the cash account down below its initial $30 balance. In other words, this condition, which overrides the other two, is intended to mean that even inventory drawdowns are to be permitted, if necessary, to cover operating deficits and, in any event, only actual net cash realized from operations may be used to restore inventory.

To render these latter conditions more precisely, we first replace the expressions (11.4) by

(13.3) $0 = -x_{SG} \qquad +x_{GC} \qquad +y_{GC}$
$\quad 0 = \qquad -x_{SR} \qquad +x_{RC} \qquad +y_{RC}$

wherein positive values of y_{GC} or y_{RC} correspond to deficiencies in replacing inventories, which are allowed to occur, if necessary, in order to conserve cash.

Inserting the constraints (13.1) through (13.3) in place of their corresponds in (12) and imposing non-negativity requirements on the ranges of admissible values, we can now complete the proposed L.P. formulation by means of a minimizing objective stated in terms of the following functional — *viz.*,

(14)   Minimize $M_1 y_{RC} + M_2 y_{GC}$.

The coefficients of y_{RC} and y_{GC} are not numerically specified. They are defined by $M_2 \rangle\rangle\rangle M_1$ where "$\rangle\rangle\rangle$" is intended to mean that no positive

---

[33] This term is borrowed from the literature on queuing (waiting line) analysis in operations research.

number $k > 0$, however large, can produce $kM_1 > M_2$. Thus, $M_2 \rangle\rangle\rangle M_1$ and $M_1 \rangle\rangle\rangle k$, where k is any positive number whatsoever, accords M_2 and M_1 the status of "relative infinites."[34]

The way in which this formulation impounds the indicated preemptive priorities on inventory maintenance may, perhaps, be given a clearer operational significance by discussing how the solution routines of L.P. could proceed, in principle, to utilize these M_1 and M_2 coefficients. Because the objective is minimization, they could first attempt to make $y_{GC}^- \geq 0$ as small as the constraints allow. Then, without allowing any increase in y_{GC}^-,[35] these routines would drive y_{RC}^- to its smallest value, and so on.

The adjusted constraints for (12) are arranged so that $y_{GC}^- = 0$ is attainable, provided the variable $y_{RC}^- \geq 0$ is assigned non-zero values. Because of the indicated preemptive priorities (impounded in $M_2 \rangle\rangle\rangle M_1$) this will always be done irrespective of the increases in y_{RC}^- values that are needed to bring $y_{GC}^- = 0$ about. After $y_{GC}^- = 0$ has been attained, the minimization process then determines $y_{RC}^- = \$1.00$ as the smallest net depletion in Raw Material inventory which the constraints permit, sacrificing any of the x variable values, as required, to bring this about.

By relaxing the constraints in one way or another it would be possible, of course, to effect a still smaller net depletion. Alternatively, the constraints could be tightened by stipulating maximum amounts of net inventory depletion by, for example, introducing extra inequalities on some of the other variables. This is to say, of course, that the even more urgent cash requirements are incorporated in the constraints so that, at least in the present case,[36] even the dominating preemptions associated with M_2 and M_1 for the inventory depletion terms are not allowed to prevail against the requirement for maintaining the opening cash balance.

By tightening or loosening the constraints, or by undertaking suitable further alterations in the model, it is possible to accord different degrees of reflection to managerial requirements. This can all be done in a highly flexible manner although, of course, an approach via constraint alterations will almost necessarily entail a mathematical analysis to establish that the essential properties are, indeed, present in the model. If particular accounts or relations between accounts deserve it, the model can even be arranged to produce contradictions (nonsolvability) as a means of vividly directing managerial attention to danger spots before any operations are undertaken. It is worth noting that even such nonsolution-possibility needs can make managerial sense, under indicated circumstances. These are readily accommodated by L.P. methods that will even order (or arrange) the relative amounts of contradiction (deviations from solution values) which occur,

[34] See pp. 756–757 in [9] for a more precise characterization.
[35] Because, as the preceding discussion should make clear, any increase in y_{GC}^-, however small it might be, would necessarily drastically worsen the already achieved solutions.
[36] I.e., with the data given in (12).

at best, when multiple accounts and stipulations must simultaneously be accorded such an "urgent-immediate-management-review" status.[37]

Extending the Spread Sheet

All of these points may now be drawn together and sharpened by spread sheeting the solution for $x_{EC} = \$4.50$ in order to show how the results of the L.P. model might be employed in accounting applications to production and financial budgeting. In order to do this in a convenient way it is first desirable to extend the ordinary spread sheet in certain respects. Thus, as in Table 4, certain extra rows and columns are adjoined to the format that was employed in Table 3. (See the new rows and columns which appear outside the heavy lined portion of Table 4.) These are labelled "Beginning Balance" and "Ending Balance" and employed according to conventions that will now be described.

Consider, first, the Beginning Balance row and column. These are treated in a manner that is analogous to the way a set of books is ordinarily closed. The entries in the Beginning Balance column represent the net amounts of Cash, Goods and Raw Materials carried forward from the preceding period. Similarly, the $50 balance for Net Worth is carried forward by the entry shown in the Beginning Balance row.

Discussion of the Ending Balance row and column is best delayed until after the results of the L.P. solution are entered within the heavy lined portion of Table 4. Because, by assumption, all transactions are effected on a

TABLE 4

Spread Sheet Extension

Credits / Debits	Beginning	Cash	Goods	Raw Materials	Net Worth	Sales	Ending Balance	Total
Beginning Balance					50.00			50.00
Cash	30.00					10.25		40.25
Goods	10.00	3.00						13.00
Raw Materials	10.00	2.75						12.75
Net Worth		4.50					49.00	53.50
Sales			3.00	3.75	3.50			10.25
Ending Balance		30.00	10.00	9.00				49.00
Total	50.00	40.25	13.00	12.75	53.50	10.25	49.00	228.75

[37] *Vide* Chapter VI in [9].

cash basis, the solution of (10) is also the solution in this case. Thus, after first adjusting the constraints in (12) to accord with (13.1)–(13.3), a substitution of $x_1 = 2$, $x_2 = 3$ can be made to generate the following entries in Table 4. Credits to cash are effected to replace Goods and Raw Materials inventories in the respective amounts of $3.00 and $2.75 and, in addition, the $4.50 entry shown in the Cash column represents the debit to Net Worth for facilities rental during the period. Turning to the Cash row, it is seen that the $10.25 entry originates from a credit to the Sales column. Finally, two debits of $3.00 and $3.75 are entered in the Sales row to reflect the cost of merchandise sold from Goods and Raw Materials inventories.

The $3.50 entry that is also shown in the Sales row is the entry that closes the nominal account, profit and loss, into Net Worth at the end of this period. This closing is, in fact, obtained by calculating the difference between total sales and cost of merchandise sold and effecting the indicated entry in a manner which brings the total debits and credits to Sales into balance.

At this point we total the debits to all *asset* accounts only. These amounts are then transferred to the foot of the corresponding account column. The difference between each such transferred amount and the total of the credit entries in each such column is next obtained. The result is then entered in the Ending Balance row. Notice, for instance, that the total of all credits in the Cash column is $10.25. Total debits to Cash amounted to $40.25, as shown by the relevant row total, and the Ending Balance (this difference) is therefore $30.00. This is the same as the Beginning Balance so that, via the constraints, a breakeven level on Cash account was achieved in accordance with the stated policies of management. Also, the dominant priority assigned to M_2 succeeded in achieving breakeven on Goods by bringing this account's Beginning and Ending Balances to equality. The result on the Raw Materials inventory is a drawdown of $y_{RC}^- = 1.00 as is verified by observing that the $10.00 Beginning Balance in this account is reduced to the $9.00 figure shown under the Materials column in the Ending Balance row.

To finish this discussion we observe that all credit balance accounts are treated in a fashion that is analogous to the previous treatment of debit balance accounts, except that the column footings are first obtained and then transferred into the corresponding account as a row total. Thus, the $53.50 figure was first obtained by totaling the Net Worth column and then transferring this same amount to the Net Worth row. The one transaction in this row appears as a $4.50 credit to Cash and so the entry for Net Worth in the Ending Balance column appears as $49.00 = $53.50 − $4.50.[38]

---

[38] It is not the case, of course, that the indicated row-column adjunctions represents the only way (or even the best way) of completing the spread sheet in this manner. Entries along the diagonal of cells stretching from the upper left to the lower right hand portion of Table 3 could also be used but this would require recourse to discussions of the suitable ways in which the resulting double counts could be eliminated. Therefore to avoid any further lengthening of the present discussion, we will not examine this or other possibilities and simply refer the reader to [45.1] where another possibility is discussed in terms of balanced-margin tables of so-called Paciolo-Stevinus type.

Reading from the Ending Balance rows and columns we now readily perceive that the end-of-the-period balance sheet will appear as follows:

Balance Sheet
End of Period Two

Cash......................	$30	Net Worth..................	$50*
Goods.....................	10	Less: Deficit for Period.......	(1)
Raw Materials	9		
Total....................	$49		$49

* From Beginning Balance row.

Next, the following operating statement is also obtained:

Operating Statement
For Period Two

Sales..		$10.25
Less: Cost of Mdse. Sold:		
Goods...	$3.00	
Raw Materials....................................	3.75	
Total...		6.75
Gross Margin..		$3.50
Deduct: Rent on Facilities.....................................		4.50
Profit or Loss, Carried to Net Worth............................		($1.00)

Then, to round out the roster of this firm's financial statements (as projected by the indicated solution), we exhibit the following version of a funds-flow analysis (recast as a Cash Flow):

Statement of Sources and Uses of Cash
For Period Two

Sources:		
Gross Sales.......................................	$10.25	
Working Capital (Raw Materials Inventory)............	1.00	
Total Sources...		$11.25
Applications:		
Goods inventory..........................	$3.00	
Raw Materials Inventory...................	2.75	
Total to Inventory...............................	$5.75	
Equipment Rental................................	4.50	
Reduction in Net Worth...........................	1.00	
Total Applications..		$11.25

In the first case, then, the accounting device of a spread sheet (when suitably extended) can be used to systematize the results of a L.P. solution in order to generate all of the statements that are ordinarily used for the financial aspects of budgetary planning. Of course, there is no need for a cash budget in this example since, by assumption, neither accruals, like depreciation, nor credit transactions are involved. But it is also obvious that the cash budget can always be derived, when needed, either from the spread sheet or, in the usual manner, by an adjusted flow of funds analysis.

The production planning budgets are also present, in principle, by virtue of the machine constraints that were incorporated in (12). Neither labor nor other raw materials, union or supplier restrictions (e.g., lead times on delivery) are present in this example, but the model can evidently be extended in these directions whenever there is a need to do so. Similar remarks also apply when extensions to the marketing aspects of budgetary planning need to be considered and, indeed, suitable allowances for lead times and other aspects of transportation and distribution can be effected whenever the value of such extensions warrants the complications and elaborations that might thereby be entailed in the model's structure.[39]

Conclusion

By means of very simple examples, the preceding sections have endeavored to show how L.P. might be joined with accounting in order to produce a coordinated budgetary planning model. This is, of course, only an "in principle" illustration and it should not be interpreted to mean that a literal translation and extension of this particular model should be undertaken in every conceivable circumstance.[40] Further research, especially on the network aspects of these accounting models, will probably be necessary in order to devise suitable artifacts that will avoid unwieldiness and achieve the efficiency that will undoubtedly be needed when actual applications to large-scale management problems are essayed. However, considerable progress has been made (and is being made) on the uses of L.P. in other areas — e.g., production scheduling — and there does not appear to be any obvious reason why similar kinds of research should not be equally successful when oriented in the direction of accounting. In fact, the incidence (network) models of L.P. have been the most successful of all so-called "model types"

[39] See the reports [29] and [36] for examples which effect some of the indicated extensions to production, marketing and distribution budgets.

[40] The models (12) ff. can also be simplified, of course, by suitable mathematical manipulations. This was not done because (a) the methods for effecting such simplifications are fairly evident and (b) the objective was, rather, to secure a full display of all pertinent accounting details.

in producing especially efficient solution methods[41] and simplifying arti-facts.[42] And this, of course, was one of the reasons that the model (12) was oriented so that its double-entry accounting aspects could be brought into a network analogy in the sharpest possible manner.

It is also worth observing that mathematical research[43] has established that every L.P. model carries along with it another problem, called its dual. These mathematically established duality relations can also be used to ef-fect still further simplifications. Furthermore, the standard methods of L.P. automatically,[44] and without extra effort, supply solutions to both the model and its dual. This has proved to be especially useful in supplying guides whereby top management can evaluate the implications of its various policies as these are reflected by the constraints that are thereby imposed on subordinates.[45] Thus, still another feature of the budgetary coordination that can be secured from this quarter is brought into view by reference to the top- and down-the-line information guides that are simultaneously ob-tained when L.P. methods are employed that simultaneously solve both an original problem and its dual.[46]

We now briefly examine some of the possible relations between mathe-matics and accounting. First we observe that, from a purely technical standpoint, the trial balance is the most fundamental of all accounting documents. It is, in fact, "the chart of accounts with the relevant entries exhibited on its face."[47] But the extended spread sheet that we have just exhibited is only an alternate way of drawing up a trial balance and so it, too, achieves this same fundamental status.

Next we observe that, from a mathematical standpoint, any spread sheet is simply a matrix.[48] Linear programming also rests heavily on the mathe-matical theory of matrices and so the spread sheet idea provides a very

[41] The so-called "transportation models" of L.P. are probably the best known members of this class of model types. See Chapters II and XIV in [9].

[42] The critical path scheduling techniques (of J. L. Kelley) which are discussed in [8] may provide a good enough illustration of such artifacts.

[43] Conducted by D. Gale, H. W. Kuhn and A. W. Tucker, under the auspices of the U. S. Office of Naval Research, and published as Chapter XIX in [41]. (This is the same volume in which G. B. Dantzig's fundamental paper on the simplex method of solving L.P. problems was also first published after it had been developed, at an earlier date, while Dr. Dantzig was employed, on the staff of M. K. Wood, in the Comptroller's office of the U. S. Department of the Air Force.)

[44] E.g., the simplex method of G. B. Dantzig.

[45] See [10] and [71] for discussions of dual solutions that are relevant to the present context.

[46] See [36] for examples of the kinds of "managerial accounting" statements that can be prepared for higher level executives who are thereby enabled to determine the "oppor-tunity cost" implications of altering financial policies, plant conditions, contract re-quirements, etc.

[47] We are indebted to Professor N. C. Churchill for giving effect to our thoughts in this manner.

[48] We should also perhaps note that matrix mathematics provides a very natural language when dealing with electronic computers. Indeed, our colleague, G. L. Thompson, has remarked to us that this fact alone will tend to weigh very heavily in biasing future elec-tronic computer applications to accounting in this direction.

natural bridge between mathematics and accounting.[49] This does not necessarily mean, of course, that either L.P. or the theory of matrices will be the only mathematics that could prove useful in accounting. This has not been true in the past and the future is not likely to prove more confining than past history has already suggested on those occasions when accounting and mathematics have been joined together.

There is, of course, a past tradition of association between mathematical developments and management practices. Werner Sombart, for example, the great German historian, virtually dates the origin of capitalist (industrial) development from the translation and extension of the Hindu-Arabic number system as published (in the *Liber Abacci*) by the Italian mathematician Leonardo Pisano[50] in 1202. This mathematical theory, which was thereby made available for use in western commercial enterprises, almost certainly constituted a necessary precondition for the development of accounting in its many modern aspects.[51]

The first clear and systematic exposition of double-entry accounting (at least for the modern Western world) was published in a tract on mathematics[52] — Fra Luca Paciolo's *Suma de Arithmetica, Geometria, Proportione, et Proportionalita*[53] — and it is possible that historical research will yet reveal that the development of accounting was rather closely attended by the work of other mathematicians.[54] Writings by Fibonacci and Paciolo

---

[49] For another example of the application of matrix ideas to accounting problems see [12].

[50] Better known as Fibonacci in the literature of modern mathematics. See [66].

[51] *Vide*, Sombart, in the source cited in footnote 1, *supra*, where (cf. pp. 129 ff.) he strongly emphasizes that Pisano (also called Leonardo da Pisa) in fact provided the basis for "an exact science of commercial calculation." See also G. E. M. de Ste. Croix, "Greek and Roman Accounting," pp. 62 ff. in [44.2].

[52] The divisions of Paciolo's book are given by R. Emmett Taylor, in [44.4], p. 179, as follows:

1. Arithmetic and Algebra
2. Their Use in Trade Reckoning
3. Book-keeping
4. Money and Exchange
5. Pure and Especially Applied Geometry.

See also, *loc. cit.* p. 180 for Paciolo's recognition of his debt to Leonardo da Pisa.

[53] An English translation of Paciolo's treatise on bookkeeping may be found in *Introduction to Contemporary Civilization in the West* (New York: Columbia University Press, 1946) as adapted from [11]. D. Rosenblatt has, in this connection, also called our attention to another important (but less widely known) book by Paciolo, called *De Divina Proportione*, which was illustrated by Leonardo da Vinci. (No English translation of this appears to be available but the *Quellenschriften für Kuntsgeschichte und Kunsttechnik des Mittelalters und der Neuzeit* provides a German accompaniment to the original in *Fra Luca Pacioli DIVINA PROPORTIONE*, Constantin Winterberg, Wien, 1889. See also Sarton [59] pp. 222, 230 and 236.)

[54] Standard American writings on accounting history have not always been even wholly aware of the issues raised by European historians of capitalism with respect to the roles they have assigned to accounting and related developments — e.g., Hindu-Arabic arithmetic — in achieving a widespread rationalistic view towards business capital along with an ability to reckon and control the processes of capital accumulation. See, e.g., Littleton [43]. It is also true, of course, that these historians did not always pay adequate attention to the developments in American accounting. Sombart, for example, relies heavily on Leo Gomberg's *La Science de la comptabilité et son système scientifique* and also his *Histoire Critique de la Théorie des Comptes*. One reason is, perhaps, that Gomberg, by reasoning

already occupy a position of prominence and the somewhat later work by Simon Stevin[55] appears to be achieving a greater degree of recognition.[56]

There are other mathematicians whose work might have influenced — or been influenced by[57] — accounting and managerial developments (and problems).[58] But this would not be the place to dilate at length on this topic even if the evidence were at hand. We can, instead, close with the following statement by Arthur Cayley, 19th century mathematician, and one of the founders of modern matrix algebra:[59]

"Bookkeeping is one of the two perfect sciences."

Perhaps Cayley meant that, at bottom, the two are only one. In any event, from a mathematical standpoint, the notions of optimality, equilibrium, breakeven and linearity are all closely related to one another.[60] So are the concepts of matrices and double-entry principles.

Bibliography

1. ANTON, HECTOR R.: "Activity Analysis of the Firm: A Theoretical Approach to Accounting (Systems) Development," *Liiketaloudellinen Aikakauskirja* (*The Journal of Business Economics*), IV, 1961, pp. 290–305.

2. BARIDON, FELIX E.: "Profit and Loss Budget by Volume," *NAA Bulletin*, Sec. 1, Nov., 1960, pp. 83–89.

3. BERGE, C.: *The Theory of Graphs and Its Applications* (New York: John Wiley and Sons, Inc., 1962).

---

from accounting considerations only, had already achieved an explicit recognition of the fact that the double-entry principle carried with it a splitting apart of ownership and control which, only at a later date, was formulated by the American lawyer-economist, A. A. Berle.

[55] Cf., e.g., 0. ten Have in [44.5].

[56] This statement is drawn from Sarton [59], p. 254, in his discussion of Stevin's *Livre de compte de prince à la manière d'Italie*. . . . The references in [65] were called to our attention by D. Rosenblatt and pp. 1–24 of [65.1] contain an excellent sketch of Stevin's life and work.

[57] *Vide*, pp. 9–11 in [42].

[58] Allowance should perhaps also be made for negative as well as positive influence. See, for instance, the reference on p. 65 in [44.2], to the *Arte dei Cambi*, the guild regulations of 1299 which forbade the use of Arabic-Hindu numerals in the accounts of Florentine bankers. See also [66], p. 105. Another vivid example of delayed effects, and missed opportunities, is supplied by Charles Babbage, the British mathematician, whose early work on computing machines has now aroused a new interest in his other work on management. See, e.g., [26], or, for an extended treatment, see [33].

[59] From A. C. Littleton, [43]. See also [6], Volume VIII, p. XXIV in Biography, where it is noted that "Financial matters and accounts interested him [Cayley]; and only a few months before his death he published a brief pamphlet on book-keeping by double entry, which he had been known to declare one of the two perfect sciences. He could not resist some reference to the subject in his Presidential Address; making the remark that the notion of a negative magnitude 'is used in a very refined manner in book-keeping by double entry'."

[60] *Vide* the references to Cronhelm's and Jocet's equations on pp. 311 ff. in [44].

4. BRUMMET, R. L.: *Overhead Costing* (Ann Arbor: University of Michigan, 1957).

5. BURCHARD, JOSEPH R.: "A Critical Look at the Marginal Graph Technique," *NAA Bulletin*, May, 1961.

6. CAYLEY, ARTHUR: *The Collected Mathematical Papers of Arthur Cayley*, (Cambridge: University Press, 1895) Vols. I-XIII plus index volume.

7. ——,: *The Principles of Book-keeping by Double Entry* (Cambridge: University Press, 1907); available from Cambridge University Press Warehouse.

8. CHARNES, A. AND W. W. COOPER: "A Network Interpretation and a Directed Sub-Dual Algorithm for Critical Path Scheduling," *Journal of Industrial Engineering*. **XIII**, No. 4, July-August, 1962, pp. 213-219.

9. —— AND ——: *Management Models and Industrial Applications of Linear Programming* (New York: John Wiley and Sons, Inc., 1961).

10. ——, —— AND M. H. MILLER: "Application of Linear Programming to Financial Budgeting and the Costing of Funds," *Journal of Business*, **XXXII**, No. 1, Jan., 1959.

11. CRIVELLI, PIETRO: *An Original Translation of the Treatise on Double-Entry Book-Keeping by Frater Lucas Pacioli*. Published by the Institute of Book-Keepers, Ltd.; 133, Moorgate, London, E.C.2, 1924.

12. CYERT, R. M., JUSTIN DAVIDSON, AND G. L. THOMPSON: "Estimation of the Allowance for Doubtful Accounts by Markov Chains," *Management Science*, April, 1962.

13. DEAN, JOEL: "Cost Structure of Enterprises and Break-Even Charts," *American Economic Review Supplement*, Vol. 38, 1948, pp. 153-164.

14. ——: "Managerial Economics," William Grant Ireson and Eugene L. Grant, eds., *Handbook of Industrial Engineering and Management* (Englewood Cliffs, N. J.: Prentice-Hall, Inc., 1955).

15. ——: "Methods and Potentialities of Break-Even Analysis," *The Australian Accountant*, **XXI**, Nos. 10 and 11, Oct. and Nov., 1951, reproduced in [64].

16. D'EPENOUX: "Sur un Problème de Production et de Stockage dans l'Aléatoire," *Revue Française de Recherche Opérationnelle*, 4e Annee 1er trimestre, 1960, Numero 14, pp. 3-17.

17. DE GHELLINCK, GUY: "Application de la Théorie des Graphes Matrices de Markov et Programmes Dynamiques," *Cahiers du Centre de Recherche Opérationnelle*, 3, No. 1, 1961, pp. 5-35.

18. ——: "Aspects de la Notion de Dualité en Théorie des Graphes," *Cahiers du Centre de Recherche Opérationnelle*, 3, No. 2, 1961, pp. 94-123.

19. ——: "Les Problèmes de Décisions Séquentielles," *Cahiers du Centre d'Etudes de Recherche Opérationnelle*, No. 2, 1960, pp. 161-179.

20. DE ROOVER, R.: "Aux Origines d'une Technique Intellectuelle: La Formation et l'Expansion de la Comptabilité à partie double," *Annales d'Histoire Economique et Sociale*, Vol. IX, No. 44-45, 1937.

21. DEVINE, CARL T.: "Boundaries and Potentials of Reporting on Profit-Volume Relationships," *NAA Bulletin*, Sec. 1, Jan., 1961, pp. 5-14.

22. EASTWOOD, R. PARKER: "The Break-Even Chart as a Tool for Managerial Control," in *Practical Uses of Break-Even and Budget Controls*, Production Series No. 186 (New York 18, American Management Association, 330 W. 42nd St., 1949).

23. EDWARDS, R. S.: *A Survey of French Contributions to the Study of Cost Accounting During the 19th Century*, Publication No. 1 of the Accounting Research Association (Lo ∙ on: Gee and Co., 1937).

24. ECKHOLDT, JOHN L.: "Using the Break Even Chart in Product-Line Decisions," *NAA Bulletin*, July, 1960, pp. 43–50.

25. GARDNER, FRED V.: *Profit Management and Control* (New York: McGraw-Hill Book Co., Inc., 1955) especially Section II, Chapters 12–27.

26. GARNER, S. PAUL: "Historical Development of Cost Accounting," *The Accounting Review*, XXII, No. 4, Oct., 1947, pp. 385–389.

27. ——: "Has Cost Accounting Come of Age?," *NA(C)A Bulletin*, XXIII, No. 3, Nov., 1951, pp. 287–292.

28. ——: *Evolution of Cost Accounting to 1925* (Alabama: University of Alabama Press, 1954).

29. GASSNER, L. M., E. B. MAGEE AND E. R. MAURER: "Linear Programming as a Method for the Analysis of the Break-Even Point of Sales Volume." Ditto, Term project for the course, Advanced Business and Engineering Economics, at the Graduate School of Industrial Administration. (Pittsburgh: Carnegie Institute of Technology, May, 1955.)

30. GEIJSBEEK-MOLENAAR, L. B.: *Ancient Double Entry Bookkeeping* (Denver, Colorado, 1914).

31. HACHIGIAN, JACK: "Some Further Results on Functions of Markov Processes," Ph.D. Thesis (Bloomington: Indiana University Department of Mathematics, June, 1961).

32. HATFIELD, HENRY RAND: "An Historical Defense of Book-keeping," *Journal of Accountancy*, 37 (April, 1924), pp. 241–253, reprinted in W. T. Baxter, ed., *Studies in Accounting* (London: 1950).

33. HOAGLAND, JOHN: "Charles Babbage — His Life and Works in the Historical Evolution of Management Concepts," Ph.D. Dissertation (Columbus: Ohio State University, 1946).

34. HOWARD, R.: *Dynamic Programming and Markov Processes* (New York: McGraw-Hill Book Co., Inc., 1960).

35. IJIRI, YUJI: *An Application of Input-Output Analysis to Some Problems in Cost Accounting*, Unpublished Term Paper (Minneapolis: University of Minnesota, 1960).

36. ——, F. LEVY AND R. LYON: "A Linear Programming Model for Budgeting and Financial Planning." *Journal of Accounting Research*, Vol. 1, No. 2 (Autumn, 1963), pp. 198–212.

37. JAEDICKE, ROBERT K.: "Improving B-E Analysis by Linear Programming Techniques," *NAA Bulletin*, Sec. 1, March, 1961, pp. 5–12.

38. ——: "Some Notes on Product-Combination Decisions," *The Accounting Review*, 33, No. 4, Oct., 1958, pp. 596–601.

39. JODKA, JOHN: "PERT — A Recent Control Concept," *NAA Bulletin*, Sec.1, Jan., 1962, pp. 81–86.

40. KOHLER, ERIC L.: *A Dictionary for Accountants* (Englewood Cliffs, N. J., Prentice-Hall, Inc., 1952).

41. KOOPMANS, T. C., ed.: *Activity Analysis of Production and Allocation* (New York: John Wiley and Sons, Inc., 1951).

42. LEONTIEF, W. W.: *The Structure of the American Economy*, 1919-1939 (New York: Oxford University Press, 1951).

43. LITTLETON, A. C.: *Accounting Evolution to 1900* (New York: American Institute Publishing Co., 1933).

44. —— AND B. S. YAMEY, eds.: *Studies in the History of Accounting* (Homewood, Ill., Richard D. Irwin, Inc., 1956).
    (44.1) YAMEY, B. S.: "Introduction."
    (44.2) DE STE. CROIX, G. E. M.: "Greek and Roman Accounting."
    (44.3) DE ROOVER, RAYMOND: "The Development of Accounting Prior to Luca Pacioli According to the Account-books of Medieval Merchants."
    (44.4) TAYLOR, R. EMMETT: "Luca Pacioli."
    (44.5) TEN HAVE, O.: "Simon Stevin of Bruges."

45. MACHOL, R. E., ed.: *Information and Decision Processes* (New York: McGraw-Hill Book Co., Inc., 1960).
    (45.1) ROSENBLATT, D.: "On Some Aspects of Models of Complex Behavioral Systems."
    (45.2) ROSENBLATT, M.: "An Aggregation Problem for Markov Chains."

46. MATTESSICH, RICHARD: "Budgeting Models and System Simulation," *Accounting Review*, July, 1961, pp. 384–397.

47. ——: "Towards a General and Axiomatic Foundation of Accountancy, with an Introduction to the Matrix Formulation of Accounting Systems," *Accounting Research*, Oct., 1957, pp. 328–355.

48. MAY, P. A.: "Profit Polygraph for Product Mix Analysis," *NA(C)A Bulletin*, Nov. 1955.

49. PATRICK, A. W.: "Some Observations on the Break-Even Chart," *The Accounting Review*, 33, No. 4 (Oct., 1958), pp. 573–580.

50. PERAGALLO, EDWARD: *Origin and Evolution of Double Entry Bookkeeping* (New York: American Institute Publishing Co., 1938).

51. PIGMAN, NATHANIEL M., JR.: "Simplified Financial Research — An Example in Profit Maximization," *NAA Bulletin*, Sec. 2, Jan., 1962, pp. 87–92.

52. PYE, M. L.: "How to Determine Break-Even Points with Simple Algebraic Formulas," *Journal of Accountancy*, August, 1948, pp. 133–137.

53. RANKIN, BAYARD: "The Concept of Enchainment," Ph.D. Thesis (Cambridge, Mass.: Massachusetts Institute of Technology Department of Mathematics, 1961).

54. RAUTENSTRAUCH, W. AND R. VILLERS: *The Economics of Industrial Management* (New York: Funk and Wagnalls Company, 1949).

55. RICHARDS, ALLEN B.: "Input-Output Accounting for Business," *The Accounting Review*, XXXV, July, 1960, pp. 429–436.

56. ROSENBLATT, D.: "On Aggregation and Consolidation in Finite Substochastic Systems, I, II, III, IV," Abstracts, *Annals of Mathematical Statistics*, 28, No. 4 (Dec., 1957), pp. 1060–1061.

57. ——: "On Aggregation and Consolidation in Linear Systems," Technical Report C, Office of Naval Research Contract Nonr-1180(00), NR-047-012 (Washington, The American University Department of Statistics, August, 1956). ASTIA Ref. No.: AD-117-944.

58. ROSENBLATT, M.: *Random Processes* (New York: Oxford University Press, 1962).

59. SARTON, GEORGE: Six Wings, *Men of Science in the Renaissance* (Bloomington: Indiana University Press, 1957).

60. SHILLINGLAW, GORDON: "Problems in Divisional Profit Measurement," *NAA Bulletin*, Sec. 1, March, 1961, pp. 33–43.

61. SMITH, D. E.: *A Source Book in Mathematics*, (Dover, 1959).

62. ——: *History of Mathematics* (New York: Dover Publications, Inc., 1951).

63. SMITH, JOHN H.: "The Use of Simultaneous Equations in Business Problems," *The Journal of Business*, University of Chicago, XI, No. 2, April, 1938, pp. 188–198.

64. SOLOMONS, DAVID, ed.: *Studies in Costing* (London: Sweet and Maxwell, Ltd., 1952).

65. STEVIN, SIMON: *The Principal Works of Simon Stevin:*
    I. *Mechanics*, edited by a committee of the Royal Netherlands Academy of Sciences; translation by Miss C. Dikshoorn, under editorial direction of E. J. Dijksterhuis (Deventer, Holland, Jan de Lange, 1955).
    II. A. and B, *Mathematics*, D. J. Struik, ed. (Amsterdam: C. V. Swets and Zeitlinger, 1958).

66. STRUIK, D. J.: *A Concise History of Mathematics*, 2nd ed. (New York: Dover Publications, Inc., 1948).

67. TAYLOR, R. EMMETT: *No Royal Road: Luca Pacioli and His Times* (Chapel Hill: University of North Carolina Press, 1942).

68. TSE, JOHN Y. D.: *Profit Planning through Volume Cost Analysis* (New York: The Macmillan Co., 1960).

69. VANCAMP, H. K.: "The Use of the Product Profit and Loss Budget for Marginal Sales Decisions," *NAA Bulletin*, Sec. 1, Nov., 1960, pp. 5–16.

70. VICKERS, DOUGLAS: "On the Economics of Break-Even," *The Accounting Review*, 35, No. 3, July, 1960, pp. 405–412.

71. WEINGARTNER, H. M.: *Mathematical Programming and the Analysis of Capital Budgeting Problems* (Englewood Cliffs, N. J.: Prentice-Hall, Inc., 1963).

72. WHINSTON, A.: *Price Coordination in Decentralized Systems*, Ph.D. thesis (Pittsburgh: Carnegie Institute of Technology, 1962.)

73. WILLSON, JAMES D.: "Practical Applications of Cost-Volume-Profit Analysis," *NAA Bulletin*, Sec. 1, Vol. 41, No. 7, March, 1960, pp. 5–18.

74. WOLFE, P. AND G. B. DANTZIG: "Linear Programming in a Markov Chain," *Operations Research* 10, No. 5, Sept.–Oct., 1962, pp. 702–710.

17

Cost accountants use cost-volume-profit analysis as a tool to aid them in choosing an optimal course of action in solving a managerial problem. CVP is a limited analysis since it does not fulfill all the needs of management in determining the optimal strategy. Factors pertinent to the choice of the optimal strategy under uncertainty are variable, although traditional CVP treats these factors as constants. Hence an approach to CVP where pertinent factors necessary for decision-making are considered variables is more desirable than traditional CVP.

By introducing uncertainty, it is also beneficial to broaden CVP to fulfill the following desire of management: Should management choose a course of action based only on its own estimates of the decision parameters, or is it advisable to postpone a terminal decision until it obtains additional information about the decision parameters? A more sophisticated CVP method solves this problem with the aid of Bayesian decision theory for the choice of the optimal course of action in the face of uncertainty.

An Approach to Cost-Volume-Profit Analysis under Uncertainty*

Jeffrey E. Jarrett†

Introduction

Cost-Volume-Profit analysis is used by business management as a basis for choosing among alternative administrative strategies. Decisions concerning the required sales volume to attain a target profit level and the

* *From* Decision Sciences, *Vol. 4, No. 3 (July, 1973), pp. 405–420. Reprinted by permission of the editor.*

† The author appreciates the aid of William Cron, Ernest Kurnow, and the referees for valuable suggestions on earlier drafts of this manuscript. However, the author assumes full responsibility for its content.

maximum profitable combination of products to produce and market are typical decision problems where C-V-P analysis is useful.

Traditionally, C-V-P analysis is limited because it does not attempt to meet the needs of management in choosing an optimal strategy from among several strategies. Factors pertinent to the choice of an optimal strategy such as the fixed cost of an investment, variable cost per unit of production, price, and unit sales are items subject to managerial discretion. These factors are usually considered as certainties or constant values in C-V-P analysis, resulting in a naive model for decision making. The above factors are variables with expected values and standard deviations which can be estimated by management through its knowledge of the costs of new projects and its assessment of the market for the products produced by a newly proposed business activity.

The purpose of this paper is to consider the broadening of C-V-P analysis to fulfill the following desire of management. Should management base a decision on its own estimates of the parameters or should it postpone a terminal decision until further research into estimating the parameters for costs, price, and demand is accomplished? The broadening of C-V-P permits management to consider this question with the aid of probability theory for the choice of the optimal decision under the condition of uncertainty.

A Traditional C-V-P Analysis

A firm is contemplating the introduction of two products, both requiring initial capital investments. Based on plans for capital expansion and management's assessment of the feasibility of these projects, management determines the profit functions for three possible administrative strategies.

The first strategy is to produce product A, which requires a fixed investment and incremental costs per unit (a linear cost function). Since selling price times unit sales equals total revenues, the revenue function is also linear. Expressing profits as the difference between revenues and costs yields the following linear profit function for strategy 1:

$$(1) \qquad V_1 = P_1 S_1 - (F_1 + I_1 S_1),$$

where

$V_1 = $ profits for strategy 1, i.e., to produce product A,
$P_1 = $ price of product A,
$I_1 = $ variable cost per unit for product A,
$S_1 = $ unit sales of product A,
$F_1 = $ fixed cost of product A.

The function can be transformed to become

$$(2) \qquad V_1 = S_1(P_1 - I_1) - F_1,$$

where $(P_1 - I_1)$ is the marginal contribution to total profits created by selling one additional unit of product A after fixed cost (F_1) is covered. Strategy 2 is the strategy of producing product B. The profit function is the same as equation (2), but with the subscript 2 rather than 1, for each parameter of the equation. A third strategy is defined as neither producing product A nor product B, i.e., the strategy of noninvestment, and having a profit function given by:

$$(3) \qquad\qquad V_3 = 0$$

At this point, traditional C-V-P analysis will find break-even points or unit sales levels where profits equal zero for each strategy. Assume management, based on its past experience and knowledge of costs and the feasibility of each project, assesses fixed costs (F) for both strategies 1 and 2 at \$200,000, variable cost per unit (I) for strategies 1 and 2 at \$3, and the selling price (P) at \$5 per unit. The break-even point for strategy 1 and 2 is established at 100,000 units (See Figure 1). Profits for strategy 3 always equal zero and are invariant to the level of unit sales.

Previous studies indicated several shortcomings in the above analysis. First, fixed cost, variable cost, price, and unit sales are not certainties. They are random variables with risks associated with the distributions of

FIGURE 1

Simple Linear Breakeven Analysis

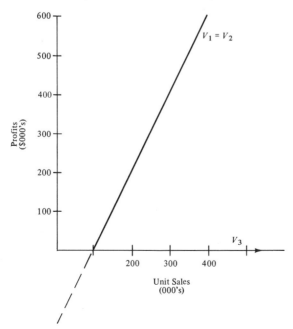

these random variables.[1] Second, profit functions may be nonlinear in form, requiring the determination of break-even points by varying methods of successive approximation.[2] Third, the integration of break-even analysis and other mathematical techniques for the solution of product line problems has also indicated that the traditional C-V-P must be widened in scope.[3] Last, the introduction of the different effects of different costs of capital further broadened C-V-P to relate it to the economists' concept of profit and loss.[4]

The purpose of this paper is to introduce practicing accountants to the methods of modern (Bayesian) statistical analysis as it applies to C-V-P. By considering price, fixed cost, and variable cost as random variables, Bayesian analysis can be applied easily to the above problem. Also, application of Bayesian analysis to nonlinear problems will be indicated.

To Introduce Uncertainty

If the criterion of choice between strategies 1 and 2 above is to choose the one with higher expected sales, management simply estimates sales. Assuming management has enough prior knowledge to make these estimates, no survey research is required. Upon estimating sales for product A to be 115,000 units, and expected sales for product B to be 110,000 units, management would choose strategy 1. Expected profits of strategy 1 is $30,000, which is larger than expected profits for the two other strategies.[5]

Since future sales as well as price, fixed cost, and variable cost are uncertain, the accountant must take on the role of a statistical consultant in advising management on how to assess probability distributions for these quantities. The method is well established and calls for information concerning average values, the possible range of values for each factor, and ideas as to the chances that the various possible values will be attained.[6] For major managerial decisions, this requires a substantial in-

---

[1] Jaedicke and Robichek [11] introduced risk into linear break-even analysis by assuming that [all] of the pertinent factors were normally distributed independent random variables.

[2] Goggans [7], Givens [6], and Morrison and Kaczka [17] solved for break-even points with curvilinear functions by differential calculus. More traditional approaches are shown by Keller [12], McFarland [16], and Beyer [1, Chapter 7].

[3] Efforts to integrate C-V-P with mathematical programming were introduced by Jaedicke [10], and Charnes, Cooper, and Ijiri [2]. Mathematical programming techniques are particularly useful in solving problems involving product-line and mix decisions.

[4] Manes [14] integrates C-V-P and microeconomic theory by using the principle of cost of capital.

[5] Expected profits are calculated as follows:

$$\overline{V}_1 = (115{,}000)(\$5 - \$3) - \$200{,}000 = \$30{,}000$$
$$\overline{V}_2 = (110{,}000)(\$5 - \$3) - \$200{,}000 = \$20{,}000$$
$$\overline{V}_3 = 0.$$

[6] The method is outlined by D. B. Hertz [9]. More recent studies include the two papers by R. Winkler [19], [20].

vestment in time and energy to pinpoint information about these relevant factors. Such an analysis can yield a subjective probability distribution of the type desired.

For this illustration, assume that the resulting distribution for profits is normal with a finite variance. The precise shape for the resulting distribution for profits will obviously affect the methods for computing the quantities desired for decision making.[7] Further, assume that for both strategies 1 and 2, the expected fixed price is $5 and its standard deviation is $2; expected fixed costs are $200,000 and its standard deviation is $10,000; expected incremental cost per unit is $3 and its standard deviation is $1 for both products A and B. Expected sales volume is 115,000 units for A and 110,000 units for B, with a standard deviation of 12,000 units for A and 6,000 units for B, expected profits are $20,000.[8] The standard deviation of profits[9] for strategy 1 is $259,000 and for strategy 2

---

[7] In the break-even problem where all quantities are variables, the resulting distribution for profit is often quite difficult to find. Decision theorists, for this reason, may not attempt to formulate a break-even analysis by establishing the break-even point as a random variable. However, the break-even analysis described in this paper holds (1) if sales volume was assumed constant and solutions found for various "possible" values for sales volume, and (2) where the distribution for profits is known to be approximated by a normal or some other well-known distribution. Even in the event that the shape of the distribution is unknown, probabilities can be estimated by implementing Chebyshev's inequality. Last, for this paper, we shall assume normality and leave the technical problem for others. See Marsaglia [15, pp. 193–204].

[8] The expected level of profits is given by:

$$\overline{V} = \overline{S} \, (\overline{P} - \overline{I}) - \overline{F}$$

where

$\overline{V} =$ expected level of profits (V),
$\overline{S} =$ expected level of sales (S),
$\overline{P} =$ expected selling price (P),
$\overline{F} =$ expected fixed cost (F),
$\overline{I} =$ expected variable cost per unit (I).

[9] The standard deviation of profits is:

$$\sigma_v = [\sigma_s^2 \, (\sigma_p^2 + \sigma_I^2) + \overline{S}^2(\sigma_p^2 + \sigma_I^2) + \sigma_s^2(\overline{P} - \overline{I})^2 + \sigma_f^2]^{\frac{1}{2}}$$

where

$\sigma_s =$ standard deviation of unit sales,
$\sigma_p =$ standard deviation of price,
$\sigma_I =$ standard deviation of incremental cost per unit,
$\sigma_f =$ standard deviation of fixed cost,

and $\overline{I}$, $\overline{S}$, and $\overline{P}$ are expected values for the variables defined previously. The above formulation can easily be determined by the methods of finding the variance of independent random variables. Previously, Jaedicke and Robichek, *op. cit.* solved for the above standard deviation; however, there is a printing error in their specification. Further, the Jaedicke-Robichek, *op. cit.,* solution is premised on another assumption that unit sales, price, incremental cost, and fixed cost are mutually uncorrelated. For many decision problems, these four variables are mutually uncorrelated and the above formulation is correct. In the event that at least two variables are related, solutions for the standard deviation of profits are available. One such solution is suggested by Kim [13]. For a further discussion of the variance of a product see Deming [4, pp. 53–59].

is $247,000. By the equation for the standard normal deviate we have:

$$(4) \qquad Z = \frac{V - \overline{V}}{\sigma_v}$$

where

V = a level of profits,
$\overline{V}$ = expected or mean level of profits,
σ_v = standard deviation of profits.

From equation (4) and a table for the normal distribution function, the probability of a loss (i.e., profits being less than zero) is determined to be 0.4522 for strategy 1 and 0.4681 for strategy 2.[10] Hence, the probability of a loss for both strategies 1 and 2 is almost as great as the probability of profits being greater than zero. This great increase in the risk factor from the previous approach is due to the consideration of fixed cost, variable cost, and price as random variables as well as considering unit sales as a random variable. The result is to increase the size of the risk measure, i.e., the standard deviation of total profits.

Since the relatively large probabilities of a loss for strategies 1 and 2 exist, strategy 3, the decision to produce neither product A nor product B, becomes a very appealing strategy to follow, especially if one adds two standard deviation limits to the break-even chart (see Figure 2). Strategy 3 is without risk since it is known with certainty that profits will be zero. However, by choosing strategy 3, an act without risk, management is avoiding the opportunity to gain additional profits. Perhaps the solution is to consider the possibility of postponing a terminal decision until research into the existing uncertainty of future events can be done. C-V-P analysis should now be concerned with the problem of determining the benefits that could be achieved by survey research.

A More Comprehensive Bayesian Probabilistic Approach

A comprehensive approach would determine whether a final decision with respect to the three strategies should be made now or postponed until more information can be obtained concerning the probability distributions for profits. In essence, a procedure to determine the costs and value of

---

[10] For strategy 1, the standard normal deviate is found by appropriate substitution in (4) as follows:

$$Z = \frac{V - \overline{V}}{\sigma_v} = \frac{0 - \$30,000}{\$259,000} = -.12$$

The probability of Z being less than $-.12$ is .4522 (from any table of the cumulative lower tail values for the standard normal deviate). Similarly, for strategy 2, we find

$$Z = \frac{0 - \$20,000}{\$247,000} = -.08,$$

and the probability is .4619.

FIGURE 2

Linear Breakeven Analysis with Two Sigma Control Limits

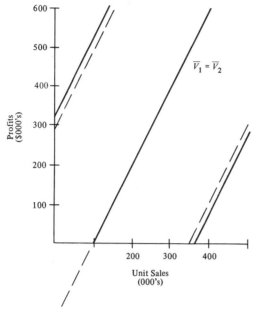

NOTE: Dashed lines represent control limits for strategy 2 and solid lines represent control limits for strategy 1.

additional information concerning the expected level of profits and its standard deviation is needed. These procedures come under the name of Bayesian Decision Theory.

Assuming that the information already obtained about the mean and standard deviations of sales price, fixed cost, variable cost per unit, and unit sales are based on the discretion of management, C-V-P analysis should find the expected level of profits if the future could be predicted with certainty. This is analogous to the situation of having a competent predictor of future events with the ability to tell management exactly what should be the optimal strategy to choose. Hence, management would always choose the optimal alternative course of action based on the particular profit levels that are predicted.

To find expected profits under certainty, first let us restate the function for the expected profits of each strategy:

(5)   Strategy 1: $V_1 = S_1(P_1 - I_1) - F_1$
(6)   Strategy 2: $V_2 = S_2(P_2 - I_2) - F_2$
(7)   Strategy 3: $V_3 = 0$,

where the symbols are defined as before. Defining strategy 1 as the decision to produce A, strategy 2 as the decision to produce B, and strategy

3 as the decision not to produce either product, and assuming (as before) that same information with regard to the expected levels of sales, prices, incremental and fixed costs, the following levels of profits are:

Strategy 1: $\overline{V}_1 = (115,000)(\$5 - \$3) - \$200,000 = \$30,000$
Strategy 2: $\overline{V}_2 = (110,000)(\$5 - \$3) - \$200,000 = \$20,000$
Strategy 3: $\overline{V}_3 = 0.$

Also, the standard deviation of expected profits are:

$$\sigma_{v_1} = \$259,000$$
$$\sigma_{v_2} = \$247,000$$
$$\sigma_{v_3} = 0.$$

If we denote $\overline{V}_m$ as the expected value of profits under certainty, i.e., the expected profits if a predictor of future events was available to management, $\overline{V}_m$ is given by:[11]

(8) $$\overline{V}_m = \overline{V}_o + \overline{V}_u$$

where

$\overline{V}_o =$ the expected profits of the optimal strategy, i.e., strategy 1 in this illustration,

$\overline{V}_u =$ the differential between $\overline{V}_m$ and $\overline{V}_o$ called the expected cost of uncertainty, or often referred to in statistical literature as the expected value of perfect information.

The expected cost of uncertainty is the maximum amount that management would pay to hire a predictor of future events to advise management as to the optimal strategy to choose. In essence, it is the price paid for not having perfect knowledge of future events.

The expected cost of uncertainty is composed of two elements: (1) the expected cost resulting from uncertainty in the choice between the optimal strategy, i.e., strategy 1, and strategy 3, and (2) the expected cost resulting from the uncertainty in the choice between strategy 1 and strategy 2. Summing these two values yields the total expected cost of uncertainty, $\overline{V}_c$. Thus, the procedure requires the measurement of the expected cost from each source of uncertainty and is given by the following equation:[12]

[11] Since the expected cost of uncertainty cannot be measured directly for this illustration, equation (8) becomes the expression for measuring the expected cost by finding the value of its parts. Equation (8) is from W. S. Peters and G. W. Summers [18, p. 233].

[12] For the discussion of the proof of this equation, and for the precise meaning for the unit normal loss integral, see T. R. Dyckman, S. Smidt, and A. K. McAdams [5, pp. 579–583]. Equations (9) and (10) are adaptations of the equations for determining the expected value of perfect information for the three action problems appearing in Peters and Summers, *op. cit.*, page 238. The problem described by Peters and Summers has one random variable — unit sales — whereas the model described here has four random variables.

(9) $$\overline{V}_c = [\sigma_{v_i} - \sigma_{v_j}] \cdot N(D), \text{ for } i \neq j,$$

where

$\sigma_{v_i} - \sigma_{v_j}$ = the difference in the standard deviations of expected profits for strategies (i) and (j), and

$N(D)$ = the unit normal loss integral for the segment of the normal loss function commencing at the point where $V_i = \overline{V}_j$.

The value for the unit normal loss integral is determined by first calculating the indifference value for the standard normal deviate (denoted by D) and then determining the normal loss value from a table of the normal loss function. The indifference value for D is given by:

(10) $$D = \frac{\overline{V}_j - \overline{V}_i}{\sigma_{v_i} - \sigma_{v_j}}, \text{ for } i \neq j.$$

By substitution in equations (9) and (10), the sources of the expected cost of uncertainty are measured below:

Source I: Strategies 1 and 3

$$\text{By (10), } D = \frac{20,000 - 30,000}{259,000 - 247,000} = -.83,$$

and from a table for the unit normal loss integral, $N(D) = .1140$[13]. Hence, by (9),

$$\overline{V}_c = (259,000 - \$247,000)\,(.1140) = \$1370.$$

Source II: Strategies 2 and 3

$$D = \frac{0 - 30,000}{259,000} = -.12, N(D) = .3418.$$

$$\overline{V}_c = (\$259,000)\,(.3418) = \$88,530.$$

The above results indicate that the expected cost of uncertainty is $89,900, i.e., $\overline{V}_u = \$89,900$. Since management cannot obtain perfect or certain information, management must reduce uncertainty by obtaining additional imperfect information.

The additional information permits a better choice of the optimal strategy in the face of uncertainty. Hence, since perfect prediction of future events is not possible, the realistic approach is to reduce the expected costs of uncertainty through the gathering of additional information through survey research. The device for the reduction in the cost of uncertainty is provided by the revision of the prior mean and standard for profits by sample information, i.e., the application of Bayes' theorem. The revision of a subjective prior standard deviation in the light of additional sample evidence will always result in a posterior (revised) standard deviation

---

[13] Values for the unit normal integral are found in Peters and Summers, *op. cit.*, Appendix H, pp. 484–485.

smaller in magnitude than its prior counterpart. Smaller posterior standard deviations result in smaller values for the expected cost of uncertainty. Hence, the purpose of survey research is to reduce the cost of uncertainty, thereby allowing management to choose the optimal strategy with greater assurance that the terminal decision is truly optimal.

Since most medium-sized business firms will not be capable of completing the job of survey research on their own, the firm in this example will try to engage a managerial research consultant. Thus, management must decide whether it is better (1) to come to a terminal decision with regard to the choice of the strategy to implement now, or (2) to postpone a terminal decision until after the survey research is completed.

The purpose of this step of the Bayesian procedure is to evaluate the prospective survey research and compare it to the expected cost of the survey research. The benefit from survey research would be the reduction in the expected costs of uncertainty. Since the expected cost of uncertainty is dependent on the expected profits from strategies 1, 2, and 3, and the standard deviations in the expected profits of these strategies, management must ask the consultant what the expected results of survey research are. It is assumed that the consultant can give management some information with respect to the standard deviation of expected profits (based on the survey) for the several strategies.

By the following equation, one can revise a prior standard with sample information:[14]

$$(11) \qquad \sigma_R = \frac{\sigma_v^2 \cdot \sigma_{\bar{x}}^2}{\sigma_v^2 + \sigma_{\bar{x}}^2}$$

where

σ_R = posterior (revised) standard deviation based on the combined evidence of prior and sample information,

$\sigma_{\bar{x}}$ = the standard deviation of total profits from sample information, i.e., in classical statistics, the standard error of mean,

and σ_v = standard deviation of profits from prior information as defined before.

If the consultant estimates that the standard deviation of profits from sample information for both strategies 1 and 2 can be limited to $100,000 by sampling 200 customers, then by equation (11) the revised standard deviations are estimated. Also, the sources of the expected cost of uncertainty conditioned on the estimates of the consultant are calculated by,

$$(12) \qquad \overline{V}_c^* = [\sigma_{R_i} - \sigma_{R_j}] \cdot N(D^*) \text{ for } i \neq j,$$

where $\overline{V}_c^*$ is the conditional expected cost of uncertainty; $\sigma_{R_i} \cdot \sigma_{R_j}$ are the estimated revised standard deviations of total profits for strategies (i) and (j); and $N(D^*)$, the unit normal loss integral for the revised estimates. Then, by equation (11) we find $R_1 = \$93,300$, $R_2 = \$92,700$, and

---

[14] Adapted from the equations for the revision of a prior variance on the basis of sample information, Peters and Summers, *op. cit.,* pp. 184–186.

$R_3 = 0$. Hence, by substitution of these revised values in equation (12) for the two sources of uncertainty, the conditional expected cost of uncertainty $\overline{V}_u^*$ is measured.

Source I: Strategies 1 and 2

$$D = \frac{\overline{V}_2 - \overline{V}_1}{\sigma_{R_1} - \sigma_{R_2}} = \frac{20,000 - 30,000}{93,300 - 92,700} = 16.7$$

$$\overline{V}_c^* = [\sigma_{R_1} - \sigma_{R_2}] \cdot N(D^*) = (600) \cdot (0) = \$0$$

Source II: Strategies 1 and 3

$$D^* = \frac{\overline{V}_3 - \overline{V}_1}{\sigma_{R_1} - \sigma_{R_3}} = \frac{-30,000}{93,300} = -.32$$

and $\quad \overline{V}_c^* = [\sigma_{R_1} - \sigma_{R_3}] \cdot N(D^*) = 93,000 \cdot (.2592)$

$$\overline{V}_c^* = \$24,180.$$

The above results indicate that survey research will reduce each source of the expected cost of uncertainty. The expected benefit of survey research is its function as an uncertainty reducer. Since management wishes to measure the expected value of survey research given the estimates of the managerial research consultant, then management finds the difference between the expected cost of uncertainty prior to sampling and the conditional expected cost of uncertainty. Letting V_s denote the expected value of sampling or survey research, then we have

(13) $$\overline{V}_s = \overline{V}_u - \overline{V}_u^* \; [15]$$

and for this illustration,

$$\overline{V}_s = \$89,900 - \$24,180 = \$65,720.$$

Knowledge of the expected value of sample information permits management to place a monetary value on the information that would be received from the managerial consultant if the survey research is completed. Although strategy 1 is optimal under uncertainty, it is likely from the above results that a survey would be beneficial since it is expected that the information received is worth $65,720 (see Figure 3).

At this point, management must decide whether to implement strategy 1 or postpone the terminal decision until the consultant completes his work. If the expected value of sample information is greater than the cost of completing the survey research, then management should postpone the terminal decision; management is wiser to implement the optimal strategy when the survey costs are greater than the expected value of the sample

---

[15] $\overline{V}_u^*$ is taken to be $24,180 because this was the higher value. Hence, the expected value of sample research is at least $65,720 and could be assumed to be more if the average of $0 and $24,180 was chosen to be $\overline{V}_u^*$. It is management's view of uncertainty and risk that should determine this computation.

FIGURE 3

Breakeven Analysis for Decision to Sample

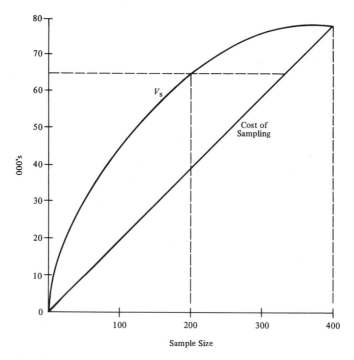

Sample Size

Note: V_s = value of information

information. Thus, an objective of C-V-P is to decide if the cost of reducing the uncertainty through survey research is greater than the monetary value of the benefits derived from that research. In this illustration, if the costs of sampling, as estimated by the managerial consultant, are less than $65,720, then the terminal decision should be postponed.

In the likely event that further research is desirable, management will revise its prior estimates of the parameters of the strategies based on the information received from the consultant. The combined evidence will yield an optimal decision under uncertainty, but the uncertainty involved in implementing this strategy is less than the uncertainty involved in implementing the optimal strategy based only on prior information. The benefit derived from the additional sample information is this ability to predict future events with more certainty. Thus, although the optimal strategy after additional research is often the same as the optimal strategy prior to the research, the research is still beneficial because the decision to conduct a survey was the best strategy to adopt at the time management adopted it.

FIGURE 4

Nonlinear Profit Functions

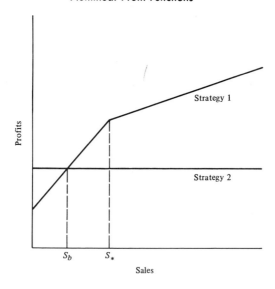

Note: S_b = breakeven point
S_* = segmentation point

Nonlinear Profit Functions

Nonlinear profit functions are common in decision problems where the actions are nonequivalent. When the profit function is nonlinear, the management decision maker resorts to evalualing the cost of uncertainty for each action. For example, suppose a two-action problem involves profits as indicated in Figure 4.

The profit from strategy 1 is nonlinear for all levels of demand, and, hence, the use of expected profits alone cannot be followed to find the optimal course of action. The function for the costs of uncertainty for Figure 4 are given in Figure 5, but here there is a break in the function at S_*. Thus, the function for the cost of uncertainty for strategy 1 has three sections. It is zero for values less than the break-even point, S_b; it is equal to the expected cost of uncertainty of strategy 1 between the S_b and S_*; and for values greater than S_* it is the last portion of the function. Solutions for computing this piecewise linear function as well as other nonlinear profit functions have been found.[16] Once the computations are completed, the decision problem becomes similar to the previous decision problem involving linear profit functions.

[16] See Dyckman, Smidt, and McAdams, *op. cit.*, Chapter 12, or DeGroot [3, Chapter 11].

FIGURE 5

Cost of Uncertainty
Involving a Nonlinear Profit Function

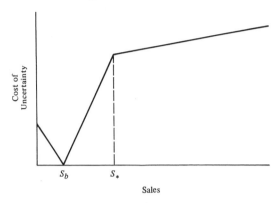

A Final Note

The Bayesian approach to C-V-P analysis can be extended to the case where management will decide to do its own survey research. Hence, management may wish to find methods for determining the optimal sample size to be examined. Procedures are available for finding the optimal sample size and are easily included into the general Bayesian Decision procedures. C-V-P analysis, consequently, becomes a generalized method of decision making for the determination of the products to be included or not included in a firm's product line.

Furthermore, problems in implementing C-V-P analysis in multiple product or product-line decisions again make Bayesian analysis more complex but not unusable. However, product-line decisions have always been more complex than single product decisions resulting in more complex C-V-P solutions. Multiple piecewise functions which often depict product-line profit functions are more difficult but not impossible to work as indicated above.

References

1. Beyer, R., *Profitability Accounting for Planning and Control,* The Ronald Press Company, 1963, Chapter 7.
2. Charnes, A., W. W. Cooper, and Y. Ijiri, "Breakeven Budgeting and Programming to Goals," *Journal of Accounting Research,* 1 (Spring, 1963), pp. 16–41.
3. DeGroot, M. H., *Optimal Statistical Decisions,* McGraw-Hill, 1970, Chapter 11.
4. Deming, W. W., *Sample Design in Business Research,* John Wiley & Sons, Inc.

5. Dyckman, T. R., S. Smidt, and A. K. McAdams, *Management Decision Making under Uncertainty,* MacMillan Company, 1969.

6. Givens, H. R., "An Application of Curvilinear Break-even Analysis," *The Accounting Review,* 41 (January, 1966), pp. 141–143.

7. Goggans, T. P., "Break-even Analysis with Curvilinear Function," *The Accounting Review,* 40 (October, 1965), pp. 867–871.

8. Hansen, M., W. Hurwitz, and W. Madow, *Sample Survey Methods and Theory, Vol. II,* John Wiley & Sons, Inc., 1953, pp. 53–59.

9. Hertz, D. B., "Risk Analysis in Capital Investment," *Harvard Business Review,* 42 (January–February, 1964), pp. 95–106.

10. Jaedicke, R. K., "Improving Breakeven Analysis by L. P. Technique," *N.A.A. Bulletin,* March, 1961, pp. 5–12.

11. Jaedicke, R. K., and A. A. Robichek, "Cost-Volume-Profit Analysis under Conditions of Uncertainty," *The Accounting Review,* 39 (October, 1964), pp. 917–926.

12. Keller, I. W., "Controlling Contribution," *Management Accounting,* 45 (June, 1967), pp. 23 and 28.

13. Kim, C., "A Stochastic Cost-Volume-Profit Analysis," *Decision Sciences,* Vol. 4, No. 3, 1973.

14. Manes, R., "A New Dimension to Breakeven Analysis," *Journal of Accounting Research,* 4 (Spring, 1966), pp. 87–100.

15. Marsaglia, G., "Ratios of Normal Variates and Ratios of Sums of Uniform Variables," *Journal of American Statistical Association,* March, 1965, pp. 193–204.

16. McFarland, W. B., *Concepts for Management Accounting,* (National Association of Accountants, 1966), p. 69.

17. Morrison, T. A., and E. Kaczka, "A New Application of Calculus and Risk Analysis to Cost-Volume-Profit Changes," *The Accounting Review,* 44 (April, 1969), pp. 330–343.

18. Peters, W. S., and G. W. Summers, *Statistical Analysis for Business Decisions,* Prentice-Hall, 1968.

19. Winkler, R., "The Assessment of Prior Distributions in Bayesian Analysis," *Journal of the American Statistical Association,* 62 (September, 1967), pp. 776–800.

20. ———, "The Quantification of Judgements: Some Methodological Suggestions," *Journal of the American Statistical Association,* 62 (December, 1967), pp. 1105–1120.

Supplemental

Readings

to Part Four

American Accounting Association. "Report of the Committee on Cost and Profitability Analyses for Marketing." *The Accounting Review,* XLVII (1972), 576–615.

Sets forth appropriate cost and revenue concepts and reporting techniques for planning, control, and decision-making in marketing, including physical distribution systems that may encompass the totality of production and marketing.

Battista, G. L., and G. R. Crowningshield. "Cost Behavior and Breakeven Analysis — A Different Approach." *Management Accounting,* 48, No. 2 (October 1966), 3–15.

Shows that break-even analysis based on historical cost data can be misleading because perfect control must be assumed.

Brault, Réjean. "Utility of the Classical Break-even Chart: A Critique." *Cost and Management,* 43, No. 3 (March–April 1969), 24–27.

For those not using direct costing, presents a chart that shows the operating results of both manufacturing and sales functions.

Brightly, Donald S. "A Statistical Tool for the Cost Accountant." *Management Services,* 2, No. 5 (September–October 1965), 13–17.

Presents statistical tools for the management accountant to use in analyzing fixed and variable costs.

Butler, John J. "Joint Product Analysis." *Management Accounting,* LIII, No. 6 (December 1971), 12–14, 38.

Presents a "composite product" approach. The illustrations given make it appear to be a very workable approach to profitability analysis of joint products.

Colantoni, Claude S., Rene P. Manes, and Andrew Whinston. "Programming, Profit Rates and Pricing Decisions." *The Accounting Review,* XLIV, No. 3 (July 1969), 467–481.

Explains linear programming models for perfect competition and monopoly, as well as a full-cost pricing linear programming model for price fixers.

Devine, Carl T. "Boundaries and Potentials of Reporting on Profit-Volume Relationships." *NAA Bulletin,* XLII, No. 5 (January 1961), 5–14.

Relates profit-volume analysis to reporting objectives and related procedures.

Harper, W. M. "Cost Profiles." *Accountancy,* LXXX (July 1969), 524–527.
Discusses prediction of future costs and activity levels as one of management accounting's contributions to decision-making processes.

Ijiri, Yuji, and Hiroyuki Itami. "Quadratic Cost-Volume Relationship and Timing of Demand Information." *The Accounting Review,* XLVIII, No. 4 (October 1973), 724–737.
Analyzes the effect of the timing of perfect information on the total cost of a firm and shows that there is a law of increasing marginal loss with respect to information delay.

Jaedicke, Robert K., and Alexander A. Robichek. "Cost-Volume-Profit Analysis under Conditions of Uncertainty." *The Accounting Review,* 39, No. 4 (October 1964), 917–926.
Considers the effects of uncertainty on cost-volume-profit analysis.

Jenkins, David O. "Cost-Volume-Profit Analysis." *Management Services,* 7, No. 2 (March–April 1970), 55–57.
Uses a basic equation to provide proper data for cost-volume-profit analysis in any size organization.

Jensen, Daniel L. "The Role of Cost in Pricing Joint Products: A Case of Production in Fixed Proportions." *The Accounting Review,* XLIX, No. 3 (July 1974), 465–476.
Examines the information requirements of the pricing decision for joint production in fixed proportions.

Johnson, Glenn L., and S. Stephen Simik. "Multiproduct C-V-P Analysis under Uncertainty." *Journal of Accounting Research* (Autumn 1971), 278–286.
Discusses the effect of correlation among products and among the C-V-P variables under conditions of uncertainty.

Killough, Larry N., and Thomas L. Souders. "A Goal Programming Model for Public Accounting Firms." *The Accounting Review,* XLVIII, No. 2 (April 1973), 268–279.
Demonstrates that goal programming, as shown by a planning model, can be used effectively where the firm has multiple, incompatible, and incommensurable goals.

Lee, Sang M. "Decision Analysis Through Goal Programming." *Decision Sciences* (April 1971), 172–180.
Presents the concept, solution method, and application potential of goal programming.

Liao, Mawsen. "Model Sampling: A Stochastic Cost-Volume-Profit Analysis." *The Accounting Review,* L, No. 4 (October 1975), 780–790.
Demonstrates the application of model sampling coupled with a curve-fitting technique to two hypothetical CVP analysis problems for a more complete and precise analysis.

Manes, Rene. "A New Dimension to Breakeven Analysis." *Journal of Accounting Research,* 4, No. 1 (Spring 1966), 87–100.
Adds capital costs to break-even analysis.

Morrison, Thomas A., and Eugene Kaczka. "A New Application of Calculus and Risk Analysis to Cost-Volume-Profit Changes." *The Accounting Review,* XLIV, No. 2 (April 1969), 330–343.
> Extends traditional break-even analysis by using differential calculus for analysis of volume and price changes.

Raun, Donald L. "Volume-Cost-Analysis — The Multiple Regression Analysis Aproach." *Management Accounting,* 48, No. 4 (December 1966), 53–55.
> Applies multiple regression and curvilinear techniques to volume-cost analysis.

Solomons, David. "Breakeven Analysis under Absorption Costing." *The Accounting Review,* XLIII, No. 3 (July 1968), 447–452.
> Clarifies assumptions underlying the classical break-even chart and adapts the break-even chart to a situation in which absorption costing is being used.

Weiser, Herbert J. "Break-even Analysis: A Re-evaluation." *Management Accounting,* 50, No. 6 (February 1969), 36–41.
> Presents break-even analysis as an extension of marginal analysis.

Additional
Bibliography
to Part Four

Anderson, Lane K. "Expanded Breakeven Analysis for a Multi-product Company." *Management Accounting,* LVII, No. 1 (July 1975), 30–32.

Berman, Norman D. "Profit Analysis Practices in an Oil Refinery Company." *NAA Bulletin,* XLII, No. 11 (July 1961), 63–68.

Chasteen, Lanny G. "Shadow Prices: A Graphical Approach." *Management Accounting,* LIV, No. 3 (September 1972), 27–29.

Dickerhoof, Wilford L. "Cutting Costs . . . Not Worth." *Management Accounting,* LIV, No. 2 (August 1972), 20–22.

Drake, Louis S. "Effect of Product Mix Changes on Profit Variance." *NAA Bulletin,* XLIII, No. 2 (October 1961), 61–70.

Fehr, Francis W. "Some Points to Watch in Studying the Fluctuation of Cost with Volume." *NAA Bulletin,* XLI, No. 7 (March 1960), 67–76.

Ferrara, William L. "Breakeven for Individual Products, Plants, and Sales Territories." *Management Services,* 1, No. 3 (July–August 1964), 38–47.

Greer, Willis R., Jr. "Theory Versus Practice in Risk Analysis: An Empirical Study." *The Accounting Review,* XLIX, No. 3 (July 1974), 496–505.

Harris, William T., Jr., and Wayne R. Chapin. "Joint Products Costing." *Management Accounting,* LIV, No. 10 (April 1973), 43–47.

Hartley, Ronald V. "Decision Making When Joint Products Are Involved." *The Accounting Review,* XLVI, No. 4 (October 1971), 746–755.

Hilliard, Jimmy E., and Robert A. Leitch. "Cost-Volume-Profit Analysis under Uncertainty: A Log-Normal Approach." *The Accounting Review,* L, No. 1 (January 1975), 69–80.

Hobbs, James B. "Volume-Mix-Price/Cost Budget Variance Analysis: A Proper Approach." *The Accounting Review,* XXXIX, No. 4 (October 1964), 905–913.

Johnson, Glenn L., and S. Stephen Simik. "The Use of Probability Inequalities in Multiproduct C-V-P Analysis under Uncertainty." *Journal of Accounting Research* (Spring 1974), 67–79.

Kim, Chaiho. "A Stochastic Cost Volume Profit Analysis." *Decision Sciences,* 4, No. 3 (July 1973), 329–342.

Liao, Mawsen. "Equal Cost Analysis." *Management Accounting,* LVII, No. 11 (April 1976), 51–53.

McClenon, Paul R. "Cost Finding Through Multiple Correlation Analysis." *The Accounting Review,* XXXVIII, No. 3 (July 1963), 540–547.

Moore, Carl L. "An Extension of Break-even Analysis." *Management Accounting,* 50, No. 9 (May 1969), 55–58.

Raun, Donald L. "The Limitations of Profit Graphs, Breakeven Analysis and Budgets." *The Accounting Review,* XXXIX, No. 4 (October 1964), 927–935.

Ricketts, Donald E., and Robert K. Zimmer. "A Dynamic Optimization Model for Planning in a Multi-product Environment." *Decision Sciences,* 6, No. 2 (April 1975), 274–283.

Robbins, Sidney M. "Emphasizing the Marginal Factor in Break-even Analysis." *NAA Bulletin,* XLIII, No. 2 (October 1961), 53–60.

Tucker, Spencer A. "A System of Managerial Control Using 'Live' Ratios and Control Charts." *NAA Bulletin,* XLIII, No. 12 (August 1962), 5–24.

Vatter, William J. "Toward a Generalized Break-even Formula." *NAA Bulletin,* 43, No. 4 (December 1961), 5–10.

Voller, Charles P. "Developing the Profit Planning Procedure." *NAA Bulletin,* XLII, No. 3 (November 1960), 31–40.

Walton, Horace C. "Profit Control and Measurement Through Statistical Correlation." *The Controller,* XXVII, No. 9 (September 1959), 410–411, 430–431.

Wilson, James D. "Practical Applications of Cost-Volume-Profit Analysis." *NAA Bulletin,* XLI, No. 7 (March 1960), 5–18.

PART FIVE

Standard Costs

and Performance Evaluation

T he concept of standard costs and their role within the accounting system — from product costing to cost control and performance evaluation — is generally well known. However, awareness of the concomitant behavioral issues and the techniques of analyzing variances from standard and budgeted figures is not so widespread. The articles selected for this section discuss and expand on basic standard cost and performance evaluation topics.

Horngren's article, for example, re-examines the volume or capacity variance as a measure of capacity use and corresponding performance evaluation. Horngren develops the existing practice, in which capacity variance relies on historical cost, into a volume variance based on a lost contribution margin concept that will "directly measure the effects of volume on profits." Thus performance evaluation is based on a current opportunity cost, not a past historical cost, analysis.

The increasing sophistication of variance analysis is reflected in much of contemporary literature and practice. Dopuch, Birnberg, and Demski illustrate one extension of variance analysis beyond conventional process and performance control to an evaluation of the decision model itself. Not only can sophisticated models be developed to signal critical variances but these models can actually be monitored by the cost system. The authors assert that most standard cost systems are designed to analyze and distinguish between deviations from expected performance that are merely random fluctuations and those that represent a temporary deviation, that is, the traditional "controllable" variances that ought to be investigated and adjusted in the next period. The authors extend the standard cost system to distinguish a third kind of deviation that results from a permanent rather than temporary change in process, and they assess its effect on the decision model being used.

Methods for applying cost-effectiveness tests to the process of variance analysis and the identification of temporary, controllable, and permanent variances have also been advanced. Kaplan's article surveys techniques that are useful for assessing the significance and potential investigation of cost variances. Using a simple 2×2 matrix classification, Kaplan distinguishes between (1) techniques that consider both the costs and benefits of investigation and those that do not, and (2) single-period and multi-period investigation models. He also exposes and evaluates relevant positions developed in the accounting literature. Based on this survey, he proposes a system to track cost variances for short-run and long-run solutions. For the former, he advocates the industrial engineering technique of cusum charts; for the latter, he urges a continuous-state model.

Finally, the article by Labick and Surges is included as an example of an increasingly important extension of traditional cost accounting concepts from the familiar product costing of the manufacturing industry in the private sector to the vast field of service-oriented industries in both private and public sectors. The authors explicitly demonstrate how an operational, cost accounting information system has been integrated in a particular banking service institution. Benefits to management include data on the expense of providing specific services and the profitability of specific customers.

18

Maximization of current net income depends on the proper utilization of acquired capacity. But the traditional accounting measure of capacity utilization, the volume variance, is based on historical cost and is "little more than a bookkeeping bridge between the control and product costing purposes of the cost accounting system." The unit fixed historical cost measure may be a useful device for looking backward to evaluate past capital budgeting decisions, but it has little relevance for planning and control. A better, forward-looking measure is the "lost contribution margin."

To measure "lost contribution margin," a framework involving practical capacity, master budgeted sales, scheduled and actual production is suggested. Variances computed, in physical terms, are expected idle capacity, total volume, marketing, and production. These variances are transformed by a dollar unit contribution margin factor into a total lost contribution margin — which represents an approximation of opportunity cost.

The author suggests that accounting systems will best tie in with decisions regarding capacity utilization if a reporting system is defined with regard to a specific, well-defined decision model.

A Contribution Margin
Approach to the Analysis
of Capacity Utilization*

Charles T. Horngren

The analysis of variances is one of the major topics in our cost accounting courses. The volume (capacity) variance, which supposedly gauges the utilization of capacity, probably gets the prize as the most

* *From* The Accounting Review, *Vol. XLII, No. 2 (April, 1967), pp. 254–264. Reprinted by permission of the American Accounting Association and the author.*

baffling measure[1] that is produced by variance analysis. What does it mean? Why should we compute it?

This article develops a conceptual framework that may prove better than traditional volume variance analysis because it (1) distinguishes long-range and short-range factors, (2) demonstrates the weaknesses of existing practices, (3) sharply pinpoints responsibility in relation to the purposes of short-range planning and control and separates the role of physical measures of capacity[2] from the role of valuation of that capacity, and (4) indicates how a contribution-margin or opportunity-cost approach to valuation is superior to a unitized historical-cost approach.

Long-Range and Short-Range Factors

Two Aspects of Capacity: Acquisition and Utilization

Organizations assemble human and physical resources that provide the capacity to produce and sell. These commitments often require heavy expenditures that affect performance over long spans of time. The implications for managers are two-fold. First, careful planning is obviously crucial to the wise acquisition of fixed resources. Second, the acquired capacity should be properly utilized if current net income[3] is to be maximized.

Many fixed costs result from capital budgeting decisions, reached after studying the expected impact of these expenditures on operations over a number of years. The choice of a capacity size may be influenced by a

---

[1] Don T. DeCoster, "Measurement of the Idle-Capacity Variance," Accounting Review (April, 1966), pp. 297–302, discusses the "disparity that exists within accounting literature in quantifying the idle-capacity variance."

[2] A thorough study of capacity would include a rigorous operational definition of the word "capacity." This is not attempted here because such a definition is subordinate to the major purpose of this article. See Research Report 39, *Accounting for Costs of Capacity* (New York: National Association of Accountants, 1963), pp. 10–11. On page 10, Report 39 observes: "Capacity planning requires definition and measurement of capacity in a manner relevant to questions which arise in the planning process. This problem has two aspects. First, it is necessary to specify capacity in terms of how much the company should be prepared to make and to sell. Second, the capacity of specific facilities available or to be acquired must be determined. . . . A variety of alternative combinations of capacity and operating patterns is usually possible." There are many other difficulties of definition that are not being dealt with exhaustively in this article. *Variable cost, fixed cost,* and *contribution margin* are examples of concepts that raise difficult but not insurmountable practical problems of definition and measurement. Contribution margin is defined here as the excess of revenue over all variable costs of manufacturing and non-manufacturing.

[3] The focus here will be on the maximization of current net income, although long-run effects and other goals could be incorporated by extending the analysis. The expected inter-play of current net income and future net income obviously affects current decisions (e.g., pricing) even though these effects are seldom explicitly quantified.

combination of two major factors, each involving trade-off decisions and each heavily dependent on long-range forecasts of demand, material costs, and labor costs:

1. Provision for seasonal and cyclical *fluctuations* in demand. The trade-off is between (a) additional costs of physical capacity versus (b) the costs of stock-outs and/or the carrying costs of safety stocks of such magnitude as to compensate for seasonal and cyclical variations, the costs of overtime premium, sub-contracting, and so on.

2. Provision for upward *trends* in demand. The trade-off is between (a) the costs of constructing too much capacity for initial needs versus (b) the later extra costs of satisfying demand by alternative means. For example, should a factory designed to make color television tubes be 100,000, 150,000, or 200,000-tube level?

ACQUISITION OF CAPACITY AND FOLLOW-UP

Suppose that management decided to build a factory that can produce 200,000 units yearly. Also suppose that the expected demand used to justify the size of the factory was a long-run average of 160,000 units for five to ten years. The larger factory was built because management decided that this was the most economical way to provide for seasonal, cyclical, and trend factors that may result in a demand at a peak rate of 200,000 units per year (practical capacity) during certain times.

A follow-up or audit of planning decisions is needed to see how well actual utilization harmonizes with the activity levels used in the plan that authorized the acquisition of the facilities. The follow-up helps evaluate the accuracy of management's past long-range planning decisions and should improve the quality of similar decisions in the future. The pertinent base for comparison is a particular year's activity level used in the capital budget that authorized the acquisition of facilities. Comparison should be done on a project-by-project basis to see whether the predictions in the capital budgeting schedules are being fulfilled. Such comparisons need not be integrated in the over-all information system on a routine basis.

Normal activity, 160,000 units in our example, is the rate of activity needed to meet average sales demand over a period long enough to encompass seasonal and cyclical fluctuations; it is the average volume level used as a basis for long-range plans. In our example, a comparison of currently budgeted sales or actual sales with the 160,000-unit normal activity might be suggested as the best basis for auditing and assessing the impact of long-range planning decisions. However, normal activity is an average that has little or no significance with respect to a follow-up for a particular year.

Moreover, normal activity should not be a reference point for judging current performance (i.e., the volume variance so often computed using historical costs). This is an example of misusing a long-range average measure for a short-range particular purpose. The acquisition of facilities and other fixed resources requires a planning and control horizon of many years — a horizon that fluctuates because various resources are often obtained piecemeal or on a project-by-project basis. In contrast, our concern here is with the planning and control of current operations; we shall see that the notion of normal activity has no bearing on this problem.

Weakness of Existing Practices

Unitizing Historical Costs

How do accountants actually apply dollar measures to the utilization of capacity? They "unitize" historical fixed manufacturing costs and use the resultant unit rate to measure a volume variance (and to cost products). In our example, suppose that manufacturing costs are $131,200 per year. The accountant would relate this cost to the number of units to get a predetermined unit cost. He might select from several possible rates. Let us consider two:

Alternative A — Use practical capacity as a base:

$$\text{Unit cost} = \frac{\text{Total Fixed Manufacturing Costs}}{\text{Practical Capacity in Units}} = \frac{\$131,200}{200,000 \text{ units}} = \$.656 \text{ per unit}$$

Alternative B — Use budgeted sales as a base:

$$\text{Unit cost} = \frac{\text{Total Fixed Manufacturing Costs}}{\text{Budgeted Sales in Units}} = \frac{\$131,200}{164,000 \text{ units}} = \$.80 \text{ per unit}$$

He would use one or the other of these unit costs for costing product and for measuring volume variances.

There are numerous drawbacks to using a historical-cost approach for management planning and control. Historical costs have no particular bearing on the management problem of obtaining desired current utilization of existing capacity. For instance, let us compare the dollar results of using the above two historical unit costs:

Alternative A — Use a historical cost unitized at $.656 per unit:

Practical capacity 200,000 units; fixed costs to account for	$131,200
Actual production and sales, 140,000 units at $.656 .	91,840
Volume variance, 60,000 units × $.656	$ 39,360

Alternative B — Use a historical cost unitized at $.80 per unit:

Master budget* sales of 164,000 units; fixed cost to account for	$131,200
Actual production and sales, 140,000 units at $.80 .	112,000
Volume variance, 24,000 × $.80	$ 19,200

EFFECT OF NUMERATOR AND DENOMINATOR

Note that the fixed cost rate as traditionally computed depends on a numerator of historical manufacturing costs only. Fixed selling and administrative costs, which often can be huge, are not incorporated in the volume variance or in the cost of the product.

The unit cost is also affected by the denominator selected. Practical capacity as a denominator results in one unit cost, while master budgeted sales as a denominator results in another unit cost. The choice of the denominator thus affects the amount of the variances (and, incidentally, computed product costs). In our example, the volume variance is either $39,360 or $19,200, depending on whether practical capacity or master budgeted sales is selected as the denominator. Such variety in quantification is difficult to justify and explain.

CHARACTERISTICS OF THE VOLUME VARIANCE BASED ON HISTORICAL COSTS

Most cost accounting systems simultaneously try to (1) accumulate costs for planning and control and (2) apply costs to product for inventory valuation and income determination. The approach to (1) and (2) for variable costs usually entails the use of unit costs for direct material, direct labor, and the variable manufacturing overhead. No volume variances arise because the total variable costs incurred are equal to the total variable costs applied to product. However, analytical troubles begin when the same approach is attempted with fixed costs.

A volume variance arises because of the conflict between accounting for control (via budgets) and accounting for product costing (via unit costing rates for applying overhead to product). The development of a product-costing rate results in an artificial transformation. Traditionally, for product-costing purposes, all costs rank abreast; no distinctions between cost behavior patterns are appropriate. Thus, the fixed cost is accounted for in product costing *as if it were a variable cost*. A volume variance appears whenever the activity level actually encountered fails to coincide with the

---

* "Master budget" is used here to designate the overall, comprehensive financial and operating plans for the year.

original activity level used as a denominator in the computation of a product-costing rate.

In a sense, the volume variance based on historical costs is little more than a bookkeeping bridge between the control and product costing purposes of the cost accounting system. It is difficult to see how such a variance could have been invented solely for purposes of current planning and control, our major concern here. Fixed costs and variable costs have different frames of reference, timing, and control features. Fixed costs simply are not divisible like variable costs. Fixed costs usually come in big masses, and they are related to providing big chunks of sales or production capacity rather than to the production of a single unit of product. To use parallel analytical devices (e.g., variances, unit costs) for costs with unlike patterns of behavior is illogical and is a reflection of the product-costing purpose's immense influence on cost accounting systems.

EFFICIENCY VARIANCES AND FIXED COSTS

Consider another example of the attempts to analyze variable costs and fixed costs in a parallel manner. Students of cost accounting are familiar with the usual way of computing efficiency variances for variable costs such as direct material, direct labor, and variable overhead:

$$
\begin{matrix} \text{Variable cost} \\ \text{efficiency} \\ \text{variance} \end{matrix} = \left(\begin{matrix} \text{Actual hours of input} \\ \text{minus} \\ \text{Standard hours allowed} \\ \text{for units produced} \end{matrix} \right) \times \text{Hourly rate}
$$

The same approach is commonly taken to the computation of an efficiency variance for fixed overhead:

$$
\begin{matrix} \text{Fixed} \\ \text{overhead} \\ \text{efficiency} \\ \text{variance} \end{matrix} = \left(\begin{matrix} \text{Actual hours of input} \\ \text{minus} \\ \text{Standard hours allowed} \\ \text{for units produced} \end{matrix} \right) \begin{matrix} \text{Hourly fixed} \\ \times \text{ overhead} \\ \text{rate} \end{matrix}
$$

But the resulting variance should be distinguished sharply from the efficiency variances for material, labor, and variable overhead, because efficient usage of these three factors can affect total actual cost incurrence, whereas short-run fixed overhead cost incurrence is not affected by efficiency. Moreover, the managers responsible for inefficiency will be aware of its existence through reports on variable costs control; so there is little additional management information to be gained from expressing ineffective utilization of fixed factory overhead factors in historical dollar terms.

LACK OF ECONOMIC SIGNIFICANCE

The unit fixed historical cost measure has little direct economic significance for current planning and control. It is conceptually inferior to the lost contribution margin per unit notion, which will be examined in a later section. Unlike variable costs, total fixed costs do not change as volume fluctuates. Fixed cost incurrence often entails lump-sum outlays based on a pattern of expected recoupment. But ineffective utilization of existing facilities has no bearing on the amount of fixed costs currently incurred. The economic effects of the inability to reach target volume levels are directly measured by lost contribution margins, even though these often are approximations. The historical cost approach to current planning and control fails to emphasize the useful distinction between *fixed cost incurrence,* on the one hand, and the objective of *maximizing the total contribution margin,* on the other hand. These are separable management problems, and the utilization of existing capacity is more closely related to the latter. This

EXHIBIT 1
Summary Framework for Analyzing Utilization of Capacity

Time of Computation and Use			
When the master budget is prepared	P = Practical Capacity M = Master budgeted sales	200,000 164,000	36,000 units expected idle capacity variance (1)
At the end of the period, when results are being evaluated	M = Master budgeted sales S = Scheduled production (sales orders received) A = Actual production (and sales)	164,000 148,000 140,000	16,000 units, marketing variance (2a) 8,000 units, production variance (2b) — 24,000 units volume variance (2)

(1) *P-M* = Expected idle capacity variance, a measure of the anticipated idle capacity.

(2) *M-A* = Volume variance, the difference between master budgeted sales and actual sales. (Note that this is the same as the volume variance that is traditionally computed — provided that master budgeted sales, and not practical capacity or "normal or average" sales, is used as a basis for the computation.)

(2a) *M-S* = Marketing variance, a measure of the failure of the sales force to get orders equal to the current sales forecast in the master budget.

(2b) *S-A* = Production variance, a measure of the failure of the production departments to adhere to production schedules.

historical cost approach may possibly be useful in looking backward for an evaluation of past capital budgeting decisions. But the contribution margin approach is more useful in looking forward for current planning and control.

Short-Range Planning and Control[4]

MEASURING ACTIVITY

What information about capacity can help management in planning and controlling operations? The analytical framework in Exhibit 1, expressed in physical terms only, should be useful.

$P = $ *Practical capacity or practical attainable capacity* is the maximum level at which the plant or department can realistically operate efficiently, 200,000 units in our example. When an organization has provided a given amount of practical capacity, little can be done in day-to-day operations to affect the total level of the associated fixed costs. The practical capacity acts as a constraint on subsequent performance. Practical capacity is ideal production capability less allowances for unavoidable operating interruptions such as repair time, waiting time (down time) because of machine set-ups, and operator personal time. N.A.A. *Research Report No. 39* describes one company's approach:

> . . . practical attainable *hourly* capacity is developed by one company. Daily, monthly, and annual capacity is determined by multiplying the number of working hours in these periods by the practical attainable hourly capacity. Additional allowances are made for events which occur during a day, month, or year, but not hourly. For example, an allowance may be required for cleaning up equipment at the end of each day and for model change-over time once a year. Industry practice and current management policy determines the number of shifts, number of hours worked per week, holidays, reserve capacity provided for contingencies, and other allowances entering into the number of working hours per period. It may be noted that this company measures annual practical attainable capacity both with and without use of premium wage time. Thus management knows how much additional production can be obtained by use of premium wage rate time.[5]

$M = $ *Master budgeted sales* is that volume of activity employed in formulating the master budget for the period. In this example, it represents

---

[4] Many of the notions in this and the next section originally appeared in Charles T. Horngren, *Accounting for Management Control: An Introduction,* (Englewood Cliffs, N.J.: Prentice-Hall, Inc., 1965), Chapter 10. However, a number of changes and embellishments have been incorporated in the present paper.

[5] Op. cit., p. 22.

management's best single estimate[6] of expected sales for the period, 164,000 units.

$S = Scheduled\ production$ is that volume of sales orders received and assigned for production in the immediate current period[7], 148,000 units in this case. This may not agree with the master budgeted sales because the marketing department may eventually fail to sell the budgeted number of 164,000.

$A = Actual\ production\ (and\ sales\ delivered\ to\ customers)$ is self-explanatory, 140,000 units in this case.

For clarity, the framework in Exhibit 1 simplifies matters by making the following assumptions:

a. There are no changes in inventory levels; that is, all units currently produced are currently sold.

b. The single product, single department case is examined here. The same fundamental analysis is applicable (but not without difficulty) in more complex cases on a product-by-product, department-by-department basis.[8]

EXPECTED IDLE CAPACITY VARIANCE

The expected idle capacity variance $(P\text{-}M)$ should be computed when the original master budget is prepared. Management may then (a) obtain a specific measure of anticipated idle capacity early enough (b) to adjust plans in light of possible uses for the expected idle capacity. This may be a give-and-take process, in which the initial master budget is altered (for example, prices may be changed) in light of the initial expected idle capacity.

---

[6] The use of probabilities in estimating sales and in the analysis of variances is germane but is not discussed here. For examples, see Robert K. Jaedicke and Alexander A. Robichek, "Cost-Volume-Profit Analysis Under Conditions of Uncertainty," THE ACCOUNTING REVIEW, October 1964, pp. 917–926; and Harold Bierman, Jr., Lawrence E. Fouraker, and Robert K. Jaedicke, "A Use of Probability and Statistics in Performance Evaluation," THE ACCOUNTING REVIEW, July 1962, pp. 409–417.

[7] For simplicity we shall assume throughout the subsequent discussion that all orders received are immediately scheduled and that production should occur immediately upon being scheduled; in other words, there are no lags between orders, schedules, and expected production. In this way, we will not have to bother with some messy technical adjustments in the analysis of variances caused by, say, an order being booked in November, scheduled in February, and produced in April. These adjustments may be difficult to construct in a particular company, and they impede practical application of these ideas.

[8] The linear programming model, using dual evaluators, will help management decide which combination of products will be most profitable when a given capacity must be utilized for their production or sale. When the primal solution shows the optimal production mix, the dual evaluators (shadow prices) of the constraining factors are the opportunity costs of their marginal products.

The responsibility for such a variance may be partially attributable to the sales department for inability to penetrate all possible market potential and partially attributable to the managers who may have wisely or foolishly over-built facilities to meet future demand. Other possible explanations may include general economic conditions or particular competitive circumstances.[9] The point is that the alternatives available under current planning and control are constrained by the past decisions which provided the present facilities. Current plans should concentrate on the optimum utilization of given facilities.

Note the difference in timing and in the frame of reference for evaluating different decisions. Practical capacity becomes important in the course of preparing the master budget. At the end of the period, however, the master budgeted sales is the key to the evaluation of results.

N.A.A. *Research Report No. 39* (p. 24) advocates evaluating performance by comparing practical capacity with scheduled production because it "measures the additional output that could be attained without incurring additional capacity costs." Advocates of practical capacity as a basis for the evaluation of performance rightly maintain that management should be regularly aware of all idle facilities. However, when do they need this information? The critical time is probably at the master budget planning stage, not the evaluation of performance stage. The master budgeted sales is the relevant base for analysis at the latter stage. The point is developed more fully below.

TOTAL VOLUME VARIANCE

The measurement system may be designed to follow up on various versions of capacity, each serving a different purpose. To continue our example, production for the current year was 140,000 units, although current production schedules called for 148,000 units. What measures would help management in the evaluation of current results? Variances should help pinpoint responsibility. Exhibit 1 shows a total volume variance (M-A), the overall difference between budgeted sales and actual sales. In turn, this volume variance is subdivided into marketing variance (M-S) which, to the extent that it can be assigned, is usually the responsibility of

[9] Conceivably, this variance could be sub-divided into two parts: (1) the difference between practical capacity and the activity level used for that particular year in a past capital budget; (2) the difference between the latter and the master budget. These subdivisions might help the evaluation of long range planning, particularly when excess facilities were deliberately acquired.

In this context, where excess capacity is deliberately acquired, the opportunity costs of bearing this capacity could be regularly compared to the costs of its elimination (e.g., overtime premium, second shift premium, sub-contracting, etc.). Then management could choose whether to eliminate the capacity through disposition or lease.

the sales manager, and the production variance $(S\text{-}A)$, which is usually the responsibility of the production manager.

Marketing Variance (M-S). The 16,000-unit deviation from the master budgeted sales (164,000 units less 148,000 units scheduled) is a measure that is primarily traceable, at least initially, to the sales arm of the organization. This *marketing variance* should be computed on a routine basis because it integrates the master budget with the results and helps explain the differences between original expectations and results. "Results," as far as the marketing department is concerned, consists of getting sales orders. That is why scheduled production (sales orders received) rather than actual production (sales delivered to customers) is used as the measure of results. Possible explanations of the variance include ineffective advertising or sales promotion, unexpected changes in economic or competitive conditions, poor estimates, and an understaffed or inefficient sales force.

The master budgeted sales, rather than practical capacity, is more germane to the evaluation of current results. Managers, particularly the sales executives, will feel much more obligated to reach the master budgeted sales, which should have been conscientiously set in relation to the optimum opportunities for sales in the current period. To have any meaning, marketing variance must at least crudely reflect the existence of a bona fide opportunity to sell. Consequently, on the operating firing line the marketing variance is much more meaningful than a variance related to practical capacity. For example, a practical capacity variance could be computed by subtracting scheduled production from practical capacity in Exhibit 1. But this would blend two unlike items: the marketing variance plus the expected idle capacity variance.

Production Variance (S-A). The production manager has two major responsibilities: to maximize efficiency and to meet production schedules.

The efficiency is monitored with the aid of standards and budgets for the variable cost factors, while the ability to meet production schedules is metered by some quantification of the difference between scheduled production and actual production.

The attainment of production schedules is a mutual effort by the producing departments and the production planning and control department. Common reasons for failure to meet schedules include poor direction of operations by factory supervisors; operating inefficiencies caused by untrained workmen, faulty machines, or inferior raw material; lack of material or parts; and careless scheduling by production planners. These reasons may be lumped together as possible explanations for a production variance.

Failure to meet a schedule would result in an unfavorable production variance. This is the most commonly encountered situation. However, it may happen that actual production exceeds scheduled production. In such a case, technically the variance would be favorable. But all unusual variances are supposed to be investigated, and the findings may or may not substantiate a favorable label in the layman's sense of the word. That is, sometimes unwanted excess production occurs because of misunderstandings of production schedules.

A common explanation for the bulk of the production variance is labor inefficiency, that is, inability to meet currently attainable standards. To pursue the example further, assume that the standard time allowance per unit is one direct labor hour, and that 148,000 actual direct labor hours were used but labor inefficiencies resulted in the production of only 140,000 good units. In such a case, the entire production variance may be attributable to inefficient labor rather than faulty scheduling or some other reason.

However, favorable or unfavorable variances in labor performance may not be necessarily related to the production variance. Departures from schedule could be caused by machine breakdowns, material shortages, poor production planning, or some other reason. Conversely, a manager can adhere to production schedules, but still produce the units inefficiently.

Expressing Variances in Dollars Rather than in Physical Measures

LIMITATIONS AND USES OF MONETARY MEASURES

Supposedly, once a certain capacity is provided, the addition of one unit of product to sales will increase net income by the unit contribution margin. The fixed costs in the short run will be unaffected by changes in volume, so failure to utilize capacity fully represents a lost opportunity to increase net income by the contribution margin associated with the unsold capacity.

So far, we have deliberately avoided expressing variances in dollar terms for two reasons. First, it is often unnecessary and confusing to express control measures in dollars when the operating personnel being judged think in physical terms only. The general guide is to express a measure in terms best understood by the individuals affected. The object is to help managers operate effectively and efficiently. If this can be achieved without converting data into dollar terms, so much the better. Second, the approximation of opportunity costs, which are the pertinent dollar measures, is hampered by many practical difficulties. For instance, a uniform unit contribution margin is often assumed. In many cases, of course, the increases in unit volume may be attained only by reducing unit prices or by accepting orders that would entail extraordinary incremental costs. In these instances, the dollar measure of the variance would have to be adjusted accordingly. The main objective is to approximate the probable impact on current net income of the best alternative uses of available capacity.

USING CONTRIBUTION MARGINS AS APPROXIMATIONS OF OPPORTUNITY COSTS

What is the best way to measure the cost of unutilized capacity? The total fixed costs will be the same regardless of whether production is 140,000 or 164,000 units. Therefore, from a short-run total operating cost viewpoint, unutilized capacity will not affect costs as they are ordinarily recorded by accountants. However, from an economic viewpoint, there may be an opportunity cost as measured by the contribution margins foregone by failure to utilize capacity. This opportunity cost may be zero, particularly if the sales force has done everything possible to market the products and if there is no alternate use for the otherwise idle facilities. An example of alternate use would be doing sub-contracting work for some other manufacturer. However, to demonstrate the general idea, assume that uniform unit contribution margins per unit can be validly used.

In our example, assume a sales price of $10.00 less unit variable costs of $8.00, or $2.00 unit contribution margin. Exhibit 2 expresses the variances in dollar terms.

Contribution margins as an approximation of the opportunity cost notion may be especially pertinent when the master budget sales forecast is hovering near practical capacity. For example, production could be master budgeted *and* scheduled at the practical capacity level of 200,000 units, but, say, inefficiencies result in only 194,000 units being produced. The economic impact of this production variance is best measured by the lost contribution margin per unit times the difference between the 200,000 and the 194,000 good units produced ($2.00 × 6,000 units = $12,000 lost contribution margin).

HELPING THE BUDGETARY PROCESS

The variances described above can also be useful in evaluating and revising the budget as the year unfolds. Even if the variances were not used to evaluate marketing and production management, they still could be useful to the budgetary process because they stress careful estimation in the first place — emphasizing consideration of alternative opportunities before the master budget is adopted. Interim follow-up could prompt a revised master budget,[10] as is now done in practice. That is, although the illustration used a year as a time span for analysis, the same approach is applicable to monthly or quarterly periods.

---

[10] This is akin to changing the optimal mix in linear programming in light of changes in constraints, prices, etc.

EXHIBIT 2

Analysis of Volume Variance Using Contribution Margins

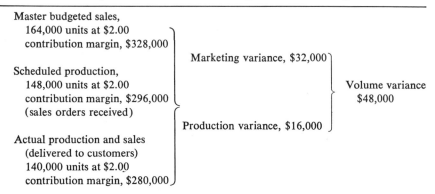

Master budgeted sales,
  164,000 units at $2.00
  contribution margin, $328,000

  Marketing variance, $32,000

Scheduled production,
  148,000 units at $2.00
  contribution margin, $296,000
  (sales orders received)

  Production variance, $16,000

Volume variance
$48,000

Actual production and sales
  (delivered to customers)
  140,000 units at $2.00
  contribution margin, $280,000

Somewhere in the reporting scheme, management will probably want an explanation of why the target net income is not achieved. The above analysis dovetails well with the income statement. Assume that total fixed costs are $200,000. A summary analysis follows:

	Master Budget 164,000 units	Actual Results 140,000 units	Variance
Sales at $10.00	$1,640,000	$1,400,000	
Variable costs at $8.00	1,312,000	1,120,000	
Contribution margin at $2.00	$ 328,000	$ 280,000	$48,000U
Fixed costs	200,000	200,000	
Net Income	$ 128,000	$ 80,000	$48,000U*

* EXPLANATION OF VARIANCE: Failure to reach volume level originally budgeted resulted in inability to obtain the contribution margin originally budgeted:

Marketing variance:
  Sales department failed to obtain enough orders (164,000 units budgeted − 148,000 units scheduled for production) × $2.00 .... $32,000
Production variance:
  Production departments failed to meet production schedules (148,000 units scheduled − 140,000 units produced and sold) × $2.00 16,000
Total volume variance, which *in this case* wholly explains the difference in net income $48,000

THE OPPORTUNITY COST APPROACH

The illustrations in this paper highlight the essence of the problem of assessing how well capacity is being utilized. However, the use here of the lost contribution margin, a single product, and a single constraint over-simplifies the real world difficulties of trying to obtain variances which are the best available measures of opportunity costs. Most companies have many products and many constraints. Interactions are manifold:

> "Alfred Marshall asked the question, which blade of scissors does the cutting? If you analyze one blade at a time, you will never find out how a scissors cuts a piece of paper. There is interaction between two blades, which is the crucial element for cutting.
>
> Many kinds of business and government phenomena that we observe can not be analyzed effectively one variable at a time. If you can analyze effectively one variable at a time, that is, by all odds, the means to use. But the crux of systems analysis is the application of the situation when you cannot explain the behavior of the system by looking at it one variable at a time — even if you exhaust all the variables, which may be many millions."[11]

How can an accounting system be designed that will tie in best with the decisions regarding the utilization of capacity? A logical first step is to try to formulate a reporting system that dovetails with a specific, well-defined decision model. Demski has developed what he calls an ex post model, based on the linear programming model, which envelopes shifts in the original master budget. It "compares what a firm actually accomplished during some planning period with what it deems on the basis of hindsight it should have accomplished — where accomplishments are measured in terms of the objective function in the firm's planning model. It is an opportunity cost approach in the sense that what a firm actually accomplished during some planning period is compared with what it should have accomplished by the ex post optimum program."[12] He ably demonstrated the feasibility of his model by applying it to the operations of an oil refinery. His approach was truly an opportunity cost approach because it considered the simultaneous changes in all relevant variables (mutatis mutandis) rather than one variable at a time (ceteris paribus). It produced variances that signaled the existence of opportunities and their exact sources and effects, as near as could be determined. The existence of well-defined decision models, such as linear programming, inventory, and queuing models, enhances the likelihood of implementing an ex post opportunity cost approach in practice.

---

[11] Comments by W. W. Cooper in Thomas J. Burns (ed.), *The Use of Accounting Data in Decision-Making* (unpublished, The Ohio State University, 1966), p. 228.

[12] Joel S. Demski, *Variance Analysis: An Opportunity Cost Approach with a Linear Programming Application,* unpublished Ph.D. dissertation, University of Chicago, 1966. Also, see J. M. Samuels, "Opportunity Costing: An Application of Mathematical Programming," *Journal of Accounting Research,* Autumn 1965, pp. 182–191.

Summary

Distinctions between long-range and short-range factors and between hierarchies of responsibility in an organization help to develop a conceptual framework for analyzing the utilization of capacity.

For purposes of current planning and control, physical measures of capacity should suffice in many instances, at least at lower levels of the organization. If dollar measures are sought, opportunity costs, even if they have to be crudely approximated via unit contribution margins, are superior to historical costs for measuring the effect on net income of the utilization of existing facilities.

Lost contribution margins directly measure the effects of volume on profits. Therefore, they are a better basis for the computation of volume variances than historical fixed costs, which unitize total costs that are not affected by current fluctuations in volume. The volume variance based on historical fixed costs has little, if any, economic significance for current planning and control.

The development in many firms of more sophisticated management control systems, which often are linked with formal, well-defined decision models, will facilitate attempts to produce variances that better approximate opportunity costs.

19

This trail-breaking article extends variance analysis beyond conventional process and performance control to an evaluation of performance of decision models. Not only is a change required in the types of variances which should be calculated and in the methods of assessing their significance, but there are essential differences in management response to observed variances. Random deviations should evoke no response; deviations reflecting a change in the process should.

Effective control systems can be accomplished if they are designed around the formal decision models used by the firm, if specific control limits are established for critical variances, and if the system distinguishes between random deviations and those caused by process change.

Procedures for monitoring the decision process are described, with discussions focusing on measurement of random fluctuations, sensitivity analysis, inventory, allocation, and capital budgeting models, and on the problem of jointness.

An Extension of Standard Cost Variance Analysis*

Nicholas Dopuch, Jacob G. Birnberg, and Joel Demski

Previous efforts to improve the usefulness of standard cost variance analysis have tended to focus on one of two related problems. Proposals have been offered that had as their objective either an improvement in the types of variances the accountant should calculate or in his methods for analyzing the significance of observed variances. An early paper by Solomons[1] and a more recent one by Samuels[2] reflect proposals of the first type.

* *From* The Accounting Review, *Vol. XLII, No. 3 (July, 1967), pp. 526–536. Reprinted by permission of the American Accounting Association and the authors.*

[1] David Solomons, "Standard Costing Needs Better Variances," *N.A.A. Bulletin,* December 1961, p. 39.

[2] J. M. Samuels, "Opportunity Costing: An Application of Mathematical Programming," *Journal of Accounting Research,* Autumn 1965, pp. 182–91; we would also classify the following efforts in this same class: R. S. Gynther, "Improving Separation of Fixed and Variable Expenses," *N.A.A. Bulletin,* June 1963, pp. 29–38; and R. B. Troxel, "Variable Budgets Through Correlation Analysis: A Simplified Approach," *N.A.A. Bulletin,* February 1965, pp. 48–55.

The application of statistical models in setting control limits is illustrative of the second type of proposal.

Significantly, these previous efforts have concentrated on the control of processes and individual performances. Our purpose in this paper is to demonstrate how similar types of analyses may be applied to a second level of control — the control of the application and performance of formal decision models. As we will illustrate later, a systematic control of formal decision models will require changes in both the types of variances the accountant should calculate and in his methods for assessing the significance of these variances.[3]

The essential difference between process control and model control lies in the type of response management should make to an observed variance. The appropriate response by management depends upon the expected source of the deviation. In this respect, we note that when management implements a particular decision model, it is uncertain about (a) the appropriateness of the model relative to the specification of the decision problem, (b) the estimates of the decision variables which are critical to the implementation of the model, and (c) after the model is in operation, whether the actions specified by the model are being performed within the prescribed limits.

An observed variance from expected performances may reflect any one of the following conditions:[4]

> *Type 1 Deviation:* The deviation resulted from the random aspect of the process being controlled. Assuming the deviation is not statistically significant, no response by management is necessary.
>
> *Type 2 Deviation:* The deviation resulted from a temporary or permanent change in the process. Further investigation is required to determine whether:
>
> a. The deviation is temporary in the sense that performance levels can be adjusted in the next period. This is the general definition of a controllable deviation.
>
> b. The deviation resulted from a permanent change in the process. If this is established, management must review the decision process in order to assess the effect of the deviation on the decisions it has adopted and/or the decision model being implemented. The deviation is noncontrollable, but, nevertheless, a response may be required.

Traditionally, standard cost systems have concentrated on the analysis of type 1 and type 2-a deviations. These systems have not been designed to indicate when and if type 2-b deviations are critical to the decision process. These type 2-b deviations are central to the control of decision models.

---

[3] This relationship is also noted in Z. S. Zannetos, "Standard Costs as a First Step to Probabilistic Control: A Theoretical Justification, an Extension and Implications," THE ACCOUNTING REVIEW, April 1964, pp. 296–304.

[4] We are ignoring measurement errors per se, i.e., deviations arising from imperfect methods of measurement.

An effective control over decision models can be accomplished if the following rules are observed. First, the control system should be designed around the formal decision models used by the firm. The form of the model indicates the critical decision variables for which variances need to be calculated. Second, specific control limits should be established for these critical variances. These control limits can be built into the system to signal when and if changes in the estimates of the critical variables call for different decisions. Finally, the system should provide some mechanism for distinguishing between type 1 and 2 deviations since type 1 deviations are not significant to the decision process.

In the remainder of the paper we will describe procedures for monitoring the decision process. We will also comment on the basic problems in designing control systems that can monitor both performances and the decision process. As a first step, however, we wish to discuss further the relationship between type 1 and type 2 deviations.

The Measurement of Random Fluctuations

If a process being controlled can be described by $y_i = x_i + e_i$, where:

$y_i =$ the observed level of performance in the ith period,
$x_i =$ the level at which the stationary process is operating in the ith period, and
$e_i =$ the random fluctuations occurring in the ith period,

then we desire a control system that can distinguish between fluctuations in y_i due to e_i and those due to a change in the x_i. This is essentially a problem in statistical analysis, for it is assumed that the random fluctuations can be identified by reference to the probability distribution of the y_i. A statistical analysis of deviations is preliminary to the control of decision models since management should respond to a deviation only if it represents a change in the estimates of the decision variables. Therefore, an effective control system depends first of all upon the efficiency with which we can eliminate the effect of type 1 (random) deviations.

In general, we are more confident in the analysis if we can work with a known distribution of the y_i. Bierman, Fouraker, and Jaedicke illustrate the procedures which can be followed whenever we can use an explicit prior distribution of the y_i to set control limits.[5] If the nature of the distribution is not known, we must fall back on a proposal by Zannetos which consists of using Chebyshev's inequality as the basis for setting the control

---

[5] H. Bierman, J. L. E. Fouraker, and R. K. Jaedicke, "A Use of Probability and Statistics in Performance Evaluation," THE ACCOUNTING REVIEW, July 1961, pp. 416–17.

limits.[6] This inequality can be applied regardless of the nature of the distribution of the y_i, but the analysis will be less efficient than one derived from a known distribution. Chebyshev's inequality represents the lower limit in the efficiency of our statements about the distribution. For example, if the distribution of the y_i can be described by the normal curve, 95% of the observations can be expected to fall within two standard deviations about the mean. An observation outside of this interval could be accepted as a signal of a change in the x_i because it has such a low probability of occurrence. However, the application of Chebyshev's inequality would only justify the expectation that at least 75% of the observations will fall within two standard deviations of the mean of the distribution.

The importance of an efficient method for analyzing type 2 deviations[7] follows from the nature of the final decision to investigate an observed deviation. The final decision to investigate must balance three factors: the probability that the deviation represents a non-random event, the costs of making the investigation, and the benefits expected from the investigation. Bierman, Fouraker, and Jaedicke illustrate the construction of a decision chart, given different estimates of these factors. A critical variable in the construction of the chart is the expected benefits from investigation. Thus, "we have to determine C (costs) and L (benefits) to compute the critical probability."[8] In another work, Bierman constructs the chart on the assumption that adjustments in performance levels are the benefits which will result from the investigation.[9] In effect, he has linked the statistical analysis to the investigation of type 2-a deviations.

However, recall that a deviation may be statistically significant but still non-controllable, i.e., it may represent a permanent change in a decision variable. Under these conditions, an investigation into the nature of the

---

[6] The Chebyshev inequality states the lower and upper bounds of the probabilities, P, that the difference between the observed value, X, and the mean, μ_x, is a certain distance, c, times the standard deviation, σ_x. Thus, as Zannetos shows:

$$P(|x - \mu_x|) \leq c\sigma_x \geq 1 - \frac{1}{c^2}$$

and

$$P(|x - \mu_x|) \geq c\sigma_x \leq 1 - \frac{1}{c^2}.$$

Zannetos, op. cit., p. 298.

[7] This includes related aspects of statistical analysis; e.g. see Paul R. McClenon, "Cost Finding Through Multiple Correlation Analysis," THE ACCOUNTING REVIEW, July 1963, pp. 540–47, and A. J. Duncan, "The Economic Design of X Charts Used to Maintain Current Control of a Process," *Journal of the American Statistical Association*, June 1956, pp. 228–242.

[8] See his *Topics in Cost Accounting and Decisions* (McGraw-Hill Book Company, 1963), p. 22. Actually it is possible to solve for a critical "L" if values of the other parameters are given. However, even in this case, we will have to have some means of assessing the likely value of "L", given actual observations.

[9] Loc. cit.

deviation can produce benefits only from changes in the firm's decisions or in the models it is employing. We now want to illustrate how the significance of these type 2-b deviations can be measured.

Sensitivity Analysis and Control Systems

A firm should adjust its decisions in response to permanent changes in the estimates of decision variables if the magnitude of change in a single estimate or in a group of estimates has significant effect on the firm's optimal decisions. A significant effect is measured by the positive difference between the opportunity costs incurred by the firm if it does not respond to the change and any organizational costs incurred if it does respond to the change. The difference between the two costs is the net benefit from a response to a permanent change in the estimate of a decision variable.

The extent of the opportunity costs incurred by the firm will depend on the sensitivity of the firm's decision model(s) to observed deviations. Therefore, the procedures necessary to determine the significance of type 2-b deviations consist mainly of the techniques for evaluating the sensitivity of the firm's decision models to assumed changes in the estimates of decision variables.

Our illustrations of these techniques will be quite similar to those found in the field of operations research. For many years an extensive use has been made of sensitivity analysis as a basis for improving the planning phase of a model's implementation. We see no reason why the same techniques cannot also be used in the control of these models. For obvious reasons, sensitivity analysis is meaningful only in the implementation of formal decision models. Our discussion is developed around two specific decision models — an inventory model and a resource allocation model. Later, we will comment on the difficulty of using sensitivity analysis to control less formal models, e.g., capital budgeting models.

Inventory Models and the Control System

An earlier proposal linking the control system to an inventory model was made by Gordon.[10] However, he was concerned only with the improvement in the evaluation of type 2-a or performance deviations. We will use the general form of the EOQ model as the basis for illustrating the evaluation of the inventory decisions. The following definitions apply to the model.[11]

[10] M. J. Gordon, "Toward a Theory of Responsibility Accounting Systems," *N.A.A. Bulletin,* December 1963, pp. 8–9.

[11] These symbols and the derivations of the optimal order quantities are based upon those found in C. W. Churchman, R. L. Ackoff, and E. L. Arnoff, *Introduction to Operations Research* (John Wiley and Sons, Inc., 1957), pp. 205–206.

C_p = cost of purchasing (per order)
C_s = cost of storage (per time period)
C_o = cost of stock-outs (per time period)
D = total demand for inventory during time period T
q = the amount of inventory to be ordered per order placed (q^* represents the optimal order quantity)
D/q = the number of orders placed during time period T.
t_s = the length of time required for the inventory to go from a level of q to the receipt of the next order, or

$$t_s = \frac{T}{D/q} = \frac{T \cdot q}{D}.$$

Exhibit 1 represents the sequence of inventory cycles.

EXHIBIT I

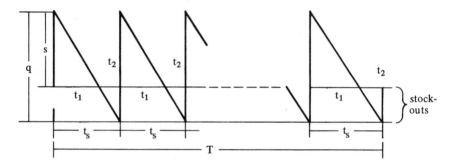

The total expected cost during time period T is:

$$T.C. = \left(\frac{s}{2} C_s t_1 + \frac{q - s}{2} C_o t_2 + C_p\right) \frac{D}{q}.$$

That is, Total Cost = (storage costs during time period t_1 + stock-out costs during time period t_2 + purchase order costs) times the number of orders, D/q. After some simplifying substitutions, the total cost equation can be differentiated with respect to s and q to obtain:[12]

$$q^* = \sqrt{\frac{2DC_p}{C_s T}} \cdot \sqrt{\frac{C_s + C_o}{C_o}}$$

$$s^* = \sqrt{\frac{2DC_p}{C_s T}} \cdot \sqrt{\frac{C_o}{C_s + C_o}}.$$

As the cost of stock-outs, C_o, becomes infinitely large, the expressions:

$$\sqrt{\frac{C_s + C_o}{C_o}} \quad \text{and} \quad \sqrt{\frac{C_o}{C_s + C_o}}$$

approach unity, and we have the EOQ model.

[12] Ibid., pp. 224–25.

Assume then that a firm faces a demand (D) of 3,600 units a year, that its purchase costs are \$10 per order, that its storage costs are 20 cents per month per unit, and that its stock-out costs are an estimated 45 cents per unit per month. The inventory policies would be based on the following:

$$q^* = \sqrt{\frac{2C_pD}{C_sT}} \cdot \sqrt{\frac{C_s + C_o}{C_o}}$$

$$= 173\sqrt{\frac{.20 + .45}{.45}}$$

$$= 173(1.20)$$

$$\approx 208 \text{ units.}$$

$$s^* = \sqrt{\frac{2C_pD}{C_sT}} \cdot \sqrt{\frac{C_o}{C_s + C_o}}$$

$$= 173\sqrt{\frac{.45}{.20 + .45}}$$

$$= 173(.832)$$

$$\approx 143 \text{ units.}$$

This results in the following set of policies: order 208 units; allow back-orders of 65 units per cycle (i.e., stock-outs of 65 units will be permitted); and carry a maximum of 143 units (after back-orders are filled).

The total cost for this set of inventory policies can be determined by the equation:

$$T.C. = \sqrt{2DC_sTC_p} \cdot \sqrt{\frac{C_o}{C_s + C_o}}$$

$$= 415(.832)$$

$$= \$345 \text{[13]}$$

If we assume that a control system has been designed to include these standard inventory costs of C_p, C_s, and C_o, this model can serve as the basis for assessing the significance of any deviations from these standards.

Consider the effect of a 50 per cent deviation in the actual purchase order costs (C_p). If we substituted the new cost, C_p', into our equations and resolved for $q^{*\prime}$ and $s^{*\prime}$, $T.C.'$ would be \$423. Thus, the 50 per cent change has caused in increase in costs of \$78 $(423 - 345)$. This is the change in the *yearly costs* of this new set of inventory policies.

Notice, however, that if the firm did not change its inventory policies in response to the new purchase order costs, the total purchase cost deviation for the year would be $(5)(17.3) = \$86.5$. The total yearly costs

[13] Specifically, this set of policies results in approximately 17.3 orders; if we assume a rate of usage of 10 units per day, the total stock-out time will be approximately 114 days or 3.8 months. This will produce a total cost of approximately \$54. The average units on hand, 72 units, will be held for about 8.2 months. This will cost the firm approximately \$118. Add the purchase order costs of \$173 and the total is \$345.

would be $345 + $86 = $431. Thus, the firm gains only $8 per year by changing its set of policies. This net benefit from change-over would have to be compared to any costs of change-over before the firm could determine its appropriate response.

A similar analysis may be performed assuming 50 per cent increases in storage costs (C_s) and stock-out costs (C_o). The effect of a 50 per cent change in storage costs is as follows: (1) order 183 units (19.6) orders; (2) stock a maximum of 109 units; and (3) permit stock-outs of 74 units. The new total cost, *T.C.'*, would be $394. However, if the firm did not shift its policies, its total cost would increase by $59 to a total of $404. Hence, the net benefit of a shift is only $10. A 50 per cent increase in stock-out costs would also result in a net benefit from shifting of only $10. That is, *T.C.'* would equal $366, but if the firm did not alter its policies, its inventory costs would increase only to $376.

We do not want to leave the impression that this inventory model will always be more sensitive to storage costs and stock-out costs than to purchase-order costs. Our results are partially dependent upon the original values we assigned to the three cost inputs. The general form of the equations for determining changes in total costs for different changes in each of the standards is given in the appendix . . .

We can conceive of a control system for a firm which incorporates a . . . set of graphs for its inventory costs. The significance of deviations from any one of the three inventory standards could be determined by referring to the effect of the change on the total costs of the inventory system. In this manner, the benefit of shifting to a new solution could be measured by comparing the total costs if the inventory policies are altered to the opportunity costs of not changing the firm's decisions.

Certainly, there are some practical problems involved in trying to design such a control system. Our analysis considered the effect on only one change at a time. Some multiple changes have been analyzed in the literature,[14] and it is conceivable that a firm could construct graphs based upon multiple changes in its standards. But these would have to be based upon management's a priori judgment as to which set of multiple changes is likely to occur. We also found it practical to examine these issues relative to a rather simple kind of inventory model. The control system would have to be based upon whatever inventory model the firm uses.[15] Finally, we assumed that the firm can and would be willing to measure storage,

[14] See Eliezer Naddor, *Inventory Systems* (John Wiley and Sons, Inc., 1966), pp. 52–53 and 68.

[15] We know of no survey which indicates the kinds of models firms do employ. However, in one informal study, the following was noted: "Since the companies chosen for interviews were largely those that had demonstrated an interest in modern methods of inventory management, it must be concluded that the actual use of these techniques is less frequent than the literature on this subject might lead one to believe." National Association of Accountants, "Techniques in Inventory Management," *N.A.A. Research Report No. 40* (1964), p. 2.

purchase-order, and stock-out costs. Regarding the latter, Hadley and Whitin have said that the general procedure is "for someone to make a guess as to what they are."[16]

Allocation Models and the Control System

In terms of the present discussion we view the allocation problem as consisting of the determination of the best use to be made of the capital equipment available to the firm. For a single product firm, the decision variables are the various prices obtained for different output levels, the different combinations and types of inputs which can produce various output levels, and their input prices. A sensitivity analysis for a single-product firm would follow a procedure suggested by Zannetos. Specifically, he states:[17]

> Whenever prices change, or at the latest, whenever price variances appear, the system will be instructed to develop the new price ratios and search for the proper input-mix solution that is *stored*. If as a result of the comparison between the suggested and existing methods of operations input substitutions are dictated, the system will signal the need for such a change and also provide all the necessary details for its implementation.

We will extend this notion to a multi-product firm. The methods we will use and the issues we will raise will be similar to those discussed in the previous section. For illustration, we have selected a simple linear programming problem.

Consider a firm which produces two products, x_1 and x_2; the products pass through two facilities, b_1 and b_2, which have fixed capacities of 1.0 (million) and .9 (million) hours respectively.

Product x_1 requires 8/10 hour of resource b_1 and 5/10 hour of b_2; similarly, x_2 requires 5/10 hour of b_1 and one hour of b_2. Each unit of x_1 contributes (revenues − variable costs) \$960 and each unit of x_2 contributes \$875. The entire problem can be expressed as:

$$\text{Max. } z = 960x_1 + 875x_2$$

Subject to

$$8/10x_1 + 5/10x_2 \leq 1.0$$
$$5/10x_1 + 1x_2 \leq .9$$
$$x_1, x_2 \geq 0.$$

We can convert these inequalities into equations by using the variables x_3 and x_4, which represent unused capacity of b_1 and b_2 respectively. The initial and final solutions (I and II respectively) to this problem are indicated below in simplex tableau form, in Exhibit 2.

---

[16] G. Hadley and T. M. Whitin, *Analysis of Inventory Systems* (Prentice-Hall, Inc., 1963), p. 420.

[17] Z. S. Zannetos, op. cit., p. 303.

EXHIBIT 2

x_J			x_1	x_2	x_3	x_4	
C_J			960	875	0	0	
x_B	C_B	b_1					
x_3	0	1.00	8/10	5/10	1	0	
x_4	0	.90	5/10	1	0	1	
$z, z_J - C_J$		0	-960	-875	0	0	I
x_1	960	1.00	1	0	20/11	$-10/11$	II
x_2	875	.400	0	1	$-10/11$	16/11	
$z, z_J - C_J$		1310	0	0	950	400	

The sensitivity of this solution to changes in input or output prices can be assessed if we refer to the imputed values of the scarce resources. In the second tableau above, these prices are located in the z, $z_j - c_j$ row under the slack-variable columns; i.e., the values are \$950 and \$450 respectively.

The criterion followed in the simplex method is that if a negative value appears in the $z_j - c_j$ row, then the solution is not optimal. Therefore, we must determine changes in the contribution margins of C_1 and C_2 which will alter the solution shown in the second tableau.

Looking back at Tableau II, we note that the value 950 is obtained by multiplying 960 (20/11) and adding the result to 875 ($-10/11$). Similarly, the value 400 is the sum of 960 ($-10/11$) + 875 (16/11). Let us consider the effect of an increase in C_1 which we will denote as C_1'.

In the x_3 column, C_1 has the positive coefficient 20/11. Therefore, an increase in C_1 will have a positive effect on the $z_3 - c_3$ value. However, a sufficient increase in the C_1 will change $z_4 - c_4$ to a negative value since C_1 has the negative coefficient of ($-10/11$) in column x_4. We can determine this critical value of C_1' by solving the equation:

$$C_1'(-10/11) + 875(16/11) = 0$$
$$C_1' = 16/10(875)$$
$$= 1400.$$

Thus, an increase of 440 is a critical upper limit for C_1 since any additional increase will change the optimal solution.

If we apply the same analysis to an increase in C_2, the critical limit is an increase of 1045. Alternatively, a decrease in C_1 to 437.50 will cause x_3 to replace x_1 in the solution, and a decrease in C_2 to 600 will cause x_4 to replace x_2.

Hence, the upper and lower limits for C_1 are $437.50 \le C_1 \le 1400$, and those for C_2 are $600 \le C_2 \le 1920$, provided the changes in C_1 and C_2 are completely independent. If both contribution margins changed at the same time, the limits we calculated would not be valid. However, it is possible to analyze multiple changes provided that we specify which contribution margins are to be changed.

Since the contribution margins summarize both revenue and variable cost changes, these limits are sufficient to analyze changes in output prices, input prices, and to some extent changes in the technical coefficients of producing the different units of output. There are techniques for analyzing other changes as well, but we will not illustrate these.[18]

As in the previous section, a calculation of these limits represents only the first step in the analysis. A change in the solution to the linear programming problem might be indicated, but the firm would still not wish to alter its output combination of $1.0x_1$ and $.4x_2$. For example, suppose C_1 drops to \$435 per unit. This would result in a change in the optimal solution as follows: $x_2 = .900$ and $x_3 = .550$; $x_1 = x_4 = 0$. Total contribution margin would be: $.900 (875) + .550 (0) = 787.50$. However, if the firm did not alter its solution and continued to produce $1.0x_1$ and $.4x_2$, its total contribution would be: $1.0 (435 = C_1') + .400 (875) = 775$. If there are organizational costs in making a solution shift, this decrease in C_1 would not be sufficient to warrant a change to the optimal solution.

It is obvious that the use of sensitivity analysis to establish limits for type 2-b deviations is much more difficult in terms of the allocation decisions of a firm. In the inventory analysis, we had to consider only three variables. However, linear programming models may involve hundreds of products of output. We cannot establish whether it is practical to control large programs unless we examine the properties of a firm's allocation model in its actual setting. More will be said about this later.

We should also stress another implication of the linking of the control system to a linear programming model. The sensitivity analysis we employed implies a different set of "variances" than the price and quantity variances normally calculated by the accountant. It is conceivable that some of the critical deviations illustrated in a sensitivity analysis will supplement, and perhaps even circumvent, the traditional standard cost variances. Indeed, the imputed values of the scarce resources have been used by Samuels to develop a different kind of capacity variance.[19]

Type 2-a and Type 2-b Deviations and the Jointness Problem

Thus far we have discussed the groupings of type 2-a and type 2-b deviations separately. However, the measurement of a particular financial variance may serve as an index of both sources of deviations. For example,

[18] For example, see S. I. Gass, *Linear Programming* (McGraw-Hill Book Company, 1964).
[19] J. Samuels, op. cit.

a price deviation could indicate either inefficient purchasing policies or a change in the prices quoted to the firm. Suppose the deviation is significant in terms of some decision of the firm. The decision should be changed only if a change in prices has taken place and this change is expected to hold for at least another decision cycle. We know of no formal method for distinguishing between sources of deviations. Yet, the benefits from investigating a deviation cannot be measured unless the source is ascertained in advance.

The solution to this problem may require a less formal methodology. We would not expect both types of deviations to have the same critical limits of significance. As one possibility, the limits for type 2-a deviations might be considerably tighter than those for type 2-b deviations. Any deviation which fell in this narrower band would be considered a type 2-a deviation. If the deviation is large enough to be significant in terms of both sets of responses, further investigation would be necessary. The firm might still wish to establish the same priority regardless, i.e., always investigate for type 2-a causes first.

Capital Budgeting Models and the Control System

Although a more complete discussion would result from a consideration of the sensitivity of capital budgeting models, we believe that, in general, it is impractical to design control systems around specific capital budgeting decisions. The decision to acquire long-lived assets is presumably made on the expectation that the net receipts generated by the utilization of the asset have a present value equal to or greater than the expenditure involved. In many instances the favorable decision implies that the firm will also commit itself to a sequence of operating and future capital budgeting decisions.

Regarding the first stage of the control problem, it is unlikely that management would be able to develop a probability distribution around the set of expected receipts which could be used to separate type 1 from other types of deviations. The uniqueness of capital budgeting decisions prevents a firm from developing a history of cash flows which could be used as a basis for predicting future cash flows. An alternative approach would be to apply a Bayesian analysis to the decision problem. However, an acceptable theory linking Bayesian analysis and capital budgeting remains to be developed.

We can also expect to encounter some major problems in trying to measure whether the expectations of specific capital budgeting decisions are being realized. The results of any capital budgeting decision become interwoven with the current operations of the firm. Consequently, it would be almost impossible to determine when and if a change in decision variables required new decisions. A more practical procedure is merely to control the current operations of the firm and let the significant deviations noted in this procedure signal the need to review capital budgeting decisions.

The Evaluation of Decision-Models

We have purposefully avoided any explicit references to an investigation of the appropriateness of the decision models used by the firm. We do not know of any formal analysis which can be employed to determine which of several available decision models is the appropriate one for the firm. The efficiency of different decision models can be evaluated only by comparing the effects of using alternative models to solve the same kind of problem. The motivation for making these comparisons develops primarily out of management's dissatisfaction with the results of the models implemented. Unsatisfactory results are reflected initially in excessive amounts of error in the estimates of the decision variables. Therefore, a control system may provide an index of the efficiency of the firm's decision models by accumulating a history of the magnitude and frequency of type 2-b deviations.

Conclusions

Our main conclusion is that the method of analysis we have described permits an extension of the standard cost system so that the system can monitor both performances and the decision process. This monitoring is achieved by structuring the control system around the formal decision models used by the firm. We recognize that there are some practical problems in implementing this type of analysis. Many of these are speculative, however, since the degree to which it will be practical to control decision models will vary from firm to firm. We know of only one accounting study aimed at describing the problems inherent in designing a control system around the linear programming model of a firm.[20] Similar studies might be conducted in the area of inventory models.

The use of formal decision models within a firm can be expected to increase as computers yield solutions to more sophisticated models. The firm's control system must be expanded to encompass these new models as they are adopted by the firm.

---

[20] Indeed, this study was initiated on the assumption that an analytical approach is not yet feasible. See Joel Demski, "Accounting for Capacity Utilization: An Opportunity Cost Approach," Ph.D. dissertation, University of Chicago, Graduate School of Business, 1967. For an example of how an analytical approach might be used in studying this problem see Yuji Ijiri, *Management Goals and Accounting for Control* (Chicago: Rand McNally and Company, 1965), especially Chapter VI.

Appendix

Changes in:
$$T.C. = (2DC_sTC_p)^{1/2}\left(\frac{C_o}{C_s + C_o}\right)^{1/2}$$

A. Change in C_p to $C.P.'$

$$T.C.' = (2DC_sTC_p')^{1/2}\left(\frac{C_o}{C_s + C_o}\right)^{1/2}$$

$T.C.' - T.C.$

$$= \left[(2DC_sTC_p')^{1/2}\left(\frac{C_o}{C_s + C_o}\right)^{1/2} - (2DC_sTC_p)^{1/2}\left(\frac{C_o}{C_s + C_o}\right)^{1/2}\right]$$

$$= \left(\frac{C_o}{C_s + C_o}\right)^{1/2}[(2DC_sTC_p')^{1/2} - (2DC_sTC_p)^{1/2}]$$

$$= \left(\frac{C_o}{C_s + C_o}\right)^{1/2}(2DC_sT)^{1/2}[(C_p')^{1/2} - (C_p)^{1/2}]$$

B. Changes in C_s to C_s'

$$T.C.' = (2DC_s'TC_p)^{1/2}\left(\frac{C_o}{C_s' + C_o}\right)^{1/2}$$

$T.C.' - T.C.$

$$= \left[(2DC_s'TC_p)^{1/2}\left(\frac{C_o}{C_s' + C_o}\right)^{1/2} - (2DC_sTC_p)^{1/2}\left(\frac{C_o}{C_s + C_o}\right)^{1/2}\right]$$

$$= (2DTC_p)^{1/2}\left[(C_s')^{1/2}\left(\frac{C_o}{C_s' + C_o}\right)^{1/2} - (C_s)^{1/2}\left(\frac{C_o}{C_s + C_o}\right)^{1/2}\right]$$

$$= (2DTC_p)^{1/2}\left[\left(\frac{C_s'C_o}{C_s' + C_o}\right)^{1/2} - \left(\frac{C_sC_o}{C_s + C_o}\right)^{1/2}\right]$$

C. Change in C_o to C_o'

$$T.C.' = (2DC_sTC_p)^{1/2}\left(\frac{C_o'}{C_s + C_o'}\right)^{1/2}$$

$T.C.' - T.C.$

$$= \left[(2DC_sTC_p)^{1/2}\left(\frac{C_o'}{C_s + C_o'}\right)^{1/2} - (2DC_sTC_p)^{1/2}\left(\frac{C_o}{C_s + C_o}\right)^{1/2}\right]$$

$$= (2DC_sTC_p)^{1/2}\left[\left(\frac{C_o'}{C_s + C_o'}\right)^{1/2} - \left(\frac{C_o}{C_s + C_o}\right)^{1/2}\right]$$

When should cost variances be investigated? This paper uses a simple taxonomy in providing a comprehensive survey of techniques that assess the significance of cost variances. With an interdisciplinary emphasis, the author integrates industrial quality-control techniques, including the cusum chart, with the accounting literature. He also points out a number of fundamental errors and hidden assumptions in the established accounting cost variance literature. From this literature review he introduces and advocates as relevant to the variance investigation decision a model that is unique to accounting cost variance analysis.

The Significance and Investigation of Cost Variances: Survey and Extensions*

Robert S. Kaplan†

1. Introduction

Standard cost systems can produce as many variances each period as there are accounts for which standards are set, since actual costs for a period will rarely equal the standard or budgeted cost for any process worth controlling.[1] Nevertheless, no one seriously advocates taking action

* *From* Journal of Accounting Research, *Vol. 13, No. 2 (Autumn, 1975), pp. 311–337. Reprinted by permission of the editor.*

† Many helpful comments on an earlier draft were received from Professors Nicholas Dopuch, Thomas Dyckman, Robert Magee, and Roman Weil. The opinions and interpretations still remaining in this paper are solely the author's responsibility.

[1] I am excluding the budgeting of expirations of accrued costs such as depreciation or prepaid expenses which should equal planned levels in each period. These expenses represent allocations of prior expenditures and, hence, are not interesting to control on an item-by-item basis each period.

and investigating every cost variance that occurs each period. Managers recognize that many variances are insignificant and caused by random, noncontrollable factors. Since any investigation will involve a certain expenditure of effort and funds, managers will attempt to take action on only the most significant and correctible variances. An investigation should only be undertaken if the benefits expected from the investigation exceed the costs of searching for and correcting the source of the cost variance.

Many articles have appeared in statistical and accounting journals that directly deal with determining whether a process is in or out of control and, hence, whether it is worthwhile to intervene in the process. Despite the widespread use of quality control techniques in industry, however, the application of these ideas in actual standard cost accounting settings can generously be characterized as minimal. For example, in 1968, Koehler reported that "in some general inquiry from some prominent corporations, I was unable to find a single use of statistical procedures for variance control."[2] He attributes this paucity of applications not to the inherent inapplicability of such procedures but to "the fact that accountants have not recognized a conceptual distinction between a significant and an insignificant variance."[3] Koehler proceeds to advocate the use of a simple testing procedure which I will consider later in the paper.

In contrast to Koehler's view, that the fault lies with the lack of formal statistical training among practicing accountants, other observers conclude that statistical procedures are rarely used in practice because the procedures themselves are inappropriate for assessing the significance of accounting variances. For example, Anthony, in a review article on management accounting, observed that "researchers continue to explore the possibility of finding a mathematical way of stating whether a variance between planned and actual cost is or is not significant."[4] He concludes, though, that

> The differences between the data on a production process that is repeated several times a day and data on the overall costs of a department that are measured once a month are so great that few if any managers believe that statistical techniques in the latter case are worth the effort to calculate them. They prefer either to establish control limits by judgment or to run down the report item by item and determine, without any numerical calculation, whether a difference between planned and actual costs is worth investigation.[5]

He also states that "attempts to be even more sophisticated and to apply Bayesian probability theory or dynamic programming to the control chart idea do not strike me as being very promising." [6]

---

[2] Koehler (1968): 35.
[3] *Ibid.*, p. 35.
[4] Anthony (1973): 52.
[5] *Ibid.*, p. 52.
[6] *Ibid.*, p. 51.

The final judgment on the appropriateness of formal statistical and mathematical models for cost variance analysis must be based on empirical studies. To date little such evidence is available. There are reasons to believe, however, that some form of screening model would be beneficial to managers by eliminating the need for them to examine extensive variance reports item by item in order to detect a significant variance. A formal screening model could also scan detailed variance reports more efficiently than a manager, thereby permitting a more disaggregate collection of costs. Moreover, there is extensive evidence in the psychological literature[7] that persons consistently underestimate the importance of sample evidence in forming probability judgments about events. In other words, a manager with strong prior beliefs that everything is all right with a given process will interpret sizable variances as still being consistent with an in-control situation, whereas a statistical model would clearly signal a low probability that such large deviations could arise from an in-control situation. A statistical model may also indicate that an occasional large variance is consistent with fluctuation that has occurred in the past so that immediate action may not be warranted.

The purpose of this paper is to provide a comprehensive survey of techniques that are potentially useful for assessing the significance of cost variances. A simple taxonomy of various approaches will be described which should help to classify the basic assumptions and purpose of each type of proposed procedure. Important techniques commonly used in industrial quality control will be briefly surveyed and related to proposals made in the accounting literature. Several widely referenced articles in the accounting literature will be reviewed and a number of fundamental errors and hidden assumptions in some of these papers will be noted. Finally, I will suggest extensions and describe a model, new to the accounting literature, that may eventually prove useful for aiding the variance investigation decision.

Before embarking on this survey, it is useful to indicate some aspects of the variance investigation decision I will *not* be considering. First, since I will deal only with a single process and a single variance reported from this process, then models which are designed to identify or isolate the most important variances from a large set [see Lev (1969)] will not be

---

[7] For surveys of this literature, see Edwards (1968) and Slovic and Lichtenstein (1971). The evidence seems very strong that persons do not process sample evidence very well in complex environments. For example, Slovic and Lichtenstein conclude (p. 714), "[Man as an] intuitive statistician appears to be quite confused by the conceptual demands of probabilistic inference tasks. He seems capable of little more than revising his response in the right direction upon receipt of a new item of information (and the inertia effect is evidence that he is not always successful in doing even this)." Also (p. 724), "We find that judges have a very difficult time weighting and combining information, be it probabilistic or deterministic in nature. To reduce cognitive strain, they resort to simplified decision strategies many of which lead them to ignore or misuse relevant information."

treated. I will not be involved with the actual investigation process [Demski (1970)] and methods for aggregating variances to enhance the reporting and investigation process [Ronen (1974)]. As an aside, Demski (1970), classifies five separate sources of cost deviations and after assuming that we are able to estimate the time to investigate each source as well as the prior probability that the deviation came from each source, describes an algorithm which will minimize the expected time until the source is uncovered. In a more general setting, DeGroot (1970) describes an algorithm when there is a cost, c_i, of investigating each source as well as a probability, α_i, of not detecting the cause even when investigating the true source of the deviation (i.e., imperfect investigation).[8]

I will also deal only briefly with relating the significance of the accounting variance to possible changes in decision models.[9] I am assuming that the significant variances being considered here are, for the most part, correctible and hence should not require changes in the firm's decisions but this point will be mentioned again in Section 6B.

2. A Taxonomy of Variance Investigation Models

All the papers and models that will be reviewed in this paper can be classified along two dimensions. The first dichotomy is whether the investigation decision is made on the basis of a single observation or whether some past sequence of observations, including the most recent one, is considered in the decision. I refer to this distinction as single-period versus multi-period models. An example of a single-period model is a control chart approach in which a variance is investigated if it falls outside a pre-specified limit, e.g., 2σ or 3σ from the expected value. An example of a multi-period approach occurs if all the most recent observations are used to estimate the current mean of the process to determine whether the process is within its control limits. The second dichotomy is whether or not the model explicitly includes the expected costs and benefits of the investigation in determining when to investigate a variance. A simple control chart or hypothesis test with preset (and arbitrary) levels of a Type I error is an example of a model which does not explicitly include decision relevant costs in the analysis. Economically designed control charts, however, in which control limits are set as a function of the cost of an investigation as well as the cost of making Type I and Type II errors would be an example of a model that included relevant costs in the analysis. Models which use statistical decision theory approaches such as Duvall (1967), Kaplan (1969), and Dyckman (1969) are other examples of this type of model.

[8] DeGroot (1970): 423–29; and Kadane (1971).
[9] This topic is developed in Dopuch, Birnberg, and Demski (1967) and Demski (1967).

Thus, we may classify the papers on the variance investigation decision into a 2×2 table as shown below. An additional sub-classification is useful in the lower right-hand category of multi-period decision theory models.

A Taxonomy of Deviation Investigation Models

	Costs and Benefits of Investigation not Considered	Costs and Benefits of Investigation Considered
Single-Period	Zannetos (1964) Juers (1967), Koehler (1968) Luh (1968), Probst (1971) Buzby (1974)	Duncan (1956) Bierman, Fouraker, and Jaedicke (1961)
Multi-Period	Cumulative-Sum Chart as in Page (1954). Also Barnard (1959) Chernoff and Zacks (1964)	Duvall (1967) Kaplan (1969) Dyckman (1969) Bather (1963)

Some models, such as Kaplan (1969) and Dyckman (1969), assume that the process being controlled can only be in a discrete set of states. Typically, only two states are assumed (in control and out of control) but it is also possible to use a finer classification in which discrete amounts of "out-of-controlness" are allowed. In fact, models such as Duvall (1967) and Bather (1963) allow the mean of the process to vary continuously so that there is an infinite set of states for the process. This leads to slightly different procedures to estimate the current state of the process and, hence, it is useful to introduce this sub-classification of discrete versus continuous process states. In the remainder of the paper, we analyze each compartment in the table, including the sub-classification just described, to indicate the assumptions, strengths, and weaknesses of the proposed models.

3. Decision Models Based on a Single Observation; No Costs of Investigation or Misclassification

In the simplest control formulation, the objective is to determine whether a shift in the probability distribution of the process generating outputs has occurred. Usually, the shift is identified with a change in the location parameter (e.g., the mean) of the distribution though it is, of course, possible to test for any shift in the distribution [see Luh (1968)]. No costs of misclassification are considered and information from previous observations on the process is ignored. The classic example of such a procedure is the simple $\bar{x}$ chart suggested by Shewhart (1931) and widely used in industry. With this procedure, a target mean is established and a standard deviation, σ, is estimated for the process when it is in control. Control limits are typically set so that the probability of an in-control process with normally distributed outcomes producing a signal beyond these limits (a Type I error) is very small (e.g., .01 or .002). In practice, Shewhart charts are modified on an ad hoc basis to detect a run of observations in excess of 1σ or 2σ, but there is no generally accepted modification to the classic Shewhart control chart.

Many articles in the accounting literature are essentially variations of a simple Shewhart chart in which a distribution is assumed under the null hypothesis that the process is in control. An investigation is signaled when the probability that any single observation could have come from this in-control distribution falls below a given level, usually assumed to be .05. For example, the papers by Buzby (1974), Juers (1967), Koehler (1968), Luh (1968), Probst (1971), and Zannetos (1964) are all of this type. Some of these papers [Buzby (1974), Zannetos (1964)] also suggest the use of Chebyschev's inequality to compute the probability of an extreme observation if one does not believe that observations from the in-control distribution are normally distributed (or some other parametric form).

Luh's paper is at a much more disaggregate form of analysis from any of the other papers. Rather than dealing with the total or average cost of a period, he assumes that we will measure the components of actual cost (usage and rate; material and labor) of every item that is produced in a period. The distribution of outcomes from each cost component is then compared with the assumed in-control distribution via a goodness-of-fit test (Kolmogorov-Smirnov or Chi-squared) to see if a significant shift in the distribution has occurred. Thus, Luh is able to detect not only shifts in the mean of the distribution but also shifts in the shape or scale of the distribution. This test will, therefore, signal an investigation much more often than a system which only monitors potential shifts in the mean. In addition, Luh's system requires the collection of far more detailed information than is typically required for traditional control chart-like systems so that the cost of operating this procedure may become a significant factor, especially relative to the incremental benefits the procedure might offer.

To summarize, procedures described in the papers referenced in this section only control for the distribution of outcomes when the process is in control. They test for significant departures from this null distribution based on a single-period's observation. Previous observations are not aggregated together when the statistical test is performed, and no costs of investigation or of failing to correct an out-of-control process are explicitly considered.

4. Decision Models Based on Multiple Observations;
No Costs of Investigation or Misclassification

The procedures described in the previous section treat successive observations from the same process as being independent samples. No attempt is made to combine the information from previous observations with the current observation to reach a statistical conclusion as to whether the process is currently in control. These procedures, therefore, ignore a lot of the potentially useful information available from a systematic examination of trends. The use of prior observations should enable a mean shift to be detected much earlier than by successively testing single observations at a low α (probability of Type I error) risk.

The cumulative sum (cusum) procedure, introduced by Page (1954), is the most common procedure that uses previous observations for detecting a shift in the mean of a process. With this procedure, the target mean, μ, is subtracted from the current observation, x_r, and a series of partial sums formed, S_r, where

$$S_r = \sum_{i=1}^{r} (x_i - \mu).$$

Under the null hypothesis, these partial sums should follow a random walk with zero mean. But if a shift in the mean has occurred (away from μ), the partial sums will start to develop a positive or negative drift. While an analytic test to detect a drift is not hard to develop, many writers advocate a graphical approach for the cusum technique. Successive partial sums, $S_r = S_{r-1} + x_r - \mu$, are plotted ($S_r$ on the vertical axis, r along the horizontal axis) and a V-mask applied from the most recent observation (see figure 1). If any previous cumulative sum ($S_i, i = 1, \cdots, r - 1$) is covered by the V-mask, a significant shift in the mean is deemed to have occurred. Cusum charts can be made sensitive to small changes in the mean of a process since these will cause the trajectory of cumulative sums to drift away from previous observations until one limb of the V-mask cuts across a prior point to signal an out-of-control condition.

The two design parameters of a cusum V-mask are the offset distance, d, and the angle of mask, θ. These can be set based on (1) an assumed shift in the mean of the process of μ, (2) the average run length in control before a false investigate signal is generated, and (3) the average run length out of control (mean shift of μ) before an investigate signal is given [see Ewan and Kemp (1960) and Goldsmith and Whitfield (1961)]. In practice, these parameters are frequently set by experimenting with different values for d and θ on charts derived from past data from the process being controlled until the right incidence of false and true signals is achieved.

A more formal model of a multi-period nonstationary process is described by Barnard (1959) who formulates the control problem as one of

Cumulative Sum Procedure

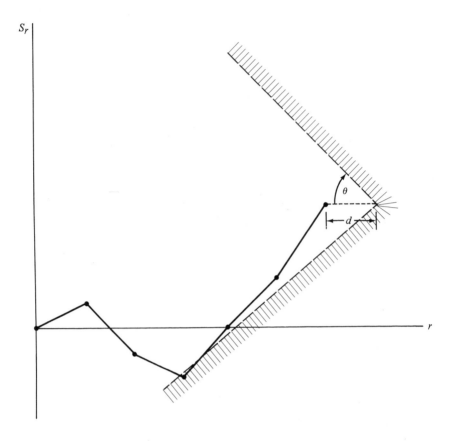

estimation rather than hypothesis testing. In order to use all the past data to estimate the current mean of the process, a specific stochastic process of how mean shifts occur needs to be formulated. Barnard assumes that shifts or jumps in the mean occur according to a Poisson process. Conditional on a jump occurring, the amount of the jump is assumed to be a normally distributed random variable with a zero mean and known variance. From this process, Barnard derives an expression for a mean likelihood estimator (the maximum likelihood estimator would be very difficult to estimate) which is a weighted mean of recent observations with the weights decreasing over time and decreasing if there is a large jump between successive observations. Barnard also suggests an approximate graphical procedure to obtain an estimate of the current mean of the process. Perhaps the most important message from Barnard's paper is to realize that when we wish to aggregate prior observations to estimate or test the current mean of the process, we need to specify a formal stochastic model of how changes in the mean occur. For the nonstationary processes we are considering in this paper, simple unweighted aggregations of past data, such as sample means and variances, will not be good estimates of the current parameters of the process. We will return to this point later when discussing some of the proposals made in the accounting literature.

Other papers in the statistical literature have also dealt with estimating the change in mean of a noisy process. For example, Chernoff and Zacks (1964), Hinich and Farley (1966), and Farley and Hinich (1970) treat a model in which the output of the process is given by

$$x(t) = \theta(t) + n(t)$$

where $n(t)$ is a Gaussian distributed noise with zero mean and known co-variance function.[10] The mean process, $\theta(t)$, is assumed to undergo discrete shifts according to a Poisson distributed process. These papers assume that the total observation time is less than the mean time between jumps so that the possibility of two or more jumps in the observed interval can be ignored. Efficient estimators of the mean process, $\theta(t)$, are developed as a function of the sequence of observations. These papers and Barnard's can be used to develop an estimator of the current mean of a noisy nonstationary process. Within a standard cost accounting context, such an estimate would correspond to the current level of average cost for the process being controlled. Presumably, if this current level were sufficiently far away from the standard level, an investigation would be signaled. Note, however, that neither the cost of an investigation nor the value of waiting for additional sample information is explicitly included in this analysis.

To date, no article in the accounting literature has advocated the use of the cusum or the other sophisticated statistical techniques described in this section which make use of the entire history of observations to signal an out-of-control situation. Such procedures do represent an improvement over simple control charts and successive hypothesis tests on single observations since they specifically model the stochastic dependence of successive observations. Nevertheless, they are still an incomplete representation of the problem since they do not include the cost and benefit structure of the investigation decision.

5. Decision Models Based on a Single Observation; Cost of Investigation and Misclassification Included

A third category of papers generalizes the simple hypothesis testing ideas described first to include the cost of investigation and the potential benefit to be achieved from an investigation. In the quality control literature, Duncan (1956) devised a scheme for the economic design of x charts. Duncan's model assumed the following types of benefits and costs: (i) Income when the process is in control, (ii) Income when the process is out of control, (iii) Cost of looking for a cause when none exists, (iv) Cost of looking for a cause when one exists, and (v) Cost of charting. With

---

[10] For the processes discussed in this paper, we have assumed that successive observations are statistically independent so that the covariance matrix would be diagonal.

these costs and assuming a specific alternative hypothesis (i.e., a mean shift of known magnitude) Duncan computed control limits that approximately maximized average income per period. Duncan's analysis was subsequently extended by Goel, Jain, and Wu (1968) and Gibra (1971). Note that even though their approaches minimized costs or maximized income over extended periods of time, the decision to investigate is still based on whether the most recent observation falls outside the control limits. Thus, information from previous observations is not used in the investigation decision.

In the accounting literature, Bierman, Fouraker, and Jaedicke (BFJ) (1961) were the first to introduce the costs and benefits of an investigation into the investigation decision. Their paper treated a single-period model and assumed, as did the papers listed in section 3, that management could specify the distribution of outcomes when the process is in control. Given a particular observation, the probability, p, that this observation came from the null (in-control) distribution was computed. With an investigation cost of C and a potential benefit from correcting an out-of-control situation of L, an investigation was signaled if $C < (1 - p)L$. One problem with this formulation is the difficulty of estimating or even interpreting L. BFJ do not devote much discussion to estimating L but in a footnote explain, "In situations where the inefficiency will be repeated, L should be defined as the present value of the costs that will be incurred in the future if an investigation is not made now." [11] Unfortunately, these future cost savings are not easy to estimate. In situations where the inefficiency will be repeated, one would have opportunities in the future to correct the process. Therefore, the discounted future costs assuming no future investigation is an overestimate of L. But L will not equal the one-period costs, assuming an investigation occurs next period, since a good realization may occur next period even when operating somewhat inefficiently so that no investigation would be signaled. Therefore, the benefit, L, depends upon future actions, and models which do not specifically include the consequences of future actions will have a hard time defining, much less estimating, what is the benefit from current actions. BFJ could reply that they are dealing with one-period nonrepetitive situations so that future costs and actions are not relevant. Such situations do occur in practice. But some of the papers to be discussed in the next section purport to treat multi-period aspects and still fail to deal with this crucial aspect of estimating the incremental benefits from an investigation now rather than in future periods.

Dyckman[12] has criticized the BFJ model for basing the investigation decision on only the most recent observation, thereby ignoring prior information — either sample information from previous periods or subjectively determined priors. To the extent that the outputs from the process

---

[11] Bierman, Fouraker, and Jaedicke (1961), footnote 1, pp. 414–15.
[12] See "A Correction," pp. 114–15 in Ozan and Dyckman (1971).

are believed to be dependent random variables from a stochastic process, then a reasonable decision should make use of prior observations as well as the most recent one. We turn now to a discussion of such procedures.

6. Discrete State Decision Models with Multiple Observations; Cost of Investigation and Misclassification Included

CONTROL CHARTS

We have already described cusum charts which can signal an investigation based on the relation of the current observation with all prior observations. In a manner analogous to that done by Duncan for $\bar{x}$ charts, Taylor (1968) and Goel and Wu (1973) develop procedures to design cusum charts that minimize long-run average cost. Both papers assume a cost structure similar to Duncan's and a process in which a single shift in the process mean of known magnitude occurs at a random time. Economically determined values of d, the V-mask offset distance, and θ, the angle of the V-mask, are determined based on the magnitude of the shift, the parameters of the distribution of time the process remains in control, the investigation costs, and the costs of operating in or out of control. The optimal design of control charts, however, is optimal in only a special sense. In effect, the form of the optimal policy is predetermined by the characteristics of the control chart, and only the parameters of the control chart are optimized. It is analogous to finding the optimal (s, S) policy in an inventory problem even though an (s, S) policy is not the globally optimal one.

Traditional control charts tend to be non-Bayesian in that no prior information about in- or out-of-control probabilities is combined with sample evidence. An exception is provided by Girshick and Rubin (1952) who considered a two-state model (in and out of control) with a Markov chain describing transitions between the two states in successive periods. Assuming a constant cost of investigation and a constant cost per period for operating out of control, an optimal investigation policy was determined that minimized long-run average cost.

KAPLAN'S MODEL

Kaplan (1969) adapted the Girshick and Rubin procedure for the accounting variance investigation decision. Rather than having to derive a cost from operating out of control, Kaplan used the actual costs when operating in or out of control to derive optimal policies. Thus, a decision to delay investigating for one period incurred the risk of operating one more period out of control, that is, obtaining a cost realization from the higher cost, out-of-control distribution, rather than from lower cost, in-control distribution. Balanced against this risk was the certain cost of an investigation which might find that the system was still in control. Note that the loss function in the accounting variance setting arises directly from the nature of the problem. In the control chart approach, the cost of operating in or out of control must be imputed. In the accounting setting, the incremental costs of operating out of control arise directly from the higher costs that accrue when operating away from standard. Thus the cost variance decision may be more amenable to an economically based decision theory treatment. Dynamic programming was used to compute optimal policies that minimized discounted future costs. Discounted future cost was used as the criterion, rather than long-run average cost as used by Girshick and Rubin, because the time interval between successive accounting reports made the time value of money a relevant consideration. But since the computation of optimal policies in this situation is not very sensitive to the assumed discount rate, the long-run average cost criterion could be achieved simply by using a discount factor of unity (or arbitrarily close to unity) and adopting the policy to which the n-period optimal policy converges.

A key feature of the two-state Markov model used by Girshick and Rubin and by Kaplan is that all the relevant information from the prior observations, since the last investigation was made, could be summarized by a single state variable — the probability that the system is currently operating in control. This variable is updated after each observation via Bayes' theorem to incorporate information from the most recent observation. Assuming a specific form for the transition matrix — in this case geometric distribution for the time until the system goes out of control — provides a tremendous reduction in the amount of information that must be stored about previous realizations of the process. One could even relax the geometric distribution assumption of constant probability of going out of control without a great increase in the complexity of the procedure. Of course, this would require more information about the specific probabilities of going out of control as a function of time. In general, one could define g_k as the probability that, in period k, the system will remain in control given that it was in control at the start of the period. For the geometric distribution, $g_k = g$ for $k = 1, 2, \cdots$, with an arbitrary distribution for going out of control, the discrete state variable k would be appended to the state description and the optimization done with respect to this state variable as well as the one summarizing the current probability that the system is in control. The main difference would be that the operator $\tau_x q^{13}$ which updates the probability, q, of being in control after re-

---

[13] See pp. 34–35 in Kaplan (1969).

ceiving an observation x would now become a function of k — the number of periods since the last investigation; i.e.,

$$\tau_{x;k}q = g_k[1 + \lambda(x)(1 - q)/q]^{-1}$$

where $\lambda(x) = f_2(x)/f_1(x)$ is the likelihood ratio of the out-of-control distribution to the in-control distribution. The functional equation for $C_n(q)$ then becomes one for $C_n(q; k)$, where $C_n(q; k)$ is the minimum expected discounted cost with present estimate of q of being in control and k periods since the last investigation. The steady state equation for $C_n(q; k)$ is given by

$$C(q; k) = \min \{K + \int [x + \alpha C(\tau_{x;\,0}g_0; 1)]f_{g_0}(x) \, dx;$$
$$\int [x + \alpha C(\tau_{x;\,k}q; k + 1)]f_q(x) \, dx\}$$

where K is the cost of the investigation, α is the discount rate and $f_q(x) = qf_1(x) + (1 - q)f_2(x)$, a weighted sum of the in-control and out-of-control density functions.

The first set of terms (before the semi-colon) is the current and expected future costs when an investigation is made now. The second set represents the expected costs when no investigation is made now. The derivation of the functional equation is along the lines developed in Kaplan (1969). Roughly speaking, the density function $f_q(x)$ gives the probability of getting an observation x when q is the probability the observation comes from, the in-control density function. After an investigation, the system is reset so that there is a probability g_0 (perhaps equal to 1) that the system will remain in control for one full period after an investigation has taken place. This is why the probability is g_0 that the observation immediately after an investigation comes from the in-control distribution. To solve the equation, some reasonable upper bound on k must be assumed. Perhaps the value such that the a priori probability is .95 or .99 that the system will be out of control after that number of periods is a reasonable upper bound for k.

The infinite period function equation serves as a convenient approximation to a long but unspecified planning horizon. In fact, the infinite period optimal policy is typically very similar to the optimal policy with only 10 or 15 periods remaining. In any case, the infinite period optimal policy is computed as the limit of the finite horizon optimal policies so that one has the information to use the policy optimal for whatever planning horizon one thinks is appropriate.

There are at least two other assumptions that may limit the applicability of this approach. One is the heroic simplification of the process to a two-state system, in control and out of control, with sudden transitions between the states. While we have seen that this model is frequently used in the quality control literature, the process by which a controllable cost process suddenly moves from in control to out of control is rather difficult to articulate. Intuitively it is more appealing to consider a process that gradually drifts away from standards through an evolutionary process of neglect and lack of proper supervision. In such a case, the forced dichotomy between in control and out of control may be an unrealistic aggregation of reality. One solution is to expand the number of states to allow for varying degrees of out of controlness. For example we might allow S states ($S = 5$ or 10, say) with state 1 representing perfectly in control, state 2 representing slight deterioration, and state S being well out of control. Each state would be associated with a different distribution of cost outcomes, with the average cost increasing from state 1 to state S. For each state s in S, we would have a density function $f_s(x)$ of outcomes arising from a process while in state s. We could then define an $S \times S$ Markov matrix, P, describing how one-period transitions are made from state to state. If the process is expected to just deteriorate over time, P would be an upper block triangular matrix with no entries below the main diagonal. Unfortunately, the state space would require $S - 1$ states ($q_1, q_2, \cdots, q_{s-1}$) with q_i being the current probability that the system is in state i.[14] Given an observation, x, the posterior probabilities, $q_i^*(x)$, that the system was in state i when observation x was produced could be computed from

$$q_i^*(x) = \frac{f_i(x)q_i}{\sum\limits_{j=1}^{S} f_j(x)q_j}.$$

These posterior probabilities $\mathbf{q}^* = (q_1^*(x), \cdots, q_s^*(x))$ would then be multiplied by the transition matrix P to yield the q_i's for the system in the next period. While this procedure is not difficult to describe, optimal policies may become difficult to compute for S larger than 4 or 5.

An extended version of such a model was treated by Ross (1971). He assumed that a process could be in a countable number of states i, ($i = 0, 1, 2, \cdots$), with quality a function of the state. He assumed that costs of production, inspecting, and revision were all functions of the current state, i. A Markov chain described the movement from state to state of the process for each transition. The state variables of the system consisted of the probability vector $\mathbf{q} = (q_0, q_1, \cdots)$ where q_i is the current probability that the system is in state i. Three actions are possible — produce without inspection, produce with inspection (to learn the current state), and revise the process, to state 0. For this very general formulation, Ross was able to obtain only the most general results. He determined that the steady state optimality function $V(\mathbf{q})$ is concave in $\mathbf{q}$ and that the inspection and revision regions are convex. Some more specific results are obtained for a two-state process (good and bad) in which he demonstrated an example for which the "produce without inspection" region could consist of two

---

[14] Since the q_i's must sum to one, we only need to explicitly consider $S - 1$ probabilities. The omitted probability is determined implicitly by subtracting the sum of $S - 1$ probabilities from 1.

disjoint regions, a region being defined by those values of q, the probability that the system is in the good state at the start of the period, for which a given action is optimal ($0 \leq q \leq 1$).

In addition to the two-state limitation of Kaplan's model, the model is also limited by the assumption that the process can always be returned to the in-control distribution. The decision model is based on the assumption that if an out-of-control situation is discovered, the process can be corrected so that future costs will likely arise from the in-control cost density function, $f_1(x)$. But, occasionally, fundamental shifts in the process may occur that are not reversible even after discovery. Prices may have risen or operating procedures developed which may be impossible or at best difficult to reverse. Therefore, an investigation undertaken in anticipation of realizing the benefits from a restoration to the historical standard cost may never realize these benefits and, hence, the benefits expected from the investigation will have been overestimated. This feature represents one of the fundamental differences between the traditional quality control setting for which most of the described techniques have been developed and the cost variance setting considered in this paper. The physical processes being monitored in the quality control environment can almost always be reset from an out-of-control situation to the desired setting once such a situation is discovered. The benefits from investigating these processes can, therefore, be measured by the almost certain return to the in-control state.

The feature of the cost variance setting in which the previous standard may no longer be attainable seems difficult to capture in a simple practical model. One could always define a probability that an out-of-control situation is not correctible but then one would have to be concerned with controllable and noncontrollable deviations from the new, but still not completely known, standard and the problem rapidly escalates. About the only ameliorating factor here is that there is some benefit in learning about a fundamental shift in the cost or technology of a process. Such a shift may affect the firm's decision model[15] and thereby effect some savings, though not as much as had been anticipated at the time the investigation decision was made. In a similar vein, the model has difficulty capturing the benefits that may accrue from investigating a below-average cost. If a lower than expected cost performance can be made permanent by resetting the cost standard to adjust to the more efficient process, then a long-term benefit can be achieved. This benefit is ignored in the model which assumes that the process is always returned to its original cost standard. Also, the model in its present formulation does not adequately handle problems with below-average costs due to use of lower-quality materials or labor. It always assumes that lower cost is better than higher cost, i.e., it assumes the quality of output remains constant.

---

[15] See Dopuch, Birnberg, and Demski (1967) and Demski (1967).

The above situations describe one set of reasons why the system may not always be returned to the in-control state after an investigation has occurred. It is also possible to consider the situation in which the investigation fails to detect an out-of-control situation when one exists. This possibility is not considered in Kaplan's model but an extension to allow for imperfect investigations will be discussed shortly. Other extensions to the basic model are discussed in Kaplan (1969). These extensions allow (1) for a delay between the time the investigation decision is made and the time the system is restored to the in-control state, (2) the system to be self-correcting, and (3) the cost of investigation to be a function of the state the system is actually in.

DYCKMAN'S MODEL

Dyckman (1969) dealt with a model very similar to Kaplan's except that the multi-period cost structure was suppressed. The stochastic process with a Markov chain describing transitions between an in-control state and out-of-control state was used with Bayesian updating of the probability of being in either state after each observation from the process. Thus the limitations of the two-state process, just described, apply to this model too.

As in the single-period BFJ model, though, Dyckman assumes a constant saving, *L,* from investigating an out-of-control situation. Dyckman does not offer much more guidance as to the interpretation or estimation of *L.* He calls it the "present value of the savings obtainable from an investigation when the activity is out of control," then notes that "where a corrective action is not forever binding, the calculation of *L* needs to be adjusted to reflect the possibility of future out-of-control periods" and then concludes that "the precise determination of the savings for each future period is not an easy matter."[16]

The difficulty, of course, arises because Dyckman suppresses the sequential decision-making nature of the problem and therefore cannot evaluate the benefits from delaying the investigation for another period when more sample evidence may be obtained. Difficulties with interpreting what *L* represents, similar to those expressed here, were raised by Li (1970) who observes that "dynamic programming is more appropriate to use under this situation."[17] Dyckman's reply concurs with the logic of this suggestion but claims that "the difficulties attendant on solving large and complex real dynamic programming problems can limit the successful application of this technique."[18] It is true that dynamic programs are difficult to solve when there are a large number of state variables. But the

[16] Dyckman (1969): 218.
[17] Li (1970): 283.
[18] Dyckman's reply, in Li (1970): 283.

model treated by Dyckman can be summarized by a single-state variable [see Kaplan (1969)] and dynamic programs with a single-state variable are quite easy to solve. Therefore, computational costs should not be high relative to the benefits from including the effect of future decisions and actions into the analysis.

Dyckman eventually concludes that L should be measured by the savings over the planning horizon which is taken to be the minimum of the average time until the process goes out of control again and the time until standards need to be revised.[19] This does not settle the issue, however, since some problems inherently remain in his nonsequential decision model. For one thing, L must then be a function of n, the number of periods since the process started. If L is the discounted savings over the planning horizon, then as a number of periods pass, there are fewer periods remaining in the planning horizon so the potential savings last for fewer periods. Hence, L must decrease with increasing n. Dyckman extends in Some Extensions, Section A (pp. 228–30) the traditional two-action space (Investigate, Don't Investigate) model by allowing for an exploratory investigation which costs less than a full investigation but has probability h, with $h < 1$, of detecting an out-of-control situation when one exists. This is certainly a worthwhile extension and can easily be incorporated into the dynamic programming framework already developed. There are two outcomes from the exploratory investigation; either an out-of-control situation is discovered or it is not. If the probability that the system is in control is q, then the probability of finding it out of control with the exploratory investigation is $(1 - q)h$. When the process is found to be out of control, it is reset and a new cycle starts. Conversely, the probability that the system is not found to be out of control by the exploratory investigation is $1 - (1 - q)h$. But in this case, the investigation is not a complete failure since we get some new information about the probability that the system is in control. If q was the probability of the system being in control before the unsuccessful exploratory investigation, the posterior probability of being in control can be obtained via Bayes theorem as $q/[1 - h(1 - q)]$ which is greater than q. Therefore, the decision to undertake an exploratory investigation must include not only the potential benefit from cheaply discovering an out-of-control situation but also the expected future benefits to be achieved by an increase in our estimate of the probability of being in control. Formally, if K' is the cost of the limited investigation, the expected infinite horizon future cost from undertaking an exploratory investigation is given by:

$$K' + (1 - q)h \int [x + \alpha C(\tau_x g)]f_g(x)\, dx$$
$$+ [1 - (1 - q)h] \int [x + \alpha C(\tau_x q')]f_{q'}(x)\, dx$$

with $q' = q/[1 - h(1 - q)]$ and $g =$ one-period probability of going out

---

[19] *Ibid.*; also in Ozan and Dyckman (1971): 98.

of control. Dyckman recognizes that the probabilities of being in or out of control should be revised to reflect the exploratory investigation outcome but advises against this if it will raise one of the probabilities.[20] He incorrectly neglects the value of this anticipated revision (in effect the expected value of sample information) in his decision to conduct the exploratory investigation.

For a more general treatment still, we might let the amount of money spent on an investigation be a continuous variable, z, and define a function $h(z)$ as the probability of detecting an out-of-control situation when one exists. Presumably $h(0) = 0$, $\lim_{z \to \infty} h(z) = 1$ and $h(z)$ is a nondecreasing function of z. The decision then becomes one of not only deciding whether to investigate or not but how much to spend on the investigation. If q is the prior probability that the system is in control, an amount z is spent on an investigation and an out-of-control situation is not found, the posterior probability that the system is in control (after the investigation) is

$$q'(z) = q/[1 - h(z)(1 - q)].$$

Therefore, we may formulate the infinite horizon decision problem as:

$$C(q) = \min_{z \geqslant 0} \{z + (1 - q)h(z) \int [x + \alpha C(\tau_x g)]f_g(x)\ dx$$
$$+ [1 - (1 - q)h(z)] \int [x + \alpha C(\tau_x q')]f_{q'}(x)\ dx\}$$

where q' is a function of z as defined above and setting $z = 0$ with $h(0) = 0$ and $q'(0) = q$ yields the expected cost when no investigation is undertaken.

Returning to Dyckman (1969), in Some Extensions, Section C (pp. 231–33), n consecutive observations are used to develop posterior probabilities about the states of the process. The sample mean, $\bar{x}$, of these n observations is used as a sufficient statistic to summarize these sample results. But the sample mean of a normal process (with known variance) can only be the sufficient statistic of a *stationary process*. That is, the procedure of combining n sample results into a sufficient statistic, $\bar{x}$, is valid only if one assumes that the process is in a given state at the start of the string of observations and *remains* in that state for all n observations. But since we are dealing with a nonstationary process, the sample mean cannot summarize all the information contained in the first n observations.[21] When drawing statistical conclusions from the observations on a process whose mean can shift over time, the order in which the observations occur provides important information.

A subsequent paper by Ozan and Dyckman (1971) expands on Dyckman's model by defining different types of controllable and noncontrollable variances. Some guidance is offered as to how to estimate some of the many different probabilities this model requires but the formulation

---

[20] *Ibid.*, p. 230.
[21] A similar error is made by Duvall (1967) and will be discussed in the next section.

is still in terms of using myopic decision rules which entails the difficulties already discussed. Ozan and Dyckman (1971) eventually derive a reward function similar to that used by Duvall (1967) in a paper discussed in the following section.

In conclusion, attempting to reduce an essentially multi-period problem to a simplified single-period one may produce more difficulties than any potential benefits gained from the simplification. While there are some limitations to the two-state dynamic programming approach, as previously discussed, these still remain under the model with single-period decision rules introduced by Dyckman. Since dynamic programming over a uni-dimensional state space, especially in a two- or three-action space setting, is straightforward and easy to implement, I am skeptical that adopting single-period decision rules will produce a net benefit in situations where the two-state model is a reasonable representation of reality.

7. Continuous State Decision Models with Multiple Observations, Cost of Investigation and Misclassification Included

DUVALL'S MODEL

Duvall (1967) develops an interesting model which allows the state of the system to be the level of controllable costs, a continuous variable. He assumes, as is traditional, that in-control costs are normally distributed with mean μ, equal to standard cost, and variance equal to σ_w^2. An observed deviation away from standard therefore consists of a noncontrollable component, w, (with $w \sim N(0, \sigma_w^2)$) and a controllable component y. The controllable component, y, is also assumed to be normally distributed and statistically independent of the noncontrollable component, w. Duvall develops procedures which allegedly allow the parameters of the distribution of y to be estimated from the observed deviations.

Duvall's reward function from an investigation is a direct function of the continuous variable, y, and I find this an appealing feature of the model. In particular, future savings are assumed to be proportional to the size of the deviation, y. This allows for savings to occur if the deviation is negative, representing the value of resetting standards at lower cost levels. It is intuitively appealing that the savings from an investigation be made a function of the degree of out-of-controlness of the system, and this procedure gets us away from having to impose a simplified discrete state world on an inherently continuous process. There is still a problem as to how to measure the savings from an investigation, since this model does not incorporate the possibility of investigations in the future; e.g., Duvall writes, "Conceptually, it is easy to say that if an investigation revealed that a certain amount could be saved each time period for the life of the project, then the present value of these future savings could be obtained."[22] But this assumes a constrained model in which the current time is the only possible opportunity for an investigation. Nevertheless, there may be circumstances in which this is not an unreasonable assumption.

There are more fundamental problems with Duvall's procedure, however, which raise questions about the validity of his entire procedure. Duvall uses a sequence of 25 observations to compute a sample mean and standard deviation. Just how we know that 25 is the right number of observations to be taken for estimating sample means and standard deviations is never discussed. Nor are we told what to do if some of the early observations indicate an out-of-control situation. Must we still wait until we get the full 25 observations before taking action? These difficulties arise because Duvall has not developed a sequential strategy that, after each observation, compares the value of obtaining additional information with the cost of operating another period at a too high, controllable cost level. But even granting the static nature of the analysis and the heuristic of estimating from an arbitrary number of observations, Duvall's procedure is not even internally consistent. Duvall uses the sample mean and standard deviation of departures from standard, $(\bar{x}, \sigma_x^*)$, computed from these 25 observations to estimate the mean and standard deviation of the distribution of controllable costs, y. Since the mean of noncontrollable costs, w, is assumed to be zero, the mean of y is estimated as the sample mean; i.e., $\mu_y^* = \bar{x}$. Also, with y and w assumed to be statistically independent, the variance of y is estimated from sample variance as

$$\sigma_y^{*2} = \sigma_x^{*2} - \sigma_w^{*2}$$

where σ_w^{*2} has been previously estimated from an arbitrary period of time during which it was somehow determined that standard conditions prevailed $(y = 0)$. This procedure, however, is only valid if the mean, μ_y, of the controllable cost distribution shifted before the first observation was taken. The above procedures treat each observation equally and symmetrically and this can only be done for a stationary process, one in which the parameters do not shift over the course of the observation period. I find this to be an unrealistic assumption. It seems far more likely that a shift in the distribution of y will occur arbitrarily in the interval and it even seems reasonable that multiple jumps could have occurred (recall Barnard's model in Section 4) during the observation period.

After describing the estimation procedure, an inference is done on only the most recent observation, and it is claimed that this inference will enable us to determine whether to investigate or not. While the previous assumption of stationarity might be classified as unrealistic, the procedure of basing an investigation decision on only the most recent observation is

[22] Duvall (1967): 638.

obviously inconsistent. For if the process is stationary, then the investigation decision should be based on all the observations, not just an isolated one. But if the most recent observation is deemed to be more informative than prior observations, there is a strong presumption of nonstationarity which implies that the procedure to estimate the parameters of the process is incorrect.

Duvall's problems arise because he failed to specify the stochastic process which leads to changes in the distribution of y. As previously noted, when we deal with noisy nonstationary processes it is vital that we identify the source of the nonstationarity before we estimate the parameters of the process. Otherwise we will be unable to separate out the effects of normal fluctuations (noise) from changes in the level of the process.

BATHER'S MODEL

In fact, a model which overcomes the previously described difficulties in Duvall's procedure had already appeared in the statistics literature. Bather (1963) describes a process which, like Duvall's, has a state described by a single continuous variable which represents the performance level of the process. Costs are similarly assumed to be a function of this continuous variable. Let y_t be the unknown performance level of the system at time t (assume that $y_t = 0$ is the state representing no deviation from standard) and let x_t be the observation at time t. As before, we assume that $x_t \sim N(y_t, \sigma^2)$.[23] Bather, however, postulates a process by which the performance level changes from period to period:

$$y_t = y_{t-1} + z_t,$$

where $z_t \sim N(0, \rho^2)$; i.e., the process mean undergoes a random walk without drift over time. Successive changes in the process mean are independent and identically distributed with zero mean and constant standard deviation, ρ. This process is the limit of the Barnard Poisson jump process as the Poisson parameter, λ, goes to infinity to yield a continuous string of infinitesimal changes.

Assume, initially, that the process is reset with some error to the standard level of performance so that $y_0 \sim N(0, v_0)$ where v_0 is the initial level of uncertainty in the current mean of the process. Then, since y_t is the sum of independent normally distributed random variables, $y_t \sim N(u_t, v_t)$, with u_t and v_t to be determined from $(x_1, \cdots, x_t)$, the observed values. The conditional distribution of y_{t+1} given just $(x_1, \cdots, x_t)$ is

$$y_{t+1} \mid (x_1, \cdots, x_t) \sim N(u_t, v_t + \rho^2)$$

and the distribution of x_{t+1} given y_{t+1} is

[23] This notation denotes that x_t is normally distributed with mean y_t and variance σ^2.

$$x_{t+1} \mid y_{t+1} \sim N(y_{t+1}, \sigma^2).$$

Therefore, by Bayes' theorem,

$$y_{t+1} \mid (x_1, \cdots, x_{t+1}) \sim N(u_{t+1}, v_{t+1})$$

where

$$\frac{1}{v_{t+1}} = \frac{1}{v_t + \rho^2} + \frac{1}{\sigma^2}$$

and

$$\frac{u_{t+1}}{v_{t+1}} = \frac{u_t}{v_t + \rho^2} + \frac{x_{t+1}}{\sigma^2}.^{24}$$

Since the sequence $v_0, v_1, \cdots, v_t$ is deterministic (not affected by sample outcomes, x_t), u_t by itself is a sufficient statistic for this process. Note that u_t is *not* the sample mean. Even though the process outcomes are normally distributed, the nonstationarity of the process causes the sample mean to be an uninteresting characterization of the process. The posterior variance v_t converges (geometrically) to v, with

$$v = \frac{1}{2} \rho^2 \left[\sqrt{1 + \frac{4\sigma^2}{\rho^2}} - 1 \right]$$

which represents the long-run tracking variance of the process. In effect, it represents a minimal level of uncertainty of the current mean of the process which cannot be reduced even by taking longer sequences of observations. If we make the simplifying and not unreasonable assumption that the process is reset with an uncertainty equal to this tracking variance (i.e., that $v_0 = v$), then we have the convenient result:

$$v_t = v \qquad \text{for all } t$$

and

$$u_t = \frac{v}{v + \rho^2} u_{t-1} + \frac{v}{\sigma^2} x_t.$$

Defining $\gamma = v/(v + \rho^2)$, so that $1 - \gamma = v/\sigma^2$, we have

$$u_t = (1 - \gamma)(x_t + \gamma x_{t-1} + \cdots + \gamma^{t-1} x_1),$$

an exponential moving average of prior observations.

Define $k(y)$ to be the cost of investigation and subsequent repair when the true process mean is y. This is a more general treatment than previous cost investigation papers which assumed this function to be a constant [but see Ross (1971)]. Let $g(y)$ be the cost of continuing to operate, for one period only, when the present state is y. We will assume the following sequence of events for the Bather model: A cost report is received, followed

---

[24] This development is analogous to the Bayesian analysis on the mean of a stationary normal process; see DeGroot (1970): 167. A more detailed derivation appears in the Appendix.

by an immediate decision whether to investigate the process or allow it to operate for another period. If the process is investigated, it is assumed that the process can always be reset back to the desired initial state in which $y_0 \sim N(0, v)$. Thus the previously mentioned difficulties of modeling situations for which it is impossible to reset the standard back to the desired level and for which it is possible to reset the standard to a lower cost level for the future are still not captured by the Bather model.

If u is the best estimate of the current mean of the process, the expected investigation cost is

$$K(u) \equiv \int k(y) f_N(y \mid u, v) \, dy$$

where $f_N(\cdot \mid u, v)$ is the density function of a normally distributed random variable with mean u and variance v. The expected one-period cost of operating when the best estimate of the current mean of the process is u will be denoted $G(u)$ with

$$G(u) \equiv \int g(y) \, f_N(y \mid u, v) \, dy.$$

The only remaining term needed for the dynamic programming equation is the prediction of the next period's state variable given the current period's state variable. We know that

$$u_{t+1} = \gamma u_t + (1 - \gamma) x_{t+1}$$

and we can write x_{t+1} as

$$x_{t+1} = y_t + (y_{t+1} - y_t) + (x_{t+1} - y_{t+1}).$$

Each of the three terms on the right is, by assumption, normally and independently distributed with means and variances given, respectively, by: (u_t, v); $(0, \rho^2)$; and $(0, \sigma^2)$. Therefore $x_{t+1} \sim N(u_t, v + \rho^2 + \sigma^2)$ and

$$E(u_{t+1} \mid u_t) = u_t.$$

Also,

$$\begin{aligned} \text{Var} \, (u_{t+1} \mid u_t) &= (1 - \gamma)^2 \, \text{Var} \, (x_{t+1}) \\ &= (1 - \gamma)^2 (v + \rho^2 + \sigma^2) \\ &= \rho^2 \end{aligned}$$

where the last equality follows from the definition of γ.[25] We therefore

---

[25] Since $1 - \gamma = \dfrac{v}{\sigma^2} = \dfrac{\rho^2}{v + \rho^2}$, we have that

$$(1 - \gamma)^2 \, (v + \rho^2 + \sigma^2) = \frac{v}{\sigma^2} \frac{\rho^2}{v + \rho^2} \, (v + \rho^2 + \sigma^2)$$

$$= v \rho^2 \left[\frac{1}{\sigma^2} + \frac{1}{v + \rho^2} \right]$$

$$= \rho^2 [(1 - \gamma) + \gamma]$$
$$= \rho^2.$$

have that

$$u_{t+1} = u_t + z \qquad \text{with} \qquad z \sim N(0, \rho^2).$$

While Bather computes optimal policies to minimize expected (undiscounted) costs per unit time I will reformulate the problem to minimize total expected discounted costs in the future. For convenience in notation, I assume an infinite horizon problem with a discount factor, α, less than one. Some mild regularity conditions on the cost functions $k(\cdot)$ and $c(\cdot)$ will ensure the geometric convergence of the finite period optimality functions to a unique steady state minimum expected cost function, $C(u)$. We can write $C(u)$ as

$$C(u) = \min \{K(u) + C(0); G(u) + \alpha E[C(u + z)]\}.$$

The first term in the minimization is the expected investigation cost, $K(u)$, and the effect of immediately resetting the process to its desired mean, 0. The second term consists of the expected costs of operating for one period at the current level plus the discounted expected future costs, one period in the future. The expectation of this latter term is taken with respect to the random variable z defined above $[z \sim N(0, \rho^2)]$. Of course, the actual state variable, u', for the next period will become known after the next period's cost report, x, is received:

$$u' = \gamma u + (1 - \gamma)x.$$

The solution to the above functional equation can be easily obtained by taking the limit of the optimal policies of the finite horizon optimality equation:

$$C_n(u) = \min \{K(u) + C_n(0); G(u) + \alpha E[C_{n-1}(u + z)]\}.$$

The preceding formulation could represent only the starting point for more elaborate models. Additional features such as adding a third action alternative of an exploratory investigation could be included as we have already discussed. Also, if one wanted to assume a gradual increase in controllable costs over time, the distribution of z could have a small positive mean. In a private communication, Dyckman has suggested the possibility that y_t be modeled as a mean reverting process, rather than a random walk, due to corrective actions undertaken by subordinates. A particularly interesting possibility to pursue would involve attempting to model the reduction in future cost due to investigating a process whose mean has drifted below the previously set standard. If such a procedure could be developed, we might similarly be able to model those situations for which a higher current level of costs would become the new standard because of our inability to reset the process back to its original standard. These extensions represent opportunities for further research. Carter (1972) has already extended Bather's model to allow for assignable causes to occur at exponentially distributed inter-arrival times rather than continuously.

8. Summary and Conclusions

This paper has surveyed papers in the accounting, statistics and management science literature dealing with the significance and investigation of realizations from a process which deviates from preset standards. A simple 2 x 2 classification scheme was developed which distinguished (i) models using only the most recent observation for decisions from those that used all observations since the last action time, and (ii) models which were mainly concerned with estimation or hypothesis testing from those whose actions were imbedded in a decision model which attempted to assess the costs and benefits from alternative actions. A number of questions were raised with respect to some models that have been proposed for the accounting cost variance decision and, it is hoped that, at the very least, the key assumptions and limitations behind all these models have been identified.

To gain some closure on this issue, suppose a hypothetical situation in which I must design a system that would track cost variances. Given the large number of alternative models surveyed in this paper and their limitations and assumptions, which would I choose to implement in a real-life ongoing situation? My short-range solution would probably be to install a cusum chart to track the accounting variances. This procedure is already widely used in quality control and would likely be reasonably robust with respect to the causes of nonstationary behavior. Initially, I would set the parameters of the cusum chart using prior data from the processes to establish the right tradeoff between false alarms and failures to detect changes quickly. With more time, I would try to estimate the cost and benefits from an investigation and use these to design "economic optimal" cusum charts [Taylor (1968), Goel and Wu (1973)]. In the long run, I would attempt to develop a continuous state model (e.g., along the lines of Bather) by attempting to directly model the source of nonstationary behavior and build this into the decision model.

My bias therefore is to first implement a procedure that systematically and sensibly processes the current data with all prior observations (i.e., the cusum chart). With this as a benchmark, I would then attempt to develop models that are closer to being "right" from a cost-benefit analysis. As more experience and data develop from such a process, I would then feel more comfortable about directly modeling the underlying stochastic process and implementing procedures which are optimal for that particular stochastic process. For the present, our most pressing need is for empirical research to uncover a set of plausible stochastic processes to describe the accounting cost variance environment.

Appendix

DERIVATION OF SUFFICIENT STATISTICS (u_t, v_t) IN BATHER'S MODEL

Assume that $y_t \mid \mathbf{x}_t \sim N(u_t, v_t)$, with u_t, v_t to be determined from $\mathbf{x}_t = (x_1, x_2, \cdots, x_t)$. Since $y_{t+1} = y_t + z_{t+1}$ with $z_t \sim N(0, \rho^2)$ and with y_t and z_{t+1} independently distributed, we have that

$$y_{t+1} \mid \mathbf{x}_t \sim N(u_t, v_t + \rho^2).$$

Also, $x_{t+1} \mid y_{t+1} \sim N(y_{t+1}, \sigma^2)$ by definition. Therefore, the likelihood function for y_{t+1} given $(x_1, x_2, \cdots, x_{t+1}) \equiv \mathbf{x}_{t+1}$ (denoted by $\Lambda(y_{t+1} \mid \mathbf{x}_{t+1})$) can be written (using the rule of conditional probability and Bayes Theorem) as

$$\Lambda(y_{+1} \mid \mathbf{x}_{t+1}) = k_1 \Lambda(y_{t+1}, x_{t+1} \mid \mathbf{x}_t)$$
$$= k_2 \Lambda(x_{t+1} \mid y_{t+1}) \Lambda(y_{t+1} \mid \mathbf{x}_t)$$

(where k_1 and k_2 are known constants). We write the two likelihood functions on the right-hand side of the above equation as:

$$\exp -\frac{1}{2}\left[\frac{1}{\sigma^2}(x_{t+1} - y_{t+1})^2\right] \exp -\frac{1}{2}\left[\frac{1}{v_t + \rho^2}(y_{t+1} - u_t)^2\right]$$

$$= \exp -\frac{1}{2}\frac{1}{\sigma^2(v_t + \rho^2)}\left[(v_t + \rho^2)(x_{t+1} - y_{t+1})^2 + \sigma^2(y_{t+1} - u_t)^2\right]$$

$$= \exp -\frac{1}{2}\left[\frac{1}{\sigma^2} + \frac{1}{v_t + \rho^2}\right]\left[y_{t+1} - \frac{(v_t + \rho^2)x_{t+1} + \sigma^2 u_t}{v_t + \rho^2 + \sigma^2}\right]^2 + k_3$$

where the last expression is obtained by completing the square and rearranging terms, and k_3 is a complicated expression involving terms such as v_t, ρ, x_{t+1}, etc., but *not* y_{t+1}.

Therefore if we identify u_{t+1} as

$$u_{t+1} = \frac{(v_t + \rho^2)x_{t+1} + \sigma^2 u_t}{v_t + \rho^2 + \sigma^2} \qquad \text{and} \qquad \frac{1}{v_{t+1}} = \frac{1}{\sigma^2} + \frac{1}{v_t + \rho^2}$$

we may write

$$\Lambda(y_{t+1} \mid \mathbf{x}_{t+1}) = k_4 \exp -\frac{1}{2}\left[\frac{1}{v_{t+1}}(y_{t+1} - u_{t+1})^2\right]$$

so that $y_{t+1} \mid \mathbf{x}_{t+1} \sim N(u_{t+1}, v_{t+1})$ with u_{t+1} and v_{t+1} defined above. Thus the posterior distribution of y_{t+1} conditional on the previous realizations $(x_1, x_2, \cdots, x_{t+1})$ is a normal distribution with mean u_{t+1} and variance v_{t+1}.

References

Anthony, R. N. "Some Fruitful Directions for Research in Management Accounting." In N. Dopuch and L. Revsine (Eds.), *Accounting Research 1960–1970: A Critical Evaluation* (Center for International Education and Research in Accounting: University of Illinois), 1973.

Barnard, G. A. "Control Charts and Stochastic Processes." *Journal of the Royal Statistical Society, Series B* XXI (1959): 239–57.

Bather, G. A. "Control Charts and the Minimization of Costs." *Journal of the Royal Statistical Society, Series B* XXV (1963): 49–70.

Bierman, H. and T. Dyckman. *Managerial Cost Accounting* (New York: Macmillan), 1971.

———, L. E. Fouraker, and R. K. Jaedicke. "A Use of Probability and Statistics in Performance Evaluation." *The Accounting Review* XXXVI (July 1961): 409–17.

Buzby, S. L. "Extending the Applicability of Probabilistic Management Planning and Control Systems." *The Accounting Review* XLIX (January 1974): 42–49.

Carter, P. "A Bayesian Approach to Quality Control." *Management Science* XVIII (July 1972): 647–55.

Chernoff, H. and S. Zacks. "Estimating the Current Mean of a Normal Distribution which Is Subjected to Changes in Time." *Annals of Math. Statistics* XXXV (December 1964): 999–1018.

DeGroot, M. H. *Optimal Statistical Decisions* (New York: McGraw-Hill), 1970.

Demski, J. "An Accounting System Structured on a Linear Programming Model." *The Accounting Review* XLII (October 1967): 701–12.

———. "Optimizing the Search for Cost Deviation Sources." *Management Science* (April 1970): 486–94.

Dopuch, N., J. G. Birnberg, and J. Demski. "An Extension of Standard Cost Variance Analysis." *The Accounting Review* XLII (July 1967): 526–36.

Duncan, A. "The Economic Design of $\bar{x}$ Charts Used to Maintain Current Control of a Process." *Journal of the American Statistical Association* LI (June 1956): 228–42.

Duvall, R. M. "Rules for Investigating Cost Variances." *Management Science* XIII (June 1967): 631–41.

Dyckman, T. R. "The Investigation of Cost Variances." *Journal of Accounting Research,* Vol. 7 (1969): 215–44.

Edwards, W. "Conservatism in Human Information Processing." *Formal Representation of Human Judgment,* B. Kleinmuntz, Ed. (New York: Wiley), 1968.

Ewan, W. D. and K. W. Kemp. "Sampling Inspection of Continuous Processes with No Autocorrelation Between Successive Results." *Biometrika* XLVII (1960): 363–80.

Farley, J. and M. Hinich. "Detecting 'Small' Mean Shifts in Times Series." *Management Science* XVII (November 1970): 189–99.

Gibra, I. N. "Economically Optimal Determination of the Parameters of $\bar{X}$-Control Charts." *Management Science* XVII (May 1971): 635–46.

Girshick, M. A. and H. Rubin. "A Bayes Approach to a Quality Control Model." *Annals of Math. Statistics* XXIII (1952): 114–25.

Goel, A. L., S. C. Jain and S. M. Wu. "An Algorithm for the Determination of the Economic Design of $\bar{X}$-Charts Based on Duncan's Model." *Journal of the American Statistical Association* LXIII (1968).

———— and S. M. Wu. "Economically Optimum Design of Cusum Charts." *Management Science* XIX (July 1973): 1271–82.

Goldsmith, P. L. and H. Whitfield. "Average Run Lengths in Cumulative Chart Quality Control Schemes." *Technometrics* III (February 1961): 11–20.

Hinich, M. and J. Farley. "Theory and Application of an Estimation Model for Time Series with Nonstationary Means." *Management Science* XII (May 1966): 648–58.

Juers, D. A. "Statistical Significance of Accounting Variances." *Management Accounting* XLIX (October 1967): 20–25.

Kadane, J. "Optimal Whereabouts Search." *Operations Research* XIX (July–August 1971): 894–904.

Kaplan, R. S. "Optimal Investigation Strategies with Imperfect Information." *Journal of Accounting Research,* Vol. 7 (1969): 32–43.

Koehler, R. W. "The Relevance of Probability Statistics to Accounting Variance Control." *Management Accounting* L (October 1968): 35–41.

Lev, B. "An Information Theory Analysis of Budget Variances." *The Accounting Review* XLIV (October 1969): 704–10.

Li, Y. "A Note on 'The Investigation of Cost Variances'." *Journal of Accounting Research,* Vol. 8 (1970): 282–83.

Luh, F. "Controlled Cost: An Operational Concept and Statistical Approach to Standard Costing." *The Accounting Review* XLIII (January 1968): 123–32.

Ozan, T. and T. Dyckman. "A Normative Model for Investigation Decisions Involving Multi-origin Cost Variances." *Journal of Accounting Research,* Vol. 9 (1971): 88–115.

Page, E. S. "Continuous Inspection Schemes." *Biometrika* XLI (1954): 100–15.

Probst, F. R. "Probabilistic Cost Controls: A Behavioral Dimension." *The Accounting Review* XLVI (January 1971): 113–18.

Ronen, J. "Nonaggregation Versus Disaggregation of Variances." *The Accounting Review* XLIX (January 1974): 50–60.

Ross, S. "Quality Control under Markov Deterioration." *Management Science* XVII (May 1971): 587–96.

Shewhart, W. A. *The Economic Control of the Quality of Manufactured Profit* (New York: Macmillan), 1931.

Slovic, P. and S. Lichtenstein. "Comparison of Bayesian and Regression Approaches to the Study of Information Processing in Judgment." *Organizational Behavior and Human Performance* VI (November 1971): 649–744.

Taylor, H. M. "The Economic Design of Cumulative Sum Control Charts for Variables." *Technometrics* X (August 1968): 479–88.

Zannetos, Z. A. "Standard Cost as a First Step to Probabilistic Control: A Theoretical Justification, An Extension and Implications." *The Accounting Review* XXXIX (April 1964): 296–304.

21

The author develops a standard cost accounting information system for a service business to address the following management problems: Do you really have any idea of the costs involved in operating your bank?; the expenses involved in providing a particular service?; the profitability (or unprofitability) of a certain customer? In analyzing these issues, the author brings forth performance measures for service personnel, specifically clerical employees.

Standard Cost Accounting for Banks*

James S. Labick and Frank C. Surges

In recent years, the operating costs of most banks have risen sharply. In spite of the fact that the dollar after-tax profits of insured banks increased more than 70 percent from 1960 to 1969, their after-tax return on average capital fell by nearly 9 percent.[1] This situation has given added food for thought to those bank managers who have long considered — but never really started — the installation of bank cost and profitability control systems. In carefully analyzing the business problems that directly contribute to the falling after-tax return on investment, forward thinking bank managers are now quickly realizing that they are the victims of a lack of information.

Most bankers feel, at one time or another, that certain customers are unprofitable, in total, even though they maintain relatively large DDA balances. Their inability to accurately measure the "overall" profitability of "assigned" customers has justifiably caused much concern among profit conscious bankers.

Today, many bankers realize that certain problems have been caused by the recent headlong rush for growth for growth's sake. Among these is

* *Reprinted from* The Bankers Magazine, *Spring 1971, Copyright © 1971, Warren, Gorham, and Lamont, Inc., 210 South Street, Boston, Mass. All rights reserved.*
[1] David W. Cole, "Profitability and the Cost of Interest-bearing Bank Funds," The Bankers Magazine, Winter 1970.

392

the situation where a bank is "forced" to provide new services and "service lines" without accurately evaluating their inherent costs. A group of bankers attending a recent AMA Seminar were asked: "How many of you are satisfied with the results of your new Bank Credit Card service line?" Out of approximately thirty bankers representing many areas of the country, only one was pleased with the results. Most felt they were too hasty in their initial decision to provide that service and indeed, many complained: "Our accounting and control systems did not provide enough information to enable us to make a rational decision, but since all of the other banks were doing it, we felt that it must be good." While this small sample of bankers cannot be considered to represent the whole banking industry, their accounting systems are probably typical. This is a sad commentary on the quality of financial information currently available for decision-making.

Also, the problem of how to measure the performance of bank officers has been raised in recent writings.[2] Other industries have solved this problem long ago through systems that use the "profit center," "investment center," and "cost center" concepts.[3] These systems have only recently been seriously applied to banks.

Finally, another problem that contributes to the reduction in the return on investment, and is particularly timely in light of the current profit squeeze, is the lack of effective control of operating costs. Clerical salaries is the most costly item of expense and yet, most banks have no method to adequately control it. A system that provides true performance measurement of clerical employees is rare in banking circles.

Having recognized and considered some or all of these problems, modern bankers invariably raise important questions: What is the best way to solve these problems? Can a well-designed cost accounting system really aid in the solution to each of these problems? Does a solution require reorganization and reassignment of responsibilities? Will a solution have a large impact on future profits? The answers to these and other frequently asked questions are contained in the balance of this article.

Standard Cost Accounting?

The term, "standard cost accounting," invariably brings to mind a manufacturing industry and the need for a system to provide performance measurement capability, pricing information, and the ability to properly value inventory. Only recently has its applicability in service industries, such as banking, been recognized. The basic difference between these industries

[2] Clarence R. Reed, "Evaluating the Performance of Commercial Loan Officers," *The Bankers Magazine,* Summer, 1970.
[3] See Chapters 5, 6, 7, *Management Control Systems, Cases and Readings,* R. Anthony, J. Dearden, R. Vancil, Irwin, 1965.

is that banks primarily sell services, or the time of employees and facilities, while manufacturers sell a tangible product. Actually, this difference is immaterial from a cost accounting point of view, and standard cost accounting can be an equally valuable tool in the banking industry.

DEFINITION OF STANDARD COST

Standard Cost Accounting is a special type of cost accounting. A text book definition sums it up nicely: "A standard cost is a predetermined cost, an explicit statement of what cost should be under the most efficient methods of operation which can be attained and sustained. It is actually the product of two factors determined separately — quantity and price."[4]

The important words in this definition are "what cost should be" and "predetermined." Standard costs allow the comparison of the actual cost incurred with a determination of the cost that should have been incurred, at the actual level of activity. If the standard includes a component for fixed overhead, the comparison will enable the determination of unused capacity, or "volume" variance.

USE IN BANKS[5]

Through the years, most of the developments in cost accounting have originated in the manufacturing industries. It was not until the middle 1930's and on into the 1940's that writers began discussing cost accounting in relation to banks. Marshall C. Corns wrote a series of ten articles in *The Bankers Magazine* in 1936.[6] Harold Randall's thesis written in 1939 was considered for many years as one of the most authoritative sources on the subject.[7] Other writings of the 1940's were those of Kennedy[8] and Anderson.[9]

The first edition of the NABAC (now Bank Administration Institute) book, entitled *Bank Costs,* was published in 1962. This is one of the more comprehensive and detailed works currently available on the subject of bank cost accounting.

All of these publications present techniques for historical cost account-

---

[4] Robert Beyer, *Profitability Accounting for Planning and Control,* The Ronald Press Company, New York, 1963, p. 101.

[5] See *Bank Costs for Decision Making,* John R. Walker, Bankers Publishing Co., Boston, 1970.

[6] Marshall C. Corns, *The Bankers Magazine,* February through December, 1936.

[7] Harold Randall, *Cost Accounting Procedure for Banks,* The Stonier Graduate School of Banking, Rutgers, New Jersey, 1939.

[8] James H. Kennedy, *Cost and Income Accounting and Its Practical Application to Banking,* The Stonier Graduate School of Banking, Rutgers, New Jersey, 1941.

[9] William H. Anderson, *A Practical Cost Accounting System for Large and Medium Sized Banks,* The Stonier Graduate School of Banking, Rutgers, N.J., 1948.

ing, rather than standard cost accounting. They describe methods that enable cost information to be accumulated on work sheets, using information taken from the regular bank accounting methods. Through a series of allocations, the various items of expense are assigned to the numerous services of the bank to arrive at a full absorption cost for each of these services. These procedures are quite time-consuming, and are rarely performed more often than semi-annually. Their major disadvantage is that historical cost inherently has hidden within it all the inefficiencies, waste, unused capacity, and other losses that an organization can sustain. A much better approach would be to use predetermined costs and relate them to the services performed. This is the basis of standard cost accounting.

Standard cost accounting evolved from production standards developed for manufacturing operations by industrial engineers. Cost accountants later used these standards to develop accounting systems in which both the actual cost and standard cost of production are computed and compared and then used to control expenses. Subsequently, the development of industrial engineering time standards in clerical work measurement programs lead to the introduction of standard costs in banks. Currently many medium- to large-sized banks maintain a work measurement group; indeed, a very large bank may have from fifty to one hundred persons engaged in this activity. However, the major benefit to be derived from the use of standard cost accounting in banks comes only with its integration into the other bank accounting systems. To date, very few banks have accomplished this.

MULTIPLE USES OF STANDARD COSTS

There are two fundamental objectives of an integrated financial information system using standard costs:[10]

- To provide the opportunity for profit improvement through control of clerical salaries, forms and other material, and overhead expenses.
- To provide the opportunity for profit improvement through evaluation of the accomplishment of officer and organizational goals, service line profitability, and customer profitability.

A standard cost accounting system provides the basic data necessary to accomplish these objectives. It serves as the hub around which the various necessary subsystems revolve (see Figure I).

The foundation of a standard cost accounting system for a bank rests on its direct labor standards. These are the time standards for performing the basic functions of banking. They are a logical byproduct of the clerical

[10] See "Computer-based Bank Financial Information Systems" — *The Bankers Magazine,* Autumn, 1969, by W. Ellingson, E. Kennedy, and P. Landgren Jr.

FIGURE I

Multiple Uses for Standard Costs
in an Integrated Bank System

Expense Control:
−Responsibility reporting
−Labor control reports

Profitability Control:
Customer,
Organizational
P & L

STANDARD
COSTS

Profitability Control
Service
Line
P & L

Pricing Decisions

work measurement programs banks have been involved with for years. By relating these labor standards (along with material and overhead standards discussed later) to the services provided, by customer and "service line," the integration of the standard cost system with the profitability subsystems becomes possible.

Specifically, a standard cost system provides variable budgets for the many classes of "production" employees within the bank; it facilitates labor control by providing data to compute the efficiency of small groups of employees, and it facilitates control of variable non-personnel expenses by providing a benchmark from which meaningful variances can be computed. In addition, by computing standard costs of providing specific banking services, a bank manager can determine profit (or loss) by service line, by "assigned" customer (if the transaction volume is accumulated by customer), and by contact officer. Thus, the full benefits of the various information subsystems shown in Figure I can be realized through integration of standard costs with the responsibility reporting and profitability reporting subsystems.

ADVANTAGES OF AN INTEGRATED
STANDARD COST SYSTEM

There are three major advantages of an integrated standard cost system:

1. *It facilitates the measurement of performance at the specific level of activity incurred.* Since a standard cost is a predetermined amount

per unit of activity, it follows that by multiplying the unit standard cost and the actual level of activity incurred, one can obtain a measure of what cost "should have been" at that level of activity.

2. *It segregates responsibility for operating on an efficient basis from the contact officer's responsibility for profitability.* An integrated system allows the control of operating cost performance to reside with the cost center supervisor while allowing the contact officer to "buy" these services for his customers at a standard rate. This enables the bank to measure the contact officer's performance on a "profit center" basis, free from the distortion of operating department efficiency, spending, and volume variances.

3. *It provides management with a realistic benchmark to establish prices on a competitive basis.* When standard costs are related to services provided and service lines offered (e.g., processing a checking account debit for a regular checking account), a manager has the ability to determine unit cost (in fixed and variable components) for pricing decisions. This is especially beneficial when determining the price for a contemplated new service, since once the price is established, it is usually difficult to increase it substantially. In the case of long-standing service lines, this same unit cost information can aid in the establishment of management priorities for expansion or reduction.

Management Reports

Before explaining in detail the workings of an integrated standard cost system and how its integration is achieved, we will describe the management reports that it all makes possible. One thing should be clear from the beginning: no matter how good the reporting system is, it cannot give absolute answers to problems. It can point out where the problems are, and in some cases can show what happened to cause them, but we know of no system that will make decisions automatically. In fact, nothing can replace a good manager who gets a report, spots a problem, determines what he should do to correct it, and then takes forceful and effective corrective action.

The system described here is currently being installed in a large bank on the east coast. A system similar in concept has been in operation in a midwest bank for a number of years.

The objectives of an integrated standard cost-based financial information system, as mentioned earlier, are basically cost control and profitability control. Costs are best controlled by comparing them to a realistic and equitable budget, such as one based on standard costs. The secret in making budgets work for you lies in the effectiveness of the reporting and in the insight into operations provided by variances from the budget. The results must be reported in such a manner that they gain the necessary attention from all levels of management. In many instances, before the installation of an integrated standard cost system, the bank will have to be reorganized to facilitate a clear delineation of responsibility. A premium must be put on defining the operations required to produce a service profitably, and on assigning responsibility organizationally for planning and controlling such operations efficiently.

Responsibility in budget preparation and in cost control is a major feature in a bank's control system. The responsibility reporting subsystem, described here, pinpoints responsibility for all controllable costs by individuals, and integrates standard cost accounting with the company's budgetary controls. Reports are prepared for all levels of management, from the lowest cost center head up to the president. The reporting system is designed as a tool for all supervisory levels in controlling their operations and their costs. The cost and variance totals are carried from one level of responsibility upward to the next (See Figure II). In this way, each level of responsibility receives reports in the detail necessary for control.

Responsibility Reports

A typical first level responsibility report is shown in Figure III. This report summarizes both personnel and nonpersonnel costs at a proper level of detail for effective control. Personnel costs, the largest cost item in any "production" cost center, are shown by "occupation code," or function. Accounts with a cost code of "V" are budgeted on a variable budget basis using the output from the standard cost accounting system. Budgets for the fixed accounts ("F") are set once per year based on the planned activity of the cost center and are stored on a computer master file.

The line item, "transferred costs," reflects the effect of transferring the budgeted cost of related support departments, covered later. It is shown below the "total spending" line since it is not controllable in any way by the cost center head.

The last item of significance on this report is the line entitled "standard costs absorbed." If this were a report for a manufacturing concern, this line would reflect the standard costs (both the fixed and variable components) that were absorbed into inventory. Since banks expense all costs on a current basis, there is no inventory for items "produced." This line represents the standard costs "absorbed" into the profitability subsystems. All costs incurred, including variances, find their way into the P & L statements at some level.

Figure IV shows an example of the responsibility report issued to the next higher responsibility level in the organization. The details of the Transit Section depicted in Figure III are summarized here on one line.

FIGURE II   Responsibility Reporting Flow

PRESIDENT

Current Month			Year to Date	
Actual	*B/(W)*		*Actual*	*B/(W)*
XXX	XX	Operations	XXX	XX
XXX	XX	———	XXX	XX
XXX	XX	———	XXX	XX
XXX	XX		XXX	XX

OPERATIONS DIVISION

Current Month			Year to Date	
Actual	*B/(W)*		*Actual*	*B/(W)*
XXX	XX	Central Operations	XXX	XX
XXX	XX	———	XXX	XX
XXX	XX	———	XXX	XX
XXX	XX		XXX	XX

CENTRAL OPERATIONS

Current Month			Year to Date	
Actual	*B/(W)*		*Actual*	*B/(W)*
XX	XX	Transit	XX	XX
XX	XX	Bookkeeping	XX	XX
XX	X	———	XX	XX
XX	X	———	XX	XX
XXX	XX		XXX	XX

TRANSIT

Current Month			Year to Date	
Actual	*B/(W)*		*Actual*	*B/(W)*
X	X	Proof Mach.	X	X
X	X	Messengers	X	X
X	X	———	X	X
X	X	———	X	X
XX	X		XX	X

BOOKKEEPING

Current Month			Year to Date	
Actual	*B/(W)*		*Actual*	*B/(W)*
X	X	Bookkeepers	X	X
X	X	Clerks	X	X
X	X	———	X	X
X	X	———	X	X
XX	X		XX	X

FIGURE III

XYZ Bank Responsibility Report

PERIOD ENDING XX

RESPONSIBILITY OF: A. Banker
COST CENTER NUMBER XX
AREA: Transit

	Current Month				Description	Year to Date		
	ACTUAL	BUDGET	BETTER WORSE—	COST CODE		ACTUAL	BUDGET	BETTER WORSE—
					— Personnel Spending —			
PROOF MACHINE OPERATORS	$27,200	$21,400	$5,800—	V		$227,300	$194,300	$33,000—
MESSENGERS	4,200	5,000	800—	V		33,000	43,600	10,610—
MAIL DEPOSIT CLERKS	2,000	2,100	100—	V		24,000	25,000	1,000—
UTILITY CLERKS	4,500	7,500	3,000—	V		49,000	65,100	16,100—
SECRETARIES	2,900	4,800	1,900—	F		38,000	36,000	2,000—
OTHER	1,100	400	700—	F		9,000	5,100	3,900—
OVERTIME PREMIUM	1,200	800	400—	F		15,800	11,000	4,800—
EMPLOYEE BENEFITS	9,600	9,600		V		64,000	72,000	8,000—
TOTAL PERSONNEL SPENDING	$52,700	$51,600	$1,100—			$460,100	$452,100	$8,000—
					— Non-personnel Spending —			
ARMORED SERVICE	$ 1,200	$ 1,200		F		$ 14,300	$ 14,400	$ 100—
OCCUPANCY CHARGE	5,400	5,100	$ 300—	F		42,700	41,900	800—
EQUIPMENT EXPENSE	12,700	13,100	400—	F		68,800	70,300	1,500—
OTHER	300	100	200—	F		2,700	1,000	1,700—
TOTAL NON-PERSONNEL SPENDING	$19,600	$19,500	$ 100—			$128,500	$127,600	$ 900—
* * * TOTAL SPENDING * * *	$72,300	$71,000	$1,200—			$588,600	$579,700	$ 8,900—
— TRANSFERRED COSTS —		6,300					76,000	
TOTAL COSTS		$77,400					$665,700	
— STANDARD COSTS ABSORBED —		$72,000—					$530,000—	
VOLUME VARIANCE		$ 5,400					$125,000	

FIGURE IV

XYZ Bank Responsibility Report

FOR PERIOD ENDING — XXXXXXXXXX, 19XX

COST CENTER NUMBER XXXXXX
RESPONSIBILITY OF D. BROWN
AREA — CENTRAL OPERATIONS

Current Month			Area Description	Year to Date		
ACTUAL	BUDGET	BETTER WORSE—	—SPENDING—	ACTUAL	BUDGET	BETTER WORSE—
X	X	X	BOOKKEEPING	X	X	X
72.3	71.1	1.2—	TRANSIT	588.6	579.7	8.9—
X	X	X	LOCK BOX	X	X	X
X	X	X	GENERAL	X	X	X
$243.1	$239.1	$4.0—	. . . TOTAL SPENDING . . .	$2,532.7	$2,535.2	$2.5

PERSONNEL REPORTS

In many cases, more information than is given on the responsibility report is needed to effectively control labor. The standard cost accounting system can provide the necessary data in almost any level of detail desired. The proper balance between having too many reports on the one hand, and having enough data to make decisions on the other, can be obtained by capturing and reporting labor standards at the "occupation code" or function level. Some banks may want to do this on the employee level, while others feel it will suffice to report performance on the department level. Figure V shows a typical Personnel Performance Report. This example covers the proof machine operators in the Transit Section. A comparison of this example with Figure III reveals that the report is simply an expansion of the detail shown on the first line of that report.

The Personnel Performance Report is made up of three sections: personnel utilized, services performed, and summary. The headings are self-explanatory. By multiplying the volume of each service performed by the employees in this occupation code times the standard time to perform the service (stored in a computer master file), we obtain "budget hours earned." The sum of the budget hours earned, when compared to the actual hours worked enables us to compute efficiency. In this example, 2440 hours were earned, 3050 hours were expended for an efficiency of 80 percent. The standard costs are based on a standard labor rate for the occupation code. Since each individual is likely to be paid slightly more or less than the standard, a rate variance is shown by individual. The primary function of this column, however, is to highlight variances caused by employees who are "loaned" to the occupation code on a temporary basis and are paid at a rate significantly different from the standard.

FIGURE V

XYZ Bank Personnel Performance Report

FOR THE PERIOD ENDING XXXXXXXX XX, 19XX

COST CENTER NUMBER — XXXXXX
AREA — Transit
RESPONSIBILITY OF — A. Banker
PROOF MACHINE OPERATORS

Personnel Utilized   *Services Performed*

EMPLOYEE NAME	TOTAL RATE VARIANCE FAV/ UNFAV—	— ACTUAL HOURS — OVERTIME	TOTAL	ACT. NO.	SER. NO.	DESCRIPTION	VOLUME	BUDGET HOURS EARNED	BUDGET AMOUNT EARNED
J. JONES	25.00	12.0	172.0	X	X	PROCESS CHECKING ACCT. DR.	3,150,000	X	X
R. SMITH	10.50—	0.0	160.0	X	X	PROCESS CHECKING ACCT. CR.	650,000	X	X
*P. ROTHBELL	33.00	5.0	165.0	X	X	PROCESS INTERNAL DR.	35,000	X	X
X	X	X	X	X	X	PROCESS INTERNAL CRS.	38,000	X	X
X	X	X	X			X			
X	X	X	X			X			
X	X	X	X			X			
X	X	X	X			X			
X	X	X	X			X			
X	X	X	X			X			
X	X	X	X			X			
TOTALS	$2,880.00	150.0	3,050.0					2,440	$21,440

SUMMARY

$ Variances — Favorable/Unfavorable —

ACTUAL COST	*% EFFICIENCY*		*EFFICIENCY*	*RATE*	*NON-MEASURED PERSONNEL*	*TOTAL LABOR*	*OVERHEAD ABSORBED*
	THIS MONTH	*Y-T-D*					
$27,200	80.0%	82.3%	$8,680—	$2,880	—	$5,800—	$17,000

* Loaned employee.

PROFITABILITY CONTROL

The second major objective of an integrated, standard cost-based financial information system is profitability control. As mentioned, this control is provided through evaluation of officer and organizational profit performance, customer profitability, and service line profitability.

Bankers have long debated the question of whether to require the payment of a fee for each service performed, or to provide some services free of charge in recognition of DDA balances maintained. Either alternative is acceptable, providing that the total customer relationship is profitable. Unfortunately, unless the cost of providing each service and the value of obtaining a DDA balance is known, a rational management decision cannot be made. All of the data required to make such a management decision is provided on the Customer Profitability Statement (Figure VI). On this report, the income and standard cost of services provided to a particular customer are pulled together to reveal a complete profitability picture. Note that recognition has been given to the value of the net average balance maintained.

This identification of total customer profitability is of major importance, particularly for commercial banks, since a corporate customer may have loan, trust, and other relationships within the bank, as well as the deposit relationship. The definition of a customer must be such that not only are individual accounts reported but total overall results recognized. A corporate customer may have several corporate DDA accounts to satisfy his needs. Profitability of any given account is not nearly as important as the profitability of the overall customer relationship.

If you consider the large number of assigned customers a typical bank can claim, you may wonder about the pile of reports that would result if this statement was produced monthly for each of them. It is rare that an officer would want to review the profitability of each of his accounts every month. Consequently, these reports should be generated on a "when needed" basis. The easiest way to accomplish this is to print them directly onto microfilm each month, then make copies as needed from the microfilm. Each assigned customer is, by definition, related to an officer. By combining all of the customer data for a particular officer, we obtain a profitability report depicting that officer as a "profit center." The performance of each contact officer can be measured against his monthly budget, or plan.

Profit center profitability is one important guide for top management to evaluate middle management's contribution to total bank profit. The organizational profitability subsystem reports profitability for each profit center and summarizes it, along organizational lines, to the top P & L. Figure VII (p. 408) shows an organizational profitability report for the officer in charge of a branch. It summarizes profitability for assigned accounts by responsible officer. Miscellaneous accounts (non-assigned) are summarized by major service line. A funds adjustment is recognized to give credit for the de-

FIGURE VI

XYZ Bank Customer Profitability Statement

CUSTOMER NAME: A. Brown
OFFICER NAME: J. Jones   CUST. NO.: XXX

Current Month	Description	Year-to-Date
	CUSTOMER INCOME	
X	Regular Service Charges	
X—	Waived Service Charges	X
X	Accounts Receivable Commitment Fees	X—
X	Mortgage Fees	X
X	Notes Discounted Fees	X
X		X
X		X
X		X
X	Notes Discounted Interest	X
X	Collateral Loan Time Interest	X
X	Construction Mortgage Interest	X
X	Total Income	X
	CUSTOMER AVERAGE BALANCES	
X	Regular Business Account	X
X—	Float Balance	X—
X	Time Deposit	X
X—	Reserve Requirements	X—
X—	Notes Discounted	X—
X—	Collateral Loan Time	X—
X—	Construction Mortgage	X—
X	Net Average Balances	X
X	Funds Credit or Charge	X

Volume	Cost	Customer Costs	Volume	Cost
XXX	X—	Checking Account Deposits	XXX	X—
XXX	X—	Checking Account Debit	XXX	X—
XXX	X—	Account Maintenance	XXX	X—
X	X—	Mortgage Set Up	X	X—
XX	X—	Lock Box Items	XX	X—
	X—	J. Jones — Officer Contact Time		X—
	X—	Accounts Receivable Project		X—
	X—	Total Customer Cost		X—
	X	Customer Net Income/Loss		X—

posit balances provided by an officer's customers, and to charge the officer for the use of funds he provided to his customers. The standard costs shown consist of all transactions processed for each customer of the officer, costed at standard, and transferred from the "production" departments. This is the other half of the "cost absorbed" entry on the responsibility statement.

The responsibility reporting "roll-up" technique is applicable here also. The details of the Metropolitan Branch depicted in Figure VII are summarized as one line item on the next higher profitability level — the Region.

The customer and officer profitability systems provide the bank management with data necessary to make day-to-day decisions. The service line profitability system will aid management in pricing and setting priorities to expand or reduce any of the hundreds of service lines offered by a typical commercial bank. An example of a service line profitability report is shown in Figure VIII (p. 410). This system takes the same profitability information previously reported on a "profit center" and "customer" basis and presents it by specific type of income or individual service such as lockbox, corporate payroll, or trust under agreement. These activities and services are performed for many different customers and are organizationally reported in many different profit centers. This system develops profitability by specific service line and segregates it for management analysis and control.

All banks have the opportunity of increasing profits through the pricing of the services provided to their customers. This can be accomplished by raising prices when costs increase, or even raising prices to price themselves out of an unprofitable service line. A knowledge of service line costs can also enable bank management to reduce prices, in selected service lines, to increase volume — and profits. With the rapid expansion of services now being provided, and the more extensive services that will be provided in the future, the problem of strategic pricing and its impact on total bank earnings is greatly intensified. Thus the bank that has available to it an accurate knowledge of its costs, by service line, will have a competitive advantage in the struggle for customers and profits.

COSTS AND PRICING

Service costs must be identified on a fixed-variable basis for pricing decisions. The identification of all costs related to each service line, including contact costs, general and administrative costs, and a provision for profit contribution, forms the basis for the bank's catalogue of prices. The final pricing decision can be made only after a careful review of the competitive situation. Some service lines, routine in nature and highly competitive must, out of necessity, be priced to produce a low profit margin. Others, perhaps a specialty of the bank, or ones that are possible only after high start-up costs, can justify higher mark-ups. The establishment of a bank pricing committee to make policy decisions and establish pricing parameters is essential to maximize overall bank profitability as it relates to pricing customer services. Once a pricing policy is set, it must be effectively communicated to all officers who have profit responsibility.

Marginal pricing techniques can increase profits if used intelligently.

These special situations must be controlled closely to keep them from getting out of hand. It is important to recognize the point at which marginally priced items are utilizing the time of employees and facilities that could otherwise be used more profitably.

Integrating the Standard Cost System

We have seen the type of management information that is made possible by an integrated standard cost system. Now standard costs can be covered in more detail. And it will be shown how the integration of a standard cost system into a bank management accounting and reporting system is accomplished.

COMPONENTS OF STANDARD COST

There are four basic standard cost components:

- *Unit of measure* — this relates to the "activity base" or service provided, e.g., open an account, process a debit or process a credit.
- *Standard time/material per unit* — this is a physical measurement of the amount of time or material necessary to directly provide the service. It is predetermined.
- *Variable standard rate* — a predetermined dollar rate per unit of time or material.
- *Fixed overhead rate* — the predetermined factor that will provide full absorption of cost center fixed overhead, at the planned level of activity.

The overhead portion of the standard cost can be computed in many generally acceptable ways: the base can be either dollars or hours; the dollars or hours can be related to the entire cost center or to only a portion of the cost center such as labor grade, or "occupation code." The important principle to follow is that the fixed and variable components of the total standard cost must be kept separate. Only in this way can the full analytical benefit be derived from their use.[11]

The first step in providing the necessary integration of standard costs with the various management reporting subsystems is the definition of the "Standard Cost Structure" (see Figure IX, p. 411). It starts with the iden-

[11] One method of calculation is as follows:

Variable portion + fixed portion = total standard cost
Variable portion = number units × Standard Time per unit × Variable Standard Rate
Fixed portion = number of units × standard time per unit × fixed overhead rate
Sum of the above = total standard cost.

FIGURE VII
XYZ Bank Organization Profitability

PROFIT CENTER — Metropolitan Branch
RESPONSIBILITY OF — J. Jones
PERIOD ENDING XX

PROFIT/LOSS	Description		Income — Interest	Income — Commission	Income — DDA	Fees — Other	Fees — Waived	Funds Usage — Funds Supplied	Funds Usage — Funds Used	Funds Usage — Funds Adj.	Expenses — Standard Cost	Expenses — T/D Interest	Expenses — Other
	ASSIGNED ACCOUNTS:												
X	J. JONES	CM	X	X	X	X	X–	X	X	X	X–	X–	X–
X		YTD	X	X	X	X	X–	X	X	X	X–	X–	X–
X	R. THOMPSON	CM	X	X	X	X	X–	X	X	X	X–	X–	X–
X		YTD	X	X	X	X	X–	X	X	X	X–	X–	X–
X	W. STANLEY	CM	X	X	X	X	X–	X	X	X	X–	X–	X–
X		YTD	X	X	X	X	X–	X	X	X	X–	X–	X–
XX	ASSIGNED ACCOUNT SUBTOTALS	CM	X	X	X	X	X–	X	X	X	X–	X–	X–
XX		YTD	X	X	X	X	X–	X	X	X	X–	X–	X–
	UNASSIGNED BY SERVICE LINE:												
X	DEMAND DEPOSIT	CM			X	X	X–	X		X	X–		
X		YTD			X	X	X–	X		X	X–		
X	SAVINGS	CM						X		X	X–	X–	X–
X		YTD						X		X	X–	X–	X–
X	OTHERS	CM	X	X		X	X–	X	X	X	X–	X–	X–
X		YTD	X	X		X	X–	X	X	X	X–	X–	X–
$ 18.1	TOTAL	CM	$ 36.1	$ 1.0	$ 21.5	$ .5	$ .3	$5,480.7	$7,735.4	$ 4.3–	$ 11.9–	$ 1.1–	$ 2.8–
$216.1		YTD	$403.1	$12.0	$258.3	$6.0	$2.1–	$5,768.5	$8,824.6	$52.1–	$143.7–	$13.0–	$34.1–

Variance from Plan

ASSIGNED ACCOUNTS:																
J. JONES	CM	X	X	X	X	X	X	X	X	X	X	X	X
	YTD	X	X	X	X	X	X	X	X	X	X	X	X
R. THOMPSON	CM	X	X	X	X	X	X	X	X	X	X	X	X
	YTD	X	X	X	X	X	X	X	X	X	X	X	X
W. STANLEY	CM	X	X	X	X	X	X	X	X	X	X	X	X
	YTD	X	X	X	X	X	X	X	X	X	X	X	X

FIGURE VIII

XYZ Bank Service Line Profitability

SERVICE LINE — Personal Trust
SERVICE LINE #XXX

PERIOD ENDING XX

PROFIT/LOSS	Description			Income					Funds Usage			Expenses		
						Fees			FUNDS SUPPLIED	FUNDS USED	FUNDS ADJ.	STANDARD COST	T/D INTEREST	OTHER
			INTEREST	COMMIS-SION	DDA	OTHER	WAIVED							
X	TRUST U/AGREE	CM		X		X	X—	X		X	X	X	X
X		YTD		X		X	X—	X		X	X	X	X
X	LIFE INS. TRUST	CM		X		X	X—				X	X	X
X		YTD		X		X	X—				X	X	X
X	GUARDIANSHIP	CM		X		X	X—	X		X	X	X	X
X		YTD		X		X	X—	X		X	X	X	X
X	OTHER	CM		X		X	X—				X	X	X
X		YTD		X		X	X—				X	X	X
X	TOTAL	CM		X		X	X—	X		X	X	X	X
X		YTD		X		X	X—	X		X	X	X	X
	Variance from Plan													
X	TRUST U/AGREE	CM		X		X	X	X		X	X		X
X		YTD		X		X	X	X		X	X		X
X	LIFE INS. TRUST	CM		X		X	X				X		X
X		YTD		X		X	X				X		X
X	GUARDIANSHIP	CM		X		X	X	X		X	X		X
X		YTD		X		X	X	X		X	X		X
X	OTHER	CM		X		X	X				X		X
X		YTD		X		X	X				X		X
X	TOTAL	CM		X		X	X	X		X	X		X
X		YTD		X		X	X	X		X	X		X

FIGURE IX

Typical Standard Cost Structure

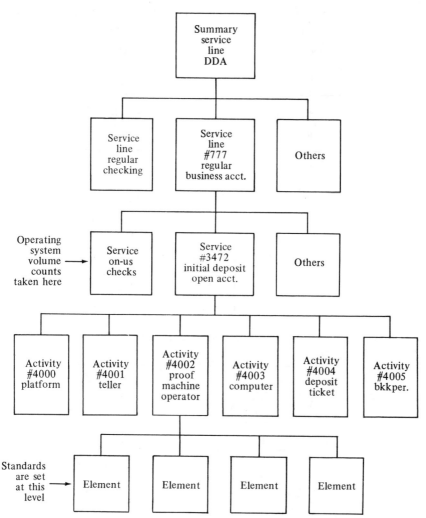

tification of all "summary service lines," such as DDA, Savings, Mortgage Loans, Trust, Investments, etc. These are further broken down into the "service lines" offered such as special checking, regular checking, pension trust, transfer agent, brokers loans. Within each service line, all unique services provided must be identified, e.g., open an account, process a debit, process a credit, and the like. A typical bank provides thousands of unique services. Many skills are involved with providing each of these services. We call the level of standard cost structure that relates to the individual "occupation codes" or skills required to provide a particular service the "activity" level. It identifies the "occupation code" or class of employee within

FIGURE X

Computer Flow Chart Explosion Cost Subsystem

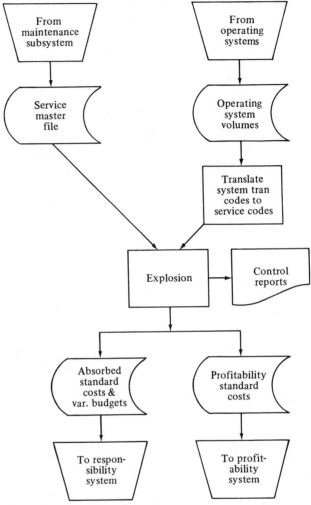

a cost center who performs a portion of the service. The lowest level of the structure is the "element." It is the level at which work measurement standards are set. In a bank of any size, of course, the sheer volume of transactions necessitates the use of a computer.

Basically the system works as follows: transaction volumes are obtained from the bank's operating system at the "service" level. These are accumulated by service line and assigned customer. These transaction volumes are fed into an "explosion" run (see Figure X), which matches them against a standards master file that relates the volume to the "activities" involved with performing the service.

Let's take an example: assume that a customer comes into the bank to

FIGURE XI

Operating System Summary Input

Service Line Code	Service Code	Customer Codes*	Volume	Profit Center Codes*
#777	#3472	XX	100	404

* If profit center and/or customer profitability information is a part of the standard cost system, then codes which will assign standard costs to customers and/or profit centers must accompany the volumes into the "explosion" run.

open a regular business demand deposit account. After the transaction has been completed, the bank computerized operating system will have the following information: The service line involved (here it is the regular business account), the particular service provided (in this example, it is the initial deposit that opens the account), the customer involved (if the customer is assigned to a specific officer, the customer code will be recorded; if not, the code will reflect "nonassigned customer"), the volume of the transaction (here it is one), and finally, the profit center to which it is related. Figure XI shows the details of a summarized operating system input relating to 100 unassigned customers. This detailed information is fed into the explosion run which matches it against a series of service master records. Figure XII shows the detail information stored on the service master record for the particular input involved. Note that for each

FIGURE XII

Service Master Record

HEADER INFORMATION
SERVICE LINE #777 — Regular Business Demand Deposit Account
SERVICE #3472 — Initial Deposit — Open Account

RECORD DETAIL

ACTIVITY	COST CENTER #	ACCOUNT CODE	ACCOUNT DESCRIPTION	STANDARD RATE PER UNIT/HOUR	OVERHEAD RATE	O H I
4000	325	0709	PLATFORM	5.00	3.00	X
4001	325	0608	TELLER	2.50	3.00	X
4002	365	0321	PROOF MACHINE OPERATOR	2.25	4.00	X
4003	390	0765	COMPUTER	65.00	10.00	X
4004	395	0897	FORMS COST	.001	—	
4005	395	0920	BOOKKEEPER	2.00	4.50	X

FIGURE XIII

Explosion Run Calculations

ACTIVITY NO.	COST CENTER #	ACCOUNT CODE	VOLUME	STANDARD HOURS OR UNITS	STANDARD RATE PER HOUR OR UNIT
4000	325	0709	100	0.30000	$5.00
4001	325	0608	100	0.00100	2.50
4002	365	0321	100	0.000122	2.25
4003	390	0765	100	0.000012	65.00
4004	395	0897	100	1.000000	.001
4005	395	0920	100	0.000400	2.00

combination of service line (777) and service (3472) there is a specific group of activities required. In this example, activities numbered 4000 through 4005. Most of these relate to direct labor functions (for example, activity 4002 relates to a proof machine operator with an "occupation code" of 0321, who works in cost center 365, has a standard wage rate of $2.25, and a related overhead rate of $4.00). Others, such as activity 4004, relate to the standard cost of material (here it is a deposit ticket). The column entitled "OHI" refers to "overhead indicator." This enables the system to determine whether overhead should be added to the standard variable cost when determining total standard cost.

The calculations involved can best be explained through use of an example (see Figure XIII). If we follow activity 4002 again, we note that by multiplying the volume times standard hours times the standard rate (columns 4x5x6) we obtain the variable standard cost of $.027. The overhead portion of the total standard cost is obtained by multiplying the volume times the standard hours times the overhead rate (columns 4x5x8). The result here is $.048. The sum of the variable standard cost and the overhead portion equals the total standard cost, or "absorbed" standard cost (column 10). Column 11 lists the variable budgets derived from the standard cost system, used for cost control purposes.

A thorough review of Figure XIII reveals that activities 4003 and 4004 do not have variable budgets posted in column 11. In addition to this, we

STANDARD COST	OVER-HEAD RATE	OVER-HEAD COSTS	STANDARD COST ABSORBED	VARIABLE BUDGETS
$150.00	$3.00	$90.00	$240.00	$150.00
.250	3.00	0.300	0.550	0.250
.027	4.00	0.048	0.075	0.027
.078	10.00	0.012	0.090	—
.100	—	—	0.100	—
0.080	4.50	0.180	0.260	0.080
			↓	↓
			Credit on Responsibility Reports	To Variable Budget Accounts on Responsibility Reports

see that activity 4004 does not have an overhead amount associated with it. These are not omissions; they are the result of provisions in the system. Activity 4003 happens to be the computer time associated with processing an initial deposit for service line No. 777. In most banks, the cost of computer rental is relatively fixed throughout the normal range of activity. One possible way to treat this situation is to provide a fixed budget to the computer department for the computer rental expense, while at the same time charge the standard cost of computer time (computed by assuming a planned level of utilization) to the customer, officer, and service line involved. Utilization is controlled by monitoring the "absorption credits" earned by the computer department. Activity 4004 relates to the cost of the initial deposit ticket. Since most of the fixed overhead incurred more closely relates to clerical salaries than to material cost, a case could be made to absorb overhead entirely on the basis of labor hours. No overhead amount, then, is associated with material cost.

Most banks do not keep a perpetual inventory record of deposit ticket use; they expense them when they are purchased. Since the actual expense recorded in the general ledger is based on bulk purchases, it would be unrealistic to compare it against the standard cost (based on predetermined use) on a monthly basis. Hence, there is no variable budget calculated for activity 4004 to be used on the responsibility reports.

Transferred Costs

In order to obtain the benefits of full absorption cost accounting, costs incurred in selected related support departments must be allocated to production cost centers. For example, the costs incurred by the chief operations officer and his staff should be allocated on some equitable basis to each of the cost centers under his control. Once transferred (allocated), these costs will be absorbed, along with the "production" centers' overhead costs, through the overhead rate of that "production" cost center. One way to obtain an equitable allocation and yet still hold the transferring cost center responsible for variances, is to transfer budgeted costs rather than the actual cost incurred.

The decision of where and how much cost to transfer to "production" cost centers is made after careful analysis of the transferring cost centers. All costs that can be logically and equitably transferred should be transferred. The balance of costs will remain in the general and administrative cost pool for inclusion in the profit and loss statement at a high level.

The above examples of standard cost techniques serve to highlight the basic principles involved. Although the examples are not all-inclusive, they do show the power of standard cost techniques and their applicability to the banking industry.

Conclusion

It should be clear that a standard cost accounting system has a definite place in the future of most banks. A banker's ambition should be to produce the best service possible to the public at the lowest cost—and still show a realistic return on the stockholders investment. In order to accomplish this, he must change his method of operation and employ modern standard cost accounting techniques that have been so effective in manufacturing industries. Within a few years, any medium- to large-sized bank that has not installed an integrated standard cost-based financial information system such as the one briefly described here will, we feel, be at a great competitive disadvantage in the quest for growth and profits.

Supplemental

Readings

to Part Five

Clayton, Henry L. "Setting Standards and Evaluating Performance." *Cost and Management,* 39, No. 5 (May 1965), 195–203.
>   Stipulates the essentials of installing and evaluating a standard cost system.

Chumachenko, Nikolai G. "Once Again: The Volume-Mix-Price/Cost Budget Variance Analysis." *The Accounting Review,* XLIII, No. 4 (October 1968), 753–762.
>   Compares methods of variance analysis used in the United States and in the USSR.

Demski, Joel S. "An Accounting System Structured on a Linear Programming Model." *The Accounting Review,* XLII, No. 4 (October 1967), 701–712.
>   Describes and gives implications of linear programming in a pilot application to the structure of an accounting control system.

———. "Analyzing the Effectiveness of the Traditional Standard Cost Variance Model." *Management Accounting,* 49, No. 2 (October 1967), 9–19.
>   Compares information provided by the standard cost variance model with that required by management, with an operational extension.

———. "Optimizing the Search for Cost Deviation Sources." *Management Science,* 16, No. 8 (April 1970), B-486–B-494.
>   Develops a model to determine the optimum sequence in which to examine the various possible causes of cost variances.

———. "Predictive Ability of Alternative Performance Measurement Models." *Journal of Accounting Research,* 7, No. 1 (Spring 1969), 96–115.
>   Discusses predictive ability as a surrogate to assess direct costing, absorption costing, and an *ex post* optimum model.

Drake, Raymond G. "Improved Control Through Flexible Budgeting in the Retail Trade." *The Canadian Chartered Accountant,* 91, No. 6 (December 1967), 429–434.
>   Explains how flexible budgeting techniques used in industry can be applied also to retail business.

Duvall, Richard M. "Rules for Investigating Cost Variances." *Management Science,* 13, No. 10 (June 1967), B-631–B-641.
>   Shows how costs of determining the reasons for variances may be treated as part of the decision to analyze variances or not.

Dyckman, T. R. "The Investigation of Cost Variances." *Journal of Accounting Research,* 7, No. 2 (Autumn 1969), 215–244.
> Develops the means for making the cost-deviation investigation decision incorporate both the cost of investigation and the expected savings.

Frank, Werner, and Rene Manes. "A Standard Cost Application of Matrix Algebra." *The Accounting Review,* XLII, No. 3 (July 1967), 516–525.
> Illustrates a matrix algebra application to calculating standard prime cost variances.

Harper, W. M. "Managerial Economic Control — IV: Profit Variance Analysis." *Accountancy,* LXXIX (August 1968), 536–540.
> Discusses overhead expenditure variances, marginal cost variances, and contribution variances.

————. "Managerial Economic Control — V: The Objection to Conventional Variance Analysis." *Accountancy,* LXXIX (November 1968), 796–799.
> Explains why fixed overhead variances have no control value.

Hasseldine, C. R. "Mix and Yield Variances." *The Accounting Review,* XLII, No. 3 (July 1967), 497–515.
> Expresses mix and yield variances in simple mathematical and graphic terms and discusses the validity of the measures obtained.

Juers, Donald A. "Statistical Significance of Accounting Variances." *Management Accounting,* 49, No. 2 (October 1967), 20–25.
> Describes statistical methods for determining the importance of a variance.

Kravitz, Bernard J. "The Standard Cost Review." *Management Controls,* 15, No. 11 (November 1968), 253–255.
> Examines the frequency at which standard costs should be revised and the form the review should take.

Lev, Baruch. "An Information Theory Analysis of Budget Variances." *The Accounting Review,* XLIV, No. 4 (October 1969), 704–710.
> Uses the concepts of information theory to supplement quality-control techniques in analyzing variances of nonrepetitive operations.

Luh, F. S. "Controlled Cost: An Operational Concept and Statistical Approach to Standard Costing." *The Accounting Review,* XLIII, No. 1 (January 1968), 123–132.
> Proposes a refinement of standard cost (controlled cost) using statistical techniques to evaluate operating efficiency and degree of control.

Magee, Robert P. "A Simulation Analysis of Alternative Cost Variance Investigation Models." *The Accounting Review,* LI, No. 3 (July 1976), 529–544.
> Indicates that (1) a rational manager who is evaluated on the basis of his or her operating results or on the number of times he or she conforms to the budget may prefer a naive cost-investigation rule, and (2) a manager who is concerned with all costs could well prefer a less complex investigation rule.

Manes, Rene P. "The Expense of Expected Idle Capacity." *Management Accounting,* 50, No. 7 (March 1969), 37–41.
> Proposes a method of considering the cost of idle capacity as a period cost, removing it from the volume variance.

Miles, Raymond E., and Roger C. Vergin. "Behavioral Properties of Variance Controls." *California Management Review,* VIII, No. 3 (Spring 1966), 57–65.

> Demonstrates how existing control theories and techniques offer a starting point for constructing a behaviorally sound and technically effective approach to control design.

Partridge, R. W. "Let's Do Right by Variance Analysis." *Cost and Management,* 40, No. 11 (December 1966), 491–498.

> Presents models that describe the behavior of the joint variance and illustrate its importance.

Ronen, Joshua. "Nonaggregation Versus Disaggregation of Variances." *The Accounting Review,* XLIX, No. 1 (January 1974), 50–60.

> Explains why the investigation and reporting decisions in variance analysis must be considered simultaneously for optimal results.

Solomons, David. "Flexible Budgets and the Analysis of Overhead Variances." *Management International,* 1961, 84–93.

> Using flexible budgets, accomplishes a four-variance analysis of overhead.

Stallman, James C. "A Framework for Evaluating Cost Control Procedures for a Process." *The Accounting Review,* XLVII, No. 4 (October 1972), 774–790.

> Presents a framework for evaluating control procedures for a manufacturing process by identifying cost changes caused by their addition to or elimination from an existing control system.

———. "Reducing the Cost of Cost Control." *Management Accounting,* LIII, No. 1 (July 1971), 59–62.

> Discusses the differences between preventive and detection-correction costs.

Wolk, Harry I., and A. Douglas Hillman. "Materials Mix and Yield Variances: A Suggested Improvement." *The Accounting Review,* XLVII, No. 3 (July 1972), 549–555.

> Proposes a different structure of raw material variances where the standard mix is intentionally abandoned in the short run because of raw material price changes, causing a different combination to be optimal.

Zannetos, Zenon S. "On the Mathematics of Variance Analysis." *The Accounting Review,* XXXVIII, No. 3 (July 1963), 528–533.

> Presents a simple mathematical approach to two- and three-variance overhead analysis, supplemented by a geometrical appendix. The author also discusses the significance of variances.

Additional
Bibliography
to Part Five

Bianchini, Frank V., and Thomas J. Cotter. "Profit Planning, Performance Reporting, Variation Analysis." *Financial Executive,* XXXI, No. 11 (November 1963), 37 ff.

Bierman, Harold, Jr., Lawrence E. Fouraker, and Robert K. Jaedicke. "A Use of Problems and Statistics in Performance Evaluation." *The Accounting Review,* XXXVI, No. 3 (July 1961), 409–417.

Cook, Mel. "Five Ways of Discrediting Standard Costs — And the Lessons They Teach." *NAA Bulletin,* XL, No. 12 (August 1959), 29–34.

Copeland, Ben R. "Analyzing Burden Variance for Profit Planning and Control." *Management Services,* 2, No. 1 (January–February 1965), 34–41.

dePaula, F. C. "Commitment Accounting for Contract Profit Control." *Accountancy* (November 1965), 1037–1040.

Ferrara, William L. "Controlling Production Overhead." *The Controller,* XXX, No. 3 (March 1962), 130 ff.

Goel, Amrit, and S. M. Wu. "Economically Optimum Design of Cusum Charts." *Management Science* (July 1973), 1271–1282.

Grinnell, D. Jacques. "Activity Levels and the Disposition of Volume Variances." *Management Accounting,* LVII, No. 2 (August 1975), 29–32, 36.

Guilfoyle, Harold B. "Measuring Production Efficiency." *The Canadian Chartered Accountant,* 85, No. 1 (July 1964), 25–28.

Itami, Hiroyuki. "Evaluation Measures and Goal Congruence under Uncertainty." *Journal of Accounting Research* (Spring 1975), 73–96.

Kahn, Louis B., and Waino W. Suojanen. "Two Simple Measures of Productivity from Accounting Data." *NAA Bulletin,* XLVI, No. 5 (January 1965), 17–23.

Kirby, Fred M. "Variance Analysis — The 'Step-through' Method." *Management Services,* 7, No. 2 (March–April 1970), 51–54.

Kollaritsch, Felix P., and Norman E. Dittrich. "Standard Sales Prices and Their Variances." *Management Services,* 1, No. 4 (September–October 1964), 30–36.

Montgomery, Douglas C., Russell G. Heikes, and Joseph F. Mance. "Economic Design of Fraction Defective Control Charts." *Management Science* (July 1975), 1272–1284.

Ozan, T., and T. Dyckman. "A Normative Model for Investigating Decisions Involving Multiorigin Cost Variances." *Journal of Accounting Research* (Spring 1971), 88–115.

Reinherr, Charles M. "Profit Fluctuations Caused by Standard Cost Variances." *NAA Bulletin,* XLII, No. 3 (November 1960), 23–30.

Shroad, Vincent J., Jr. "Control of Labor Costs Through the Use of Learning Curves." *NAA Bulletin,* XLVI, No. 2 (October 1964), 15–22.

Shultis, Robert L. "Applying PERT to Standard Cost Revisions." *NAA Bulletin,* XLIV, No. 1 (September 1962), 35–43.

Solomons, David. "Standard Costing Needs Better Variances." *NAA Bulletin,* XLIII, No. 4 (December 1961), 29–39.

Weber, Charles. "The Mathematics of Variance Analysis." *The Accounting Review,* XXXVIII, No. 3 (July 1963), 534–539.

Yoshida, Yasuo. "Cost Control in Product Feasibility Decisions." *NAA Bulletin,* XLII, No. 6 (February 1961), 27–38.

Zannetos, Zenon S. "Toward a Functional Accounting System: Accounting Variances and Statistical Variance Analysis." *Industrial Management Review,* 7, No. 2 (Spring 1966), 71–82.

Zeff, Stephen A. "Standard Costs in Financial Statements — Theory and Practice." *NAA Bulletin,* XL, No. 8 (April 1959), 5–16.

PART SIX

Cost Allocation

and Decentralization

Considerable controversy has arisen regarding the proper handling of overhead costs in both centralized and decentralized environments. Advocates of full, or absorption, costing recommend use of an estimated overhead rate to assign all overhead costs to products or services. However, as direct costing enthusiasts emphasize, this traditional procedure can result in misleading product or service cost information and, consequently, less than ideal managerial decisions. Profitable services can, for example, sometimes appear unprofitable because of the amount of fixed overhead allocated to them. Direct or variable costing avoids this kind of distortion and provides more useful managerial information by assigning to the service only those costs that fluctuate with volume and by treating fixed overhead as a period cost. This approach, however, can also be criticized for failing to recognize the opportunity costs associated with the actual delivery of one service or service mix as opposed to another. Hence direct costing tends to understate service or manufacturing costs.

Livingstone deals with this problem in an interdivisional cost-allocation situation. He develops a matrix cost-allocation model and integrates it with input-output analysis, which he presents as a superior tool for allocating costs and for planning and control. The concepts he presents, with examples and discussion, are based on Leontief's model. Livingstone pays special attention to the problem of expressing variables in physical as well as monetary terms and to the analysis of incremental and opportunity costs as an alternative to the direct-absorption cost controversy.

Morse's article, also, seeks to improve cost allocation by using the learning-curve phenomenon. He seeks to avoid the distortions of traditional cost-allocation methods by taking into account the fact that the "... ratio of actual production costs to units produced declines over the product's life cycle." The production process produces not only a physical product but also an intangible asset of production "know-how." The learning-curve cost-allocation model ". . . recognizes the existence of this know-how and modifies the amounts charged to the units produced accordingly" to achieve the cost-allocation goal of matching effort and accomplishment.

The final two articles deal with the topic of transfer pricing, which evolves naturally from the problems of cost allocation and the phenomenon of increasing decentralized organizations. Onsi elaborates on the inadequacies of using variable costs and other common methods as a basis for transfer pricing and performance evaluation in decentralized organizations. He proposes a transfer price system based on the opportunity-cost concept, taking into consideration some of the behavioral problems that attend transfer pricing when divisional performance is evaluated on a "profit center" basis.

Watson and Baumler draw more extensively on behavioral research to develop a paradigm of the social system within which the transfer pricing problem can be analyzed. The authors develop a theoretical framework integrating organizational decentralization, differentiation, and integration concepts and relate them to the role and effect of transfer pricing. Within this framework they constructively criticize mathematical programming solutions, negotiated prices, and conflict resolution approaches to the transfer pricing problem. As part of an accounting information system, appropriate transfer pricing mechanisms can enhance either organization differentiation or organizational integration, depending on the needs of the organization.

$2\mathbf{2}$ *Input-output analysis is presented as a general model, of which the matrix model is a special case, for handling interactive cost allocation problems. From unit variable and fixed costs computed for varying output volumes, breakeven analyses, flexible budgets, and overhead absorption rates can be computed for each division and for the system as a whole.*

The author illustrates and discusses the basic input-output model, its application to planning and to an analysis of incremental and opportunity costs. He also suggests that the input-output technique can be as valuable for intrafirm analysis as it has been for inter-industry and interfirm economic analysis.

Input-Output Analysis for Cost Accounting, Planning and Control*

John Leslie Livingstone†

Several articles in the recent accounting literature have dealt with the allocation of costs among interacting departments in an organization.[1] The term "interacting departments" is used here to describe departments which both make and receive allocations of costs to and from other departments. An example would be a service department which supports several operating departments and which in turn receives support from other service departments.

The articles cited make use of simultaneous linear equation systems and linear algebra to handle the interactive cost allocation problems. The purpose of this paper is to present some more powerful extensions of these

* *From* The Accounting Review, *Vol. XLIV, No. 1 (January, 1969), pp. 48–64. Reprinted by permission of the American Accounting Association and the author.*

† The author wishes to express appreciation to Gerald L. Salamon, doctoral candidate at The Ohio State University, for helpful comments on this paper.

[1] Thomas H. Williams and Charles H. Griffin, "Matrix Theory and Cost Allocation," THE ACCOUNTING REVIEW (July 1964), pp. 671–78. Neil Churchill, "Linear Algebra and Cost Allocations: Some Examples," THE ACCOUNTING REVIEW (October 1964), pp. 894–904. Rene P. Manes, "Comment on Matrix Theory and Cost Allocation," THE ACCOUNTING REVIEW (Teachers' Clinic) (July 1965), pp. 640–43.

techniques and to show their uses for planning and decision-making. This will be done through input-output analysis. It will be shown that input-output analysis is a general model, of which the matrix cost allocation model is a special case.

Matrix Cost Allocation

To show the link between matrix cost allocation and input-output analysis it is convenient to borrow the example used by Williams and Griffin.[2] This example is based on five interacting service departments and three operating departments, and is summarized as follows:

Cost Allocation Percentage

	Allocations from Service Departments				
	1	*2*	*3*	*4*	*5*
To Service Departments					
1	0	0	5	10	20
2	0	0	10	5	20
3	10	10	0	5	20
4	5	0	10	0	20
5	10	10	5	0	0
To Operating Departments					
A	25	80	20	0	10
B	25	0	30	40	5
C	25	0	20	40	5
Total	100%	100%	100%	100%	100%

Direct costs of each department, before any allocations are:

Service Departments

1	$ 8,000
2	$ 12,000
3	$ 6,000
4	$ 11,000
5	$ 13,000

Operating Departments

A	$120,000
B	$200,000
C	$ 80,000

[2] Williams and Griffin, *op. cit.*, p. 675.

The following system of simultaneous equations is formed:

$$
\begin{array}{llll}
(1) & X_1 & -.05X_3 - .10X_4, - .20X_5 = & 8,000 \\
(2) & X_2, - .10X_3 - .05X_4, - .20X_5 = & 12,000 \\
(3) & -.10X_1 - .10X_2 + X_3 - .05X_4 - .20X_5 = & 6,000 \\
(4) & -.05X_1 - .10X_3 + X_4 - .20X_5 = & 11,000 \\
(5) & -.10X_1 - .10X_2 - .05X_3 + X_5 = & 13,000
\end{array}
$$

Where X_i is the redistributed cost of the ith service department after receiving cost allocations from the other service departments. In matrix form these equations are expressed as $Ax = b$, where A is the matrix of cost allocation percentages, x is the vector of redistributed service department costs with elements $X_1, X_2, \cdots, X_5$, and b is the vector of service departments' direct costs.

The system is solved for x by premultiplying $Ax = b$ by the inverse of A, so that $x = A^{-1}b$. The result is:

$$
x = \begin{bmatrix} X_1 \\ X_2 \\ X_3 \\ X_4 \\ X_5 \end{bmatrix} = \begin{bmatrix} 13,657.46 \\ 17,503.59 \\ 13,290.64 \\ 16,368.06 \\ 16,780.64 \end{bmatrix}
$$

By summing equations (1) through (5) we get:

$$.75X_1 + .80X_2 + .70X_3 + .80X_4 + .20X_5 = \$50,000$$

so that a total of $50,000 (which is the total of service department direct costs, ΣB_i) is allocated to the operating departments.

The X_i are now distributed to operating departments, by using the matrix of percentages of service department costs allocable to operating departments to premultiply the x vector, as follows:

$$
\begin{bmatrix} .25 & .80 & .20 & 0 & .10 \\ .25 & 0 & .30 & .40 & .05 \\ .25 & 0 & .20 & .40 & .05 \end{bmatrix} \begin{bmatrix} 13,657.46 \\ 17,503.59 \\ 13,290.64 \\ 16,368.06 \\ 16,780.64 \end{bmatrix} = \begin{bmatrix} 21,755 \\ 14,787 \\ 13,458 \end{bmatrix}
$$

which, subject to some small rounding errors, gives the allocation to the three operating departments of the $50,000 of service department costs.

To the vector of redistributed service department costs we add the vector of direct costs of operating departments and arrive at the total costs — both allocated and direct — of operating departments, as follows:

$$
\begin{bmatrix} 21,755 \\ 14,787 \\ 13,458 \end{bmatrix} + \begin{bmatrix} 120,000 \\ 200,000 \\ 80,000 \end{bmatrix} = \begin{bmatrix} 141,755 \\ 214,787 \\ 93,458 \end{bmatrix}
$$

We now recast the same example in terms of input-output analysis and show the same result achieved in a single matrix multiplication instead of the three sets of matrix operations used above.

Input-output Representation

Input-output analysis summarizes transactions between all possible economic units involved, in a square matrix. For this reason we express our example in such a manner (in the table below), adding zeros to indicate the absence of cost flows from operating to service departments.

		Allocations from Departments							
		1	*2*	*3*	*4*	*5*	*A*	*B*	*C*
	(1)	0	0	.05	.10	.20	0	0	0
	(2)	0	0	.10	.05	.20	0	0	0
	(3)	.10	.10	0	.05	.20	0	0	0
	(4)	.05	0	.10	0	.20	0	0	0
To Departments	(5)	.10	.10	.05	0	0	0	0	0
	(A)	.25	.80	.20	0	.10	0	0	0
	(B)	.25	0	.30	.40	.05	0	0	0
	(C)	.25	0	.20	.40	.05	0	0	0

We refer to the above matrix as A^* and, as before, we use the vectors x (now 8 by 1, to include all departments — both service and operating) and b (also now 8 by 1).

In our matrix formulation of equations 1 through 5 earlier, the matrix A actually consisted of the service department reciprocal cost allocation percentages subtracted from an identity matrix of the same dimensions. This is seen in equations 1 through 5 by the unity coefficients along the main diagonal and negative or zero coefficients elsewhere.

We now formalize this procedure and define:

$$A = I - A^*.$$

The input-output conditions[3] for clearing all costs out of service departments into operating departments are:[4]

$$Ax = b.$$

---

[3] See R. G. D. Allen *Mathematical Economics* (Macmillan, 1963), p. 483. Our formulation is of an open (rather than closed) system.

[4] Readers can, of course, verify from our example that this equation holds.

Since we are given b and want to find x, we have:

$$x = A^{-1}b$$

and the reader who makes this computation will find that:

$$x = \begin{bmatrix} 13,658 \\ 17,503 \\ 13,290 \\ 16,368 \\ 16,780 \\ 141,755 \\ 214,787 \\ 93,458 \end{bmatrix}$$

which is the same result that we previously obtained in three steps of matrix operations.

In our example so far we have made no distinction between fixed and variable costs. Suppose that certain service departments have both fixed and variable costs. In particular, let us assume that the direct costs of departments 1 and 4 include fixed costs of $2,000 and $5,000, respectively. We can separate the fixed cost allocations by redefining the b vector for fixed costs only as:

$$b^t = [2,000 \quad 0 \quad 0 \quad 5,000 \quad 0 \quad 0 \quad 0 \quad 0]$$

and recomputing x, which we rename x'. Then:

$$x' = A^{-1}b = \begin{bmatrix} 2,624 \\ 393 \\ 631 \\ 5,261 \\ 333 \\ 1,130 \\ 2,967 \\ 2,903 \end{bmatrix}$$

Now the last three elements of b total $7,000 and represent the fixed cost portion of the aggregate costs of operating departments. It is vitally important that the fixed cost portion be separated, otherwise the model automatically unitizes fixed costs as in absorption costing but does not allow for under- or overabsorption when activity levels change. Of course, the first five elements of b represent fixed cost components of service departments' total costs. By subtracting x' from x the variable costs of each department can be found.

With this information, unit fixed and variable costs can be computed by dividing these respective costs for each department by its unit output.

From these unit variable costs, and unit fixed costs computed for varying volumes of output, there can be developed breakeven analyses, flexible budgets and absorption rates for overhead for each department and the system as a whole.

In the above example we were given b, the vector of direct cost inputs, and solved for x, the output vector. Usually the input-output model is used for the opposite purpose. Given the output vector, it is sought to determine the inputs required. The model is briefly described below, after which we will again apply it to our example — this time as a planning technique to compute resource requirements from an expected level of outputs.

The Basic Input-Output Model

The input-output model, which is due to Leontief,[5] analyzes transactions between economic activities, where an activity may represent an industry, a firm, or — as in our case — a single department or cost center. It is assumed that there is only one primary input (usually labor) and only one output for each activity. There are n activities and n output commodities, each of which may comprise a final product or an intermediate product serving as input for other activities. Production takes place through processes with fixed technological yields of constant proportionality. There is only one process used with no substitution in each activity. The use of only one process does not necessarily imply that alternative processes are non-existent. It may be that an activity has a production function that includes alternative processes, each with constant technological yields, and then elects a single, perhaps optimal, process for use. In this case the process selected is preferred only for a given set of prices.

The basis of the input-output model is a matrix of transactions (presently assumed to be in monetary terms), with a row and a column for each activity. The transactions matrix can be summarized as:

$$
\begin{array}{c}
n \text{ rows} \\[2em]
1 \text{ row}
\end{array}
\left[
\begin{array}{c|c|c}
V_{rc} & v_r & V_r \\
\hline
e_c & 0 & W
\end{array}
\right]
$$

$$
\begin{array}{ccc}
n & 1 & \text{total} \\
\text{columns} & \text{column} & \text{column}
\end{array}
$$

The amounts V_{rc} (with $r,c = 1,2,\cdots, n$) are the monetary values of output of the rth activity used as input by the cth activity. The rows thus represent distribution of the output of each activity, while the columns

[5] Wasily W. Leontief, *The Structure of American Economy, 1919–39,* second edition (Oxford University Press, 1951). A very good, concise description of the model is given in Richard Mattessich, *Accounting and Analytical Methods* (Richard D. Irwin, Inc., 1964), pp. 295–311.

represent sources of the inputs of activities. The n dimensional vector, v_r, shows the final demand for each commodity (or the "bill of goods") and V_r (n by 1) is the total output column so that:

(1)
$$V_r = v_r + \sum_c v_{rc}, \quad r = 1, 2, \cdots, n.$$

The n dimensional row vector e_c represents the costs of the primary input (say labor) to the activities, with a total of W, and thus:

(2)
$$W = \sum_c e_c$$

Fixed technological coefficients are assumed:

(3)
$$a_{rc} = v_{rc}/V_c \quad r, c = 1, 2, \cdots, n$$

which are the $(n + 1)$ elements of each column, respectively, divided by their sum, V_c, which is:

(4)
$$V_c = e_c + \sum_r v_{rc}.$$

These give an input coefficient matrix:

(5)
$$A^* = [a_{rc}], \quad \text{of order } n \text{ by } n$$

and a technology matrix:

(6)
$$A = I - A^* = \begin{bmatrix} 1 & -a_{12} & \cdots & -a_{1n} \\ -a_{21} & 1 & \cdots & -a_{2n} \\ \hline -a_{n1} & -a_{n2} & \cdots & 1 \end{bmatrix}.$$

The solution to the system, expressing the condition that all output is exactly distributed over uses (both final and intermediate) is:

(7)
$$AV_r = v_r.$$

Note that equation (7) does not directly give us e_c which can be derived as follows: Given v_r, final demand, we compute V_r, total output, and then calculate e_c. From (7) we compute V_r,

(8)
$$V_r = A^{-1}v_r.$$

Since all output is exactly distributed over uses, total inputs equal total output for each activity, i.e.,

(9)
$$V_r = V_c \quad \text{for all } r = c$$

in other words, the row total for any activity equals its column total.

Now consider any column, with subscript $c = 0$. We can rewrite (3) as:

(10)
$$a_{r0} = v_{r0}/V_0$$

and sum both sides over rows:

$$(11) \qquad \sum_r a_{r0} = \sum_r v_{r0}/V_0.$$

Similarly, (4) can be rewritten as:

$$(12) \qquad V_0 = e_0 + \sum_r v_{r0}.$$

Then, we divide (12) by V_0 and obtain:

$$(13) \qquad 1 = e_0/V_0 + \sum_r v_{r0}/V_0$$

and substitute from (11) into (13):

$$(14) \qquad 1 = e_0/V_0 + \sum_r a_{r0}$$

which can be rearranged into:

$$(15) \qquad e_0 = V_0 \left(1 - \sum_r a_{r0}\right).$$

Since V_0 is known to us from (8) and (9), and $\sum_r a_{r0}$ is given, e_0 can be computed from (15). Having set up the basic input-output model, we now

TABLE 1

Inputs

	1	2	3	4	5
(1)			1,366	683	1,366
(2)			1,750		1,750
(3)	655	1,329		1,329	665
(4)	1,637	818	818		
Outputs (5)	3,356	3,356	3,356	3,356	
(A)					
(B)					
(C)					
e_c	8,000	12,000	6,000	11,000	13,000
Total (V_c)	13,658	17,503	13,290	16,368	16,781

	A	B	C	v_r	*Total* (V_r)
(1)	3,415	3,414	3,414		13,658
(2)	14,003				17,503
(3)	2,658	3,986	2,658		13,290
(4)		6,548	6,547		16,368
Outputs (5)	1,679	839	839		16,781
(A)				141,755	141,755
(B)				214,787	214,787
(C)				93,458	93,458
e_c	120,000	200,000	80,000		450,000
Total (V_c)	141,755	214,787	93,458	450,000	977,600

apply it to our example as a planning technique to compute requirements for primary inputs from a given level of outputs.

Input-Output Applied To Planning

Input-output applications normally proceed by gathering the data for the transactions matrix and then computing the technological coefficients from these data. We will follow this procedure, using the same example as before. The dollar transactions matrix in canonical (or standard) form is shown in Table 1.

The transactions matrix in Table 1 requires some explanation. Note that it differs in form from the cost allocation model where outputs were stated in columns and inputs along rows as shown above. The standard transactions matrix is the transpose of that arrangement, with outputs stated rowwise and inputs columnwise. The vector V_r

$$V_r = \begin{bmatrix} 13,658 \\ 17,503 \\ \vdots \\ 93,458 \end{bmatrix}, \quad 8 \text{ by } 1.$$

is seen to be identical with the vector x which we computed previously in the one-step procedure for cost allocation. Note that the vector V_c of column totals is simply the transpose of the V_r vector, so that the row and column totals for any activity are equal.

The V_r vector of final demand shows the output of operating departments which, as expected, totals $450,000 and equals the scalar, W, which is the total value of primary inputs (the elements of the e_c vector). It is worth pointing out that the overall total of the table, namely $977,600, amounts to twice the total of primary inputs ($450,000) or final demand, plus the sum of interactivity transfers ($77,600), i.e.:

$2(450,000) + 13,658 + 17,503 + 13,290 + 16,368 + 16,781 = 977,600.$

Thus the table adds to the aggregate value of all transactions of all activities in the system. The familiar macro-economic quantities of gross national product, national income, consumption and so on that are used in national income accounting have their analogies at the micro level of our system of activities.

Payments to primary factors, or gross system product at factor prices, is $450,000 — the sum of the e_c row, which is also gross system income, or total consumption — the sum of the v_r column. This is the fundamental identity of the product and expenditure sides in national (or here, system) income accounting. Interactivity transactions would, of course, be excluded as double-counting since they do not represent any value added. Thus, input-output analysis can be regarded generally as a double-entry accounting technique for recording and analyzing transactions between activities in an economic system.

Finally, in explanation of Table 1, it remains to show the derivation of the v_{rc}, i.e., the amounts in the upper left hand part of the transactions matrix. These are obtained by applying the cost allocation percentages previously given to the total redistributed cost of each service department. For instance, of service department #2's total redistributed costs of $17,503, 10% (or $1,750) each is allocated to departments 3 and 5 and the remaining 80% (or $14,003) to operating department A. We now calculate the a_{rc} to obtain A^*. Applying (3) to column 1 of the transactions matrix we have:

$$
\begin{aligned}
V_1 &= 13,658 \\
a_{31} = v_{31}/V_1 &= 665/13,658 = 0.0487 \\
a_{41} = v_{41}/V_1 &= 1,637/13,658 = 0.1199 \\
a_{51} = v_{51}/V_1 &= 3,356/13,658 = 0.2457 \\
e_1/V_1 &= = 8,000/13,658 = 0.5857 \\
& \text{Total} = \underline{\underline{1.0000}}
\end{aligned}
$$

The remaining columns are treated in the same way to compute A^* and then A, which is:

$$
\begin{bmatrix}
1 & & -.1028 & -.0417 & -.0814 & -.0241 & -.0159 & -.0365 \\
& 1 & -.1317 & & -.1043 & -.0988 & & \\
-.0487 & -.0759 & 1 & -.0812 & -.0396 & -.0188 & -.0186 & -.0284 \\
-.1199 & -.0467 & -.0616 & 1 & & & -.0305 & -.0701 \\
-.2457 & -.1918 & -.2525 & -.2050 & 1 & -.0118 & -.0039 & -.0090 \\
& & & & & 1 & & \\
& & & & & & 1 & \\
& & & & & & & 1
\end{bmatrix}
$$

and

$$
A^{-1} =
\begin{bmatrix}
1.0386 & .0319 & .1391 & .0737 & .0934 & .0319 & .0217 & .0471 \\
.0424 & 1.0378 & .1734 & .0402 & .1186 & .1082 & .0056 & .0094 \\
.0767 & .0947 & 1.0410 & .0995 & .0573 & .0314 & .0238 & .0394 \\
.1312 & .0581 & .0889 & 1.0169 & .0203 & .0108 & .0348 & .0786 \\
.3096 & .2427 & .3485 & .2594 & 1.0643 & .0506 & .0235 & .0403 \\
& & & & & 1 & & \\
& & & & & & 1 & \\
& & & & & & & 1
\end{bmatrix}
$$

Now, for any given final demand vector v_r we can compute e_c, the primary input resource requirements. For instance, consider a final demand one-tenth as large as before, so that:

$$
v_r =
\begin{bmatrix}
0 \\
0 \\
0 \\
0 \\
0 \\
14{,}176 \\
21{,}479 \\
9{,}346
\end{bmatrix}
$$

Then, from (8),

$$
V_r = A^{-1}v_r =
\begin{bmatrix}
1{,}359 \\
1{,}742 \\
1{,}326 \\
1{,}636 \\
1{,}668 \\
14{,}176 \\
21{,}479 \\
9{,}346
\end{bmatrix}
$$

Note that rounding error impairs the accuracy of the computation. We know from Table 1 that the elements of V_r should be (to the nearest dollar) 1,366, 1,750 and so on rather than the 1,359, 1,742, etc., above. This is due to the use of only four decimal places in setting up the A^* matrix, a nearest-dollar v_r vector, and use of a single-precision computer routine for the inversion of A.[6] The inaccuracy is of the order of one-half of one per cent. Users wishing superior accuracy may be well advised to resort to double-precision routines.[7]

Having determined V_r, the next step is to compute e_c, the primary input resource requirements. We use expression (15), which can be expressed in matrix form as:

(16) $$e_c = V_r^T Z$$

where Z is a matrix with elements

$$\left(1 - \sum_r a_{r0}\right)$$

[6] Inversion was done using the General Electric Time-Sharing Service and one of its library routines called MATRIX***. Even though this program requires a redundant (for this purpose) matrix multiplication, its run time was 7 seconds. This run time (inefficiently used) for an 8 by 8 matrix inversion, is interesting to compare with the 10 seconds reported by Manes (*op. cit.*, p. 641) for a 5 by 5 matrix, which resulted in a loss of one-third of one per cent average accuracy.

[7] See Manes, *op. cit.*, p. 641, for a report on the use of a double-precision routine.

on the main diagonal and zeros elsewhere:

$$Z = \begin{bmatrix} \left(1 - \sum_r a_{r1}\right) & 0 & \cdots & \cdots & 0 \\ 0 & \left(1 - \sum_r a_{r2}\right) & \cdots & 0 \\ \hline 0 & 0 & \left(1 - \sum_r a_{rn}\right) \end{bmatrix}.$$

In our example we have:[8]

$$Z = \begin{bmatrix} .5857 & 0 & 0 & 0 & 0 & 0 & 0 & 0 \\ 0 & .6856 & 0 & 0 & 0 & 0 & 0 & 0 \\ 0 & 0 & .4514 & 0 & 0 & 0 & 0 & 0 \\ 0 & 0 & 0 & .6721 & 0 & 0 & 0 & 0 \\ 0 & 0 & 0 & 0 & .7747 & 0 & 0 & 0 \\ 0 & 0 & 0 & 0 & 0 & .8465 & 0 & 0 \\ 0 & 0 & 0 & 0 & 0 & 0 & .9311 & 0 \\ 0 & 0 & 0 & 0 & 0 & 0 & 0 & .8560 \end{bmatrix}$$

and using V_r corrected for rounding error,

$$e_c = [800 \quad 1{,}200 \quad 600 \quad 1{,}100 \quad 1{,}300 \quad 12{,}000 \quad 20{,}000 \quad 8{,}000],$$

which we can see from Table 1 is correct, being one-tenth of the primary input requirements in the table.

Expression (16) can be generalized and used to find any desired row of the dollar transactions matrix. The Z matrix applied to find e_c can be subscripted e. A Z matrix, Z_r, can be formulated to find any row r as follows:

$$Z_r = \begin{bmatrix} a_{r1} & 0 & \cdots & 0 \\ 0 & a_{r2} & \cdots & 0 \\ \hline 0 & 0 & \cdots & a_{rn} \end{bmatrix},$$

and then (16) in general form becomes:

(17) $$r = V_r^T Z_r.$$

For instance let $r = 2$. Then:

$$Z_{33} = .1317, \quad Z_{55} = .1043 \quad \text{and} \quad Z_{66} = .0988$$

with all other $Z_{ij} = 0$, and:

$$\text{row } 2 = V_r^T Z_2 = [0 \quad 0 \quad 175 \quad 0 \quad 175 \quad 1400 \quad 0 \quad 0]$$

which, it is seen from Table 1, is correct.

[8] Note that the $(1 - \sum_r a_{r0})$ can be obtained by summing the columns of the A matrix.

To summarize, it has been shown how any vector of expected final demand can be translated into the required vector of primary inputs. In addition, we have shown how to derive the associated interactivity transactions. Once the A^{-1} and Z matrices have been computed, so long as the mix of services is constant, they can be used again and again for any values of expected final demand, and the computational load of evaluating the effects of various final demand vectors is quite light. Therefore, the technique has advantages for planning and resource allocation purposes, and also for ensuring proper coordination of input and output requirements. In fact, it conforms to the normal budgeting procedure of commencing with expected sales and then working back to determine production and other budgets consistent with the sales forecast. However, in the standard budget procedure this internal consistency is not assured as it is in input-output analysis — where the output of any activity is consistent with the demands, both final and from other activities, for its product.

The illustration above is only the most obvious application of input-output analysis for planning. Before proceeding to more sophisticated levels, however, it is necessary to examine the model in greater detail.

Physical Coefficients and the Numeraire

The transactions matrix has so far been dealt with in terms of dollars. It can, however, be broken down into physical quantities and unit costs or prices which enables more precise planning use. The effects of price and quantity changes can then be separated in similar fashion to standard cost variance analysis.

Let there be n activities plus a final demand vector and a vector of primary inputs. Let x_{rc} be the physical amount of the output quantity X_r of the rth activity used by the cth activity. Then the physical transactions matrix is composed of elements x_{rc} and sums across rows to the vector X_r of total physical output. Let f_c be the vector of primary input quantities (say labor hours), summing to Y for all activities. Thus, the physical transactions matrix is:

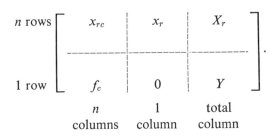

Fixed physical coefficients, t_{rc}, are assumed:[9]

(18) $$t_{rc} = x_{rc}/X_r, \text{ for all } r = c = 1, 2, \ldots, n.$$

The t_{rc} comprise an input coefficient matrix, T^*, and a technology matrix $T = I - T^*$ which is n by n in dimension. The T matrix can be expanded by adding a bottom row of labor input coefficients, $-d_c$, where:

(19) $$d_c = f_c/X_r, \text{ for all } c = r.$$

Finally we need two vectors of prices: p is the row vector of unit commodity prices, and w is the row vector of labor cost per unit of output, and both are n-dimensional.

The system takes as given T, x, and w. For all output to be exactly distributed over final and intermediate uses, the conditions are:

(20) $$TX_r = x_r$$

(21) $$pT = w.$$

Note from (21) that the prices, p, are dependent on unit labor costs, w, just as in a standard cost system amounts transferred to work-in-process and finished goods depend on standard material, labor and overhead unit costs. In other words, output prices are determined by cost-based primary input prices, as is generally the case in accounting. In addition we can compute Y, total labor hours, and S, total labor costs (which equals system gross income or aggregate final demand), as follows:

(22) $$\begin{aligned} Y &= d_c X_r \\ &= d_c T^{-1} x_r, \quad \text{substituting from (20)} \end{aligned}$$

and:

(23) $$\begin{aligned} S &= p x_r \\ &= w X_r \\ &= w T^{-1} x_r, \quad \text{substituting from (20)}. \end{aligned}$$

As mentioned before, prices of outputs are cost-determined by the w vector of labor unit costs (or — more generally — unit costs of whatever the primary input happens to be, say computer time for that matter). Since specification of w determines p, w can be called the numeraire vector, or common denominator for assigning value. Thus, w serves the same purpose as a set of standard costs, which are also exogenous, or given, in an accounting system.

[9] These are analogous to physical standards for material and labor usage in a standard cost system.

Although perhaps theoretically less acceptable, it should be noted that there is no mathematical reason for w to be given. If p is given, equation (21) is then:

$$(24) \qquad\qquad v_{rc} = p_r x_{rc}$$

recalling that the v_{rc} are the dollar elements of the dollar transactions matrix and the x_{rc} are the elements of the physical transactions matrix. From (3) we have the dollar technological coefficients, a_{rc}:

$$(25) \qquad
\begin{aligned}
a_{rc} &= v_{rc}/V_c \\
&= P_r x_{rc}/V_c \\
&= (p_r/p_c) t_{rc}
\end{aligned}$$
$$\text{since for any } c = r,\ P_c X_r = V_c.$$

Thus the relationship between a_{rc} and t_{rc} is determined by the ratio of the respective row and column unit prices. Then, given v_{rc}, the system can be solved as shown previously.

Up to now, we have followed the usual input-output approach of determining primary inputs given final demand, i.e., the last column vector of the transactions matrix is treated as exogenous (or given) and it is desired to find the last row vector (of primary inputs). However, any column vector and any row vector of the transactions matrix can be made exogenous, say the ith row and the jth column. Then the technical matrix A is reduced, by elimination of the ith row and jth column, to order $(n-1)$, and the vector V_r of total output also becomes $(n-1)$ dimensional by elimination of the ith row. Expression (7) may then be generalized to:

$$(26) \qquad\qquad AV_r = v$$

where v_j is the given column vector of inputs to the jth activity.[10]

Analysis of Incremental and Opportunity Costs

In order to illustrate the analysis in terms of physical inputs and outputs, a new example is required. This is as follows:

		Process Inputs			Final Demand x_r	Total Output X_r
		1	2	3		
	(1) (lbs.)	0	14	30	36	80
Process Outputs	(2) (gals.)	4	0	48	18	70
	(3) (cu. ft.)	16	28	0	56	100
	Labor (hrs.)	20	98	72	0	190

[10] Allen, *op. cit.*, pp. 486–488.

Using (18) we compute the t_{rc}, for instance:

$$t_{21} = 4/80 = .05, \qquad t_{31} = 16/80 = .20.$$
$$t_{12} = 14/70 = .20, \qquad t_{32} = 28/70 = .40.$$

and then the technology matrix, T:

$$T = \begin{bmatrix} 1 & -.20 & -.30 \\ -.05 & 1 & -.48 \\ -.20 & -.40 & 1 \end{bmatrix}.$$

Computation of the inverse results in:

$$T^{-1} = \begin{bmatrix} 1.13356 & .448934 & .555556 \\ .204826 & 1.31874 & .694444 \\ .308642 & .617284 & 1.38889 \end{bmatrix}.$$

From (20) we have:

$$(27) \qquad X_r = T^{-1}x_r = \begin{bmatrix} 80 \\ 70 \\ 100 \end{bmatrix},$$

which agrees with the transactions matrix above.

We now consider what it takes to produce one pound of final output from process 1. This is best shown by setting final demand accordingly, i.e.:

$$x_r = \begin{bmatrix} 1 \\ 0 \\ 0 \end{bmatrix}.$$

Then:

$$X_r = T^{-1}x_r = \begin{bmatrix} 1.13356 \\ .204826 \\ .308642 \end{bmatrix},$$

which is simply the first column of T^{-1}. Thus, the columns of T^{-1} show the total production required to end up with a single unit of output from each activity. For instance, to produce one gallon from process 2 requires 0.448934 pounds from process 1, 1.31874 gallons from process 2 and 0.617284 cubic feet from process 3.

Note that 1.31874 gallons from process 2 are needed as intermediate output, since this process requires inputs from processes 1 and 3 — both of which in turn, require inputs from process 2. Note also that the T matrix does not give this information. It shows inputs of 0.20 pounds from process 1 and 0.40 cubic feet from process 3 to produce 1 gallon from process 2. However, these are simply the direct or "first round" inputs and not the total additions to production after allowing for indirect effects through the system. The cumulative results, after all the feedback effects have worked themselves out, are therefore shown in the T^{-1} matrix. In other words, the analysis is not *ceteris paribus* but *mutatis mutandis*.[11]

By use of the T^{-1} matrix *mutatis mutandis* physical standards become available, relating the work loads of the respective process to the demands imposed by exogenous activities.[12] These standards are useful tools in planning for the logistics of changes in the future levels of activities, in budgeting for processes, activities and products, and in appraising performance for control purposes.

We now introduce monetary values to the system. It is convenient to take as given the price vector p, rather than the more usual step of determining p from a given w, the unit wage cost. Let:

$$p = [5 \quad 10 \quad 15]$$

with elements representing the dollar cost per pound, gallon and cubic foot, respectively, of the output of each process.[13] Then, from (21):

(28) $$w = pT = [1.5 \quad 3 \quad 8.7].$$

Using (19) we compute the labor input coefficients:

$$d_c = [20/80 \quad 98/70 \quad 72/100]$$
(29) $$= [0.25 \quad 1.4 \quad 0.72]$$

and from (22) we set Y, total labor hours:

(30) $$Y = d_c X_r = 190$$

which is also verified as correct from the transactions matrix. Finally, from (23), S, total labor cost is:

(31) $$S = wX_r = \$1,200.$$

Now the dollar transactions matrix can be completed:

		Process Inputs			Final Demand v_r	Total Output V_r
		1	2	3		
Outputs	(1)	0	70	150	180	400
	(2)	40	0	480	180	700
	(3)	240	420	0	840	1,500
	e_c	120	210	870	0	1,200
Total	V_c	400	700	1,500	1,200	3,800

[11] For further discussion and illustration of *mutatis mutandis* vs. *ceteris paribus* approaches see Yuji Ijiri, Ferdinand K. Levy and R. C. Lyon, "A Linear Programming Model for Budgeting and Financial Planning," *Journal of Accounting Research* (Autumn 1963), pp. 208–210.

[12] For discussion of the dependent nature of service departments on the volume demands of other activities, and for exposition of budgeting and control techniques with respect to non-interactive departments, see Gordon Shillinglaw. *Cost Accounting*, revised edition (Richard D. Irwin, Inc., 1967), pp. 481–494.

[13] Given the direct linear proportionality of cost and volume in the system, p and w represent both average and incremental unit costs.

The v_{rc} were computed as in (24), by multiplying the x_{rc} by their unit prices and similarly for the v_r and V_r vectors. The labor costs, e_c, were inserted as balancing figures,[14] which sum to $1,200 as shown in (31) above.

We now consider the effects of changes in prices. Suppose that a wage rate increase takes place in process 1. Previously, as shown in the physical and dollar transactions matrices, 20 hours of labor cost $120 giving an average wage rate of $6 an hour. Say that this average now becomes $10 an hour.

From (29) we computed the labor input coefficient[15] for process 1, d_1:

$$d_1 = 0.25$$

and multiplied d_1 by the wage rate to calculate w, the vector of labor cost per unit of output. Previously W_1 (the first element of w) was 0.25 times $6 or 1.5. Now, with an average wage rate of $10 an hour:

$$W_1 = 0.25(\$10) = 2.5$$

and

$$w = [2.5 \quad 3 \quad 8.7].[16]$$

From (23) we compute S, total labor costs:

$$S = wX_r$$
$$= \$1,280$$

which have increased from the previous $1,200 in the dollar transactions matrix. The increase of $80 is, of course, the 20 hours in process 1 multiplied by the rise of $4 an hour in the wage rate. This can be computed directly by using the change in w, which we designate w'. Then:

$$w' = [1 \quad 0 \quad 0]$$

and

$$w'X_r = \$80 = S$$

which is the increment to the total wage bill.

From the new value of w a revised dollar transactions matrix can be derived. First, from (21),

(32) $\qquad p = wT^{-1} = [6.13356 \quad 10.448934 \quad 15.555556].$

By multiplying the x_{rc}, the x_r and the X_r by these new unit prices, the revised dollar transactions matrix is found to be:

---

[14] They could be directly derived by multiplying each W_r (elements of w) with the corresponding X_r element, for instance $W_1 = 1.5$, $X_1 = 80$ and $e_1 = W_1X_1 = 1.5(80) = \$120$.

[15] Representing the hours of labor required to produce one unit of output in that process.

[16] Note, by comparison with (28), that remaining elements of w are unchanged.

		Process Inputs			Final Demand v_r	Total Output V_r
		1	*2*	*3*		
Outputs	(1)	0	85.87	184.01	220.81	490.69
	(2)	41.79	0	501.55	188.08	731.42
	(3)	248.90	435.55	0	871.11	1,555.56
	e_c	200.00	210.00	870.00	0	1,280.00
Total	V_c	490.69	731.42	1,555.56	1,280.00	4,057.67

A comparison with the previous dollar transactions matrix shows that while total wages increased by $80, total output increased by $90.69 in process 1, $31.42 in process 2, and $55.56 in process 3, amounting to $177.67 altogether. This illustrates the multiplier (or amplification) effect in the interactive system. It can be more directly analyzed by again taking the incremental approach with respect to p, where we use p' to designate the change or difference between the old and revised p vectors.

From (32):

(33) $$p' = w'T^{-1} = [1.13356 \quad .448934 \quad .555556].$$

Using p' to multiply the x_{rc}, x_r and X_r we can compute the changes in the dollar transactions matrix. These changes are, of course, the increments resulting in each input-output element of each process in the dollar transactions matrix due to the change in wage rate in process 1. Thus, for each increment in the cost of primary inputs, there is a complementary set of process opportunity costs arising in the interactive system.

It is worth glancing back at (33) and noting that the elements of p' are identical to the first row of T^{-1}. The reason for this is as follows: labor costs in process 1 went up by $4 an hour. Since 4 pounds of output are produced per hour in process 1, the increase in labor costs per pound, is $1. In other words, $W_1' = 1$ as we previously found.

Now the first row of T^{-1} shows the inputs in pounds, from process 1 required to produce one unit of output in each process. Equivalently, this row shows the increase in cost per unit of each process from a $1 per pound increase in the costs of process 1. Therefore, given the strict linear proportionality of the system, we can generalize that the ith row of T^{-1} shows the unit opportunity cost in each process per $1 increment in the unit cost of the ith process. Thus by using (33), the effects on the system of any labor rate change in any process can easily and speedily be computed. Where labor rates vary in more than one process, the effects of individual changes can be computed separately if desired and then in the aggregate.

It should be emphasized that this analysis of cost changes and their effects was made without any need to adjust the T matrix. Any adjustments to T would, of course, have required the computation of a new inverse, T^{-1}, to be used in the analysis. This is an advantage of basing the system on physical relationships and explicit independent price vectors, rather than using monetary values as the original basis.[17] If the system had been built from scratch on a dollar transactions matrix, any change in wage rates (or in any other prices) would have altered the input-output coefficients and thus required computation of a new inverse.

Note that we refer to a change in the unit cost of a primary input as an incremental cost, and to its effect on the costs of the system as the associated opportunity cost. It was also shown that the interactive nature of the system amplified the incremental cost into a larger cost[18] — which we termed opportunity cost. This is a true opportunity cost since it reflects the total sacrifice associated with the wage rate increase on a *mutatis mutandis* (rather than a *ceteris paribus*) basis. In other words, it takes into account the effects on every other activity resulting from the single change in wage rate, as opposed to the more usual approach of assuming that only one or a few effects are considered, while all others are treated as constant.

Expanding the Transactions Matrix

The analysis can be extended to take into account factors not yet considered. For instance, the notion of beginning and ending inventories has not explicitly been considered. Implicitly, however, there has been an unstated inventory assumption made in the following sense. Given a system of interacting activities, many or most of which use each other's outputs as inputs, it seems very unlikely that the system could start up or continue to operate without inventories. In the absence of inventories the situation may be likened to attempting to produce a chicken without an egg or vice versa.[19]

Extension of the system can be accomplished to include inventories and other factors by expanding the transactions matrix. Instead of a single

[17] For a more general and complete discussion of separating physical measurement and monetary valuation in accounting see Yuji Ijiri, "Physical Measures and Multi-Dimensional Accounting," in *Research in Accounting Measurement*, R. K. Jaedicke, Y. Ijiri and O. Nielsen, editors (American Accounting Association, 1966), pp. 150–164.

[18] In our example, for instance, incremental cost of the wage rate increase in process 1 was $80, while the cost of total output went up by $177.67.

[19] It is possible for activities to use their own output as input. Usually self-consumption is offset against output. For the opposite approach see Yuji Ijiri, "An Application of Input-Output Analysis to Some Problems in Cost Accounting," *Management Accounting*, (April 1968), pp. 60–61.

vector for final demand it is possible to have a series of column vectors such as the following, one for each component of final demand:

Additions to Inventory	*Outputs Sold Outside Without Further Processing*	*Outputs for Use Elsewhere in Firm*	*Sales to Customer Classes A, B ··· N*

Similarly, the vector of primary inputs can be expanded into a series of row vectors such as:

Inventory Depletion
Direct Outside Purchases
Depreciation Allowances
Materials
Labor
Variable Overhead
Fixed Overhead
Profit Margin

Thus, the expanded transactions matrix (in either physical or money terms) now consists of multiple vectors of final demand and of primary input components, in addition to the sector which states the input-output flows between processes or activities.[20] The latter sector is normally termed the processing sector.

For the purposes of performing any computations it is necessary to collapse the multiple vectors of final demand and primary input components into single vectors by addition. Then the computation is carried out as previously shown. However, after computation the computed vector (usually that of primary inputs) can be disaggregated again into its components, so that an expanded transactions matrix is made available. The disaggregation may be done by using previously established ratios between various components (such as proportionalities between materials, labor, variable overhead and profit) and/or use of constraints (such as a limit to the quantities of beginning inventory available, or a constant amount as in the case of fixed costs). A component such as inputs purchased direct from outside may serve as a slack, to provide for demands in excess of available inventory quantities.

With respect to lump sum constant items such as fixed costs and possibly depreciation and profit (unless treated as factors directly varying with output volume) the cautions previously noted must be observed. Also, it should be remembered that the transactions matrix is required to meet a symmetry condition: that total inputs match total outputs. Thus, primary

---

[20] An example of a transactions matrix expanded to include ending inventories, overhead, and profit, appears in Shawki M. Farag, "A Planning Model for the Divisionalized Enterprise," THE ACCOUNTING REVIEW, (April 1968), pp. 317–318.

input components, such as depreciation and profit for example, must have their theoretical output complements — such as "Outputs Used Elsewhere in the Firm" (perhaps in capital investment) and "Sales," respectively. Of course, the dollar totals of aggregate final demand and primary inputs must be the same.

Conclusions

As in the case of every model, input-output analysis is conditioned on strict assumptions. These were previously described, but will be briefly noted below. The would-be user is cautioned to ensure that the assumptions are met by the situation in which the model is hoped to be applied. Three critical assumptions may be summarized as follows.

(a) *One standard output for each activity:* it is required that each activity produce a single, standardized output. If individual activities were to vary their commodities produced, we would not be able to specify the fixed input-output coefficients needed to form the technology matrix. If there are joint or by-products it is necessary for them to be produced in constant combination, so that a fixed ratio exists between the quantities of each product of a process and thus this combination can be specified as a standardized single output. Also, the same commodity should not be produced by two or more processes, since this creates alternative rather than unique input-output coefficients.

(b) *Fixed input-output coefficients:* it is not permissible for the proportions among inputs used in a process to be varied. If such input substitutions are allowable it again becomes impossible to specify fixed input-output coefficients from which to derive the technology matrix.

(c) *A linear homogenous production function:* this requires the relations between inputs and outputs not only to be linear, which follows from (b) above, but also to be homogenous. The mathematical condition for linear homogeneity is:[21]

$$f(kx_1 \quad kx_2 \quad \cdots, \quad kx_n) = kf(x_1, \quad x_2, \quad \cdots, \quad x_n).$$

For instance the function $y = a_1x_1 + a_2x_2$ meets this condition since:

$$a_1kx_1 + a_2kx_2 = k(a_1x_1 + a_2x_2).$$

However, the function $y = c + a_1x_1 + a_2x_2$ does not since:

$$c + a_1kx_1 + a_2kx_2 \neq k(c + a_1x_1 + a_2x_2).$$

[21] See Allen *op. cit.,* p. 335.

In the model, each column of the technological matrix represents a process in the firm's production function. If any process is not linear homogenous due to the presence of a constant term, a different input-output coefficient would be needed for each value of the x_1 (i.e., for every possible volume of operation the technological yield would vary). Therefore, once again, we would not have fixed input-output coefficients for the technology matrix.

Subject to the assumptions outlined above, input-output analysis may usefully be applied as shown in this paper. There seems to be no reason why it cannot be as valuable a technique for intrafirm as it has been for interfirm and interindustry economic analysis.

23

The learning-curve phenomenon is well established in other disciplines and is now applied to the accounting problem of tracking production costs. The author analyzes the cost-allocation problem with the application of the learning-curve technique to a production example, which is extended into financial statements. He argues that economic income is more relevant than accounting income as are asset valuations that generate predictions closer to future economic income returns. The mathematics of learning curves are presented briefly in the appendix.

To summarize, in situations where production costs follow the learning-curve phenomenon, a cost-allocation model based on this phenomenon will better measure the relationship between efforts and accomplishments.

Reporting Production Costs That Follow the Learning Curve Phenomenon*

Wayne J. Morse

In 1964, the American Accounting Association's Concepts and Standards Research Study Committee defined "costs" as resources given up or economic sacrifices made.[1] The committee stated that costs "are incurred with the anticipation that they will produce revenues in excess of the outlay" and that "appropriate reporting of costs and revenues should therefore relate costs with revenues in such a way as to disclose most vividly the relationship between efforts and accomplishments." In order to accomplish this the committee advocated that costs should be related to revenues within a spe-

* *From* The Accounting Review, *Vol. XLVII, No. 4 (October, 1972), pp. 761–773. Reprinted by permission of the American Accounting Association and the author.*
[1] American Accounting Association, 1964 Concepts and Standards Study Committee, "The Matching Concept," *The Accounting Review* (April 1965), pp. 368 and 369.

cific period on the basis of some discernible positive correlation of such costs with the recognized revenues. In the case of costs incurred to produce goods intended for future sale, the committee recommended that the specific costs for material and labor be attached to specific units and that these costs be expensed when these units are sold.

It will be shown that in at least one production situation, in which costs are incurred with the anticipation that they will produce revenues in excess of the outlay, attaching specific costs for material and labor to specific units and expensing these costs when these units are sold does not disclose most vividly the relationship between effort and accomplishment. This situation occurs when production costs follow the learning curve phenomenon.[2] It will be shown that in this situation a cost allocation model based on the learning curve phenomenon will better disclose the relationship between efforts and accomplishments.

Nonrecognition

When the production costs of a product follow the learning curve phenomenon the ratio of actual production costs to units produced declines over the product's life cycle. The production process has two joint products, one physical and the other intangible. The physical product is the unit being produced for sale. The intangible product is the ability to produce additional units with a lower expenditure of time and materials. This intangible asset is a firm-specific, job-specific asset. It is of value because it can reduce subsequent production costs. The value of the intangible asset increases rapidly at first as the organization quickly acquires

---

[2] Appendix I contains a brief description of the mathematics of learning curves. For a discussion of the discovery, theory, and previous applications of learning curves, see F. Andres, "The Learning Curve as a Production Tool," *Harvard Business Review* (January–February 1954); C. Blair, "The Learning Curve Gets An Assist From the Computer," *Management Review* (August 1968); R. Brenneck, "The Learning Curve For Labor Hours — For Pricing," *N.A.A. Bulletin* (June 1959); R. Brenneck, "Learning Curve Techniques for More Profitable Contracts," *N.A.A. Bulletin* (July 1959); R. Brenneck, "Break-even Charts Reflecting Learning," *N.A.A. Bulletin* (January 1965); J. Broadston, "Learning Curve Wage Incentives," *Management Accounting* (August 1968); E. Broster, "The Learning Curve for Labor," *Business Management* (March 1968); K. Hartley, "The Learning Curve and Its Applications to the Aircraft Industry," *Journal of Industrial Economics* (March 1965); W. Hirschman, "Profit From the Learning Curve," *Harvard Business Review* (January–February 1964); R. Jordan, "Learning How to Use the Learning Curve," *N.A.A. Bulletin* (January 1958); F. Montgomery, "Increased Productivity in the Construction of Liberty Vessels," *Monthly Labor Review* (November 1943); and, B. Sanders and E. Blystone, "The Progress Curve — An Aid to Decision Making," *N.A.A. Bulletin* (July 1961). Also of interest is S. A. Billon, *Industrial Time Reduction Curves As Tools for Forecasting* (unpublished Ph.D. Dissertation, Michigan State University, 1960). Billon found that the learning curve phenomenon existed in a number of firms without the awareness of management.

"know how." As production becomes more efficient the rate of investment in this intangible asset declines until little or no additional investment takes place. Finally, as the product's life cycle nears its end the intangible asset loses value as the potential cost savings from its use declines. Current accounting procedures do not give recognition to this intangible asset. They attach all production costs to the units produced each period. The result is a large variation in the reported cost of units produced and the reported unit cost of goods sold. These costs are higher in early periods and lower in later periods than the average cost of all units produced. This variation in reported unit cost has implications for the economy, the firm and investors.

The economic implications may include a reduced level of competition (as firms decline to enter markets in which the selling price of products is below the early period cost of goods sold they would have to report) or overpricing to such an extent that the product cannot be sold in enough volume to attain the lower production costs which would be derived from continued production. The issues involving pricing are complex and deserve more extensive treatment than can be given here. Accordingly, for purposes of expedition, they will not be developed further. For the remainder of this article, unless stated otherwise, it will be assumed that selling prices are constant and low enough to sustain consumer demand. Dropping this assumption may lessen the generality of the following analysis but will not invalidate it.

Significance of Learning Curves for Accounting Reports

With constant selling prices, attaching actual production costs to individual units makes the reported earnings of firms whose production costs follow the learning curve phenomenon depend on the current stage of their product's life cycles. Gross margin and net income are low in earlier periods and higher in later periods. The gross margin percents and rates of return computed from the accounting reports of most firms are variable. But, to the extent that this variability is caused by accounting methods of matching costs and revenues, it is artificial.

The dangers of artificial variability in reported earnings for investors were mentioned in a recent speech by Sidney Davidson:

> [Today] there is a widespread view among managers and accountants that the market responds directly to changes in reported earnings per share, that investors . . . cannot see through the reported earning data to the underlying economic facts which the reports are supposed to depict.[3]

[3] Sidney Davidson, "Accounting and Financial Reporting in the Seventies," *The Journal of Accountancy* (December 1969), p. 30.

A study reported on in 1967 by Hamil and Hodes indicates that companies with a history of highly volatile earnings tend to trade at a much lower price-earnings multiple than other comparable companies whose growth in earnings is stable around a basic trend.[4] Assuming that investors react to increased variability by demanding an increased return, the variability in a firm's reported earnings caused by an accounting method of matching costs and revenues may lead to a lower P/E ratio for the firm's stock than the firm's underlying economic income trend warrants.

Davidson has also commented on the problems which current cost allocation techniques cause management when reported production costs decline over the production life cycle of a product and startup costs are high.

> It seems unthinkable that a wise decision by management, based on careful consideration of probable future consequences and proceeding precisely according to plan, should have the effect of reducing reported net income. It is scant comfort for management to be told that, if the program continues according to plan, reported net income will ultimately be higher, indeed higher by an amount that compensates for the earlier reported losses or understatements of income. Income measures effectiveness, and judgments on managerial effectiveness are made too frequently for managers to take much solace from the thought of compensating gains sometime in the future. It is bad enough to think of the danger of being replaced by a new management as a result of troublesome accounting reporting practices, and worse to be told that the successor management will look especially good as the compensating effect for the losses charged against current management.[5]

Davidson concluded that, "If management comes to feel that accounting practices inhibit desirable action, this indeed will present a day of reckoning for accounting."

The above problems concern the matching concept. They center around income recognition and cost allocation. They are caused by the use of reporting periods which do not coincide with either the life of a firm's products or the life of the firm. In *Accounting Research Study No. 1,* Moonitz noted that, "The problem of recognition and allocation is made more difficult because the 'events' often take longer to work themselves out than the reporting period customarily in vogue."[6] Here the "event" is a venture whose duration is the life of a product. The problem is how to match all of the costs and revenues associated with the venture.

[4] Hamil and Hodes, "Factors Influencing Price-Earnings Multiples," *Financial Analyst Journal* (January–February 1967), pp. 90–93.

[5] Sidney Davidson, "The Day of Reckoning — Managerial Analysis and Accounting Theory," *Journal of Accounting Research* (Autumn 1963), pp. 18–19.

[6] Maurice Moonitz, "The Basic Postulates of Accounting," *Accounting Research Study No. 1* (AICPA, 1961), p. 33.

Economic Income

In economic theory the problem of income measurement does not center on achieving a proper matching of costs and revenues but on asset valuation. Assets are valued on the basis of the revenues they will produce. With conditions of certainty periodic income is equal to either the rate of discount times the value of the investment at the beginning of the period or the difference in the value of the investment at the beginning and end of the period plus any withdrawals and minus any investments made during the period.

The concept of income presented above is called "economic income." This concept "is generally defined as an ideal theoretical concept which is impractical to implement because of the difficulty in an uncertain world of measuring cash flows."[7] Bierman and Davidson have noted that "since the conceptually satisfactory definition of income may not be an operational one, the accountant is forced to use measures that are estimators of this approach." However, they go on to suggest that "one way of judging these estimators is to consider whether or not they tend to be consistent with the conceptually satisfactory measure."[8]

When presented with two or more alternative accounting procedures they suggest the use of two criteria to evaluate them: first, the nearness of the reported income, under each procedure, to a "conceptually satisfactory" definition of income as the change in value of a firm between two points in time; and second, the nearness of the predicted income of a period to this conceptually satisfactory definition of income when predicted income is computed as the discount rate times the accounting valuation under each procedure at the beginning of the period.[9]

These criteria are used later to evaluate the incomes and asset values reported matching actual production costs and revenues and those reported using a cost allocation model based on the learning curve phenomenon.[10] In the example presented below it will be shown that the income reported with the use of the learning curve cost allocation model is more consistent

[7] Keith Shwayder, "A Critique of Economic Income as an Accounting Concept," *Abacus* (August 1967), p. 28. Shwayder, however, is very critical of the use of this concept as an ideal for accounting.

[8] Harold Bierman, Jr. and Sidney Davidson, "The Income Concept-Value Increment or Earnings Predictor," *The Accounting Review* (April 1969), p. 241.

[9] *Ibid.*, pp. 236–46.

[10] The desirability of matching costs with revenues is assumed in this article. This assumption is based on the 1964 report of the American Accounting Association's Concepts and Standards Research Study Committee. The purpose of this article is to improve upon current methods of matching costs with revenues. Some researchers would argue that all attempts to match costs and revenues are futile. For example, see A. Thomas, "The Allocation Problem in Financial Accounting Theory," *Studies in Accounting Research No. 3* (American Accounting Association, 1969). This author agrees that matching is difficult but denies that it is futile.

FIGURE 1

L-C Cost Allocation Model:
Diagram of Flow of Costs

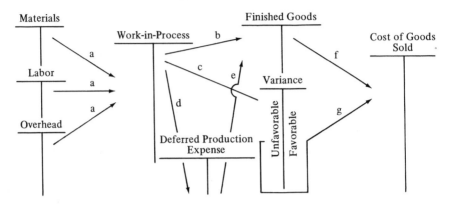

a. Actual costs.
b. Projected unit cost or expected average unit cost of all anticipated production, whichever is lower.
c. Actual less projected unit cost.
d. Excess of projected unit cost over expected average unit cost of all anticipated production.
e. Excess of expected average unit cost of all anticipated production over projected unit cost.
f. Period sold.
g. Period incurred.

with the "conceptually satisfactory" definition of income than that reported by matching actual production costs with revenues.

The Model

The learning curve (L-C) cost allocation model projects production costs over the entire anticipated life cycle of a product on the basis of cost data for the first few units of production. Using this data comparisons are made between the projected cost of each unit and the expected average unit cost of all anticipated production. As production takes place any excess of the projected cost of each unit over the expected average cost of all anticipated production is charged to a deferred production expense account[11] and inventory is charged with an amount equal to the expected average unit cost of all anticipated production. When the projected unit cost is less than the expected average unit cost of all anticipated production this difference is deducted from the deferred production expense account and inventory is charged with an amount equal to the expected average unit cost of all anticipated production. As production takes place any

---

[11] The account could be named "Production Know-How," "Improvements in Production Procedures," or a host of similar things which would indicate its nature. Because it is an intangible which will ultimately become a period cost a general reference to its ultimate demise is used.

differences between actual and projected costs are written off as a period variance unless a change in a parameter of the model occurs. In effect, the projected unit cost becomes the standard cost. Figure 1 shows the flow of costs under the L-C cost allocation model.

Figure 2 presents a series of cost curves for the example presented later. Line 1 represents the projected average unit cost at various output levels. At output N, the number of units of anticipated production, the value of line 1 is equal to the expected average unit cost of all anticipated production, line 2. Line 3 represents the calculated (projected) cost of each unit. Until output level E is reached line 3 exceeds line 2 and as production takes place the deferred production expense account is charged with the difference between lines 3 and 2. After output level E is reached the deferred production expense account is credited with the difference between lines 2 and 3. Any difference between actual production costs and line 3 is written off as a variance in the period incurred. At output level N the balance in the deferred production expense account is zero. This is true because area I is equal to area D.

FIGURE 2

Cost Curves for Example

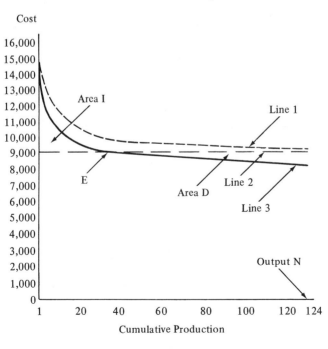

Line 1	———	Projected Average Unit Cost
Line 2	—— -	Projected Average Unit Cost of All Anticipated Production
Line 3	———	Projected Unit Cost
Output N		124 units

The effect of using the L-C cost allocation model is to decrease the amount of production costs charged to inventory and to cost of goods sold in early periods, raising reported income, and to increase the amount of production costs charged to inventory and the cost of goods sold in later periods, lowering reported income.

With constant selling prices use of the L-C cost allocation model avoids the variability in reported earnings caused when production costs decline over the life cycle of a product. A production decision by management, proceeding precisely according to plan, does not have the effect of reducing reported net income in early periods unless the project as a whole has the effect of reducing reported net income. The only factors that would change the reported unit cost of goods sold from the average cost of all anticipated production would be the existence of a cost variance as described above and/or a change in a parameter of the model.

Example

To demonstrate the operational characteristics of the L-C cost allocation model and to compare the results of its use with a model that matches actual unit production costs with revenues (actual cost model), use is made of a hypothetical corporation. The precision shown in this example is artificial but the general pattern of production costs is characteristic of those incurred in many industries.[12]

The management of the XYZ Company, after a careful consideration of anticipated costs and revenues, began construction of a new product line of sailboats in 19x1. Sales forecasts indicated that 124 of these sailboats could be sold during the next four years at a price of $10,000 each. In 19x1 XYZ built and sold 20 boats as planned.

All of XYZ's expenses are directly associated with production. Factory overhead and direct labor costs are each incurred at the rate of $5 per direct labor hour. From XYZ's production reports, information for Table 1 is obtained.

The XYZ's income statement for 19x1, prepared matching actual unit production costs with revenues, is presented in Table 2. Despite the fact that management determined that production and sales, on what was considered to be a profitable operation, were proceeding precisely according to plan, XYZ's 19x1 income statement indicated a loss of $18,950.

In 19x1 the L-C cost allocation model would have reported an income of $15,588, determined as follows:

From the production data for the first 20 units and projected sales of 124 units the average unit cost of all anticipated production is computed to be

---

[12] See references listed in footnote 2.

TABLE 1

Information from XYZ Company's Production Reports

Boat Numbers	Direct Labor Hours	Direct Labor Costs	Variable Factory Overhead	Direct Materials	Total Costs
1–4	2,890.17	$14,451	$14,451	$24,000	$52,902
5–8	2,020.26	10,101	10,101	24,000	44,202
9–12	1,784.94	8,925	8,925	24,000	41,850
13–16	1,647.48	8,237	8,237	24,000	40,474
17–20	1,552.26	7,761	7,761	24,000	39,522
					$218,950

$9,220.[13] The projected cost for units 1 through 20 is $218,950.[14] Because this is equal to the actual cost of units 1 through 20 there is no cost variance. When the production venture is completed the average cost of a lot of 20 units should be $184,412. For use in the L-C cost allocation model this information is summarized as follows:

	(Nearest Dollar)
Actual cost of units produced	$218,950
—Model based cost of units produced	218,950
Cost variance, unfavorable (favorable)	$ 0
Model based cost of units produced	$218,950
Period production × average unit cost of all anticipated production	184,412
Increase (decrease) in deferred production expense	$ 34,538

Assuming that sales and production costs proceed exactly according to plan in 19x2 through 19x4 the income statements that would be prepared

---

[13] Applying least-squares regression analysis to the production data for the first 20 units we can solve for α and β in $\log Y = \log \alpha - \beta \log X$. $\alpha = 1,001.23$ hours, $\beta = .235308$. Then, solving for Y in $Y = \alpha X^{-\beta}$ with X equal to 124 we get $Y = 322.059$ hours. This is the average production time per boat. The average cost per boat is then determined to be $9,220, ($10 × 322 + $6,000 direct materials).

[14] Solving for $T = \alpha X^\gamma$ with X equal to 20 we get $T = 9,895$ hours. So total production costs are $(9,895 × $10) + (20 × $6,000)$. (See Appendix I.)

TABLE 2

XYZ Company Income Statements (19X1 Through 19X4)

Prepared Matching Actual Production Costs with Revenues

	19X1	%	19X2	%	19X3	%	19X4	%
Sales	$200,000	100.00	$300,000	100.00	$350,000	100.00	$390,000	100.00
Cost of goods sold	218,950	109.48	280,448	93.48	309,789	88.51	334,164	85.68
Net income	$(18,950)	−9.48	$ 19,552	6.52	$ 40,211	11.49	$ 55,836	14.32

Prepared Using Learning Curve Cost Allocation Model

	19X1	%	19X2	%	19X3	%	19X4	%
Sales	$200,000	100.00	$300,000	100.00	$350,000	100.00	$390,000	100.00
Cost of goods sold	184,412	92.21	276,618	92.21	322,720	92.21	359,603	92.21
Net income	$ 15,588	7.79	$ 23,382	7.79	$ 27,280	7.79	$ 30,397	7.79
Production and sales in units	20		30		35		39	

using the actual and the L-C cost allocation models are presented in Table 2.[15]

Attaching actual production costs to each unit and matching these costs to the revenues generated by the sales of these units resulted in large variations in reported income and the income/sales ratio.[16] In 19x1, when XYZ undertook a production venture which management rightly determined would be profitable, the use of actual costs resulted in a loss being reported. The anticipation of such a loss being reported or, in a less drastic case, the anticipation of a low income/sales ratio may give management second thoughts about the desirability of this venture.

When the L-C cost allocation model is used a profit is reported in every period. Income on this production venture varies, but the variation in reported income is directly associated with the variation in production and sales.[17]

Evaluation

Assume XYZ invested $100,000 in fixed assets at the beginning of 19x1 in order to produce the sailboats and that these assets were sold for $100,000 at the end of 19x4. This assumption is necessary to determine a rate of return on the investment while avoiding the problems caused by alternative accounting procedures for determining depreciation. With the net income reported matching actual production costs to revenues representing end of year cash flows the rate of return is 18.85 percent. Further assume that this is the normal discount rate. The income and asset values reported using an economic income model under conditions of certainty are presented in Table 3. Table 3 also shows the income and asset values reported matching actual costs to revenues and using the L-C cost allocation model.

[15] The XYZ Company applied the L-C cost allocation model on the basis of direct labor hours with constant materials costs. If it is anticipated that materials costs will also decrease, due to less waste, as cumulative production increases, the model could be applied to all production costs. If it is anticipated that the decrease in production time and materials waste will occur at different rates the model could be applied separately to materials, labor and overhead costs.

In this example, the time required for all production processes declined in accordance with the learning curve phenomenon. The model can be easily adopted to situations in which the time required for some production processes do not decline. See W. J. Morse, "Learning Curve Cost Projections With Constant Unit Costs" (unpublished paper, University of Illinois, 1972).

[16] In a more general situation the reference is to the contribution margin ratio or gross margin percent. For the XYZ Company the income/sales ratio, the gross margin percent and the contribution margin ratio are the same.

[17] With variations in inventory levels the variation in reported income would be directly associated with variations in sales plus or minus any differences between projected and actual unit costs.

TABLE 3

Income and Value Under Conditions of Certainty (Nearest Dollar)

Economic Income Model

	Period				*Total Income*
	1	*2*	*3*	*4*	
Beginning of Period Value	$100,000	$137,800	$144,224	$131,199	
Income at 18.85%	18,850	25,976	27,186	24,731	$96,743[a]
Additional Investment	18,950	–0–	–0–	–0–	
Cash Withdrawn from Project	–0–	(19,522)	(40,211)	(155,836)	
End of Period Value	$137,800	$144,224	$131,199	$ 94[a]	

Actual Cost and Revenue Model

	Period				*Total Income*
	1	*2*	*3*	*4*	
Beginning of Period Value	$100,000	$100,000	$100,000	$100,000	
Income from Table 2	(18,950)	19,552	40,211	55,836	$96,649[a]
Additional Investment	18,950	–0–	–0–	–0–	
Cash Withdrawn from Project	–0–	(19,552)	(40,211)	(155,836)	
End of Period Value	$100,000	$100,000	$100,000	$ –0–	

Learning Curve Cost Allocation Model

	Period				*Total Income*
	1	*2*	*3*	*4*	
Beginning of Period Value	$100,000	$134,538	$138,368	$125,437	
Income from Table 2	15,588	23,382	27,280	30,397[a]	$97,647[a]
Additional Investment	18,950	–0–	–0–	–0–	
Cash Withdrawn from Project	–0–	(19,552)	(40,211)	(155,836)	
End of Period Value	$134,538	$138,368	$125,437	($ 2)[a]	

[a] Errors caused by rounding.

The income and asset values reported by the actual cost model and the L-C cost allocation model can now be evaluated by the two criteria suggested by Bierman and Davidson.[18] First, the accounting procedure whose reported income is closer to economic income is preferred. Second, the accounting procedure whose asset valuation at the beginning of the period

[18] Bierman and Davidson, pp. 236–46.

TABLE 4

Evaluation of Actual and Learning Curve Cost Allocation Models

	Period			
	1	*2*	*3*	*4*
Actual Cost Model				
Percent reported income from economic income	−200.54	−27.43	+47.91	+125.77
Percent predicted income from economic income	–0–	−27.43	−30.66	− 23.90
Learning Curve Allocation Model				
Percent reported income from economic income	− 17.30	− 9.98	+ 3.42	+ 22.91
Percent predicted income from economic income	–0–	− 2.37	− 4.06	+ 3.23

multiplied by the discount rate gives income predictions closer to economic income is preferred. Table 4 shows the results of this evaluation. In all periods the income reported by the L-C cost allocation model is closer to economic income than the income reported by the actual cost model. In all periods except the first, the income predicted on the basis of investment values determined by the L-C cost allocation model is closer to economic income than that determined by the use of the actual cost model. The first period's predicted income under both the L-C and the actual cost models is equal to the first period's economic income because the asset values before any transactions have taken place are equal. It is concluded that in this situation, according to the two criteria suggested by Bierman and Davidson, the L-C cost allocation model is superior to the actual cost model.

Parameter Changes

Two circumstances may indicate a need to change the parameters of the L-C cost allocation model. First, the original parameters of the model (including the estimate of total production) may be in error.[19] They were determined on the basis of limited information. Additional data available after more production has occurred may indicate the necessity of some

---

[19] α and β are estimates of the true underlying regression slope coefficients. Until all production has taken place there is no absolutely certain way of knowing what these parameters are. However, models based on the learning curve phenomenon are widely used for decision making because of the accuracy of forecasts made with them. See footnote 2.

changes being made in these parameters. Second, unexpected events subsequent to the implementation of the model may necessitate changes in its parameters. These events include such things as an early leveling off of the learning curve, a change in production costs, a partial change in the product or production process, or a change in the number of units of anticipated production.

One possible way of handling changes in the parameters of the L-C cost allocation model is to incorporate these changes into the parameters of the model and determine new values for the cumulative average cost of all anticipated production, and the unit cost, total cost, and balance in deferred production expense at various output levels.[20] These new values will serve as the basis for subsequent applications of the model. An adjustment will also have to be made to the balance in the deferred production expense account. Its current balance was determined using the old model parameters. The adjustment is necessary to bring its balance to the amount which would have been in the account if the new parameters had been used to determine its current balance. The amount of this adjustment could be treated in a number of ways. The most expedient method of handling this adjustment is to treat it as an adjustment to current income. On the income statement the nature of the adjustment should be disclosed as a "Correction to the L-C cost allocation model," or as a "Change in the L-C cost allocation model caused by . . . ."

Assume that XYZ's labor costs unexpectedly increased by 20 percent on 1/1/x3 after 50 units were produced, all other costs remaining unchanged. Table 5 shows XYZ's income statements for the years 19x1 through 19x4 using both actual production costs and the L-C cost allocation model with a 20 percent increase in labor costs at unit 51. In this particular case the effect of the increase in labor costs is hidden in the upward trend of reported earnings when actual production costs are matched with revenues. Use of the L-C cost allocation model shows a decrease in the gross margin percent, gross margin and net income. The decrease in the gross margin percent is the most significant of these figures. When compared with the gross margin percent of this project in earlier periods it indicates that the increase in labor costs will reduce the overall profitability of this project from previous expectations. The change in labor costs had an effect on the overall profitability of the project. The L-C cost allocation model brought attention to this change. The actual cost model did not.

If the increase in labor costs was anticipated, as it might under a preexisting labor contract, the anticipated increase could have been incorporated into the original parameters of the model.

---

[20] The equations necessary to do this can be easily adjusted to incorporate any number of changes. The calculations are tedious, but can be easily performed with a computer. For a complete description of procedures for handling changes in the parameters of the L-C cost allocation model see Wayne J. Morse, *The Allocation of Production Costs With the Use of Learning Curves* (unpublished Ph.D. dissertation, Michigan State University, 1971).

TABLE 5

XYZ Company Income Statements 19X1 Through 19X4 (Change in Labor Costs at Unit 51)

Prepared Matching Actual Production Costs to Revenues

	19X1	%	19X2	%	19X3	%	19X4	%
Sales	$200,000	100.00	$300,000	100.00	$350,000	100.00	$390,000	100.00
Cost of goods sold	218,950	109.48	280,448	93.48	319,767	91.36	344,179	88.25
Net income	$(18,950)	(9.48)	$ 19,552	6.52	$ 30,233	8.64	$ 45,821	11.75

Prepared Using Learning Curve Cost Allocation Model

	19X1	%	19X2	%	19X3	%	19X4	%
Sales	$200,000	100.00	$300,000	100.00	$350,000	100.00	$390,000	100.00
Cost of goods sold	184,412	92.21	276,618	92.21	328,364	93.82	365,891	93.82
Gross margin	$ 15,588	7.79	$ 23,382	7.79	$ 21,636	6.18	$ 24,109	6.18
Change in L-C cost caused by increase in labor costs	-0-		-0-		(8,597)	(2.46)	-0-	
Net income	$ 15,588	7.79	$ 23,382	7.79	$ 13,039	3.73	$ 24,109	6.18
Production and sales in units	20		30		35		39	

Production Estimates

Given the production time and/or cost data for units produced during the first accounting period and knowledge of a company's contractual obligations, the only parameter of the model which cannot be objectively determined and verified is the number of units of anticipated production. Fortunately, the costs allocated under the model are not changed materially[21] by relatively large errors in the initial estimate of the number of units of anticipated production. For example, with an 85 percent learning curve (which is approximately the curve used in the example)[22] when *all* production costs decrease in accordance with this curve, the number of units of anticipated production must be overstated by more than 56 percent before the average unit cost of all production is understated by 10 percent.[23] This is true because production costs which follow the learning curve decline rapidly at first but level off quickly (see Figure 2).

A decrease in the number of units of anticipated production will have the effect of reducing income in the year it is reported, following the adjustment procedures presented above, but information about management errors of this type is useful.

With an 85 percent learning curve, when all production costs decline in accordance with the learning curve phenomenon, the number of units must be understated by more than 33 percent before the average cost of all production is overstated by more than 10 percent.[24] This relatively minor

---

[21] Materiality is defined as a 10 percent error in the determination of the average unit cost of all anticipated production. This is an arbitrary definition. Others may argue that it should be a higher or lower percentage.

[22] See Appendix I.

[23] Let $\alpha/(N+\theta)^\beta = .90\alpha/N^\beta$, where N is the number of units actually produced and θ is the amount of the overstatement in units. The equation indicates that the average cost computed with N overstated by θ units is equal to 90 percent of the average cost computed without the overstatement:

$$(N+\theta)^\beta = N^\beta/.90,$$
$$N+\theta = N^\beta/\sqrt{.90},$$
$$\frac{\theta}{N} = 1^\beta/\sqrt{.90} - 1.$$

For a given value of β, θ/N is a constant representing the percentage overstatement in actual production required before the average cost of all anticipated production is understated by 10 percent. For an 85 percent learning curve $\beta = .23446$ and θ/N is .56732.

[24] Let $\alpha/(N-U)^\beta = 1.10\alpha/N^\beta$, where N is the number of units actually produced and U is the amount of the understatement in units. The equation indicates that the average cost computed with N understated by U units is equal to 110 percent of the average cost computed without the understatement:

$$(N-U)^\beta = N^\beta/1.10,$$
$$N-U = N^\beta/\sqrt{1.10},$$
$$\frac{U}{N} = 1 - 1^\beta/\sqrt{1.10}.$$

For a given value of β, U/N is a constant representing the percentage understatement in actual production required before the average cost of all anticipated production is overstated by 10 percent. For an 85 percent learning curve, $\beta = .23446$ and U/N is .334023.

effect on costs of a relatively large understatement of anticipated production presents a number of interesting possibilities for accountants who believe in "conservative" accounting practices. In order to avoid understating expenses in early periods because of forecasting errors, the anticipated production can be deliberately understated. The L-C cost allocation model could be used for this period of time only. Then, actual production costs could be matched with revenues. The model would still have the desired effect of increasing the early period gross margin and gross margin percent while lowering that which would be reported in some intermediate periods. The gross margin percent would rise some after the model is discontinued. The important point is that any use of a model based on the learning curve would improve the current matching of cost and revenues when production costs decline in accordance with the learning curve phenomenon.

The model presented here can be generalized and applied to varying situations where production costs follow a predictable pattern.

Conclusions

When production costs follow the learning curve phenomenon the use of the L-C cost allocation model results in a better matching of production costs with revenues than does the actual cost model. The actual cost model fails to consider the cost reducing value of the production know-how obtained early in the production process and charges all production costs to the units produced. The L-C cost allocation model recognizes the existence of this know-how and modifies the amounts charged to the units produced accordingly. Consequently, the L-C model reports income closer to economic income and asset values which results in more accurate predictions of economic income than does the actual cost model. The model also gives some immediate indication of the ultimate effects on profits of changes in the product or production process while the actual cost model may hide or cushion the effect of these changes.

The assumption of constant selling prices limits the generality of the model, as presented here, but does not eliminate it except where selling prices decline precisely in accordance with the learning curve experienced on a production venture. The model can be generalized to allow for lesser declines in selling prices. There are a number of economic issues related to whether or not selling prices can, or should, decline in a pattern similar to the learning curve. Awareness of the implications of the model and its use may result in lower prices and increased competition by reducing the likelihood that accounting reports will reflect unfavorably on management when they undertake production ventures that will ultimately be profitable.

Appendix I

MATHEMATICS OF LEARNING CURVES

If the total time to produce the first unit is 100 hours, the second unit is 80 hours, and the third and fourth units together are 144 hours, the production process is said to be following a 90 percent learning curve, when the learning curve refers to cumulative average time.[25] The decrease in cumulative average production time is further illustrated in Table 6.

The information presented in Table 6 is frequently presented in a graphic manner as in Figure 3.

TABLE 6

Ninety Percent Learning Curve

Units Produced	Group Production Time (Hours)	Group Average Production Time (Hours)	Cumulative Average Production Time	Percent Decline
1	100	100	100	—
2	80	80	90	10
3–4	144	72	81	10
5–8	259.2	64.8	72.9	10
9–16	466.4	53.8	65.6	10
17–32	844.8	52.4	59.0	10

The mathematical relationship between cumulative production and cumulative average production time in Table 6 and Figure 3 is:

(1) $$Y = \alpha/X^\beta,$$

where:

X = cumulative production (the horizontal axis);
Y = cumulative average production time (cost) (the vertical axis);
α = time (cost) required to produce the first unit (vertical axis intercept); and
β = exponent which accounts for the slope of the L-C.

---

[25] The percentage used in reference to learning curves is in reality the complement of the rate of learning. For example, with no learning the learning rate is 0 percent, but the learning curve percent is 100. With a 90 percent learning curve there is a 10 percent decrease in cumulative average hours between the first and second units of production.

FIGURE 3

Cumulative Average Production Times — Ninety Percent
Learning Curve

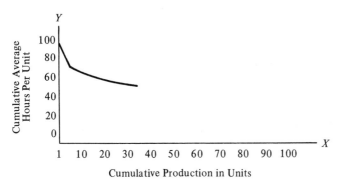

Cumulative Production in Units

Equation 1 is sometimes expressed as:

(2) $$Y = \alpha X^{-\beta},$$

or placed into a linear form by the use of logarithms:

(3) $$\log Y = \log \alpha - \beta \log X.$$

When placed in a linear form, least-squares regression analysis can be used to determine α and β on the basis of initial production data. Total production time (cost) to produce the first X units is developed from equation 1 by multiplying equation 1 by X:

(4) $$T = X \cdot \alpha / X^{\beta}.$$

Equation 4 is simplified to:

(5) $$T = \alpha X^{\gamma},$$

where:

   T = total production time (cost) for the first X units; and
   $\gamma = (1 - \beta)$.

Time (cost) to produce unit X is derived from equation 5 by finding T for X units and subtracting T for $X - 1$ units:

(6) $$U = \alpha (X^{\gamma} - (X - 1)^{\gamma}),$$

where:

   U = time (cost) required to produce unit X.

Equation 1 is asymptotic to zero. However, as is seen in Figures 2 and 3, after a number of units have been produced, the rate at which Y approaches zero as additional units are produced becomes so small that no problems are caused by this property in any practical applications of the model.[26]

Appendix II

COMPARISON OF AIRCRAFT INDUSTRY AND L-C COST ALLOCATION MODELS

Despite some apparent similarities, the aircraft industry's method of accounting for production costs differs in a number of ways from the cost allocation model presented in this article:

1. The aircraft industry leaves costs in excess of projected average unit production costs on completed units in work-in-process and does not separate the costs incurred to produce units still in production. The cost allocation model presented here uses a special account to show the unusual nature of this cost.
2. The aircraft industry does not regard a cost as excessive, and to be written-off in the period incurred, unless such a write-off is necessary to reduce work-in-process to estimated realizable value. The cost allocation model presented here recognizes production cost variances whenever actual production costs differ from model based costs. Such variances are written off to the cost of goods sold in the period incurred.
3. In the aircraft industry's cost allocation model the number of units to be produced is certain. The cost allocation model presented here does not require certainty with regard to the number of units to be produced.

[26] See footnotes 2 and 15.

24

Increasing decentralization of decision-making and creation of profit centers makes the transfer pricing problem acute. Existing accounting and economic solutions are seriously deficient. In this article, a new transfer pricing system based on the concept of opportunity cost is advocated.

The economic transfer pricing system is examined, under both the "simple maximizer" and "cooperative" cases. Behavioral problems are exposed, and suggested refinements are offered. A set of solutions involving the opportunity cost concept then is offered, with consideration given to the need for certain policy decisions at the corporate level. The use of "motivation costs" to resolve residual areas of conflict which persist in a few special cases is one of this article's significant new ideas.

A Transfer Pricing System Based on Opportunity Cost*

Mohamed Onsi

With decentralization of decision-making and creation of profit centers in multi-product organizations, the transfer pricing system becomes an acute problem. To arrive at an optimal solution, or at an approximation to it, both accounting and economic thought have recommended certain solutions.[1] However, some of the suggested solutions have shortcomings that cannot be ignored or assumed to be insignificant. The problem is material when the performance of a divisional manager is measured based on profit, and incentive compensation is so determined.

In this paper, the economic foundation of a transfer pricing system and its limitations will be briefly presented. A new transfer pricing system is

* *From* The Accounting Review, *Vol. XLV, No. 3 (July, 1970), pp. 535–543. Reprinted by permission of the American Accounting Association and the author.*

[1] See: David Solomons, *Divisional Performance* (Financial Executives Research Foundation, 1965), pp. 212–228, and Jack Hirshleifer, "Internal Pricing and Decentralized Decisions," in *Management Controls,* ed. by C. P. Bonini, R. K. Jaedicke and H. M. Wagner (McGraw-Hill, 1964), pp. 27–37.

suggested, based on an opportunity cost concept. The advantages of this approach, compared to others, will be discussed.

The Economic Transfer Pricing System

When there is a market price for intermediate goods, they are transferred according to such a price, assuming that the goods transferred are produced in a competitive market where the supplying center cannot influence the sales price in the open market by its own output decision. Pricing intermediate goods according to market price has the advantage of motivating the supplying center to reduce its cost as much as possible and emphasize innovation and research and development, since it will be to its advantage.

However, if there is no market price for the intermediate goods, then the volume which Profit Center A should produce and that which Profit Center B should demand, ideally, is at that level where the MC_A is equal to the NMR_B. Operationally, however, the profit center manager, in this case, may behave according to one of two possibilities: (1) as *a simple maximizer* of his own profit, or (2) as a *cooperator* who is concerned with maximizing total joint profits.

THE SIMPLE MAXIMIZER CASE

If the selling profit center (A) is in a monopolistic position, he will keep the price of the intermediate goods at P_2 (Exhibit 1) and will produce at a level equal to that demanded, OBd_2; that is, the volume where the buying center equates its own $NMR_B = P_2$. The profit area of Center A lies between the P_2 line and his MC_A line. This area is larger than his profit if he accepts lowering the price to P^*, where $MC_A = NMR_B$ and corresponds to the ideal volume X. On the other hand, if the buying profit center (B) is in a monopsonistic position, it will force the selling center (A) to set the price at P_1 and produce a volume OAS_1, where it equates its own $MC_A = P_1$. This results in a maximization of profit for center B, as shown in the area between the NMR_B line and P_1. This profit area is larger than that of a transfer price set at P^*. The total profit of both centers, however, is smaller than the joint profit that can be achieved if both centers set the transfer price at P^*.

THE COOPERATIVE CASE

In this second case, in which the profit center manager is a *cooperator* concerned with maximizing total joint profits; the volume produced will be optimal from the corporate point of view. Total profit will be a maximum

EXHIBIT 1
Transfer Price is Equal to $MC_A = NMR_B$

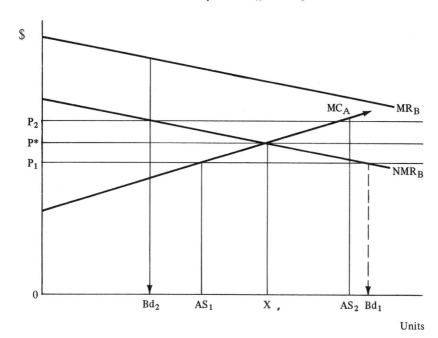

and larger than that under the first case, but the distribution of such profits is not clear-cut (see Exhibit 2 [on the following page]).

If Profit Centers A and B are conceived to maximize their combined profits, the volume of transferred goods is the quantity OX^*, for which $MC_A = NMR_B$, and the ideal price is P^*. However, in such a situation where the buyer is obliged to buy from within, there is no guarantee that the price is going to be P^*, even if they are cooperative. The transfer price, in other words, is indeterminate, i.e., between P_1 and P_2. That is to say, the transfer price can be negotiated somewhere between ANR_B and AC_A (e.g., the average net revenue for Center B and the average cost of Center A for the volume OX^*).

If the transfer price is negotiated at P_1 for the optimal volume OX^*, Center A receives zero profits and Center B receives the total joint profit. If the transfer price is negotiated at P_2, Center A will receive the total joint profit and Center B receives zero. So, operationally, the negotiated transfer price is in a range with P_2 as an upper limit and P_1 as a lower limit, and the actual transfer price somewhere in between. This negotiated transfer price is set after reaching the optimal product volume and not before.

To overcome such a limitation, it is believed that the budget committee should be in a position to receive the necessary information from each profit center, establish the volume which maximizes corporate profit (OX^*), and

EXHIBIT 2
The Paretian Optima Solution

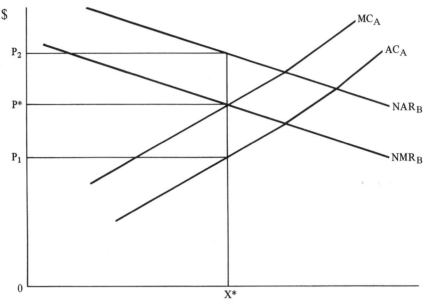

set the price at P^*. The accounting practice of pricing the transfer goods as equal to variable costs, approximating marginal costs, is felt to yield such an optimal volume. However, imposing a transfer price does not guarantee an optimal solution. The reason is that the selling profit center knows the rules of the game and, as a result, it adjusts its level of accuracy in estimating variable costs according to its belief in the accuracy of other centers' estimations. This managerial response is feasible especially when the selling profit center is not given the option to produce another product that is more profitable.

Another weakness in the economic transfer system is its failure to provide incentive for a center manager to reduce his MC below the determined level ($MC_A = NMR_B$). Suppose that the transfer price of intermediate goods is $8.00/unit.[2] If the supplying profit center discovers a new method for producing such goods at $7.00/unit, should this be the new price for transferred goods according to the $MC_A = NMR_B$? If the answer is yes, there is no motivation or reward for the innovating supplying profit center,

[2] Remember that we are assuming, in the entire discussion, no cost interdependence, i.e., MC_A is independent from the MC_B. If the marginal cost of (A) (which is P^*) depends also on the volume of output of the final product (B), through common cost savings, the level of over-all marginal costs of the final product B for the organization is not equal to the sum of MC_A & MC_B. The analysis in such a case will be different.

since the receiving profit center will reap all the profit increment, while the supplying center breaks even. Should the transfer price remain at $8.00/ unit, the receiving profit center will find no incentive to remix its production or increase its output to take advantage of the relatively cheaper input prices. As a solution to this problem, it is suggested, violating the main principle of $MC_A = NMR_B$, that the supplying profit center should charge $8.00/unit for additional units over that budgeted volume. Another solution is that the supplying center will negotiate a lump sum grant or subsidy from the receiving center as a condition for continuous cost reduction and innovation.[3] While this is a deviation from the theoretical principle (e.g., P is determined having $MC = MR$), its purposes are motivationally oriented.

Another operational difficulty stems from the assumption that there are no constraints (physical or monetary) on the resources available for each profit center in producing the volume OX^* that is optimal based on $MC = MR$. This assumption is not realistic, because each profit center has certain constraints, either manpower, capacity, etc. If these constraints are not explicitly dealt with in the system, the theoretical solution is no longer a pragmatic one.

To solve these problems, a new approach to solving the transfer price problem based on an opportunity cost concept is needed. Opportunity cost is used here with cost accounting derived surrogates. This approach takes into consideration in arriving at the optimal solution the physical and financial constraints that exist at divisional levels and at the top corporate level. While the transfer price under this system is determined based on the decomposition principle, the final suggested price is not necessarily equal to it as we will show later. Since we will not discuss the mathematical operational steps of solving a case using the decomposition principle, a bibliography at the end of this article is a representative reference for this purpose. In addition, we will show how this approach, with some motivational factors, can induce a profit center manager to act in the right direction and lessens his reason to manipulate cost estimates. This approach works as follows.

Transfer Price and Opportunity Cost

If Profit Center (A) transfers a part of its goods to Profit Center (B), and there is an outside market price, the transferred goods are priced equal to the market price, which represents the opportunity cost of not selling to outsiders.

If there is no market price, the transferred goods still should be priced equal to the opportunity cost of diverting divisional (A) resources into

[3] Jack Hirshleifer, "On the Economics of Transfer Pricing," *Journal of Business* (July 1956), pp. 172–184.

producing such goods, instead of producing another kind of goods that has an outside market. In developing the framework of this system, two cases will be differentiated.

I. Profit Center (A) transfers product X_1, that has no outside market price, to Profit Center (B). However, Profit Center (A) also produces X_2, which has a known market price.[4]

In this case, the price of the transferred product X_1 is equal to the opportunity cost or the shadow price of resources utilized in its production instead of being used to produce X_2. The following example is written in a linear programming model:

$$\text{Max } \pi = C_1 X_1 + C_2 X_2 = ?X_1 + 8X_2$$

subject to:

$$\text{Process I} \quad 3X_1 + 6X_2 \leq 60$$
$$\text{Process II} \quad 2X_1 + 4X_2 \leq 40$$
$$X_1, X_2 \geq 0$$

Since the market price of product X_1 is unknown, we will first *a priori* assume that Profit Center A will maximize its profit by producing only X_2. The optimal solution is to produce 10 units of X_2, yielding a contribution margin of $80.00 and shadow price of $W_1 = \frac{8}{10}$ and $W_2 = \frac{8}{10}$. No idle capacity is available.

If Profit Center A is to produce X_1, it will divert a portion of its resources devoted to producing X_2 to produce X_1. For example, to reduce X_2 by 1 unit, it will increase X_1 by 2 units. Such a substitution rate will maintain the total contribution margin ($80.00) at the same level. This means that if Profit Center A is to produce (X_1), it should charge Profit Center B $7.00/unit in order to maintain its profitability intact. The $4.00/unit represents the opportunity cost of profit foregone by not producing X_2, calculated as follows:

$$C_1 = a_{11}W_1 + a_{12}W_2$$
$$= \left(3 \times \frac{8}{10}\right) + \left(2 \times \frac{8}{10}\right)$$
$$= \frac{24}{10} + \frac{16}{10} = \frac{40}{10} = \$4.00$$

Sales price = Variable costs + Contribution margin = 3.00 + 4.00 = $7.00

---

[4] This is assuming that X_2 has a free competitive market, and that the organization will be able to sell all it produces of X_2. If this assumption is released, the analysis still can be applied, although it gets complicated.

If the preceding example had resulted in idle capacity with the optimal solution, it would create motivational problems that the operating manager of Profit Center A may find difficult to ignore. For example, assume that the preceding example is the same, except for a change of the coefficient a_{22}.

$$\text{Max} = CX_1 + C_2X_2$$
$$?X_1 + 8X_2$$
$$\text{subject to:} \quad 3X_1 + 6X_2 \leq 60$$
$$2X_1 + 3X_2 \leq 40$$
$$X_1, \quad X_2 \geq 0$$

The solution is to produce 10 units of X_2, with a contribution margin of $80.00. However, process II has an idle capacity of 10 hours and, accordingly, $W_2 = 0$. Process I has dual evaluator of $W_1 = 1\frac{1}{3}$. The substitution rate is still 2 units of X_1 for 1 unit of X_2, requiring X_1 to be priced at $7.00/unit. However, if Profit Center A is being asked to completely divert its resources into producing X_1, it will produce 20 units of X_1, yielding the same contribution margin of $80.00. There is no idle capacity in process II, however. The center manager will hardly accept the utilization of all of his center's resources and still receive the same contribution margin. Theoretically, this is explainable on the grounds that the idle capacity of a slack variable is considered cost-free, assuming that such idle capacity cannot be leased, rented, or have its utilization deferred to next year without a reduction in its value. If these conditions are not met, the opportunity cost concept will require that the transfer price of X_1 be more than $7.00/unit to account for such additional profit foregone. If this is not accounted for, the manager of Profit Center A may believe that top corporate policy favors Profit Center B, because it does not reward his profit foregone.

The previous example also raises a crucial problem operationally. The shadow price value of W_1 and W_2 depends on the contribution margin of X_2 per unit and its required [A] coefficients. If the CM is high, the values of the dual evaluators will be high, and vice versa, assuming that the [A]'s are the same. If it happens that X_2 is the most profitable product for Center A, the transfer price for X_1 will be so high that Profit Center B may not be able to pay. The opposite may also be possible, leaving Profit Center A at a disadvantage. While such operational problems have long-run implications for policy planning, in the short-run it is a situation to reckon with! A suggested solution is that the corporate level may use dual pricing for motivating reasons, since its total profit is still optimal because the volume of both centers is determined by the system.

It is not advisable to obtain the optimal solution for Profit Center A first, and then that of Profit Center B.[5] This procedure usually leads to dis-

---

[5] This is due to the fact that Profit Center A acts as a simple maximizer, and, as such, forces Center B to behave in the same way, leading to suboptimization. See the example illustrated above.

economies or a suboptimal solution for the company as a whole. To overcome such a difficulty, a solution for the combined efforts of both centers has to be obtained. If such an optimal solution, company-wise, put Profit Center A at a disadvantage, the system should provide a motivational solution to induce and maintain the divisional manager's motivation in the right direction, or at least minimize the chance of moving in the wrong motivational direction. Motivation costs (the difference between the center's maximization figure and that resulting from the corporate optimal solution) should be credited to Center A's profitability plan. If this is not done, conflict between the division's goal and that of the corporation moves into full gear, especially when the reward system is based on each center's profit. These points are illustrated in the following example:

Profit Center A	*Profit Center B*
Max $C_1X_1 + C_2X_2$	$C_3Y_1 + C_4Y_2$
$?X_1 + 8X_2$	$(10 - C_1X_1)Y_1 + 5Y_2$

subject to:

$3X_1 + 6X_2 \leq 60$	$4Y_1 + 5Y_2 \leq 28$
$2X_1 + 4X_2 \leq 40$	$3Y_1 + 2Y_2 \leq 14$
$X_1, X_2 \quad \geq 0$	$Y_1, Y_2 \quad \geq 0$

To solve this problem, maximizing profit from a corporate point of view, assume that the variable cost of X_1 is \$3.00/unit, and that one unit of X_1 is needed to produce one unit of Y_1. This makes the net contribution margin of $Y_1 = \$7.00$/unit.

A linear programming model based on decomposition is as follows:[6]

$$
\begin{array}{rlr}
\text{Max } \pi(X, Y) = 0X_1 + 8X_2 + 7X_1 + 5Y_2 & \\
-X_1 \qquad\qquad + Y_1 & \leq 0 \\
3X_1 + 6X_2 & \leq 60 \\
2X_1 + 4X_2 & \leq 40 & \text{Master Budget} \\
4Y_1 + 5Y_2 & \leq 28 \\
3Y_1 + 2Y_2 & \leq 14 \\
X_1 \quad X_2, \quad Y_1, \quad Y_2 & \geq 0.
\end{array}
$$

The mathematical solution of such a case is illustrated in Exhibit 3, where the feasible plans and optimal one are shown.[7] The slack variables

---

[6] See: George Dantzig and Philip Wolf, "Decomposition Principles for Linear Programming," *Operations Research* (FEBRUARY 1960); and George Dantzig, *Linear Programming and Extensions* (Princeton University Press 1963); Chapters 22–24.

[7] No top corporate constraints are assumed. If any exist, the problem can still be solved, using the decomposition principle. The operating costs of each center are assumed to be independent of the level of activity of the other center and linear. Also, any additional sales of Y's will not reduce the external demand for X_2. These two conditions are called technological independence and demand independence consecutively. However, there is a demand interdependence for Y_1 and X_1; the demand of X_1 is derived from that of Y_1. If the demand for X_2 and Y_2 is interrelated, the problem still can be solved, although it gets complicated.

EXHIBIT 3
Different Operating Profitability Plans

	Plan I			Plan II			Plan III	
Production	Center (A)	Center (B)	Production	Center (A)	Center (B)	Production	Center (A)	Center (B)
$Y_2 = 5$ units	0	$25.00	$Y_2 = 1$ units	0	$ 5.00	$Y_2 = 4$		$20.00
$Y_1 = 0$ units		0	$Y_1 = 4$ units		28.00	$Y_1 = 2$		14.00
$X_1 = 0$ units			$X_1 = 4$ units			$X_1 = 2$		
$X_2 = 10$ units	$80.00		$X_2 = 8$ units	$64.00		$X_2 = 9$	$72.00	
$S_1 = 0$ hours			$S_1 = 0$ hrs.			$S_1 = 0$		
$S_2 = 0$ hours			$S_2 = 0$ hrs.			$S_2 = 0$		
$S_3 = 3$ hours			$S_3 = 7$ hrs.			$S_3 = 0$		
$S_4 = 4$ hours			$S_4 = 0$ hrs.			$S_4 = 0$		
Divisional Profit	$80.00	$25.00	Divisional Profit	$64.00	$33.00	Divisional Profit	$72.00	$34.00
Corporate Profit	$105.00		Corporate Profit	$97.00		Corporate Profit	$106.00	

(S_1, S_2, S_3, S_4) corresponding to each plan are also shown, indicating any idle capacity in the corresponding process of each profit center.

For the corporation as a whole, plan III is optimal. However, if we look at the solution from the point of view of each profit center, do we reach the same conclusion?

From the Profit Center B's point of view, plan III is optimal. From Profit Center A's point of view, it is not, since plan I is its optimal program. Would the manager of Profit Center A accept plan III, knowing what this means for his incentive compensation at the end of the year? Will the rate of return on his divisional investment reflect a fair measure of his performance if he accepts plan III?

What is the source of the problem and how should it be solved? The problem arises from the fact that the intermediate good X_1 is priced equal to its marginal (variable) costs. No contribution margin is given to Profit Center A, meaning that Profit Center B has captured all the gains yielded from this process itself, without sharing it with Profit Center A. This reflects unfair treatment. Accounting literature argues for the distribution of the joint profit of \$7.00/unit of (X_1, Y_1) between both centers, either through bargaining or by means of an equalization rate based on the ratio of production cost in both centers related to (X_1, Y_1). This accounting solution, as seen in this example, leads to suboptimization.[8] If a fair and equitable distribtuion is to be followed, Profit Center A should be given the profit foregone as a result of producing X_1. This means that the operating budget of Center A, if plan III is adopted, should be increased by \$8.00 as motivation costs. Profit Center B's additional contribution, as a result of further processing X_1 to Y_1, is \$1.00. This is the additional gain the company obtained by encouraging the production of (X_1, Y_1). If the corporate level does not adhere to such an opportunity cost approach, budgetary conflict arises between the profit center managers and the corporate level.

The previous solution in general, however, raises two important implications:

1. If product X_2 is highly profitable, the opportunity cost of producing X_1 is high. If product Y_1, which uses X_1 as input, is not so profitable as to afford paying such opportunity costs, the company as a whole will be better off by not producing Y_1. However, if product Y_1 should be produced in order to meet a contract commitment, or as a result of a policy decision, this decision is a top corporate decision and not a center one. The profit (or loss) consequence of such a decision should be isolated. Center A should not be penalized by a decision not of its own.

---

[8] If Center A charges B a sales price of \$8.00/unit of X_1, using the accounting equalization method, Center B finds it in its best interest not to buy X_1 and not to produce Y_1. Center B will produce 5 units of Y_2 and yield CM of \$25.00, and Center A will then produce 10 units of X_2 yielding CM of \$80.00. The total of \$105.00 (equal to plan I) is a suboptimization case.

2. If product X_2 is not highly profitable, the opportunity cost of producing X_1 will be less, and Profit Center B may be in an advantageous position. Profit Center A should not blame Profit Center B for this condition. Profit Center A would be well advised, if the demand for X_2 is decreasing and profitability is declining, to shift its resources to a new product. In the short run, however, Profit Center A should not ask Profit Center B to subsidize its operation and increase its profits.

These two implications do not necessarily require that the top corporate level use motivation costs in profitability planning, as in the case above.

II. *Profit Center A produces both product X_1 and product X_2 for Profit Center B, and there are no market prices for either product.*

In this case, Profit Center A, in reality, is not a profit center. It will function the same if it is treated as a cost center,[9] or is joined with Profit Center B to compose one large profit center. The latter may require a change in the organization's structure, which may be justifiable to minimize the undesirable motivational consequence of a system based on "games" if the price of suboptimization is too high for the company to bear!

Summary

Under the assumption $MC_A = NMR_B$, the supplying profit center is not motivated to change the relative use of various factors of production in response to changes in factor prices, since these favorable effects will pass over to the buying profit center. In addition, the profit center selling the final product will be motivated either to manipulate its sales by delaying them to next year, if this year is especially profitable, or to increase its production inventory level so that a part of its overhead will be capitalized, leading to an increase of its profit if it is originally unfavorable. This will affect the production of intermediate goods. To prevent this, the corporate level watches the inventory level and asks for an explanation if it exceeds a certain level. Another solution is that the buying division commits itself to acquire a certain volume. These methods are partial solutions to the problem.

We have shown that using variable costs, approximating marginal costs, to price transfer goods has several limitations since this approach ignores several strategic factors. Also, we have shown that using the accounting equalization method leads to suboptimization and that any solution to a transfer pricing system cannot ignore the motivational conflict that is pertinent. We have used "motivation costs" to reduce the level of conflict

[9] If it is treated as a cost center, it will have a zero marginal contribution which a budgetary system should accept. Its performance can be evaluated in terms of cost control and volume attainment.

due to the transfer pricing system. As a result, arriving at an optimal solution based on oppotrunity costs from the company's point of view, accepted by profit centers, is feasible.

References on the Decomposition Principle

1. A. Charnes, and W. W. Cooper, *Management Models and Industrial Application of Linear Programming,* Vol. I, II (John Wiley & Sons, 1961).

2. G. B. Dantzig, *Linear Programming and Extensions* (1963).

3. ——— and P. Wolfe, "The Decomposition Principle for Linear Programs," *Operations Research,* Vol. 8 (1960), pp. 101–111.

4. Warren E. Walker, "A Method for Obtaining the Optimal Dual Solution to a Linear Program Using the Dantzig-Wolfe Decomposition," *Operations Research* (March-April 1969), pp. 368–370.

5. Adi Ben-Israel and Philip D. Roberts, "A Decomposition Method for Interval Linear Programing," *Management Science* (January 1970), pp. 374–387.

6. David P. Rutenberg, "Generalized Networks, Generalized Upper Bounding and Decomposition for the Convex Simplex Method," *Management Science* (January 1970), pp. 338–401.

7. William J. Baumol and Tibor Fabin, "Decomposition Pricing for Decentralization and External Economics," *Management Science* (September 1964), pp. 1–32.

8. Jerome E. Hass, "Transfer Pricing in a Decentralized Firm," *Management Science* (February 1968), pp. 310–331.

9. C. S. Colantoni, R. P. Manes and A. Whinston, "Programming, Profit Rates and Pricing Decisions," *The Accounting Review* (July 1969), pp. 467–481.

10. Andrew Whinston, "Pricing Guides in Decentralized Organization," *New Perspective in Organizational Research,* edited by W. W. Cooper, et al., (John Wiley and Sons, 1964), pp. 405–448.

11. Edwin V. W. Zschau, *A Primal Decomposition Algorithm for Linear Programming,* Ph.D. Thesis (Graduate School of Business, Stanford University, December 1966).

25

This article integrates behavioral considerations into the transfer pricing literature, which has been largely quantitative in nature, consisting primarily of mathematical programming techniques. The need to achieve both decentralization and integration goals in an organization may be facilitated by the proper use of transfer pricing. Mathematically elegant solutions to transfer pricing problems may be less than ideal in behavioral terms because decentralization is sacrificed to optimize a numerical solution. The authors advocate negotiated transfer prices to help resolve conflicts of organizational subunits. More research on the behavioral implications of transfer pricing solutions is needed.

Transfer Pricing:
A Behavioral Context*

David J. H. Watson and John V. Baumler

The accounting, management science, and economics literature contains numerous models addressing the resource allocation and transfer pricing problems. Some of the earliest statements on the transfer pricing problem are recorded by Hirshleifer (1956 & 1957), Dean (1955), and Cook (1955). These authors suggest solutions to the transfer pricing problem which reflect the analogy of the internal price problem to the determination of the (Competitive) market price of traditional economics. The advent of mathematical programming produced another stream of articles addressing the transfer price problem, especially after the relation between a decentralized firm and the Dantzig and Wolfe (1960) decomposition principle was stated by Whinston (1964) and Baumol and Fabian (1964).[1]

This paper represents an attempt to place the solutions proposed by the

* *From* The Accounting Review, *Vol. L, No. 3 (July, 1975), pp. 466–474. Reprinted by permission of the American Accounting Association and the authors.*

[1] As examples of this see the articles by Dopuch and Drake (1964); Godfrey (1971); Gordon (1970); Hass (1968); Ruefli (1971 a&b).

mathematical programming models as well as other traditional solutions in an appropriate context. Since the transfer pricing problem only arises within a recognizable social system (be it an organization or a socialist economy) the paper considers the solutions in a social system context.[2] The paradigm developed can then be used to evaluate the usefulness and limitations of the various proposed solutions.

Decentralization and Differentiation

Decentralization is one approach to organizational design. Implicit in this approach is the segmentation of the organization into various specialities. Numerous reasons are provided in the transfer price literature for decentralization. For example, Dean (1955) suggests, ". . . the modern integrated multiple product firm functions best if it is made into a miniature of the competitive free enterprise system." Dopuch and Drake (1964) suggest that the division managers are in a better position to process information concerning resource allocation. Along a similar vein Ronen and McKinney (1970) argue that the division manager's nearness to the market place provides relevant information regarding changes in prices of inputs and outputs and that more effective coordination of production factors should be obtained at the divisional level. Reasons such as size and diversity of modern corporations and the promotion of morale (because of the decision-making autonomy of managers) are also offered in support of decentralization (Godfrey, 1971). While each of these reasons may be true, none of the authors has offered a coherent theory of decentralization. Consequently, the implications that the authors see of decentralization for transfer pricing are fairly restricted and pragmatic.

We consider the central problem facing complex organizations is one of coping with uncertainty. This is the view many current organizational theorists propose. Similarly, we identify the two major sources of uncertainty for a complex organization as its technology and its environment. An organization's design, then, represents a response to these sources of uncertainty.[3] Specifically, an organization may create parts to deal with the uncertainty and thereby leave other parts to operate under conditions of near certainty, i.e., the organization will departmentalize and decentralize.[4] Decentralization is a response to uncertainty.

Decentralization, however, does not quite explain the process involved.

---

[2] In this paper we only consider an organizational context, but there seems to be a direct analogy to a planned (or socialist) economy.

[3] The exact roles technology and environment play in determining organizational design is still the subject of research: see Burns and Stalker (1961); Lawrence and Lorsch (1967); Mohr (1971); Thompson (1967); Woodward (1965).

[4] Even in the most dynamic industries manufacturing operations are often sufficiently buffered to allow the effective use of standard cost systems to control manufacturing processes.

A consequence of the segmentation of the organization into parts (departments, divisions, etc.) is that the behavior of organizational members will be influenced by the segmentation. Because of the differences in the nature of the task and in the environmental uncertainty facing various segments, the organizational members will develop different mental processes and working styles, adopt different decision criteria, and may have varying perceptions of reality. A well-known example of this differentiation at the perceptual level is the research report of Dearborn and Simon (1958) which demonstrated that different executives can interpret differently the same organizational problem. The differences in interpretation reflect the departmental identification of the executives.

Therefore, we use the term *differentiation* to include not only the segmentation of the organization into specialized parts, but also to include the consequent differences in attitudes and behavior of organizational members. Requisite differentiation is a requirement for organizational success. That is, each organizational unit must be designed so as to cope effectively with the demands of its technology and environment. Later we will discuss the role of management accounting and transfer pricing in achieving the requisite degree of differentiation between organizational units.

Organizational Integration

THE CONCEPT

Differentiation is only one design problem facing the organization. The other side of the same coin, and another design problem, is integration: the process of insuring that efforts of the several organizational units, now appropriately differentiated, do collectively attain the goals of the total organization.

Lawrence and Lorsch (1967) in their research demonstrated that the most successful firms (in terms of the traditional measures of profitability) in the various industries studied were the firms that achieved the required differentiation and were then able to integrate the diverse units. Further, the research indicates that only firms that achieve these dual requirements can be successful. However, a basic organizational dilemma is that the more successful an organization is in achieving the requisite differentiation (especially those organizations requiring significant differentiation) the more difficulty the organization has in achieving the necessary integration. But, of course, the difficulties in achieving the required degree of differentiation and then integrating the total organizational effort is not uniformly distributed over all firms and industries. Rather, the more diverse and dynamic (uncertain) the subenvironments faced by organizational units, the more differentiated they must be. The greater the degree of differentiation, the more difficult is integration.

We stated, originally, that the central problem facing organizational designers is one of coping with uncertainty. This problem has now been restated in terms of achieving requisite differentiation of organizational components while simultaneously coordinating (or integrating) their collective efforts. The magnitude of the differentiation problem is basically determined by uncertainty in technological and environmental factors. However, the magnitude of the integration problem is partly determined by uncertainty factors and partly by the state of interdependence between organizational components.[5] To summarize, the most challenging problems to those seeking integration arise when organizational components are strongly differentiated and highly interdependent. At the opposite extreme, mildly differentiated subunits which exhibit only minimal interdependencies do not pose significant integration problems.

Integrating Mechanisms

Integration is achieved by the use of integrating mechanisms of which there are obviously many. One list of such mechanisms is indicated below. This list is adapted from an article by Galbraith (1972).[6]

- Rules, routines, standardization
- Organization hierarchy
- Planning
- Direct contact
- Liaison roles

---

[5] (i) We are considering interdependence basically from technological (the actual technical processes employed) and resource allocation viewpoints, although interdependence may also arise through the environment (e.g., from operating in common input and output markets). Environmental interdependence is not excluded, although we believe the most important aspect of the environment is the uncertainty dimension.

(ii) We are using the term "interdependence" in the Thompson (1967) sense. He identifies pooled, sequential, and reciprocal interdependence. Pooled interdependence is a situation in which each part of the organization renders a discrete contribution to the whole and each is supported by the whole. The parts do not interact directly with one another. This is basically the situation where the only major common organizational link among subunits is some scarce organizational resource, e.g., capital. Sequential interdependence is a situation in which, in addition to the pooled aspect, direct interaction between the units can be pinpointed and the order of that interdependence specified. Reciprocal interdependence refers to the situation in which the outputs of two units become inputs for each other. The three types of interdependence are, in the order indicated, increasingly difficult to coordinate.

[6] (i) Galbraith actually expands this list somewhat especially with regard to organizational planning.

(ii) Thompson (1967) has provided a somewhat different list. He suggests three mechanisms for achieving integration, coordination by standardization, coordination by planning, and coordination by mutual adjustment. The first two mechanisms we present correspond to Thompson's No. 1, while mechanisms 4 to 9 (lateral mechanisms in Galbraith's terminology) correspond to Thompson's No. 3.

- Temporary committees (task forces or teams)
- Integrators (personnel specializing in the role of coordinating inter-subunit activities)
- Integrating departments (departments of integrators)
- Matrix organization (an organization that is completely committed to joint problem solving and *shared* responsibility)

The list is ordered from the least elaborate to the most sophisticated integrative mechanisms. All organizations employ the first several mechanisms on the list. These mechanisms are sufficient for integrating many organizational functions and are probably all that is needed by organizations facing minimal environmental and technological demands. However, when environmental and technological demands become more complex, organizations become more differentiated and this increases the problem of integration. Consequently, more sophisticated integrating mechanisms (the latter ones listed), in addition to the simpler mechanisms, are required.

Differentiation, Integration, and Management Accounting

The amount of differentiation required is determined primarily by technological and environmental demands, and an organization's adaptation to these demands is reflected in the first instance by the organizational design. The accountant, in designing the management accounting system, needs to consider the requisite degree of differentiation as a constraint. That is, the accountant cannot create or demand differentiation when behavioral factors dictate otherwise.

This is not to say that the management accounting system has no part to play in organizational design. In fact, the accounting system can be designed to facilitate or enhance the differentiation achieved. For example, each of the concepts — expense center, profit center, and investment center — may be employed, depending upon the differentiation required by the technological and environmental demands. When the appropriate accounting techniques are used in conjunction with required organizational design we expect the claimed benefits of decentralization to be realized.[7]

We are now in the position to consider the role of the accounting system in integration. An accounting system is a well-defined, formal information system within an organization. Basically, it is a set of rules and standard procedures. The accounting system can thus be classified as an integrating mechanism primarily of the first type listed above.[8] In more complicated

---

[7] For one listing of these claimed benefits "automatically" arising from decentralization see Horngren (1972), p. 693.

[8] Budgeting and planning are also usually considered part of the management accounting system. Notice, however, that planning has also been classed as a fairly simple or routine integrating mechanism.

integrating situations, although the accounting system (or, more precisely, the costs and prices generated by the accounting system) may be helpful in obtaining integration, this will only be *one* input to the integrating process.

Differentiation, Integration, and Transfer Pricing

Essentially we have argued that the requisite differentiation has to be taken as given by the accountant when he designs an organization's formal control and reporting subsystems. In some cases there will be a one-to-one mapping between the differentiated units and the accountant's responsibility centers, i.e., the expense, profit, and investment centers. However, when there is not this convenient mapping we would argue that the behavioral factors dominate, and that the accountant should not try to impose differentiation through the creation of artificial responsibility centers. Organizational design is a complete task. Numerous variables must be simultaneously considered. The accountant must accept the organizational structure as given. Restructuring the organization merely to facilitate the management accounting system is not recommended.

What then is the role of transfer pricing? Obviously, once responsibility centers are established, goods and services transferred among these units need to be priced. This helps separate and pinpoint responsibility for different aspects of the firms functioning. In other words, to some extent, the transfer pricing mechanism *enhances* differentiation. But, we have also demonstrated above that differentiation is only one part of the problem. Integration is another facet of this problem. Can the transfer pricing mechanism be used to help achieve the required integration? Again the answer is obviously "yes." In many cases the pricing mechanism is a routine or standardized process, a formula like, for example, standard cost, cost plus, marginal cost, a fixed price, etc. This type of transfer pricing is at least applicable in simple integrating situations, although in more complicated integrating situations it may be only one input to the integrating process.

Mathematical Programming Solutions to the Transfer Pricing Problem

As stated in the introduction to this paper many of the papers proposing programming solutions to the transfer price problem rely on the interpretation of the decomposition principle as a model of decision making in a decentralized firm. While the analogy is undoubtedly useful for analyzing some situations, the methodology appears to have some limitations.

The first limitation of these approaches is that they maintain only the facade of decentralized decision making. The last phase of the process is usually dictated by central management. For example, in the Baumol and Fabian (1964) model, although the optimal divisional plan will be a weighted average of the plans submitted by the division, the weights are entirely determined by central management. Godfrey (1971, pp. 289–90) in evaluating the Baumol and Fabian article and the more recent refinements to their model says:

> Despite the appeal of the decomposition technique, in our opinion, it is still a highly centralized decision making procedure. The divisions are at the mercy of central headquarters and would probably not agree that they enjoy the autonomy of decision making that is intended.[9]

There seems to be two explanations for this problem. The first is that many authors of the programming solutions are primarily interested in the mathematical properties (or elegance) of their solutions and only secondarily in the model's organizational implications. The second is that most authors in the transfer price literature are asking the question, "What transfer price will result in the decentralized firm maximizing joint (or corporate) profits?" Since the emphasis is on the maximization of joint profits whenever conflict arises between this goal and the decentralization philosophy, the latter tends to be sacrificed. The solution is always centralized decision making whether this is through some stated price rule, a wishful appeal to competitive market prices and their surrogates, or to mathematical programming solutions. The result is predictable since none of these authors has offered a coherent theory for decentralization. On the other hand, we have offered a theory for explaining decentralization, and under this theory it is not clear that decentralization should be sacrificed or that sacrificing decentralization will optimize decision making.

A second limitation of this approach is that they concentrate on the behaviorally simple integration problems.[10] The environments are stable and the interdependencies are of the simplest kinds. This is true even of recent articles in the area. Ruefli (1971a), for example, develops a decomposition model which can be interpreted as a representation of decision making in a three-level hierarchial organization. Ruefli greatly restricts the

---

[9] Godfrey also uses the decomposition approach in his short-run planning model but freely admits it is a centralized decision making model.

[10] (i) We are using mathematical programming models as the example. However, the same argument could be made against the economic solutions and against the traditional accounting solutions.

(ii) We are not arguing against the future development of programming models. Even the development of more efficient algorithms for handling solved problems is undoubtedly important.

degree and incidence of interdependent relationships within his tri-level hierarchy.[11]

The Case Against Negotiated Prices

The use of negotiated prices has rarely been seriously entertained by those writing in the transfer price literature. Joel Dean (1955) pressed for negotiated prices, but in such a way that they simulated a competitive market. The foundation for his recommendations really lay in the availability of markets outside the decentralized firm. Cook (1955) also discussed the use of "free negotiation" but proceeds to point out two disadvantages: (1) the amount of executive time it is likely to take, and (2) negotiated prices may distort the profit center's financial reports.[12] However, Cook (1955, p. 93) does suggest, ". . . if managers are sophisticated and equipped with good accounting data on their operations, such a free negotiation system could satisfy the basic criteria outline above; that is, a transfer price that will not lead to transfers which will reduce the company's profit but will permit and encourage any transfer which increases the company's profit."[13] Dopuch and Drake (1964, p. 13) also seem to be concerned about Cook's second point above when they state:

> In evaluating the resulting performance of the divisional managers, however, the central management may be evaluating their ability to negotiate rather than their ability to control economic variables. Accordingly, the information economies of decentralization may be more apparent than real.

Later, in their paper, when discussing the decomposition procedure solutions Dopuch and Drake (1964, p. 18) suggest:

> The relevant point is that, if this method can be applied in practice, it will provide a basis for negotiation between the departmental and central management levels. In this respect it would not be necessary for the divisional

[11] (i) Ruefli's model, as he notes, is easily generalized to an *n*-level hierarchial model.

(ii) In a second article Ruefli (1971b) does mention, with regard to behavioral externalities, the question of bidirectional effects (reciprocal interdependence) for operational units within a management unit. However, he does not propose any solution. Ruefli even proposes an integrating mechanism (a behavioral center) which he says could be a liaison arrangement, a joint planning committee, etc. However, this behavioral center seems to act very similarly to the central management unit and consequently be subject to the same "centralization" criticism.

[12] One, often mentioned, example of this is when one division occupies a monopoly position.

[13] Unfortunately, (technically) sophisticated managers and good accounting data are probably not sufficient conditions for insuring proper integration. Dean (1955) also suggests the position of "price mediator" for a company when *initially* installing his system. These ideas are similar to the concepts of an integrator which we will discuss later.

managers to negotiate with each other. This in itself may be an advantage since situations of negotiation between divisional managers may degenerate into personal conflicts.

Although there is undoubtedly some truth to each of these observations, that is, at times negotiated transfer prices may have these dysfunctional effects, we believe a very strong case can be made for the use of negotiated transfer prices. In presenting this case we will also be suggesting a way for obtaining suitable transfer prices for the complicated integrating situations.

Transfer Prices and Conflict Resolution

Lawrence and Lorsch (1967) in their research were able to isolate three conflict resolution mechanisms in the firms they studied. One of their most interesting results was that the successful firms facing uncertain environments were able to resolve effectively interdepartmental conflict, and the most important means of resolving this conflict was confrontation, i.e., negotiation.[14] This effective resolution of interdepartmental conflict seemed to be an important reason why these successful firms could achieve a high degree of integration as well as the high degree of differentiation demanded by their uncertain environment.

A second point worth noting is that within a complex organization conflict is going to be multidimensional. In a highly differentiated organization this will at times involve the transfer and pricing of goods and services within the organization. But it may also include design and engineering changes, production and delivery schedules, and quality control. Seen in this light, the transfer pricing question becomes one facet of a multidimensional conflict resolution process.[15] If the appropriate conflict resolution process is negotiation, then it appears the transfer price should be one arrived at through negotiation.[16] Specifically, determination of transfer prices could be part of the integrative process. Note that this is not a

---

[14] Forcing was also an important back-up means. Smoothing was the third method and generally was the least effective.

[15] Hence, it makes little sense to be concerned about a possible monopoly position by one department. It is unlikely, if at all possible, in uncertain environments or reciprocally interdependent situations (or both) that one department will have a monopoly position on all dimensions of the conflict.

[16] This general argument for negotiated prices could probably be extended into the simpler integrating situations. Resolving conflict in part depends upon how close the protagonists' expectations of a suitable solution point are (see Schelling for a clearly stated exposition of this point). The similarity of expectations is also a function of the complexity of the situation. Thus, it could be argued that, when environmental demands or organizational interdependencies or their interaction are least complex, expectations of a mutually agreeable solution point are closest and so the conflict is easily resolved. This seems to be, for example, the conditions when a competitive market transfer price can be established. In other words, the market-based transfer price is a limiting (or simple) case of negotiated prices. See Schelling (1963).

wholesale endorsement of negotiated transfer prices in all cases. There are undoubtedly instances in which unalterable formulas could be employed (e.g., the least difficult integration situations). Such formulas may be necessary to guard against obvious diseconomies or, more importantly, to enhance requisite differentiation. But if the requisite degree of differentiation is achievable and the problem is to obtain adequate integration, one of the integrative tools available might well be negotiating intrafirm prices. If organizational subunits seek to resolve conflict by confrontation — possibly with the aid of an integrator — and negotiate their differences, negotiated transfer prices might well be the desired result.

Implications for Research on Transfer Pricing

The obvious implication is that we need to know something about the conflict resolution processes. In particular, we would like to know how accounting data are, or can be, used in a conflict situation. It may be, for example, that accounting data are completely irrelevant or unimportant in the more difficult integrating situations. Alternatively we may find some accounting data useful and other accounting data less useful. It may even be that we need to develop new kinds of data for these tougher areas.

Let us for the moment consider a difficult integrating situation — one that requires a formal integrator to integrate successfully the differentiated units. What can we say about this situation? First, although the protagonists may have somewhat different working styles, time horizons, decision criteria, and perceptions of reality (because they are part of a differentiated firm facing different subparts of the organizational environment), they are still members of the one organization and consequently have some attributes in common. There is some basis therefore for believing agreement can always be attained. Second, successful integration will depend largely on the skill of the integrator and how the personnel in the differentiated units perceive him.[17] Third, from a strict accounting viewpoint, instead of giving point estimates to all the parties on the "correct" transfer price (as, for example, the output of a mathematical program) we may wish to provide guides to simply bound the solution area.[18] These bounds could then

---

[17] Again notice Dean (1955) argues along a similar line when discussing his successful price mediator. He suggests the prime role of the mediator is not to dictate a price but to keep the negotiations flowing until that is a settlement.

[18] (i) For example, the variable costs of the input units may represent a lower bound, and the selling price less the variable costs of the output units may represent an upper bound. We may also give the integrator various other combinations of cost data to facilitate his integrating role (e.g., full costs (plus a markup), the mathematical programming solutions, etc.).

(ii) These behavioral questions obviously require future empirical verification or falsification.

reflect other accounting restraints on the transfer price (e.g., the fact that the transfer price may be used in the evaluation of the economic performance of the units). However, within the guides set, the final transfer price is a result of the confrontation process.

If we move to a more complicated integrating situation requiring an integrating department, some members of this department may need to be experts in internal financial matters. The implications of this and the wider implications of a matrix organization, for management accounting practice, are still very open questions. We are saying that at times the management accounting process must perform more than a mere scorekeeping or attention-directing function. The integrator has one of the most crucial roles within the organization. Certain aspects of the managerial accounting system — specifically, resolving transfer price disputes — must perhaps be merged within the integrator's total activities.

Further, little empirical evidence has been gathered on how transfer prices are established in various organizations. In gathering such evidence in the future, it is suggested that assessments of the states of differentiation and integration between buyer and seller subunits, the degree of interdependence between them, and the mode of conflict resolution utilized be made. This will allow the transfer pricing techniques to be viewed in terms of the relevant organizational and behavioral variances. Finally, it might be worth while to investigate the relative trade-offs between nonoptimal transfer prices and the dysfunctional consequences of removing this subject from the integrator's purview.

Conclusion

We have attempted to place the transfer pricing question in a relevant behavioral setting. Briefly, we have suggested the management accountant needs to consider organizational differentiation a constraint in designing the management accounting system. Working within this constraint we suggested the management accounting system can be designed to enhance the organizational differentiation achieved or to facilitate organizational integration. The transfer pricing mechanism, being part of the management accounting system, can be used to enhance organizational differentiation and to facilitate organizational integration. The transfer pricing mechanisms will probably play the role of enhancing differentiation in those instances in which integration is easily attained. This may well be achieved by the use of formula pricing mechanisms. In other cases, integration will be a major organizational problem. Consequently, the transfer pricing mechanism could be utilized to facilitate integration. An appropriate transfer price mechanism in this case seems to be negotiated pricing. Further areas of research suggested by this conclusion were discussed.

References

Baumol, W. J. and Fabian, T., "Decomposition, Pricing for Decentralization and External Economics," *Management Science* (September 1964), pp. 1–32.

Burns, T. and Stalker, G. M., *The Management of Innovation* (London: Tavistock Institute, 1961).

Cook, P. W., "Decentralization and the Transfer Price Problem," *Journal of Business* (April 1955), pp. 87–94.

Dantzig, G. B. and Wolfe, P., "Decomposition Principles for Linear Programs," *Operations Research* (February 1960), pp. 101–11.

Dean, J., "Decentralization and Intracompany Pricing," *Harvard Business Review* (July–August 1955), pp. 65–74.

Dopuch, N. and Drake, D. F., "Accounting Implications of a Mathematical Programming Approach to the Transfer Pricing Problem," *Journal of Accounting Research* (Spring 1964), pp. 10–24.

Galbraith, J. R., "Organization Design: An Information Processing View," in J. W. Lorsch and P. R. Lawrence, eds., *Organizational Planning: Cases and Concepts* (Georgetown, Ontario: Irwin-Dorsey Limited, 1972).

Godfrey, J. T., "Short-Run Planning in a Decentralized Firm," *The Accounting Review* (April 1971), pp. 282–97.

Gordon, M. J., "A Method of Pricing for a Socialist Economy," *The Accounting Review* (July 1970), pp. 427–43.

Hass, J. E., "Transfer Pricing in a Decentralized Firm," *Management Science* (February 1968), pp. B-310–B-331.

Hirshleifer, J., "On the Economics of Transfer Pricing," *Journal of Business* (July 1956), pp. 172–84.

———, "Economics of the Divisionalized Firm," *Journal of Business* (April 1957), pp. 96–108.

Lawrence, P. R. and Lorsch, J. W., *Organization and Environment* (Irwin, 1967).

Mohr, L. B., "Organizational Technology and Organizational Structure," *Administrative Science Quarterly* (December 1971), pp. 444–59.

Ronen, J. and McKinney, G., "Transfer Pricing for Divisional Autonomy," *Journal of Accounting Research* (Spring 1970), pp. 99–112.

Ruefli, T. W., "A Generalized Goal Decomposition Model," *Management Science* (April 1971), pp. B-505–B-518.

———, "Behavioral Externalities in Decentralized Organizations," *Management Science* (June 1971), pp. B-649–B-657.

Schelling, T. C., *The Strategy of Conflict* (Oxford University Press, 1963).

Thompson, J. D., *Organizations in Action* (McGraw-Hill, 1967).

Whinston, A., "Pricing Guides in Decentralized Organization," in W. W. Cooper et al., eds., *New Perspectives in Organizational Research* (Wiley, 1964).

Woodward, J., *Industrial Organizations: Theory and Practice* (Oxford University Press, 1965).

Supplemental
Readings
to Part Six

Abdel-Khalik, A. Rashad, and Edward J. Lusk. "Transfer Pricing — A Synthesis." *The Accounting Review,* XLIX, No. 1 (January 1974), 8–23.
    Considers the development of transfer pricing models in the following categories: (1) the economic theory of the firm; (2) mathematical programming approaches; and (3) other analytical approaches.

Amey, Lloyd. "On Opportunity Costs and Decision Making." *Accountancy,* LXXIX (July 1968), 442–451.
    Explains opportunity costs in light of the types of decisions for which they are relevant.

Bailey, Andrew D., Jr. "A Dynamic Programming Approach to the Analysis of Different Costing Methods in Accounting for Inventories." *The Accounting Review,* XLVIII, No. 3 (July 1973), 560–574.
    Attempts to construct and solve a more general analytical model for the investigation of inventory valuation methods. It provides additional support for variable costing as the preferred internal accounting method where a multiperiod horizon is used.

———, and Warren J. Boe. "Goal and Resource Transfers in the Multigoal Organization." *The Accounting Review,* LI, No. 3 (July 1976), 559–573.
    Reviews the literature on transfer pricing and interprets the new transfer pricing models in terms of interest to accountants in providing a data net appropriate for divisional reporting and decision-making while at the same time meeting the firm's goals.

Birnberg, Jacob G., Louis R. Pondy, and C. Lee Davis. "Effect of Three Voting Rules on Resource Allocation Decisions." *Management Science,* 16, No. 6 (February 1970), B-356–B-372.
    Discusses the effect of the voting rule adopted by a capital budgeting committee on the allocation of resources among divisions.

Broster, E. J. "The Dynamics of Marginal Costing." *The Accountant,* 162, No. 4971 (March 26, 1970), 451–454.
    Explains the advantages of using marginal costing.

Churchill, Neil. "Linear Algebra and Cost Allocations: Some Examples." *The Accounting Review,* 39, No. 4 (October 1964), 894–904.
    Applies linear algebra to a problem of reciprocal cost allocation.

Cook, David E. "Inter-unit Pricing and Your New Pricing Expert: The IRS." *Management Accounting,* 51, No. 2 (August 1969), 9–11.
> Reviews regulations set up by the Internal Revenue Service regarding transfer prices.

Corcoran, A. Wayne, and Wayne E. Leininger. "Stochastic Process Costing Models." *The Accounting Review,* XLVIII, No. 1 (January 1973), 105–114.
> Develops process costing models that are based on the premise that product flows within a mass-production system can be described stochastically.

Dearden, John. "The Case Against ROI Control." *Harvard Business Review,* 47, No. 3 (May–June 1969), 124–135.
> Explores the reasons that return on investment creates conflict and is of limited use in evaluating division performance.

DeCoster, Don T., Victor Powers, and George I. Prater. "Accounting Information and Capacity Utilization." *Cost and Management,* 42, No. 10 (November 1968), 10–16.
> Illustrates the failure of traditional accounting approaches to the measurement of plant capacity and suggests an effective approach.

Demski, Joel S. "Decision — Performance Control." *The Accounting Review,* XLIV, No. 4 (October 1969), 669–679.
> Describes a broader view of the decision process, including the interaction between planning and control.

Dittman, David A. "Transfer Pricing and Decentralization." *Management Accounting,* LIV, No. 5 (November 1972), 47–50.
> Analyzes a number of pricing methods in terms of performance measurement, goal congruence, and resource allocation. Evidently, middle management gets more satisfaction from being associated with a "profit center" rather than a "cost center" even though they have no control over the reported profits.

Farag, Shawki M. "A Planning Model for the Divisionalized Enterprise." *The Accounting Review,* XLIII, No. 2 (April 1968), 312–320.
> Constructs a micro input-output model that can be used for planning the activities of divisionalized enterprises.

Feltham, Gerald A. "Some Quantitative Approaches to Planning for Multiproduct Production Systems." *The Accounting Review,* XLV, No. 1 (January 1970), 11–26.
> Illustrates a way to use linear algebra and linear programming in planning, estimation, and normative prediction in a multiproduct system.

Ferrara, William L. "Responsibility Reporting vs. Direct Costing — Is There a Conflict?" *Management Accounting,* 48, No. 10 (June 1967), 43–54.
> States a series of hypotheses that such a conflict is imaginary.

Finney, Frederick D. "Pricing Interdivisional Transfers." *Management Accounting,* 48, No. 3 (November 1966), 10–18.
> Discusses at length pricing transfers of raw materials, goods-in-process, and finished goods in an interplant setting.

Furlong, William L., and Leon H. Robertson. "Matching Management Decisions and Results." *Management Accounting,* 49, No. 12 (August 1968), 3–10.
Discusses why management's current performance should be judged by its ability to maintain the proper level of "domino" costs.

Gambling, Trevor E. "A Technological Model for Use in Input-Output Analysis and Cost Accounting." *Management Accounting,* 50, No. 4 (December 1968), 33–38.
Considers accounting aspects of technological models.

Goetz, Billy E. "Transfer Prices: An Exercise in Relevancy and Goal Congruence." *The Accounting Review,* XLII, No. 3 (July 1967), 435–440.
Explains why using incremental costs as transfer prices is the unique way to achieve congruence of goals.

Greer, Willis R., Jr. "Better Motivation for Time-constrained Sequential Production Processes." *Management Accounting,* LIV, No. 2 (August 1972), 15–19.
Develops a system that provides motivation for compliance with optimum schedules by charging responsible processes with the total-firm incremental costs that are incurred by failure to comply.

Hass, Jerome E. "Transfer Pricing in a Decentralized Firm." *Management Science,* 14, No. 6 (February 1968), B-310–B-331.
Applies a transfer pricing concept via a decomposition algorithm for quadratic programming.

Herson, Richard J. L., and Ronald S. Hertz. "Direct Costing in Pricing: A Critical Reappraisal." *Management Services,* 5, No. 2 (March–April 1968), 35–44.
Shows why direct costing is dangerous for pricing decisions — full costing is better for the long run.

Ijiri, Yuji, Robert K. Jaedicke, and John L. Livingstone. "The Effect of Inventory Costing Methods on Full and Direct Costing." *The Journal of Accounting Research,* 3, No. 1 (Spring 1965), 63–74.
Analyzes the impact of various inventory costing methods on the pattern of profit differences.

Kaplan, Robert S. "Variable and Self-service Costs in Reciprocal Allocation Models." *The Accounting Review,* XLVIII, No. 4 (October 1973), 738–748.
Illustrates cost-allocation procedures with quantitative techniques.

————, and Gerald L. Thompson. "Overhead Allocation via Mathematical Programming Models." *The Accounting Review,* XLVI, No. 2 (April 1971), 352–364.
Discusses linear programming principles and uses them to analyze the cost overhead allocation problem.

Kochenberger, Gary A. "Inventory Models: Optimization by Geometric Programming." *Decision Sciences,* 2, No. 2 (April 1971), 193–205.
Presents a brief summary of geometric programming and then illustrates its application to managerial problems by applying it to three well-known inventory models.

Moriarity, Shane. "Another Approach to Allocating Joint Costs." *The Accounting Review,* L, No. 4 (October 1975), 791–795.
> Suggests allocating cost savings as an offset to the cost of obtaining services independently and lists five advantages of this method.

Parker, John R. E. "Perspectives on Direct Costing." *The Canadian Chartered Accountant,* 78, No. 3 (March 1961), 225–232.
> Discusses why both direct and absorption costing are needed for different management purposes.

Petri, Enrico. "Holding Gains and Losses as Cost Savings: A Comment on Supplementary Statement No. 2 on Inventory Valuation." *The Accounting Review,* XLVIII, No. 3 (July 1973), 483–488.
> Discusses holding gains and losses from inventory revaluations from a managerial perspective in the specific context of cost savings.

————, and Roland Minch. "Evaluation of Resource Acquisition Decisions by the Partitioning of Holding Activity." *The Accounting Review,* XLIX, No. 3 (July 1974), 455–464.
> Applies an inventory optimization model, which the authors think overcomes some of the problems of using holding activity as a performance measurement surrogate.

Rappaport, Alfred. "A Capital Budgeting Approach to Divisional Planning and Control." *Financial Executive,* 36, No. 10 (October 1968), 47–63.
> Suggests that "discounted cash flow" is the most reasonable measure of capital productivity and that a "time-adjusted rate of return" should be determined for a division's long-range cash forecast to replace return on investment as a measure of performance.

Ruff, Fred H. "Planning for Profit." *Financial Executive,* 37, No. 7 (July 1969), 31–50.
> Explains why, if the goal of an enterprise is to "maximize profits," contribution reporting and direct costing provide the way to achieve the goal by planning for profits.

Shillinglaw, Gordon. "Toward a Theory of Divisional Income Measurement." *The Accounting Review,* XXXVII, No. 2 (April 1962), 208–216.
> Discusses the theory, which is based on the concept that divisional income (profit contribution) should reflect divisional management performance.

Slaybaugh, Charles J. "Inventory Management Program." *Management Accounting,* LIII, No. 1 (July 1971), 13–17, 22.
> Describes the inventory management program of International Heating and Air Conditioning Corporation.

Theil, Henri. "How to Worry about Increased Expenditures." *The Accounting Review,* XLIV, No. 1 (January 1969), 27–37.
> Explores ways to analyze differences between budgeted performance and actual performance using information theory concepts.

Thomas, Arthur L. *The Allocation Problem.* Studies in Accounting Research #3, American Accounting Association, 1969.
> Introduces the cost-allocation problem.

————. *The Allocation Problem: Part Two.* Studies in Accounting Research #9, American Accounting Association, 1974.

Explores further the cost-allocation problem.

Trippi, Robert R., and Donald E. Lewin. "A Present Value Formulation of the Classical EOQ Problem." *Decision Sciences* (January 1974), 30–35.

Develops solution differences and error implications using a present-value and the traditional EOQ methodologies.

Tuckett, R. F. "Combined Cost and Linear Programming Models of Industrial Complexes." *Operational Research Quarterly,* 20, No. 2 (June 1969), 223–236.

Proposes a general combined cost/LP model usable for either costing or planning.

Weiser, Herbert J. "The Impact of Accounting Controls on Performance Motivation." *The New York C.P.A.,* 38, No. 3 (March 1968), 191–201.

Explains why in establishing accounting controls, one should consider their significance as stimulants of motivational efforts, as well as devices for evaluation.

Williams, Thomas H., and Charles H. Griffin. "Matrix Theory and Cost Allocation." *The Accounting Review,* XXXIX, No. 3 (July 1964), 671–678.

Introduces principles of matrix theory and applies them to the cost-allocation problem.

Wormley, James T. "Ensuring the Profit Contribution of a Corporate Data Processing Department." *Management Accounting,* 48, No. 5 (January 1967), 3–12.

Explores transfer pricing policies that can be used by an EDP department.

Wright, Wilmer. "Use of Standard Direct Costing." *Management Accounting,* 48, No. 5 (January 1967), 39–46.

Compares standard direct costing with simple direct costing and illustrates the benefits of using a standard direct costing system.

Additional
Bibliography
to Part Six

Barrett, Dermot. "Centralization and Decentralization." *The Canadian Chartered Accountant,* 78, No. 5 (May 1961), 445–450.

Beyer, Robert. "Profitability Accounting: The Challenge and the Opportunity." *The Journal of Accountancy,* 117, No. 6 (June 1964), 33–36.

Bierman, Harold, Jr. "A Way of Using Direct Costing in Financial Reporting." *NAA Bulletin,* XLI, No. 3 (November 1959), 13–20.

Bows, Albert J., Jr. "Broadening the Approach to Management Reporting." *The Arthur Andersen Chronicle,* 22, No. 2 (April 1962), 7–25.

Brausch, John J. "Direct Costing: Progress or Folly?" *The Journal of Accountancy,* 112, No. 2 (August 1961), 52–60.

Brummet, R. Lee. "Direct Costing — Its Weaknesses and Strengths." *NAA Bulletin,* XLIII, No. 7 (March 1962), 61–68.

Bulloch, James, and Richard M. Duvall. "Adjusting Rate of Return and Present Value for Price-level Changes." *The Accounting Review,* XL, No. 3 (July 1965), 569–573.

Butterworth, John E., and Berndt A. Sigloch. "A Generalized Multi-stage Input-Output Model and Some Derived Equivalent Systems." *The Accounting Review,* XLVI, No. 4 (October 1971), 700–716.

Cook, Doris M. "The Effect of Frequency of Feedback on Attitudes and Performance." *Journal of Accounting Research,* 5, Supplement (1967), 213–224.

Crompton, Walter H. "Transfer Pricing: A Proposal." *Management Accounting,* LIII, No. 10 (April 1972), 46–48.

Crowningshield, Gerald R., and George L. Battista. "Fixing Responsibility Through Profit and Loss Analysis." *NAA Bulletin,* XLIII, No. 4 (December 1961), 11–27.

Dean, Joel. "An Approach to Internal Profit Measurement." *NAA Bulletin,* XXXIX, No. 7 (March 1958), 5–12.

Dearden, John. "Interdivisional Pricing." *Harvard Business Review,* XXXVIII, No. 1 (January–February 1960), 117–125.

———, and Bruce D. Henderson. "New System for Divisional Control." *Harvard Business Review,* 44, No. 5 (September–October 1966), 144–160.

DeCoster, Don T., and Kavasseri V. Ramanathan. "An Algebraic Aid in Teaching the Differences Between Direct Costing and Full-absorption Costing Models." *The Accounting Review,* XLVIII, No. 4 (October 1973), 800–801.

Dopuch, Nicholas, and David F. Drake. "Accounting Implications of a Mathematical Programming Approach to the Transfer Price Problem." *Journal of Accounting Research,* 2, No. 1 (Spring 1964), 10–24.

Dudick, Thomas S. "Direct Costing — 'Handle With Care'." *The Journal of Accountancy,* 114, No. 4 (October 1962), 45–52.

———. "Is Direct Costing the Answer?" *The New York Certified Public Accountant,* XXXIII, No. 12 (December 1963), 857–862.

Fekrat, M. Ali. "The Conceptual Foundations of Absorption Costing." *The Accounting Review,* XLVII, No. 2 (April 1972), 351–355.

Ferrara, William L. "The Contribution Approach." *NAA Bulletin,* XLVI, No. 4 (December 1964), 19–29.

Foss, Philip E., and William L. Ferrara. "The Period Cost Concept for Income Measurement — Can It Be Defended?" *The Accounting Review,* XXXVI, No. 4 (October 1961), 598–602.

Flock, Henry H. "The Change to Direct Costing in a Multi-product Company." *Management Accounting,* LIII, No. 1 (July 1971), 52–55.

Fremgen, James M. "Variable Costing for External Reporting — A Reconsideration." *The Accounting Review,* XXXVII, No. 1 (January 1962), 76–81.

Greer, Howard C. "Divisional Profit Calculation — Notes on the Transfer Price Problem." *NAA Bulletin,* XLIII, No. 11 (July 1962), 5–12.

Harper, W. M. "Managerial Economic Control — III: The Concept of Control Profit." *Accountancy,* LXXIX (June 1968), 415–417.

Hirschman, Robert W. "Direct Costing and the Law." *The Accounting Review,* XL, No. 1 (January 1965), 176–183.

Holstrum, Gary L., and Eugene H. Sauls. "The Opportunity Cost Transfer Price." *Management Accounting,* LIV, No. 11 (May 1973), 29–33.

Hopwood, Anthony G. "Leadership Climate and the Use of Accounting Data in Performance Evaluation." *The Accounting Review,* XLIX, No. 3 (July 1974), 485–495.

———. "An Empirical Study of the Role of Accounting Data in Performance Evaluation." *Empirical Research in Accounting: Selected Studies, 1972,* 156–193.

Horngren, Charles T., and George H. Sorter. " 'Direct' Costing for External Reporting." *The Accounting Review,* XXXVI, No. 1 (January 1961), 84–93.

Ijiri, Yuji. "An Application of Input-Output Analysis to Some Problems in Cost Accounting." *Management Accounting,* 49, No. 8 (April 1968) 49–61.

Jordan, Raymond B. "Learning How to Use the Learning Curve." *NAA Bulletin,* XXXIX, No. 5 (January 1958), 27–39.

Kadel, J. Henry. "Contribution Reporting." *Management Accounting,* LIV, No. 5 (November 1972), 40–46.

Kaplan, Robert S., and Ulf Peter Welam. "Overhead Allocation with Imperfect Markets." *The Accounting Review,* XLIX, No. 3 (July 1974), 477–484.

Kilbridge, Maurice. "A Model for Industrial Learning Costs." *Management Science,* 8, No. 4 (July 1962), 516–552.

Kornbluth, J. S. H. "Accounting in Multiple Objective Linear Programming." *The Accounting Review,* XLIX, No. 2 (April 1974), 284–295.

Laimon, S. "Cost Analysis and Pricing Policies." *Cost and Management,* XXXV, No. 8 (September 1961), 360–375.

Lambert, Douglas M., and Bernard J. LaLonde. "Inventory Carrying Costs." *Management Accounting,* LVIII, No. 2 (August 1976), 31–35.

Largay, James A., III. "Microeconomic Foundations of Variable Costing." *The Accounting Review,* XLVIII, No. 1 (January 1973), 115–119.

Lea, Richard B. "A Note on the Definition of Cost Coefficients in a Linear Programming Model." *The Accounting Review,* XLVII, No. 2 (April 1972), 346–350.

Leffler, William L. "Shadow Pricing." *Data and Control Systems* (July 1966), 26–29.

Li, David H. "Interdivisional Transfer Planning." *Management Accounting,* 46, No. 10 (June 1965), 51–54.

Longnecker, Ray E. "Converting to Direct Costing." *NAA Bulletin,* XLIII, No. 12 (August 1962), 25–37.

Lusk, Edward J. "Discriminant Analysis as Applied to the Resource Allocation Decision." *The Accounting Review,* XLVII, No. 3 (July 1972), 567–575.

Mahoney, Thomas A., and William Weitzel. "Managerial Models of Organizational Effectiveness." *Administrative Science Quarterly,* 14, No. 3 (September 1969), 357–364.

Manes, Rene P. "Comment on Matrix Theory and Cost Allocations." *The Accounting Review,* XL, No. 3 (July 1965), 640–643.

Marple, Raymond P. "Management Accounting Is Coming of Age." *Management Accounting,* 48, No. 11 (July 1967), 3–16.

McGrail, George R., and Daniel R. Furlong. "Absorption Break-even." *Management Accounting,* LV, No. 4 (October 1973), 31–35.

McNeill, Winfield I. "Groping Through the Accounting Maze." *The Controller,* XXX, No. 12 (December 1962), 610–615.

Miller, Robert D., and Terry L. Robinson. "Performance Reports Based on Direct Costing: A Case Study." *Management Accounting,* 51, No. 10 (April 1970), 43–47.

Moffitt, Henry K. "Controlling Indirect Costs of Research and Development." *The Controller,* XXX, No. 10 (October 1962), 486–491.

Piper, A. G. "Internal Trading." *Accountancy* (October 1969), 733–736.

Raiborn, Mitchell, and William T. Harris. "Integration of Inventory and Product Sales — Mix Models." *Decision Sciences,* 5, No. 4 (October 1974), 664–668.

Robinson, Bruce, and Chet Lakhani. "Dynamic Price Models for New-product Planning." *Management Science* (June 1975), 1113–1122.

Schiff, Michael. "Physical Distribution: A Cost Analysis." *Management Accounting,* LIII, No. 8 (February 1972), 48–50.

———. "Reporting for More Profitable Product Management." *The Journal of Accountancy,* 115, No. 5 (May 1963), 65–70.

———, and Joseph Schirger. "Incremental Analysis and Opportunity Costs." *Management Services,* 1, No. 3 (July–August 1964), 13–17.

Shillinglaw, Gordon. "Problems in Divisional Profit Measurement." *NAA Bulletin,* XLII, No. 7 (March 1961), 33–43.

Skinner, R. C. "Return on Capital Employed as a Measure of Efficiency." *Accountancy,* LXXVI (June 1965), 530–533.

Sorensen, James E., and David D. Franks. "The Relative Contribution of Ability, Self-esteem and Evaluative Feedback to Performance: Implications for Accounting Systems." *The Accounting Review,* XLVII, No. 4 (October 1972), 735–746.

Spinetto, Richard D. "Fairness in Cost Allocations and Cooperative Games." *Decision Sciences,* 6, No. 3 (July 1975), 482–491.

Sunder, Shyam. "Properties of Accounting Numbers under Full Costing and Successful-efforts Costing in the Petroleum Industry." *The Accounting Review,* LI, No. 1 (January 1976), 1–18.

Thomas, Arthur L. "Useful Arbitrary Allocations (With a Comment on the Neutrality of Financial Accounting Reports)." *The Accounting Review,* XLVI, No. 3 (July 1971), 472–479.

Wright, Wilmer R. "Direct Costs Are Better for Pricing." *NAA Bulletin,* XLI, No. 8 (April 1960), 17–26.

———. "Why Direct Costing is Rapidly Gaining Acceptance." *The Journal of Accountancy,* 114, No. 1 (July 1962), 40–46.

PART SEVEN

Emerging Areas

in Managerial Accounting

Even a casual reading of recent accounting journals will alert the reader to two exciting trends in accounting. First, there is an increasing awareness in accounting of the significance of research and concepts other disciplines have developed and a greater willingness to incorporate these insights into the analysis of accounting issues. The previous sections are replete with examples of the application of behavioral science concepts and mathematical techniques to accounting problems. Second, there is a thrust toward expanding the scope of accounting beyond traditional boundaries.

Accountants have recently directed their attention toward management information systems and their role in designing such systems. Ackoff develops basic principles of management information system (MIS) design by discussing five common, erroneous assumptions underlying it. If these fallacies are not corrected, major problems result in the MIS. To avoid these problems, Ackoff suggests a procedure for designing an MIS and illustrates it with an actual market-area control system.

Gordon and Miller draw on literature from organization theory and management policy to broaden the horizon of factors that should be considered in MIS design. By examining environmental (government regulations, strikes, shortages), organizational (decentralization, differentiation, resources), and management decision style variables and analyzing their impact on the "... requisites of the accounting information system," the authors provide a contingency framework, or model, for a system design that will meet the specific needs of an organization. They then use this model to evaluate and improve MIS in three archetypal organizations.

The "Report of the Committee on Human Resource Accounting" is indicative of the second major trend in accounting, the extension of traditional discipline boundaries. It provides an introduction into the emerging field of human resource accounting. The committee surveys the major models that have been developed for measuring the cost and value of people to organizations. The report explores, among others, the works of Flamholtz ("positional replacement costs"), Lev and Schwartz (discounted future salaries), and Likert (determinants of a group's value to an organization). It also investigates the cognitive and behavioral impacts of human resource accounting on management thinking and decision-making.

There are some who seriously question the extension of the accountant's functions into new areas, particularly into the area of social program assessment. Birnberg and Gandhi clarify and evaluate the issues raised by this hotly debated topic. They emphasize that the accountant need not be concerned with broad social experiments but only specific operational social programs. An interdisciplinary approach may be required where accountants track relevant costs and other professionals track corresponding social outcomes with a joint assessment of program results.

The final article by Sorensen and Grove examines such an interdisciplinary approach in the mental health program evaluation area. First they outline deficiencies with common not-for-profit performance evaluation approaches such as social indicators, program planning, budgeting systems, and cost-benefit analysis. Then they develop operational cost-outcome and cost-effectiveness models as not-for-profit performance evaluation techniques. These models are illustrated with applications to mental health program data. The models in this example rely on costs that accountants provide and outcomes that psychologists provide. Such joint efforts are necessary as the scope of accounting expands to meet the needs of society.

26 *Five assumptions commonly made by designers of management information systems are identified. It is argued that these are not justified in many (if not most) cases and hence lead to major deficiencies in the resulting systems. These assumptions are: (1) the critical deficiency under which most managers operate is the lack of relevant information, (2) the manager needs the information he wants, (3) if a manager has the information he needs his decision making will improve, (4) better communication between managers improves organizational performance, and (5) a manager does not have to understand how his information system works, only how to use it. To overcome these assumptions and the deficiencies which result from them, a management information system should be imbedded in a management control system. A procedure for designing such a system is proposed and an example is given of the type of control system which it produces.*

Management Misinformation Systems*

Russell L. Ackoff

The growing preoccupation of operations researchers and management scientists with Management Information Systems (MIS's) is apparent. In fact, for some the design of such systems has almost become synonymous with operations research or management science. Enthusiasm for such systems is understandable: it involves the researcher in a romantic relationship with the most glamorous instrument of our time, the computer. Such enthusiasm is understandable but, nevertheless, some of the excesses to which it has led are not excusable.

Contrary to the impression produced by the growing literature, few computerized management information systems have been put into operation. Of those I've seen that have been implemented, most have not matched

* *From* Management Science, *Vol. 13, No. 12 (December, 1967), pp. 147–156.* *Reprinted by permission of the publisher and the author.*

expectations and some have been outright failures. I believe that these near- and far-misses could have been avoided if certain false (and usually implicit) assumptions on which many such systems have been erected had not been made.

There seem to be five common and erroneous assumptions underlying the design of most MIS's, each of which I will consider. After doing so I will outline an MIS design procedure which avoids these assumptions.

Give Them More

Most MIS's are designed on the assumption that the critical deficiency under which most managers operate is the *lack of relevant information.* I do not deny that most managers lack a good deal of information that they should have, but I do deny that this is the most important informational deficiency from which they suffer. It seems to me that they suffer more from an *overabundance of irrelevant information.*

This is not a play on words. The consequences of changing the emphasis of an MIS from supplying relevant information to eliminating irrelevant information is considerable. If one is preoccupied with supplying relevant information, attention is almost exclusively given to the generation, storage, and retrieval of information: hence emphasis is placed on constructing data banks, coding, indexing, updating files, access languages, and so on. The ideal which has emerged from this orientation is an infinite pool of data into which a manager can reach to pull out any information he wants. If, on the other hand, one sees the manager's information problem primarily, but not exclusively, as one that arises out of an overabundance of irrelevant information, most of which was not asked for, then the two most important functions of an information system become *filtration* (or evaluation) and *condensation.* The literature on MIS's seldom refers to these functions let alone considers how to carry them out.

My experience indicates that most managers receive much more data (if not information) than they can possibly absorb even if they spend all of their time trying to do so. Hence they already suffer from an information overload. They must spend a great deal of time separating the relevant from the irrelevant and searching for the kernels in the relevant documents. For example, I have found that I receive an average of forty-three hours of unsolicited reading material each week. The solicited material is usually half again this amount.

I have seen a daily stock status report that consists of approximately six hundred pages of computer print-out. The report is circulated daily across managers' desks. I've also seen requests for major capital expenditures that come in book size, several of which are distributed to managers each week. It is not uncommon for many managers to receive an average of one journal a day or more. One could go on and on.

Unless the information overload to which managers are subjected is reduced, any additional information made available by an MIS cannot be expected to be used effectively.

Even relevant documents have too much redundancy. Most documents can be considerably condensed without loss of content. My point here is best made, perhaps, by describing briefly an experiment that a few of my colleagues and I conducted on the OR literature several years ago. By using a panel of well-known experts we identified four OR articles that all members of the panel considered to be "above average," and four articles that were considered to be "below average." The authors of the eight articles were asked to prepare "objective" examinations (during thirty minutes) plus answers for graduate students who were to be assigned the articles for reading. (The authors were not informed about the experiment.) Then several experienced writers were asked to reduce each article to $\frac{2}{3}$ and $\frac{1}{3}$ of its original length only by eliminating words. They also prepared a brief abstract of each article. Those who did the condensing did not see the examinations to be given to the students.

A group of graduate students who had not previously read the articles were then selected. Each one was given four articles randomly selected, each of which was in one of its four versions: 100%, 67%, 33%, or abstract. Each version of each article was read by two students. All were given the same examinations. The average scores on the examinations were then compared.

For the above-average articles there was no significant difference between average test scores for the 100%, 67%, and 33% versions, but there was a significant decrease in average test scores for those who read only the abstract. For the below-average articles there was no difference in average test scores among those who had read the 100%, 67%, and 33% versions, but there was a significant *increase* in average test scores of those who had read only the abstract.

The sample used was obviously too small for general conclusions but the results strongly indicate the extent to which even good writing can be condensed without loss of information. I refrain from drawing the obvious conclusion about bad writing.

It seems clear that condensation as well as filtration, performed mechanically or otherwise, should be an essential part of an MIS, and that such a system should be capable of handling much, if not all, of the unsolicited as well as solicited information that a manager receives.

The Manager Needs the Information That He Wants

Most MIS designers "determine" what information is needed by asking managers what information they would like to have. This is based on the assumption that managers know what information they need and want it.

For a manager to know what information he needs he must be aware of each type of decision he should make (as well as does) and he must have an adequate model of each. These conditions are seldom satisfied. Most managers have some conception of at least some of the types of decisions they must make. Their conceptions, however, are likely to be deficient in a very critical way, a way that follows from an important principle of scientific economy: the less we understand a phenomenon, the more variables we require to explain it. Hence, the manager who does not understand the phenomenon he controls plays it "safe" and, with respect to information, wants "everything." The MIS designer, who has even less understanding of the relevant phenomenon than the manager, tries to provide even more than everything. He thereby increases what is already an overload of irrelevant information.

For example, market researchers in a major oil company once asked their marketing managers what variables they thought were relevant in estimating the sales volume of future service stations. Almost seventy variables were identified. The market researchers then added about half again this many variables and performed a large multiple linear regression analysis of sales of existing stations against these variables and found about thirty-five to be statistically significant. A forecasting equation was based on this analysis. An OR team subsequently constructed a model based on only one of these variables, traffic flow, which predicted sales better than the thirty-five variable regression equation. The team went on to *explain* sales at service stations in terms of the customers' perception of the amount of time lost by stopping for service. The relevance of all but a few of the variables used by the market researchers could be explained by their effect on such perception.

The moral is simple: one cannot specify what information is required for decision making until an explanatory model of the decision process and the system involved has been constructed and tested. Information systems are subsystems of control systems. They cannot be designed adequately without taking control in account. Furthermore, whatever else regression analyses can yield, they cannot yield understanding and explanation of phenomena. They describe and, at best, predict.

Give a Manager the Information He Needs and His Decision Making Will Improve

It is frequently assumed that if a manager is provided with the information he needs, he will then have no problem in using it effectively. The history of OR stands to the contrary. For example, give most managers an initial tableau of a typical "real" mathematical programming, sequencing, or network problem and see how close they come to an optimal solution. If their experience and judgment have any value they may not do badly, but they will seldom do very well. In most management problems there are too many possibilities to expect experience, judgment, or intuition to provide good guesses, even with perfect information.

Furthermore, when several probabilities are involved in a problem the unguided mind of even a manager has difficulty in aggregating them in a valid way. We all know many simple problems in probability in which untutored intuition usually does very badly (e.g., What are the correct odds that 2 of 25 people selected at random will have their birthdays on the same day of the year?). For example, very few of the results obtained by queuing theory, when arrivals and services are probabilistic, are obvious to managers; nor are the results of risk analysis where the managers' own subjective estimates of probabilities are used.

The moral: it is necessary to determine how well managers can use needed information. When, because of the complexity of the decision process, they can't use it well, they should be provided with either decision rules or performance feed-back so that they can identify and learn from their mistakes. More on this point later.

More Communication Means Better Performance

One characteristic of most MIS's which I have seen is that they provide managers with better current information about what other managers and their departments and divisions are doing. Underlying this provision is the belief that better interdepartmental communication enables managers to coordinate their decisions more effectively and hence improves the organization's overall performance. Not only is this not necessarily so, but it seldom is so. One would hardly expect two competing companies to become more cooperative because the information each acquires about the other is improved. This analogy is not as far fetched as one might first suppose. For example, consider the following very much simplified version of a situation I once ran into. The simplification of the case does not affect any of its essential characteristics.

A department store has two "line" operations: buying and selling. Each function is performed by a separate department. The Purchasing Department primarily controls one variable: how much of each item is bought. The Merchandising Department controls the price at which it is sold. Typically, the measure of performance applied to the Purchasing Department was the turnover rate of inventory. The measure applied to the Merchandising Department was gross sales; this department sought to maximize the number of items sold times their price.

Now by examining a single item let us consider what happens in this system. The merchandising manager, using his knowledge of competition and consumption, set a price which he judged would maximize gross sales. In doing so he utilized price-demand curves for each type of item. For each

FIGURE 1

Price-Demand Curve

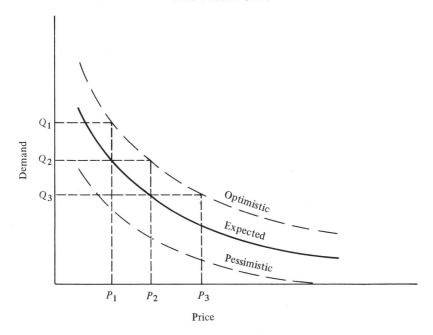

Price

price the curves show the expected sales and values on an upper and lower confidence band as well. (See Figure 1.) When instructing the Purchasing Department how many items to make available, the merchandising manager quite naturally used the value on the upper confidence curve. This minimized the chances of his running short which, if it occurred, would hurt his performance. It also maximized the chances of being over-stocked but this was not his concern, only the purchasing manager's. Say, therefore, that the merchandising manager initially selected price P_1 and requested that amount Q_1 be made available by the Purchasing Department.

In this company the purchasing manager also had access to the price-demand curves. He knew the merchandising manager always ordered optimistically. Therefore, using the same curve he read over from Q_1 to the upper limit and down to the expected value from which he obtained Q_2, the quantity he actually intended to make available. He did not intend to pay for the merchandising manager's optimism. If merchandising ran out of stock, it was not his worry. Now the merchandising manager was informed about what the purchasing manager had done so he adjusted his price to P_2. The purchasing manager in turn was told that the merchandising manager had made this readjustment so he planned to make only Q_3 available. If this process — made possible only by perfect communication between departments — had been allowed to continue, nothing would have been bought and nothing would have been sold. This outcome was avoided by prohibiting communication between the two departments and forcing each to guess what the other was doing.

I have obviously caricatured the situation in order to make the point clear: when organizational units have inappropriate measures of performance which put them in conflict with each other, as is often the case, communication between them may hurt organizational performance, not help it. Organizational structure and performance measurement must be taken into account before opening the flood gates and permitting the free flow of information between parts of the organization. (A more rigorous discussion of organizational structure and the relationship of communication to it can be found in [1].)

A Manager Does Not Have to Understand How an Information System Works, Only How to Use It

Most MIS designers seek to make their systems as innocuous and unobtrusive as possible to managers lest they become frightened. The designers try to provide managers with very easy access to the system and assure them that they need to know nothing more about it. The designers usually succeed in keeping managers ignorant in this regard. This leaves managers unable to evaluate the MIS as a whole. It often makes them afraid to even try to do so lest they display their ignorance publicly. In failing to evaluate their MIS, managers delegate much of the control of the organization to the system's designers and operators who may have many virtues, but managerial competence is seldom among them.

Let me cite a case in point. A Chairman of a Board of a medium-size company asked for help on the following problem. One of his larger (decentralized) divisions had installed a computerized production-inventory control and manufacturing-manager information system about a year earlier. It had acquired about $2,000,000 worth of equipment to do so. The Board Chairman had just received a request from the Division for permission to replace the original equipment with newly announced equipment which would cost several times the original amount. An extensive "justification" for so doing was provided with the request. The Chairman wanted to know whether the request was really justified. He admitted to complete incompetence in this connection.

A meeting was arranged at the Division at which I was subjected to an extended and detailed briefing. The system was large but relatively simple. At the heart of it was a reorder point for each item and a maximum allowable stock level. Reorder quantities took lead-time as well as the allowable maximum into account. The computer kept track of stock, ordered items when required and generated numerous reports on both the state of the system it controlled and its own "actions."

When the briefing was over I was asked if I had any questions. I did.

First I asked if, when the system had been installed, there had been many parts whose stock level exceeded the maximum amount possible under the new system. I was told there were many. I asked for a list of about thirty and for some graph paper. Both were provided. With the help of the system designer and volumes of old daily reports I began to plot the stock level of the first listed item over time. When this item reached the maximum "allowable" stock level it had been reordered. The system designer was surprised and said that by sheer "luck" I had found one of the few errors made by the system. Continued plotting showed that because of repeated premature reordering ,the item had never gone much below the maximum stock level. Clearly the program was confusing the maximum allowable stock level and the reorder point. This turned out to be the case in more than half of the items on the list.

Next I asked if they had many paired parts, ones that were only used with each other; for example, matched nuts and bolts. They had many. A list was produced and we began checking the previous day's withdrawals. For more than half of the pairs the differences in the numbers recorded as withdrawn were very large. No explanation was provided.

Before the day was out it was possible to show by some quick and dirty calculations that the new computerized system was costing the company almost $150,000 per month more than the hand system which it had replaced, most of this in excess inventories.

The recommendation was that the system be redesigned as quickly as possible and that the new equipment not be authorized for the time being.

The questions asked of the system had been obvious and simple ones. Managers should have been able to ask them but — and this is the point — they felt themselves incompetent to do so. They would not have allowed a handoperated system to get so far out of their control.

A Suggested Procedure for Designing an MIS

The erroneous assumptions I have tried to reveal in the preceding discussion can, I believe, be avoided by an appropriate design procedure. One is briefly outlined here.

1. ANALYSIS OF THE DECISION SYSTEM

Each (or at least each important) type of managerial decision required by the organization under study should be identified and the relationships between them should be determined and flow-charted. Note that this is *not* necessarily the same thing as determining what decisions *are* made. For example, in one company I found that make-or-buy decisions concerning parts were made only at the time when a part was introduced into stock and was never subsequently reviewed. For some items this decision had gone unreviewed for as many as twenty years. Obviously, such decisions should be made more often; in some cases, every time an order is placed in order to take account of current shop loading, underused shifts, delivery times from suppliers, and so on.

Decision-flow analyses are usually self-justifying. They often reveal important decisions that are being made by default (e.g., the make-buy decision referred to above), and they disclose interdependent decisions that are being made independently. Decision-flow charts frequently suggest changes in managerial responsibility, organizational structure, and measure of performance which can correct the types of deficiencies cited.

Decision analyses can be conducted with varying degrees of detail, that is, they may be anywhere from coarse to fine grained. How much detail one should become involved with depends on the amount of time and resources that are available for the analysis. Although practical considerations frequently restrict initial analyses to a particular organizational function, it is preferable to perform a coarse analysis of all of an organization's managerial functions rather than a fine analysis of one or a subset of functions. It is easier to introduce finer information into an integrated information system than it is to combine fine subsystems into one integrated system.

2. An Analysis of Information Requirements

Managerial decisions can be classified into three types:

(a) Decisions for which adequate models are available or can be constructed and from which optimal (or near optimal) solutions can be derived. In such cases the decision process itself should be incorporated into the information system thereby converting it (at least partially) to a control system. A decision model identifies what information is required and hence what information is relevant.

(b) Decisions for which adequate models can be constructed but from which optimal solutions cannot be extracted. Here some kind of heuristic or search procedure should be provided even if it consists of no more than computerized trial and error. A simulation of the model will, as a minimum, permit comparison of proposed alternative solutions. Here too the model specifies what information is required.

(c) Decisions for which adequate models cannot be constructed. Research is required here to determine what information is relevant. If decision making cannot be delayed for the completion of such research or the decision's effect is not large enough to justify the cost of research, then judgment must be used to "guess" what information is relevant. It may be possible to make explicit the implicit model used by the decision maker and treat it as a model of type (b).

In each of these three types of situation it is necessary to provide feedback by comparing actual decision outcomes with those predicted by the model or decision maker. Each decision that is made, along with its predicted outcome, should be an essential input to a management control system. I shall return to this point below.

3. AGGREGATION OF DECISIONS

Decisions with the same or largely overlapping informational requirements should be grouped together as a single manager's task. This will reduce the information a manager requires to do his job and is likely to increase his understanding of it. This may require a reorganization of the system. Even if such a reorganization cannot be implemented completely what can be done is likely to improve performance significantly and reduce the information loaded on managers.

4. DESIGN OF INFORMATION PROCESSING

Now the procedure for collecting, storing, retrieving, and treating information can be designed. Since there is a voluminous literature on this subject I shall leave it at this except for one point. Such a system must not only be able to answer questions addressed to it; it should also be able to answer questions that have not been asked by reporting any deviations from expectations. An extensive exception-reporting system is required.

5. DESIGN OF CONTROL OF THE CONTROL SYSTEM

It must be assumed that the system that is being designed will be deficient in many and significant ways. Therefore it is necessary to identify the ways in which it may be deficient, to design procedures for detecting its deficiencies, and for correcting the system so as to remove or reduce them. Hence the system should be designed to be flexible and adaptive. This is little more than a platitude, but it has a not-so-obvious implication. No completely computerized system can be as flexible and adaptive as can a man-machine system. This is illustrated by a concluding example of a system that is being developed and is partially in operation. (See Figure 2.)

The company involved has its market divided into approximately two

FIGURE 2

Simplified Diagram
of a Market-area Control System

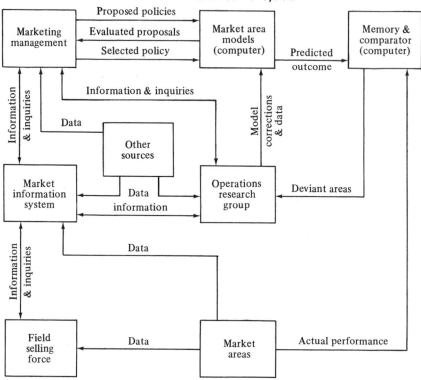

hundred marketing areas. A model for each has been constructed as is "in" the computer. On the basis of competitive intelligence supplied to the service marketing manager by marketing researchers and information specialists he and his staff make policy decisions for each area each month. Their tentative decisions are fed into the computer which yields a forecast of expected performance. Changes are made until the expectations match what is desired. In this way they arrive at "final" decisions. At the end of the month the computer compares the actual performance of each area with what was predicted. If a deviation exceeds what could be expected by chance, the company's OR Group then seeks the reason for the deviation, performing as much research as is required to find it. If the cause is found to be permanent the computerized model is adjusted appropriately. The result is an adaptive man-machine system whose precision and generality is continuously increasing with use.

Finally it should be noted that in carrying out the design steps enumerated above, three groups should collaborate: information systems specialists, operations researchers, *and managers*. The participation of managers in the design of a system that is to serve them, assures their ability to evaluate its performance by comparing its output with what was predicted. Managers who are not willing to invest some of their time in this process are not likely to use a management control system well, and their system, in turn, is likely to abuse them.

Reference

1. Sengupta, S. S., and Ackoff, R. L., "Systems Theory from an Operations Research Point of View," *IEEE Transactions on Systems Science and Cybernetics,* Vol. 1 (Nov. 1965), pp. 9–13.

2 7 *Most of the research to date concerning the de-*
sign of an accounting information system has
taken a rather narrow and inflexible view of accounting information.
The primary intent of this paper is to provide a broader and more
adaptive framework for designing such systems. The authors advo-
cate a contingency approach, which takes into account the environ-
ment, organizational attributes, and managerial decision-making
styles. In this context, they offer several hypotheses on the requisites
of an accounting information system.

A Contingency Framework
for the Design
of Accounting
Information Systems*

Lawrence A. Gordon and Danny Miller†

Problems of designing an accounting information system (A.I.S.) have long received the attention of management accountants. For the most part, the efforts to date have been directed at searching for the single most desirable method of generating financial data to promote effective decision making. Little attention has been given to the need for considering environmental, organizational, and decision making style attributes in the design of an A.I.S. Also overlooked in much of the previous work is the contingent nature of most decision making. Accordingly, this paper represents the

* *From* Accounting, Organizations and Society, *Vol. 1, No. 1 (June, 1976), pp. 59–69. Reprinted by permission of the editor.*

† The authors wish to thank all the participants at the 1975 McGill Symposium entitled "Behavioral Models and Processing Accounting Information," for their comments on a draft paper which contained some of the initial thoughts leading up to this manuscript. Subsequent comments on earlier versions of the paper by M. Bariff, J. Birnberg, H. Falk, W. Frank, D. Marshall, and an anonymous referee are also greatly appreciated.

FIGURE 1

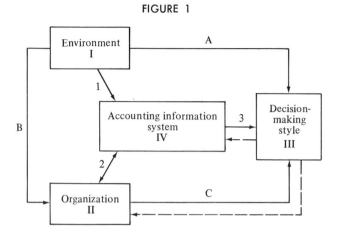

results of an effort to fill some of these gaps. Our objective is to provide a framework for designing accounting information systems which consider the *specific needs* of the organization. In order to accomplish this objective, we have drawn on the literature of organization theory, management policy, and accounting so as to isolate the environmental, organizational, and decision making variables which have been shown to be critical to organizational performance. We examine the impact of these variables upon the requisites of the accounting information system. The specific relationships considered are indicated by the solid lines in Fig. 1.[1]

The characteristics of the accounting information system, to which the environmental, organizational and decision making variables will be related are: information load, centralization of reporting, cost allocation methods (with reference to both amount and timing), frequency of reporting, method of reporting (e.g. statements, raw data, charts, pictures), time element of information (e.g. *ex ante* vs *ex post* data), performance evaluation, measurement of events (e.g. financial vs nonfinancial data and external vs internal data), and valuation methods (e.g. historical cost vs market value vs price level adjusted information).

We will also briefly discuss the relationships hypothesized in the literature among environmental, organizational, and decision style variables (links A, B, C in Fig. 1). Our discussion of these latter relationships will highlight the non-random nature of the required organization attributes and decision making styles, given the nature of the environment.

In the third section of the paper we discuss three "archetypes" empirically derived by Miller (1976) which characterize common clusterings of

---

[1] The relationships indicated by the dashed lines will not be discussed in this paper. However, we do not believe that this restriction will mitigate the thrust of the paper. Further work by the authors, now underway, does include explicit consideration of these relationships.

environmental, organizational and decision style traits. The thrust of this discussion is to relate these archetypes to the A.I.S. requisites which we hypothesize to be effective under each circumstance. The first archetype discussed is an "adaptive" firm, while the second and third portray "running blind" and "stagnant bureaucracy" firms respectively. Implications are drawn about the required features of the A.I.S. under each circumstance. These archetypes are intended to illustrate that different information systems are required according to each situation and that these systems should be designed employing a total conception of the firm and its administrative tasks. However, it must be emphasized that we are attempting to provide a *framework for analyzing* the needs of A.I.S., rather than prescribing a unique system. In fact, due to the contingent nature of a well designed A.I.S., we believe that no one prescribed system could ever be effective in all circumstances. However, we do offer several hypotheses on the A.I.S. characteristics which may be appropriate under certain conditions.

The Links of the Model

A. THE ENVIRONMENT OF THE FIRM AND THE REQUISITES OF THE ACCOUNTING INFORMATION SYSTEM

The environment of an organization can be characterized by at least the following three key dimensions: (1) dynamism, (2) heterogeneity, and (3) hostility. A discussion of each of these dimensions and their relationships with the accounting system follows.

Environmental Dynamism. Some organizations sell their products in environments where consumer tastes are stable and predictable, the technology required to produce goods or render services remains the same (or almost the same) as time passes, and competitors behave in a predictable fashion in their product-market orientations. Other firms face much more dynamic environments. In these settings, consumer tastes shift rapidly and unpredictably, new technologies and sources of supply often arise, and competitors introduce many radically new products. The same accounting information system cannot serve the needs of both these groups of firms equally well. Thus, we propose the following hypotheses: As environmental dynamism increases, the effective A.I.S.:

(a) begins to incorporate more nonfinancial data to provide managers with information on competitor actions, consumer tastes, and shifting demographic factors. Financial data alone will not provide information which is sufficiently precise to inform managers of important trends before they become crises.

(b) increases the frequency of reporting. Although Cook (1967) implies that an increase in the frequency of feedback will in general increase managerial performance, it is our contention that the relationship between frequency of feedback and performance becomes more crucial in a dynamic environment than in an unchanging environment.

(c) makes greater use of forecast information, again to inform managers of trends and important issues before they become difficult problems.

(d) is more conservative in the allocation of expenses; for example it expenses, rather than capitalizes, costs for such things as R & D, to help inform managers of the additional risk associated with projects having a long-term payoff. Thus we would tend to concur with the FASB's recommendation (1974) to expense, rather than capitalize, R & D under these conditions. On the other hand, with a stable (unchanging) environment, the wisdom of their recommendation seems questionable.

Environmental Heterogeneity. The environment of an organization might be homogeneous in terms of the required product-market orientations, consumer characteristics, production technologies, and raw materials markets. As pointed out by Lawrence and Lorsch (1967), Thompson (1967) and Khandwalla (1972a), for some organizations the environment may be extremely diverse in these respects. For example, a large conglomerate, such as I.T.T., deals in very different markets, with very different products and different required technologies, i.e., a heterogeneous environment. We hypothesize that, as the level of environmental heterogeneity increases, the effective A.I.S.:

(a) does more to tailor specific parts of the system to the sub-segments of the environment. In other words, there is greater need for more decentralized as opposed to centralized accounting systems. Some divisions of a firm may require an elaborate A.I.S. to cope with a dynamic setting, whereas others may cope with a simple system if they operate in a stable environment.

(b) compartmentalizes information so that it is possible for central management to assess the performance of the separate divisions and the personnel responsible for them. Cost, profit and investment centers are some of the compartmentalization techniques available by which to accumulate accounting information.

Environmental Hostility. A dimension closely related to environmental dynamism is that of hostility (Hermann, 1969). Hostility results from threatening actions of competitors (e.g. cut-throat competition) or threatening shortages of scarce resources due to strikes, governmental regulations or credit squeezes. We hypothesize that, as hostility increases, the effective A.I.S.:

(a) provides more frequent reports to inform managers of impending dangers.

(b) provides substantial nonfinancial data to characterize the variables most sensitive to, and indicative of, threats in the environment. As pointed out by Mintzberg (1975) one of the existing impediments to managerial use of data gathered in formal information systems is that the information is too limited in scope. Presumably this recommendation would tend to offset this impediment.

(c) employs a fairly sophisticated cost accounting and control system. Khandwalla's study (1972b), where he points out that the sophistication of a firm's control system is highly correlated with the intensity of competition in that firm, clearly shows that many firms have already recognized this requisite of the A.I.S.

B. THE ORGANIZATION AND THE REQUISITES OF THE A.I.S.

The literature on organization theory is replete with findings on the types of organizational structures required given the conditions in the environment. Woodward (1965), Lawrence and Lorsch (1967), Burns and Stalker (1961), Thompson (1967), Perrow (1970), and a host of others, have pointed to the need for more "sophisticated" organizational devices as the degree of environmental dynamism, heterogeneity, and hostility accelerate. Typical devices used by firms to cope with these more complex environments include uncertainty reduction mechanisms such as decentralization, divisionalization, differentiation of organizational sub-units, and integration of these diverse orientations via committees, rules and policies. We shall discuss five organizational attributes which derive from increased environmental dynamism, heterogeneity, and hostility, and focus upon the characteristics of the A.I.S. which are required for increasing levels of these organizational traits. The attributes, which are intended to be illustrative rather than exhaustive, are as follows: (1) decentralization, (2) differentiation, (3) integration, (4) bureaucratization, and (5) resources.

Decentralization. As the administrative task becomes more complex, sub-tasks and responsibilities must be delegated to lower levels of management to ease the burden of decision making. Thus increased environmental dynamism, heterogeneity and hostility must often be accompanied by decentralization of power and responsibilities. Such decentralization might take the form of divisionalization and/or departmentalization. Under these conditions, the A.I.S. may have to become more sensitive and sophisticated since the progress of divisions must be monitored at the top of the organization. There is an increased requirement for formal controls to replace informal controls. We hypothesize that under decentralization the effective A.I.S.:

(a) produces more explicit reports on the performance of organizational sub-units (i.e. the accounting system itself must become decentralized). As pointed out by Benston (1963), many have argued that this type of reporting system is not only the result of, but is in fact a prerequisite to, decentralization.

(b) develops substantial supporting information to enable sub-unit performance evaluation. For example, the development of a transfer pricing system will facilitate sub-unit profit evaluation. Other ways of facilitating performance evaluation, as pointed out by Abdel-Khalik & Lusk (1974), include analysis of costs and measurement of physical units of output.

(c) encompasses a sophisticated planning and control system. Decentralized firms must carefully consider how they will allocate and control their resources among divisions so that the maximum return is achieved without negating the potential motivational benefits to be derived from decentralization. In this regard, Godfrey (1971) has suggested a short run planning model for use in a decentralized firm, which recognizes the need for corporate allocation of scarce resources and also promotes divisional autonomy.

Differentiation. Some firms have sub-units which are quite similar to one another in terms of their modus operandi, time horizons, goal orientations, and the interpersonal habits of their staff. Others contain sub-units which are very different in these respects. The latter group of firms is referred to as being highly differentiated (Lawrence & Lorsch, 1967). Clearly the administrative control tasks and internal communication of the organization become much more difficult if managers with different orientations must come into contact with one another. Since they often perceive issues very differently (Lawrence & Lorsch, 1967), we hypothesize that the effective A.I.S. can help meet the challenge posed by these communication and control problems by:

(a) providing the different sub-units with an A.I.S. suited particularly to their needs. Accordingly the accounting system should be of a decentralized nature. For example, Watson & Baumler (1975) discuss the role the A.I.S. can play in facilitating the requisite degree of differentiation among organizational units via the appropriate transfer pricing system.

(b) gathering data from sub-units in a manner such that executives can assess the *relative* performance of each sub-unit. To the extent that units are very different, data collected for the top management must be chosen carefully so as not to mix "apples with oranges." Also, care must be taken so as to prevent information overload from occurring. As discussed by much of the accounting literature (e.g. Miller & Gordon, 1975; Driver & Mock, 1975; Revsine, 1970), more information is not necessarily desirable.

Integration. As the level of organizational differentiation increases, there is a greater need for more integrative devices to assure a consistent and coordinated strategic effort and avoid interdivisional conflict (Lawrence & Lorsch, 1967). Khandwalla (1972a) lists an array of integrative devices, such as: participative management, coordinative committees, explicit policies and group objectives. Thompson (1967) speaks of various modes of interdepartmental coordination, such as rules and reciprocal feedback mechanisms, which become required as the degree of environmental uncertainty (dynamism and hostility) increases. The A.I.S. can serve as a powerful coordinative device, particularly if the degree of organizational differentiation is quite high. We postulate that under these conditions the effective A.I.S.:

(a) incorporates plans and budgets which represent overall corporate targets to which each sub-unit must contribute. However, achieving goal congruency (Bierman & Dyckman, 1971) among sub-units is easier said than done and thus the difficulty of implementing this suggestion should not be under-estimated.
(b) presents information to managers of sub-units on some vital matters or parameters concerning other units. Such information should help to encourage joint problem solving among the managers of separate units, which in turn can serve to foster invaluable inter-unit communication.

Bureaucratization. Bureaucratization refers to the extent to which organizational activities are structured, programmed, specialized, and narrowly prescribed. Formal rules abound and traditional modes of operation severely limit the individual discretion of lower level managers in highly bureaucratic settings.[2] Argyris (1964), Burns & Stalker (1961), and Bennis (1966) have indicated some dysfunctional side effects of bureaucratization, such as insensitivity to the need to change strategies and employee dissatisfaction. These are particularly dangerous in dynamic environments in which individual initiative at lower levels is very much required to prompt the

---

[2] Pugh *et al.* (1963) have denoted this situation as "structuring" of activities.

organization to adjust to its external context. We hypothesize that some of the ill effects of bureaucratization can be countered by an effective A.I.S.:

(a) the A.I.S. can provide upper level managers with financial and non-financial information on the external environment. This type of information may indicate important trends requiring more flexible and situational organizational responses. Specifically, the information presented can to some extent alert the executives and motivate them to eliminate some dysfunctional bureaucratic traditions or rules. The A.I.S. can act as a "change agent."

(b) the A.I.S. can provide price level adjusted and/or market value statements, as well as forecast statements, to inform managers of conditions which require the departure from traditional modes of operation. Unlike many proponents of market value accounting (see, e.g. Romano, 1975) and price level adjusted statements (e.g. AICPA, 1969) we believe that the virtues of these valuation methods depend on the specific organizational traits of the firm in question.

Resources. While some firms have an abundance of slack resources such as managerial expertise, technocratic skills, and financial and material resources, others may experience grave shortages. We hypothesize that the effective A.I.S. can help managers to cope with these shortages as follows:

(a) if managerial expertise is known to be deficient in any area, the accounting system can be used to provide data which could better inform managers about things they otherwise would not have been able to fully understand. For example, if managers are unfamiliar with the behavior of their customers, the A.I.S. should be particularly thorough and informative in terms of the information which it provides about market characteristics and buyer purchasing patterns. Recent efforts in the area of human resource accounting (see, e.g. Flamholtz, 1974) may eventually go a long way in helping to isolate those areas where managerial expertise is, in fact, deficient.

(b) if technocratic expertise is lacking, then the A.I.S. could provide more detailed costing information such as quantity and cost variances, percentage of total costs due to scrap or poor quality, and number of units rejected because of production flaws. Such statistics would help to inform managers about the areas where production methods could be improved.

(c) scarcities in material and financial resources may also be reflected in the A.I.S. Such resources could be carefully monitored by the information system through sophisticated costing techniques, profit plans, resource allocation plans, resource utilization forecasts, and key indicators of the conditions prevailing in the financial markets.

C. THE DECISION MAKING STYLE OF EXECUTIVES AND THE REQUISITES OF THE A.I.S.

The decision making style which an executive employs to adjust his organization's orientation to the needs of the environment is critical to the well being of the enterprise. For example, where the environment is dynamic, decision makers are sometimes required to be more proactive in their decision making (Ackoff, 1969). Perrow (1970) and Thompson (1967) claim that decision making must become more sensitive and adaptive to external requirements under these circumstances. Thompson & Tuden (1959) and Wheelright (1970) argue that a simpler, less analytical, more short run oriented type of decision making will tend to take place where environments are dynamic and heterogeneous. Organizational attributes also determine the types of decision styles needed. Normann (1971) and Allison (1971) indicate how structuring of activities reduces adaptiveness and innovativeness. Cyert & March (1963) indicate how decentralization might result in less integrated, more bargaining oriented, decision styles.

We shall focus on the ability of the A.I.S. to influence the following six dimensions of decision making styles: (1) analysis, (2) time horizons, (3) multiplexity, (4) adaptiveness, (5) proactivity, and (6) consciousness or explicitness of strategies and objectives. In other words, we shall examine the manner in which the A.I.S. may eventually *change* a manager's style of decision making behavior (Hofstedt & Kinard, 1970).[3]

Analysis of Decisions. The executives of some organizations spend a great deal of time and effort studying their environment and the problems and opportunities which confront the organization. Other managers tend to make "seat of the pants" decisions on the basis of their intuition, scarcely regarding the objective characteristics of the situation. Although Mock *et al.* (1972) suggest that the payoffs from "analytical" decision making will in general exceed those accruing to "seat of the pants" executives, it is our contention that such payoffs will depend on a host of environmental and organizational variables. For example, under an extremely stable environment, the incremental costs associated with an analytical rather than "seat of the pants" approach to decision making may well be more than the incremental benefits derived. On the other hand, where environmental dynamism and hostility are substantial, a more analytical approach to decision making may become necessary for survival (although difficult to implement). In the latter case, we hypothesize that the effective A.I.S.:

(a) provides substantial non financial data on key operating trends.
(b) provides a graphical presentation of information which compares

[3] Hopwood (1974) discusses a relationship of another direction — i.e., the manner in which leadership climate, another dimension of decision making style, influences the way managers use accounting information in performance evaluation.

actual with forecasted (budgeted) figures and clearly indicates historical trends. This type of presentation may stimulate managers to further explore key issues.

(c) stores adequately detailed financial information so that in-depth analysis can be performed where deemed appropriate.

Decision Time Horizons (Futurity). Managers concerned only with day-to-day operating matters neglect to consider the long-term repercussions of their immediate decisions. It may be crucial to give serious attention to the long-term implications of decisions. Certain environmental and organizational conditions (e.g. a relatively stable environment, where certain key material resources are steadily being depleted) increase the feasibility and need for managers to take a long-term approach to decision making. Under such conditions, to provoke executives to look into the future, we hypothesize that the effective A.I.S.:

(a) presents trends, as well as data points.

(b) provides forecasts of expected events and financial variables which are critical to the operating performance of the firm. The recent (February, 1973) decision by the SEC in the U.S. to permit the filing of forecasted earnings statements should have interesting implications towards fostering the generation of this type of information.

(c) presents information on objective setting procedures which force managers to think more about goals, programs, and the future of the organization.

Multiplex Decision Making. Some corporate executives consider very few factors in making strategic decisions. For example, a manager may begin to introduce a new product on the basis of forecasted market demand, neglecting to examine such things as detailed estimates of product costs, production methods, and staff requirements. Other managers adopt a much more multiplex approach. In some environments, such as ones which are *extremely* heterogeneous and/or dynamic, a multiplex decision making orientation is probably not feasible. On the other hand, in a moderately dynamic and heterogeneous environment, multiplex decision orientation may be both feasible and desirable. Assuming the latter situation exists, the effective A.I.S. may be able to foster multiplexity by:

(a) providing both financial and nonfinancial data.

(b) supplying top level executives with information which pertains to a number of functions (e.g. marketing, finance, production) in the organization.

(c) allowing only the very crucial facts to appear on centralized reports, since, in order to prevent information overload, there is a need to sacrifice depth and detail for breadth.

(d) providing sub-unit heads with information, financial and non-financial, on the activities of other sub-units.

Adaptiveness. As dynamism increases, there is a greater need to track what competitors are doing and how consumers are behaving. Some corporate managers are quite adaptive to changes in the organization's environment, while others are not. The A.I.S. can be an extremely vital vehicle for promoting adaptiveness to external factors and internal needs. We hypothesize that, in promoting adaptiveness, an effective A.I.S. will:

(a) supply managers with information on what is going on in the external environment. Examples include information on the market share of the firm's various products, and reports of customer attitude surveys.

(b) increase the frequency of reporting so as to provide information or critical conditions before they become problems.

(c) highlight cost and budget variances and point to situations in which things are not going smoothly.

Proactivity. Proactivity is defined as the tendency to be ahead of competitors in taking certain actions. Its opposite is reactiveness in which decisions are only made upon provocation. Many managers tend to be overly conservative in their approach to decision making. They introduce new products or embark upon programs to execute technological innovations in the production process only when they have very clear evidence that they are in trouble. The absence of proactivity is especially serious in dynamic environments where it is extremely easy to fall behind the competition. To promote a proactive decision making style, we hypothesize that the effective A.I.S.:[4]

(a) includes information on the activities of competing firms. Information should be supplied on new product introductions and technological innovations being implemented in the industry. While this is hardly a standard sort of information for an A.I.S., it is likely to pay off handsomely in making managers more aware of the need for change.

(b) reports product demand forecasts (translated into forecasted revenues) and the long-run prospects for the costs of production. Such forecasts should help executives to think in terms of promising new markets and technologies which might be exploited before the old ones become uneconomical.

---

[4] Although our discussion has been concerned with the impact that the A.I.S. can have on a given decision making style, it should be apparent that this relationship is like a two edged sword. For example, Sorter *et al.* (1964) have provided evidence showing how a corporation's conservative management can unfavorably affect that part of the accounting system related to depreciation policy.

Consciousness of Strategies. Lindblom (1968) describes a type of decision making which is disjointed such that organizational decisions are made more or less independently. It is difficult under this mode to ensure that the actions of organizational sub-units are congruent with overall organizational objectives. Executives tend to maximize short term objectives and parochial interests at the expense of strategic goals and long term plans. In an environment characterized by heterogeneity, an explicit and conscious conception of decision making is difficult to achieve but is most desirable. In an effort to facilitate such an orientation towards decision making, the effective A.I.S.:

(a) incorporates a system of targets and objectives which must be met by each department. Targets relating to costs and profits, quality control, customer satisfaction and market share are all potential candidates. The objective setting process may be a participative one, with information coming from all relevant departments.

(b) compares actual results with targeted or budgeted objectives so that the performance of organizational sub-units can be appraised in light of overall organizational objectives.

Archetypal Organizations and Requisite Qualities of the A.I.S.

By now it should be clear that an accounting information system should be designed in light of the contextual variables surrounding the specific organization. Our discussion thus far was intended to generate some conceptual anchor points and related hypotheses which might provide a basis for future research and which eventually designers might use as examples in the design of their own systems. We did not attempt to prescribe a panacea system. Instead, we have been trying to establish the point that a contingency approach must be taken in designing an organization A.I.S.

In this section we discuss three "archetypal" firms discovered by Miller (1976) which represent typical agglomerations of environmental, organizational, and decision style traits. The three archetypes are (1) adaptive, (2) running blind, and (3) stagnant bureaucracy. We then relate these archetypes to the A.I.S. requisites which we hypothesize to be effective under each circumstance.

Based on Miller's analysis of the cases, *it seems that environmental, organizational, and decision style traits are not distributed randomly but actually cluster together to form commonly occurring configurations.* Thus, rather than having to worry about an unmanageable number of permutations of the variables discussed in the previous section, it appears that the designer of an A.I.S. may have only to focus on a few select variables from which a host of peripheral factors generally follow. Our emphasis here is not, however, on the derivation of the archetypes (since this is discussed at length in Miller & Friesen, forthcoming); but rather with the generation of hypotheses concerning the requisites of the A.I.S. given the existence of such archetypes.

A. THE ADAPTIVE FIRM

Several of the cases studied involved firms whose environments have been quite dynamic for a substantial length of time while heterogeneity is only moderate. In these firms, there exists much decentralization of authority, moderate to low differentiation and more than adequate integration. Managerial, technocratic, and financial resources are quite abundant. Decision making styles are characterized by great multiplexity, substantial analysis of strategic issues, an adaptive and responsive orientation to important trends in the environment, and an explicit and well defined strategy. Executives tend to be quite innovative and proactive in that they seize upon opportunities in their environment rather than waiting until they are in trouble before acting. The performance level in these firms is high.[5] A large part of the apparent success of these "adaptive" firms seems to be due to the type of information and intelligence systems which they employ.

Individuals designing accounting information systems for these firms have apparently done their jobs fairly well. The main information system characteristics which are hypothesized to be effective for such firms are:[6]

   (a) a capacity for gathering information on the external environment. Environmental dynamism makes this a particularly important feature to incorporate into the A.I.S. in firms of this sort.
   (b) the collection of non-financial, as well as financial, information (e.g. information on inflationary trends, new product ideas, technological ideas, and consumer taste trends). Again, environmental dynamism increases the importance of nonfinancial information in tracking the environment.
   (c) a uniform accounting system across sub-units. Since differentiation is low in these firms, the same type of information system can be used across the firms' divisions. A centralized, rather than decentralized, A.I.S. seems more appropriate.
   (d) an unimpeded and timely internal flow of information to departments (laterally) and levels of authority (vertically). This is important due to environmental dynamism and is feasible because of moderate heterogeneity and differentiation.
   (e) a *low* level of detail in data presented to top management. Because

[5] Performance ratings were based on growth in revenues and profits, and return on invested capital.

[6] Accounting information system characteristics were not measured by Miller (1976) in his analysis of cases. We are hypothesizing these attributes in the light of the environmental, organizational, and strategy making attributes of the firm.

decentralization has been operating successfully and resources are plentiful, top level executives need not be overly concerned with the minutia of lower level operating matters.

(f) a *broad* array of information provided to managers. This can be effective since managers in these firms tend to be multiplex, adaptive, and analytically inclined. Thus executives will themselves seek more information (which the A.I.S. can store but not distribute) if and when they feel it is needed.

B. THE RUNNING BLIND FIRM

Several of the cases studied involved firms in heterogeneous markets whose environments change markedly over a relatively short period of time. The tremendous dynamism and heterogeneity in some of these firms is created by the actions of competitors. In others, it comes about because executives have rapidly acquired new firms in very different types of markets. The organization structure of these companies is rather peculiar. Power is tightly centralized in the hands of a few top level executives. Organizational differentiation is, however, extremely high because of the manifest differences among departments, divisions, and subsidiaries. Therefore, the various orientations are not easily reconciled through integrative devices. Separate and sometimes conflicting objectives seem to be pursued by the various organizational sub-units.

The decision making styles of the managers of these firms are characterized by low multiplexity, intuitive rather than analytical decision making, and an insensitivity to conditions in the environment. Perhaps most notably, managers in these firms are quite entrepreneurial — they are proactive and take substantial risks. For example, new product lines, which require a radically new or different type of technology, are often introduced with little in-depth analysis. Also, large new subsidiaries are often acquired in businesses which are strange to the old entity.

Performance in these firms is low. The intelligence system seems to be inadequately suited to the emergent environmental conditions. The environment is scanned infrequently and only for a few select cues (e.g. acquisition candidates) by top level personnel. Controls which can inform managers of the performance of their divisions — old and new — are often lacking. Communication seems to run one way — from top level managers down to subordinates. Individual divisions in these firms are quite isolated from one another and top managers usually do not know what is happening in the divisions until crises arrive.

Designers of the A.I.S. can ostensibly go a long way in helping to reduce some of the problems in these firms. For instance:

(a) it is critical that facts be gathered about situations out of control and be sent to top management in timely fashion.

(b) information on the new products and technological innovations of competitors should be provided to help facilitate an effective style of decision making.

(c) if a great deal of power centralization makes information overload a potential problem, the onus is on the information system to provide the top managers only with critical data which reveal a situation to be out of kilter. For example, only aggregated data for each division (e.g. total expenses) should be submitted to top managers, since they can quickly scan this information. If a problem is revealed, they can ask subordinates to investigate the situation in more detail.

(d) substantial environmental dynamism requires that the information system be oriented towards gathering data on external trends (e.g., changing national economic conditions, buying trends, and competitor moves) and forecasted financial variables.

(e) the high degree of organizational differentiation and the absence of effective integrative measures make necessary the employment of coordinative mechanisms in the A.I.S. For example, profit objectives and resource allocation plans may be set up on a company-wide basis which should encourage "goal congruency" within the organization. Such an effort should foster discussions between top and divisional managers, as well as between divisional managers themselves, thus leading to greater resolution of conflicts of interests among organizational sub-units.

(f) to enable assessment of divisional performance, adequate attention should be given to developing information on sub-unit costs, profits and physical output.

(g) to help eliminate the ill effects of pursuing divisional, rather than organizational, objectives a well designed cost accounting and control system should be set up.

C. THE STAGNANT BUREAUCRACY

Several of the cases studied involved firms which have been in an extremely stable and homogeneous environment. However, dynamism and heterogeneity have recently been increasing and, unfortunately, structural and decision-making styles are still geared to conditions of the past. Organizational differentiation is very low and integration is achieved by rigid rules and programs. Power is highly centralized in the hands of top managers. Managerial and technocratic expertise seems to be lacking. Decision-making styles are characterized by low multiplexity, poor analysis, unresponsiveness to external trends in the environment, and excessive conservatism. The performance level of these firms is low. The intelligence system seems to be totally inadequate. The environment is rarely scanned for new problems or opportunities, controls are not sufficiently sensitive to highlight important trends before they become extremely troublesome, and internal communication is held to a minimum and is of an exclusively top-down nature.

The main role of the A.I.S. in these firms should be to make the enterprise more responsive to its changing environment. For example,

(a) there should be a move towards gathering information on external factors such as the conditions of the economy, new products, and trends in the market share of the firm. These factors are increasingly relevant under conditions of accelerating turbulence.

(b) reports should provide timely information on encroaching problematic trends with comparisons of future expectations to historical events.

(c) in an effort to invoke a performance orientation on the part of departments, and thus elicit pressure for change from below, a profit planning system could be established. Lower level managers will thus be motivated to change sub-optimal operating practices by putting pressure on a relatively complacent top management.

(d) price-level and/or market value statements may help provide some idea of the firm's growth potential.

(e) forecasted statements should also focus management's attention on upcoming changes in the organization's environment.

Conclusion

Most of the research to date concerning the design of an accounting information system (A.I.S.) has taken a rather narrow and inflexible view of accounting information. The primary intent of this paper has been to provide a broader and more adaptive framework for designing such systems. A contingency approach, which takes into account the environment, organizational attributes, and managerial decision making styles was advocated. In this context, several hypotheses were offered concerning the requisites of the A.I.S.

In the process of describing our framework, we have tried to integrate a small portion of the existing accounting and related literature. One thing which became apparent in the accounting literature is the fragmentary nature of the research to date. This was also noted by Hofstedt & Kinard (1970, p. 45). Hopefully, this paper will help to stimulate work on an overall framework for integrating this literature and more importantly, for coordinating future research. Indeed one logical extension of our work is the further development and testing of the hypotheses suggested.

A secondary implication of this paper is that in some circumstances the A.I.S. could act as an agent of change to improve organizational performance. In other words, it seems possible for a custom designed A.I.S. to improve poorly functioning organizations by providing information most relevant to the key organizational problems and opportunities.

We discussed the three "archetypal" firms which represent typical agglomerations of environmental, organizational, and decision style attributes. We showed that the requisites of the A.I.S. under each of these common conditions could vary greatly. These archetypes reinforced our point that a contingency approach must be taken in designing accounting information systems.

Bibliography

Abdel-Khalik, R. A. & E. J. Lusk, Transfer Pricing: A Synthesis. *The Accounting Review* (January, 1974), pp. 8–23.

Ackoff, Russell L., *A Concept of Corporate Planning* (New York: Wiley–Interscience, 1969).

Allison, G., *Essence of Decision* (Boston: Little, Brown, 1971).

American Institute of Certified Public Accountants, *Statement of the Accounting Principles Board No. 3,* Financial Statements Restated for General Price-Level Changes, 1969.

Argyris, C. *Integrating the Individual and the Organization* (New York: J. Wiley & Sons, 1964).

Bennis, W. *Changing Organizations* (New York: McGraw-Hill, 1966).

Benston, G. J., The Role of the Firm's Accounting System for Motivation. *The Accounting Review* (April, 1963), pp. 347–354.

Bierman, Harold Jr. & Thomas R. Dyckman, *Managerial Cost Accounting* (New York: Macmillan Company, 1971).

Burns, T. & G. Stalker, *The Management of Innovation* (London: Tavistock, 1961).

Cook, Doris, The Effect of Frequency of Feedback on Attitudes and Performance. *Empirical Research in Accounting* (1967), pp. 213–224.

Cyert, R. & J. March, *A Behavioral Theory of the Firm* (Englewood Cliffs, N.J.: Prentice-Hall, 1963).

Driver, Michael J. & T. J. Mock, Human Information Processing, Decision Style Theory, and Accounting Information Systems. *The Accounting Review* (July, 1975), pp. 490–508.

Financial Accounting Standards Statement of Financial Accounting Standards No. 2, Accounting for Research and Development's Costs (October 1974).

Flamholtz, Eric, *Human Resource Accounting* (Encino, California: Dickenson Publishing Co., Inc., 1974).

Godfrey, James T., Short-Run Planning in a Decentralized Firm. *The Accounting Review* (April, 1971), pp. 286–297.

Hermann, C. International Crisis as a Situational Variable, in J. Rosenau, *International Politics and Foreign Policy* (Free Press, 1969).

Hofstedt, Thomas R. & James C. Kinard, A Strategy for Behavioral Accounting Research. *The Accounting Review* (January, 1970), pp. 38–54.

Hopwood, Anthony G., Leadership Climate and the Use of Accounting Data in

Performance Evaluation. *The Accounting Review* (July, 1974), pp. 485–495.

Khandwalla, Pradip, Environment and its Impact on the Organization. *International Studies of Management and Organization* (Fall, 1972a), pp. 297–313.

Khandwalla, Pradip, The Effect of Different Types of Competition on the Use of Management Controls. *Journal of Accounting Research* (Autumn, 1972b), pp. 276–285.

Lawrence, P. & J. Lorsch, *Organization and Environment* (Harvard University Press: 1967).

Lindblom, C., *The Policy Making Process* (Englewood Cliffs, N.J.: Prentice-Hall, 1968).

Miller, Danny, Towards a Contingency Theory of Strategy Formulation. *Academy of Management Proceedings* (1975), pp. 66–68.

Miller, Danny, Strategy Making in Context: Ten Empirical Archetypes. Doctoral dissertation, McGill University (1976).

Miller, Danny & Peter H. Friesen, Archetypes of Strategy Formation, *Management Science,* forthcoming.

Miller, D. & L. A. Gordon, Conceptual Levels and The Design of Accounting Information Systems. *Decision Sciences* (April, 1975), pp. 259–269.

Mintzberg, Henry, *Impediments to the Use of Management Information* (New York: National Association of Accountants, 1975).

Mock, T. J., T. Estrin & M. Vasarhelyi, Learning Patterns, Decision Approach, and Value of Information. *Journal of Accounting Research* (Spring, 1972), pp. 129–153.

Normann, R. Organizational Innovativeness: Product Variation and Reorientation. *Administrative Science Quarterly* (Vol. 16, 1971), pp. 203–215.

Perrow, C., *Organizational Analysis: A Sociological View* (London: Tavistock, 1970).

Pugh, D., D. Hickson, C. Hinnings, K. Macdonald, C. Turner & T. Lupton, A Conceptual Scheme for Organizational Analysis. *Administrative Science Quarterly* (June, 1963), pp. 289–315.

Revsine, Lawrence, Data Expansion and Conceptual Structure. *The Accounting Review* (October, 1970), pp. 704–711.

Romano, M. B., Goodwill: A Dilemma, *Management Accounting* (July, 1975), pp. 39–44.

Sorter, G. H., S. Becker, T. Archibald & W. Beaver, Corporate Personality as Reflected in Accounting Decisions: Some Preliminary Findings. *Journal of Accounting Research* (Autumn, 1964), pp. 183–192.

Thompson, J., *Organizations in Action.* (McGraw-Hill, N.Y., 1967).

Thompson, J. & A. Tuden, Strategies, Structures and Processes of Organizational Decision, *Readings in Managerial Psychology* (Chicago, 1969).

Watson, D. J. & J. V. Baumler, Transfer Pricing: A Behavioral Context. *The Accounting Review* (July, 1975), pp. 466–474.

Wheelright, S., An Experimental Analysis of Strategic Planning Procedures, *Research Paper #26,* INSEAD, 1970.

Woodward, J., *Industrial Organization: Theory and Practice* (London: Oxford University Press, 1965).

2 8 *This report addresses the issues raised in the charge to the Committee ". . . to identify, examine, and propose alternative methods for human resource accounting. Consideration should be given to measurement and implementation problems. Special attention should be given to related research reports from economics and behavioral science publications." The report organizes and reviews issues developed in the existing literature according to three major objectives of human resource accounting: measurement, applications, and cognitive-behavioral impacts. A final section is directed toward future research strategies.*

Report of the Committee on Human Resource Accounting*

American Accounting Association
Committee on Human Resource Accounting†

Introduction

Corporate management has long suggested that the employees of an organization constitute a valuable resource. Until about a decade or so ago, however, little systematic consideration was given to the measurement of the cost or value of the human resources to an organization. The economists were the first group to show interest in the area of human resource measurement. The thrust of recent work on human capital in economics

* *From* The Accounting Review, *Vol. XLVIII, No. 1 (Supplement, 1973), pp. 169–185. Reprinted by permission of the American Accounting Association.*

† *Members:* Roger H. Hermanson, Chairman, University of Maryland; R. Lee Brummet, University of North Carolina; Nabil Elias, University of Manitoba; Eric G. Flamholtz, Columbia University; Robert R. Irish, University of Toledo; Carl G. Kretschmar, University of South Carolina; Gary A. Luoma, Emory University; Joshua Ronen, University of Chicago; Michael J. Vertigan, The University of Alberta.

has been towards the quantification of human resources at the macro level rather than from the point of view of the individual or the firm. Interest has focused on particular facets of human capital, such as investments in education and in medical care.

During the early and mid 1960's, shortly after the economists became interested in human capital, some accountants became concerned at the potential impact of ignoring a resource as significant as human capital when making financial decisions. This concern has led to the development of a new field of inquiry in accounting called Human Resources Accounting (H.R.A.).[1] H.R.A. is defined by the Committee as follows:

> the process of identifying and measuring data about human resources and communicating this information to interested parties.

The purpose of H.R.A. is to improve the quality of financial decisions made both internally and externally concerning an organization. With respect to internal decisions, H.R.A. data should result in a widening of the scope of present decision-making by permitting the consideration of a larger set of variables or improving the basis on which these variables are currently considered in decision making. Internal decision-making in an organization generally ignores the impact of human resources on both short run and long run decisions or, at best, considers the human resources on a subjective rather than a quantitative basis. The availability of quantitative data on human resources should permit their impact to be readily incorporated in the decision-making structure. This is particularly relevant so far as the capital budgeting decision is concerned. The development of an H.R.A. system should provide the data necessary to convert the "qualitative" decision-making inherent in the management of human resources into a somewhat more quantitative framework.

External users, particularly investors, *could* benefit from H.R.A. through the provision of information on the extent to which the human assets of the organization have been increased or have diminished during the period. Likert, for example, has suggested that it is possible for a firm to increase profits in the short run by actions which result in the liquidation of human assets.[2] The end result of this behavior is lower profits in later periods. Thus, the conventional accounting treatment of human resource outlays tends to distort both the asset base and the income of an organization in the year in which human resources are being liquidated.

Although some of the literature on H.R.A. refers to its use solely for

---

[1] The traditional practice of considering all human resource cost outlays as expenses is only one way of accounting for human resources. The focus of human resource accounting, however, is reflected in the definition of H.R.A. provided in the introduction.

[2] Likert, Rensis, *The Human Organization: Its Management and Value* (New York: McGraw-Hill Book Company, 1967), pp. 84–95.

management decision-making, the Committee considers this viewpoint to be unduly restrictive and considers that the development of H.R.A. should fully take into account its potential usefulness to external parties. The Committee recognizes, however, that H.R.A. will, in most circumstances, be implemented for internal purposes somewhat in advance of its use for external reporting.

The development of H.R.A. is part of the overall movement which questions the ability of accounting reports prepared under the traditional accounting model to meet the needs of the user groups. The accepted practice of regarding all expenditures on human capital formation as an immediate charge against income is inconsistent with the treatment accorded comparable outlays on physical capital. The practice of assigning a zero value to an asset was the subject of criticism in *A Statement of Basic Accounting Theory*. One of the specific recommendations contained in the Statement was that costs should be capitalized when they were incurred in order to yield future benefits and when such benefits can be measured.[3] Expenditures on personnel recruitment and training were explicitly referred to as part of this recommendation.

The field of H.R.A., being relatively new, has no clearly established boundaries. As a result, each researcher interested in the field has identified what he interprets to be the major problem areas independently from other researchers. This makes H.R.A. difficult to explain to those just becoming interested in the field. The purpose of this committee report, therefore, is to identify the objectives of H.R.A., to summarize the research conducted to date as it relates to these objectives, and to indicate areas where further research is needed. Recognizing the fact that the fruits of many suggested ideas and research in H.R.A. are yet to be obtained, this report will not be concerned with evaluating the work that has been done in this area. By summarizing the existing work in the field, it is hoped that this report will serve as a useful starting point to stimulate new research.

FRAMEWORK

The purpose of the committee's report is to deal with the major issues posed by Human Resource Accounting (H.R.A.). Broadly stated, our approach is to identify the objectives of H.R.A. and to summarize and present the work dealing with each objective. There appear to be three major objectives of H.R.A.:

1. *Measurement:* To develop valid and reliable models and methods for measuring the cost and value of people to organizations (including both monetary and non-monetary measurements),

[3] AAA Committee, *A Statement of Basic Accounting Theory* (American Accounting Association, 1966), p. 35.

2. *Applications:* To design operational systems to apply (implement) these measurement methods in actual organizations, and
3. *Cognitive and behavioral impact:* To determine the behavioral impact of the human resource accounting measurements and frameworks on human attitudes and behavior (decisions and performance).

In the subsequent discussion, the research dealing with each of these objectives will be examined.

Measurement

The statement "our loyal employees are our greatest assets," frequently made by executives, is mostly a reflection that, although these assets do not appear on the balance sheet per se, they are, nonetheless, very important to the operation of the firm. While valuable assets exist in the form of the human organization, many believe that the nature of these assets is such that any attempt to quantify them may be unreliable, costly or fruitless. We have seen, however, that more and more individuals and firms are becoming interested in quantifying this asset in some way. Several measurement models and methods have been suggested in the literature and some of them have been implemented in practice. Although a thorough evaluation of these models or methods is yet to be made, a review of the suggested measurement approaches provides an initial step.

The following is a brief discussion of measurement methods classified under cost, value and non-monetary measurement. It should be stated at the outset that although this classification is convenient, it is somewhat arbitrary. In addition, these measurement sets are not mutually exclusive. For example, opportunity cost is included as a cost measurement, although it would be equally appropriate to include it as a "value" measurement.

Cost

Historical or Acquisition Cost. According to at least one author, and probably reflecting the sentiments of a large number of accountants of today, "the development of an outlay cost system for human resource accounting should be viewed as a first step or the providing of an important first installment of a useful set of human resource information."[4]

This historical cost method has actually been used to accumulate the amount invested in human resources by at least one firm, the R. G. Barry

[4] Brummet, R. L., "Accounting for Human Resources," speech at the annual convention of the American Accounting Association, South Bend, Indiana, August 26, 1969, quoted in the *New York Certified Public Accountant,* July 1970.

Corporation.[5] Generally, the costs included in accounting for the human asset are those associated with recruiting, selecting, hiring, training, placing and developing the employees of the firm. Once capitalized, these costs are amortized over the expected useful life of the asset involved. If the asset is liquidated prematurely, losses will be recorded. If the useful life is recognized to be longer than originally expected, revisions are made in the amortization schedule. If additional costs are incurred that can be expected to increase the future benefit to be derived from the asset, these are capitalized to be amortized over the remaining life. This is, of course, the time-honored approach to accounting for the majority of assets presently recognized by firms.

Such a system for human resource accounting provides interesting implications for management decision-making. In particular, it should provide a base for evaluating a company's return on its investment in human resources and it should create an awareness of the importance of the human organization by management. The technique is easily recognizable by members of management and by accountants, and can probably be relatively objectively applied to the costs to be capitalized.

There are however, several drawbacks to the use of these measurements, not the least of which is the subjectivity associated with the appreciation and amortization of these assets once capitalized. Such a system would have to be in operation for a number of years before the total accumulation reasonably could be expected to represent the firm's total investment in human assets. Additionally, the real economic value of human assets may be significantly higher or lower than their cost.

Replacement Cost. Replacement cost of human resources has been suggested as an alternative to, and in some cases in addition to, historical cost. This is a measure of the cost to replace a firm's existing human resources. Included would be the costs to the firm to recruit, hire, train, and develop replacements to the level of proficiency and familiarity with the organization and its operations presently experienced with existing employees. Flamholtz states that such measures have at least two major classes of potential uses for management:

> First, they are useful in a variety of phases of the manpower planning and control process as principal measures of the cost of replacing people *per se.* Second, they are also *potentially* useful in developing valid and reliable surrogate measures of the value of people to formal organizations.[6]

---

[5] The system used by this firm has been described in a number of articles including Pyle, W. C., "Human Resource Accounting," *Financial Analysts Journal,* September–October, 1970.

[6] Flamholtz, Eric, "Human Resource Accounting: A Review of Theory and Research," *Academy of Management Proceedings,* Thirty-Second Annual Meeting, August 13–16, 1972.

In his dissertation, Flamholtz develops a model for measuring the cost of replacing individuals occupying specified organizational positions ("positional replacement costs"), describes an application of this model in an insurance company, and presents the data derived.[7] He has discussed the implications to accounting of such an approach and stated:

> At this point, one must admit that the data are probably relatively crude, first approximations .... It can also be argued that if such data have face-validity to management, and are used for *internal* purposes, then the standard of "relevance," as defined by the Committee to Prepare a Statement of Basic Accounting Theory, should receive greater weight than the standards of "verifiability" or "freedom from bias."[8]

Brummet states that:

> the estimated replacement costs may be monitored as added measures within the accounting system, or they may be integrated within a single system to provide the type of information most suitable to a particular management's needs.[9]

The usefulness of the measure for management purposes seems well established in accounting for all types of assets. The problem of subjectivity in the application of the technique, apparent in assessments of the approach to accounting for assets presently recognized by accountants and members of management, appears even more critical here. For example, Likert and Bowers reported that when managers were asked to estimate the cost of completely replacing their human organization, the estimates ranged from two to ten times their annual payroll.[10]

Hekimian and Jones indicate that:

> Though current replacement cost comes close to being an ideal method of asset valuation, it suffers from two deficiencies:
>
> 1. Management may have some particular asset which it is unwilling to replace at current cost, but which it wants to keep using because the asset has a value greater than its scrap value. There must be some method of valuing such an asset.
> 2. There may be no similar replacement for a certain existing asset. This situation is caused either by a changing technology, where an asset has to

[7] Flamholtz, Eric, "The Theory and Measurement of an Individual's Value to an Organization," unpublished Ph.D. dissertation, The University of Michigan, 1969.

[8] Flamholtz, "Human Resource Accounting: A Review," *op. cit.*

[9] Brummet, *op. cit.*

[10] Likert, R. and Bowers, D. G., "Organizational Theory and Human Resource Accounting," *American Psychologist,* September 1968, p. 588.

be replaced by a "new model," or by the simple fact that the asset is custom-made. We feel that a proper system of asset valuation must include a methodology for valuing assets in these circumstances.[11]

Opportunity Cost. As a solution to the deficiencies in the replacement cost method of measurement, Hekimian and Jones propose a competitive bidding process that is closely related to the concept of opportunity cost.[12]

This proposal involves an investment center manager bidding for any scarce employee he desires. The successful bidder includes the bid price in his investment base. Only scarce employees are subject to a bid price and thus only scarce employees form the asset base of the investment center. It is only when the employment in one division of an individual or group denies this kind of talent to another division that the human resource can be called scarce. Employees easily hired from the outside are *not* assets under this approach.

These authors believe that such an approach to the measurement of human resources would provide for more optimal allocation of personnel and would set the quantitative base for planning, evaluating, and developing the human assets of the firm.[13]

Elovitz takes exception to this approach and states:

> ... while I applaud the attempt to improve the generally poor job we do of utilizing the human resources available to us, the approach suggested (by Hekimian and Jones) seems to me so artificial as to impair its effectiveness.[14]

He then goes on to suggest that, as an alternative,

> top management can best demonstrate its dedication to the development of the company's human resources by recognizing each manager's moral obligation to give of himself to build his subordinates . . . .[15]

This approach, of course serves to complement the quantification of human resource variables and value.

Discounted Future Salaries. Hermanson[16] suggests a method of measuring the human resources which he calls the "adjusted present value method." It involves the discounting of expected wage payments over the

[11] Hekimian, James S. and Jones, Curtis H., "Put People on Your Balance Sheet," *Harvard Business Review,* January–February 1967, p. 108.

[12] *Ibid.,* pp. 108–9.

[13] *Ibid.,* p. 108.

[14] Elovitz, David, "From the Thoughtful Businessman," *Harvard Business Review,* May–June 1967), p. 59.

[15] *Ibid.*

[16] Hermanson, Roger H., *Accounting for Human Assets,* Occasional Paper No. 14, Bureau of Business and Economic Research, Graduate School of Business Administration, Michigan State University, 1964.

next five years at the most recent "normal" rate of return, and then modifying the result by a weighted average of the effectiveness of performances over the last five years, or what Hermanson calls "efficiency ratio."

Lev and Schwartz[17] describe the economic concept of recognizing humans as wealth — sources of income — and discuss the measurement of such wealth as the present value of future income streams. The authors suggest that such information will be valuable in determining (1) the ratio of human to nonhuman capital within the firm, (2) information about changes in the structure and age of the labor force.

This "human capital" accounting would follow the pattern of accounting for leases — the recording of both an asset and a liability in equal amounts at the present value of future wage or salary payments. The arguments once used against accounting for leases in this manner could be applied here against accounting for human resources in such a fashion. More important, however, is the distinction between the two — a lease is based upon pre-established, contractually agreed upon, future outlays for a given number of years. Subjectivity here enters only to the extent that discount rates must be determined.

In the case of human resources, added subjectivity would need to be introduced regarding level of future salary and length of expected employment within the firm. Does the discounted amount then reflect the present value of future cost to the firm from the utilization of this particular resource, or is it, instead, a conglomerate of future cost and other highly subjective considerations?

VALUE

A knowledge of the present economic value of human resources should be quite interesting and useful both to a firm's management and to interested outside parties. Economic value has been defined differently by various authors, but most authors in the human resource accounting area have defined it in terms of the discounted present value of the expected future earnings attributable to human resources.

Hermanson, for example, has developed an approach to the discounting of excess earnings of an organization, attributing this excess to the "unidentified assets," which include the human resources. The author claims benefits from the adoption of his proposal in the following areas: (1) more efficient allocation of funds, (2) closer tie-in between financial statements, (3) rejuvenation of the position statement, and (4) aid in financial analysis for internal purposes.[18]

---

[17] Lev, Baruch and Schwartz, Aba, "On the Use of the Economic Concept of Human Capital in Financial Statements," *The Accounting Review,* January, 1971, pp. 103–112.

[18] Hermanson, *op. cit.,* pp. 32–42.

Drawing upon economic value theory (and the foundation laid by Hermanson) Brummet, Flamholtz and Pyle have suggested an approach to the valuation of human resources.[19] Their approach is to forecast future earnings, discount them to determine the firm's net present value, and allocate a portion to human resources, based on their relative contribution.

Using Likert's work as a source, they have suggested using social-psychological measurements as a means of forecasting changes in future earnings. Specifically, Likert has argued that changes in so-called causal variables produce (with a lag) changes in intervening variables which, in turn, produce (also with a lag) changes in end results such as earnings.[20] Based upon these hypothesized interrelationships, Likert has suggested that if such relationships can be *validated,* then "by using appropriate statistical procedures, relationships can be computed among the causal, intervening, and such end result variables as costs and earnings. The resulting mathematical relationships will enable one to estimate the productive and earnings capacity of any profit center, or smaller unit, based upon its present scores on the causal and intervening variables." According to Likert:

> These estimates of probable subsequent productivity, costs, and earnings will reveal the earning power of the human organization *at the time* the causal and intervening variables were measured, even though the level of estimated subsequent earnings may not be achieved until much later. These estimates of probable subsequent productivity, costs, and earnings provide the basis for attaching to any profit center, unit, or total corporation a statement of the present value of its human organization.[21]

Flamholtz has focused on the problem of measuring an individual's value to an organization.[22] He has conceptualized the individual valuation problem as a stochastic process with rewards, and has presented a stochastic model for the monetary valuation of individuals. The model is based on the notion that a person is not valuable to an organization in the abstract, but in relation to the roles (service states) he is expected to occupy.

Flamholtz has assessed the convergent and discriminant validity of the model in a field study.[23] The model was operationalized in a medium-sized mutual insurance company for groups of sales and claims personnel, using

[19] Brummet, R. Lee, Flamholtz, Eric G., and Pyle, William C., "Human Resource Measurement — A Challenge for Accountants," *The Accounting Review,* April, 1968, pp. 222–23.

[20] This will be described in some more detail later in this section under the "non-monetary measurement" subsection.

[21] Likert, Rensis, *The Human Organization: Its Management and Value,* New York: McGraw-Hill Book Company, 1967, p. 150.

[22] Flamholtz, Eric, "A Model for Human Resource Valuation: A Stochastic Process with Service Rewards," *The Accounting Review,* April 1971, pp. 253–267.

[23] Flamholtz, Eric, "The Theory and Measurement of an Individual's Value to an Organization," *op. cit.,* pp. 46–113.

surrogate measures of the value of service states. The findings of this exploratory study were that replacement cost, compensation, and sales revenue each possess convergent and discriminant validity as surrogate measures of an individual's value at an ordinal level of measurement.

NON-MONETARY MEASUREMENTS

It is recognized that non-monetary measurements are and can be used for decision-making. The Committee's definition of H.R.A. does not exclude non-monetary measurements.

Although certainly not of the same nature as the items that have been discussed to this point in this section of the report, one non-monetary "measure" of the human resources of the firm relates to a simple inventory of skills and capabilities of people within the organization. This technique involves an inventory of human resources and, as such, is certainly a useful technique for purposes of personnel assignment within a firm. Similar to this approach, but usually externally oriented, is the listing of key people in an organization with some of their personal credentials, or the listing of the academic personnel of a college or university with their earned and honorary degrees and other professional recognitions.

Several authors have suggested that we might find some non-monetary behavioral measurements useful to H.R.A. The behavioral science area deals with the description and explanation, measurement and prediction of human behavior. This includes peoples' attitudes and motives as well as their actions. Most behavioral science research deals with an examination of the activities and attitudes of people and groups of people in order to discover causal relationships capable of prediction. An example of a behavioral science approach to human resource measurement has come from Rensis Likert and several of his associates.[24]

The basic thrust of Likert's work has been to investigate the relationship between the system of management used by a firm and the productivity of the organization.[25] As a result of his studies, Likert has attempted to formulate a model of the variables which determine the effectiveness of a firm's "human organization" (the groups of people that comprise the firm), and, in turn, the effectiveness of the enterprise as a whole. Since the resulting model identifies the determinants of the productive capability of the human organization, it thus reflects the value of that human organization.

This model is comprised of three classes of variables: "causal," "intervening," and "end-result." They are defined as follows:[26]

---

[24] For example, see Likert and Pyle, "Human Resource Accounting — A Human Organizational Approach," *Financial Analysts Journal,* January–February, 1971, p. 82.

[25] This model is the product of work that was first described in Likert's *New Patterns of Management* (New York: McGraw-Hill Book Co., 1961) and *The Human Organization,* (New York: McGraw-Hill Book Co., 1967).

[26] Likert and Bowers, *op. cit.*

1. The *causal* variables are independent variables which can be directly or purposely altered or changed by the organization and its management and which, in turn, determine the course of development within an organization.
2. The *intervening* variables reflect the internal state, health, and performance capabilities of the organization, e.g., the loyalties, attitudes, motivation, performance, goals, and perceptions of all members and their collective capacity for effective action, interaction, communications, and decision making.
3. The *end-result* variables are the dependent variables which reflect the results achieved by that organization, such as its productivity, costs, scrap loss, growth, share of the market, and earnings.

According to Likert, the causal and intervening variables describe the internal state of the organization as a human system. Causal variables (which include organizational structure, managerial leadership styles, and organizational policies) are believed to affect "the quality and capabilities of the human organization." In this model, the "quality and capability" of the human organization are defined in terms of certain organizational processes such as decision-making, communication, and coordination. Other so-called intervening variables are motivation and perception. Thus the causal variables influence the intervening variables, which, in turn, determine the organization's end results. (See Figure 1).

Likert states that a certain pattern of causal variables yields certain levels of intervening variables which in turn lead to certain levels of end-result variables. Furthermore, he has some research evidence to support this belief. He contends that a management style he refers to as participative management, where managers support their subordinates rather than dictate to them, yields more favorable attitudes as measured by such intervening variables as confidence and trust in superiors, ease and accuracy of communication, and group loyalties.

He has found significant relationships but feels that the end-result variables currently in use can distort the analysis by failing to include measures of changes in human resources. He further believes that human resources can ultimately be measured by predicting a firm's future earnings based on the current status of causal and intervening variables and then discounting to net present value and allocating a portion of this value to human assets. As an interim step, Likert has recommended that the status of a firm's causal and intervening variables be measured and reported periodically so that their impact can at least be considered subjectively.[27]

Flamholtz attempts to develop and empirically assess the validity of a model of an *individual's* value to an organization. This model identifies

[27] Likert, Rensis, and Pyle, W. C., "Human Resource Accounting — A Human Organizational Approach," *Financial Analysts Journal,* January–February, 1971, p. 82.

FIGURE 1

Likert's Model of Determinants
of a Group's Value to an Organization:
Schematic Relationships Among Causal, Intervening,
and End Result Variables

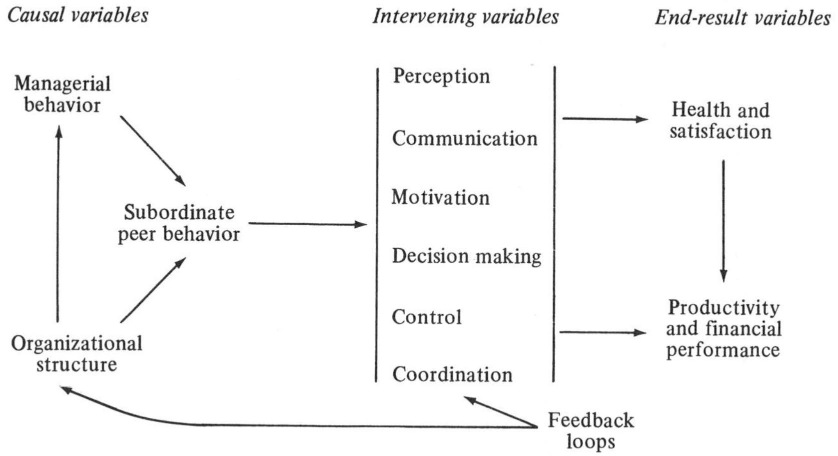

From "Organizational Theory and Human Resource Accounting," by Rensis Likert and David G. Bowers, American Psychologists, *Vol. 24, pages 585–592 (June 1969) p. 587. Copyright 1969 by the* American Psychological Association. *Reprinted by permission.*

social and psychological as well as economic determinants of a person's value to an organization.[28]

Although the model is complex, it can be described briefly: The individual brings certain attributes to the organization: cognitive abilities such as intelligence; and personality traits such as need for achievement. These individual attributes are the source of work-related value determinants: the person's skills, activation level (motivation), and attitudes. However, the individual is not valuable to a firm in the abstract; he is valuable in relation to the roles (positions) he can or will potentially occupy. Organizational attributes of structure and management style determine the roles and rewards available within the organization; and these organizational determinants interact with the individual determinants to produce the elements of conditional value (productivity, promotability, and transferability) and the person's satisfaction with the organization. Satisfaction and the latter variable (conditional value) produce the ultimate construct — the person's expected realizable value. The model is graphically portrayed in Figure 2.

[28] Flamholtz, Eric, "Toward a Theory of Human Resource Value in Formal Organizations," *The Accounting Review,* October 1972, and Eric Flamholtz, "Assessing the Validity of a Theory of Human Resource Value: A Field Study," *Empirical Research in Accounting: Selected Studies, 1972.*

FIGURE 2

**Revised Model of the Determinants
of an Individual's Value to a Formal Organization**

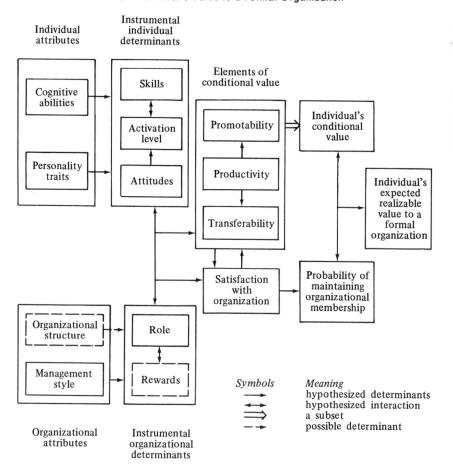

From "*Assessing the Validity of a Theory of Human Resource Value: An Exploratory Field Experiment/Study,*" *by Eric G. Flamholtz,* Empirical Research in Accounting: Selected Studies, 1972, p. 257.

Like the Likert model, most of these variables can be measured in non-
monetary terms using social and psychological measures. Thus, they can
be used as non-monetary measures of changes in the value of human
resources.

Applications of Human Resource Accounting

At present, H.R.A. is in a developmental stage. Consequently, there
have been few attempts to implement its concepts and methods. Two dif-
erent approaches have been taken in applying human resource accounting.

One approach involves the development of general purpose systems of accounting for human resources (i.e. accounting for investments in people). The other approach is to apply H.R.A. on a partial or a problem-oriented basis (e.g. for layoff decisions).

The first reported attempt to develop a system of accounting for investments in people was made at the R. G. Barry Corporation. The firm attempted to identify the cost of its investment in human resources (such as costs of recruiting, hiring, training, experience, and development). These costs were then capitalized (rather than expensed) and amortized as the value of the asset was consumed.[29] This traditional cost tracing procedure has been a useful starting point for the actual measurement of human resources.

Stimulated by the work at R. G. Barry Corporation, the Montreal office of Touche Ross & Co., Chartered Accountants, has also developed a system of accounting for investments in human resources.[30] Like the R. G. Barry system, this system is also intended primarily as a managerial tool. It has been reported that the system assists management in planning manpower needs, directing training efforts and allocating staff.

A.T. & T. is one of the organizations that has applied H.R.A. on a problem-oriented basis. As Flanders reports, they have used it in designing a system of "human resource accountability." This is a system for increasing managerial effectiveness in developing and retraining employees. "It accomplishes this," states Flanders, "by treating employee-replacement costs (hiring, training, benefits, etc.) as if they were capital investment rather than operating expense, and holding managers directly accountable for those segments of the investment that fall within their area of responsibility."[31]

Other applications of human resource accounting are also in progress. For example, Flamholtz is engaged in research at Lester Witte & Company, Certified Public Accountants, to develop an operational system of accounting for the value of people to the firm.[32]

Cognitive and Behavioral Impact

H.R.A. is expected to have both a cognitive and behavioral impact. First, it is expected to influence management's thinking about people as resources.

[29] For a further description of the R. G. Barry case, see Brummet, R. Lee, Flamholtz, Eric G., and Pyle, William C., "Human Resource Measurement — A Challenge for Accountants," *Accounting Review,* April 1968, pp. 217–224 and Pyle, William C., "Human Resource Accounting," *Financial Analysts Journal,* Sept.–Oct., 1970, pp. 69–78.

[30] For a discussion of the Touche Ross System, see Alexander, Michael O., "Investments in People," *Canadian Chartered Accountant,* July 1971, pp. 38–45.

[31] Flanders, Harold, "The A.T. & T. Company Manpower Laboratory, Circa 1971," *Academy of Management Proceedings,* 31st Annual Meeting, August 15–18, 1971, p. 205.

[32] See Flamholtz, Eric, "Human Resource Accounting: A Review," *op. cit.*

This involves attitudes toward viewing people as "resources" as well as placing a monetary value on individuals or groups of "human resources." In addition, it is expected to influence management's thinking about the management of people as organizational resources. Second, H.R.A. is expected to have an impact on decision-making involving human resources. The basic issue here is: "Will decisions be made differently if measurements of human resource cost and value are available as decision inputs?" There has been some work, including general theorizing, on both of these dimensions of the behavioral impact of human resource accounting, as examined below.

IMPACT ON MANAGEMENT THINKING

Recently, a few writers have argued that the concepts of human capital and human resource value will be the stimulus for a new way of thinking about the management of people in organizations. As Flamholtz has stated:

> At present, the management of human resources in organizations is less effective than it might be because it lacks a unifying framework to guide it. Managers have neither a valid criterion to guide decisions affecting people nor a methodology for assessing the anticipated or actual consequences of such decisions. . . .
>
> The notion of "human resource value" seems to provide one possible solution to these problems. It can serve as the *raison d'etre* of human resource management: it can simultaneously provide the goal and criterion for the management of human resources. More specifically, the aim of human resource management can be viewed as the need to contribute to the value of the organization as a whole by optimizing the value of its human assets; the effectiveness criterion can be the measured change in the value of the organization's human resources.[33]

While Flamholtz has argued that the notion of human resource *value* will lead to a new paradigm for managing people, another writer, Robert Wright, has stated that the notion of *capitalizing investments* in human resources will also lead to a new way of thinking about managing man. In his article, "Managing Man as a Capital Asset," Wright suggests that:

> A new way of thinking about the human resource is emerging. It is apparent that this reconceptualization of the only vital factor of production will have a profound impact on the way managers manage. The new set of concepts is coming as an outgrowth of the design of accounting systems adequate to measure the cost of human resources and to report manpower as a capital asset.[34]

[33] Flamholtz, Eric, "Model for Human Resource Valuation," *op. cit.*, p. 267.
[34] Wright, Robert, "Managing Man as a Capital Asset," *Personnel Journal*, April 1970, p. 290.

Wright argues that the accounting treatment of investments made in man as assets rather than as expenses will also cause management to recognize that people are truly assets possessing expected future benefits. Similarly, it will make managers more conscious of the intangible benefits created by investment in training.

IMPACT ON DECISION-MAKING

At present, there has been very little research on the impact of human resource accounting on decision making. Instead, most of the researchers in this area have either assumed the relevance and usefulness of human resource accounting data or suggested the need for future research to test its utility.

In the only published study on this problem, Elias attempted to empirically test the effects of including human asset accounting data in financial statements on investor decisions in a field experiment.[35] Elias' study focused upon three related questions:

1. Will the reporting of human assets in the financial statements on the historical cost basis cause investment decisions to be different?
2. When human assets are reported in financial statements, will investment decisions be the same for different groups with different levels of sophistication in accounting and different orientations?
3. Related to the previous question, what are the background or moderating variables that may cause decisions to be different?

Elias found that for his experimental groups, the inclusion of human asset data did affect the decisions of certain groups of subjects, but not all of the subjects. Although the differences observed were statistically significant, Elias also measured the strength of the relations among the variables by the contingency coefficient and found that it was not very strong. Finally, the attempt to identify background variables that might explain differences in decisions produced no statistically significant results.

Avenues for Future Research in Human Resource Accounting

The preceding sections of the report have identified and summarized prior research in human resource accounting. The purpose of this section

---

[35] Elias, Nabil, "The Effects of Human Asset Statements on the Investment Decision: An Experiment," *Empirical Research in Accounting: Selected Studies, 1972.*

is to indicate the future research which is required for the development of H.R.A.[36]

In brief, the areas requiring future research correspond to all the objectives of research in human resource accounting. Thus future research is required 1) to develop valid and reliable methods of measuring human resource cost and value, 2) to develop operational systems of accounting for human resource cost and value, and 3) to study the cognitive and behavioral impact of H.R.A. The specific research needs are discussed below.

MEASUREMENT OF HUMAN RESOURCE COST AND VALUE

Human Resource Cost Measurement. A major area of future research is the need to assess the reliability and validity of models and methods developed by measuring the *original* and *replacement* cost of human resources. At present, no reported attempt has been made at R. G. Barry Corporation to assess the reliability and validity of its system or the data derived. Similarly, there has been no reported attempt to test Flamholtz's positional replacement cost model. This research is an essential prerequisite to the application of these models in actual organizations.

Human Resource Value Measurement. The basic research need in the area of human resource valuation is for empirical testing of proposed methods. In other words, it is necessary to test the reliability and validity of proposed methods for measuring human resource value.

It will be necessary to test the method first proposed by Likert and later adapted by Brummet, Flamholtz, and Pyle for using social-psychological variables to value the human organization. Before this method can be used in the proposed way, it will be necessary 1) to test the validity of Likert's model, and 2) to develop techniques to operationalize the model and use it to forecast future earnings from changes in social-psychological variables.

Bowers and Taylor have recently tested Likert's model. Specifically, they tested the validity of the model's hypothesized relationships. Their findings suggest: 1) the need to reconceptualize the model because some of its hypothesized relations were not found to be valid, and 2) that the general hypothesized relation between causal and intervening variables (social-psychological variables) and end-result variables (economic performance variables) is valid. Bowers and Taylor concluded that further testing and refinement of the model is required.[37]

In order to apply this method, however, additional future research will be required. Once the model's variables have been validated, it will be

---

[36] This section draws upon Chapter 8 of Eric Flamholtz's book *Human Resource Accounting,* Dickenson Publishing Company (forthcoming), by permission of the publisher.

[37] Bowers, David G., and Taylor, James, *The Survey of Organizations* (Ann Arbor: Institute for Social Research, 1972), forthcoming.

necessary to develop methods to translate changes in causal and intervening variables into economic end results.

It is also necessary for further empiric testing of the validity of the stochastic rewards valuation model proposed by Flamholtz. Preliminary results from a test of the model's validity were reported by Flamholtz in his doctoral dissertation.

IMPLEMENTATION OF HUMAN RESOURCE ACCOUNTING

Although a few companies have pioneered the development and implementation of accounting for investments in human resources, a great deal of future research is required in this area. Research is needed to develop systems in different types of industries and determine the generalizability of models and methods used.

Although there are a few reported accounts of systems of accounting for human resource costs, there is presently no reported research on systems to account for human resource value.

COGNITIVE AND BEHAVIORAL IMPACT OF HUMAN RESOURCE ACCOUNTING

Cognitive Impact. As summarized above, several researchers have hypothesized that human resource accounting will have an impact on management's attitudes and beliefs. Others have suggested that it may have an impact on the attitudes of people being valued.

At present, there is no published work in this area. Research is needed to answer the following types of questions: Does the availability of measurements of human resource cost and value increase managements' awareness of the importance of human resources? Are managers influenced by knowing the human resource value of their staff? If so, in what ways?

Behavioral Impact. At present, the only published research on the impact of human resource accounting on decision making is Elias' study, cited previously. Further research is required to determine the impact of various human resource measurements on various types of decisions made by the different users of accounting data.

Bibliography

This bibliography is not inclusive, but it contains most of the references in the literature on Human Resources Accounting.

Alexander, Michael O., "Investments in People," *Canadian Chartered Accountant,* July, 1971.

Andrews, Frederic, "Proposed Measurement of Corporate Goodwill May Curb Acquisitions," *Wall Street Journal,* February 27, 1970, p. 1.

1969 Annual Report: R. G. Barry Corporation, Columbus, Ohio.

1970 Annual Report: R. G. Barry Corporation, Columbus, Ohio.

1971 Annual Report: R. G. Barry Corporation, Columbus, Ohio.

Arnold, John D., "Consider the 'acquired' executive," *Financial Executive,* January, 1970, pp. 18–23.

Bailey, Andrew D. Jr., and Gray, Jack, "A Study of the Importance of the Planning Horizon on Reports Utilizing Discounted Future Cash Flows," *Journal of Accounting Research,* Spring, 1968, pp. 98–105.

Becker, Gary S., *Human Capital.* (New York: Columbia University Press, 1964).

————. "Investment in Human Capital: A Theoretical Analysis," *The Journal of Political Economy,* Supplement, October, 1962, pp. 9–49.

Berg, Ivar, *Education and Jobs: The Great Training Robbery.* (New York: Praeger Publishers, 1970), Chapter 9.

Blaine, E., and Stanbury, W. T., "Accounting for Human Capital," Education and Training, Gray, G. C. P., editor, *Canadian Chartered Accountant,* January, 1971, pp. 68–72.

Blaug, M., *Economics of Education: A Selected Annotated Bibliography.* (Oxford: Pergamon Press, 1966).

Bowers, D. G., and Seashore, S., "Predicting Organizational Effectiveness with a Four Factor Theory of Leadership," *Administrative Science Quarterly,* 1966, 11(2), pp. 238–263.

Bowman, Mary Jean, "The Human Investment Revolution in Economic Thought," *Sociology of Education,* Spring, 1966, pp. 111–137.

Brummet, R. Lee, "Accounting for Human Resources," *Journal of Accountancy,* December, 1970, pp. 62–66.

————. " Accounting for Human Resources," *The New York Certified Public Accountant,* July, 1970, pp. 547–555.

————. "Human Resource Management," *Exploring the Frontiers of Administration.* Ed. Edwards, George A. (Toronto: Faculty of Administrative Studies, York University, 1970), pp. 25–32.

————. Flamholtz, Eric G., and Pyle, William C., "Human Resource Measurement — A Challenge for Accountants," *The Accounting Review,* April, 1968, pp. 217–224.

————., ————., ————. "Accounting for Human Resources," *Michigan Business Review,* March, 1968, pp. 20–25.

————., ————., ————. *Human Resources Accounting: Development and Implementation in Industry.* (Ann Arbor: Foundation for Research on Human Behavior, 1969).

————., ————., ————. "Human Resource Myopia," *Monthly Labor Review,* January, 1969, pp. 29–30.

————., ————., ————. "Human Resource Accounting in Industry," *Personnel Administration,* July-August, 1969, pp. 34–46.

————., ————., ————. "Human Resource Accounting: A Tool to Increase Managerial Effectiveness," *Management Accounting,* August, 1969, pp. 12–15.

"How Much is the Help Worth?" *Business Week,* December 27, 1969, p. 37.

Catlett, George R. and Olson, Norman O., *Accounting for Goodwill.* AICPA Accounting Research Study No. 10 (New York: AICPA, 1968).

Cullather, James L., "The Missing Asset: Human Capital," *Mississippi Journal of Business and Economics,* Spring, 1967, pp. 70–73.

Dean, Joel, "Does Advertising Belong in the Capital Budget," *Journal of Marketing,* October 1966, p. 17.

Denison, Edward F., "Education, Economic Growth, and Gaps in Information," *Journal of Political Economy,* Supplement, October, 1962, pp. 124–128.

Doty, Jack H., "Human Capital Budgeting: Maximizing Returns on Training Investment," *Industrial Engineering,* March–April, 1965, pp. 139–145.

Eggers, H. C., "The Evaluation of Human Assets," *Management Accounting,* November, 1971, pp. 28–30.

Elias, Nabil S., *The Impact of Accounting for Human Resources on Decision-Making: An Exploratory Study.* Unpublished Doctoral Dissertation, University of Minnesota, 1970.

————. "Some Aspects of Human Resource Accounting," *Cost and Management,* November–December, 1971, pp. 38–43.

————. "The Effects of Human Asset Statements on the Investment Decision: An Experiment," *Empirical Research in Accounting: Selected Studies,* 1972 (forthcoming).

————. "Human Resource Measurement and Socio-Psychological Variables," A paper presented at the 56th Annual Meeting of the American Accounting Association, Salt Lake City, Utah, August, 1972.

Elovitz, David, "From the Thoughtful Businessman," *Harvard Business Review,* May–June, 1967, p. 59.

Flamholtz, Eric G., *The Theory and Measurement of an Individual's Value to an Organization.* Unpublished Doctoral Dissertation, University of Michigan, 1969.

————. "A Model for Human Resource Valuation: A Stochastic Process With Service Rewards," *The Accounting Review,* April, 1971, pp. 253–267.

————. "On the Use of the Economic Concept of Human Capital in Financial Statements: A Comment," *The Accounting Review,* January, 1972, pp. 148–152.

————. "Toward a Theory of Human Resource Value in Formal Organizations," *The Accounting Review,* 1972 (forthcoming).

————. "Assessing the Validity of a Theory of Human Resource Value: A Field Study," *Empirical Research in Accounting: Selected Studies,* 1972 (forthcoming).

————. "Human Resource Accounting: A Review of Theory and Research," *Academy of Management Proceedings,* Thirty-Second Annual Meeting, August 13–16, 1972 (forthcoming).

————. "Should Your Organization Attempt to Value Its Human Resources?" *California Management Review,* Winter, 1971, pp. 40–45.

Flanders, Harold, "The A.T. & T. Company Manpower Laboratory, Circa 1971," *Academy of Management Proceedings,* 31st Annual Meeting, August 15–18, 1971.

————. "As I See It," *Forbes,* April 1, 1970.

Gilbert, Michael H., "The Asset Value of the Human Organization," Management Accounting, July 1970, pp. 25–28.

Gynther, Reg. S., "Some Conceptualizing on Goodwill," *Accounting Review,* April, 1969, pp. 247–255.

Hansen, W. Lee, "Total and Private Rates of Return to Investment in Schooling," *Journal of Political Economy,* April, 1963, pp. 128–140.

Hekimian, James S. and Jones, Curtis H., "Put People On Your Balance Sheet," *Harvard Business Review,* January–February, 1967, pp. 105–113.

————., ————. "From the Thoughtful Businessman," *Harvard Business Review,* May–June, 1967, p. 59, 188–189.

Hermanson, Roger H., *Accounting For Human Assets,* Occasional Paper No. 14 (East Lansing: Bureau of Business and Economic Research, Michigan State University, 1964).

————. *A Method for Reporting All Assets and the Resulting Accounting and Economic Implications,* Unpublished Doctoral Dissertation, Michigan State University, 1963.

Hyatt, Jim, "R. G. Barry Includes Its Employees' Value on Its Balance Sheet," *The Wall Street Journal,* April 3, 1970, p. 14.

Kelley, Roger T., "Accounting in Personnel Administration," *Personnel Administration,* May–June, 1967, pp. 24–28.

Kiker, B. F., "The Historical Roots of the Concept of Human Capital," *Journal of Political Economy,* October, 1966, pp. 481–499.

————. *Investment in Human Capital.* (Columbia, S. C.: University of South Carolina Press, 1971).

Kollaritsch, Felix P., "Future Service Potential Value," *Journal of Accountancy,* February, 1965, pp. 57–62.

Lev, Baruch and Schwartz, Aba, "On the Use of the Economic Concept of Human Capital in Financial Statements," *The Accounting Review,* January, 1971, pp. 103–112.

————, ————. "On the Use of the Economic Concept of Human Capital in Financial Statements: A Reply," *The Accounting Review,* January, 1972, pp. 153–154.

Likert, Rensis, *New Patterns of Management* (New York: McGraw-Hill, 1961).

————. *The Human Organization: Its Management and Value* (New York: McGraw-Hill, 1966).

————. "A Technique for the Measurement of Attitudes," *Archives of Psychology,* 1932, 140, pp. 1–55.

————. "Measuring Organizational Performance," *Harvard Business Review,* March–April, 1968, pp. 41–50.

————. "Human Organizational Measurements: Key to Financial Success," *Michigan Business Review,* May, 1971, pp. 1–5.

Likert, Rensis and Bowers, David G., "Organizational Theory and Human Resource Accounting," *American Psychologist,* September, 1968, pp. 585–592.

Likert, Rensis, Bowers, David G. and Norman, Robert M., "How to Increase a Firm's Lead Time in Recognizing and Dealing with Problems of Managing Its Human Organization," *Michigan Business Review,* January, 1969, pp. 12–17.

Likert, Rensis and Seashore, Stanley E., "Making Cost Control Work," *Harvard Business Review,* pp. 96–108.

Likert, Rensis and Pyle, William C., "A Human Organizational Measurement Approach," *Financial Analysts Journal,* January–February, 1971, pp. 75–84.

————., ————. "People are Capital Investments at R. G. Barry Corp.," *Management Accounting,* November, 1971, pp. 53–55, 63.

Maslow, Abraham H., *Eupsychian Management* (Homewood: Richard D. Irwin, Inc. and the Dorsey Press, 1965), pp. 216–219.

Miles, Raymond E., "Human Relations or Human Resources?" *Harvard Business Review,* July–August, 1965, pp. 148–163.

Mincer, Jacob, "On-the-Job Training: Costs, Returns, and Some Implications," *Journal of Political Economy,* Supplement, October, 1962, pp. 50–79.

Mullins, Peter L., "The Price Tag on Employee Transfers," *Personnel,* March–April, 1969, pp. 34–39.

Mushkin, "Health as an Investment," *Journal of Political Economy,* Supplement, October, 1962, pp. 129–157.

Norton, Hugh S. and Kiker, B. F., "The Public Utility Concept and Human Capital," *Public Utilities Fortnightly,* April 11, 1968, pp. 15–21.

Oi, Walter Y., "Labor as a Quasi-Fixed Factor," *Journal of Political Economy,* December 1962, pp. 538–555.

Paine, Frank T., "Human Resource Accounting: The Current State of the Question," *The Federal Accountant,* June, 1970, pp. 57–67.

Pyle, William C., "An Accounting System for Human Resources," *Innovation,* Number 10, 1970, pp. 46–54.

————. "Monitoring Human Resources — on Line," *Michigan Business Review,* July, 1970, pp. 19–32.

————. "Human Resource Accounting," *Financial Analysts Journal,* September–October, 1970, pp. 69–78.

————. "Customer Resource Accounting," May, 1968 (Institute for Social Research, The University of Michigan, Unpublished Report).

Radar, Lawrence Al, "A Stock in a Company is People," *Financial Analysts Journal,* September–October, 1969, pp. 105–108.

Report To Management, "Price-Tagging Company's Human Resources," *The Iron Age,* April 25, 1968, p. 25.

Richmond, Herbert J., "People Building," *Financial Executive,* June 1970, pp. 23–29.

Rosen L. S. and Schneck, R. E., "Some Behavioral Consequences of Accounting Measurement Systems," *Cost and Management,* October, 1967, pp. 6–16.

Schoonmaker, Alan N., "Why Mergers Don't Jell: The Critical Human Elements," *Personnel,* September–October, 1969, pp. 39–48.

Schultz, Theodore, W., "Investment in Human Capital," *American Economic Review,* March, 1961, pp. 1–17.

———. "Reflections on Investment in Man," *Journal of Political Economy,* Supplement, October, 1962, pp. 1–8.

———. *Investment in Human Capital: The Role of Education and of Research* (New York: The Free Press, 1971).

———. "Capital Formation by Education," *Journal of Political Economy,* December, 1960, pp. 571–584.

Singer, Henry, A., "The Impact of Human Resources on Business," *Business Horizons,* April, 1969, pp. 53–58.

Sjaastad, Larry A., "The Costs and Returns of Human Migration," *Journal of Political Economy,* Supplement, October, 1962, pp. 80–93.

Smith, William H., "Putting People in the Financial Statement is the Aim of Human Resource Accounting," *The Carolina Financial Times,* June 8, 1970, p. 1.

Spencer, Daniel L. and Woroniak, Alexander, *The Transfer of Technology to Developing Countries,* Chapter 6, Training and Human Capital by Neil W. Chamberlain. (New York: Frederick A. Praeger, Publishers).

Stigler, "Information in the Labor Market," *Journal of Political Economy,* Supplement, October, 1962, pp. 94–105.

Thurow, Lester, *Investment in Human Capital (Belmont: Wadsworth, 1970).*

Weisbrod, Burton A., "Education and Investment in Human Capital," *Journal of Political Economy,* Supplement, October, 1962, pp. 106–123.

———. "The Valuation of Human Capital," *Journal of Political Economy,* October, 1961, pp. 425–36.

Woodruff, R. L., Jr., "Human Resource Accounting," *Canadian Chartered Accountant,* September, 1970, pp. 156–161.

———. "What Price People," *The Personnel Administrator,* January–February, 1969.

Woodruff, Robert L. Jr., and Whitman, Robert G., "The Behavioral Aspects of Accounting Data for Performance Evaluation at the R. G. Barry Corporation (With Special Reference to Human Resource Accounting)," *The Behavioral Aspects of Accounting Data For Performance Evaluation.* Ed. Thomas J. Burns. (Columbus: College of Administrative Science, The Ohio State University, 1970), pp. 1–33.

Woodruff, Robert L. Jr., Whitman, Robert G., and Brummet, R. Lee., "Discussion: R. G. Barry Human Resource Accounting," *The Behavioral Aspects of Accounting Data For Performance Evaluation.* Ed. Thomas J. Burns. (Columbus: College of Administrative Science, The Ohio State University, 1970), pp. 35–47.

Wright, Robert, "Managing Man as a Capital Asset," *Personnel Journal,* April, 1970, pp. 290–298.

29

A conflict currently exists in accounting concerning the propriety of extending the accountant's function to include the assessment of social programs. This paper attempts to clarify the issues of debate and evaluate the various points of view. The first two sections discuss the social science literature on evaluation problems and activities. The following two sections focus on the accountant's role in various evaluation activities. The concluding section offers a schema of the process that can be applied in the evaluation of social programs.

Toward Defining the Accountant's Role in the Evaluation of Social Programs*

Jacob G. Birnberg and Natwar M. Gandhi

Currently a debate is surging on in the accounting literature concerning the extension of the accountant's functions into the area of assessment of programs. On one side of the debate we have enthusiastic accountants who have declared that "as it has done for the private sector of the economy, the accounting profession can help significantly to enhance efficiency in the public sector. . . . For CPAs to participate in this aspect of our rapidly evolving social structure, we should aggressively seek out the challenges. By so doing, we will demonstrate our ability to make significant contributions to social measurement." (Linowes, 1968, p. 42) They also contend that "the American accounting profession and business management — working in tandem for the first time with the social scientists — have all the know-how needed to begin a 'turn-around' for the public sector. Together they can create social investments that can finally begin showing desperately needed profits: improving the quality of life in the United States." (Linowes, 1971, p. 14)

* *From* Accounting, Organizations and Society, *Vol. 1, No. 1 (June, 1976) pp. 5–10. Reprinted by permission of the editor.*

On the other side of the debate, however, there are those who take a different and dim view of the accountant's role in the evaluation of social programs. For example, Francis (1973) contends that the accountant has no professional training or acknowledged expertise to understand social ills. He therefore will be a poor guide in the processes of planning as well as of evaluation of social programs designed to eradicate these ills. Further he has too limited a stock of statistical skills to attest professionally to the veracity of data collected in conjunction with the evaluation of social programs. Thus, Francis (1973, p. 250) concludes that "the question is, given that independent auditing bodies should be established, does the accountant possess the training or experience to qualify him over others to audit in the social arena? The evidence seems to indicate that the answer to this question is negative."

Such a position predictably led to a series of comments from accountants (see Granof & Smith, 1974; McRae, 1973). They for their turn enumerated the strengths of accountants and after the rejoinder by Sobel & Francis (1974) we are at an impasse. The basic issue in this debate concerning the accountant's role in evaluation of the social programs is a very simple one: How well can we transplant the well-tested accounting evaluation techniques of the profit-oriented business entities into the environment of the not-for-profit social programs? Is there anything sufficiently unique about social programs such that the accounting evaluation process which flourishes in a profit-oriented business environment would necessarily languish in them?

In this paper we intend to clarify the issues and assess the appropriateness of various views so that the benefits of such an interdisciplinary exchange are not lost in partisan rancor. To do this we will return in the first section to some of the earlier literature on evaluation research and place arguments in perspective. In the second section we will review the current issues and in the final section we will suggest that evaluation research and the management of social programs require the combined talents of all parties to the discussion.

A Brief Review of Evaluation Research

The literature concerned with the evaluation of social programs considers two types of evaluation decisions. One is the program's *effectiveness* wherein the primary question is: Did the program achieve its goals? The other is the program's *efficiency* wherein the primary question is: At what economic costs were the program goals achieved? (For a discussion see Rossi & Williams, 1972.) It is therefore of significance that at the outset we separate any evaluation discussion into its two components — effectiveness and efficiency. These are separable issues measurable in different ways and in different dimensions.

EVALUATION PROBLEMS

It is also instructive to note what the evaluation literature does *not* discuss. The authors in that area have little concern for the fiduciary aspects inherent in the funding of any social program (see for example, Perloff *et al.,* 1975). Moreover, once the activity is no longer classified as a program — something that is experimental or tentative in nature — the evaluation researchers are not likely to find it of much interest. Their interests are primarily in research evaluation and not in administrative evaluation where the focus is primarily retrospective and the assessment is in terms of specific practices and decisions, operating costs and immediate pay-offs, and statutory compliance and efficiency. In research evaluation, however, the focus is on the future and primary emphasis is on the generalizable knowledge. Thus for the social scientists–researchers the administration of the programs is something of an inconvenience that they must tolerate. As Nelson (1975, p. 707) complains of the psychologist-researchers, they assume "an arrogant, distant, and academic stance, involving themselves with occupying nonadministrative functions."

Further, even in research evaluation the social scientists have yet to solve certain fundamental problems whose solutions are crucial to the evaluation of the effectiveness of any social programs. Gorham (1967) has identified these problems, and we summarize them below:

1. Problem of Definition of the Objectives. In many programs from their broad social objectives mandated in the enabling legislation it is not clear *what* precisely should be the outcome of the programs and *what* precisely should an evaluator measure as benefits of the programs. The identification of the specific program benefits is a prerequisite both to the program administration as well as to the program evaluation.

2. Problem of Measurement of the Results. Even if we were able to specify what specific benefits a program should strive for the problem of their measurement still remains. The measurement problem is two-fold: (a) Many of these programs are wide in scope and diversity. They reach a variety of people in different socioeconomic segments in various geographic locations. Each recipient segment has a different utility function for the program benefits. Thus, there is a need for devising a measurement scheme which would attach different weights to the benefits accruing to different groups. (b) In the social arena we have a variety of programs dealing in such diverse fields as health, education, welfare, housing, etc. Even though they all have to compete against each other for funding, their benefits are in different dimensions and inherently incommensurable. "The incommensurability of the benefits makes it difficult for cost–benefit analysis to contribute greatly to the choices that must be made. . . ." (Gorham, 1967, p. 7)

3. Problem of the Lack of Follow-up Information. Even if we were to solve the problems identified in (1) and (2) above, there is just not enough relevant information now available concerning the effects of the social programs to conduct an effective evaluation process. Even in case of certain programs which are several years old by now, there is no relevant data-base available from which the evaluation indicators can be derived. As Drew (1967, p. 11) puts it so well: "Whatever the files and computers do contain, there is precious little in them about how many and whom the programs are reaching, and whether they are doing what they are supposed to do."

EVALUATION ACTIVITIES

It would appear that there are four evaluation activities which are ongoing in the not-for-profit sector as social programs are developed, implemented, evaluated, rejected or continued on a relatively permanent basis. These are:

(1) Assessing program *effectiveness.* Measuring the discrepancy, positive or negative, between the program's broad social objectives and its accomplishments. This is a macro-level analysis.

(2) Assessing *program efficiency.* Measuring the operating performance by which the program utilized its resources in pursuing the objectives discussed in (1). This is a micro-level analysis.

(3) Assessing program *compliance* with statutory requirements. Checking whether the program is carried out in accordance with the legislative mandate and guidelines.

(4) Assessing administrative *efficiency.* Evaluating the administrative performance with a concern for the behavior of personnel rather than a program as discussed in (2). This is also a micro-level analysis.

As Wholey (1972) suggests, the evaluative activities are generally carried on at two levels in the hierarchy: (i) From the perspective of the policy makers, i.e. top-administrators and/or legislators, who are concerned with the legislative changes and budget levels; and (ii) from the perspective of the program managers who are concerned with the immediate planning–management-control processes.

From the perspective of the policy makers the evaluation generally concentrates on both assessing the total impact of the existing programs and analyzing the results of field experiments and demonstration projects which may be the forerunners of new programs. This evaluation is holistic in nature, and what impact it has on the actual administration of these programs is purely a matter of conjecture. For example, in the case of the

Labor Department, according to Wholey (1972, p. 363), evaluation of the impact of national programs plays almost no part in their day-to-day administration. Worse yet, "even *if* reliable and valid data *were* being generated in the national program impact studies being done, such studies are not appropriate support for the types of decisions actually made within the Labor Department. National program impact evaluation studies circulate from office to office in the Labor Department without being acted upon or in most cases even read, because Labor Department administrators do not make the types of decisions which these studies are designed to support."

The most salient point emerging from the literature is that even the most relevant evaluation studies conducted to assess the effectiveness of the social programs are quite seriously limited in their impact on the crucial decisions concerning resource allocation. There are powerful political as well as structural forces which bear heavily on these decisions when they are being deliberated upon in the legislative as well as administrative bodies. In general the aims of a social policy or well-documented warnings of an appropriate evaluation are subordinated to the exigencies of political considerations. Thus the real enemy of even the most valuable evaluation studies is the very nature of American political process. As Coleman (1973) points out: "Probably because of the fragmentation of power, the principal deliberations in the formulation of policy are often deliberations about what strategies will generate enough support to enable passage of legislation, rather than deliberations about social consequences of the legislation."

The Accountant and Various Evaluation Activities

It is clear from the outset that Francis (1973, pp. 249–250) is concerned with the first evaluation activity — assessing the program effectiveness as a social experiment at the macro-level. Her interests are in research evaluation and not in administrative evaluation. Her stressing of the limitations of the accountant as a social scientist and statistician are most telling on this point and would appear to carry the point to even the most reluctant critic. Significantly, even Granof & Smith (1974, pp. 824–825) carefully qualify conditions under which the accountant could assist. These qualifications deal with data certification not data analysis, and the latter is an important problem in the evaluation of any social experiment.

In the second evaluation activity — program efficiency — there appears to be a question of definition. When does a social program of an experimental nature end and a social program on a relatively permanent basis begin? If, for purposes of discussion, we suppose that program efficiency refers to the period during which the macro-level statistical analysis of the program effectiveness is ongoing, then Francis (1973) is correct and the accountants have little part in evaluating the efficiency of the programs.

The accountant's function is at best fiduciary and this is quite different from assessing the efficiency of the program. However, it must be noted that judging from the past records even the social scientist is in a blind alley too when it comes to the evaluation of the experimental programs.

The third evaluative activity — assessing program compliance with the statutory requirements — is fiduciary in nature and clearly the province of accountants and lawyers. This is an area where accounting expertise is needed. As Thomas (1975, pp. 8–10) quite correctly points out, in the conduct of social programs the higher social goals should be obtained not by ignoring the requirements specified in the enabling legislation but only within the statutory guidelines provided. The fiduciary reporting and financial controls are important parts of the evaluation process. This is particularly so when Federal funds are involved but the actual expenditure of funds is in the local hands. For example, "the best that can be said for the manpower programs that engaged private employers is that the performance record is mediocre. The firms that accepted performance contracts to teach the hard-to-teach have folded their tents and slipped away. There are many reports of sharp practices, shoddy workmanship, and outright fraud involving real estate brokers and builders working with federal funds to provide housing for poor families." (Ginzberg & Solow, 1974, p. 218)

Given the decentralized nature of so many social programs the assessing of statutory compliance is important to the proper management of social programs. Funding authorities must encourage the proper utilization of resources and take the necessary steps to ensure this. Toward this end the Federal government typically provides funds and sets forth basic guidelines as to how these funds are to be used. The funds and guidelines are disseminated to the operating units and the management of the program is generally left in the hands of local officials. Thus to make a social program operationally viable requires not only the cooperation of the local beneficiary population but also of the local authorities for it may be the latter who actually operate the programs.

Further, the local authorities operating the program may have a different perception of the social ills and of the goals of the program designed to eradicate the ills than the Federal government who originated, designed and funded the program. This critical delegation of responsibility between the design stage and the implementation stage may be a fatal blow to the original purposes of the program unless the strong fiduciary controls exist to ensure the statutory compliance. Here the accounting function can provide regular feedback information concerning the actual administration of the program and assure its adherence to the statutory guidelines.

The fourth evaluative activity — assessing the administrative efficiency — is usually ignored by the social scientist-researchers. It is realistic to assume that the managerial accountant is in a position to assist the program managers. Indeed a significant literature has already evolved in this area as accountants identified with "for-profit" firms shift their attention in varying degrees to the not-for-profit agencies (e.g. Anthony & Herzlinger, 1975; Livingstone & Gunn, 1974). It would appear to belabor the obvious to argue in favor of the role of the accountant in this area.

Toward a Cooperative View of the Evaluation Process

What then is the essence of the exchanges? First, that the accountant's role is not in assessing the effectiveness of the social programs is clear. This is the province, as Francis (1973, pp. 249–250) has noted, of a particular subset of social scientists who are adequately trained in *both* the social sciences and the appropriate statistical techniques. The resource allocation issue to which Francis (1973, p. 245) alludes is not a measurement of program effectiveness. Rather, it is a question of social policy and politics where the issues are complex and there is little firm knowledge available on which to base policy.

Granof & Smith (1974, pp. 824–825) are correct in stressing the relevance of the accountants in the compliance function when the goals can be stated operationally. This can create a potential conflict between the researchers for whom the efficacy of the program is open to question and the auditor for whom compliance is of essence. This conflict which is stressed by Sobel & Francis (1974, pp. 829–830) is the crux of the difference between the evaluation of a program's effectiveness as a social experiment and a compliance audit by the G.A.O. Perhaps it is on this point that the orientation of the two groups may never be reconcilable.

In the arena of social programs at this juncture, given the state of evaluation art and the overwhelming political nature of decision-making, we contend that the evaluation process should be reoriented. There should *also* be a major emphasis on the micro-level analysis and statutory compliances as identified in the evaluation activities (2), (4) and (3) respectively. We believe that the accountant can contribute most to these evaluation activities which together form what may be described as "administrative evaluation" as distinguished from "research evaluation."

However, as Granof & Smith (1974, p. 825) point out, "the accountant can make a substantial contribution to the evaluation of social programs so long as their goals are stated operationally." Thus there is an operational bias in the accountant's view of the evaluation. His evaluation role will be at the operating level and primarily for the program managers, who as Wholey (1972) points out, can use detailed information concerning what works best and under what conditions. We consider this a significant contribution because even many social scientist–researchers (e.g. Binner, 1973; Wholey, 1972) now believe that it is this kind of evaluation which provides the primary pay-off in terms of decisions actually influenced.

Finally, all of the discussants have viewed the accountant as a potential social auditor. Yet, it is as an assistor of management that he can do his most useful work. As resources for social programs become more scarce, their efficient utilization becomes even more important. It is in the area of efficient utilization of resources that the accountant can help the not-for-profit social programs and agencies.

Some Concluding Observations

Figure 1 provides a general evaluation scheme that could be applied in the evaluation of social programs. As it can be seen from the figure we view the whole process of social programs in two phases. In the first phase the primary emphasis is on the formulation of social policy where politics plays a dominant role in deciding which social objectives are to be achieved,

FIGURE 1

Two Phases of Social Programs

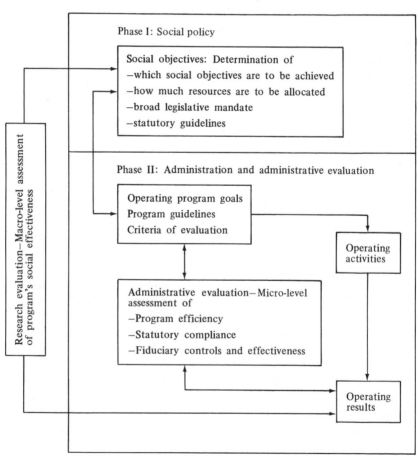

how much of national resources are to be devoted to their achievement, and what legislative mandate and guidelines are to be provided. The accountant's role at this stage in social programs is minimal and indirect at best.

The second phase of the process is operational and deals with the actual administration and evaluation of the programs. The transition from the first to the second phase, that is the reduction of the broad social objectives into operating program goals, is a function of social planners and is very crucial both to the program administrators as well as to the program evaluators. This is also a very frustrating function because there is no guarantee that a successful completion of the program goals would necessarily lead to the achievement of mandated social objectives.

It should be noted that this is quite in contrast with the profit-oriented business enterprises. In the business organizations most operating activities are well-structured, meaning that there are identifiable and measureable objectives as well as operational goals and activities. The causal linkage among all these is more clearly defined and also is so perceived by those who are concerned with it. Thus we have a structure of established relationships in the profit-oriented businesses. What is more important, these objectives, goals and activities can be measured on the accountant's unidimensional monetary scale. An established structure of causal relationships and its amenability to the unidimensional measurement scale are what make the accountant's evaluation task most effective in the profit-oriented business enterprises.

However, the accountant's unidimensional monetary measurement is quite inoperative when it comes to the measurement of a multidimensional phenomenon like a social objective (Gandhi, 1975). That is why "operationalization" of the social program — reduction of a broad social objective into measurable and verifiable operating goals, activities and evaluation criteria — is a crucial prerequisite to the accountant's entry into the evaluation of a social program. In this regard Granof & Smith (1974, p. 824) correctly point out that "accountants should avoid becoming involved in evaluating social programs until policy-makers are able to establish operational objectives."

Bibliography

Anthony, Robert N. & Herzlinger, Regina, *Management Control in Nonprofit Organizations* (Richard D. Irwin, Inc., 1975).

"Coleman cites NIMH, OE, NIH waste of Policy Research Funds." *APA Monitor* (February, 1973), p. 6.

Drew, Elizabeth B., HEW Grapples with PPBS. *The Public Interest* (Summer, 1967), pp. 9–29.

Francis, M. E., Accounting and the Evaluation of Social Programs: A Critical Comment. *The Accounting Review* (April, 1973), pp. 245–257.

Gandhi, Natwar, The Emergence of the Post-Industrial Society and the Future of the Accounting Function. Working Paper 110, Graduate School of Business, University of Pittsburgh, 1975.

Ginzberg, Eli & Solow, Robert M., Some Lessons of the 1960's. *The Public Interest* (Winter, 1974), pp. 210–220.

Gorham, William, Notes of a Practitioner. *The Public Interest* (Summer, 1967), pp. 4–8.

Granof, Michael H. & Smith, Charles, H., Accounting and the Evaluation of Social Programs: A Comment. *The Accounting Review* (October, 1974), pp. 822–825.

Linowes, David F., Accounting for Social Progress. *The New York Times* (March 14, 1971) Section 3, p. 14.

————, Socio-Economic Accounting. *The Journal of Accountancy* (November, 1968), pp. 37–42.

Livingstone, John Leslie & Gunn, Sanford E., *Accounting for Social Goals: Budgeting and Analysis of Nonmarket Projects* (Harper & Row, Publishers, 1974).

McRae, Thomas, Social Auditing Questioned. *The Journal of Accountancy* (December, 1973), pp. 92–94.

Nelson, Ronald H., Psychologists in Administrative Evaluation. *American Psychologist* (June, 1975), pp. 707–708.

Perloff, Robert, Perloff, Evelyn & Sussna, Edward, Program Evaluation. *Annual Review of Psychology*, 1976, in press.

Rossi, P. H. & Williams, W., eds., *Evaluating Social Programs* (Seminar, 1972).

Sobel, E. L. & Francis, M. E., Accounting and the Evaluation of Social Programs: A Reply. *The Accounting Review* (October, 1974), pp. 826–830.

Thomas, Arthur L., The EESP Debate: What's Really at Issue, unpublished paper.

Wholey, Joseph S., What Can We Actually Get From Program Evaluation? *Policy Sciences* (3, 1972), pp. 361–369.

30 *Starting with the increased role of nonprofit organizations and mounting pressures for accountability, this paper reviews several contemporary approaches used to achieve performance evaluation in nonprofit service organizations. An analysis of the deficiencies of social indicators, PPB systems, and cost-benefit analysis leads to prospective cost-analytic solutions focusing on costs and outcomes of service programs. In developing these solutions, the authors emphasize cost outcome as fundamental to building viable cost-effectiveness analyses for service program evaluation and accountability. Conceptual discussions of related outcome issues follow. A detailed mental health example illustrates the application of the combined cost-outcome and cost-effectiveness methodology in assessing nonprofit performance for decision-making purposes. A summary of benefits and related admonishments completes the paper.*

Cost-outcome and Cost-effectiveness Analysis: Emerging Nonprofit Performance Evaluation Techniques*

James E. Sorensen and Hugh Grove

As the United States gradually shifts from an industrial to a service economy, nonprofit organizations are providing an increasing proportion of the national income. In 1971, for example, nonprofit organizations such as government (all levels), health, education, nonprofit associations,

* *From* The Accounting Review, *Vol. LII, No. 3 (July, 1977). Reprinted by Permission of the American Accounting Association and the authors.* (Ed.'s note: This article appeared in substantially the same form in the cited journal.)

and research agencies collectively accounted for over 20% of the total national income (Anthony and Herzlinger, 1975, p. 7). In 1973 these same nonprofit organizations had grown from five to eight times their 1950 income levels (Anthony and Herzlinger, 1975, p. 8). Since nonprofit organizations exist to provide a service rather than earn a profit and because services often are more difficult to measure than profits, choices among alternative courses of action and evaluation of accomplishments become problematic. The increase in services (especially in human services) by nonprofit organizations has created new pressures for more effective performance evaluation and may heighten the roles of both the accountant in gathering appropriate data and the auditor in attesting to such data. A manifestation of these pressures is reflected in the recent General Accounting Office (GAO) statement on performance audit standards which requires a review of efficiency and economy in the use of resources and an evaluation as to whether desired results are being effectively achieved (Controller of the United States, 1972). The GAO standards specify that the performance audit shall include the following:

- The relevance and validity of the criteria used by the audited entity to judge effectiveness in achieving program results;
- The appropriateness of the methods followed by the entity to judge effectiveness in achieving program results and reliability;
- The accuracy of the results obtained (Controller of the United States, 1972).

Demands for nonprofit performance evaluation are not all from external sources. Internally, nonprofit service program managers are often faced with limited or decreasing resources and require evaluation of programs for planning and controlling program operations. These managers need a wide range of analyses ranging from

- Assessments of population or client needs, demands for services or incidence of a problem within a specified population or geographic area
- Formulation of organizational objectives and development of program structure to deliver services
- Identification of amounts of resources devoted to or budgeted for services rendered and how they are consumed; assessment of patterns of services and development of aids to monitor service programs
- Evaluation of outcome of specific programs or services on clients or beneficiaries and assessment of impact on larger social systems.

The American Accounting Association has sensed the emerging demand for nonprofit service programs. Several special committees have focused on

- Not-for-Profit Organizations (1971 and 1974 *Accounting Review* Supplement)

- Nonfinancial Measures of Effectiveness (1971 *Accounting Review* Supplement)
- Measures of Effectiveness for Social Programs (1972 *Accounting Review* Supplement).

While the accountant's role has not traditionally required active involvement in formulating models to evaluate nonfinancial outcomes and impacts, nor has the auditor been expected to attest to such information, the GAO standards, various nonprofit decision needs, and the AAA committee reports signal a new kind of involvement for the accountant and the auditor. A widespread literature, focused upon profit-oriented organizations, has left the accounting literature with few operational techniques which are responsive to nonprofit service performance evaluations. In addressing this problem, this paper is accordingly divided into three major parts:

- a brief discussion of problems identified with established performance evaluation techniques
- a general introduction to emerging cost-analytic methods and related outcome assessment issues, and
- a specific development and application of cost-outcome and cost-effectiveness techniques in a mental health example to illustrate a methodology for nonprofit performance evaluation

Problems with Established Nonprofit Performance Evaluation Techniques

Major established nonprofit performance evaluation techniques are social indicators, program-planning-budgeting systems (PPBS), and cost-benefit (C/B) analyses. None of these have been widely adopted for performance evaluation purposes in service programs.

Two major problems impede the application of social indicators. First, the method of data compilation may lead the user to question the meaning of the final social indicator statistic. For example, petty thefts over $100 comprise about 40% of the Federal Crime Index. With increasing affluence in society, many more personal property items over $100 are now owned and susceptible to theft. Therefore, if the Federal Crime Index goes up, it may be an indication of increasing affluence rather than just crime increases.

The second major problem with social indicators is that they are often either inadequate proxies (unrepresentative of the social impact being analyzed) or they are too general to aid in specific performance evaluation. Suicide, for example, is a poor indicator of mental health problems in general (Mechanic, 1975). Continuing the crime index example, an increase or decrease in the index by itself cannot evaluate the effectiveness of a single police program such as a program which uses boy scouts and girl scouts with binoculars on rooftops to spot potential crimes. Rather, a detailed index of crime occurrences in the specific areas at the specific surveillance times is needed. Only these types of specific social indicator statistics can help one attempting to assess the outcomes of various non-profit and service programs.[1]

Two established techniques which attempt to relate costs to outcome assessment are PPBS and C/B analysis. Cost collection and allocation systems are well established and are the strong points of these two techniques. The crucial weakness which has impeded general use of these methods is outcome measurement. PPBS has fallen into disuse because its required specification of objectives, such as nuclear parity, cannot be readily transformed into operational outcome quantities or statistics, i.e., how operational and meaningful is a maximum kill ratio from nuclear bombings? C/B analysis has not been generally applied because of its fixation with the improbable: transformation of essentially nonmonetary outcomes, such as lives saved or sicknesses cured, into monetary outcomes, such as the present value of all future earnings of the person whose life is saved. Consequently, both the PPBS and C/B analysis endeavors have often resulted in relatively meaningless and not too useful monetary outcome statistics.[2]

Cost-outcome and Cost-effectiveness Methods for Improving Performance Evaluation Applications

Effective program management requires program evaluation. Program evaluation, an important part of any systematic approach to program management (Wholey et al., 1970; Zusman and Wurster, 1975):

- Assesses the effectiveness of an onging program in achieving its objectives
- Relies on the principles of research design to distinguish a program's effects from those of other forces working in a situation
- Aims at program improvement through modification of current operation.

Measuring program outcomes is a vital linkage in assessing program effectiveness. Hargreaves and Attkisson (1974) suggest three reasons why program outcomes are important in program management.

---

[1] A taxonomy with related discussion of social indicators is provided by Biderman (1966, pp. 81–153). An extensive strategy for improving social indicators is provided by Gross (1966, pp. 154–271).

[2] Extensive development of PPBS and cost-benefit approaches is provided in Hinricks and Taylor (1969).

One of the most useful occasions for an outcomes study is when it can aid management and clinical staff in making a specific decision about program change. These are generally time-limited special projects . . . . A second reason to examine outcomes is to routinely detect relative strengths and weaknesses in a system of delivering services. Finally, program managers often need to demonstrate their program's overall effectiveness to funders and other groups who have a stake in the . . . [organization]. For these latter purposes, routine monitoring and public accountability, some simple outcome assessment can be a useful part of an integrated management information system.

The brief review of well-known problems of existing nonprofit performance evaluation techniques poses a perplexing question which emphasizes the role of outcome measures: Can performance measures which *avoid* the

- generality or incompleteness of most social indicator outcome measures
- nonoperational PPBS outcome measures
- hindrance of monetary outcome measures sought by cost-benefit analysis

be developed while providing meaningful cost and outcome information to be used in program evaluation and program management?

One possible solution might be to relate monetary inputs (or costs) to *non*monetary outcomes for specific programs. Newer forms of effort-accomplishment measurement systems have recognized the problem of monetary output measurements and have shifted to linking monetary inputs to nonmonetary output measurements to analyze the benefits produced by specific programs in a cost analytic perspective.

GENERAL EVALUATION STRATEGY: COST-ANALYTIC TECHNIQUES

When examining various ways to perform evaluation in service programs, three general strategies for evaluation emerge (Tripodi, Fellin, and Epstein, 1971):

- Monitoring techniques
- Social research techniques
- Cost-analytic techniques

Monitoring techniques include accountability or administrative audits as well as time and motion studies. Heavy emphasis is usually given to resource input and process activities. Service delivery statistics currently exist and can be applied. Process measures deal with an examination of the service process and whether the applied process is appropriate. Historically in human service programs, for example, this has meant:

- Audit of records (e.g., case-by-case evaluation)
- Direct observation of staff/program activities
- Examination of client/patient conditions

- Testing of professional staff (with hypothetical cases)
- Comparisons of actual and desired (or normative) profiles or ratios.

Social research techniques include experiments or quasi-experiments, surveys (e.g., of client satisfaction concerning service processes and results), and case studies (Davis et al., 1973; Tripodi et al., 1971; Campbell and Stanley, 1969). The objectives and properties of various performance indicators which may be used as process and outcome measures are reviewed in Table 1.

Cost-analytic techniques include approaches where resource consumption is a common element of the analysis. These approaches range from cost accounting and cost-finding for programs, units of services, and episodes (e.g., spell of illness) to techniques which link resource consumption to nonmonetary outcome or benefit. These techniques are thus responsive to the performance evaluation strategy relating monetary costs to nonmonetary outcomes.

In developing cost-analytic techniques, service accountability measurement must be broken down into manageable measurement problems:

- Identification of specific service attributes (such as outpatient mental health care)
- Identification and measurement of specific service delivery networks such as the relation of input efforts (e.g., mental health care costs) and outcome rewards (e.g., mental health improvements).

Two types of cost-analytic techniques, cost-outcome and cost-effectiveness (Quade, 1967; Goldman, 1967; Levin, 1974; Fishman, 1974; Yates, 1975), are explored in the paper as a combined operational approach to nonprofit performance evaluation:

- Cost outcome defined as the programmatic resources consumed to achieve a change in a relative measure of performance (e.g., health symptoms, social or role performance)
- Cost-effectiveness defined as the comparison of cost-outcomes to identify the most beneficial outcome to cost of programs, modalities, or treatment techniques (e.g., economy versus intensive day care programs).

Using cost-outcome information as building blocks, cost-effectiveness emerges as the last of five sequential steps:

- Identifying the objective to be achieved (or treatment goals to be achieved) for specific target groups, e.g., social functioning of neurotic depressives in a catchment area admitted to a Community Mental Health Center (CMHC)
- Specifying optional (or alternative) treatment programs to be used (e.g., random assignment to individual vs. group therapy)
- Determining the costs of each program, cost per unit of service, and

amounts of service rendered (e.g., use of accrual accounting, operating statistics, cost-finding, and rate-setting)

• Assessing the effect or outcome of the program intervention on the target group (e.g., pre-intervention vs. post-intervention assessment)
• Combining cost and outcome information to present cost-outcome and cost-effectiveness analyses.

While development of appropriate costing for nonprofit services is a challenging task,[3] the accountant is more likely to understand the issues of cost accounting than the issues embedded in assessing outcomes. Because nonprofit performance evaluation currently implies *nonmonetary* outcome assessment, the discussion turns to major issues in outcome assessment.

OUTCOME ISSUES

In profit organizations decision making is focused on: "What is the impact on profits?" This single, all-encompassing, widely-understood measure organizes the consideration of multiple resource factors and facilitates comparisons among varying organizational units (Anthony and Herzlinger, 1975). No such comprehensive measure exists for nonprofit organizations; to date, there are few good ways of estimating whether additional inputs (or resources) will produce commensurate outputs. The central problem is the *inadequacy of output measures,* and assessing outcomes is a first step in remedying this deficiency. The following aspects of outcome measurement are briefly analyzed: time patterns, multiple outcomes, effects among different populations, simple vs. complex evaluations, and research design questions.

Time Patterns. Effectiveness in human service organizations should be measured at multiple points in time. A specific drug treatment program may be evaluated at several points in time with each time frame revealing varying levels of effectiveness. Choosing an appropriate time frame is important. Should it be three months? six months? five years? If the time period is too short, changes may not be observable; but if the period is too long, important dynamics may be masked, missed, or identified too late for decision maker intervention. Similar to financial reporting, periodic assessment (e.g., quarterly) with cumulative restatements (e.g., year-to-date) may be one workable compromise.

Multiple Outcomes. All human service programs have multiple outcomes. A drug abuse program may decrease the use of heroin and increase

[3] For examples, see Sorensen and Phipps (1972) and Sorensen (1976). Although beyond the scope of this paper, there are significant unresolved cost issues in the nonprofit area, such as the major conceptual issue of whether expense or expenditure is the proper cost measure.

TABLE 1

Properties of Service Performance Indicators

Focus of Measure	Conceptual Content	Tells	Examples
Availability	Amount and type of service provided	What can be obtained	List of services Number of units of service rendered
Awareness	Knowledge of user population and other agencies (especially referral agencies) of existence, range, and conditions for which services are appropriate	Who knows what agency services	% of user group aware of agency service Patterns of referrals Sources of individuals referred to other agencies
Accessibility	Indicates if services can be obtained by appropriate groups	Ease of reaching service	Availability of city transportation Sloping curbs to accommodate wheelchairs Average travel time Hours of service available by day of week
Extensiveness	Compares quantity of services rendered to backdrop of problem	"How much," but not "How well"	Students enrolled in public schools Clients in outpatient programs Number and rate of catchment area resident's use of service
Appropriateness	Correct type and amount of service rendered for presenting problem	Proper use and quality of service	Length of stay in hospital exceeded criterion Mismatch between diagnosis and services received

Efficiency	Compares resource inputs to specified process or output variable	How much resource was used such as "How many hours of staff time was used per served client" "How much something cost per unit" "How much something cost in total"	Chargeable professional staff hours Cost per person riding RTD Cost per client served Cost per spell or episode of illness
Effectiveness	Compares accomplishment to goals (or what was intended) — qualitative — comparative	Characteristics Duration Content Effect Proportions served Variance from standards, budgets, or goals Ranking of options	Number of patients cured Number of trainees employed Number of clients avoiding institutionalization Traffic accidents per thousand vehicle miles Unduplicated count of clients served to total number of clients in a specified group Ratio of actual outcome to planned outcome
Outcomes/ Benefits/ Impacts	Identifies social or economic benefit	Monetary effects Nonmonetary effects	Changes in earnings Welfare payments Decreases in noise levels or air pollution levels Change in level of social functioning after treatment Change in arrests for driving while intoxicated
Acceptability	Assess match of service to client/citizen preferences	User satisfaction with services and prediction to use services	Number of complaints Willingness to refer friends to service

SOURCE: Adapted from Woy, J. Richard, "The New Community Mental Health Center Law (PL 94–63) and Its Implications for Program Evaluation" (mimeographed), Department of Health, Education and Welfare, National Institute of Mental Health, Region II, New York, 1976.

the use of alcohol. So which outcome or aggregation of outcomes should be used? A theoretical response might be "include measures of all outcomes produced with each outcome weighted by decision maker judgments of value." A practical response might be "identify the most important outcomes using simple unweighted measures." While each approach is fraught with conceptual and methodological pitfalls, operational techniques should be stressed in additional research.

Effects Among Different Populations. Who receives the benefits of a program? The benefits of a program to develop early reading skills may not be uniform across all socio-economic levels. In this example, the program effects may be expected at two levels: (1) improved levels and lower variance in reading skills in the *target group* of children from lower socio-economic status and (2) improved levels and lower variance in reading skills among *all* children entering primary schools. Identification of goals for various recipients and corresponding outcome assessment is needed.

Simple vs. Complex Evaluations. The distinction between the evaluation of complex programmatic approaches and simple program operations should be drawn clearly. A long-term study examining the cost-effectiveness of short-term hospitalization as an alternative to long-term hospitalization for schizophrenic patients requires an elaborate design using classical evaluation procedures (Glick, Hargreaves, and Goldfield, 1974). However, ascertaining if a given mental health center target group received services that achieved a treatment plan objective and at what cost during the past three months may be accomplished with less complicated approaches.

Research Design Issues. Simple designs should not be shoddy, however. Controlled evaluations of accomplishment are required whether the evaluations are complex or simple. While this is not a treatise on research design, a few research guidelines seem worth repeating.

- The results of the program should be observable (Gruenberg, 1966; MacMahon, Pugh, and Hutchinson, 1961). This requirement has directed the front line evaluator in mental health and vocational rehabilitation, for example, to examine variables such as social functioning and problem manifestation.
- In any comparison of populations, treatment and comparison samples must be created by random or systematic allocation of individuals to groups (MacMahon et al., 1961; Fishman, 1974). While other procedures can be used (such as matched samples and analysis of covariance), complexity and possible contaminants arise quickly. Randomization avoids self-selection or biased selection, increases objectivity, and offsets variables beyond the control of the experimenter

(Gilbert, Light, and Mosteller, 1975). Conducting such studies is far more preferable than just "fooling around with people" in service delivery systems that gather unreliable and misleading data on effectiveness.

• Analysis of improvements of a specific target group must be supported by comparison with similar groups which (may) have received different interventions. In this way, changes which are simply concurrent with treatment during a time span are controlled or randomized for the treatment and comparison group (Campbell and Stanley, 1963).

• Evaluation instruments must be assessed for reliability, especially for inter-rater agreement and for validity (Nunnally and Durham, 1975). If the inter-rater agreement as to the actual service delivery is poor, for example, reliability and the resulting information are bound to suffer. Validity should be examined at the level of local service delivery to assure that measures are reflecting what was intended to be measured.

• Observed differences (Gilbert et al., 1975) are often small. New programs usually create only modest effects and large "slam-bang" effects will be few.

In brief, while highly sophisticated research designs may still be required in program evaluation, these traditional, usually expensive and complex, approaches are not likely to be the ones used by programmatic practitioners and administrators. In the following mental health example, the cost-effectiveness research design is advocated as a pragmatic, operational solution.

Outcome Issues Summary. Usable outcome evaluations should honor the constraints of simplicity, economy, and utility:

Evaluations . . . are designed to fit within the operating budget of a service facility . . . used by persons with varying degrees of experience with research methods . . . (and) are to reinforce effective service and to signal the need for changes in delivery techniques or policies (Davis et al., 1973).

As the conceptual approach and role of outcome assessment become clearer, improvements in the quality of the output side of the cost-outcome approach can be expected to meet vital external and internal service accountability demands.

Cost-outcome and Cost-effectiveness Performance Evaluation: Mental Health Example

The last major section of the paper develops and applies specific cost-outcome and cost-effectiveness evaluation techniques to a mental health example. An activity flow chart for human service performance evaluation (Table 2) suggests desired service activities to be delivered to target groups in three time frames. The following discussion will emphasize the emerging nonprofit performance evaluation activities in Table 2:

- outcome assessment (activities 2 and 5)
- cost-outcome calculation (activity 9)
- cost-effectiveness calculation (activity 10) and corresponding assessment (activity 11)

OUTCOME ASSESSMENT

In this mental health care output scaling example, the output measurers are the mental health professionals who determine the degree of client (patient) impairment or level of functioning at successive points in time. In one such ordinal (ranking) scale procedure, the patients are rated on

TABLE 2

Activity Flow Chart of Human Service Performance Evaluation:
Mental Health Example

Time Frame	Activity
One	1. Specification of objectives and corresponding programs for target groups which are identified by random assignment or matched comparisons
	2. Assessment of level of functioning at intake or beginning of time period (Table 3)
Two	3. Delivery of program services
	4. Update Management Information System files for services rendered and resources consumed
Three	5. Assessment of level of functioning after intervention (Table 3)
	6. Comparison with Time One level to determine change
	7. Compute costs for units of service
	8. Calculate costs per episode/time frame by using cost per unit of service received
	9. Plot cost-outcome on matrix (Figure 1)
	10. Plot cost-outcome program results on cost-effectiveness matrix (Table 4)
	11. Statistically assess relative cost-effectiveness of competing programs for decision purposes (Tables 5–8)

SOURCE: Adapted from Fishman, Daniel B., "Development of a Generic Cost-Effectiveness Methodology for Evaluating Patient Services of a Community Mental Health Center," National Conference on Evaluation in Alcohol, Drug Abuse, and Mental Health Programs (Washington, D.C., February, 1975) and Carter, Dale, and Newman, Frederick, *A Client-Oriented System of Mental Health Service Delivery and Program Management: A Workbook and Guide,* Department of Public Welfare, Commonwealth of Pennsylvania (Philadelphia, Penn., 1975).

four major criteria, personal self-care, social functioning, vocational and/or educational functioning, and evidence of emotional stability and/or stress tolerance. These four criteria are used to rate the patients on a nine-point ordinal scale with respect to their level of functioning.[4] Table 3 presents the scale.

The final determination of these ratings is based upon consensus among the professional evaluators. The reliability and validity of such ratings are checked with special emphasis on the consensus concept. A number of professionals are asked to rate a number of cases and analysis of variance is performed on the results. The amount of variance caused by the different cases is isolated from the variance caused by the different raters. This case variance is determined as a percentage of total variance. This percentage is the reliability coefficient for the professional raters where a low percentage indicates low rater reliability and a high percentage indicates high rater reliability.[5] Validity is investigated through reference to external behavioral criteria from other rating procedures, i.e., a concurrent validity approach.[6] These types of reliability and validity verifications may be applied to help determine output aspects in the cost-effectiveness approach.

When such an estimate is made of a client's level of functioning at each clinical encounter, summaries can describe the changes which may have taken place in a specific group over a given period of time. Adequate cost-finding procedures will enable accumulation of the service costs for the same group of clients during the period of time associated with the changes in level of functioning.

COST-OUTCOME MATRIX

The matrix of costs and outcomes in Figure 1 was drawn from an adult mental health program using a nine-point level of functioning scale. Clients, grouped by level of functioning, may be traced over time utilizing the matrix.[7]

The matrix mechanics are as follows:

- All clients are assessed at the beginning of the period and placed in the appropriate diagonal cell (e.g., a pre-rating of 3 would place a client in the 3,3 diagonal matrix cell)
- All clients are reassessed at the end of the period and placed in the appropriate horizontal cell (e.g., using the previous example, a post-

---

[4] There are numerous mental health scales. Weissman (1975) has a useful review of the global scales currently available; Waskow and Parloff (1975) have a comprehensive analysis of psychotherapy change measures. This specific nine-point scale has been used successfully in actual CMHC operations (Carter and Newman, 1975).

[5] Refer to Carter and Newman (1975, pp. 231–240) for a detailed seventeen-step procedure for computing this reliability coefficient based upon Cronbach et al. (1972); also see Nunnally and Durham (1975).

[6] Refer to the nine-step validity procedure in Carter and Newman (1975, pp. 250–253).

[7] This example uses the nine-point level of functioning scale developed earlier.

TABLE 3

Nine-point Scale for Rating by Level of Functioning

Definitions of the Nine-scale Levels of Functioning

With regard to the balance of the four criteria (personal self-care, social, vocational/educational, and emotional symptoms/stress tolerance), the person's ability to function autonomously in the community is at "Level X," where "X" can assume one of the following nine (9) levels.

Level I: Dysfunctional in all four areas and is almost totally dependent upon others to provide a supportive protective environment.

Level II: Not working; ordinary social unit cannot or will not tolerate the person; can perform minimal self-care functions but cannot assume most responsibilities or tolerate social encounters beyond restrictive settings (e.g., in group, play, or occupational therapy).

Level III: Not working; probably living in ordinary social unit but not without considerable strain on the person and/or on others in the household. Symptoms are such that movement in the community should be restricted or supervised.

Level IV: Probably not working, although may be capable of working in a very protective setting; able to live in ordinary social unit and contributes to the daily routine of the household; can assume responsibility for all personal self-care matters; stressful social encounters ought to be avoided or carefully supervised.

Levels 5 through 8 describe persons who are usually functioning satisfactorily in the community, but for whom problems in one or more of the criteria areas force some degree of dependency on a form of therapeutic intervention.

Level V: Emotional stability and stress tolerance is sufficiently low that successful functioning in the social and/or vocational/educational realms is marginal. The person is barely able to hold on to either job or social unit, or both, without direct therapeutic intervention and a diminution of conflicts in either or both realms.

Level VI: The person's vocational and/or social areas of functioning are stabilized, but only because of direct therapeutic intervention. Symptom presence and severity is probably sufficient to be both noticeable and somewhat disconcerting to the client and/or to those around the client in daily contact.

Level VII: The person is functioning and coping well socially and vocationally (educationally); however, symptom reoccurrences are sufficiently frequent to maintain a reliance on some sort of regular therapeutic intervention.

Level VIII: Functioning well in all areas with little evidence of distress present. However, a history of symptom reoccurrence suggests periodic corespondence with the center; e.g., a client may receive a medication check from a family physician who then contacts the center monthly, or the client returns for bi-monthly social activities.

Level IX: The person is functioning well in all areas and no contact with the MH/MR services is recommended.

SOURCE: Carter and Newman, *op. cit.*

FIGURE 1

A Sample Cost-Outcome Matrix
for Target Group of Mental Health Adults, Ages 45–64,
January 1, 19xx to March 31, 19xx

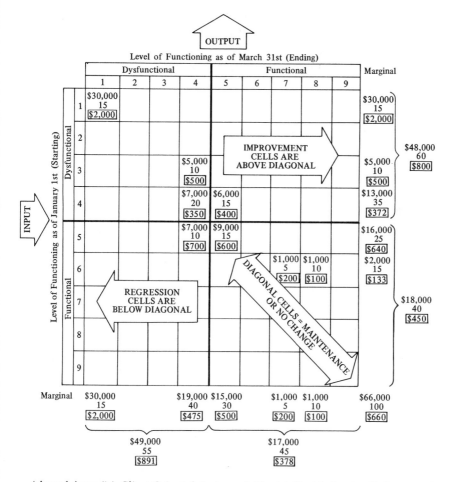

Adapted from "A Client-Oriented System of Mental Health Service Delivery and Program Management: A Workbook and Guide," by Dale Carter and Frederick Newman, Department of Public Welfare, Commonwealth of Pennsylvania.

rating of 4 would place the client in the 3,4 matrix cell, indicating improvement, a post-rating of 1 places the client in the 3,1 cell, indicating regression, a post-rating of 3 leaves the client in the 3,3 cell, indicating no change)

• in summary:

• improvement is indicated by horizontal movement to right of diagonal

• regression is indicated by horizontal movement to left of diagonal
• no change is indicated by remaining in the diagonal
• vertical movement is not allowed.

Cost data are accumulated by:

• initially computing costs by units of services provided to individuals
• aggregating these unit costs by various programs for the target group at each functional level
• summing these program costs at each functional level.

Observe the kinds of questions that can be answered using this approach:

• How many individuals are in the target group (age 45–64) and what was the average cost of service during the quarter? ($N = 100$; average cost = $660)
• How many individuals were dysfunctional at the end of the time period? ($N = 55$) How many were functional? ($N = 45$) Did these two groups consume the same amount of resources? (No, the dysfunctional consumed almost three times as much as the functional: $891 vs. $378 on the average and $49,000 vs. $17,000 in total)
• How many individuals were dysfunctional at the beginning of the quarter? ($N = 60$) How many were functional? ($N = 40$) How much in total was spent on each group? ($48,000 and $18,000 respectively) On the average? ($800 and $450 respectively)
• How many individuals were simply maintained over the quarter? ($N = 15 + 20 + 15 = 50$) At what average cost? ($30,000 + $7,000 + $9,000/50 = $920)
• How many improved? ($N = 10 + 15 + 5 + 10 = 40$) At what average cost? ($5,000 + $6,000 + $1,000 + $1,000/40 = $375)

To determine if these types of changes in the cost-outcome analysis are significant, chi-square analysis of frequency distributions can be applied. For comparability with other cost-outcome matrices, contingency coefficients can also be computed (Sorensen and Newman, 1976).

Using the foregoing illustration, the cost-outcome approach can be generalized to provide useful insights on questions such as (Carter and Newman, 1975; Burwell, Reiber, and Newman, 1975):

• Did varying target groups receive the services planned for specified levels of functioning?
• How much improvement did members of a target group achieve? At what cost?
• Where are the high and low cost services being used?
• Did the services delivered have the expected impact?
• What are the average values and are certain values out-of-line?

In this example, by combining target groups and programs, the clinician's assessment of client movement from one functional level to another, and costs into a cost-outcome matrix, a basic decision-making system has been formed for effective client and resource management and accountability.

COST-EFFECTIVENESS MATRIX

Cost-effectiveness builds on cost-outcome measurement procedures and strengthens the service measurement and evaluation procedure by correcting the design for a deficiency in the cost-outcome approach. The deficiency is that "there is not a way of scientifically documenting whether such change is actually caused by the treatment or is simply concurrent with it" (Fishman, 1975).

The correction in the research design is simple: use a control group. Potential intervening variables, such as history or selection bias, can be randomized or controlled by using two groups of similar patients which are exposed to different types of treatments, such as token-economy or intensive therapeutic day care. Ideally, the treatment variable is isolated as the only difference between the two groups:

> At the level of cost-effectiveness analysis, the causal relationship between intervention and change over time can be investigated. For example, if two groups of comparable patients each receive different interventions and then are assessed with standard procedures at follow-up, any differences between the two groups at follow-up can be ascribed to the difference between the treatments (Fishman, 1975).

This research design is similar to one of Campbell and Stanley's (1963) "true experimental designs," the pretest-posttest control group design, modified to reflect two different sets of treatments:

$$\text{Group 1: } R \; O \; X_1 \; O$$
$$\text{Group 2: } R \; O \; X_2 \; O$$

Where

R = randomization of clients or patients into two groups or matched samples or covariance analysis (Glick, Hargreaves, and Goldfield, 1974)

O = process of observation or measurement, for example, the functioning level rating at the beginning and the end of the period

X_1 = exposure of first group to a specific type of therapeutic treatment, such as a special token-economy day care program

X_2 = exposure of second group to a different type of therapeutic treatment, such as an intensive day care program

The research design is pragmatic in acknowledging real world demands of human service clients (i.e., immediate service needs) which preclude utilizing the true control group where no treatment is given during the research period.

TABLE 4

Cost-effectiveness Matrix

Effectiveness of A Relative to B	Cost of A Relative to B		
	A Is Less Costly	A Is as Costly	A Is More Costly
A Is Less Effective	11 ?	12 Choose B	13 Choose B
A Is as Effective	21 Choose A	22 No Difference	23 Choose B
A Is More Effective	31 Choose A	32 Choose A	33 ?

SOURCE: Adapted from Fishman, *op. cit.*

Table 4 summarizes the logical relationships and choice points for comparing treatments *A* and *B*. The decision criteria, based upon this measurement information, is to maximize output at minimum cost, and seven choices are self-explanatory. Because the binary choice in cells 1 and 9 is not obvious, the analysis could proceed along statistical lines by testing for the significance of outcome and cost differences and choosing the treatment outcome or cost with the highest level of significance using a nonorthogonal comparison test (such as Scheffe or Tukey).

The subsequent example statistically assesses the results of one cost-effectiveness matrix example, including the binary choice problem in cells one and nine. The nontechnical reader may desire to skip this section.

COST-EFFECTIVENESS ASSESSMENT

Cost-effectiveness leads to ranking of optional choices, e.g., *A* is more cost-effective than *B* for decision purposes. *A* and *B* may be competing programs within a human service organization (HSO) or they may be the same program, but are in two different HSOs. The ranking process may be changed depending on the type of measure or statistical analysis employed as well as the level of experimental control. To illustrate, assume the following data in Table 5 using social-functioning measures of outcome.

Using the cost-effectiveness matrix in Table 4 and the *changes,* or perhaps more desirably the percent of change, in social functioning in Table 5, Program *A* does not appear to be significantly different from Program *B* on

TABLE 5

T-Tests Between Treatment Programs

Comparison	Program A Mean (N = 30)	S.D.	Program B Mean (N = 30)	S.D.	Level of Confidence t (Mean)	F (S.D.)
Social Functioning:						
Time 1	4.90	1.062	6.10	1.155	.99	.67
Time 2	6.00	.91	7.40	.814	.99	.72
Changes in Social Functioning:						
Time 1 — Time 2	+1.10	0.84	+1.30	0.794	.64	.63
Costs:						
Time 1 — Time 2	$500	50.86	$550	25.43	.99	.99

outcome ($p \geq .64$). On the cost-effectiveness matrix, this outcome condition is identified in Row 2. Program *A* also appears to be significantly less expensive than Program *B* ($p \geq .99$). On the cost-effectiveness matrix, this cost condition is identified in Column 1. The intersection of Row 2 and Column 1 is Cell 21, which indicates that Program *A* is chosen for cost considerations.

If the measure is shifted to social functioning at *Time 2* (a cross-sectional approach without any time series considerations or where clients have been randomly assigned to treatment programs), the statistical comparison suggests Program *B* is superior on outcome ($p \geq .99$). Row 1 of the cost-effectiveness matrix is chosen. Since the costs did not change, Column 1 is chosen again. Row 1 and Column 1 intersect at Cell 11, which does not indicate a clear decision. Program *A* has lower outcomes but also is less costly. Since both cost and outcome are significantly different, the decision is still open.

A troublesome aspect is the significant difference on the *entry* levels of functioning between the two programs. If the differences between Program *A* and Program *B* at Time 1 and Program *A* and Program *B* at Time 2 are materially unequal, an *interaction* between the levels of functioning in the various programs and the time of measurement may be expected. Analysis of variance (with repeated measures) reveals significant effects on programs, social functioning, but *no* interaction between program and time of measurement. (Only program and social functioning *F*-ratios were significant in Table 6. Program *A* may appear to have lower initial levels of functioning than Program *B,* but this condition was not revealed in the analysis of variance interactions.)

A further statistical test, analysis of covariance of Time 2 social func-

TABLE 6

Analysis of Variance with Repeated Measures on Social Functioning
Time 1 Versus Time 2

Source of Variation	SS	df	MS	F
			Social Functioning	
Between Subjects:				
Program	1.690	1	1.690	30.92*
Subjects Within Groups	3.170	58	0.055	
Within Subjects:				
Social Functioning	1.440	1	1.440	128.49*
Program × Functioning	0.010	1	0.010	0.89
Functioning × Subjects				
Within Groups	0.650	58	0.011	

* Level of Significance $< .01$.

tioning, can investigate the apparent initial difference between the two treatment programs by adjusting for the initial condition at Time 1. The covariance analysis suggests significant differences between program outcomes ($p \geq .95$), with Program *B* achieving higher outcomes even after adjusting for differing initial conditions (Tables 7 and 8).

TABLE 7

Analysis of Covariance of Time 2 Social Functioning*
(Where Initial Condition = Covariate)

Source	df	YY	SS (about)	df	MS
Treatment					
(Between)	1	29.40			
Error					
(Within)	18	43.20	23.18	57	0.40
Total	19	72.60	29.92	58	
Differences					
(for testing					
adjusted means)			6.74	1	6.74

$$F(1,57) = 16.554$$
$$p < .05$$

* To use multiple measure requires analysis of covariance using repeated measures.

TABLE 8

Table of Adjusted Means and Standard Error
(Covariate = Initial Social Functioning)

Time	Treatment	Mean	Adjusted	Adjusted SE
Time 2	A	6.00	6.31	.125
	B	7.40	7.08	.125

Program B still seems to be superior on outcomes and the choice between A and B is yet unresolved. However, if there were no significant differences in outcomes of Programs A and B from this covariance test, then Program A, which costs less, would have been chosen as the more effective method. In this situation, the choice would revert to Cell 21 in the cost-effectiveness matrix, which then indicates the selection of Program A. These illustrations demonstrate how different concepts of "outcomes" can lead to different decisions: in one case to choose A, another shows indecision, and a third case indicates the choice of B.

A different conceptualization of cost-effectiveness may change the ranking, however, assuming that the following measure is used (Hanson et al., 1974):

$$\text{Cost-effectiveness} = \frac{\text{Average cost per episode}}{\text{Average change in global impairment per episode}} = \text{Cost per unit of change in global impairment}$$

When applied to the illustrative data, the results are:

$$\text{Program } A = \frac{\$500}{1.10} = 454.54 \approx 455$$

$$\text{Program } B = \frac{\$550}{1.30} = 423.07 \approx 423$$

Observe that this analysis ranks Program B as more cost-effective (viz., lower cost per unit of change) although no test of statistical significance was applied.

By comparisons of two or more cost-outcome statements (Step 11 in Table 2), the effectiveness of costs for achievement of programs, modalities, or techniques can be assessed. The cost-effectiveness model emerges as the summary technique which incorporates the fundamental service accountability information requirements.

Summary

In summary, the cost-effectiveness approach uses the cost-outcome measurement procedures and severely restricts the possibility that the outcome was caused by nonservice factors occurring concurrently in the treatment period. This advancement in service measurement is achieved by identifying specific types of services or treatment costs with specific results or outcomes and statistically investigating the results of such programs. Decision-making information about service measurement and evaluation are improved accordingly. But the variety, complexity, and difficulties of interpretation of cost-effectiveness measures should not be underestimated. The approach offered here is neither easy nor obvious when extended in realistic programmatic decision making and accountability environments.

References

Anthony, Robert N. and Herzlinger, Regina, *Management Control in Nonprofit Organizations* (Richard D. Irwin, Inc., 1975).

Biderman, Albert D., "Social Indicators and Goals," in Raymond A. Bauer, ed., *Social Indicators* (The M.I.T. Press, 1966), pp. 68–153.

Burwell, Barbara, Sue Reiber and Frederick Newman, "The Client-Oriented Cost/Outcome System of the Fayette County Mental Health/Mental Retardation," Statewide Conference on Cost Analysis Systems in MH/MR Programs (Hershey, Penn., June 25, 1975).

Campbell, Donald T. and Julian C. Stanley, *Experimental and Quasi-experimental Designs for Research* (Rand McNally, 1963).

Carter, Dale and Frederick Newman, *A Client-oriented System of Mental Health Service Delivery and Program Management: A Workbook and Guide,* Department of Public Welfare, Commonwealth of Pennsylvania (Philadelphia, Penn., 1975).

Committee on Accounting for Not-for-profit Organizations, *The Accounting Review,* Supplement to Vol. 46 (1971), pp. 81–164.

Committee on Measures of Effectiveness for Social Programs, *The Accounting Review,* Supplement to Vol. 47 (1972), pp. 337–398.

Committee on Nonfinancial Measures of Effectiveness, *The Accounting Review,* Supplement to Vol. 46 (1971), pp. 165–212.

Committee on Not-for-profit Organizations, 1972–73, *The Accounting Review,* Supplement to Vol. 49 (1974), pp. 225–249.

Controller General of the United States, United States General Accounting Office, *Standards for Audit of Governmental Organizations, Programs, Activities, and Functions* (1972).

Cronbach, L. J., G. C. Gleser, N. Nanda, and H. Rajartnam, *The Dependability of Behavioral Measurements: Theory of Generalizability for Scores and Profiles* (John Wiley and Sons, 1972).

Davis, Howard R., Carol Weiss, Karen Louis, and Janet Weiss, *Planning for Creative Change in Mental Health Services: Use of Program Evaluation,* U.S. Department of Health, Education and Welfare, National Institute of Mental Health, Publication #(HSM) 71–9057 (Rockville, Maryland, 1973).

Fishman, Daniel B., "Development of a Generic Cost-effectiveness Methodology for Evaluating Patient Services of a Community Mental Health Center," National Conference on Evaluation in Alcohol, Drug Abuse, and Mental Health Programs (Washington, D.C., April 3, 1974).

———, "Suggested Guidelines for Utilizing 2% Evaluation Funds in the Emergent Community Mental Health Center Legislation: A Cost-effectiveness Approach," National Council of Community Mental Health Centers (Washington, D.C., February, 1975).

Gilbert, John P., Richard J. Light, and Frederick Mosteller, "Assessing Social Innovations: An Empirical Base for Policy," in R. Zeckhauser et al., eds., *Benefit-Cost and Policy Analysis, 1974* (Aldine Publishing Company, 1975), pp. 3–65.

Glick, Ira D., William A. Hargreaves, and Michael D. Goldfield, "Short vs. Long Hospitalization," *Archives of General Psychiatry,* Vol. 30 (March 30, 1974), pp. 363–369.

Goldman, Thomas A., ed., *Cost-effectiveness Analysis* (Frederick A. Praeger Publishers, 1967).

Gross, Bertram, "The State of the Nation: Social Systems Accounting," in Raymond A. Bauer, ed., *Social Indicators* (The M.I.T. Press, 1966), pp. 154–271.

Gruenburg, Ernest M., ed., "Evaluating the Effectiveness of Mental Health Services," *Milbank Memorial Fund Quarterly,* Vol. 44, No. 1 (1966), Part 2.

Hanson, Marshall R., Henry H. Horn, Jr., Katherine Ruland, Edward D. Shafer, and Melvin H. Voyles, *Final Report: Five County Cost-effectiveness Study,* Department of Health, State of California (October, 1974).

Hargreaves, William A. and C. Clifford Attkisson, "Outcome Studies in Mental Health Program Evaluation," (University of California, 1973).

Hinricks, Harley H., and Graeme M. Taylor, eds., *Program Budgeting and Benefit-Cost Analysis* (Goodyear Publishing Co., 1969).

Levin, Henry M., "Cost-effectiveness Analysis in Evaluation Research," Evaluation Consortium (Stanford University, 1974), pp. 8–10.

MacMahon, B., T. F. Pugh, and G. B. Hutchinson, "Principles in the Evaluation of Community Mental Health Programs," *American Journal of Public Health,* Vol. 51, No. 7 (1961), p. 963.

Mechanic, David, "Evaluation in Alcohol, Drug Abuse, and Mental Health Programs: Problems and Prospects," in J. Zusman and C. Wurster, eds., *Program Evaluation* (D. C. Heath and Co., 1975), pp. 3–25.

Nunnally, J. C. and Robert Durham, "Validity, Reliability and Special Problems in Evaluation Research," in E. L. Struening and M. Guttentag, eds., *Handbook of Evaluation Research,* Vol. 1 (Sage Publications, Inc., 1975), pp. 289–352.

Quade, Edward S., "Introduction and Overview," in T. A. Goldman, ed., *Cost-effectiveness Analysis* (Praeger Publishers, 1967), pp. 1–16.

Sorensen, James E., "Uniform Cost Accounting in Long-term Care," in J. H. Murnaghan and K. L. White, eds., *Long-term Care Data,* Supplement to *Medical Care,* Vol. 13 (1976).

——, and Frederick L. Newman, "Using Cost-Outcome Analysis to Develop Cost-effectiveness for Program Evaluation," (Unpublished paper, University of Denver, 1976).

——, and David W. Phipps, *Cost-finding and Rate-setting for Community Mental Health Centers,* U.S. Department of Health, Education and Welfare, National Institute of Mental Health, Publication #(HSM) 72–9138 (Rockville, Maryland, 1972).

Tripodi, Tony, Phillip Fellin, and Irwin Epstein, *Social Program Evaluation* (F. E. Peacock, 1971).

Waskow, Irene E., and Morris B. Parloff, eds., *Psychotherapy Change Measures,* U.S. Department of Health, Education and Welfare, publication #(ADM) 74–120, National Institute of Mental Health (Rockville, Maryland, 1975).

Weissman, Myrna M., "The Assessment of Social Adjustment," *Archives of General Psychiatry,* Vol. 32 (March, 1975), pp. 357–365.

Wholey, Joseph S., John W. Scanlon, Hugh G. Duffy, James S. Fukumoto, and Leona M. Vogt, *Federal Evaluation Policy: Analysis of Effects of Public Programs* (Washington, D.C.: The Urban Institute, 1970).

Woy, J. Richard, "The New Community Mental Health Center Law (PL94–63) and Its Implications for Program Evaluation" (mimeographed), Department of Health, Education and Welfare, National Institute of Mental Health, Region II, New York, 1976.

Yates, Brian, "Towards Cost-effectiveness Analysis in Applied Psychology: Compiling Cost-effectiveness Indices for Behavioral Treatment" (Western Psychological Association, April, 1975).

Zusman, Jack, and Cecil R. Wurster, *Program Evaluation* (D. C. Heath and Co., 1975).

Supplemental
Readings
to Part Seven

Ashton, Robert H. "User Prediction Models in Accounting: An Alternative Use." *The Accounting Review,* L, No. 4 (October 1975), 710–722.
Establishes human information processing systems from behavioral research.

Burns, Thomas J., ed. *Behavioral Experiments in Accounting.* The Ohio State University, 1972.
Presents eight behavioral experiments in accounting prepared by accounting researchers and discussed and evaluated by social scientists.

Butterworth, John E. "The Accounting System as an Information Function." *Journal of Accounting Research* (Spring 1972), 1–27.
Applies concepts of information value and decision models to the accounting system structure. The author uses matrices to represent double-entry accounting.

Charnes, A., C. Colantoni, W. W. Cooper, and K. O. Kortanek. "Economic, Social, and Enterprise Accounting and Mathematical Models." *The Accounting Review,* XLVII, No. 1 (January 1972), 85–108.
Characterizes double-entry accounting, input-output analysis, and other topics through mathematical representations that help exhibit underlying relations as well as suggest new extensions in each case.

Dermer, Jerry, and Jacob P. Siegel. "The Role of Behavioral Measures in Accounting for Human Resources." *The Accounting Review,* XLIX, No. 1 (January 1974), 88–97.
Discusses a study conducted to determine if behavioral measures could play a role in human resource accounting. The results indicated they cannot play such a role.

Dickhaut, John W. "Alternative Information Structures and Probability Revisions." *The Accounting Review,* XLVIII, No. 1 (January 1973), 61–79.
Considers the individual's ability to adjust his or her personal probability estimates when he or she receives just one accounting report as against that when he or she receives two accounting reports.

Dilley, Stephen C., and Jerry J. Weygandt. "Measuring Social Responsibility: An Empirical Test." *The Journal of Accountancy* (September 1973), 62–70.
Evaluates current approaches to social accounting and puts forth and tests empirically a nonmonetary approach.

Elias, Nabil, and Marc Epstein. "Dimensions of Corporate Social Reporting." *Management Accounting,* LVI, No. 9 (March 1975), 36–40.
Reviews and analyzes the different thrusts that social reporting has taken in the recent past, as applied by a number of US corporations.

Feltham, Gerald A. *Information Evaluation.* Studies in Accounting Research #5, American Accounting Association, 1972.
Develops an information evaluation model and applies it to accounting systems.

Flamholtz, Eric. "A Model for Human Resource Valuation: A Stochastic Process with Service Rewards." *The Accounting Review,* XLVI, No. 2 (April 1971), 253–267.
Focuses on the measurement of an individual's value to a specified organization and presents a normative model for the economic valuation of individuals.

———. "Toward a Theory of Human Resource Value in Formal Organizations." *The Accounting Review,* XLVII, No. 4 (October 1972), 666–678.
Presents a model of the nature and determinants of a person's value to an organization. Its main purposes are (1) to identify a set of variables that purport to explain a person's value to a firm, and (2) to discuss the variables' interrelationships.

Francis, M. E. "Accounting and the Evaluation of Social Programs: A Critical Comment." *The Accounting Review,* XLVIII, No. 2 (April 1973), 254–257.
Reviews and criticizes some of the recommendations for the accountant to play an important role in social reporting. Accounting knowledge might be helpful in improving the accuracy of the data but would do little in improving the relevance and reliability. Also, accountants lack the necessary statistical knowledge for this type of job.

Gorry, G. Anthony, and Michael S. C. Morton. "A Framework for Management Information Systems." *Sloan Management Review* (Fall 1971), 55–70.
Elaborates on a basic MIS design framework.

"Human Resource Accounting." *Accounting Organizations and Society* (August 1976).
Devotes the entire issue to human resource accounting articles.

Ijiri, Yuji. *Theory of Accounting Measurement.* Studies in Accounting Research #10, American Accounting Association, 1975.
Develops measurement theory concepts in an accounting context.

Jaggi, Bikki, and Hon-Shiang Lau. "Toward a Model for Human Resource Valuation." *The Accounting Review,* XLIX, No. 2 (April 1974), 321–329.
Criticizes the Flamholtz and Lev/Schwartz valuation models and suggests valuating human resources on a group basis and applying the Markov chain to this purpose.

Jones, Phillip A., Sr. "The Computer: A Cost-Benefit Analysis." *Management Accounting,* LIII, No. 1 (July 1971), 23–25, 51.
Reviews cost-benefit factors related to computerization, with special emphasis on the implications for small businesses.

Lev, Baruch. *Accounting and Information Theory.* Studies in Accounting Research #2, American Accounting Association, 1969.
Introduces the concepts of information, entropy, and aggregation in an accounting system context.

Mason, Richard. "Basic Concepts for Designing Management Information Systems." University of California, Los Angeles, Research Paper No. 8 (October 1969).

Elaborates on basic MIS design concepts.

McDonough, John J. "The Accountant, Data Collection and Social Exchange." *The Accounting Review,* XLVI, No. 4 (October 1971), 676–685.

Examines how the financial management function has adapted to corporate growth, which has resulted in the increase of diversification, decentralization, and use of technology.

Mervin, Michael N. "Robinson-Patman Act Cost Justifications and CPAs." *The Journal of Accountancy* (June 1971), 59–62.

Discusses the "novel accounting requirements" of the Robinson-Patman Act and explains that once simple and clear accounting standards are established, every business entity with price differentials will use cost justifications to prove their legality.

Mitroff, Ian I., John Nelson, and Richard O. Mason. "On Management Myth-information Systems." *Management Science* (December 1974), 371–382.

Compares mythic (personalistic) and nonmythic (nonpersonalistic) information systems experimentally and advocates further research on mythic information systems.

Mock, Theodore J. *Measurement and Accounting Information Criteria.* Studies in Accounting Research #13, American Accounting Association, 1976.

Develops measurement theory concepts and applies them to accounting information systems.

———. "The Value of Budget Information." *The Accounting Review,* XLVIII, No. 3 (July 1973), 520–534.

Develops a series of business game experiments with the primary objective of generating empirical evidence as to the value of an information structure based on the budget variance concept of feedback.

Norgaard, Corine T. "Operating Auditing: A Part of the Control Process." *Management Accounting,* LIII, No. 9 (March 1972), 25–28.

Describes an operational audit and compares it to a financial audit.

Ramanathan, Kavasseri V. "Toward a Theory of Corporate Social Accounting." *The Accounting Review,* LI, No. 3 (July 1976), 516–528.

Develops a theoretical framework consisting of a proposed set of social accounting objectives and concepts in the areas of valuation, measurement methods, and reporting standards.

Smith, Charles H., Roy A. Lanier, and Martin E. Taylor. "The Need for and Scope of the Audit of Management: A Survey of Attitudes." *The Accounting Review,* XLVII, No. 2 (April 1972), 270–283.

Reports the results of a field study done in connection with the audit of management. The survey focused on the need for a management audit by a CPA, the scope of such an audit, and the audit standards required.

Ullmann, Arieh A. "The Corporate Environmental Accounting System: A Management Tool for Fighting Environmental Degradation." *Accounting, Organizations and Society* (June 1976), 71–79.

Develops an accounting system that provides corporate management (and governmental authorities) with a comprehensive assessment system of the annual environmental effects of a corporation's business activities.

Additional
Bibliography
to Part Seven

Ackoff, Russell L. "Towards a System of Systems Concepts." *Management Science* (July 1971), 661–671.

Abdel-Khalik, A. Rashad. "The Entropy Law, Accounting Data, and Relevance to Decision-making." *The Accounting Review,* XLIX, No. 2 (April 1974), 271–283.

American Accounting Association. "Report of the Committee on Nonprofit Organizations." *The Accounting Review,* XLX (1975), 1–39.

―――. "Report of the Committee on Measures of Effectiveness for Social Programs." *The Accounting Review,* XLVII (1972), 336–396.

―――. "Report of the Committee on Internal Measurement and Reporting." *The Accounting Review,* XLVIII (1973), 208–241.

―――. "Report of the Committee on Accounting for Social Performance." *The Accounting Review,* XLXI (1976), 37–69.

―――. Report of the Committee on Accounting for Not-for-profit Organizations." *The Accounting Review,* XLVI (1971), 80–163.

―――. "Report of the Committee on Concepts of Accounting Applicable to the Public Sector, 1970–71." *The Accounting Review,* XLVII (1972), 76–108.

―――. "Report of the Committee on Information Systems, 1970–71." *The Accounting Review,* XLVII (1972), 186–213.

―――. "Report of the Committee on Not-for-profit Organizations." *The Accounting Review,* XLIX (1974), 224–249.

―――. "Report of the Committee on Social Costs." *The Accounting Review,* XLX (1975), 50–89.

―――. "Report of the Committee on Accounting for Human Resources." *The Accounting Review,* XLIX (1974), 114–124.

―――. "Report of the Committee on Measurement of Social Costs." *The Accounting Review,* XLIX (1974), 98–113.

―――. "Report of the Committee on Management Information Systems." *The Accounting Review,* XLIX (1974), 140–155.

————. "Report of the Committee on Foundations of Accounting Measurement." *The Accounting Review,* XLVI (1971), 1–48.

————. "Report of the Committee on Non-financial Measures of Effectiveness." *The Accounting Review,* XLVI (1971), 164–211.

————. "Report of the Committee on Accounting and Information Systems." *The Accounting Review,* XLVI (1971), 286–350.

Ashton, Robert H. "The Predictive-Ability Criterion and User Prediction Models." *The Accounting Review,* XLIX, No. 4 (October 1974), 719–732.

Berck, Wayne R. "Evaluation of Subcontractor Performance." *Management Accounting,* LIII, No. 11 (May 1972), 34–36.

Birnberg, Jacob G., and Raghu Nath. "Implications of Behavioral Science for Managerial Accounting." *The Accounting Review,* XLII, No. 3 (July 1967), 468–479.

Brummet, R. Lee, Eric G. Flamholtz, and William C. Pyle. "Human Resource Measurement — A Challenge for Accountants." *The Accounting Review,* XLIII, No. 2 (April 1968), 217–224.

Charnes, A., W. W. Cooper, and G. Kozmetsky. "Measuring, Monitoring and Modeling Quality of Life." *Management Science* (June 1973), 1172–1188.

Churchman, C. West. "On the Facility, Felicity, and Morality of Measuring Social Change." *The Accounting Review,* XLVI, No. 7 (January 1971), 1–16.

Demski, Joel S. "Implementation Effects of Performance Measurement Models." *The Accounting Review,* XLVI, No. 10 (April 1971), 268–278.

Driver, Michael, and Theodore Mock. "Human Information Processing, Decision Style Theory, and Accounting Information Systems." *The Accounting Review,* L, No. 3 (July 1975), 490–508.

Elias, Nabil. "Behavioral Impact of Human Resource Accounting." *Management Accounting,* LVII, No. 8 (February 1976), 43–45, 48.

Epstein, Marc, Eric Flamholtz, and John J. McDonough. "Corporate Social Accounting in the United States of America: State of the Art and Future Prospects." *Accounting, Organizations and Society* (June 1976), 23–42.

Estes, Ralph W. "Socio-economic Accounting and External Diseconomies." *The Accounting Review,* XLVII, No. 2 (April 1972), 284–290.

Etter, William L. "Benjamin Franklin and Prudential Algebra." *Decision Sciences* (January 1974), 145–147.

Fellingham, John C., Theodore J. Mock, and Miklos A. Vasarhelyi. "Simulation of Information Choice." *Decision Sciences,* 7, No. 2 (April 1976), 219–234.

Flamholtz, Eric G. "Assessing the Validity of a Theory of Human Resource Value: A Field Study." *Empirical Research in Accounting: Selected Studies, 1972,* 241–282.

Foran, Michael F., and Don T. DeCoster. "An Experimental Study of the Effects of Participation, Authoritarianism, and Feedback on Cognitive Dissonance in a Standard Setting Situation." *The Accounting Review,* XLIX, No. 4 (October 1974), 751–763.

Gilbert, Michael H. "The Asset Value of the Human Organization." *Management Accounting* (July 1970), 25–28.

Haseman, William D., and Andrew B. Whinston. "Design of a Multidimensional Accounting System." *The Accounting Review,* LI, No. 1 (January 1976), 65–79.

Heimann, Stephen R., and Edward J. Lusk. "Decision Flexibility: An Alternative Evaluation Criterion." *The Accounting Review,* LI, No. 1 (January 1976), 51–64.

Hindman, William R., and Floyd F. Kettering. "Integrated MIS: A Case Study." *Management Accounting,* LV, No. 2 (August 1973), 20–27.

Hofstedt, Thomas R. "Behavioral Accounting Research: Pathologies, Paradigms and Prescriptions." *Accounting, Organizations and Society* (June 1976), 43–58.

Jauch, Roger, and Michael Skigen. "Human Resource Accounting: A Critical Evaluation." *Management Accounting,* LV, No. 11 (May 1974), 33–36.

Keller, T. F., and D. J. Laughhunn. "An Application of Queuing Theory to a Congestion Problem in an Outpatient Clinic." *Decision Sciences,* 4, No. 3 (July 1973), 379–393.

King, William R. "Methodological Analysis Through Systems Simulation." *Decision Sciences* (January 1974), 1–9.

———, and David I. Cleland. "The Design of Management Information Systems: An Information Analysis Approach." *Management Science* (November 1975), 286–297.

Libby, Robert. "The Use of Simulated Decision Makers in Information Evaluation." *The Accounting Review,* L, No. 3 (July 1975), 475–489.

Lieberman, Arthur Z., and Andrew B. Whinston. "A Structuring of an Events-accounting Information System." *The Accounting Review,* L, No. 2 (April 1975), 246–258.

Lucas, Henry C., Jr. "An Empirical Study of a Framework for Information Systems." *Decision Sciences,* 5, No. 1 (January 1974), 102–113.

———. "The Use of an Accounting Information Systems Action and Organizational Performance." *The Accounting Review,* L, No. 4 (October 1975), 735–746.

Marshall, Ronald M. "Determining an Optimal Accounting Information System for an Unidentified User." *Journal of Accounting Research* (Autumn 1972), 286–307.

Mattessich, Richard. "The Incorporation and Reduction of Value Judgments in Systems." *Management Science* (September 1974), 1–9.

Miller, Danny, and Lawrence A. Gordon. "Conceptual Levels and the Design of Accounting Information Systems." *Decision Sciences,* 6, No. 2 (April 1975), 259–269.

Mock, Theodore J. "Concepts of Information Value and Accounting." *The Accounting Review,* XLVI, No. 4 (October 1971), 765–778.

Ogan, Pekin. "A Human Resource Value Model for Professional Service Organizations." *The Accounting Review,* LI, No. 2 (April 1976), 306–320.

————. "People Are Capital Investments at R. G. Barry Corp." *Management Accounting,* LIII, No. 5 (November 1971), 53–55, 63.

Prakash, Prem, and Alfred Rappaport. "Informational Interdependencies: System Structure Induced by Accounting Information." *The Accounting Review,* L, No. 4 (October 1975), 723–734.

Ritzman, Larry P., and Leroy J. Krajewski. "Multiple Objectives in Linear Programming — An Example in Scheduling Postal Resources." *Decision Sciences,* 4, No. 3 (July 1973), 364–378.

Ronen, Joshua. "Some Effects of Sequential Aggregation in Accounting on Decision-making." *Journal of Accounting Research* (Autumn 1971), 307–332.

————, and Gideon Falk. "Accounting Aggregation and the Entropy Measure: An Experimental Approach." *The Accounting Review,* XLVIII, No. 4 (October 1973), 696–717.

Savich, Richard S., and Keith B. Ehrenreich. "Cost/Benefit Analysis of Human Resource Accounting Alternatives." *Human Resource Management* (Spring 1976), 7–18.

Seago, W. E. "Medicare: Accounting Methods and Social Goals." *The Journal of Accountancy* (August 1971), 46–53.

Spier, Leo. "A Suggested Behavioral Approach to Cost-Benefit Analysis." *Management Science* (June 1971), B-672–B-693.

Swanson, E. Burton. "Management Information Systems: Appreciation and Involvement." *Management Science* (October 1974), 178–188.

Appendix

Background Sources
For Selected Articles

Quantitative Method	Suggested Sources	Part	Article
Correlation and regression analysis	Spurr, W. A., and C. P. Bonini. *Statistical Analysis for Business Decisions*, rev. ed. Irwin, 1973.	2	Forecasting and measuring with correlation analysis, Knapp.
	Neter, J., and W. Waserman. *Fundamental Statistics for Business and Economics*, 4th ed. Allyn and Bacon, 1973.	4	Multiple regression analysis of cost behavior, Benston.
Simulation	McMillan, C., and R. F. Gonzalez. *Systems Analysis: A Computer Approach to Decision Models*, 4th ed. Irwin, 1977. Spurr and Bonini.	3	Evaluating simplified capital-budgeting models using a time-state preference metric, Sundem.
Goal programming	Charnes, A., and W. W. Cooper. *Management Models and Industrial Applications of Linear Programming*. Wiley, 1961.	4	Break-even budgeting and programming to goals, Charnes, Cooper, and Ijiri.
Bayesian decision theory	Bierman, H., C. P. Bonini and W. H. Hausman. *Quantitative Analysis for Business Decisions*, 5th ed. Irwin, 1977. Spurr and Bonini.	4	An approach to cost-volume-profit analysis under uncertainty, Jarrett.

Topic	Reference		Description
Statistical control models	DeGroot, M. H. *Optimal Statistical Decisions.* McGraw-Hill, 1970. Spurr and Bonini.	5	The significance and investigation of cost variances: survey and extensions, Kaplan.
Matrix algebra and input-output analysis	Levin, R. I., and C. A. Kirkpatrick. *Quantitative Approaches to Management,* 3d ed. McGraw-Hill, 1975. Corcoran, W. *Mathematical Applications in Accounting.* Harcourt, Brace, 1961. Allen, R. G. D. *Mathematical Economics.* MacMillan, 1963.	6	Input-output analysis for cost accounting, planning, and control, Livingstone.
Learning curves	Jordan, R. "Learning How to Use the Learning Curve." *NAA Bulletin* (January 1958).	6	Reporting production costs that follow the learning curve phenomenon, Morse.
Linear programming	Bierman, Bonini, and Hausman. Levin and Kirkpatrick.	6	A transfer pricing system based on opportunity cost, Onsi.
Analysis of variance and covariance analysis	Kerlinger, F. N. *Foundations of Behavioral Research,* Holt, Rinehart, Winston, 1973. Hays, W. L. *Statistics for the Social Sciences.* Holt, Rinehart, Winston 1973.	7	Cost-outcome and cost-effectiveness analysis: emerging nonprofit performance evaluation techniques, Sorensen and Grove.